D1593432

Religious War and Religious Peace in Early Modern Europe

Religious War and Religious Peace in Early Modern Europe presents a novel account of the origins of religious pluralism in Europe. Combining comparative historical analysis with contentious political analysis, it surveys six clusters of increasingly destructive religious war between 1529 and 1651, analyzes the diverse settlements that brought these wars to an end, and describes the complex religious peace that emerged from two centuries of experimentation in accommodating religious differences. Rejecting the older authoritarian interpretations of the age of religious wars, the author uses traditional documentary sources as well as photographic evidence to show how a broad range of Europeans – from authoritative elites to a colorful array of religious "dissenters" – replaced the cultural "unity and purity" of late-medieval Christendom with a variable and durable pattern of religious diversity, deeply embedded in political, legal, and cultural institutions.

Wayne P. Te Brake is Professor of History Emeritus at Purchase College, SUNY, and the author of *Shaping History: Ordinary People in European Politics, 1500–1700.*

Cambridge Studies in Contentious Politics

Editors

Books in the Series

Ronald Aminzade, *Race, Nation, and Citizenship in Post-Colonial Africa: The Case of Tanzania*

Ronald Aminzade, et al., *Silence and Voice in the Study of Contentious Politics*

Javier Auyero, *Routine Politics and Violence in Argentina: The Gray Zone of State Power*

Phillip M. Ayoub, *When States Come Out: Europe's Sexual Minorities and the Politics of Visibility*

W. Lance Bennett and Alexandra Segerberg, *The Logic of Connective Action: Digital Media and the Personalization of Contentious Politics*

Amrita Basu, *Violent Conjunctures in Democratic India*

Clifford Bob, *The Marketing of Rebellion: Insurgents, Media, and International Activism*

Charles Brockett, *Political Movements and Violence in Central America*

Valerie Bunce and Sharon Wolchik, *Defeating Authoritarian Leaders in Postcommunist Countries*

Lars-Erik Cederman, Kristian Skrede Gleditsch, and Halvard Buhaug, *Inequality, Grievances, and Civil War*

Christian Davenport, *How Social Movements Die: Repression and Demobilization of the Republic of New Africa*

Christian Davenport, *Media Bias, Perspective, and State Repression*

Gerald F. Davis, Doug McAdam, W. Richard Scott, and Mayer N. Zald, *Social Movements and Organization Theory*

Donatella della Porta, *Clandestine Political Violence*

Mario Diani, *The Cement of Civil Society: Studying Networks in Localities*

Todd A. Eisenstadt, *Politics, Identity, and Mexico's Indigenous Rights Movements*

Daniel Q. Gillion, *The Political Power of Protest: Minority Activism and Shifts in Public Policy*

(continued after index)

Religious War and Religious Peace in Early Modern Europe

WAYNE P. TE BRAKE
Purchase College, SUNY

CAMBRIDGE
UNIVERSITY PRESS

University Printing House, Cambridge CB2 8BS, United Kingdom

Cambridge University Press is part of the University of Cambridge.

It furthers the University's mission by disseminating knowledge in the pursuit of education, learning and research at the highest international levels of excellence.

www.cambridge.org
Information on this title: www.cambridge.org/9781107459229

© Wayne P. Te Brake 2017

First published 2017

Printed in the United States of America by Sheridan Books, Inc.

A catalogue record for this publication is available from the British Library

ISBN 978-1-107-08843-6 Hardback
ISBN 978-1-107-45922-9 Paperback

In memory of David D. Bien and Charles Tilly

Contents

Figures, Illustrations, and Tables

x   *List of Figures, Illustrations, and Tables*

TABLES

Preface

This work presents a novel account of religious war, religious peace, and the origins of religious pluralism in Europe. Combining comparative historical analysis with contentious political analysis, I survey the history of six clusters of increasingly destructive religious war between 1529 and 1651, analyze the very diverse settlements that eventually brought each of these wars to an end, and describe the complex religious peace that emerged from two centuries of experimentation in accommodating religious differences. Rejecting the older authoritarian interpretations of the age of religious wars, this work uses traditional documentary sources as well as photographic evidence to show how a broad range of European political actors – from authoritative elites to a colorful array of religious "dissenters" – replaced the cultural "unity and purity" of late-medieval Christendom with a variable and durable pattern of peaceful religious coexistence, deeply embedded in political, legal, and cultural institutions. I conclude with some thoughts on how we might envision and work for religious peace in our own age of religious wars.

A book this ambitious takes a very long time to research and write, and I can well imagine that it will not be easy for nonexperts to read. Thus at the end of my long journey, I am pleased both to acknowledge the many people and institutions that have helped me on my way and to offer some simple advice to readers on how to approach the consumption of this book. The latter may seem gratuitous to my scholarly peers, but I have learned from my students, some of whom valiantly read these chapters when they were still in process, that with a little help, those who are not burdened by graduate training and scholarly aspirations can find something useful in my often dense prose. Indeed, it is my students at Purchase College whom I would like to thank first of all for their patience, hard work, and creativity, which helped me enormously in shaping this book.

Generous grants from two foundations encouraged me to ask bold questions about Europe's religious wars and their aftermath. A research grant from the

Harry Frank Guggenheim Foundation (1995–1996) made it possible for me to explore the relationship between religious solidarity, violence, and large-scale political change and to complete a book on popular politics and state formation. Between 1999 and 2004, a series of exploratory and project grants from the Ford Foundation allowed me to organize an international collaboration on the theme of accommodating religious differences and to begin collecting visual and photographic evidence of peaceful religious coexistence in the most unlikely places. The collaboration took the form of a preliminary conference in 2000 at the Italian Academy for Advanced Studies in America, at Columbia University, followed by a much larger conference in 2001 at the Netherlands Institute for Advanced Studies in the Humanities and Social Sciences, in Wassenaar, the Netherlands, which confirmed for me that peaceful religious coexistence was the rule, rather than the exception, in post-Reformation Europe. I am deeply indebted to my program officer at the Ford Foundation, Dr. Constance H. Buchanan, who provided precious financing as well as a dynamic intellectual community among her grantees, which proved to be critically important in how the project developed. I am also very grateful to the Italian Academy and Netherlands Institute for Advanced Studies (NIAS) for providing both conference facilities and a stimulating intellectual home away from home for extended periods of time.

For thirty-six years, Purchase College, which provides an extraordinary combination of liberal arts education and professional arts education within the State University of New York, provided me with an institutional context in which I could be myself and go my own way as a scholar, without disciplinary or departmental constraints. My colleagues in the School of Humanities were consistently indulgent of my requests for research leaves of absence, and in the later stages of this project, the college provided critical support in the form of the Kempner Distinguished Professorship, which provided a research stipend, and two paid research leaves toward the end of my teaching career. My *compagnon* in European history, Geoffrey Field, was not only the ideal colleague but an inspiration. I only wish that my colleague Robert M. Stein, who also defied disciplinary boundaries and helped me in so many ways, could have seen me bring this project to completion.

A very large number of scholars, most of whom I do not know personally, have made the completion of this broadly comparative book possible; their names populate the many footnotes and the large bibliography. I only hope I have not left anyone out! Several scholars deserve special mention, however. Keith Luria, Randolph Head, Karen Barkey, and Darwin Stapleton have read all or parts of the manuscript, offering sage intellectual advice as well as saving me from embarrassing errors; the mistakes that remain are all mine! My dear friend, Maxine Gaddis, will not claim to be a scholar, but she plowed through the manuscript for me nevertheless, offering valuable warnings and suggestions for improving its clarity along the way. My brother Bill, who is also a specialist on the Low Countries, was not as involved in this book as he was in its predecessors, but he knows his support and advice have always been treasured. Two anonymous scholars, who evaluated my book proposal for Cambridge University Press, offered extraordinarily helpful suggestions for the improvement of the book, for which I am very grateful; they may also be said to be responsible for increasing the size of the text by fifty percent and more than tripling the number of photographs. My commissioning editor at Cambridge University Press, Lewis Bateman, announced at a very early date that he would like to publish my book, and he was true to his word. That kind of confidence and support is a scholar's dream come true!

Two extraordinary scholars, teachers, and mentors were crucial to the course of my life as a historian: David D. Bien (1930–2015) and Charles Tilly (1929–2008). Together, they sponsored my work as a graduate student at The University of Michigan in a field of specialization that neither knew very much about; in the process, they showed me how to ask and answer important questions, comparatively and historically, without getting hopelessly entangled in the intellectual politics of received traditions. And while I could never come close to matching the precision of David's scholarship or the enormous breadth of Chuck's knowledge and analysis, their intellectual fingerprints are all over this work. It is my fond hope that both of them would have found it "interesting" and been proud of the fact that I finally got it done. For my part, I am proud to dedicate it to their memory.

My family – my wife, Nelva Lagerwey; our grown children, Martin, Maria, and Nicholas; and now our first grandchildren, Carter and Jenna – have, in various configurations, always been my anchor, both in my private and in my professional life. They have put up with me, nursed me through some significant challenges, and always brought me immense joy. I suppose I could have dedicated this work to them, but I think they will understand the choice I made; besides, they got the last one.

* * * *

And now some advice for the reader. I have always taught my undergraduates that reading an academic book like this one requires a strategy – one that doesn't necessarily involve reading every word from the beginning to the end. In general, one should start with the introduction and then turn to the conclusion for the simple reason that academics are not very good at alerting their readers to where the book will actually take them; how one then reads what comes in between depends on one's purpose, interests, and background. In this case – a book aimed at multiple audiences – the strategic choices are especially important.

In the body of this work, I am principally concerned with three problems: (1) How did Europe's religious wars start, and how did they develop over time? (2) How did the wars end, and what did their settlements look like? (3) What did religious peace actually look like, and how did it come into being? I try to answer each of these questions in each of the three parts of the book, which cover, roughly, the first half of the sixteenth century, the second half of the sixteenth century, and the seventeenth century, respectively. Altogether, the central chapters of the book tell a story of dramatic cultural change, account for similarities and differences that were evident in the various cases that are discussed, and suggest "who done it," not in the sense of a mystery with a surprise ending (go ahead and read the conclusion early on), but in the deliberate identification of the kinds of historical actors, many of whom remain nameless, who made the story unfold the way it did.

In order not to get lost in the historical weeds, I encourage readers to skip ahead or around if the story or analysis gets too dense at times; after all, one can read beginnings and endings of particular chapters just as one reads the beginnings and endings of books. For those who are particularly interested in the religious wars and how they changed over time, Chapters 2, 5, and 9 will be most important; those who are interested in military history, as such, will be disappointed because the emphasis here is on how the wars started and ended and not on how they were prosecuted. For those who are specifically interested in how wars end and what successful settlements look like, Chapters 3, 6, 7, and 10 will be most interesting; those who are interested in the peace-negotiation process, as such, will be disappointed because the emphasis here is on the outcome or product of negotiations, broadly defined as both formal and informal, lasting and ephemeral.

Those who are interested in the historical experiences of particular polities or places or in specific conflicts or peace agreements can use the index to read these chapters selectively. Those who are interested in how specific, recurrent mechanisms combine differently to produce different kinds of wars or peace settlements can also use the index to read selectively. Throughout the text and, by extension, in the index, I have italicized the various mechanisms that recurrently combined to produce politically salient religious identities, religious conflicts (including wars), and peace settlements of various kinds; I have done the same with the mechanisms that account for the survival of religious dissenters under active repression.

My hope is that all readers will be especially interested in my description and account of the variant forms of peaceful religious coexistence that emerged during these two centuries of religious controversy and conflict and constituted a durable and pervasive religious peace in Europe north of the Alps and Pyrenees. In order to envision a more peaceful world for ourselves, I believe that we need to develop a more realistic – that is, historically informed – understanding of what religious peace actually looks like. In this regard, Chapters 4, 8, 11, and 12 are most important, and while I would like to think that all the historical details are important, even these chapters can be read selectively, using the index to focus on the nature of religious peace in particular polities or places, or to explore the prevalence of the variant forms of religious coexistence In both the text and the index, I have used **boldface** to highlight the principal forms of religious coexistence that were widely dispersed throughout Europe.

In some sense, I have lived and wrestled with the questions that inform this book my whole life. I distinctly remember being haunted as a teenager, growing up in a Dutch Calvinist household in rural Minnesota, by the words of Luke 19:42: "Would that even today you knew the things that make for peace! But now they are hid from your eyes." What *are* the things that make for peace, and why should they be *hidden*? Isn't it our responsibility to seek them out and make them visible? As a young adult at Calvin College, I was confronted by the moral ambiguity and the grim reality of the Vietnam War; despite the bellicose example of my Dutch forebears, I decided to become a conscientious objector, having reached the conclusion, under the pressure of the draft, that in our time, war is the problem, not the solution to our problems. As a graduate student, I began a career-long study of the role of violence, in its various collective forms, in the process of political and social change – first in the age of democratic revolutions, then in the process of early modern state formation, and now in the cultural transformations of Reformation and post-Reformation Europe. At the end of this journey, then, all I can do – having chosen to approach the problems of our world, not as an activist, but as a teacher and a writer – is offer this work to you, the reader, in the hope that it will encourage you to question the facile association of "religious diversity" with "disorder" and "violence" and to envision a more peaceful future.

Ossining, New York
November 2015

I

Religion and Violence, War and Peace

In the winter of 1562, France was on the brink of civil war. An official attempt to reconcile theological differences between representatives of the established French Church and the recently organized Reformed churches had failed in the autumn of 1561. Then, rather than fostering peace as it was intended to do, the Edict of Saint-Germain (January 1562), which granted limited legality to Reformed Protestant worship, had produced even greater uncertainty about government policy and further polarization between the religious factions. What many regard as the first shots of civil war were fired on March 1, when troops raised by the Catholic partisan, Charles, duke of Guise, attacked unarmed Reformed worshipers near the town of Vassy. A month later, a national Reformed Synod, which included lay and clerical representatives, responded to the "massacre" at Vassy by proclaiming Louis, prince of Condé, the protector of all Protestant churches in the kingdom, thus linking their churches with mobilization for war.

Meanwhile, Reformed partisans began executing plans to seize power in towns throughout France. In Rouen, for example, on the night of April 15, a group of armed Huguenots – as the French Reformed Protestants came to be called during the civil wars – took over the Hôtel de Ville and the city gates and began securing their political and military domination of the city. In early May, in a wave of iconoclasm, zealous Huguenots physically destroyed the sacred symbols – altars, baptismal fonts, statues, pews – associated with Catholic worship in the city's churches and precipitated a significant Catholic exodus from Rouen.[1]

In the southern city of Toulouse, however, an attempted coup by Huguenot partisans failed miserably. The local Huguenot coalition could count on

---

[1] For a general introduction to the religious wars in France, see Arlette Jouanna, et al., *Histoire et dictionaire des Guerres de Religion* (Paris: Robert Laffont, 1998) and Mack P. Holt, *The French Wars of Religion, 1562–1629*, New Approaches to European History (Cambridge: Cambridge University Press, 1995); for Rouen, see Philip Benedict, *Rouen during the Wars of Religion* (Cambridge: Cambridge University Press, 1981).

considerable support within the municipal administration, which had always been keen to defend local political self-regulation, but was staunchly opposed by the judges of the sovereign royal court – the *parlement* – which only registered the January Edict of Saint-Germain under royal order and actively worked to undermine its provisions. In early April 1562, Toulouse first experienced serious sectarian violence when Catholics, celebrating the feast of Saint-Salvador, disrupted a Protestant funeral; in the melee that ensued, a number of Huguenots were killed or wounded. Still, local mediation produced a truce that lasted until the leaders of the newly organized Reformed congregation decided, amid gathering evidence of civil war elsewhere, to take immediate, preemptive action on the night of May 11. Having already smuggled arms and men into the city, the Protestant forces occupied the Hôtel de Ville and several colleges of the city's university and quickly assembled barricades to fortify those parts of the city where they were strongest. Although momentarily surprised, the much larger Roman Catholic coalition, organized earlier in the year by means of a *syndicat*, was nevertheless ready to meet the challenge of Protestant insurrection. Following four days of very destructive urban warfare, a truce was arranged on May 16, which amounted to a capitulation by the Huguenots' forces. The Protestants, who had suffered heavy casualties, were granted limited safe conduct in order to leave the city by the evening of the seventeenth, but amid the chaos of the Protestant exodus, the truce broke down, and many more Protestants were killed by vengeful Catholics outside the city's gates. By the time the dust had settled, perhaps as many as 4,000 people, or nearly ten percent of the city's population, had died.[2]

* * * * *

By all accounts, the long series of civil wars that began in France in the late winter and spring of 1562 can be considered religious wars – indeed, they were among Europe's most violent and destructive – and even this brief sketch highlights some of the dynamics that we might expect to find in the run-up to religious war in Reformation and post-Reformation Europe: that is, apparently irreconcilable theological differences, widespread politicization of religious controversies, popular mobilization and collective action on behalf of religious causes, political brokerage that connects popular religious movements with military specialists, and so on. Not all of Europe's religious wars were as violent and destructive as the civil wars in France; yet considered together, they reveal a great deal about the political dynamics that lead recurrently to religious war.

---

[2] On the events in Toulouse and their immediate aftermath, see Mark Greengrass, "The Anatomy of a Religious Riot in Toulouse in May 1562," *Journal of Ecclesiastical History* 34 (1983): 367–91, and Joan Davies, "Persecution and Protestantism: Toulouse, 1562–1575," *The Historical Journal* 22 (1979): 31–51.

Although it may be relatively easy to sketch how a complex series of religious wars began, it is rather more difficult to suggest how they ended. In the short term, the French civil war that began in early 1562 was ended by the Peace of Amboise on March 19, 1563, with the accompanying Edict of Amboise spelling out more precisely than the original Edict of Saint-Germain had done the limited toleration that would be granted to Protestant worship within the kingdom of France. Yet civil war broke out again briefly in September 1567, with the Peace and Edict of Longjumeau of March 23, 1568, reiterating more precisely still the terms of the Edict of Amboise. And so it went through a series of seven starts and stops between 1562 and 1580, with most of the intervals of war and peace lasting two years or less. Beginning in 1585, however, a much longer round of war ended thirteen years later on April 30, 1598, with the Peace and Edict of Nantes, by far the most complex of all the peace settlements, which many scholars regard as the end of the French civil and religious wars.[3] Still, an intermittent war started again in the 1620s following the assassination of King Henry IV, and ended finally on June 16, 1629, with the Peace and Edict of Alais. The Edict of Alais reaffirmed the terms of the religious settlement but revised the security arrangements of the Edict of Nantes.[4]

So precisely when and how did the French civil and religious wars actually end? In some sense, the answer is that the religious conflicts were never really settled because, from the 1630s onward, the royal government of France continued to encroach on the liberties it had guaranteed to French Protestants until, by the Edict of Fontainebleau in October 1685, King Louis XIV formally revoked the Edict of Nantes. This official revocation of the terms of France's most enduring peace settlement precipitated not only a massive exodus of Protestants from France but eventually a new civil war in 1702 to eliminate militarily the continued challenge of the Protestant "Camisards" in the south of France; this War of the Camisards, which may in some sense be considered the last of the French wars of religion, ended indecisively with no formal settlement in 1706. Despite the eventual failure of all of France's peace settlements, even this brief sketch highlights one of the principal dynamics that led recurrently toward peace in early modern Europe: negotiated political settlements that made peace possible, though not necessarily durable. Not all of Europe's religious wars proved to be as difficult to settle as the French wars, but considered together, their varied settlements reveal a great deal about the political dynamics that have recurrently led away from religious violence and war toward more or less durable patterns of peace.

---

[3] See the very useful table in Philip Benedict, "Settlements: France," in *Visions, Programs and Outcomes*, vol. 2 of *Handbook of European History, 1400–1600*, ed. Thomas A. Brady, Heiko A. Oberman, and James D. Tracy (Leiden: E. J. Brill, 1995), 436–8; see also Table 5.1 in this volume.

[4] See Holt, *French Wars*, which includes this seventeenth-century extension of the Wars of Religion.

In the chapters that follow, I will use comparative historical analysis to explore the dynamic mechanisms and historical processes that account for religious violence and war in order to explore, by extension, those mechanisms and processes that account for religious peace. Understanding religious war and religious peace is a tall order, of course, but the history of early modern Europe provides a very solid foundation on which to build this kind of comparative analysis for the simple reasons that the religious wars of the sixteenth and seventeenth centuries are generally well documented, and the historical literature on a broad range of cases allows us to see not only how Europe's religious wars began, but also how they ended, or in some cases, kept on beginning and ending. As I see it, the intellectual and moral challenge that the resurgent phenomenon of religious war presents us with in our own time is to connect beginnings of religious wars with possible endings – that is, to imagine how a world engulfed in religious conflict and war might once again find peace and what that peace might look like.

UNDERSTANDING RELIGIOUS WAR

How will we recognize and account for religious war when we see it? It is tempting, perhaps even conventional, to identify religious war in terms of the motives and intentions of the combatants. By this criterion, the series of European Crusades to conquer the Holy Land from the Muslim "infidels" who ruled it are likely to enjoy pride of place as Europe's most obvious and sensational religious wars.[5] And by extension today, some commentators are inclined, using this criterion, to identify ours as a new age of religious war, given the obvious religious motives of radical Islamic groups (among many others) that have, in various places around the globe, declared a holy war on the evil forces of Western modernization and secularism.[6] By this criterion, too, historians often suggest that Europe's age of religious wars only ended when economic competition replaced religious competition as the principal motive for war toward the end of the seventeenth century.[7]

---

[5] There is an enormous literature on the history of the Crusades, but see especially the work of Norman Housley, who links the religious warfare of the later Crusades with the early modern wars of religion in *Religious Warfare in Europe, 1400–1536* (Oxford: Oxford University Press, 2002).

[6] See, for example, Mark Juergensmeyer, *Terror in the Mind of God: The Global Rise of Religious Violence* (Berkeley: University of California Press, 2000), and Andrew Sullivan, "This Is Religious War," *The New York Times Magazine*, 7 October 2001. Cf. Mohammed Ayoob, *The Many Faces of Political Islam: Religion and Politics in the Muslim World* (Ann Arbor: University of Michigan Press, 2008).

[7] See, for example, T. K. Rabb, *The Struggle for Stability in Early Modern Europe* (Oxford: Oxford University Press, 1975); Richard S. Dunn, *The Age of Religious Wars, 1559–1715*, The Norton History of Modern Europe (New York: Norton, 1979); and Mark Konnert, *Early Modern Europe: The Age of Religious War, 1559–1715* (Peterborough, Ont., Canada; Orchard Park, NY, USA: Broadview Press, 2006).

There are obvious and perhaps insurmountable difficulties, however, in determining the real or essential motives of the multiple historical actors who account for the kind of warfare that swept France in the second half of the sixteenth century. Where will we get reliable evidence of motives and intentions? Which actors' motives and intentions count? How will we know whether stated intentions represent real motives? Which, in a complex mixture of motives, might we consider the most significant or decisive? Because these questions are so difficult to answer, the individual, cognitive dimensions of religious conflict and violence are unlikely to serve as a reliable guide for either contemporary or historical analysis.[8] In any case, we know from a broad range of historical research, especially on the nature of violent conflict and revolution, that the intentions of particular actors are notoriously unreliable predictors of outcomes in complex political processes.

Since violent religious conflict is, at bottom, a relational problem, not simply a cognitive problem, we will be much better served, I believe, to highlight as our point of departure the more readily visible and verifiable social and relational dimensions of religious war. For our present purposes, we can regard as *religious* any warfare or ongoing conflict in which (1) the forces in conflict *identify their enemies* in terms of religious beliefs, practices, or affiliations; (2) mobilization for the conflict invokes broader networks of support and solidarity based on *religious identities*.[9] These simple criteria highlight the ways in which contentious political actors use their religious identities and affiliations to mark both their political oppositions and their political alignments.[10] Despite their being more specific and demanding in the sense that they require us to attend to the interactions of multiple combatants, these criteria are nevertheless capacious enough to include not only the medieval Crusades, but also a number of recent conflicts, both in Europe and beyond. Applying these criteria to early modern Europe, we can readily identify six distinct, yet interrelated, clusters of religious war (Table 1.1). At once familiar to scholars and clearly depressing to even the most casual observer, Table 1.1 suggests that there was religious war somewhere in Europe north of the Alps and the Pyrenees almost continuously for well over a century between 1529 and 1651.[11]

---

[8] Cf. Konrad Repgen, "What Is a 'Religious War'?" in *Politics and Society in Reformation Europe. Essays for Sir Geoffrey Elton on His Sixty-Fifth Birthday*, ed. E. I. Kouri and Tom Scott (London: Macmillan Press, 1987), 311–28. Repgen, too, rejects an inquiry into the motives of the protagonists; he focuses instead on public legitimations for war, which still privileges the cognitive activities of rulers and their agents and offers no practical guidance for understanding the political processes involved in either war making or peacemaking.

[9] Compare the more restrictive version of this definition in Wayne Te Brake, *Shaping History: Ordinary People in European Politics, 1500–1700* (Berkeley and Los Angeles: University of California Press, 1998), 115.

[10] On the importance of attending to alignments as well as oppositions in the study of contentious politics, see Te Brake, *Shaping History*, 13–17.

[11] I should point out, however, that the list of wars in Table 1.1 is more inclusive than most accounts of Europe's religious wars in that it includes the less violent and destructive wars in

TABLE 1.1 *The principal clusters of religious war in early modern Europe*

War	Geographic Area	Inclusive Dates
Kappel wars	Swiss Confederation	1529–1531
Schmalkaldic wars	German-Roman Empire	1545–1555
Civil/religious wars	France	1562–1629
Eighty Years War	Low Countries	1568–1648
Thirty Years War	German-Roman Empire	1618–1648
Civil wars	British Isles	1638–1651

Altogether these relational criteria are useful for comparative historical research, because following Charles Tilly's approach to collective violence, they do not assume that religious wars are fundamentally different from other forms of lethal conflict and coordinated destruction. In his most recent work on the politics of collective violence, Tilly wrote that in lethal contests,

at least two organized groups of specialists in coercion confront each other, each using harm to reduce or contain the others' capacity to inflict harm. War is the most general label for this class of coordinated destruction, but different variants go by the names of civil war, guerrilla, low-intensity conflict, and conquest.[12]

In addition to *lethal contests* or war, the other major forms of coordinated destruction that Tilly identifies are *"campaigns of annihilation* [in which category he includes genocide] when one contestant wields overwhelming force or the object of the attack is not an organization specialized in the deployment of coercive means," and *"conspiratorial terror* when a small but organized set of actors begins attacking vastly more powerful targets by clandestine means – assassinations, kidnappings, bombings, and the like."[13]

Situating and explaining the incidence of coordinated destruction within the larger framework of an integrated analysis of the politics of collective violence, Tilly emphasizes shades of variation rather than hard and fast boundaries among such heavily freighted concepts as war, genocide, and terror. Distinctions among these categories, he suggests, rest on the relative degree of

Switzerland and Germany prior to the French civil and religious wars, which often serve as the touchstone for definitions of religious war in Europe. The analytic value of the more inclusive approach I am adopting here should become evident in later chapters.

[12] Charles Tilly, *The Politics of Collective Violence*, Cambridge Studies in Contentious Politics (Cambridge: Cambridge University Press, 2003), 104.

[13] Tilly, *Collective Violence*, 104. It is important to distinguish Tilly's later work on collective violence from his earliest work, which identified often rigid historical typologies; cf. Charles Tilly, "Collective Violence in European Perspective," in *The History of Violence in America: Historical and Comparative Perspectives*, ed. Hugh Davis Graham and Ted Robert Gurr (New York: F. A. Praeger, 1969).

inequality among the contestants, who prominently include incumbent governments as well as challengers to their authority. In general,

[c]oordinated destruction occurs when well organized incumbents strike down resistance to their demands, when incumbents use force of arms to extend their jurisdictions, and when excluded parties organize on a sufficient scale to challenge incumbents' own armed force. These effects become stronger when the parties on either side of the boundary polarize – when cooperative arrangements and overlapping actors disappear – and/or when uncertainty about the other side's future actions increases on either or both sides.[14]

Tilly's relational approach to collective violence, in general, and war, in particular, shuns universal explanations of closely defined categorical phenomena; instead he underscores variable trajectories and historical contingency, and he focuses on the causal mechanisms and processes that help us to account for the complexity of specific historical developments, such as the incidence of religious war in Reformation and post-Reformation Europe.[15] With regard to France's descent into religious war in 1562, for instance, Tilly's work alerts us to the family resemblance among different sorts of coordinated destruction without requiring that we choose between terms such as "war" and "civil war," or even "low-intensity conflicts." What started out as a civil war in France in 1562 easily escalated into an interstate war in the coming years as both sides sought and received the help of external allies, but it also frequently settled locally or regionally into low-intensity conflicts, as was the case in Rouen, or even veered off into something like a campaign of annihilation in the case of Toulouse following the collapse of the Protestant cause in 1562. Nationally, however, we can safely say that France's violent religious conflicts remained in or near the realm of coordinated destruction, with notable interludes of relative peace following negotiated truces, for decades to come.[16]

UNDERSTANDING RELIGIOUS PEACE

How, in turn, will we recognize and account for religious peace when we see it? It is tempting, perhaps even conventional, to set a high standard for religious peace: real peace, we are often told, is much more than the simple absence of war; rather, it can only be predicated on reconciliation and/or justice. This high standard might even seem historically appropriate to early modern Europe inasmuch as many of those who actually drafted reasonably effective, but

---

[14] Tilly, *Collective Violence*, 105.

[15] For comparative historians, identifying and measuring broadly operative mechanisms can be critically important to the development of new and more precise understandings of the variations evident among recurrent phenomena. See Doug McAdam, Sidney Tarrow, and Charles Tilly, *Dynamics of Contention* (New York: Cambridge University Press, 2001), and Doug McAdam, Sidney Tarrow, and Charles Tilly, "Methods of Measuring Mechanisms of Contention," *Qualitative Sociology* 31, no. 4 (December 2008): 307–31.

[16] For a specification of the various French wars between 1562 and 1629 and the negotiated truces that ended them, see Table 5.1 and Chapters 5, 6, and 7 in this volume.

often messy, peace settlements saw their work as provisional – that is, as a temporary necessity, an unfortunate compromise, until such time as a purer ideal, religious reconciliation, could be achieved. Indeed, many of the participants in Europe's religious wars appear to have yearned for the restoration of an imagined religious unity and/or purity of an earlier day; whether that earlier day was the Latin Christendom of the Middle Ages or the prophetic and persecuted Church of Antiquity spoke volumes, of course, about the religious politics of the participant. By this standard, however, we would, in fact, find little evidence of religious peace in early modern Europe, or in any other time and place for that matter.

For our purposes, we will do well to adopt a more clearly relational standard. *Religious peace* may be identified with two conditions: (1) the more-or-less durable *absence of the coordinated destruction of religious war*, as defined earlier, and (2) the continued *presence of some form of religious coexistence.*[17] By this less exacting standard, we will not expect to see the absence of religious contention, as such, or even of episodic religious violence, as long it does not escalate to the level of coordinated destruction, conspiratorial terror, or campaigns of annihilation. Like the relational criteria for religious war, this simple standard for religious peace highlights the relational, as opposed to the cognitive, aspects of the historical problem. More fundamentally, it turns our attention toward the kinds of settlements that were actually produced and reproduced in early modern Europe – messy and fragile though they might be – and eventually laid the foundations of religious pluralism in the modern West. Thus the intellectual and moral challenge, as I see it, is to describe and account for the ways in which historical actors, despite their professed ideals of religious unity and purity, have learned to manage and ultimately to live with the kinds of religious differences that have recurrently served as the principal markers of political enmity and whose activation in specific settings recurrently set the stage for religious war.

So how did the clusters of religious war listed in Table 1.1 actually end? Table 1.2 offers a summary answer to this question. Now, in the minds of those who prosecute them, wars and other lethal contests are undoubtedly about winning and losing, and a survey of more than seventy civil wars worldwide between 1940 and 1992 indicates that approximately sixty percent ended in decisive military victories.[18] Yet, as Table 1.2 suggests, it is strikingly difficult to discern clear winners and losers at the end of Europe's religious wars. With the exception of the last case – the cluster of civil wars in the composite monarchy of England, Scotland, and Ireland – all of the most prominent wars of religion ended

[17] Cf. Penny Roberts, "The Languages of Peace during the French Religious Wars," *Cultural and Social History* 4, no. 3 (2007): 305: "Peace is more than simply the absence of war; it requires a process by which pacification can be maintained."

[18] See table A.1 in Barbara F. Walter, *Committing to Peace: The Successful Settlement of Civil Wars* (Princeton: Princeton University Press, 2002), 169–70.

TABLE 1.2 *Europe's religious wars and their settlements*

Religious War	Military Outcome or Peace Settlement
Kappel wars (Switzerland) (1529, 1531)	National Peace [*Landfrieden*] of Kappel (1529), **Second National Peace of Kappel** (1531)
Schmalkaldic wars (Germany) (1545–1555, intermittently)	[Peace of Nürmberg (1532)], Augsburg Interim (1548), Treaty of Passau (1552), **Religious Peace [*Religionsfriede*] of Augsburg** (1555)
Civil/religious wars (France) (1562–1629, intermittently)	Separate edicts ended each of the nine wars; the most successful was the **Edict of Nantes** (1598), which was revoked by Louis XIV (1685)
Eighty Years War (Low Countries) (1568–1648)	The Pacification of Ghent (1576), Peace of Religion (1578), Twelve Year Truce (1609–1621), and the (first) Treaty of Münster, which was part of the **Peace of Westphalia** (1648)
Thirty Years War (Germany) (1618–1648)	The Treaty of Osnabrück and the (second) Treaty of Münster, which were part of the **Peace of Westphalia** (1648)
Civil wars (Scotland, Ireland, England) (1638–1651)	No formal settlement; war ended in England with the capture, trial, and execution of Charles I (1649); war ended in Ireland and Scotland with Oliver Cromwell's military campaigns (1649–1651); monarchy restored in 1660

with some form of political compromise that was expressed in the text of a truce, an edict, or a treaty.

Even in the exceptional cases, however, winning and losing was not as clear or as unambiguous as it might at first seem. In the civil wars in England, the rebellious New Model Army under the command of Oliver Cromwell won a decisive victory over the forces of King Charles I in 1648. Then, having executed the king, abolished the monarchy, and disestablished the Anglican Church in 1649, the revolutionary forces went on to crush both the Irish Confederates and the Scottish Covenanters in order to consolidate their power in all three of the kingdoms that constituted the composite British state. But military success by 1651 was followed, within just a few years, by political failure and gave way not only to a restoration of the monarchy in all three kingdoms, but the reestablishment of the Anglican Church.[19] Indeed, unambiguous winners and losers are hard to find in Europe's religious wars.

[19] See Martyn Bennett, *The Civil Wars in Britain and Ireland, 1638–1651* (Oxford: Blackwell Publishers, 1997); Austin Woolrych, *Britain in Revolution, 1625–1660* (Oxford: Oxford University Press, 2002); and Allan I. Macinnes, *The British Revolution, 1629–1660*, British

If the bulk of the religious wars ended formally with some kind of negotiated settlement, it was certainly not without difficulty. Between the first shocks of the "Luther question" in 1517 and the Peace of Westphalia in 1648, many attempted settlements went wrong and gave way to renewed violence; still, in the process of trying and often failing, the forces in conflict were eventually able to strike a series of political compromises that made enduring peace possible. The first of these compromise settlements – the *Landfrieden* (National Peace) in Switzerland and the *Religionsfriede* (Religious Peace) of Augsburg in Germany – institutionalized a pattern of fragmented cultural sovereignty that mirrored the fragmentation and layering of political sovereignty in both the Swiss *Eidgenossenschaft* (Oath Confederation) and the German *Reich*. The French Edict of Nantes, by contrast, preserved the unitary political sovereignty of the French monarchy by recognizing legally what many in Latin Christendom at the time considered unthinkable: the coexistence of two separate and protected institutional churches, the Roman and the Reformed. Of the three treaties that constituted the Peace of Westphalia, only the Treaty of Osnabrück addressed specifically the religious differences that divided the empire; although much more elaborate as a whole, its provisions for the religious peace in Germany in many ways simply amplified or made adjustments to the earlier *Religionsfriede* of Augsburg, especially with regard to the question of religious sovereignty. However, it included as well an explicit guarantee of the individual's freedom of religious conscience, which legitimated religious diversity, not only among the constituent territories of the empire, but within them. By contrast, the conspicuous silence on religious matters in the First Treaty of Münster – by which both Spain and the Dutch Republic gave up on their long-standing goals of reuniting the seventeen Low Countries territories, both religiously and politically – validated without specification the religious diversity that had emerged as facts on the ground in the course of eight long decades of inconclusive military struggle.

Historians have traditionally glossed the pattern of territorial religious differentiation that was shaped by these settlements in starkly authoritarian terms – *cuius regio eius religio* (whose the rule, his the religion)[20] – and the

Studies Series (Houndmills, Basingstoke, Hampshire; New York, NY: Palgrave Macmillan, 2005).

[20] This simple, thus memorable, epigram with its unambiguously authoritarian thrust has been a staple of Western civilization textbooks and undergraduate history education for more than a century, but I should note that it does not actually appear in any of the official documents relating directly to the religious wars or their negotiated settlements; it is rather a retrospective characterization, coined in the late sixteenth century by J. Stephani, an Evangelical canonist from Greifswald, in northern Germany. See Martin Heckel, *Staat und Kirche nach den Lehren der evangelischen Juristen Deutschlands in der ersten Hälfte des 17. Jahrhunderts*, Jus ecclesiasticum, vol. 6 (München: Claudius-Verlag, 1968); cf. Thomas A. Brady Jr., "Settlements: The Holy Roman Empire," in *Visions, Programs and Outcomes*, vol. 2 of *Handbook of European History, 1400–1600*, ed. Thomas A. Brady, Heiko A. Oberman, and James D. Tracy (Leiden: E. J. Brill, 1995), 352–3. *Cuius regio eius religio* gained common currency among historians only in

recently dominant "confessionalization" paradigm in early modern historiography clearly built on and reinforced that ruler-centered, authoritarian interpretation of the religious peace.[21] In order to understand more precisely how these very diverse agreements actually made peace possible, it is necessary to reject the cultural absolutism of *cuius regio eius religio* as a point of departure and to take a fresh look at the negotiated settlements – both the successes and the failures – in relation to the very different wars they sought to end. We need to ask how the political compromises they entailed disrupted or deflected the historical mechanisms that led recurrently to religious war.

In principle, some form of theological reconciliation might have solved the problem of religious war by eliminating the underlying theological issues and erasing the religious identity boundaries associated with them. In the absence of a religious reconciliation, however, we will need to attend to very different historical processes to describe and account for religious peace. Those who undertook to negotiate an end to the religious wars invariably sought ways to reduce the political salience of their enduring religious differences by offering mutual recognition, pledging mutual security, and adopting formal procedures to mediate or adjudicate conflicts that activated religious boundaries. The thrust of the negotiated settlements was, thus, to create a variety of politically acceptable spaces for religious diversity and coexistence, despite the continuing "intolerance" of many of the individual historical actors.

TOWARD A COMPARATIVE HISTORY OF WAR AND PEACE

The chapters that follow will explore the frequent alternations between religious war and religious peace in early modern Europe by means of a series of three paired historical comparisons: (1) the Kappel and Schmalkaldic wars in Switzerland and Germany and their settlements; (2) the civil/religious wars in France and the Eighty Years War in the Low Countries and their settlements; and (3) the Thirty Years War in Germany and the civil wars in Scotland, Ireland, and England and their settlements. The goal of these paired comparisons is twofold. On the one hand, as a social scientist, I want to demonstrate how a limited set of recurrent mechanisms and processes can help us to describe and account for the incidence of both religious war and religious peace in early modern Europe, although my more precise ambition, following the lead of

the second half of the nineteenth century; see Archibald S. Foord, "Historical Revisions: The Peace of Augsburg," *New England Social Studies Bulletin* 9 (1952): 1–7.
[21] For a summary of the confessionalization perspective, see Heinz Schilling, "Confessional Europe," in *Visions, Programs and Outcomes*, vol. 2 of *Handbook of European History, 1400–1600*, ed. Thomas A. Brady, Heiko A. Oberman, and James D. Tracy (Leiden: E. J. Brill, 1995), 641–81. For an excellent summary and a review of the most important critiques of the confessionalization paradigm, see Ute Lotz-Heumann, "The Concept of 'Confessionalization': A Historiographical Paradigm in Dispute," *Memoria y Civilizacion* 4 (2001): 93–201. See also Philip S. Gorski, *The Disciplinary Revolution: Calvinism and the Rise of the State in Early Modern Europe* (Chicago: University of Chicago Press, 2003), 15–22.

Doug McAdam, Sidney Tarrow, and Charles Tilly in *Dynamics of Contention*, is "to show how different settings, sequences, and combinations of mechanisms produce contrasting political processes and outcomes."[22] On the other hand, as a historian, I want to tell stories of change over time, both in the patterns of religious violence and war and, perhaps more controversially, in the nature of religious peace. As I see it, the clusters of religious war and the settlements that eventually brought them to an end – thus, making durable peace possible – constitute important episodes in the larger history of religious freedom and human rights. Unfortunately, this important history has been largely obscured by the traditional deference that historians have given to the claims and aspirations of rulers and the equally limiting tendency toward narrow geographic and chronological specialization in historical studies. My goal is not to displace the Peace of Westphalia as the touchstone of modern politics, but to redefine the political and cultural modernity that it played an important role in creating.[23]

The comparative historical analyses that follow will emphasize a limited number of historical mechanisms and processes that, I will argue, recurrently combined to produce and reproduce the alternations between religious war and religious peace that are at the heart of this analysis. By mechanisms, social scientists denote a delimited class of events or interactions that alter the relations among historical actors in identical or closely similar ways across a variety of situations. Processes, by extension, are clusters or concatenations of mechanisms that recurrently alter the relations of historical actors over longer periods of time and in a variety of situations with a limited range of variant outcomes. By way of introduction, then, let me identify three important clusters of mechanisms that recurrently combined to produce: (1) politically salient religious identities; (2) religious conflicts, including religious war; and (3) religious peace, in variant forms of religious coexistence.

Like politically significant identities more generally, religious identities provide collective answers to such questions as Who are you? Who are we? and Who are they?[24] When the answers that political actors give to these questions invoke important elements of religious belief, ritual behavior, or sectarian affiliation, we can call them *religious identities*. Conceived in this way, religious identities are relational and subject to challenge, revision, and negotiation; they entail boundaries separating "us" from "them," social relations within as well as across the boundaries, and stories about what those boundaries mean and where the boundaries come from. Thus, contrary to

---

[22] McAdam, Tarrow, and Tilly, *Dynamics of Contention*, 83; this goal is part of the larger "uncommon foundations" strategy of paired comparisons articulated on pages 80–4. See also, Sidney Tarrow, "The Strategy of Paired Comparison: Toward a Theory of Practice," *Comparative Political Studies* 43, no. 2 (2010): 230–59.

[23] See Chapters 10 and 11.

[24] Cf. Charles Tilly, "Political Identities in Changing Polities," *Social Research* 70 (2003): 1301–15.

a familiar thread of traditional wisdom, religious identities are neither "immutable" nor the "essential" characteristics of particular groups or individuals. Indeed, as the early history of the Protestant Reformation demonstrates, on some remarkable occasions politically salient religious identities almost seem to appear out of thin air or change overnight. Consider the following sequence.

In the fall of 1517, the young German theologian Martin Luther famously issued his public challenge to debate a series of ninety-five propositions in which, having previously outlined a bold new theology of the core Christian concept of grace, he attacked the validity of specific religious practices, especially the sale of indulgences, rooted in the late-medieval sacramental system.[25] In very short order, Luther found himself enmeshed in a variety of ongoing debates and controversies that came quickly to be known as the "Luther question." When his opponents refused to concede his debating points, Luther appealed to a higher authority, and when the Papacy condemned some of his core ideas, he symbolically burned the papal bull that declared his work suspect. In 1521, Luther was summoned to defend himself before the German *Reichstag* (imperial diet) meeting at Worms; there, confronted by Emperor Charles V's resolute defense of religious unity and papal orthodoxy, Luther stated equally firmly in his own defense: "Here I stand. I can do no other."[26] When the diet, the highest political authority in the German-Roman Empire, issued a condemnation of Luther's teachings in the Edict of Worms, a sophisticated set of religious ideas had become thoroughly politicized, and a new seed bed of religious identities had been opened up.

Not all of the seedlings grew to maturity, of course; in fact, some were crowded out by sturdy perennials such as "heretic" and "reformer." In the early years of the struggles, however, the identities and the boundaries they indicated remained remarkably fluid. Although there was a long history of reform movements in Western Christendom, "reformer" took on new, more specific meanings in the context of the "Luther question." Generically it indicated those who attacked corruption in the Church, with significant variations such as "Lutheran," "Zwinglian," or later "Calvinist." Over time,

---

[25] For general surveys of the Reformation, see Euan Cameron, *The European Reformation* (Oxford: Clarendon Press, 1991); James D. Tracy, *Europe's Reformations, 1450–1650*, Critical Issues in History (Lanham, MD: Rowman and Littlefield, 1999); and Diarmaid MacCulloch, *The Reformation* (New York: Viking, 2004). Cf. Robert Wuthnow, *Communities of Discourse: Ideology and Social Structure in the Reformation, the Enlightenment, and European Socialism* (Cambridge, MA: Harvard University Press, 1989); Wuthnow emphasizes the importance for the *success* of culturally critical movements of going beyond simple criticism of the status quo to suggest concrete forms of symbolic or figural action that followers might undertake to indicate their allegiance; Luther's theses, as well as his many sermons and pamphlets, may be said to have done that much more concretely than his theological discourses.

[26] The classic account is in Roland Bainton, *Here I Stand: A Life of Martin Luther* (New York: Abingdon-Cokesbury Press, 1950).

the related term "Reformed" came to designate specific movements and churches modeled on the Swiss-based Zwinglian-Calvinist example, as distinct from the Lutheran churches of Germany and Scandinavia, and in official French usage this eventually became "the so-called Reformed Religion."

The most inclusive identity of all – "Protestant" – didn't come into existence until there was a formal, organized "protest" in 1529 among the highest circles of German politics against the authoritarian drift of imperial policy; thus it had more clearly a political than a theological meaning before it was gradually applied to all those who challenged the established Church. Still, both the Religious Peace of Augsburg in 1555 and the Peace of Westphalia in 1648 identified the German Protestants simply as the adherents of the "Augsburg Confession," which was a descriptive apologia of Lutheran religious practices that had been presented to the imperial diet in 1530. Among the various Protestant movements, all of which were roundly condemned as "heretical" by the established Church, some new identities betrayed specific theological positions, such as the generic "Anabaptists" (i.e., "re-baptizers" who did not recognize the validity of infant baptism) and church-institutional positions, such as "Presbyterians" and "Independents." Others originated as terms of derision that later became badges of pride, including the French "Huguenots," the Dutch "Beggars," and the English "Quakers."[27]

On the other side of the coin, those who defended the established Church from attack struggled to find a common identity, although their enemies commonly identified them as "papists" and "idolaters." Monarchs typically swore to defend the Church and true religion in their coronation oaths, and the French kings, in particular, proudly laid claim to the title "Most Christian King." Even Henry VIII of England earned the title "Defender of the Faith" by attacking Luther's ideas before eventually breaking with Rome for dynastic reasons. Subsequently, the massive popular mobilization in 1536 that condemned the "heresies of Luther" and defended the established Church in England against Henry VIII's modest Reformation styled itself as a "Pilgrimage of Grace." As late as 1555, the *Religionsfriede* of Augsburg referred simply to "the old religion" while the broad coalition that eventually formed to defend the established Church in France in the course of the religious wars called itself the *Sainte Union* (Sacred Union or League). In the end, the geographical location of the Church's institutional center at Rome and its explicit claim to universality informed the label that historians most often use retrospectively, but the principal actors themselves were for a long time reluctant to trade an inclusive, universalist "Christian" identity for something as parochial as "Roman Catholic."

The religious identities at play in the conflicts of the Reformation and post-Reformation eras were, thus, many and various; they remained fluid and

---

[27] On the origins of terms "Huguenots" and "Beggars," see Chapter 5. On the "Quakers," see Chapters 10 and 12.

fundamentally relational in the sense that those which stuck were the ones that were most effectively descriptive of the differences of religious belief, practice, and affiliation that the historical actors used to describe themselves and others. The politically salient religious identities that we will encounter – and, in turn, adopt for descriptive purposes – may be considered the historical residue of a number of recurrent mechanisms. At bottom, they are rooted in controversy regarding theological ideas, ritual practices, and/or religious authority that awakened opposition or resistance, as was evident in the case of Martin Luther. Although they are often innovative in some important sense, the points of contention need not be entirely novel; on the contrary, they were often framed by their advocates as revivals of ancient ideals or practices that had been corrupted over time. In any case, it is in the combined mechanisms of *innovation* and *disputation* – usually in the realm of religious specialists such as Martin Luther, Huldrych Zwingli, Jean Calvin, and their similarly specialized opponents – that we see the gestation of new religious identities and the boundaries of difference that they entail. These differences were recurrently *politicized* when third parties – especially competitive rulers, such as Emperor Charles V and members of the German Imperial Estates, as well as their various political subjects – chose sides in the religious disputes, which served both to sharpen the differences and to increase the stakes of the controversy. The nascent identities recurrently grew to political maturity when political actors on both sides of the controversies *mobilized* for collective action on behalf of their chosen cause. In short, the mechanisms of *innovation* and *disputation* recurrently combined with the mechanisms of *politicization* and *mobilization* to produce and reproduce a wide variety of politically salient religious identity boundaries throughout the early modern period.

In seeking to explain struggles characterized by recourse to coordinated destruction, Charles Tilly counsels us to be particularly attentive to three complementary and recurrent mechanisms.[28] One is the *activation* in specific settings of political identities and the boundaries associated with them; in sixteenth-century France this occurred, for example, when limited toleration emboldened previously secretive Protestant worshiping communities to become public challengers to the religious domination of the established Church in specific communities, thus activating the boundary between Protestants (Huguenots) and Catholics. A second mechanism is the *escalation* that occurs when networks of support segregate on either side of this boundary and redefine the dispute as categorical; this was evident in France when Protestant churches created and activated new networks of support in the form of regional and national assemblies, and Catholics activated or revitalized long-standing institutions of traditional Catholic piety, such as confraternities, to counter the Protestant challenge and reinforce the categorical Protestant/Catholic boundary. The third mechanism is the *brokerage* of political entrepreneurs

---

[28] Tilly, *Collective Violence*, 119–20.

who connect people and groups who were previously unconnected; this was evident in France when political entrepreneurs such as the duke of Guise and the prince of Condé linked networks of zealous Catholics and Protestants, respectively, to specialists of coercion in the form of mercenary armies on the eve of and throughout the many decades of religious war. To these I will add a fourth: *polarization*, which occurs when actors on either side of an identity boundary police that boundary and make peaceful transactions or cooperation across that boundary more difficult; this was evident in France when the contending parties, mobilizing for armed struggle, both locally and nationally, made routine social interactions and collaborative governance among "heretics" and "papists" more difficult, if not impossible.

Together, then, the dynamics of identity-boundary *activation, polarization* in relation to those activated boundaries, network-based *escalation*, and political *brokerage* help us to describe and account for particular occurrences of coordinated destruction. When the identities that are activated are politically salient religious identities, these clusters of mechanisms recurrently produce a variety of religious conflicts, including religious wars. Because these common mechanisms combined differently in different settings, however, the wars they produced were also decidedly different. Still, it is in recognizing the common mechanisms and recurrent processes that we will be able to frame a more telling discussion of their obvious differences.

Theological reconciliation might have disrupted the various concatenations of the mechanisms that led recurrently to religious war by depoliticizing the underlying theological issues and eliminating the religious identity boundaries, but in its absence we will need to attend to a very different set of mechanisms to describe and account for religious peace. The first and most obvious is *negotiation*, by which a variety of political actors sought an end to the religious wars; the negotiators routinely sought ways to reduce the salience of their religious identities as markers of political difference and to prevent the escalation of local conflicts into categorical struggles by adopting formal procedures to mediate or adjudicate conflicts that activated religious boundaries. The thrust of the negotiated settlements was, thus, to create a variety of politically acceptable spaces for religious diversity and coexistence. But the negotiated settlements, which institutionalized a variety of forms of religious coexistence, also depended on a certain degree of political, social, or geographic *segregation*, which can reduce the potential for contentious or violent interactions and separate religious movements from their military allies. Moreover, as we will see, the political or cultural *domination* entailed by military victories or institutionalized inequality could bring order to otherwise violent and chaotic situations, but domination was invariably counterbalanced, from the point of view of the subordinated or vanquished groups, by a considerable degree of *subversion* of the harshest implications of defeat or negotiated inequality. Indeed, in the cases of England and the Dutch Republic – perhaps the most visibly diverse and eventually

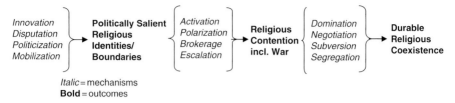

FIGURE 1.1: Recurrent processes and variable outcomes

"tolerant" of the religious regimes in early modern Europe – the domination of one religious group over all others was the most obvious outcome of the military struggle, whereas widespread subversion mitigated the worst effects of that outcome for those who were identified as "dissenters."

In sum, I will argue that the dynamics of both formal and informal *negotiation*; geographic, social, and/or and institutional *segregation*; political and/or military *domination*; and political and cultural *subversion* combined recurrently to lead a variety of violent political actors away from religious war and make durable religious peace possible. Because these common mechanisms combined differently in different settings, the religious peace they made possible took decidedly different forms. Still, it is in recognizing the common mechanisms and recurrent processes that we will be able to frame a more telling discussion of their obviously different outcomes.

Altogether, these three sets of common mechanisms, constituting three distinct, yet interrelated and recurrent historical processes, will frame the comparative historical analysis of religious war and religious peace that follows. Although Figure 1.1 summarizes this analytic vocabulary, it reveals little of the specific history of political and cultural change in early modern Europe, except to suggest that the ultimate outcome of these combined processes is durable religious coexistence. Meanwhile, although Table 1.2 summarizes the principal struggles, along with their settlements, that constituted the history of religious war and peace in early modern Europe, it also does not specify the nature of the more-or-less durable religious peace that had emerged in Europe by the second half of the seventeenth century.

DESCRIBING RELIGIOUS PEACE

What did religious peace actually look like in early modern Europe? Where will we find it, and how will we recognize it when we encounter it? The minimalist formal definition of religious peace that I have offered – the absence of coordinated destruction combined with the continued presence of religious diversity – suggests only generally what we should be looking for. Meanwhile, the negotiated settlements that we will be analyzing will certainly suggest where we might look and what the signatories of these agreements thought peace should look like. But as we have already seen, not all wars ended with negotiated settlements, and in any case, the negotiated settlements we have to work with are at best prescriptive, rather than descriptive. Meanwhile, the "confessionalization" literature in European historiography offers an essentially hegemonic ruler-centered perspective on the religious peace, with its emphasis on official attempts to promote and enforce religious *unity* and *purity* in the face of unwanted diversity. Indeed, given the reality of official intolerance and active confessionalization, religious diversity was as often as not deliberately hidden from view.

Just as the conventional history of state formation is transformed when we take ordinary people seriously as intentional and consequential actors,[29] so also the conventional history of religious authoritarianism is transformed when we take religious dissenters seriously as intentional and consequential actors. In order to describe and account for the history of religious diversity, then, historians must necessarily move beyond the official story that is privileged in governmental archives and actively seek out what James Scott calls the "hidden transcript"[30] – the informal testimony of those who lost the lethal contests and/ or accepted secrecy or formal subordination as the cost of survival in a deeply divided and recurrently violent world. Discovering that hidden transcript and documenting the largely hidden history of religious diversity is a daunting task, to be sure, but recent historical research that incorporates the perspectives and experiences of religious dissidents and dissenters has clearly shown that religious coexistence – that is, religious diversity within as well as among Europe's largely composite states – was the rule rather than the exception in post-Reformation Europe.[31]

[29] See Te Brake, *Shaping History*.
[30] James C. Scott, *Domination and the Arts of Resistance: Hidden Transcripts* (New Haven: Yale University Press, 1990).
[31] A project grant from the Ford Foundation, which supported my research, underwrote an international, interdisciplinary conference at the Netherlands Institute for Advanced Studies in 2001. A series of important books by participants in that project eloquently represents both the breadth and the sophistication of the transformative conversation that has informed my work ever since. See Keith P. Luria, *Sacred Boundaries: Religious Coexistence and Conflict in Early Modern France* (Washington: Catholic University of America Press, 2005); Benjamin J. Kaplan, *Divided by Faith: Religious Conflict and the Practice of Toleration in Early Modern Europe* (Cambridge, MA: Harvard University Press, 2007); Stuart B. Schwartz, *All Can Be Saved: Religious Tolerance and Salvation in the Iberian Atlantic World* (New Haven: Yale University Press, 2008); Karen Barkey, *Empire of Difference: The Ottomans in Comparative Perspective* (Cambridge; New York: Cambridge University Press, 2008). See also, C. Scott Dixon, Dagmar Freist, and Mark Greengrass, eds., *Living with Religious Diversity in Early Modern Europe* (Farnham, England: Ashgate Publishing, 2009), 53–79, which includes essays by many of my collaborators and references the growing literature, and Thomas Max Safley, ed., *A Companion to Multiconfessionalism in the Early Modern World*, Brill's Companions to the Christian Tradition, vol. 28 (Leiden; Boston: Brill, 2011). An important complement to these discussions of religious diversity is Mark Greengrass, *Christendom Destroyed: Europe 1517–1648* (New York: Viking Penguin, 2014), which appeared after most of this work was completed.

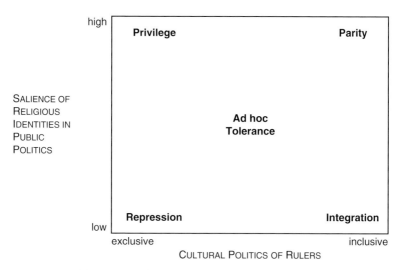

FIGURE 1.2: Variable patterns of religious coexistence

A comprehensive description of the pervasive pattern of religious coexistence in central and western Europe as well as the British Isles is, of course, beyond the ken of a single scholar and certainly beyond the compass of a relatively small volume.[32] In order to describe the varied outcomes that our comparative histories seek to account for, I will deploy a new typology of religious coexistence that I think comprehends the broad variety of historical experience and the perspectives of both rulers and their religiously diverse subjects. Since the retrospective authoritarian characterization – *cuius regio eius religio* – cannot be said in any meaningful sense to describe the outcome, I propose a more clearly relational set of descriptors, emphasizing both the variable claims of rulers and the variable visibility of religious dissidents, and by extension the salience of religious differences, in public life.[33] Figure 1.2 summarizes the range of variation graphically.

On the inclusive side of the diagram, in the upper-right quadrant, **parity** describes the relationships among rulers and subjects in political regimes that were formally inclusive of multiple, publicly visible religious or "confessional" groups; in very different parts of Europe, north of the Alps and Pyrenees, parity

---

[32] A collaborative catalogue of coexistence in the German Empire alone runs to no less than seven volumes; see Anton Schindling and Walter Ziegler, eds., *Die Territorien des Reichs im Zeitalter der Reformation und Konfessionalisierung: Land und Konfession 1500–1650*, Katholisches Leben und Kirchenreform in Zeitalter der Glaubensspaltung, vol. 49–53, 57 (Münster: Aschendorff, 1989–97).

[33] For a brief summary of the literature as well as a preview of this typology, see Wayne Te Brake, "Emblems of Coexistence in a Confessional World," in *Living with Religious Diversity in Early Modern Europe*, ed. C. Scott Dixon, Dagmar Freist, and Mark Greengrass (Farnham, England: Ashgate Publishing, 2009), 53–79.

among religious groups might take the form of shared churches, shared urban spaces, or carefully balanced political institutions. In the lower-right quadrant, **integration** describes the experiences of religiously different groups in political regimes that were formally inclusive of multiple religious identities, but in these situations, religious identities were largely "invisible" and thus not a salient feature of the social and political relations of specific institutions and/or public spaces; in early modern Europe, political integration might be the relatively rare experience of the privileged members of corporate bodies or of a broad range of religious groups, none of which enjoyed formal preference over the others in public life.

On the exclusive side of the diagram, in the lower-left quadrant, **repression** describes the relations between subordinate religious groups and political/religious authorities that excluded "dissidents" and actively sought to eliminate religious diversity as a visible, thus salient, feature of public life; in such circumstances, which recurred at least episodically for a wide variety of religious groups throughout Europe, religious differences survive only by means of subterfuge, secrecy, or at least formal invisibility. In the upper-left quadrant, **privilege** describes the relations of rulers and subjects in political regimes that formally elevated one religious group over all others and formally discriminated against "dissidents," who were willing to incur the cost of the public expression of their religious differences; regimes of privilege, however, did not forcefully seek to eliminate those differences through active repression. In early modern Europe, this relationship of public privilege/subordination was the routine experience of a wide range of Protestants and Catholics alike.

Finally, in the middle of the diagram, **ad hoc tolerance** describes the experience of specific religious groups, who were granted a clearly delimited space for self-regulation, and thus were neither fully included nor fully excluded, and whose differences were at least partially visible, yet not fully salient, in public life; ad hoc tolerance, which Europe's rulers granted as formal exceptions to otherwise operative rules, was the "privileged" experience of specific groups of both Christians and Jews, but not Muslims, in various parts of early modern Europe.[34] Although exceptional by definition, ad hoc tolerance is nevertheless characteristic of the changing nature of religious coexistence in post-Reformation Europe, for it was in a world organized by the concept of social and political privilege that the cataclysmic cultural changes of the reform of religion took place; it was also, not surprisingly, as a series of privileged exceptions to generally operative rules that religious diversity could gradually

---

[34] For recent exploration of the generally understudied place of Muslims in "Christian" Europe north of the Alps and Pyrenees, see Benjamin J. Kaplan, *Muslims in the Dutch Golden Age: Representations and Realities of Religious Toleration*, Fourth Golden Age Lecture (Amsterdam: Universiteit van Amsterdam, 2007). The most prominent example of ad hoc tolerance in early modern Europe was in Ottoman Europe, which is outside the scope of this analysis; see Barkey, *Empire of Difference*.

be incorporated into the political and cultural landscape of previously exclusionary regimes.

Throughout this work, I will use the descriptive vocabulary of Figure 1.2 to survey the contours of religious peace that emerged in central and western Europe between 1500 and 1700. As a complement to the relatively dry language of this typological map, I will also provide visual evidence illustrative of religious coexistence, especially in the "hard" cases where diversity was deliberately hidden from view. In order to visualize what religious peace actually looked like, even in the midst of war and active repression, I have amassed a large archive of photographs of what I call "emblems of coexistence." To my surprise and delight, I found that dissident religious histories, like dissenting voices more generally, can be easily located using simple Google searches on the World Wide Web. These virtual locations are invariably linked to physical sites of dissident memory, where one can find the often fragmentary remnants and ongoing commemorations of religious resistance and survival. The stories of heroic resistance, perseverance, and survival that religious dissenters gladly tell about themselves are, of course, incomplete, selective, and partial, but they are a necessary complement to the official stories of unity and purity – also incomplete, selective, and partial – that are too often privileged by historians.[35] This visual evidence allows us to explore the spatial dimensions of religious coexistence and to illustrate the inventively various forms of religious diversity. In the end, these emblems also enhance our ability to recognize the various forms of religious coexistence or simply to imagine what religious peace might look like in our own deeply conflicted world.

WHAT'S COMING

The chapters that follow divide the analysis of Europe's "Age of Religious Wars" into three overlapping phases. I use the term *phases* to suggest that whereas each paired comparison is distinctive, each successive phase built on and was informed by previous experiences. Within each phase, there are separate chapters on the histories of war making and peacemaking. Despite this organizational convenience, however, I will be at pains to demonstrate that war and peace are not alternating or mutually exclusive experiences in a chronological sequence. Rather, just as conflict and coexistence are inextricably linked in the long-term historical process of accommodating religious differences, so also are war making and peacemaking inextricably linked in the making of modern religious pluralism.

In the first phase, which is not always included in general histories of the Age of Religious Wars, we will encounter relatively limited military engagement and relatively low levels of coordinated destruction. In this early phase, we will also

---

[35] Cf. Te Brake, "Emblems of Coexistence."

encounter two formal and remarkably effective peace settlements that entailed difficult political compromises; these settlements served to manage religious competition and change while validating, at least "temporarily," religious diversity where unity and purity had previously been the official norm. In the second phase, which is often considered the "heart" of the Age of Religious Wars, we will encounter dramatically more violence and a broader range of military and popular engagement; not surprisingly, the history of peacemaking (divided into two chapters) is also more challenging to describe and account for. Although we will encounter *three* very different trajectories of change in this phase, we will also encounter considerable overlap and continuity in the practical experience of religious diversity in central and western Europe. In the third phase, which we might consider the climax and denouement of the Age of Religious Wars, we will encounter two very different clusters of occasionally very destructive military engagement; not surprisingly, we will also encounter very different political and cultural outcomes. Despite their different histories, however, these famous conflicts, which are rarely considered comparable, revealed strikingly familiar dynamics and (re) produced strikingly familiar patterns of religious coexistence; in this case, the analysis of the contours of religious peace is divided into two chapters.

In the concluding chapter, we will review the broader "lessons" that I believe we can learn from the study of religious war and religious peace in early modern Europe. After this long journey through European history, in which I am especially concerned with getting the story straight, I will step back to offer some guidance on how we might answer the BIG questions regarding the problems of religious war and religious peace – What makes religious war possible? What makes religious peace possible? What does religious peace look like? – in other times and places. In an effort to promote a "realistic," by which I mean historically grounded, vision of religious peace in our own time, I will be careful to count the costs, as well as the benefits, of religious peace. I will nevertheless underscore how the diffusion across central and western Europe of political compromises, practical arrangements, and subtle accommodations actually made religious peace possible and sustainable, despite the persistence of both official and popular forms of religious intolerance. Finally, I will highlight the less obvious emergence of an internationally sanctioned freedom of individual religious conscience, one of the hallmarks but also perhaps the most contested of modern human rights.

PHASE I

1529–1555

2

Wars and Rumors of War

Not all theological controversies or dissident calls for religious reform lead toward religious violence and war, of course. That depends in large measure on the responses of the multiple audiences who witness the debates and/or hear the calls for reform. Still, it seems clear, as Robert Wuthnow argues, that would-be reformers and their culturally critical discourses are more likely to be effective in actually bringing change and seeing their ideas for reform embedded in new institutional arrangements if they move beyond simple criticism of things as they are to suggest what kinds of *figural action* their audiences might undertake to both signal their assent to the new ideas and to bring about the changes they seek.[1]

Like John Wycliff and Jan Hus, their predecessors in the fourteenth and fifteenth centuries, Martin Luther, the brilliant German theologian, and Huldrych Zwingli, the charismatic Swiss pastor, appear to have been particularly adept at translating their theological discourses into figural action on behalf of religious reform.[2] What their followers did, in turn, was to politicize the religious controversies by choosing sides; in addition, by mobilizing for collective action, they helped immeasurably to establish the most prominent religious identity boundaries of the early Reformation era. Although it is clear in retrospect, then, that reformers such as Luther and Zwingli were critical actors in initiating the larger drama of what we term collectively the Reformation, the religious identity boundaries that we might retrospectively take for granted emerged only haltingly and with myriad variations in the course of a wide variety of political struggles initiated by

---

[1] Robert Wuthnow, *Communities of Discourse: Ideology and Social Structure in the Reformation, the Enlightenment, and European Socialism* (Cambridge, MA: Harvard University Press, 1989).

[2] For a general introduction to the larger context of late-medieval and early modern reform, see Peter G. Wallace, *The Long European Reformation: Religion, Political Conflict, and the Search for Conformity, 1350–1750*, European History in Perspective (Houndmills, Basingstoke, Hampshire; New York: Palgrave Macmillan, 2004).

their followers, most of which fell far short of the realm of coordinated destruction. Consider the following examples.

On July 1, 1523, two Augustinian monks, Hendrik Voes and Johannes van Esschen, were burned in the market square of Brussels.[3] Coming in the wake of anti-Lutheran placards and the burning of Luther's books, these judicial executions for "obstinate heresy" were merely the first of many thousands to follow over the next four decades in the Low Countries. In the short term, these executions initiated a sequence of events that included the suppression of the monastic house at Antwerp to which these "protomartyrs" of the Reformation belonged; the victims also inspired none other than Martin Luther to commemorate their execution in a sacred hymn, "Ein neues Lied," when he learned of the executions a month later.[4]

Just over seven months later, on February 14, 1524, in the Alsatian city of Strasbourg, an artisan named Strubelhans interrupted the monks who were singing the Compline in the choir of the cathedral; after a verbal exchange with the monks, in which he mocked the monks' Latin chants, Strubelhans picked up a preaching stool and attacked the monks, who in turn attacked and disarmed him and threw him out of the church. This act of anticlericalism, one of many in the early years of the Reformation, set off its own sequence of events that included a protest outside the cathedral by some 300 of Strubelhans's "companions" and an official inquiry by the Ammeister (a municipal judge) at the town hall.[5]

Later that year, on June 24, 1524, in the Swiss Thurgau, a group of twelve men invaded the parish church of Stammheim and a nearby chapel dedicated to St. Anna; they removed several sacred images, including an ancient statue of St. Anna, and later burned them. This act of iconoclasm, one of many such incidents in the early years of the Reformation era, also set off a sequence of events that included official arrests and prosecutions, popular protests and demonstrations, the occupation and partial destruction of a nearby monastery, and eventually the execution of three of the principal actors, including a local official and his son, an evangelical preacher.[6]

---

[3] Alastair Duke, "The Face of Popular Religious Dissent, 1520–30," in *Reformation and Revolt in the Low Countries* (London: Hambledon Press, 1990), 29–59.

[4] The text of this hymn, which has a ballad or storytelling form and no less than twelve verses, may be found at http://gedichte.xbib.de/Luther_gedicht_Ein+neues+Lied.htm; an English translation may be found at www.ctsfw.edu/etext/luther/hymns/homl/fain.homl. Cf. Robin A. Leaver, *Luther's Liturgical Music: Principles and Implications*, Lutheran Quarterly Books (Grand Rapids, MI: Wm. B. Eerdmans Pub. Co., 2007), 13.

[5] Lee Palmer Wandel, "Strubelhans and the Singing Monks," in *Krisenbewusstsein und Krisenbewältigung in der frühen Neuzeit: Festschrift für Hans-Christolph Rublack*, eds. Monika Hagenmaier and Sabine Holtz (Frankfurt am Main: Peter Lang, 1992), 307–15.

[6] John Maarbjerg, "Iconoclasm in the Thurgau: Two Related Incidents in the Summer of 1524," *Sixteenth Century Journal* 24 (1993): 577–93. Cf. Lee Palmer Wandel, *Voracious Idols and Violent Hands. Iconoclasm in Reformation Zurich, Strasbourg, and Basel* (Cambridge: Cambridge University Press, 1995).

These three incidents within the space of a year, yet spread geographically from the Low Countries to Switzerland, illustrate the politically contentious dimensions of the religious conflicts that have retrospectively been labeled "the Protestant Reformation." In each case, government agents were involved in the interaction, although they played varied roles. In Brussels, the local magistrates, encouraged by Charles V's promulgation of a Dutch/French version of the Edict of Worms condemning Luther's heresies, clearly weighed in as active defenders of papal orthodoxy, whereas in Strasbourg the magistrates took on a more neutral, investigative role, concerned primarily with preserving domestic peace. In the Swiss Thurgau, local officials were clearly divided, with some prosecuting offensive behavior and others being condemned to death for participating in the offenses.

Although there was no standard sequence, these incidents taken together illustrate some of the common and recurrent features of the formation of religious reform movements and politically significant Reformation coalitions.[7] Typically, it was literate and theologically educated clerics, like the Augustinian monks in Brussels, who were initially attracted to Luther's theological critique, whereas it was a wide variety of popular evangelical preachers, not all of them educated clerics, who translated the theological message into a practical call to action. Popular reform movements began to form when the preachers' audiences responded by taking a number of practical or symbolic actions, ranging from the relatively private and almost invisible decision to stop participating in religious rituals, such as the Mass, to joining public demonstrations of religious dissent and attacking both clerics and religious objects. Such movements typically became contentiously political when they began to demand that civil authorities undertake specific actions to "reform" religious practice: to promote the preaching of the "True Gospel;" to set up community charities to avoid the "corruption" of the Church's benevolent institutions and finances; to close monasteries and convents; or to reform, even abolish, the Mass. In short, popular reform movements typically grew out of the dynamic interaction of preachers and ordinary people, whereas reformation coalitions came into being when segments of the ruling elite took up the cause of religious reform or rulers acted favorably on popular demands. In these and countless other ways, the politicization of the "Luther question" yielded to a larger reformation process, which was invariably a political process whether civil authorities defended the established Church or participated in its piecemeal transformation.

A DRAMATIC PRELUDE AND THE FIRST ACT

Rulers, subjects, and competing claimants to religious authority – all of these actors were involved in the political processes of the early Reformation, and

[7] Cf. Wayne Te Brake, *Shaping History: Ordinary People in European Politics, 1500–1700* (Berkeley; Los Angeles: University of California Press, 1998), 35–44.

their shifting alignments and realignments account for a dramatic crescendo in the calls for religious reform as well as in the level of conflict.[8] As it happened, in much of upper Germany and adjacent parts of Switzerland and Austria, the escalating conflict very quickly reached the level of coordinated destruction in the second half of 1524. What is often called the Peasants' War of 1525 began when German, Swiss, and Austrian peasants rebelled, as they had been doing with increasing frequency for more than a century, against what they considered the illegitimate exactions of their lords.[9] This time the mobilization began in Germany near the Black Forest – at Stühlingen in the Hegau – in June of 1524 when several hundred disgruntled tenants of Count Siegmund von Lupfen chose as their leader Hans Müller, a former mercenary, who quickly worked out an alliance with the nearby town of Waldshut, where a popular preacher had galvanized a local opposition to their more distant Austrian overlord.[10] When these in turn allied with the city of Zürich, the authorities were forced to play for time. While the peasants of Stühlingen submitted their grievances to an imperial court, the rebel forces led by Müller forced the capitulation of the city of Freiburg-im-Breisgau. Similar scenarios were played out throughout Swabia, Franconia, Thuringia, and Tyrol – virtually all of southern Germany, with the exception of Bavaria, plus parts of modern Switzerland and Austria – as local resistance to lordly or princely rulers aggregated under the leadership of skilled soldiers, urban artisans and lawyers, and/or popular preachers. The soldiers and their military experience were critically important to the mobilization of hundreds of thousands of peasants; the artisans and lawyers were essential because they brokered the unusual political connection between town and countryside; and the preachers, with their radical religious populism, served mightily to unite otherwise very diverse people in the common cause of "godly justice."

The enormous breadth of the mobilization and the radicalism of the rebels' demands inspired Peter Blickle, the peasants' most prolific recent historian, to dub the aggregate of these many local and regional conflicts the "Revolution of the Common Man."[11] In emphasizing the common cause of "godly justice," Blickle underscores the importance of deliberative peasant assemblies, informal

---

[8] See also the diagram of the principal actors in the history of religious coexistence in Wayne Te Brake, "Emblems of Coexistence in a Confessional World," in *Living with Religious Diversity in Early Modern Europe*, eds. Scott Dixon, Dagmar Freist, and Mark Greengrass (Farnham, England: Ashgate Publishing, 2009), 65.

[9] Peter Blickle, "Peasant Revolts in the German Empire in the Late Middle Ages," *Social History* 4 (1979): 223–39.

[10] For a brief account in English of the movement's spread and the military campaigns associated with it, see the translators' introduction in Peter Blickle, *The Revolution of 1525: The German Peasants' War from a New Perspective*, trans. Thomas A. Brady Jr. and H. C. Erik Midelfort (Baltimore: Johns Hopkins University Press, 1981); for maps, essential chronology, and mobilization, see also Douglas Miller, *Armies of the German Peasants' War 1524–26*, illustrated by Angus McBride, Men-at-Arms Series (Oxford: Osprey, 2003).

[11] Blickle, *Revolution of 1525*, esp. 105ff.

alliances, and political manifestos, such as the famous "Twelve Articles of the Peasantry of Swabia." Indeed, from some 300 grievance lists, the authors of the Twelve Articles not only distilled a common list of demands concerning the disposition of communal resources, the collection of tithes, the imposition of unpaid labor services, and so forth, but they also articulated a vision of the future that could unite and inspire very diverse people across a very broad terrain.[12] To judge by the Twelve Articles, then, in a godly society, ordinary people would be both personally free and collectively in charge of their material and religious welfare while their rulers would clearly be limited by the precepts of divine justice.

For their part, the lords and princes, whom the rebels challenged, naturally had more ready access to coercive force. In some cases, of course, they could mobilize their own armies, but in this case, even though urban magistrates were not the natural allies of rural landlords, the cities of the imperial Swabian League eventually carried the day when they committed their coercive forces to the side of their fellow rulers.[13] And from the point of view of the peasants, it was both ironic and tragic that Martin Luther, whose theological challenges stimulated so much debate and conflict, emphatically chose the side of the rulers and loudly condemned the actions of the peasants in a series of widely circulated pamphlets.[14] In retrospect, it hardly seems like a fair fight. Still, even though the peasant armies were soundly defeated or just gave up without a serious fight, one is necessarily impressed by the speed with which a variety of local political challenges could escalate into the coordinated destruction of war.

Should we, then, consider the Peasants' War the first of the Reformation era's religious wars? If we were to consider manifestos such as the Twelve Articles an accurate reflection of motives and intentions of the rebels, the answer would undoubtedly be affirmative according to the traditional cognitive criteria. But in light of the relational criteria I have suggested, we need to attend to political and social relations in order to make such judgments. On the one hand, it is not obvious that divergent religious identities were as yet clearly enough articulated to serve as markers of political enmity; although "Lutheran" had quickly become synonymous with "heretic" or religious rebel, this Lutheran label could hardly be definitive of the peasant movements in light of Martin Luther's harsh condemnation. Neither is it clear that there were alternative networks of religious solidarity, as opposed to communal or political solidarity, that could be invoked in the course of the struggle. Thus, while the peasant

[12] See the full text of the Twelve Articles in Tom Scott and Bob Scribner, trans. and eds., *The German Peasants' War: A History in Documents* (Atlantic Highlands, NJ: Humanities Press, 1991), 252–7.

[13] Thomas A. Brady, *Turning Swiss: Cities and Empire, 1450–1550* (Cambridge: Cambridge University Press, 1985).

[14] See, for example, "Admonition to Peace: A Reply to the Twelve Articles of the Peasants in Swabia" and "Against the Robbing and Murdering Hordes of Peasants" in Martin Luther, *Luther: Selected Political Writings*, ed. and trans. J. M. Porter (Philadelphia: Fortress Press, 1974).

rebels framed the conflict as one pitting the "godly" against the "unjust," the political intervention of the Swabian cities on behalf of the rural nobility and the polemical support by Martin Luther of the political establishment served mightily to reframe the forces in conflict in the strictly political terms of "legitimate" rulers versus "rebellious" subjects. On the other hand, it does seem to be true that the stated claims of the rebels predicted a significant transformation of the relations of religious authority – one of the principal demands in the Twelve Articles was the local election of priests – and in the repression that followed the peasants' defeat, it became obvious that the victors were intent on undoing the religious changes that were enacted in local communities in the course of the revolt.[15] In the end, of course, the question may not be important: Whether or not we consider this a religious war, it is clearly evident in the Peasants' War that political struggles informed by the Luther question and inspired by a host of radical preachers could combine with the mechanisms and processes that account more generally for the coordinated destruction of war and, in some instances in the aftermath of peasant capitulations, campaigns of annihilation directed at the peasant rebels.[16]

Altogether we can see a variety of dynamic mechanisms at work here: the *politicization* of otherwise arcane matters of systematic theology; the *mobilization* of popular reform and social protest movements; the *activation* of clearly demarcated boundaries between lordly and imperial rulers, on one side, and their rebellious subjects, on the other; the *escalation* of the conflict as wider networks of political support transformed originally local and parochial conflicts into categorical oppositions; and the *brokerage* that linked otherwise disconnected people into larger coalitions or alliances that prominently included specialists of coercion. These processes recombined in a wide variety of settings in the Reformation era and beyond, and although they certainly did not yield the same consequences in every case, their recurrence helps us to explain the widespread incidence of warfare that invoked religious identities as the principal markers of difference and enmity. One such recurrence just a few years later threatened to destroy the Swiss Confederation.

Coming just a few years after the Peasants' War, the Kappel wars (1529 and 1531), the first of the religious wars in the Reformation era, were predicated on the political success of reformation coalitions in several city-states within the Swiss *Eidgenossenschaft* (oath confederation) under the leadership of Huldrych Zwingli.[17] On the eve of the Reformation era, the *Eidgenossenschaft* consisted

[15] On the importance of communal solidarities as well as the repression of religious transformations, see especially Peter Blickle, *Communal Reformation: The Quest for Salvation in Sixteenth-Century Germany*, trans. Thomas Dunlap (Atlantic Highlands, NJ: Humanities Press, 1992).
[16] In the end, as many as 130,000 rebels may have died in the fighting and in the repression that followed; cf. Blickle, *Revolution of 1525* and R. W. Scribner and Gerhard Benecke, eds., *The German Peasant War of 1525: New Viewpoints* (London: George Allen and Unwin, 1979).
[17] For a general survey in English, see Bruce Gordon, *The Swiss Reformation* (Manchester: Manchester University Press, 2002).

of thirteen independent and self-governing territories that were linked through a variety of treaties, connecting the rural "forest cantons" in central Switzerland to the imperial cities of the foothills, which had emerged from the late thirteenth through the late fourteenth centuries, partly in response to Habsburg efforts to exert more thorough political control in the region. In a complex history of crisis and expansion, the confederation had maintained its autonomy and blocked Habsburg efforts to reassert influence by its victory over Emperor Maximilian in 1499, and had by 1513 expanded to include six rural and seven urban members.[18] Together these confederated cities and territories ruled a series of subordinate *Gemeine Herrschaften* (shared lordships) and were affiliated or allied with other equally self-governing territories, such as Valais (Wallis) and Graubünden (Grisons).[19]

The relatively compact political spaces of self-governing cities proved to be especially conducive to the institutionalization of religious reform. The first political success of the religious reform movement came in 1523 when Zwingli crafted a solid reform coalition with a majority of the Zürich city council by means of two formal, public disputations in January and October that were intended to adjudicate the principal differences between the proponents of evangelical reform and the defenders of papal orthodoxy. In the next two years, this coalition between magistrates and the reform movement, rooted firmly in Zwingli's idea of the leading role of magistrates in guiding the Church, enacted a series of reforms that entailed the removal of sacred images from the churches and the suppression of religious and monastic houses; it culminated in the spring of 1525 in the abolition of the Mass and the adoption of a new liturgy for the celebration of the Lord's Supper.

Although the process was often more conflicted elsewhere, other cities followed Zürich's lead in establishing a new church order: St. Gallen (1527), Bern (1528), and Schaffhausen and Basel (1529). In each case, reform movements building on the success of evangelical preachers were translated into reform coalitions that brought the popular movements and their alternative claimants of religious authority together with important factions of the urban political elite.[20] Meanwhile, evangelical preachers also gained considerable followings that supported religious reforms in the more rural confederates of eastern Switzerland, especially Appenzell and Glarus, as well as in the allied

---

[18] The rural members were Uri, Schwyz, Unterwalden, Zug, Glarus, and Appenzell; the urban members were Zürich, Bern, Luzern, Fribourg, Solothurn, Basel, and Schaffhausen.

[19] Hans Conrad Peyer, *Verfassungsgeschichte der Alten Schweiz* (Zürich: Schultheis Polygraphischer Verlag, 1978).

[20] By emphasizing the compactness of the urban political spaces, I mean to denote the relative concentration of power in an urban elite or patrician oligarchy that ruled in close proximity to citizen-subjects on whose approval they implicitly depended in order to preserve domestic tranquility; geographically, city-states such as Zürich and Bern might rule over a fairly sizable hinterland, which did not participate in the same way in the dynamic interactions of urban governance, although Bern did submit its new Reformed church order to its subordinate rural communities for a vote; cf. Gordon, *The Swiss Reformation*, 107–8.

territories of Graubünden.[21] Given the republican principle of self-rule operative within the confederation, those confederates that resolutely defended the established Church – especially the five core territories, the so-called *V Orte* (Luzern, Uri, Schwyz, Unterwalden, and Zug) – were constitutionally powerless to resist or undo these urban reformations. The *Gemeine Herrschaften* represented, however, a very different political context, which was ripe for direct competition and confrontation.

The *Gemeine Herrschaften* were not self-governing members of the *Eidgenossenschaft*; on the contrary, these were territories that had been conquered collectively by the combined forces of members of the confederation and were ruled collectively by various combinations of those confederates.[22] The Thurgau, for example, to the north and east of Zürich, was conquered in 1460 by a coalition of seven of the confederates – Zürich, Luzern, Uri, Schwyz, Unterwalden, Zug, and Glarus – which consequently shared the newly acquired lordship; their authority, exercised through an appointed *Landvogt*, remained limited, as of old, by the privileges of local towns and by extensive ecclesiastical immunities. In order to share the honors and profits of this lordship, the office of *Landvogt* rotated every two years among the seven ruling confederates, but the discontinuity of the officeholders did not prevent a shared policy of expanding where possible their collective control of the territory.[23]

Even though there was considerable evidence of local popular support for religious reform,[24] the opportunities for institutionalizing communal reformations in the *Gemeine Herrschaften* were severely limited when the collective lordship of the confederates, which remained in the majority faithful to the established Church, resulted in the appointment of a "Catholic" *Landvogt*. Zürich nevertheless actively promoted the religious reform movement in the *Gemeine Herrschaften* and demanded that nothing be done to harm the

---

[21] See Gordon, *The Swiss Reformation*, 86–115, and Randolph C. Head, *Early Modern Democracy in the Grisons: Social Order and Political Language in a Swiss Mountain Canton, 1470–1620*, Cambridge Studies in Early Modern History (Cambridge: Cambridge University Press, 1995).

[22] The best work in English on the shared lordships in general is Randolph C. Head, "Shared Lordship, Authority, and Administration: The Exercise of Dominion in the *Gemeine Herrschaften* of the Swiss Confederation, 1417–1600," *Central European History* 30 (1997): 489–512; Head is justifiably reluctant to use the conventional term "Mandated Territories," which not only seems like a strange translation but does little to clarify or describe their political position within the confederation. Cf. Peyer, *Verfassungsgeschichte*.

[23] See Randolph C. Head, "Fragmented Dominion, Fragmented Churches: The Institutionalization of the *Landfrieden* in the Thurgau, 1460–1600," *Archiv für Reformationsgeschichte* 96 (2005): 117–44, who traces the institutional transformation of the territory both before and after the Reformation.

[24] Popular mobilization on behalf of evangelical reform in Thurgau, for example, predated the Peasants' War, as evidenced by sensational iconoclastic attacks at Stammheim and Ittingen in the summer of 1524. See Maarbjerg, "Iconoclasm in the Thurgau"; cf. Gordon, *The Swiss Reformation*, 93–5.

evangelicals or to prevent the preaching of the "true gospel." In the spring of 1528, officials from Zürich even arrested and eventually executed a local bailiff in Thurgau who was a staunch opponent of evangelical reform. As it happened, however, it was the arrest and execution in 1529 of an evangelical preacher, Jakob Kaiser, in the *Gemeine Herrschaft* of Gasterland by officials from Catholic Schwyz that precipitated the First Kappel War.[25]

In response to Kaiser's execution, Zürich mobilized for war and sent a citizen army of 4,000 men toward Kappel in early June 1529 where they confronted the outnumbered forces of the Catholic territories. Zürich was supported, in principle, by the other Reformed city-states, whereas their Catholic enemies had allied for their protection with Habsburg Austria, their former sovereign. Zürich's allies, however, were reluctant to fight and offered mediation instead; meanwhile, help for the Catholic coalition was not forthcoming from Austria. Thus, although war was declared, the commander of the Catholic forces quickly opted for negotiations instead of combat. Negotiations that began on June 17 concluded on June 26, 1529, with the first Swiss *Landfrieden*, or National Peace.[26] The thrust of the *Landfrieden*, which we will analyze more fully in the next chapter, was to affirm the principle that each of the confederates could abide by its own religious choice; given their apparent military superiority, Zürich and its allies also demanded that the Catholics' alliance with Austria be dissolved and that the *V Orte* (the core Catholic territories) pay reparations. Inasmuch as the evangelical coalition threatened to impose an economic blockade if the onerous reparations were not paid by the Catholic coalition, it is hardly surprising that the actual imposition of the economic blockade precipitated a second round of war two years later.

In the Second Kappel War, the previously outnumbered and underprepared forces of the Catholic coalition, now numbering 7,000 or 8,000, surprised and decimated the hastily assembled army of Zürich on October 11, 1531, killing one-quarter of Zürich's force of 2,000. Among the casualties were several of Zürich's magistrates and the charismatic reformer, Huldrych Zwingli, himself. In a second battle on October 24, a combined force from Zürich, Bern, and Schaffhausen was overrun by soldiers from Zug, leaving 800 soldiers and the commander of the evangelicals' army dead. Zürich and its allies quickly sued for peace. After another brief round of negotiations, Zürich signed a peace agreement with the *V Orte* on November 20, 1531, and four days later, Bern concluded a similar agreement.[27] Together, these documents constituted the

---

[25] Gordon, *The Swiss Reformation*, 124.

[26] Documents relating to the negotiations can be found in Johannes Strickler, ed., *Eidgenössischen Abschiede aus dem Zeitraume von 1529 bis 1532*, vol. 4, part 1b of *Amtliche Sammlung der älteren Eidgenössischen Abschiede*, ed. Johannes Strickler (Zürich: J. Schabeliz, 1876), 256–86; the text of the peace agreement is in Strickler, *Eidgenössischen Abschiede*, 1478–83.

[27] Basel and Schaffhausen signed separate and less comprehensive agreements with the *V Orte* on December 22, 1531, and January 31, 1532, respectively. Documents relating to these negotiations are published in Strickler, *Eidgenössischen Abschiede*, 1214–24, and all of the peace agreements are published in Strickler, *Eidgenössischen Abschiede*, 1567–77. A modern

Zweiter Landfrieden (Second National Peace), which served as an important constitutional foundation for managing religious differences within the Swiss Confederation for the next 125 years.

The Kappel wars lack the scale and drama, not to mention the monumental destruction of human life, of the Peasants' War, but they more clearly illustrate the way the emergence of new religious identities could combine with activation, escalation, and brokerage to produce religious war. Here I should like to highlight the effect of a series of formal, public disputations in shaping the religious identity boundary that would, in turn, inform both the religious wars and the religious peace within the Swiss Confederation. Although earlier academic debates in Germany regarding the Luther question undoubtedly served to define the theological and liturgical issues at stake in the early Reformation, the series of public disputations that were organized first in Zürich in 1523 and which culminated at Bern in 1528 were far more public and participatory. Consider the situation in Zürich in 1523.[28]

When Huldrych Zwingli had been called to be pastor at the Grossmünster Church in Zürich in 1522, he was a "foreigner" from Toggenburg who represented the kind of "evangelical" – that is, Bible-based – preaching that had come to symbolize early calls for religious change. Meanwhile, Zwingli, and by extension Zürich, was denounced in the Swiss *Tagsatzung* (national assembly) as a heretic and traitor to the staunchly conservative policies of the majority of the confederates. In an effort to clarify where Zwingli was leading them, the magistrates of Zürich called for a public disputation to be held at the end of January 1523. Since Zürich did not have a university, this was not to be a traditional academic debate; rather, Zwingli would be given the opportunity to state his views while the bishop of Constance and his representatives would have the opportunity to respond. This would afford the assembled "people" the opportunity to choose on the basis of what they heard. Invitations were sent to the other confederates to attend, and the cities of Basel, Bern, and Schaffhausen sent representatives. The bishop himself refused to attend, but he did send Johannes Fabri, the vicar-general of the diocese, "not to dispute, but to listen, advise and mediate."[29] All of the parish clergy in Zürich were also summoned to attend, and for the event, approximately 600 people were on hand.

Given the fact that Zwingli set the agenda by means of "Sixty-Seven Articles," which were later published, while the established Church decided to challenge the legitimacy of the event rather than debate the articles, it is hardly surprising that the municipal council's verdict was to exonerate Zwingli of theological error. With regard to the question of legitimacy and authority, Zwingli laid out a radical position, according to which the 600 people in

---

edition of the agreement between Zürich and the *V Orte* is published in Ernst Walder, ed., *Religionsvergleiche des 16. Jahrhunderts*, vol. 7–8 of *Quellen zur neueren Geschichte* (Bern: Verlag Herbert Lang, 1960–61), I: 5–13.

[28] The following account is based on Gordon, *The Swiss Reformation*, chapter 2.

[29] Quoted in Gordon, *The Swiss Reformation*, 58.

attendance at the Rathaus were the true church, empowered to make decisions based on Scripture. Armed with this mutual affirmation, Zwingli and the civil magistrates of Zürich began the gradual political process of religious reformation, focusing initially on religious and monastic houses, in defiance of the established Church as well as the majority of the confederates. In September 1523, the magistrates called for a second disputation in October to focus on the particularly contentious issues of the role of saints, the appropriateness of religious images, and the efficacy of the Mass. This time there were 900 people in attendance, including 300 clergy, and in the absence of a substantial delegation from the established Church, Zwingli once again carried the day and thus laid the foundations for the systematic removal of images from the churches of Zürich as well as the abolition of the Mass in 1525, which effectively placed the Zürich Church outside the Church of Rome.

The authorities in the five inner confederates, the *V Orte*, which led the opposition to Zürich's reforms, responded to the intellectual and political challenge of the Zürich disputations and Zürich's subsequent reforms by organizing a debate on their terms at Baden in May 1526.[30] Prior to the debate, Fabri and Zwingli exchanged uncompromising open letters that discredited Zwingli and questioned the authority of the confederates to try Zwingli, respectively, and in the absence of Zwingli at the debate itself, Johannes Eck, the German theologian who had debated Luther in 1519, easily dominated the proceedings. Subsequently, nine of the confederates adopted the resolutions of the Baden debate – which declared Zwingli a heretic and called for implementation of the Edict of Worms' condemnation of Luther in the *Eidgenossenschaft* – while three others (Basel, Bern, and Schaffhausen) refused to choose between the established Church and the "evangelicals" led by Zwingli and Zürich.

Meanwhile, evangelical preaching was beginning to have considerable impact in St. Gallen, Appenzell, Thurgau, and in Graubünden.[31] Following the lead of Zürich, the city of St. Gallen, which was allied with but not a full member of the confederation, followed an incremental path toward reform of the Church's institutions and liturgy, along Zwinglian lines, culminating in the celebration of the first evangelical Lord's Supper at Easter in 1527. The "evangelicals" also gained a considerable following in the rural territory of Appenzell, a full member of the confederation, and in April 1524 the *Landsgemeinde* (territorial assembly) mandated "scriptural preaching," which was quickly becoming the essential first step toward religious reform. But they also met with considerable opposition from those who defended the established Church, and in July 1524 the *Landesgemeinde* followed Zürich's tactic of holding a disputation to resolve the many contentious issues. Three

---

[30] See Irena Backus, "The Disputations of Baden, 1526 and Berne, 1528: Neutralizing the Early Church," *Studies in Reformed Theology and History* 1 (1993): 1–69.

[31] See Gordon, *The Swiss Reformation*, chapter 3.

hundred people gathered for what proved to be a poorly organized and rancorous debate that produced no resolution. Subsequently, it was decided that each community within Appenzell should be allowed to choose whether to adopt evangelical practices or remain true to the establish Church.[32] In Thurgau, which was a *Gemeine Herrschaft*, evangelical preaching produced both followers and, as we have seen, scattered religious violence, which clearly divided the authorities who shared the Thurgau lordship.[33] In the three leagues that constituted Graubünden, which was allied with but not a full member of the confederation, evangelical preaching led to a considerable reform movement in the isolated rural communities that guarded their local autonomy and resulted in the Ilanz Articles of 1524, which provided considerable lay control of Church affairs.[34] The evangelical leaders also pressed for a disputation, on the Zürich model, which took place at Ilanz in January 1526. The debate lasted for two days and proved to be inconclusive, but it resulted in the Second Ilanz Articles, which relieved the bishop of his territories and placed religious houses under political control.

The most critical and conclusive of the evangelical-inspired disputations came in the important city-state of Bern in 1528.[35] Although there was a popular reform movement within Bern, with considerable support among the guilds, between 1524 and 1528 the magistrates of Bern, seeking to avoid open conflict, remained officially uncommitted to either side in the increasingly polarized confederation. In 1527, however, the large council of Bern, following a shift in its composition, acceded to the wishes of the guilds and convened a disputation in January 1528. Eight of the confederates refused the invitation to attend the disputation in which more than 250 theologians took part. A series of ten propositions, compiled by evangelical leaders, were debated for nearly three weeks before they were finally accepted by a vote of 200 to 48. After a large gathering of Bern's inhabitants agreed to accept the municipal council's decision, the council, in early February 1528, issued a Reformation mandate, which laid out the details of a new church order. Before the end of the month, a majority of rural communities under Bern's jurisdiction – most of which had earlier opposed reform – also accepted the new religious order. In the course of 1529, the cities of Basel and Schaffhausen followed Bern's lead and adopted Reformation mandates in April and September, respectively.

In retrospect, the religious disputations in Switzerland between 1523 and 1528 may be said to have had two principal consequences. On the one hand, in

---

[32] In Glarus, which was also a full member of the confederation, the Reformation was similarly partial and inconclusive, with the result that there, too, local communities were authorized to choose for or against religious reform. See, Gordon, *The Swiss Reformation*, 98–100, and Markus René Wick, "Der 'Glarnerhandel,' Strukturgeschichte und Konfliktsoziologische Hypothesen Zum Glarner Konfessionsgegensatz," *Jahrbuch Des Historischen Vereins Glarus* 69 (1982): 49–240. See also, Chapter 3 in this volume.

[33] See Head, "Fragmented Dominion."   [34] See Head, *Early Modern Democracy*.

[35] Backus, "Disputations."

this early and very uncertain phase of the reformation process, these public performances of religious difference, which were designed to adjudicate rather than reconcile contentious issues, served mightily to clarify the theological, liturgical, and institutional issues at stake, not only within the Swiss Confederation but more broadly in Europe. On the other hand, they served very effectively to frame the stark political choices that the members of the confederation were facing in the course of the escalating religious conflict. Meanwhile, between 1527 and 1529, two competitive alliances served to divide the members of the confederation against one another over these religious issues. The Christian Civic Union joined Zürich with Bern, St. Gallen, Basel, Schaffhausen, and several German cities, whereas the Catholic Christian Union joined the *V Orte* with Ferdinand of Austria in opposition to the reformation process. These are the broader coalitions of solidarity, identified by their commitments for or against religious reform, which framed the Kappel wars and the peace agreements that followed. The fragility of the evangelical alliance was evident, however, in the First Kappel War, when Zürich's allies were reluctant to join its military mobilization, while Habsburg Austria also failed to aid the *V Orte* before it sued for peace.

What is striking, in the end, is how quickly a specific incident in a minor lordship – the arrest and execution of Jacob Kaiser in Gasterland – could ignite a broadly national conflict that invoked extensive alliances among the confederates and beyond the boundaries of the *Eidgenossenschaft*. Although there had been sporadic violence within the constituent parts of the *Eidgenossenschaft*, largely in relation to the removal of images from churches, the coordinated destruction of the Kappel wars in Switzerland pitted the deeply divided members of the *Eidgenossenschaft*, with their relatively ready access to coercive means, against one another in a struggle that threatened the future of the *Eidgenossenschaft*. Indeed, polarization within the *Tagzatsung* over matters of religion threatened to paralyze the confederation internally, while civil war that engaged larger transnational networks of religious solidarity clearly made the *Eidgenossenschaft* vulnerable to outside intervention.[36] In sum, in the Swiss case, *innovation* and *disputation* clearly combined with *politicization* and *mobilization* to clarify the issues as well as to crystalize the religious identity boundaries while *activation* of those identities in multiple contexts, *escalation* via newly created networks of religious solidarity, *polarization* among the members of the *Eidgenossenschaft*, and *brokerage* of broader military coalitions combined to produce Europe's first religious warfare.

---

[36] As Randolph Head has suggested, religious issues were not the only ones dividing the members of the *Eidgenossenschaft*; their involvement in the Italian wars, which ended catastrophically with many casualties in 1525, had already produced deep polarization, though along different lines than the religious issues produced, and threatened the ability of the *Tagsatzung* to manage disagreements (private correspondence, September 19, 2010).

A DRAMATIC INTERLUDE AND THE SECOND ACT

It is critical to note, however, that combinations of some of these dynamic mechanisms in other contexts did not necessarily yield to religious war. Consider the example of the so-called Pilgrimage of Grace in England in 1536. In this case, the politicization of religious questions combined with popular mobilization, not in favor of evangelical reform, but in defense of the established Church. Having first attacked the theology of Luther and thereby earning the papal appellation "Defender of the Faith," King Henry VIII changed course and undertook a limited ecclesiastical reformation – that is, starting in 1529, he severed the English Church from Rome and established himself as its head – for apparently dynastic reasons, but in alliance with reform-minded clerics, he also undertook some modest reforms of religious ritual and dogma.[37] Consequently, in the mid-1530s, his royal commissioners were fanning out throughout the kingdom, closing monasteries, suppressing "superfluous" saints' days and popular festivals, and allegedly confiscating the movable wealth of local churches.

In the absence of significant popular reform movements demanding change, especially in the north of England where the pilgrimage began, these negative confiscatory policies, which seemed to many to be the embodiment of Henry's religious reforms, met with various forms of popular opposition, ranging from passive resistance to massive popular mobilizations.[38] In Yorkshire in October 1536, one such mobilization, led by an obscure and somewhat mysterious lawyer named Robert Aske, mobilized more than 20,000 men who represented a significant political challenge to the ecclesiastical policies of Henry VIII. First the rebels moved on the northern city of York, and from there, marching south under the crusading symbol of the "Five Wounds of Christ," they proceeded to Pontefract, where Lord Darcy surrendered the royal castle and joined the insurrection, and then to Doncaster, where they encountered a small royal army, which they vastly outnumbered. Although some of the rebels apparently wanted to continue their self-styled Pilgrimage of Grace all the way to London, the leaders of the opposing forces agreed to a truce before any shots were fired. Subsequently, in anticipation of serious negotiations with the king, many of the rebels dispersed while hundreds of their representatives met in late November to formulate their grievances.

---

[37] For general background and context, see Christopher Haigh, *English Reformations: Religion, Politics, and Society Under the Tudors* (Oxford: Clarendon Press, 1993); cf. Te Brake, *Shaping History*, 24, 56–60.

[38] C. S. L. Davies, "Popular Religion and the Pilgrimage of Grace," in *Order and Disorder in Early Modern England*, eds. Anthony Fletcher and John Stevenson (Cambridge: Cambridge University Press, 1985), 58–91; C. S. L. Davies, "The Pilgrimage of Grace Reconsidered," in *Popular Protest and the Social Order in Early Modern England*, ed. P. Slack (Cambridge: Cambridge University Press, 1984), 16–38; Michael Bush, *The Pilgrimage of Grace: A Study of the Rebel Armies of October 1536* (Manchester: Manchester University Press, 1996).

Like the peasant grievances formulated during the Peasants' War in Germany, the demands of the English pilgrims were eclectic and broad ranging.[39] Robert Aske, in particular, highlighted the religious demands for the restoration of monasteries and the suppression of "heretical" religious practices, also formulating an oath to be sworn by both the elite leaders of the movement and the assembled pilgrims, who may have numbered more than 10,000. Despite formal negotiations in December appearing to yield significant royal concessions, the king apparently had no intention of actually satisfying the rebels' demands, and following an unsuccessful attempt to remobilize the rebels, many of the rural elites who had initially joined the broadly based regional coalition against the king's reform policies now joined in the repression of the rebels.

If the Peasants' War demonstrates how quickly local conflict could escalate into coordinated destruction, the Pilgrimage of Grace suggests that such escalations are nevertheless contingent, even when all the ingredients of a good fight appear to be present. In addition to the *politicization* of religious issues and the *mobilization* of a popular movement against reform, the pilgrimage was predicated on the *activation* of the reform/counterreform boundary in specific local arenas, the *escalation* of the conflict as regional networks of support threatened to make this a categorical fight, and the *brokerage* of connections between otherwise unconnected people, including violent specialists. Yet the escalation remained partial, and the brokered connections proved not to be durable. Thus, what might have counted as a religious war never materialized, although the repression cost the lives of nearly 200 rebel leaders, including Lord Darcy and Robert Aske.[40]

Meanwhile, in Germany, the Peasants' War of 1524–1526 undoubtedly had a chastening effect on a wide variety of political actors, many of whom appear to have worked hard to avoid the recurrence of that kind of destruction. But it did little to retard the political process of religious reform in many of the constituent political units of the empire. In the territory of Electoral Saxony, for example, Luther himself, under official protection, helped to construct a new model of the Christian community in conformity with both his dissident theology and his emergent ecclesiology, which like Zwingli's accorded a significant role to the civil authorities in reforming the Church and administering religious affairs. From numerous experiences of this sort historians have constructed a model of the top-down "princely" Reformation that placed a premium on order and social discipline.[41] Meanwhile, a more

---

[39] The text of these articles may be found in Anthony Fletcher, *Tudor Rebellions*, 3rd ed. (London: Longman, 1983).

[40] Fletcher, *Tudor Rebellions*, 37.

[41] For useful summaries in English, see R. W. Scribner, *The German Reformation* (Atlantic Highlands, NJ: Humanities Press, 1986); Euan Cameron, *The European Reformation* (Oxford: Clarendon Press, 1991); and James D. Tracy, *Europe's Reformations, 1450–1650*, Critical Issues in History (Lanham, MD: Rowman and Littlefield, 1999). Compare the slightly broader perspective in Te Brake, *Shaping History*, 50–62.

varied history of religious reform in cities and towns continued to engage
ordinary people more directly in the political process well into the 1530s.[42]
It was especially the dynamic force of popular reform movements that anchored
significant reform coalitions and propelled the installation of some form of
evangelical church order in the majority of the eighty imperial free cities, subject
only to the authority of the emperor, and in many of the more than 2,000
provincial towns under the more direct lordship of territorial princes. All of this
occurred, of course, in defiance of the *Reichstag*'s official condemnation of
Luther's teachings in 1521 and Charles V's stalwart defense of Christian unity.

The consequence was a growing political polarization within the empire
between those who promoted religious reform and those who defended the
established Church. Although this version of the identity boundary between
reformers and opponents of reform not infrequently caused tension inside the
many self-governing political units that constituted the German Empire, once
reform was a local fait accompli, these tensions quickly subsided in most cases.
Indeed, in the remarkable absence of a strong popular mobilization in defense of
the established Church, it was the variously sovereign rulers within the empire
whom this polarization engaged most directly and immediately. Their growing
estrangement from one another was evident in the formal protest at the imperial
diet in 1529 that gave birth to the term *Protestant*, and it took institutional form
in 1531 with the creation of the "Protestant" League of Schmalkalden to
counteract the domination of the emperor's "Catholic" allies in the
Reichstag.[43] Although rooted in late-medieval imperial precedents, the League
of Schmalkalden nevertheless broke new ground in that it brought various
governments throughout the empire into an alliance that opposed, rather than
supported, the emperor. As Thomas Brady describes it:

The Protestants' creation was indeed a form of governance, though not a state in any
modern sense. They fashioned a fairly effective government, constructed a European
network of diplomacy, disrupted the Imperial judicial system, and protected their own
members until the new faith was too well established to be uprooted.[44]

In short, the formation of the Protestant League, as well as a Catholic counterpart
aligned with the emperor, crystallized a political-religious division that would
have been inconceivable just fifteen years earlier.

[42] In addition to the general works cited earlier, see R. W. Scribner, *Popular Culture and Popular
Movements in Reformation Germany* (London: Hambledon Press, 1987) and Te Brake, *Shaping
History*, 35–44. Cf. Christopher W. Close, *The Negotiated Reformation: Imperial Cities and the
Politics of Urban Reform, 1525–1550* (Cambridge; New York: Cambridge University Press,
2009).

[43] For an account of the origins of the League of Schmalkalden from the perspective of a single
urban leader who was also a principal broker of the League, see Thomas A. Brady, Jr.,
The Politics of the Reformation in Germany: Jacob Sturm (1489–1553) of Strasbourg
(Atlantic Highlands, NJ: Humanities Press, 1997).

[44] Brady, *Politics of the Reformation*, 116.

Even before it took full institutional form, the League of Schmalkalden succeeded in negotiating the Peace of Nuremberg in 1532. In 1530, the evangelical polities within the empire had found a measure of theological unity under the Augsburg Confession,[45] and they now gained de facto legitimacy under the terms of the Peace of Nuremberg inasmuch as Charles suspended his legal attempts to gain restitution of ecclesiastical properties that the Protestants had confiscated, *until such time* as a general council of the Church could meet.[46] The League of Schmalkalden achieved more success in 1534 when it helped to restore the Lutheran Duke of Württemberg and in 1542 when it imprisoned the Duke of Brunswick-Wolfenbüttel and forcibly converted his duchy to Lutheranism. But as long as Charles V was distracted by other military challenges – especially the advance of the Ottomans in the east – there was no significant escalation along the now well-established Protestant/Catholic boundary within the empire. On the contrary, the popular revolution that took place in the city of Münster, *mirablile dictu*, precipitated cooperation across this religious divide in order to suppress the "radical Anabaptists," who seemed to threaten "mainline" Protestants and Catholics alike.

Between 1531 and 1533, the city of Münster experienced what might be regarded as a fairly typical urban reformation process driven by a popular reformation movement.[47] Following an armed militia challenge to the local political elite in 1532, municipal elections in early 1533 established a new guild-based political elite, which promptly issued an evangelical ordinance to consolidate the reformation of the Church. In the summer of 1533, however, the reformation coalition of moderate magistrates and more zealous popular reformers fell apart, and an influx of Anabaptists ("rebaptizers"), primarily from the Netherlands, helped to push the religious reform movement and, by

[45] The Augsburg Confession was in some sense a byproduct of the failed attempt by Philipp of Hesse in 1529 to broker a theological agreement between Luther and Zwingli in the so-called Colloquy of Marburg; although both theologians stubbornly refused to compromise on a single contentious point of disagreement – their understanding of the nature of the Eucharist – Philipp Melanchthon, Luther's colleague at the University of Wittenberg, used the fourteen points on which there was agreement as the foundation for his draft of the Augsburg Confession, which the evangelical leaders presented to the emperor at the diet at Augsburg in 1530. It subsequently became the touchstone for official identification of the evangelicals in the Religious Peace of Augsburg (1555). The full annotated text of the Augsburg Confession, in parallel Latin and English columns, may be found at www.ccel.org/ccel/schaff/creeds3.iii.ii.html. On the pivotal importance of the diet of Augsburg, see David M. Luebke, "A Multiconfessional Empire," in *A Companion to Multiconfessionalism in the Early Modern World*, ed. Thomas Max Safley, Brill's Companions to the Christian Tradition, vol. 28 (Leiden; Boston: Brill, 2011), 133–4.

[46] Although the Peace of Nuremberg was considered by all parties to be temporary, it in fact established a template for the later peace treaties of Augsburg (1555) and Westphalia (1648). See Chapters 3 and 10 in this volume.

[47] For accounts in English of the events in Münster, see R. Po-Chia Hsia, "Münster and the Anabaptists," in *The German People and the Reformation*, ed. R. Po-Chia Hsia (Ithaca: Cornell University Press, 1988), 51–69, and Sigrun Haude, *In the Shadow of "Savage Wolves": Anabaptist Münster and the German Reformation During the 1530s*, Studies in Central European Histories (Boston: Humanities Press, 2000).

extension, the whole city in a more radical direction. In 1534, for example, the new regime required the rebaptism of all citizens and forced dissidents into exile, while the prince-bishop Franz von Waldeck, the city's territorial overlord, mobilized his military resources in order to crush the rebellion and the "heresy" it represented. With the city under siege and intermittent attacks, the charismatic leadership of two Dutch immigrants, the prophet Jan Matthys and his disciple Jan of Leiden, moved the city toward social revolution, instituting the radical "community of goods" based on early Christian examples, and even polygamy. In the face of this popular revolutionary challenge, Catholic and Lutheran princes were able to put aside their differences in order to close ranks in the face of a common "radical" enemy, and the prince-bishop of Münster raised sufficient forces to cut off the flow of both food and Anabaptist reinforcements to the city. During the night of June 24, 1535, the Anabaptist "kingdom" of Münster fell to its combined Lutheran and Catholic opponents; its leaders were captured, tortured, and executed. In the end, however, the displacement of the Protestant/Catholic identity boundary by a new radical/mainline identity boundary was as short-lived as the Anabaptist kingdom.

In 1541, the famous Colloquy of Regensburg briefly revived hopes for some sort of theological reconciliation between "Protestants" and "Catholics," not just in Germany, but more broadly in Europe.[48] The ground for this conference, which met in parallel sessions with the *Reichstag* at Regensburg, had been laid in the previous months by preliminary discussions between major Catholic (e.g., Johann Eck and Johann Gropper) and Protestant (e.g., Philipp Melanchthon and Martin Bucer) theologians. During the colloquy, however, the theologians refused to compromise on a few keys points – especially the doctrine of transubstantiation in the Eucharist and the necessity of priestly confession – which doomed the enterprise to failure. Then, on December 13, 1545, the long-awaited general council of the Church finally began its meeting at Trento in northern Italy.[49] Theoretically the Council of Trent also opened up the possibility of Protestant-Catholic reconciliation, which many considered the only desirable outcome of the long-simmering conflict, but the event, which had no Protestants in attendance, only exacerbated the religious conflict by hardening both the Catholic Church's theological positions and its resolve to defeat, rather than accommodate, its critics.[50] In the meantime, it also set the

---

[48] Diarmaid MacCulloch, *The Reformation* (New York: Viking, 2004), 229–31.

[49] Hubert Jedin, *A History of the Council of Trent*, 2 vols., trans. Dom Ernest Graf (Edinburgh: Thomas Nelson and Sons, 1957).

[50] The council met intermittently from 1545 to 1563 for the expressed purpose of reforming the Church and securing reconciliation with Protestants. Both Lutherans and Calvinists declined to attend, however, and in the end the Tridentine decrees served to attack old abuses – e.g., clerical absenteeism, pluralism (holding more than one office), and simony – by strengthening and centralizing ecclesiastical discipline and prescribing the "proper" belief of all Catholics in the *Roman Catechism*. See *Canons and Decrees of the Council of Trent*, trans. and ed. Henry Joseph Schroeder (Rockford, IL: Tan Books and Publishers, 1978). An English translation of the Catechism may be found at www.cin.org/users/james/ebooks/master/trent/tindex.htm.

increasingly polarized context both for Germany's religious wars and for the peace agreement that followed.

Against this backdrop, Emperor Charles V finally went to war against the League of Schmalkalden in 1545 for apparently political reasons: in order to execute an imperial judgment against the Elector of Saxony and the Landgrave of Hesse, two of the league's leading members, for their attack on Brunswick-Wolfenbüttel in 1542.[51] In April 1547 the emperor's forces decisively defeated the Saxons at Mühlberg, and the elector and the landgrave were imprisoned. Although this victory seemed to assure Charles's political dominance for the future, the conflict escalated again when Maurice of Saxony broke with Charles and reconstituted the Protestant alliance in 1550. The Protestant forces restarted the war in 1552, but in the absence of decisive military campaigns by either side, the conflict stalemated until Charles gave his brother, Ferdinand, archduke of Austria, a free hand to mediate what would become the *Religionsfriede* (Religious Peace) of Augsburg, which brought religious war in the empire to an end and annulled the 1521 Edict of Worms.

In Germany, as is Switzerland, then, the religious identity boundaries of the early Reformation served especially to divide the rulers of a composite state into two factions, each with ready access to coercive means. In both of these closely related cases, *politicization* and popular *mobilization* helped to define new religious identities that were clearly *activated* in a variety of contexts. *Polarization*, which tends toward the restriction of routine cooperation, was evident in both of these composite polities as the religiously divided constituents of the Swiss *Tagsatzung* and German *Reichstag* were recurrently unable to transact the routine business of governance. Meanwhile, the *brokerage* of new political alliances that included officials with ready recourse to violent means aided the *escalation* of local conflicts into categorical conflicts defined by networks of religious solidarity and trust.[52] Still, the limited level of destruction hardly confirms the notion that religious war is always characterized by extreme bitterness and unrestrained bloodletting; indeed, the Pilgrimage of Grace may have entailed more drama and uncertainty than either of these instances of religious war. That pattern changed dramatically, however, when similar processes yielded to much more violence and destruction under very different circumstances in France and the Low Countries. But before we turn our attention to the second phase of Europe's religious wars, we will examine how these first, limited wars of religion came to an end.

[51] On Charles's effort to disguise his religious motives, see Konrad Repgen, "What Is a 'Religious War'?" in *Politics and Society in Reformation Europe. Essays for Sir Geoffrey Elton on His Sixty-Fifth Birthday*, eds. E. I. Kouri and Tom Scott (London: Macmillan Press, 1987), 319; cf. Wim Blockmans, *Keizer Karel V: De utopie van het keizerschap* (Leuven: Van Halewyck, 2000).
[52] For vivid examples of the importance of solidarity and trust in the escalation of the conflict in Germany, see Brady, *Politics of the Reformation*, 108ff.

3

Managing Conflict, Validating Diversity

Article IX. And since we both parties have agreed upon these articles as stated above, which were negotiated and concluded between us and accepted by both parties to hold in good faith, therefore upon this all feuds, hostility, division, envy, hate and all bad feelings that may have arisen between the parties during or before this war, through words or deeds, shall be gone, dead and down, [so that] we shall not consider or think about each other with bad or evil opinions, but rather all things shall be forgiven and henceforth, (may God wish it), we shall hold one another to be good companions and loyal dear Confederates, and treat one another as loyal dear Confederates in open commerce and in all other ways.

Swiss *Landfrieden*, November 20, 1531

With these hopeful, even noble, intentions, a very diverse group of delegates concluded the first relatively successful settlement of a religious war in early modern Europe. Although good intentions are notoriously unreliable predictors of specific outcomes of historical processes, the people who tried in good faith to end Europe's religious wars in the sixteenth and seventeenth centuries sometimes got it right, and the settlements they crafted actually made enduring religious peace possible. As it happened, the recurrent intention that "all things shall be forgiven" was rarely, if ever, fulfilled, and "hostility, division, envy, hate, and all bad feelings" usually remained long after the dust and smoke of war had settled. Still, early modern Europeans did manage to make peace possible after each phase of the religious wars. The purpose of this chapter is to examine comparatively the legal principles and the relational dynamics of the peace settlements that ended the first phase of religious war in Switzerland and Germany. We will both analyze the specific ways in which the Swiss *Landfrieden* and the German *Religionsfriede* ended the coordinated destruction of these relatively limited wars and describe in Chapter 4 the varied patterns of an enduring, if messy, religious peace that the well-intentioned negotiators made possible.

MANAGING RELIGIOUS CONFLICT IN SWITZERLAND

Coming quickly in the wake of the Peasants' War, the Kappel wars in Switzerland were predicated on the political success of evangelical reform coalitions, especially in the city-states of the Swiss Confederation. The relatively compact political spaces of self-governing cities proved to be especially conducive to the institutionalization of religious reform, and in Zürich, St. Gallen, Bern, Schaffhausen, and Basel, reform movements building on the success of evangelical preachers were translated, between 1525 and 1529, into reform coalitions that brought the popular movements and their alternative claimants of religious authority together with important factions of the urban political elite.[1] Given the republican principle of self-rule operative within the *Eidgenossenschaft*, those confederates that resolutely defended the established Church – especially the five core territories, the so-called *V Orte*: Uri, Schwyz, Unterwalden, Luzern, and Zug – were constitutionally powerless to resist or undo these urban reformations. As we saw in the previous chapter, however, the *Gemeine Herrschaften* represented a very different political context that was ripe for direct competition and confrontation. And having provided the spark for war, they were, not surprisingly, the greatest challenge for those who sought to make peace possible.

After the First Kappel War was aborted before it really got started, peace negotiations that began on June 17 concluded on June 26, 1529, with the first Swiss *Landfrieden*, or National Peace.[2] The foundation of this unprecedented agreement was the Swiss republican principle that each of the full members of the *Eidgenossenschaft* should regulate its own affairs and should, therefore, determine its own religion. In the slightly awkward language of the first article, the *Landfrieden* declared,

First of all, regarding the word of God: since no one should be coerced into the faith, that therefore the *Orte* and their subjects should also not be coerced.[3]

The eighth article amplified this point, especially with regard to the religious changes that had been made by the evangelicals: it stated specifically that the agreements and mandates for change

shall stand and remain in effect … And where one also has removed and abolished the Mass, images, church decorations, and other related services to God, that also

---

[1] By emphasizing the compactness of the urban political spaces, I mean to denote the relative concentration of power in an urban elite or patrician oligarchy that ruled in close proximity to citizen-subjects on whose approval they implicitly depended in order to preserve domestic tranquility; geographically, city-states such as Zürich and Bern might rule over a fairly sizable hinterland, which did not participate in the same way in the dynamic interactions of urban governance.

[2] Documents relating to the negotiations can be found in Johannes Strickler, ed., *Eidgenössischen Abschiede aus dem Zeitraume von 1529 bis 1532*, vol. 4, part 1b of *Amtliche Sammlung der älteren Eidgenössischen Abschiede*, ed. Johannes Strickler (Zürich: J. Schabeliz, 1876), 256–86; the text of the peace agreement is in Strickler, *Eidgenössischen Abschiede*, 4, 1b, 1478–83.

[3] Strickler, *Eidgenössischen Abschiede*, 4, 1b, 1479. I am deeply grateful to Prof. Randolph Head for helping me puzzle my way through this document and for providing these translations.

everyone ... should remain unchallenged on this account ...; but in this matter, no one shall be coerced into faith.[4]

But in the *Gemeine Herrschaften*, where competition between evangelicals and Catholics, who shared political authority, had led to war, the *Landfrieden* specified that questions of religious authority and affiliation would be decided at the local level, within each village. Continuing, the first article of the *Landfrieden* sets out these parameters, again in the tortured language of a difficult compromise:

[B]ut concerning the subsidiary allies and the domains where one rules together, where these have abolished the Mass and burned or taken down images, that they shall not be punished in their bodies, honor or goods. Where, in contrast, the Mass and other ceremonies are still present, those people should not be forced, and no preachers should be sent, established or given [to them] unless it is so recognized by the majority; rather, whatever is voted among the members of the parish to set up or take down, also [what they decide about] foods that God has not forbidden them to eat, that is how it should be done at the pleasure of the parish members, and no party should either deprecate or punish the other because of their faith.[5]

In subsequent articles, Zürich and the other evangelical confederates insisted that the Catholic alliance with Ferdinand of Austria be dissolved and that separate meetings of only some members of the *Eidgenossenschaft* be prohibited. In the thirteenth article, the issue of reparations for damage caused during the war was referred to further arbitration by the delegates who were conducting the negotiations, but with the proviso that in the absence of a satisfactory resolution of this contentious issue, the evangelical confederates could impose an economic embargo on the *V Orte*.[6] Not surprisingly, it was the subsequent economic blockade that precipitated a second round of war two years later.

In the Second Kappel War, the previously outnumbered and underprepared forces of the Catholic coalition surprised and decimated the hastily assembled army of Zürich on October 11, 1531. In a second battle on October 24, a combined force from Zürich, Bern, and Schaffhausen was overrun by soldiers from Zug. After another brief round of negotiations, November 14–20, 1531, Zürich signed a peace agreement with the *V Orte* (the core Catholic territories) on November 20, 1531, and four days later, Bern concluded a similar agreement.[7] Together, these documents constituted the *Zweiter Landfrieden*

[4] Strickler, *Eidgenössischen Abschiede*, 4, 1b, 1480.
[5] Strickler, *Eidgenössischen Abschiede*, 4, 1b, 1479; Ernst Walder also includes this critical article in his edition of the second peace: Ernst Walder, ed., *Religionsvergleiche des 16. Jahrhunderts*, vol. 7–8 of *Quellen zur neueren Geschichte* (Bern: Verlag Herbert Lang, 1960–61), 5.
[6] Strickler, *Eidgenössischen Abschiede*, 4, 1b, 1481.
[7] Basel and Schaffhausen signed separate and less comprehensive agreements with the *V Orte* on December 22, 1531, and January 31, 1532, respectively. Documents relating to these negotiations are published in Strickler, *Eidgenössischen Abschiede*, 4, 1b, 1214–24, and all of the peace agreements are published in Strickler, *Eidgenössischen Abschiede*, 4, 1b, 1567–77. A modern

(Second National Peace), which served as an important constitutional foundation for managing religious differences within the Swiss *Eidgenossenschaft* for the next 125 years.

Although the third article of this new *Landfrieden* formally abrogated the terms of the original *Landfrieden*, it was a surprisingly similar agreement; indeed, the *Zweiter Landfrieden*, though somewhat shorter, elaborated the basic provisions of the *Erster* more fully, without changing their essence. Article I, for example, spelled out the mutual recognition of religious differences among the sovereign confederates in more specific detail, with the opposing coalitions of confederates pledging to leave one another "in the unchallenged and undisputed practice" of their faith.[8] The critical article II specified the parameters of religious coexistence in the *Gemeine Herrschaften* in a long series of subclauses, which may be paraphrased as follows:

a) That the privileges of the confederates sharing the lordships should be maintained.

b) That those communities – i.e., "parishes, communes or domains ... by whatever name they might go" – that had chosen for the "new faith" would be able to maintain their practice of it.

c) That those communities that had adopted the new faith but now wished to return to the "old true Christian faith" would be allowed to do so.

d) That those individuals who had not disavowed the old faith, "in secret or in public," should "remain with their old faith unattacked or unhated" in communities that had adopted the new faith.

e) That groups that wished to "reestablish and carry out the seven sacraments, the office of the Holy Mass, and other elements of Christian Church ceremonies" in communities that had adopted the new faith should be allowed to do so.

f) That in divided communities, Church properties and endowments should be divided proportionally, "according to the number of armed men."

g) And finally that "[n]either party should either degrade or defame the other on account of belief, and he who would transgress this command shall be punished directly by the bailiff of that place on account of it, according to the nature of the matter."[9]

The most pronounced difference between the two peace settlements, with regard to the *Gemeine Herrrschaften*, was that, in addition to the greater specificity, the second provided for protection of Catholic minorities within Reformed communities in the *Gemeine Herrschaften*. That the settlement did

---

edition of the agreement between Zürich and the *V Orte* is published in Walder, *Religionsvergleiche*, I: 5–13.

[8] Strickler, *Eidgenössischen Abschiede*, 4, 1b, 1568, and Walder, *Religionsvergleiche*, I, 7. Quotations are from Walder, and translations are generously provided by Randolph Head.

[9] Strickler, *Eidgenössischen Abschiede*, 4, 1b, 1568–9, and Walder, *Religionsvergleiche*, I, 8–9.

not include an equivalent protection for evangelical or Reformed minorities in Catholic communities suggests the extent to which the tables had been turned militarily, but it does not alter the essential political compromises of the religious peace: mutual recognition, mutual security guarantees, and commitment to mediation of future disputes.

The third article reaffirmed the confederates' commitment to the "sworn alliances and letters, as well as everything that developed under our pious ancestors and came to us from old times," with Zürich pledging, in particular, noninterference "in any domain that does not pertain to us and where we have no dominion." Article IV enjoined *both sides* to give up newly created alliances, based on religious affiliations, "with anyone within our Confederation or with outside lords or cities."[10] This provision evokes, of course, the well-known principle of Swiss neutrality in European affairs, but in the early sixteenth century, this was still very much an untested policy in formation.[11] Under article V, Zürich was obliged to return reparations paid earlier by the V *Orte*, but in response to generalized complaints by the V *Orte* "that in various churches and houses of God the images and decorations were destroyed, broken, and burned," Zürich accepted responsibility only in some specific cases whereas the other damage claims, including damage resulting from the war, were subjected to further investigation and mediation. Finally, article VI provided that

from now on, whenever one party might have or later come to have any charges against the other, whether against one Confederate or several, or against spiritual or secular persons, that the same charging party shall be satisfied with the legal process, and will pursue and carry through its claims at law, in accordance with our sworn alliances.[12]

In order to restore peace within the *Eidgenossenschaft* and to secure their collective political future, then, all parties to the Swiss *Landfrieden* explicitly recognized and validated the coexistence of two competitive religious organizations within the same confederated polity and established some basic political rules by which their religious differences could be managed. These were, to be sure, circumstances that no one considered desirable, but in order to avoid political polarization across the reform/counterreform identity boundary that had occasioned political paralysis at the national level – that is, within the *Tagsatzung*, the meetings of the central political authority of the *Eidgenossenschaft* – the republican principle of territorial self-regulation would apply to the religious affairs of all the full members of the *Eidgenossenschaft*. This meant that cultural or religious sovereignty would mirror the fragmentation of the *Eidgenossenschaft*'s political sovereignty,

---

[10] Strickler, *Eidgenössischen Abschiede*, 4, 1b, 1569, and Walder, *Religionsvergleiche*, I, 9.
[11] Cf. Edgar Bonjour, *Swiss Neutrality, Its History and Meaning*, trans. Mary Hottinger (London: G. Allen & Unwin, 1946).
[12] Strickler, *Eidgenössischen Abschiede*, 4, 1b, 1570; Walder, *Religionsvergleiche*, I, 11.

while the religious differences of the confederates would be neutralized in national politics.[13]

Within the *Gemeine Herrschaften*, however, the territorial principle that regulated the affairs of the full members of the *Eidgenossenschaft* would have threatened to reignite confrontations among religiously different confederates that shared political sovereignty. Consequently the peace settlement provided that final, enforceable decisions for or against the reformation of religion in the *Gemeine Herrschaften* would be made at the community or parish level. This meant that cultural sovereignty would be even more radically fragmented in these politically peripheral jurisdictions than it was at the *Eidgenossenschaft*'s core.

Altogether, then, the Swiss *Landfrieden* outlined parameters for decision making in the realm of religious politics without freezing a status quo ante or specifying the outcome of the political process. This open-ended, process-oriented quality, Randolph Head argues, allowed the *Zweiter Landfrieden* to function, not simply as a truce, but as a constitutional foundation for managing change within the religiously divided *Eidgenossenschaft*.[14] In terms of the political processes that led recurrently toward war in Reformation Europe, then, what the Swiss *Landfrieden* did was, on the one hand, to deactivate or suppress the reform/counterreform identity boundary at the national level; thus, the scale and, by extension, the political salience of religious competition, or worse yet, *polarization*, was shifted to the territorial or local level in the interest of renewed cooperation among the free and self-regulating confederates in the *Tagsatzung*. On the other hand, the *Landfrieden* worked to block the (re)*escalation* of local religious conflicts into national, categorical struggles by (1) *channeling religious competition* into enforceable decision-making processes at the local level and judicial procedures at the national level and (2) *prohibiting domestic and international alliances* based on religious solidarity. In principle, then, straightforward rules adjudicated by competent authorities would replace coercive means, both to regulate decision making and to manage the distribution of resources that the coexistence of competitive religious organizations within common political boundaries entailed.

---

[13] I use the term "sovereignty" in the sense of the authority to make binding, enforceable decisions within a given territory or domain. This usage, which regards both cultural and political sovereignty as eminently divisible, contrasts sharply with the more absolute, indivisible sense that was developed later by theorists such as Jean Bodin in response to the ravages of the French civil wars. See Jean Bodin, *The Six Books of a Commonweale*, ed. and trans. Kenneth Douglas McRae (Cambridge, MA: Harvard University Press, 1962), and compare the work of his contemporary Johannes Althusius, *The Politics of Johannes Althusius*, trans. and ed. Frederick S. Carney (London: Eyre & Spottiswoode, 1964). On the divisibility of political sovereignty in early modern Europe more generally, see Wayne Te Brake, *Shaping History: Ordinary People in European Politics, 1500–1700* (Berkeley and Los Angeles: University of California Press, 1998).

[14] Randolph C. Head, "Negotiating Co-Existence through Institutions and Practice in Early Modern Europe: The Thurgau, 1520–1712." Paper presented to a conference on "Accommodating Difference: The Politics of Cultural Pluralism in Europe" at the Netherlands Institute for Advanced Study (Wassenaar, The Netherlands, 2001).

How well did the Swiss manage the processes of religious conflict and change under the provisions of the *Zweiter Landfrieden*? On the face of it, reasonably well, inasmuch as the Swiss *Eidgenossenschaft* was not again wracked by religious war – that is, coordinated destruction among religiously different members of the *Eidgenossenschaft* – until the second half of the seventeenth century. This is not to say, of course, that religious conflict disappeared altogether. On the contrary, religious contention continued to bedevil the Swiss *Eidgenossenschaft* for decades, even centuries, to come. Here it will be instructive to look at some examples of religious polarization and conflict at both the local level, in Thurgau and Baden, and the territorial level, in Basel, Glarus, and Appenzell; these were often difficult conflicts that nevertheless failed to reignite civil and religious war within the *Eidgenossenschaft*.

In the *Gemeine Herrschaft* of Thurgau, the hilly region of modern Switzerland just south of Lake Constance, Randolph Head has surveyed parish-level narratives of the post-Reformation era in order to discern the institutional contexts within which religious conflict and coexistence were managed.[15] By the time of the Second Kappel War, a substantial majority of the communities in Thurgau had opted for some kind of Protestant worship, but under the guidelines laid out in the second article of the *Zweiter Landfrieden*, which clearly disadvantaged the Reformed churches, a succession of Catholic governors worked hard to regain some of the ground the Catholics had lost. The result, in the first two decades after 1531, was a variety of hybrid forms of worship, including the sharing of many parish churches, within biconfessional communities, many of which did not, in fact, permanently divide the resources of the Church in accordance with the second article of the *Landfrieden*.[16] Beginning in the 1550s, however, increasing friction and polarization among the confederates that shared sovereignty in Thurgau fostered "numerous incidents of harassment, insult, vandalism, and litigiousness" reflecting especially local concerns about spiritual purity – for example, concerning the burial of "heretics" in consecrated graveyards and the use of baptismal fonts.[17] In addition, a succession of governors, both Catholic and Protestant, "spurred consciousness of religious differences by emphasizing confessional discipline and the obligation of subjects to conform and obey."[18] Still, local conflict rarely resulted in escalation or coordinated violence because at the national level, where the most contentious issues would be appealed and finally resolved under the *Landfrieden*, "politics rather than purely religious interests played a determining role."[19]

[15] See Randolph Head, "Fragmented Dominion, Fragmented Churches: The Institutionalization of the *Landfrieden* in Thurgau, 1460–1600," *Archiv für Reformationsgeschichte* 96 (2005): 117–44.
[16] Examples of *simultankirchen* (simultaneous churches) that have been shared by Protestants and Catholics since the sixteenth century may still be found in Ermatingen and Güttingen near the Bodenzee. See Chapter 4 in this volume.
[17] Head, "Fragmented Dominion," 134.   [18] Head, "Fragmented Dominion," 137.
[19] Head, "Fragmented Dominion," 138.

Similarly, Daniela Hacke examines the communication dynamics of a Protestant/Catholic conflict over baptismal fonts in the early seventeenth century in the *Gemeine Herrschaft* of Baden.[20] Like Thurgau, Baden was a confessionally mixed territory in which the shared sovereignty of the confederates was in the majority Catholic (of the eight confederates that shared the sovereignty, five were Catholic). Under the principles of the Catholic Reformation following the Council of Trent, Catholic priests were urged to lock their baptismal fonts lest the holy water be contaminated. In 1603, then, the Reformed Protestants in the village of Zurzach petitioned to be allowed to install their own baptismal font within the parish church that the Catholic and Reformed communities shared. This request ran up against Catholic opposition on the grounds that any alteration of a shared-church interior, and especially those undertaken by the Reformed community, was considered a breach of the *Landfrieden*. This, in turn, set off a protracted negotiation among a wide range of political actors within the *Eidgenossenschaft*. Following a series of written communications, by which the confederates negotiated their differences, it was finally decreed in 1605 "that the members of the Reformed congregation in Zurzach may place a font in the church of the said town for the conduct of their Christian services."[21] Still, this permission did not specify *where* the baptismal font should be placed within the church, and after a further round of negotiations did not produce a consensus, Protestant Zürich, the leader of the Reformed confederates, forced the issue and ordered the font to be installed, in accordance with Reformed Protestant principles, in front of the pulpit. Although Zürich's action drew loud Catholic complaints, it did not force a confrontation between the Catholic and Reformed confederates, and in the end, the new baptismal font remained in place. As Haeke concludes,

An awareness of the delicacy of the position of the *Gemeine Harrschaften* as far as Confederate harmony was concerned was a key ingredient in contemporary political perceptions. As the Catholic and Reformed Confederates sought to de-escalate conflicts, so diplomatic language and communicative processes took on special significance.[22]

Through their complex communications/negotiations under the auspices of the *Landfrieden*, the confederates maintained peace and unity at the national level by ensuring that denominational conflicts, even at the local level in the *Gemeine Herrschaften*, remained negotiable.

At the territorial level, managing religious conflict and coexistence was a different matter altogether. By pledging in the second article of the *Landfrieden* to leave one another "in the unchallenged and undisputed practice" of their faith, the confederates were clearly asserting the principle of

---

[20] Daniela Haeke, "Church, Space and Conflict: Religious Co-Existence and Political Communication in Seventeenth-Century Switzerland," *German History* 25, no. 3 (2007): 286–312.

[21] Quoted in Haeke, "Church, Space and Conflict," 304.

[22] Haeke, "Church, Space and Conflict," 312.

territorial self-regulation in matters of religion. In most cases, this meant that prior decisions either for or against the reformation of religion would stand, leaving territorial authorities to enforce conformity to such either/or decisions without outside interference. Under this principle the majority (seven) of the thirteen confederates – Uri, Schwyz, Underwalden, Luzern, Zug, Solothurn, and Fribourg – remained Catholic, while just four confederates – Zürich, Bern, Basel, and Schaffhausen – were officially Reformed. In some of the Catholic confederates, such as Luzern, Zug, and Solothurn, emerging evangelical movements were forcefully repressed, especially after the second war.[23] In the larger Reformed confederates, such as Zürich and Bern, extending the Reformation to the countryside and enforcing a new religious uniformity turned out to be a formidable task. Zürich forcibly expelled many of its Anabaptist dissidents early on, but the authorities had to remain vigilant in the face of religious "dissent" in the countryside.[24] Similarly, Bern, despite the strenuous efforts of its ecclesiastical courts, was ultimately unable to eradicate either its Catholic or its Anabaptist minorities.[25] In other words, whereas *negotiation* and *segregation* characterized the peace at the national level, *domination* and *subversion* were both clearly operative at the local level within the various confederates. In Basel, by contrast, the will to enforce Protestant uniformity outside the city itself, within the territory of the Catholic Bishopric of Basel, was apparently lacking; indeed, the Reformed municipal authorities developed a modus vivendi with their Catholic neighbors, repeatedly passing up opportunities to extend Protestantism more forcefully in the dependent bishopric, for the sake of peace and harmony.[26]

In Glarus and Appenzell, however, choosing either for or against the reformation of religion turned out to be extremely difficult, and the challenge of managing religious conflict and coexistence there remained particularly vexing. In both of these largely rural territories, the participatory *Landesgemeinde* (meetings of all full citizens) empowered each parish or community to choose either for or against religious reforms, and in consequence, both became thoroughly biconfessional, not unlike the *Gemeine Herrschaften*. But since Glarus and Appenzell were full members of the *Eidgenossenschaft*, their mixed-confessional makeup had the potential to

[23] Bruce Gordon, *The Swiss Reformation* (Manchester: Manchester University Press, 2002), 119–22.

[24] See Gordon, *The Swiss Reformation*, 135–8, 228ff.

[25] See Gordon, *The Swiss Reformation*; Heinrich Schmidt, *Dorf und Religion: Reformierte Sittenzucht in Berner Landgemeinden der Frühen Neuzeit*, Quellen und Forschungen Zür Agrargeschichte (Stuttgart: Gustav Fischer, 1995); and Mark Furner, "The Repression and Survival of Anabaptism in the Emmental, Switzerland, 1659–1743" (Ph.D. diss., Cambridge University, 1998). See also Chapter 4 in this volume.

[26] See Hans Berner, *"Die gute Correspondenz": die Politik der Stadt Basel gegenüber dem Fürstbistum Basel in den Jahren 1525–1585*, Basler Beiträge zur Geschichtswissenschaft, vol. 158 (Basel: Helbing & Lichtenhahn, 1989).

trouble the often polarized politics of the *Eidgenossenschaft*, more directly and in ways that the *Landfrieden* did not anticipate.

In order to stem a rising tide of conflict and violence that accompanied Glarus's inability to resolve the question of religion in 1528 and 1529, the *Landesgemeinde* of Glarus decided in May 1529, just before the outbreak of the First Kappel War, that each community should be allowed to choose its form of worship.[27] In the wake of the First Kappel War, Zürich continued to push for a complete reformation of the Church in Glarus, but in the wake of the Second Kappel War, it was the *V Orte* that demanded a return to the "old faith." Although the evangelicals appear to have been in the majority, they were weakened by the lack of external support from Zürich, which had been defeated in the second war, and in 1532 the deeply divided parties began meeting in separate *Landesgemeinden*. In order to preserve domestic peace, however, the contending parties agreed to the *Landesvertrag* (First Glarus Peace) of 1532, which validated the separate meetings of the *Landesgemeinde*, granting each a half-vote in the *Tagsatzung*; declared that the Catholics and evangelicals would not preach against one another; and provided that only one village, Linthal, be returned to Catholicism.[28] This arrangement provided stability until the mid-1550s, when Reformed worship was established in the village of Linthal in the absence of a Catholic priest. The *V Orte* considered this a violation of the agreement, and in 1559 they mobilized for military action to expel the Reformed and forcibly reestablish Catholicism in all of Glarus. Although the *V Orte* refused to recognize the Reformed in Glarus for several years, outside mediation in the 1560s finally convinced the two factions to restore the peace agreement of 1532, thereby sparing the *Eidgenossenschaft* a third round of religious war, at least for the time being. Indeed, religious polarization in Glarus extended well into the seventeenth century, but each new round of open conflict ended in a new/old agreement or *Landesvertrag*, the fifth and last coming in 1687. In short, mediation and *negotiation* recurrently prevented the *escalation* of territorial conflict into coordinated destruction on the national level.

In Appenzell, too, the *Landesgemeinde* decided to have each community choose for or against the reform of religion.[29] As early as April 1525, the *Landesgemeinde* had mandated "biblical" preaching by all priests, but a subsequent religious disputation ended in rancor rather than resolution.

[27] Markus René Wick, "Der 'Glarnerhandel,' Strukturgeschichte und konfliktsoziologische Hypothesen zum Glarner Konfessionsgegensatz," *Jahrbuch des Historischen Vereins Glarus* 69 (1982): 49–240; see especially the extended chronology on pp. 201–21. In English, see Gordon, *The Swiss Reformation*, 98–100, 167–8, and passim.

[28] The text of this agreement is published in Walder, *Religionsvergleiche*, I, 34–8.

[29] See P. Rainhald Fischer, Walter Schläpfer, and Franz Stark, *Das ungeteilte Land (Von der Urzeit bis 1597)*, vol. 1 of *Appenzeller Geschichte* (Appenzell: Regierungen der beiden Halbkantone Appenzell, 1964). I am deeply grateful to Prof. Peter Blickle, formerly of the University of Bern, and his staff for helping me to puzzle my way through this singularly complex and sad history of religious polarization and paralysis.

As Bruce Gordon describes, the Appenzell decision to empower local choice meant "[t]here could be only one form of worship in each church and that was to be chosen by the people, with the minority being allowed to attend the nearest church of their faith."[30] As it turned out, however, the local decision making took on a rather clear geographic pattern with the *Innere Roden* (inner or core districts) by and large retaining the "old faith" and the *Aussere Roden* (or peripheral districts) embracing Reformed worship. Although this geographic *segregation* proved to be less volatile than the more intermingled biconfessional pattern in Glarus, *polarization* between the two parties recurrently paralyzed the politics of this classically participatory confederate to the extent that it could no longer function as a full member of the *Eidgenossenschaft*.[31] Finally, in 1597, the *Landesgemeinde* ruefully decided to divide the territory into two half-confederates, with each having a half-vote in the affairs of the *Eidgenossenschaft*.[32] In this case, then, *negotiation* combined with segregation to produce a territorial modus vivendi that preserved peace and harmony on a national scale.

Although these examples are hardly exhaustive, they are illustrative of the relational dynamics, rooted in provisions of the *Landfrieden*, that made enduring peace possible in the Swiss *Eidgenossenschaft*. At bottom, the signatories to the Swiss *Landfrieden* of 1531 committed themselves to three essential principles that appeared recurrently in the settlements of Europe's religious wars in the early modern period: (1) mutual recognition among mutually intolerant religious groups; (2) pledges of nonaggression and security; and (3) commitment to mediation or legal procedures to resolve future conflicts. Within these parameters, then, the ongoing management of religious conflict within the Swiss *Eidgenossenschaft* in the aftermath of the Kappel wars combined all of the relational dynamics that recurrently made peace possible in early modern Europe.

The most obvious mechanism at work here is *negotiation*, by which I mean to denote not only the brief negotiations that produced the formal settlements, but also the ongoing mediation, legal processes, and consensual decision making that recurrently prevented the escalation of local or territorial conflicts into the coordinated destruction of civil and religious war. Equally obvious is the dynamic of *segregation*, by which I mean to denote not only the various forms of institutional, political, and geographic segregation of the contentious religious parties, which reduced the opportunities for direct conflict, but also the dissolution of larger alliances and coalitions, including prominently specialists in coercion, that recurrently facilitated civil and religious war in post-Reformation Europe. At the same time, we see the dynamic of *domination*,

---

[30] Gordon, *The Swiss Reformation*, 93.

[31] The dysfunctional quality of Appenzell's politics is readily evident in its official documents: Traugott Schiess, ed., *Von der Aufname Appenzells in den Eidgenössischen Bund bis zur Landesteilung, 1514–1597*, vol. 2 of *Appenzeller Urkundenbuch* (Trogen: O. Kübler, 1934).

[32] The text of this agreement is published in Walder, *Religionsvergleiche*, I, 21–32.

which is evident in the unequal power relations between the confessions as a result of either/or decision making with regard to religious reform, both at the territorial and the local level. But by the same token, we see the countervailing dynamic of *subversion*, both in the sharing of churches and in the cohabitation of territories, despite the aspiration for unity and purity that domination often entailed. In sum, though it would be hard to consider the relatively modest Kappel wars the model for religious destruction to come, the Swiss *Landfrieden*, I would like to suggest, both anticipates the basic principles of future peace settlements and illustrates the recurrent relational dynamics that made enduring religious peace possible, even in the absence of formal religious settlements.

VALIDATING RELIGIOUS DIVERSITY IN GERMANY

Following the Peasants' War, religious war was much slower to (re)develop in the German Empire than in Switzerland, and when it did, it lacked the urgency and immediacy of the military confrontations between locally mobilized citizen armies in Switzerland. Still, religious war threatened the political viability of the composite German *Reich*, just as it did the Swiss *Eidgenossenschaft*, and the same mechanisms that were operative in the Swiss *Landfrieden* are evident in the more famous *Augsburger Religionsfriede* (Religious Peace of Augsburg) in 1555. In retrospect, however, what seems distinctive about the peace process that ended the Schmalkaldic Wars in Germany is that the template for this peace was visible long before its final negotiation.

Given the hundreds of more-or-less self-governing polities that constituted the empire, it is even more difficult to narrate the "progress" of evangelical reform in Germany than in Switzerland. At one time or another, more than three-fourths of the empire's eighty imperial free cities – that is, cities subject only to the emperor and directly represented in the imperial *Reichstag* – plus a large number of the more than 2,000 territorial cities, and a large swathe of principalities, especially in northern and central Germany, adopted some form of reformed church regulation – thereby institutionalizing the changes in religious ritual, belief, and governance that we associate with the Protestant Reformation – prior to the outbreak of the Schmalkaldic Wars.[33] All of this was done, however, in open defiance of the will of the emperor, Charles V, and the Edict of Worms, which had condemned Lutheran teachings in 1521!

[33] For a brief analysis of the political dynamics of both the urban and princely reformations, see Te Brake, *Shaping History*, 35–49. The standard work on the urban reformations, which are the best studied, is Bernd Moeller, *Imperial Cities and the Reformation: Three Essays*, eds. H. C. E. Midelfort and M. U. Edwards (Philadelphia: Fortress Press, 1972); see also Christopher W. Close, *The Negotiated Reformation: Imperial Cities and the Politics of Urban Reform, 1525–1550* (Cambridge; New York: Cambridge University Press, 2009). The best survey in English of the entire process is Euan Cameron, *The European Reformation* (Oxford: Clarendon Press, 1991); see especially Cameron's very useful table of the princely reformations in Germany on p. 269 as well as his map of the religious complexion of the major German territories on pp. 264–5.

Meanwhile, in Bavaria, the lands under direct Habsburg rule, the territories controlled by the major prince-bishops, and most of the other ecclesiastical states, the established Church retained its dominant position. Thus, the religious politics of the empire were characterized by a growing polarization between two distinct factions of rulers, which began to form defensive alliances. Indeed, as Euan Cameron suggests, for more than thirty years, beginning in the early 1520s, the reformation of religion became *the* issue in the meetings of the *Reichstag*.[34]

Between 1521 and 1555, there were, to be sure, frequent attempts to resolve the religious issues that divided the rulers of Germany. In principle, a theological reconciliation between the established Church and the reformers would have depoliticized the religious issues and averted armed conflict; indeed, whenever the defenders of papal unity and orthodoxy demanded a halt to "unauthorized" religious innovations, the proponents of reform invariably asked for suspension of any and all attempts to turn back the clock *until such time* as the Church could convene a general council to resolve the underlying religious differences. Increasingly polarized in two uncompromising factions, and in the absence of a general council to resolve their religious differences, then, the Estates of the empire repeatedly failed to take decisive action. In the *Reichstag* at Speyer in the summer of 1526, for example, Archduke Ferdinand, who was Charles V's brother and the presiding officer of the assembly, called for immediate implementation of the Edict of Worms. The imperial free cities declared, however, that they were unable to comply with the edict, and in the end the assembly simply resolved that each of the Estates would govern their own affairs "as [they] hope and trust to answer to God and his Imperial Majesty."[35] Thus, as in the Swiss *Eidgenossenschaft*, the idea of devolving the authority for decisions over religious matters to the level of the territories and cities that constituted the imperial Estates emerged at a very early date. The difference here was that the counterargument for Christian unity was being made by Europe's most successful composite state maker, Charles V.

The *Reichstag* at Speyer in 1529 was less sympathetic to the reformers' cause, and in April the majority resolved that errors with regard to the sacraments would not be tolerated and that religious changes should be halted. In response to this apparent abrogation of the earlier resolution from 1526, the minority group of "Lutheran" princes and cities submitted its famous *Protest*, which gave rise to the term *Protestants*, even though the unsympathetic majority did not even allow the *Protest* to be registered among the official acts of the

---

[34] See Cameron's succinct survey of the building political crisis in imperial politics in *The European Reformation*, 339–49; see also the list of the various Protestant leagues on p. 271. Compare A. F. Pollard, "The Conflict of Creeds and Parties in Germany," in *The Reformation*, vol. 2 of *The Cambridge Modern History*, eds. A. W. Ward, G. W. Prothero, and Stanley Leathes, reprint, 1934 (Cambridge: Cambridge University Press, 1903), 206–45, which is chock full of both useful information and early twentieth-century prejudice.

[35] Quoted in Cameron, *The European Reformation*, 341.

session.[36] At the *Reichstag* in Augsburg in 1530, with Charles V himself present, the Lutheran princes supported by the cities of Nuremberg and Reutlingen submitted a *Confession*, which defended the Lutherans from the charge of extreme heresy and formulated their position as near as possible to the Church's traditions.[37] The "Catholic" response to the Augsburg Confession was a *Confutation*, which served only to produce stalemate rather than reconciliation.

It was in this context that the Protestant leaders formed the League of Schmalkalden in 1531 as a more-or-less permanent vehicle for their mutual defence, which greatly enhanced the potential for armed confrontation. Still, the military advance into Hungary of Suleiman the Magnificent, the sultan of the Ottoman Empire, led to the Peace of Nuremberg on July 23, 1532 – that is, before an armed confrontation had even developed.[38] This "temporary" agreement suspended the implementation of the Edict of Worms and, in particular, halted legal suits that were intended to recover Church property and assets that had been seized in the reformation process; thus, it allowed Charles V to win the tangible support of men and arms from his Protestant "enemies" for a common struggle against "The Infidel Scourge of God" in the east.[39] As Thomas Brady argues, "The peace [of Nuremberg], which was renewed in 1534 and again in 1539, also provided the Protestant powers with the time and security to bring their churches under control and to deal with religious radicalism in the form of Anabaptism."[40] Indeed, even though the League of Schmalkalden's forcible restoration of the Lutheran Duke of Württemberg in 1534 clearly violated the status quo, common enemies such as the Ottoman Turks and the Anabaptist revolutionaries at Münster repeatedly brought the opposing leagues of German rulers into "temporary" agreements that implicitly validated their existing religious differences *until such time* as a general council of the Church could resolve the underlying issues of theology, ritual practice, and ecclesiastical assets.

---

[36] The list of the "Protesters" can be found in Cameron, *The European Reformation*, table 16.2, p. 271.

[37] Four other south-German cities – Strasbourg, Constance, Lindau, and Memmingen – aligned more clearly with Zürich and Zwingli, submitted their own confession, called the *Tetrapolitana*, which reflected theological differences between Luther and Zwingli; in 1536, however, representatives of the two groups glossed over the differences between the Augsburg Confession and the *Tetrapolitana* in the "Wittenberg Accord" so that henceforth they could constitute a united front as the proponents of the Augsburg Confession.

[38] The Latin text of this agreement may be found in B. J. Kidd, ed., *Documents Illustrative of the Continental Reformation* (Oxford: Clarendon Press, 1911), 302–4.

[39] For the fierce rhetorical construction of this Muslim "menace," see, for example, John W. Bohnstedt, "The Infidel Scourge of God: The Turkish Menace as Seen by German Pamphleteers of the Reformation Era," *Transactions of the American Philosophical Society*, New Series 58, part 9 (1968).

[40] Thomas A. Brady, Jr., *The Politics of the Reformation in Germany: Jacob Sturm (1489–1553) of Strasbourg* (Atlantic Highlands, NJ: Humanities Press, 1997), 117–18.

In the first round of the Schmalkaldic Wars, Charles V defeated his Protestant enemies decisively at Mühlberg in 1547 and proceeded unilaterally to publish a provisional peace called the Augsburg Interim (1548),[41] which seemed to satisfy no one. The interim required, for example, that Protestant territories and cities readopt traditional Catholic religious practices, such as the seven sacraments, but it also allowed Protestant clergy to marry. Not surprisingly, the interim awakened strong opposition from both sides. At the same time, Charles's autocratic and coercive, yet ineffective, attempts to implement the Augsburg Interim led the Protestant leaders to reconstitute the Schmalkaldic League in 1550 and to restart the war in 1552. After Charles was driven from Innsbrück, the Treaty of Passau (1552), concluded by Elector Maurice of Saxony and Ferdinand, Charles's brother, once again postponed a resolution of the religious issues until the next *Reichstag*.[42] But in 1554, Charles, thoroughly exhausted and discouraged, left the forthcoming negotiations entirely to his brother and eventually retreated to a monastery in Spain. When the *Reichstag* finally met at Augsburg, it produced what proved to be a remarkably durable peace agreement that was promulgated by Ferdinand on September 25, 1555.[43]

The opening paragraph of the *Augsburger Religionsfriede* offers eloquent testimony to the sense of weariness and resignation with which the rulers of the composite German Empire came at long last in 1555 to accept the obvious fact of their religious differences as the necessary foundation for their common political future:

Whereas, at all the Diets held during the last thirty years and more, and at several special sessions besides, there have often been negotiations and consultations to establish between the Estates of the Holy Empire a general, continuous and enduring peace in regard to the contending religions; and several times terms of peace were drawn up, which, however, were never sufficient for the maintenance of peace, but in spite of them the Estates of the Empire remained continually in bitterness and distrust toward each other, from which not a little evil has its origin: inasmuch then, as in continued division of religion a comprehensive agreement and treaty of peace, regarding both religions and profane and secular things, was not undertaken ... so that the Estates and subjects could not be sure of continual and abiding safety, but everybody had continually to stand doubtfully in unbearable danger: to remove such serious uncertainty, and to secure again

---

[41] See Joachim Mehlhausen, ed., *Das Augsburger Interim von 1548*, Texte zur Geschichte der evangelischen Theologie (Neukirchen-Vluyn: Neukirchener Verlag, 1970).

[42] The German text is in Christoph Lehmann, *De pace religionis acta publica et originalia, das ist, Reichs-Handlungen, Schriften und Protocollen über die Reichs-Constitution des Religion-Friedens*, 3 vol. (Franckfurt am Main: Christian Genschens Buchhandlung, 1707–10), I, 1–7.

[43] The definitive, critical edition of the German text of the Religious Peace of Augsburg can be found in Karl Brandi, ed., *Der Augsburger Religionsfriede vom 25 Sept. 1555: Kritische Ausgabe des Textes* (München: Rieger'sche Universitäts-Buchhandlung, 1896). See also Lehmann, *De pace religionis*, II, 62–5. An English translation (remarkably difficult to find for such an important document) based on the Lehmann edition can be found in Henry Clay Vedder, ed., *The Peace of Augsburg*, Historical Leaflets, no. 5 (Chester, PA: Crozer Theological Seminary, 1901).

peace and confidence in the minds of Estates and subjects toward each other, and to save the German nation, our beloved Fatherland, from final dissolution and ruin, We [King Ferdinand], on the one hand, have united and agreed with the Electors and the regular Princes and Estates present ... as they on the other hand with Us.[44]

Accordingly, the agreement began by declaring a permanent cessation of hostilities: "We therefore establish, will and command, that from henceforth no one ... shall engage in feuds, make war upon, rob, seize, invest or besiege another."[45] The heart of the settlement, however, was an explicit recognition by the members of the imperial diet of their obvious religious differences. On one hand,

the Imperial Majesty, and We [King Ferdinand], and the Electors, Princes and Estates of the Empire, will make war on no Estates of the Empire on account of the Augsburg Confession and the doctrine, religion and faith of the same, nor injure, nor do violence to, or in any other ways invade it, against conscience, knowledge and will, where the religion, faith, church-usages, ordinances and ceremonies of the Augsburg Confession have been established or may hereafter be established in their principalities, lands and dominions. ...

On the other hand, the Estates that have accepted the Augsburg Confession shall suffer his Imperial Majesty, Us and Electors, Princes and other Estates of the Holy Empire, adhering to the old religion ... to abide in like manner by our religion, faith, church-usages, ordinances and ceremonies.[46]

The thrust here was not so much to manage an ongoing and extremely volatile process, as the *Landfrieden* did in the early stages of the Swiss Reformation, but rather to validate relatively stable "facts on the ground" by means of pledges of mutual recognition. The deeply divided rulers of Germany were, thus, guaranteeing one another the legitimacy and security that had eluded them for more than three decades.

The most explicit expression of the signatories' urge to preserve the status quo, and by extension the security and authority of territorial rulers, comes later in the document in the form of an injunction against the kind of cross-territorial support or interference that so readily fostered *escalation*: "No [members of the] Estates shall endeavor to urge another or the subjects of the same to his religion, nor against his authority take them under his protection and care, nor annoy in any way."[47] An earlier draft proposal for the treaty had further stipulated that

if the subjects of one or more Estates should determine to rebel against their true overlords upon pretext of religion, or should determine to burst forth and undertake any innovation in their religion, without the knowledge and approval of their true

---

[44] Brandi, *Augsburger Religionsfriede*, 16; Vedder, *The Peace of Augsburg*, 1–2.
[45] Brandi, *Augsburger Religionsfriede*, 16; Vedder, *The Peace of Augsburg*, 2.
[46] Brandi, *Augsburger Religionsfriede*, 17–18; Vedder, *The Peace of Augsburg*, 3.
[47] Brandi, *Augsburger Religionsfriede*, 31; Vedder, *The Peace of Augsburg*, 7. In the Brandi edition this is numbered as paragraph 10, whereas in Vedder's translation this is paragraph 11; there are no paragraph numbers in the Lehmann edition.

overlords, then upon the strength of this Peace the other Estates should give their true overlords earnest and true support, aid and assistance until those disobedient subjects shall again be persuaded and reduced to obedience.[48]

This unambiguously authoritarian provision did not, however, make it into the final draft, which suggests the extent to which the *Religionsfriede* sought simultaneously to validate diversity and preserve stability rather than to assert unequivocally and guarantee collectively the religious sovereignty of territorial rulers. Indeed, the limited gesture toward mutual nonaggression that was actually adopted was immediately softened in the final version by the assurance in the following paragraph that when individual subjects

adhering to the old religion or to the Augsburg Confession, for the sake of their religion wish to go with wife and children to another place in the ... Holy Empire, and settle there; such going and coming, and the sale of property and goods ... shall be unhindered, permitted and granted, and on our honor and faith shall in no way be punished.[49]

Historians have traditionally described this narrowly as the formal right of emigration (*ius emigrandi*), but it could just as plausibly be understood as an early, if limited, assertion of the individual's freedom of religious conscience in the face of authoritarian claims to religious uniformity.[50]

The *Religionsfriede* also includes the infamous exclusion of "other" Christians that is often cited to account for the agreement's ultimate failure: "Yet all others if they are not adherents of either of the above mentioned religions, are not intended in this peace, but shall be altogether excluded."[51] Some variants of an earlier draft of the treaty specify the "others" as "sacramentarians [i.e., Zwinglians or Swiss Reformed], anabaptists and other suchlike sects,"[52] and the inclusion of such a specification in the final treaty would have had serious repercussions for cities such as Strasbourg, which were allied with the Swiss reformers. In the absence of such a specification, however, the verbal gymnastics of the "Wittenburg Accord," which in 1536 had glossed over the doctrinal differences between the Lutheran Augsburg Confession and the Zwinglian *Tetrapolitana*,[53] could continue to provide cover for all

---

[48] See Brandi, *Augsburger Religionsfriede*, 11–12. This translation comes from Archibald S. Foord, "Historical Revisions: The Peace of Augsburg," *New England Social Studies Bulletin* 9 (1952): 2; unfortunately Foord, who sees this passage as a strong confirmation of the authoritarian principle, mistakes the draft version for the final version, where it was clearly eliminated.

[49] Brandi, *Augsburger Religionsfriede*, 32; Vedder, *The Peace of Augsburg*, 7.

[50] See David M. Luebke, "A Multiconfessional Empire," in *A Companion to Multiconfessionalism in the Early Modern World*, ed. Thomas Max Safley, Brill's Companions to the Christian Tradition, vol. 28 (Leiden; Boston: Brill, 2011), 135: "Forcible conversion was forbidden categorically; non-conformists were given the right to emigrate in an orderly manner." See also Christoph Link, "Ius Emigrandi," in *Religion Past & Present: Encyclopedia of Theology and Religion*, ed. Hans Dieter Betz (Leiden; Boston: Brill, 2007–13), vol. 6, 626.

[51] Brandi, *Augsburger Religionsfriede*, 21; Vedder, *The Peace of Augsburg*, 4.

[52] See Brandi, *Augsburger Religionsfriede*, 7.

[53] See Cameron, *The European Reformation*, 161–6, 343, and note 37 above.

"mainline" Protestants – that is, still excluding the dreaded Anabaptists – as adherents to the Augsburg Confession.

Like the Swiss *Landfrieden*, then, the *Religionsfriede* recognized and validated religious differences among the constituent elements of a larger composite state in order to ease the enduring religious *polarization* that had intermittently paralyzed imperial governance for three decades. But in this case the devolution of religious sovereignty came at the obvious expense of – indeed, as a resounding defeat of – the emperor's countervailing claim to a centralized, imperial religious sovereignty, which he regarded as a necessary complement to his claims to imperial political sovereignty, hence, Charles's personal retreat from German politics in order to avoid an unacceptable compromise.

The *Religionsfriede* also implicitly frustrated pious hopes on all sides for a final reconciliation of the theological differences that divided Protestants from Catholics – the idealized *sine qua non* of "true peace," the prospect of which the Protestants had skillfully used to forestall repression that might have been justified by the Edict of Worms.[54] Although the agreement clings rhetorically to the possibility of that ideal resolution sometime in the future, the negotiators could hardly avoid the probability that, after several decades of division and conflict, reconciliation might never occur:

Where then such settlement will not ensue by means of general councils, national synods, colloquies and imperial acts, then shall this state of peace [i.e., the *Religionsfriede*] in all the aforesaid points and articles no less continue and remain in force, until a final settlement of religion and matters of faith. And herewith in the manner aforesaid, and in all ways besides, they shall establish, conclude and remain an enduring, constant, unbroken and perpetual peace.[55]

Here the tortured language of the text suggests again just how difficult it had been for the politically privileged parties to this agreement to accept compromise, to validate the status quo, and to embrace the obvious fact of religious diversity as the foundation for an enduring peace.

The *Religionsfriede* most explicitly embraces religious diversity, at the expense of authoritarian uniformity, in a paragraph that spells out the political implications of the peace agreement for the imperial free cities, the overwhelming majority of which had adopted some form of Protestant worship:

But moreover in many free and imperial cities both religions, namely, our old religion and the Augsburg Confessional religion, have hitherto come into vogue and practice; the same shall remain hereafter and be held in the same cities, and citizens and inhabitants of the same free and imperial cities, spiritual ranks and secular, shall peacefully and quietly dwell with and among one another, and no party shall venture to abolish the religion, church-customs or ceremonies of another, or persecute them therefor; but each party shall permit the other, in virtue of this peace, to remain in a peaceful and friendly manner

[54] Cf. Henry Clay Vedder, ed., *The Decree of Worms*, Historical Leaflets, no. 3 (Chester, PA: Crozer Theological Seminary, 1901).
[55] Brandi, *Augsburger Religionsfriede*, 33–4; Vedder, *The Peace of Augsburg*, 8.

in [the enjoyment of] their religion, faith, church-usages, customs and ceremonies, and of their goods and chattels, and all else that the Estates of the Empire have decided and commanded above concerning religion.[56]

Coming in the wake of three decades of competition and conflict, this ringing endorsement of the viability and sustainability of peaceful religious coexistence, not just among the territories of the empire but within its urban communities, suggests how fundamentally the German political and cultural landscape had been transformed in the course of nearly four decades of religious struggle.

There remained, however, two important points on which the parties to the *Religionsfriede* could not agree. The first involved the thorny question of what would become of ecclesiastical properties, incomes, and rights "when one or more of the spiritual Estates [i.e., the holders of (arch)bishoprics, prelatures, or benefices] should abandon the old religion." Since the Protestants would not agree to the Catholics' demands, Ferdinand simply declared in his own name that "where an archbishop, bishop, prelate or other spiritual incumbent shall depart from our old religion, he shall immediately abandon, without any opposition or delay, his archbishopric, bishopric, prelature, and other benefices, with the fruits and incomes that he may have had from it."[57] Given the Protestants' rejection of this so-called Ecclesiastical Reservation, it is hardly surprising that this issue remained divisive, and this provision was repeatedly violated in the decades to come.

The second issue on which compromise could apparently not be reached had to do with the position of Protestants within ecclesiastical states that had remained Catholic. In order to assure Protestant assent to the *Religionsfriede* as a whole, Ferdinand issued a supplementary declaration, which he proclaimed to be an integral and unassailable part of the religious peace; again in his own name and on the authority delegated to him by Charles V, he declared

[t]hat the spiritual [Estates] shall not, on account of religion, faith, church-usages, and ceremonies, hereafter persecute through anybody their knights, cities and communes, which long time ago became adherents of the Augsburg Confession and its religion, and have openly professed and practiced the said religion, faith, church-usages, ordinances and ceremonies; but shall permit them to be undisturbed in the same, until the aforesaid Christian settlement of religion.[58]

Like the ecclesiastical reservation, this declaration of free religious conscience and practice on behalf of Protestants within ecclesiastical jurisdictions remained contentious, and both of King Ferdinand's declarations were frequently violated in the decades to come. Still, such violations did not, in fact, restart the processes that recurrently led to war.

Altogether, then, the *Augsburger Religionsfriede*, like the Swiss *Landfrieden* before it, reduced the salience of religious identities in the political affairs of the

[56] Brandi, *Augsburger Religionsfriede*, 35; Vedder, *The Peace of Augsburg*, 8–9.
[57] Brandi, *Augsburger Religionsfriede*, 23–4; Vedder, *The Peace of Augsburg*, 4–5.
[58] Lehmann, *De pace religionis*, I, 55–6; Vedder, *The Peace of Augsburg*, 13.

Reichstag by means of pledges of mutual recognition and security; in doing so, it shifted the scale of religious sovereignty – which is to say, final decision-making authority with respect to the possible reform of religious belief and practice – to the territorial or local level. Where possible, it also sought to prevent the (re)*escalation* of local conflicts by channeling disputes over ecclesiastical resources into mediation and formal adjudication procedures.[59] This is not to say, of course, that it enunciated anything like the authoritarian principle of *cuius regio eius religio*, which does not appear in any of the original texts.[60] On the contrary, the *Religionsfriede* very pragmatically asserted important limitations on the religious authority of all political leaders and, thereby, embraced religious diversity as the only viable foundation of religious peace *until such time* as the underlying theological and ecclesiastical differences could be resolved.

Like the Swiss *Landfrieden*, the German *Religionsfriede* was a relatively successful settlement. Although religious war broke out again within the empire in 1618, the *Religionsfriede*, having validated the diversity that had existed for some time, did provide a framework within which those who professed the Augsburg Confession and those who maintained the "old religion" could live in relative peace, though not necessarily harmony, for more than six decades. Indeed, there were multiple challenges to the status quo, which the *Religionsfriede* had, on the whole, not envisioned. On the one hand, there was a series of princely conversions that changed the confessional map of the empire, including the conversion of Electors of the Palatinate and Brandenburg to Calvinism. On the other hand, there were a number of contests between territorial rulers and their subjects that certainly called into question the rulers' claims to the so-called *ius reformandi*, which claim historians have traditionally seen as the foundation of an essentially authoritarian peace.[61] In the East Frisian city of Emden, for example, a combined municipal and ecclesiastical revolution successfully resisted an aggressively Lutheran prince and preserved the local Calvinist church.[62] Similarly, the Lutheran city of Lemgo successfully resisted the Count of Lippe's attempt to impose his newly adopted Calvinism in the 1610s.[63] At the same time, Protestantism seemed also

[59] See, for example, paragraph 9 (in the Brandi edition; paragraph 10 in the Vedder translation), which provides for appointment of arbiters to resolve disputes over eccleisastical resources intended to support ministers, schools, hospitals, and the poor. Brandi, *Augsburger Religionsfriede*, 30; Vedder, *The Peace of Augsburg*, 6–7.

[60] See Chapter 1, note 20, in this volume.

[61] See Bernd Christian Schneider, *Ius reformandi: die Entwicklung eines Staatskirchenrechts von seinen Anfängen bis zum Ende des Alten Reiches*, Jus ecclesiasticum, vol. 68 (Tübingen: Mohr Siebeck, 2001). See also Chapters 9 and 10 in this volume.

[62] Heinz Schilling, *Civic Calvinism in Northwestern Germany and the Netherlands: Sixteenth to Nineteenth Centuries*, Sixteenth Century Essays and Studies, vol. 17 (Kirksville, MO: Sixteenth Century Journal Publishers, 1991).

[63] Heinz Schilling, "Between Territorial State and Urban Liberty. Lutheranism and Calvinism in the County of Lippe," in *The German People and the Reformation*, ed. R. Po-Chia Hsia (Ithaca: Cornell University Press, 1988), 263–83.

to flourish even in the patrimonial lands of the Austrian Habsburgs; indeed, in 1609, Rudolf II promulgated the "Letter of Majesty" in Bohemia, which provided religious guarantees to the many Protestant groups that were thriving there.[64] All of these cases highlighted the significant ways in which the authoritarian claims of Germany's rulers could be challenged by determined subjects within the empire without precipitating a new cycle of religious war.

In the relative success of the *Religionsfriede*, then, we can discern a combination of legal principles and relational dynamics that is strikingly similar to those we found in the Swiss *Landfrieden*. On the one hand, the signatories to the *Religionsfriede* agreed to the three basic principles that were to be recurrently present in early modern peace settlements: mutual recognition, pledges of mutual security, and a commitment to mediation or legal processes to resolve outstanding issues. On the other hand, the religious politics of the German-Roman Empire under the provisions of the *Religionsfriede* reveal the recurrent combination of four complementary dynamics: negotiation, segregation, domination, and subversion. We can see the dynamic of *negotiation*, not only in the production of this seminal peace agreement, but in the ongoing political interactions and struggles through which various rulers and their religiously contentious subjects worked out accommodations of differences that were not envisioned in the settlement itself. The dynamic of *segregation* is apparent in both the checkerboard pattern of territorial religious differentiation that the agreement validated and in the (temporary) dissolution of religiously competitive coalitions or military alliances that had facilitated the start of the religious wars. The dynamic of religious and political *domination* is readily evident in the authoritarian claims of territorial and some municipal rulers, both Protestant and Catholic, and the policies that historians have recently characterized as producing a long-term "confessionalization," which by disciplining and educating the laity served to accentuate religious differences among the constituent parts of the composite empire and within biconfessional communities. But the countervailing dynamic of *subversion* is also readily evident in the stories of successful resistance to princely conversions in Emden, Lemgo, and eventually Brandenburg.[65] When we turn our attention in the next chapter to the patterns of religious coexistence that emerged in the context of these wars and their settlements, we will find that *subversion* is a far more significant dynamic in the stories of "survival" that religious dissenters – those whose religious choices are different from that of their rulers – have to tell.

[64] See J. V. Polisensky, *The Thirty Years War* (Berkeley: University of California Press, 1971); R. J. W. Evans, *The Making of the Habsburg Monarchy, 1500–1700: An Interpretation* (Oxford: Oxford University Press, 1979); and Winfried Eberhard, "Reformation and Counter-Reformation in East Central Europe," in *Visions, Programs and Outcomes*, vol. 2 of *Handbook of European History, 1400–1600*, eds. Thomas A. Brady, Heiko A. Oberman, and James D. Tracy (Leiden: E. J. Brill, 1995), 551–605.

[65] Bodo Nischan, *Prince, People and Confession: The Second Reformation in Brandenburg* (Philadelphia: University of Pennsylvania Press, 1994).

4

The Contours of Religious Peace I

Central Europe

Together the Swiss *Landfrieden* and the German *Religionsfriede* served to make a remarkably durable pattern of religious peace possible in central Europe north of the Alps. What kind of peace did these settlements make possible? Would we recognize religious peace if we saw it? Above all, it can be said that the religious peace in Switzerland and Germany validated and preserved a pattern of religious diversity that was extremely varied and more than a little messy. What the previously warring parties could agree on, finally, was the necessity of less than comfortable political compromises *until such time* as reconciliation could resolve the religious issues at stake and dissolve the religious identity boundaries that marked their enduring enmities.

When the second *Landfrieden* stopped the fighting in Switzerland in 1531, the religious diversification of the European cultural landscape was very much a work in progress, but by the time the German *Reich* adopted the *Religionsfriede* in 1555, some basic elements of a durable religious peace were coming more clearly into focus in central Europe. To be sure, neither of these agreements actually describes what diversity looked like on the ground, but in their prescriptions for a more peaceful future, they tell us *where* we might look for diversity. Both of these agreements sought, above all, to restore comity and cooperation to the institutions of national and imperial governance, in anticipation, in the words of the *Landfrieden*, that "we shall hold one another to be good companions and loyal dear Confederates, and treat one another as loyal dear Confederates in open commerce and in all other ways." To that end, they devolved final decision-making authority regarding religious belief and practice to the territorial or local level and adopted legal procedures and impartial institutions to resolve future conflicts, if and when they bubbled back up to the national level. In doing so, they reduced the salience of their religious differences in the routine functioning of the *Tagsatzung* and the *Reichstag*, and in principle, they established the conditions for what Figure 1.2 calls **integration**. Political integration across a previously unknown identity boundary was more clearly an aspiration than a fait accompli, in 1555 as well as 1531, as religious conflicts continued to bedevil the internal politics of Swiss and German elites at the national or imperial level. Still, these frictions did not immediately trigger new rounds of coordinated destruction, and the peace held.

Accommodating religious differences at the territorial or local level was a bit more complicated and messy, and it is surely safe to say that the many actors involved in this early phase – subjects and rulers as well as cultural authorities – were faced with challenges for which there were no established scripts or well-known strategies. How they muddled through the political challenges of religious diversification within constituent units of the Swiss *Eidgenossenschaft* and the German *Reich* is not always readily evident, but there are enough vivid cases that illustrate for us the range of variation. In order to describe and account for the complex and messy contours of the religious peace that emerged in the second half of the sixteenth century, then, it is important to explore the divisions within as well as among the constituent parts of these late-medieval composites and to recognize the dynamics of the contentious political processes that produced and reproduced religious diversity where we might least expect to find it.

INCLUSION AND EXCLUSION IN THE EARLY REFORMATION

Since Protestant dreams of reforming the whole of Latin Christendom, in the face of Catholic resistance, very quickly dissolved into more "realistic" aspirations to reform specific communities and territories one by one, historians are accustomed to thinking about the outcomes of the early reformations in Germany and Switzerland in terms of geographic differentiation: a "patchwork quilt" or a "checkerboard" of variously Protestant and Catholic territories. Indeed, it was the *limited* success of the early religious reform movements in institutionalizing official or magisterial reformations that framed both the enmities of the first round of religious wars and the negotiated terms of the religious peace. Thus, in their explicit validation of territorial religious differentiation, both the *Landfrieden* and the *Religionsfriede*, as "national" settlements, were formally inclusive of religious differences that were previously unimaginable, and the patchwork or checkerboard imagery may be usefully emblematic of the national inclusiveness of these pioneering settlements.

Still, the process of religious differentiation, of which the official reformations were certainly an important part, was a good deal more complex and messy than any geographic map of "The Reformation" could ever reflect, even if a map could do justice to the intense fragmentation of authority that characterized these composite states.[1] The fact is that the implementation of official reformations was in most places an incremental and often attenuated process with a limited

[1] On the confusing futility of religious mapping, see Benjamin J. Kaplan, *Divided by Faith: Religious Conflict and the Practice of Toleration in Early Modern Europe* (Cambridge, MA: Harvard University Press, 2007), 150–1.

reach. As we saw in the early example of Zürich in Chapter 2, the advent of "scriptural" preaching was followed by formal disputations, the "cleansing" of churches, the closure of religious institutions or the seizure of church properties, the replacement of recalcitrant priests with evangelical pastors, experimentation with new forms of worship, and as a sort of culmination, the abolition of the Mass. In the case of Zürich, these official changes were enacted very quickly, within the space of just a few years, but implementation of these prescriptions across the whole of its territory took decades.[2] In Germany, as C. Scott Dixon suggests, the reformation process more commonly took the better part of a century![3] Consider the example of Electoral Saxony.

Electoral Saxony, which included the city and university of Wittenberg, the base of Luther's operations, may in many ways be considered the prototype of an official territorial reformation.[4] Although Elector Frederick "the Wise" (1486–1525) both protected Luther, following his excommunication and the proclamation of an imperial ban against him in 1521, and allowed experimentation with a new order of worship in the castle church of Wittenberg, it was only under his successor, Johann "the Steadfast" (1525–1532) that a Lutheran service replaced the Mass, Catholic clergymen were replaced by evangelical pastors, Church wealth was appropriated by the government, and a new system of Church governance replaced the episcopal system. In 1528, the first Saxon Church Order (*Kirchenordnung*) was promulgated, which served as a model for later reformations in Württemberg (1534), Albertine Saxony (1539), and Brandenburg (1540). Perhaps the most important feature of the implementation of the official reformation in Saxony, and elsewhere, was the so-called visitation process, which began in 1528 and entailed a parish-by-parish assessment of local religious practices, but efforts to extend or enforce Lutheran uniformity into rural parishes remained tentative in most places until the *Religionsfriede* finally afforded the "princes" the security they needed to assert the top-down process of confessionalization.[5] Thus, as the process slowly unfolded, there was still considerable space for the development of a variety of "hybrid" religious practices or the perpetuation of "Catholic superstitions" in the interstices of time and authoritative space through the end of the century.[6]

---

[2] Cf. Bruce Gordon, *The Swiss Reformation* (Manchester: Manchester University Press, 2002).

[3] See C. Scott Dixon, *The Reformation in Germany*, Historical Association Studies (Oxford, England; Malden, MA: Blackwell Publishers, 2002), esp. chapter 4.

[4] On the patterns and politics of "princely reformations," see Dixon, *The Reformation in Germany*, 114–39.

[5] On the process of reformation in rural parishes, see C. Scott Dixon, *The Reformation and Rural Society; The Parishes of Brandenburg-Ansbach-Kulmbach, 1528–1603* (Cambridge: Cambridge University Press, 1996).

[6] For an excellent summary of the varieties of religious coexistence in the German Empire, see David M. Luebke, "A Multiconfessional Empire," in *A Companion to Multiconfessionalism in the Early Modern World*, ed. Thomas Max Safley, Brill's Companions to the Christian Tradition, vol. 28 (Leiden; Boston: Brill, 2011), 129–54. Luebke distinguishes six general types of coexistence: hybrid, subcutaneous, entrenched, liminal, coequal, and concentric. Although these

A similarly attenuated reformation process was visible in the imperial free city of Strasbourg.[7] Originally permissive of a variety of "scriptural" preachers, the city's leaders did not formally adopt the Augsburg Confession until 1536 in order to align themselves with their Saxon allies. Two years later, one of the city's leading evangelical preachers, Martin Bucer, published *On True Care of Souls* in an effort to clarify the roles of the new Church and its ministers; at the same time, the city issued a mandate against "radicals" like the Anabaptists, whose notions of reform seemed to threaten disorder, especially in the wake of the debacle at Münster in 1535. Meanwhile, there remained a visible, resident community of Catholics who gained new legitimacy in the *Religionsfriede*, which urged the preservation of religious coexistence in cities; they were joined shortly by a steady stream of evangelical refugees who were fleeing persecution in France and the Low Countries. As Dixon describes the situation in Strasbourg, "A plurality of religious cultures in Lutheran Strasbourg remained the norm throughout the century, each with a unique understanding of faith and community."[8] Thus, even in polities that experienced official or magisterial reformations, the attenuated process and the independent choices of both residents and refugees recurrently left a residue of often unwanted and certainly unintended religious diversity.

Something analogous may be said of polities that retained the "old faith" during the early reformation and in the wake of the first peace settlements. In the small Swiss Catholic territory of Schwyz, for example, there is strong evidence of a pocket of religious nonconformists, who were sometimes labeled "Anabaptists" by their enemies, in the village of Arth that persisted well into the seventeenth century.[9] The controversial "Declaration" that Ferdinand appended to the *Religionsfriede*, in his own name and on his authority as Charles V's designee, clearly speaks to the existence of "knights, cities and communes, which long ago became adherents of the Augsburg Confession and its religion" within the many ecclesiastical jurisdictions in the empire. Even in the duchy of Bavaria, the rare secular principality that remained Catholic, the government worked very hard, under the long reign of Duke Maximilian (1573–1651), in collaboration with Jesuit and Capuchin

descriptive types are compatible with the descriptors I use in Figure 1.2, it is not entirely clear what kinds of variation they are meant to identify.

[7] On the reformation in Strasbourg, see L. J. Abray, *The People's Reformation; Magistrates, Clergy and Commons in Strasbourg, 1500–1598* (Ithaca: Cornell University Press, 1985), Lorna Jane Abray, "Confession, Conscience, and Honor: The Limits of Magisterial Tolerance in Sixteenth-Century Strassburg," in *Tolerance and Intolerance in the European Reformation*, eds. Ole Peter Grell and Bob Scribner (Cambridge: Cambridge University Press, 1996), 94–107, and Thomas A. Brady, Jr., *The Politics of the Reformation in Germany: Jacob Sturm (1489–1553) of Strasbourg* (Atlantic Highlands, NJ: Humanities Press, 1997).

[8] Dixon, *The Reformation in Germany*, 113.

[9] See Mark Furner, "The 'Nicodemites' in Arth, Canton Schwyz, 1530–1698" (Master's thesis, University of Warwick, 1994). I am very grateful to Mr. Furner for sharing this unpublished work with me.

missionaries to eradicate Lutheranism, but was never completely successful. This officially Catholic state had also to accommodate Lutheran enclaves within its territory – the imperial free city of Regensburg and the small county of Ortenburg – because they were subordinate only to the emperor and not to the duke.[10]

In terms of the descriptive typology laid out in Figure 1.2, then, the religious peace that emerged in central Europe in the second half of the sixteenth century was formally inclusive and exclusive at the same time. On the one hand, by the general terms of the *Landfrieden* and the *Religionsfriede*, both the Swiss Confederation and the German Empire, as composite states, were officially biconfessional, which would situate them on the right side of the diagram. On the other hand, the formal claims that territorial rulers made in terms of the putative *ius reformandi*, or the right of reformation, were at least formally exclusive and would locate them generally on the left side of the diagram. This is not to say, of course, that the constituent territories represented or actually achieved religious uniformity. On the contrary, both Catholic and Protestant rulers governed populations that were religiously diverse in a variety of ways. In order to visualize the nature of that variety, it will be instructive to look at the contours of religious diversity and coexistence in a series of local examples that illustrate both the range of variation and introduce to us some modular strategies for accommodating difference. We will start out in the German city of Bautzen and end up in the Swiss Emmental.

SHARING SPACE AND CROSSING BORDERS

Evangelical preachers first came to the provincial city of Bautzen, the historic capital of Upper Lusatia, near the modern borders of Germany, Poland, and the Czech Republic, sometime in 1520 or 1521.[11] A popular reform movement very quickly succeeded in coaxing the formal appointment in 1523 of a Lutheran preacher, Michael Arnold, who then led the city council toward a bold, formal declaration in 1524 for evangelical reform within the city of Bautzen. The city council did not, however, dispossess the cathedral chapter of St. Peter, which left the deacon of the cathedral chapter in possession of the cathedral church of St. Peter (St. Petri Dom) and spiritually responsible for the Sorbian population of the surrounding Lusatian countryside.[12] Since St. Peter's Cathedral was the only parish church in Bautzen and its immediate environs, the deacon, fearing for the welfare of his parishioners, should he lose control of the cathedral,

---

[10] Dixon, *The Reformation in Germany*, 148–9; Kaplan, *Divided by Faith*, 152–3.

[11] See Jan Mahling, "Die evangelishe Kirche – Gemeindegeschichte seit 1523," in *Von Budissin nach Bautzen: Beiträge zur Geschichte der Stadt Bautzen*, ed. Manfred Thiemann (Bautzen: Lusatia Verlag, 2002), 122–33.

[12] For the Catholic perspective, see Siegfried Seifert, "Die katholische Kirche nach der Reformation," in *Von Budissin nach Bautzen: Beiträge zur Geschichte der Stadt Bautzen*, ed. Manfred Thiemann (Bautzen: Lusatia Verlag, 2002), 110–21.

invited the new evangelical community in Bautzen to share "his" beautiful worship space. With this, the evangelicals and Catholics of Bautzen began a long experiment in religious coexistence.

The relationship between evangelicals and Catholics was fraught with tension as the majority of the city and the Lusatian countryside turned gradually, but decisively, toward Lutheranism in the coming decades, but the bold experiment in sharing a sacred space was apparently successful enough that the city council and the cathedral chapter drew up a formal contract in 1543 to share the St. Petri Dom permanently – this in the context of rising polarization among German elites and on the eve of the First War of Schmalkalden. By this agreement, the church was divided in two parts at the point where the nave takes a slight bend (Illustration 4.1); the Catholics retained exclusive use of the front of the nave and the choir, plus the side chapels around it, and the evangelicals worshiped exclusively in the rest of the nave. This contract specified that each Sunday, the evangelicals would worship between the hours of 6:00 AM and 8:30 AM and between noon and 2:00 PM,[13] and although the specific worship times have since changed, this basic agreement to share the use of the cathedral remains in effect to this day (Illustration 4.2). At some point, the two parts of the church were formally separated by a screen – originally this screen was four meters high, but today there is only a low railing – and it appears as if a larger portal on the north side of the church was replaced by two smaller entries on either side of the division (Illustration 4.3).

At first blush, creating a shared sacred space (in German, a *Simultankirche*) may seem like a sensible, even obvious, negotiated solution to the "problem" of religious differentiation. The case of Bautzen, however, highlights the fact that it could also be a profoundly subversive practice. In the first place, Bautzen was only a provincial city, subject historically to the margrave of Lusatia, whose sovereignty had reverted to the king of Bohemia in the fifteenth century; in 1526, following the death of King Louis II of Bohemia in the Battle of Mohacs against the Ottoman Turks, Upper Lusatia was incorporated into the territorial domains of none other than the Habsburg Archduke of Austria, Ferdinand, Charles V's brother and the future emperor, who actively resisted the spread of evangelical reform. In addition, the deacon of the cathedral chapter – between 1526 and 1546, the whole period of experimentation, the deacon was Paul Küchler – was clearly acting, in the place of a nonresident bishop, in defiance of both official Church policy, which forbade compromise with "heretics," and the emperor, who had condemned Lutheran teaching in the Edict of Worms.

But religious coexistence was not limited to the sharing of sacred space in St. Peter's Cathedral. The *modus vivendi* that evangelicals and Catholics developed in their formal agreement to share the Petri Dom also had significant, but indirect, ramifications for the coexistence of the two faith communities more generally in the city and in the countryside. As more and

---

[13] Mahling, "Die evangelishe Kirche," 122.

ILLUSTRATION 4.1: St. Peter's Cathedral in Bautzen is divided internally where the nave takes a slight turn; Evangelicals worship in the back of the nave and Catholics in the front of the nave and the choir with its side chapels. (Photo Wayne Te Brake)

ILLUSTRATION 4.2: Though the worship times have changed, the original contract to share Bautzen's only parish church has not changed fundamentally for nearly 500 years. (Photo Wayne Te Brake)

ILLUSTRATION 4.3: In order to accommodate two congregations on either side of a four-meter screen (now only a small railing), two separate entries appear to have replaced a larger portal in St. Peter's in Bautzen. (Photo Wayne Te Brake)

more rural communities committed to evangelical reform, the continued existence of the cathedral chapter presented a vantage point for the representation of Catholic interests both inside and outside the jurisdiction of the city.[14] It also offered a place of refuge for those who chose to remain Catholic in the sense that rural Catholics could travel to the city to attend Catholic worship services at the Petri Dom. Again, traveling temporarily from one jurisdiction to another in order to worship in the manner of one's choice – a practice the Germans called *Auslauf* – might seem like a perfectly sensible, even obvious solution to the "problem" of religious diversity, but in a world

[14] Seifert, "Die katholische Kirche," 110–12.

where rulers claimed the authority to determine the religious practices of their subjects, it could easily be construed as an act of religious and political defiance. Permanent migration – the so-called *ius emigrandi* – was, of course, recognized in the *Religionsfriede* as a legal remedy to those whose religious choice differed from the local norm. As Benjamin Kaplan writes, however, "Unlike emigration, Auslauf enabled people of different faiths to live in the same towns and villages."[15]

Thus, the complex and messy relationships between evangelicals and Catholics in Bautzen, and more generally in Upper Lusatia, introduce us to two practices by which local rulers, competitive claimants to religious authority, and ordinary political subjects of different faiths managed to accommodate their religious differences in very different circumstances. When, in the volatile and unprecedented context of religious differentiation, an experiment that evolved into a formal agreement resulted in the long-term sharing of a church, as it did in Bautzen, it may be described as **parity**, a relationship among equals, on the inclusionary side of Figure 1.2. When the same process of religious differentiation replaced one form of worship with another, as it did more generally in the countryside of Upper Lusatia, it looks more like confessional **privilege**, a decidedly unequal relationship, on the exclusionary side of Figure 1.2. Both *Simultankirchen* and *Auslauf* were common-sense strategies for dealing with these obvious, but variable, facts of religious diversity. Recall, however, that these complex facts on the ground were taking shape in a territory that was subject to a Catholic prince who opposed reform, but clearly had to make his peace with the coexistence that emerged in Upper Lusatia. Certainly retrospective claims of *ius reformandi* or *cuius regio eius religio* cannot be said either to describe or to account for these facts on the ground.

Although innovative and distinctive, the ongoing experience of religious coexistence in Bautzen and Upper Lusatia is hardly unique in its complexity. In a number of German cities and territories that formally adopted evangelical reforms, Catholic worship was preserved by means of a variety of institutions – cathedral chapters, church foundations, monasteries, and the like – that managed to maintain their corporative independence, despite the destruction or disruption of the Catholic episcopal hierarchy.[16] In the Swabian city of Biberach, St. Martin's Church – like St. Peter's in Bautzen, the city's only parish church – was also shared by evangelicals and Catholics (Illustration 4.4).[17] Although

---

[15] Kaplan, *Divided by Faith*, 162. Kaplan's exploration in chapter 6 of the practice of *Auslauf*, which he regards as a "bona fide form of toleration" that entails "an agreement between dissenters, authorities and members of the official church," is to my knowledge the best available anywhere.

[16] Anton Schindling, "Neighbours of a Different Faith: Confessional Coexistence and Parity in the Territorial States and Towns of the Empire," in *Politics, Religion, Law and Society*, vol. 1 of 1648: *War and Peace in Europe*, eds. Klaus Bussmann and Heinz Schilling (Münster/Osnabrück: Veranstaltungsgesellschaft 350 Jahre Westfälischer Friede, 1998), 446.

[17] Kaplan, *Divided by Faith*, 198–204.

ILLUSTRATION 4.4: St. Martin's Church in Biberach is, like St. Peter's in Bautzen, a very prominent feature of a small urban environment with only one parish. (Photo Wayne Te Brake)

St. Martin's is sometimes said to be the one of the oldest *Simultankirchen* in Germany, it's shared use was not the product of local experimentation and subversive negotiation as was the case in Bautzen; instead, in the wake of the First Schmalkaldic War, under the terms of the hated Augsburg Interim (1548), the Lutheran city of Biberach, like the other imperial free cities of Swabia, was required to reestablish Catholic worship, which resulted in an agreement to share St. Martin's Church. In this case, the entire nave was shared by the two congregations in very complicated alternations on Sundays, which occasioned the installation of a large clock to monitor the sequence; the choir and its associated chapels were claimed exclusively by the Catholics (Illustration 4.5). In 1561, after the *Religionsfriede*, a Catholic foundation in Wetzlar, a small imperial free city in Hesse, which had adopted evangelical reforms very early in

ILLUSTRATION 4.5: High above its elaborately decorated nave, St. Martin's Church in Biberach has a clock to regulate the intricate alternations between Evangelical and Catholic use of the worship space. (Photo Wayne Te Brake)

1524, also came to an agreement with the Lutheran community to share the St. Marien Church.[18]

Finally, we should note an interesting variation on the theme of shared sacred space in the important south-German city of Augsburg, which was at once an imperial free city and the seat of a resident bishop. Popular evangelical preaching came to Augsburg in the early 1520s, and when the bishop tried to discipline the preachers, the city council obstructed his efforts and failed to enforce imperial

[18] Schindling, "Neighbours of a Different Faith," 466.

mandates, even though they had them published.[19] In the summer of 1524, however, the council surreptitiously removed from the city a radical Franciscan monk who criticized both spiritual and temporal authorities and attracted large crowds of followers. When a large crowd protested this action, the magistrates were compelled to use their authority to appoint a different evangelical preacher to the post in the Franciscan church – as it turned out, a "Zwinglian," rather than a "Lutheran" – who was acceptable to both the urban authorities and the parishioners. Thus it was that the municipal authorities began to use their long-standing authority to appoint the pastors of specific churches within Augsburg to introduce Protestant religious practices incrementally while the bishop used his direct authority over other churches, including the Cathedral Church of Our Lady, to ensure that there would still be spaces for Catholic worship.

One of the sacred spaces that the council traditionally controlled was a small chapel dedicated to St. Ottmar in the courtyard of the Augustinian Priory of the Holy Cross, very near the larger church of the priory.[20] In 1525, the municipal authorities appointed a Zwinglian preacher to the post at the priory chapel in order to secure more space for the large number of Augsburgers who chose to worship as Protestants. Thus, the St. Ottmar Chapel became a Lutheran "preaching house," much to the chagrin of both the prior and the bishop, and the Catholics and Protestants of this famously biconfessional city began a long experiment in sharing the sacred space of the priory courtyard. What is striking in this case is that the Protestants and the Catholics could not agree on who owned or controlled the rights over the property they shared, but they agreed to share it nevertheless out of a common sense of "good neighborliness" (*gueter Nachparschafft*). By the 1530s, the Protestant city council had taken firmer control over the religious affairs of the city, and in 1537 they proscribed all Catholic worship services altogether. Still, those sacred spaces controlled by the bishop, including the priory church, remained empty rather than being appropriated for Protestant use. In 1547, during the First Schmalkaldic War, Augsburg became officially Lutheran, but under the Augsburg Interim (1548), Catholic worship was reinstated not only in the cathedral, but also in the priory church. After the second war, the *Religionsfriede* (1555) confirmed Augsburg's biconfessional status, and "good neighborliness" once again allowed the two mutually intolerant faith communities to share (with a few contentious interruptions) the keys to the only door to the priory courtyard; they also shared the bell tower to announce their services, and for a long time the

---

[19] See P. Broadhead, "Popular Pressure for Reform in Augsburg, 1524–1534," in *Stadtbürgertum und Adel in der Reformation*, eds. W. J. Mommsen, P. Alter, and R. W. Scribner (Stuttgart: Klett-Cotta, 1979), 80–7, and P. Broadhead, "Politics and Expediency in the Augburg Reformation," in *Reformation Principle and Practice; Essays in Honour of A. G. Dickens*, ed. P. N. Brooks (London: Scolar Press, 1980).

[20] The following account of the shared spaces of the Priory of the Holy Cross is based on Emily Fisher Gray, "Good Neighbors: Architecture and Confession in Augsburg's Lutheran Church of Holy Cross, 1525–1661" (Ph.D. diss., University of Pennsylvania, 2004).

caretakers of the two churches shared an on-site residence. Complicated and messy this certainly was, but it proved to be an entirely workable form of shared space until well into the Thirty Years War.

Taken together, these varied examples of shared spaces in Germany – shared urban spaces as well as shared sacred spaces – are undoubtedly what the framers of the *Religionsfriede* had in mind when they wholeheartedly endorsed the viability and sustainability of religious coexistence in German cities.[21] The sharing of political and sacred spaces in order to accommodate emergent religious differences took slightly variant forms in Switzerland. There the second *Landfrieden* empowered the constituent cities and territories of the *Eidgenossenschaft*, the confederates, to make "un-coerced" choices for or against reform (article I), while in the *Gemeine Herrschaften*, those decisions were to be made at the local, community level (article II).[22] As we saw earlier, however, two of the thirteen confederates, Glarus and Appenzell, eventually devolved religious sovereignty to the local level and, over time, developed two different patterns of segregated diversity (**parity**) within their territories, which resulted in two divided votes and separate delegations in the *Tagsatzung*. Meanwhile, in the *Gemeine Herrschaften* many local communities, as we saw in Thurgau and Baden, also frustrated the expectation of either/or decision making by deciding to share their local churches; one assumes that these communities shared their churches generally for reasons of practical necessity rather than comity, inasmuch as their disagreements regarding the sharing of sacred spaces recurrently threatened the religious peace in the early years. Still, like the sharing of the St. Peter's in Bautzen and St. Martin's in Biberach, some of these arrangements have endured for centuries, long outlasting the practical considerations that may have brought them into being.[23] Naturally, the sharing of small village churches looks somewhat different than larger urban churches or cathedrals. In the village of Güttingen, in Thurgau, for example, evangelicals, who were in the majority, shared the village church with the minority Catholics, whose interests were powerfully protected by the nearby Kreuzlingen Abbey, which retained the right to appoint the local priest (see Illustration 4.6). While the two faith communities share, to this day, most of the interior space of this modest church, except for the apse, which contains the Catholic altar (Illustration 4.7), they preserve separate burial grounds on either side of the church building (Illustrations 4.8 and 4.9).

[21] Henry Clay Vedder, ed., *The Peace of Augsburg*, Historical Leaflets, no. 5 (Chester, PA: Crozer Theological Seminary, 1901), 8–9.

[22] Ernst Walder, ed., *Religionsvergleiche des 16. Jahrhunderts*, vol. 7–8 of *Quellen zur neueren Geschichte* (Bern: Verlag Herbert Lang, 1960–61), I, 7.

[23] Many of the churches that were shared in the sixteenth and seventeenth centuries are no longer shared because one of the two congregations subsequently built its own sacred space. Thus, the *Simultankirche* in Zurzach, in Baden, whose baptismal fonts occasioned much turmoil at the beginning of the seventeenth century (see Chapter 3, p. 51, in this volume), is no longer shared by evangelicals and Catholics, but there are still excellent examples of shared churches in Ermatingen and Güttingen in Thurgau.

ILLUSTRATION 4.6: The *Simultankirche* at Güttingen in Thurgau sits high on a bluff overlooking Lake Contance. (Photo Wayne Te Brake)

Like St. Peter's in Bautzen, the *Simultankirchen* of the *Gemeine Herrschaften* are emblematic of a broader, multifaceted relationship of **parity** (on the inclusive side of Figure 1.2) between two religiously distinct and competitive faith communities at the local level, whereas the cases of Glarus and Appenzell are examples of **parity** at the territorial level. But in this extremely fragmented political context, this kind of publicly visible, negotiated coexistence was not always the case.[24] Consider the

---

[24] See Frauke Volkland, "Katholieken und Reformierte im Toggenburg und im Rheintal," in *Frühe Neuzeit*, vol. 4 of *Neue St. Galler Kantonsgeschichte* (2003), 131–46. There is also a broader social and political study of the very contentious, sometimes violent, relationship between the Abbey of St. Gall, as the dominant political authority, and the evangelical "resistance" to that authority in Toggenburg; see Bruno Z'Graggen, *Tyrannenmord im Toggenburg. Fürstäbtische Herrschaft und protestantischer Widerstand um 1600* (Zürich: Chronos Verlag, 1999).

ILLUSTRATION 4.7: At Güttingen, the Reformed and Catholic congregations shared the body of the church, while the apse was reserved for Catholic use. (Photo Wayne Te Brake)

ILLUSTRATION 4.8: The Protestant cemetery at Güttingen has as many modest plaques as independent grave monuments. (Photo Wayne Te Brake)

ILLUSTRATION 4.9: The Catholic burial ground at Güttingen, on the opposite side of the church from the Protestant, has highly decorated grave makers. (Photo Wayne Te Brake)

complex case of St. Gallen and the subject territory of Toggenburg. In the 1520s, the city of St. Gallen, which was allied with, but not a full member of, the *Eidgenossenschaft*, followed an incremental path toward religious reform along Zwinglian lines. Meanwhile, in the adjacent territory of Toggenburg, which was subject to the political authority of the Abbey of St. Gallen, the cause of evangelical reform, which enjoyed considerable popular support, was opposed by its Catholic overlord. Despite the fact that the Abbey of St. Gallen expressly forbade the practice, many local communities incorporated "illegal" evangelical congregations within officially Catholic churches. In the small village of Oberhelfenschwil, for example, the lovely parish church (Illustration 4.10), with its beautifully preserved medieval frescos (Illustration 4.11), resembles the shared spaces of *Simultankirchen* in Thurgau (Illustration 4.12); its survival is nevertheless emblematic of a more subversive political dynamic that brought it into being. In the case of Toggenburg, then, we encounter a form of coexistence, located on the exclusive side of Figure 1.2, somewhere between **privilege** and **repression**, depending on how forcefully the abbey was enforcing its counter-Reformation vision of unity and purity.

All in all, if we were to consider the sharing of a sacred space as a form of collective action, then the evidence from this first phase of conflict and coexistence in early modern Europe is that it was, to borrow Sidney Tarrow's apt use of the concept, "modular," which is to say, adaptable to a variety of

ILLUSTRATION 4.10: The Church at Oberhelfenschwil is one of the few still used as a *Simultankirche* in Toggengurg; there is another nearby in Mogelsberg. (Photo Wayne Te Brake)

circumstances.[25] Indeed, whereas Bautzen may have been the earliest example of a *Simultankirche* in the Reformation era, it is clear that this form of collective action emerged more or less simultaneously in Switzerland and Germany and could be adopted and adapted by a variety of actors in a variety of political contexts.[26] What's more, the sharing of sacred spaces eventually became

[25] See Sidney Tarrow, *Power in Movement. Social Movements, Collective Action and Politics*, 2nd ed., Cambridge Studies in Comparative Politics (Cambridge: Cambridge University Press, 1997), 31–47. Tarrow defines "modularity" as "the capacity of a form of collective action to be utilized by a variety of social actors, against a variety of targets, either alone, or in combination with other forms" (p. 33).

[26] The best thematic work on *Simultankirchen* and mixed-confessional communities in Switzerland is by Frauke Volkland, to whom I am deeply indebted for her generous help and personal guidance in my own excavation of the history of shared spaces. See, for example, Frauke Volkland, "Reformiert sein 'unter' Katholiken. Zur religiösen Praxis reformiert

ILLUSTRATION 4.11: The *Simultankirche* at Oberhelfenshwil has a series of partially restored medieval frescos. (Photo Wayne Te Brake)

a routine or familiar feature of Europe's religious peacemaking repertoire: although they were not evident everywhere in Europe, shared churches remained an important feature of European peacemaking in the last, climactic phase of religious war making and peacemaking (see Chapter 11), and they remain a feature of the religious landscape today.[27] The same might be said of the practice of *Auslauf*; as Benjamin Kaplan suggests:

Gläubiger in gemischtkonfessionellen Gemeinden der Alten Eidgenossenschaft im 17. Jahrhundert," in *Ländliche Frömmigkeit. Konfessionskulturen und Lebenswelten 1500–1850*, eds. Norbert Haag, Sabine Holtz, and Wolfgang Zimmermann (Stuttgart: Thorbeke, 2002), 159–77; Volkland, "Katholieken und Reformierte im Toggenburg und im Rheintal"; and Frauke Volkland, "Konfessionelle Abgrenzung Zwischen Gewalt, Stereotypenbildung und Symbolik: Gemischtkonfessionelle Gebiete der Ostschweiz und die Kurfalz Im Vergleich," in *Religion und Gewalt: Konflicte, Rituale, Deutungen (1500–1800)*, eds. Kaspar von Greyerz and Kim Siebenhüner (Göttingen: Vandenhoek & Reprecht, 2006), 343–65.

[27] See, for example, the brief survey and the works cited in the German article "Sumultankirche" at http://de.wikipedia.org/wiki/Simultankirche. Also, the Institute for Religion, Culture, and Public Life at Columbia University has an ongoing project on shared sacred spaces, focusing especially on the territories of the Ottoman Empire; see http://ircpl.org/projects/cdtr/shared-sacred-spaces.

ILLUSTRATION 4.12: As in many shared churches, the apse of the church at Oberhelfenschil was occupied by the Catholic altar; note the two separate baptismal fonts in the lower right of this image. (Photo Wayne Te Brake)

In different periods and varied forms, dissenters can be found performing Auslauf in Switzerland, Germany, Austria, Poland, Transylvania, Hungary, the northern and southern Netherlands, France, and Ireland. It is not that the inhabitants of these lands copied or learned from one another: rather, facing a common predicament, they lighted on a common solution.[28]

Modularity indeed!

THE LIMITS OF INCLUSION

The active repression of religious differences, such as occurred episodically in Toggenburg, but not in Lusatia, is often associated with Catholic authorities, especially in southern Europe where inquisitorial courts were active, but also in France and the Low Countries, as we will see in the next chapter. Here, however, it will be instructive to highlight the history of repression in the evangelical city-state of Bern and to uncover the deliberately hidden history of Anabaptist survival in the Emmental. We have, of course, already encountered radical Anabaptists in Münster between 1533 and 1535, when the repression of their violent, revolutionary "kingdom" occasioned the temporary collaboration

[28] Kaplan, *Divided by Faith*, 162.

of otherwise polarized Protestant and Catholic authorities (see Chapter 2). In Switzerland, the active repression of Anabaptists began earlier, when the followers of Konrad Grebel broke with Huldrych Zwingli over a range of issues, including the pace of reform, the legitimacy of infant baptism, and the authority of magistrates, who were Zwingli's powerful allies in Zürich. In January of 1526, the radical critics of magisterial reform symbolically signaled their break with the newly "Reformed" Church in Zürich when they performed the first "rebaptisms" of adult believers, which earned them the derisive title of "Anabaptists" (rebaptizers). The civil and religious authorities in Zürich struck back quickly, banning the Anabaptists and threatening capital punishment for anyone who had been rebaptized.[29]

Following their expulsion from Zürich, the Anabaptists dispersed in several directions within the *Eidgenossenschaft*: to the village of Zollikon and more generally the countryside of Zürich; to St. Gallen and Schaffhausen; and to Bern, especially the relatively remote Emmental. In 1527, a conference of Swiss "Brethren," as they called themselves, meeting at the village of Schleitheim in Schaffhausen, adopted a series of seven articles of faith that were intended to give a common voice to the Anabaptist movements in Switzerland and southern Germany.[30] The "Schleitheim Confession" underscored the importance of believer baptism (rejecting infant baptism as a papal "abomination"), strict separation of believers from unbelievers, the rejection of coercive force (the "sword") and magisterial office, and the refusal to swear oaths.[31] Although there were many variations on these Anabaptist themes, their common rejection of infant baptism (a very long Christian tradition that both Catholics and most Reformers could agree on) as well as civil authority made even the pacifistic Brethren appear to be deeply dangerous and worthy of active repression. Indeed, in August of 1527, the cities of Zürich, Bern, and St. Gallen issued a concordat against the Swiss Brethren that imposed fines for sympathizers and condemned pastors, leaders, and persistent offenders to death by drowning.[32]

One simple measure of the seriousness of the Anabaptist repression is the number of people who were executed. Claus-Peter Clasen found a total of 845 "known or probable" executions of Anabaptists in southern Germany, Switzerland, and Habsburg territories in Tyrol and Austria between 1525 and

---

[29] For a broad outline of the history of "The Radical Challenge" in Switzerland, see Gordon, *The Swiss Reformation*, 191–227.
[30] See James M. Stayer, "The Swiss Brethren: An Exercise in Historical Definition," *Church History* 47, no. 2 (1978): 174–95.
[31] An English translation of the Schleithiem Confession may be found online at www.anabaptists .org/history/the-schleitheim-confession.html.
[32] Samuel Geiser, "Concordat of the Cities of Zürich, Bern, and St. Gall (Switzerland)." *Global Anabaptist Mennonite Encyclopedia Online*, 1953, available at http://gameo.org/index.php? title=Concordat_of_the_cities_of_Z%C3%BCrich,_Bern,_and_St._Gall_(Switzerland)&oldid=11 7977.

1614.[33] Approximately half of these were in Catholic Habsburg lands, but of the seventy-three executions he found it Switzerland, well over half (forty) were in the city-state of Bern. Anabaptism had first appeared in Bern in 1525 when itinerant preachers began to gain a popular audience, and having agreed to the Concordat in 1527, officials in Bern carried out the first executions of three radical Brethren in 1529. Thirty more executions followed in the 1530s, with as many as twenty-two in 1537 and 1538, following the Anabaptist debacle in Münster. Thereafter, the executions tapered off and virtually stopped, but to judge by an enumeration of the various mandates issued by the Bernese authorities in the coming decades and generations, the determination of the Bernese authorities to eradicate the Anabaptist "weeds," especially in the Emmental, never really abated. Even as late as the eighteenth century, the Bernese authorities appointed official Anabaptist "hunters" and organized large-scale "hunts" that often sent the Anabaptist faithful fleeing into neighboring territories.[34]

Over decades and centuries, the official repression of Anabaptists occasioned a good deal of emigration from the Emmental. In the sixteenth century there was a significant migration toward Moravia, where there was hope for a safer haven; in the seventeenth century there was a significant migration toward the United Provinces, whereas in the eighteenth century many descendants of Emmental Anabaptists migrated to the New World. All the same, there were also periods when there were significant flows of Anabaptists into Bern, when under worsening conditions elsewhere, the Brethren found refuge in the remote valleys of Emmental. Thus, the official repression of Anabaptists in the Emmental and more generally in Switzerland is only part of the story. Its counterpoint – the history of Anabaptist survival in the face of active repression – is a good deal more difficult to excavate and reconstruct, in part because critical records from the sixteenth century are missing, but more fundamentally because this history was, for a very long time, deliberately hidden for the sake of survival. Still, the broad outlines of this history are both readily evident today and a necessary counterpoint to the official stories of unity and purity.

In earlier work on what I consider the "hard" cases of religious coexistence, I have identified seven recurrent mechanisms that help us to understand the survival of religious dissidents under conditions of active repression (Table 4.1),[35] and I believe that most of these are readily evident in the history of Emmental.

[33] Claus-Peter Clasen, "Executions of Anabaptists, 1525–1618; A Research Report," *Mennonite Quarterly Review* 47 (1973): 115–52; see also, C. P. Clasen, *Anabaptism: A Social History, 1525–1618* (Ithaca, NY: Cornell University Press, 1972).

[34] See A. J. Amstutz-Tschirren and Isaac Zürcher-Geiser, "Emmental (Switzerland)," *Global Anabaptist Mennonite Encyclopedia Online.* 1990. Web. 14 Apr 2014. http://gameo.org/index.php?title=Emmental_(Switzerland)&oldid=121031.

[35] See Wayne Te Brake, "Emblems of Coexistence in a Confessional World," in *Living with Religious Diversity in Early Modern Europe,* eds. C. Scott Dixon, Dagmar Freist, and Mark Greengrass (Farnham, England: Ashgate Publishing, 2009), 68–73.

TABLE 4.1 *Mechanisms in the "survival" of religious diversity*

Mechanism	Type	Effect
Secrecy	Relational	Hides group differences, either of necessity or to keep up appearances
Dissimulation	Relational	Protects individuals from detection/prosecution
Casuistry	Cognitive	Relieves group members from strict norms
Private education	Cognitive	Counteracts official ideology and reaffirms group identity
Indifference	Relational	Protects "others" from detection
Connivance	Relational	Undercuts official prosecution
Toleration	Cognitive	Defends diversity and its effects

Reprinted from Wayne Te Brake, "Emblems of Coexistence in a Confessional World," in *Living with Religious Diversity in Early Modern Europe*, edited by C. Scott Dixon, Dagmar Freist, and Mark Greengrass (Farnham, England: Ashgate Publishing, 2009), p. 73. Copyright © 2009.

According to James M. Stayer, at some point between the late 1530s – the era of the most severe repression – and the end of the sixteenth century, the Anabaptists who survived in Switzerland and elsewhere in Europe made a fundamental transition from a radical movement seeking an all-or-nothing and immediate transformation of society to a more discreet movement of "conforming nonconformists"; as Stayer describes it simply, "these people chose life rather than death."[36] In very practical terms, this meant that the Brethren in the Emmental began practicing *secrecy* – keeping their organizations and worship clandestine and thus invisible – and *dissimulation* – appearing to conform to Reformed practices in "nonessential" matters so as to cover up their more fundamental nonconformity – thereby reducing the likelihood of negative interactions with authorities, such as arrest and interrogation.[37] At the same time, they had to abandon or at least to adjust some of their original ideals concerning "pure" Christian behavior for the sake of survival in exceptional circumstances – a practice that Mark Furner very aptly describes as "lay casuistry."[38] Still, survival is never a solo performance; rather,

[36] James M. Stayer, "The Passing of the Radical Moment in the Radical Reformation," *Mennonite Quarterly Review* 71, no. 1 (1997): 147–52.

[37] I am deeply indebted, here, to the unpublished dissertation research of Mark Furner at Cambridge University, which he very generously shared with me early on in my own work; see especially chapter 5 ("Anabaptists and the Villagers") of Mark Furner, "The Repression and Survival of Anabaptism in the Emmental, Switzerland, 1659–1743" (Ph.D. diss., Cambridge University, 1998). On the survival strategies of Anabaptists more generally, see the research in progress of Mathilde Monge, "Clandestinité, dissimulation, détachement du monde. Les anabaptistes en Europe occidentale, des xvie-xviie siècles," *Hypothèses* (2006): 35–44.

[38] I have borrowed the term "casuistry" – which I use to denote the ideological and theological adjustments that persecuted groups make in order to rationalize their failure to meet strictest norms of public witness and ritual purity – from Mark Furner; see "Lay Casuistry and the Survival of Later Anabaptists in Bern," *Mennonite Quarterly Review* 75 (2001): 429–70.

as Furner's research shows, the Anabaptists of the Emmental were dependent both on the general *indifference* of family, friends, and neighbors, who refused to betray nonconformity to the authorities, and the active *connivance* of local officials who either failed to prosecute offenders or warned them of danger.

Although this dynamic history was once largely hidden, since the nineteenth century it has become increasingly visible, not only in a substantial body of historical scholarship, but in the many memorials and commemorations of the movement's descendants. Today, the town of Langnau boasts the oldest continuously existing Mennonite Church in the world, having been organized in 1530,[39] and various sites in the Emmental, such as the castle prison at Trachselwald where many Anabaptists were held captive, are prominent stops on the many Anabaptist/Mennonite "discovery tours" that converge on Europe each year. As an especially fitting emblem of this remarkable history of repression and survival, however, I would like to suggest the *"Täuferversteck"*, an Anabaptist hiding place built into a massive hayloft of Hinter-Hütten farm near Trub, to the northeast of Langnau (Illustrations 4.13 and 4.14). A simple box, approximately one meter by two meters, which is only accessible under removable planks in the floor of the hayloft, the hideout was constructed in the late seventeenth century to shelter Christen Fankhaus, a Mennonite leader whose descendants still work the farm. As their simple website advertises, Simon and Regula Fankhauser, the current residents, are pleased to welcome visitors who want to learn about the *Täuferversteck* and the history of Anabaptism.[40] The *Täuferversteck* – which is also a prominent stop on virtually all Mennonite discovery tours and is even promoted by local tourist organizations – is emblematic, I believe, of at least two essential features of the larger history of the survival of the Anabaptists of Emmental: the secrecy that was necessary to protect the Anabaptist pastors and leaders who were most at risk of harm, and the clandestine networks of support that sustained the Brethren for decades and centuries.

Although distinctive, the history of Anabaptist repression and survival in the Emmental is hardly unique.[41] As we will see, repression and survival were

---

[39] See http://gameo.org/index.php?title=Emmental_Mennonite_Church_%28Kanton_Bern,_Swit zerland%29. To call this a Mennonite church as early as 1530 is, of course, anachronistic since the Mennonite movement was not born until after the debacle at Münster. On Menno Simons and the birth of the Mennonite movement, see Chapter 5 in this volume.

[40] See www.taeuferversteck.ch. I am very grateful to Heinrich Schmidt and his wife who very generously took my wife and me on a day-long guided tour of Anabaptist sites in the Emmental more than a decade ago.

[41] Even in Bern, the Anabaptist experience was not unique in the sense that the Bernese authorities also had a "Catholic problem" in the Berner Oberland. See Heinrich Schmidt, *Dorf und Religion: Reformierte Sittenzucht in Berner Landgemeinden der Frühen Neuzeit*, Quellen und Forschungen Zür Agrargeschichte (Stuttgart: Gustav Fischer, 1995), and Heinrich Richard Schmidt, "Morals Courts in Rural Berne During the Early Modern Period," in *The Reformation in Eastern and Central Europe*, ed. Karin Maag (London: Scolar Press, 1997), 155–81. Although the unsuccessful repression of persistent Catholicism is well documented in the morals courts of the Reformed authorities, the lived experience of the Catholic population is not as well preserved in popular memory as that of the Anabaptist population.

ILLUSTRATION 4.13: Hinter-Hütten farm, near Trub in the Emmental, has a hidden space, accessible only via the hayloft, to shelter Anabaptist leaders and pastors during times of danger. (Photo Wayne Te Brake)

ILLUSTRATION 4.14: The *Täuferversteck*, built into the hayloft of Hinter-Hütten farm, is a regular stop on Mennonite "discovery tours" to Europe. (Photo Wayne Te Brake)

recurrent themes in the history of both Protestant and Catholic "dissidents" in the sixteenth and seventeenth centuries. Together with the histories of *Simultankirchen* and *Auslauf*, it is usefully illustrative of the varied and messy religious peace that the Swiss *Landfrieden* and the German *Religionsfriede* made possible in central Europe.[42] Although religious peace in its various forms was not always pretty, religious coexistence was pervasive – not by any means the rare exception to authoritarian unity and purity, but the pluralistic rule.

THE VARIETIES OF COEXISTENCE

If we use Figure 1.2 as a template to plot the variation, we can see in Figure 4.1 that the various examples of religious coexistence I have highlighted here represent a broad range of variation, from **parity** and **integration** to **privilege** and **repression**.

In the upper-left quadrant I have located both the territories of Electoral Saxony and Upper Lusatia and the city of Strasbourg, although the **privilege** of

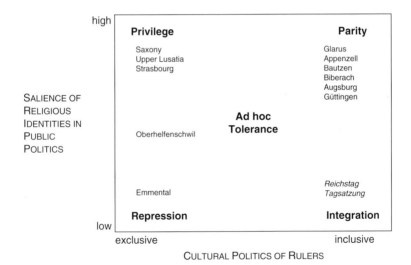

FIGURE 4.1: Patterns of religious coexistence in central Europe

[42] To be sure, many observers, like my students, will bristle at the notion that repression and survival may be considered a form of peaceful coexistence, but against the backdrop of intermittent war and the initial wave of violent repression, especially of Anabaptist leaders, the ongoing interactions of Reformed authorities and subversive Anabaptists after the 1530s appears to have resembled more clearly a ritual Kubuki dance that maintained appearances than a sustained campaign of annihilation; see especially Furner, "The Repression and Survival of Anabaptism."

their Lutheran churches was the residue of very different contentious political processes, official, subversive, and consensual, respectively. If this were intended to be a complete catalogue of this complex and messy peace, it would undoubtedly locate a large number of German territories and Swiss confederates in the upper left, with privileged "confessions" dominating but not actively persecuting subordinate dissident groups. In these places, *Auslauf* often afforded opportunities for dissidents to worship freely in adjacent jurisdictions. In the upper-right quadrant I have situated a longer list of examples: Glarus, Appenzell, Bautzen, Biberach, Augsburg, and Güttingen. This very diverse list bespeaks both the modularity of the practice of sharing sacred space and the scalability of both formal and informal **parity** arrangements. The lower half of the diagram is strikingly less populated: the *Reichstag* and the *Tagsatzung* in the lower right, as examples of **integration**, and Oberhelfenschil and the Emmental in or near the lower left, as examples of varying levels of active **repression** and survival. Whereas integration and repression will become more prominent in the wake of the next clusters of war making and peacemaking (see Chapters 8 and 11), for now it is striking that when German and Swiss actors learned to accommodate their new and largely unprecedented religious differences, these differences generally became very visible and thus salient features of public life. By contrast, the relative absence of active repression, with the notable exception of "radicals" such as Anabaptists, is perhaps a byproduct of the relatively limited nature of the religious wars, which flowed more clearly from the polarization of ruling elites than the direct polarization or militarization of popular religious movements (see Chapters 8, 11, and 12). In any case, all of the local and regional accommodations that our illustrative cases represent were subject to changes and adaptations that defy any kind of *definitive* conceptual or geographical mapping; rather they may be said to represent merely the first of several overlays that illustrate the increasingly dense accumulation over time of a limited range of historical outcomes.

As we will see in the chapters that follow, a broad range of variation in the patterns of religious coexistence will reappear during and after the next two phases of conflict. Compared to the Kappel and Schmalkaldic wars, the next rounds of religious war were both longer and more destructive. At the same time, the patterns of peacemaking were more clearly national and international in scope, whereas in the contours of religious peace both active repression and political integration will emerge more prominently alongside ad hoc adjustments to otherwise exclusive policies. Still, the religious peace that emerged in these later phases of religious war was just as varied and messy, and the persistence of religious diversity and the durability of religious coexistence remained the rule rather than the exception.

PHASE II

1562–1609

5

Religious War Unleashed

In the first phase of Europe's religious wars, in Switzerland and Germany, we saw that a limited level of coordinated destruction was predicated on the relative success of reformation coalitions. That is to say, collaborations between established rulers and popular reform movements succeeded in institutionalizing some form of "Lutheran" or "Reformed" theology, liturgical practice, and ecclesiastical structure locally or territorially within two late-medieval composite states: the Swiss *Eidgenossenschaft* and the German *Reich*. In the second phase of Europe's religious wars, we encounter much longer and more destructive religious wars that were predicated on the failure of reformation coalitions to accomplish anything like a piecemeal pattern of religious reform on the local or territorial level.

The civil/religious wars in France and the Eighty Years War in the Low Countries were, in their origins, both similar and closely linked to one another;[1] in both cases, religious polarization affected local as well as national politics, and broad military alliances effectively internationalized the scale of religious war at critical junctures. In addition, in the long duration of these struggles, the coordinated destruction of religious warfare served not only to transform the political geography of religious differences, but to make compromise and, by extension, durable peace more difficult to achieve. But

---

[1] There have been a number of attempts to compare the French wars and the Dutch Revolt; see, for example, Henk van Nierop, "Similar Problems, Different Outcomes: The Revolt of the Netherlands and the Wars of Religion in France," in *A Miracle Mirrored: The Dutch Republic in European Perspective*, eds. Karel Davids and Jan Lucassen (Cambridge: Cambridge University Press, 1995), 26–56; J. J. Woltjer, "Violence during the Wars of Religion in France and the Netherlands: A Comparison," *Nederlands Archief Voor Kerkgeschiedenis* 76, no. 1 (1996): 26–45; and Philip Benedict, et al., *Reformation, Revolt and Civil War in France and the Netherlands 1555–1585* (Amsterdam: Koninklijke Nederlandse Akademie van Wetenschappen, 1999). For a comparison of the French and Netherlandic examples from the perspective of popular politics and state formation, see Wayne Te Brake, *Shaping History: Ordinary People in European Politics, 1500–1700* (Berkeley and Los Angeles: University of California Press, 1998), 63–108.

by the beginning of the seventeenth century, these two wars yielded not two, but three dramatically different outcomes in France, the southern Netherlands and the United Provinces of the Northern Netherlands. In order to understand how these extended religious wars and their eventual settlements differed from the wars and settlements in Switzerland and Germany as well as from one another, we will have to describe and account for the emergence of two new and politically potent religious identities, commonly labeled the "Huguenots" and the "Beggars."

Early on, there had been considerable interest in Luther's theology in France and the Low Countries, but determined and initially more effective efforts to criminalize religious dissent and punish dissenters, as illustrated by the execution of the Augustinian monks in Brussels in 1523, characterized the official response.[2] Whereas Charles V's constitutional and political limitations as emperor prevented him from taking truly effective action against "Lutheran heresies" in Germany, his more direct overlordship of a collection of territories in the Low Countries allowed him greater latitude to develop and enforce repressive policies. Since the Low Countries quickly became an important center of evangelical publishing outside Germany, Charles's government issued a placard to regulate the book trade in 1520; in 1521 he promulgated a special Dutch/French edition of the Edict of Worms; in 1525 the government proscribed attendance at gatherings where Scriptures were read; in 1526 all those who possessed vernacular versions of the Scriptures were ordered to surrender them; by 1529 all those who possessed a wide variety of forbidden books faced the death penalty; and so on. The governments of both Charles V and Philip II, his son and successor as king in Spain and lord in the Netherlands, followed up this repressive legislation with pressure on local officials to pursue judicial action, producing the most sustained and destructive persecution of Protestants anywhere in Europe. Although the records are incomplete, Alastair Duke estimates that at least 1,300 and perhaps as many as four or five times that number were executed between 1523 and 1566.[3]

Although the institutional structure of his political sovereignty was significantly different, King Francis I of France, and his successor Henry II, pursued similar policies in order to suppress religious dissent and experimentation. Through successive waves of government action in the 1520s, 1530s, and 1540s, French policy criminalized a variety of beliefs as well as behaviors, so that by the 1550s heretical belief could legally be inferred from the behaviors of the subject. Thus, interpreting Scripture without official sanction, attending secret meetings, attacking sacred images, selling and distributing forbidden books, even possessing letters from Calvinist Geneva were equated with public unrest and sedition and were punishable by

---

[2] See Chapter 2, p. 26, in this volume.
[3] Alastair Duke, *Reformation and Revolt in the Low Countries* (London: Hambledon Press, 1990), esp. 29–59, 71–100.

death.[4] Despite there being probably fewer judicial executions in France than in the Low Countries, there were tens of thousands of indictments, and in Provence in 1543 judicial persecution spilled over into official violence. Apparently fearing that the Waldensians (*Vaudois*) – religious dissidents who were the followers of Peter Vaudes, a twelfth-century preacher condemned as a heretic – who lived peacefully in remote mountain villages in the southeast would "turn Swiss" and rebel, the *parlement* of Aix-en-Provence ordered preemptive strikes on the Vaudois villages.[5] This infamous campaign of annihilation, which provoked an international outcry, resulted in the wholesale massacre of Waldensians.

As determined as this repression was in both the Low Countries and France, it served not so much to eliminate "Lutheran heresies" as to deprive popular reform movements of their most prominent leaders and to drive the "dissenters" underground. Under these conditions, publicly successful reformation coalitions linking local political elites with popular reform movements, as they had in Switzerland and Germany, were virtually impossible, although in some places elite protection did allow some room for "private" dissent and clandestine religious experimentation. In the meantime, however, theological innovation and disputation did not cease with the institutionalization of Lutheran and Reformed churches inspired by Martin Luther and Huldrych Zwingli. Among the next generation of theologians and reformers, two are particularly relevant to the history of France and the Low Countries: Menno Simons and Jean Calvin.

Menno Simons was a Catholic priest in the territory of Friesland along the North Sea coast, which had submitted to Habsburg control in the early sixteenth century.[6] Following the debacle of the revolutionary Anabaptists in Münster in 1535, Simons joined and quickly became an important leader of the "peaceful" Anabaptists of the northern Netherlands. Under his leadership, the "Mennonites" embraced not only adult (re)baptism but also a strict separation of church and state, refusing to swear oaths and take up arms

---

[4] David Nicholls, "France," in *The Early Reformation in Europe*, ed. Andrew Pettegree (Cambridge: Cambridge University Press, 1992), 120–41; Mark Greengrass, *The French Reformation*, Historical Association Studies (Oxford: Blackwell, 1987).

[5] Euan Cameron, *The Reformation of the Heretics: The Waldenes of the Alps 1480–1580* (Oxford: Clarendon Press, 1984); Gabriel Audisio, *Les Vaudois de Luberon: Une Minorité de Provence, 1460–1560* (Gap: Mérindol, 1984); Gabriel Audisio, *The Waldensian Dissent: Persecution and Survival, c. 1170–c.1570*, trans. Clair Davison, Cambridge Medieval Textbooks (Cambridge: Cambridge University Press, 1999).

[6] Classic biographies include Karel Vos, *Menno Simons, 1496–1561, Zijn Leven en Werken en Zijne Reformatorische Denkbeelden* (Leiden: E. J. Brill, 1914), and John Horsch, *Menno Simons, His Life, Labors, and Teachings* (Scottdale, PA: Mennonite Publishing House, 1916); see also, B Rademaker-Helfferich and S. Zijlstra, *Een leven vol gevaar: Menno Simons (1496–1561) leidsman der dopers*, Catalogue of an exhibit at the Fries Museum, Leeuwarden (Amsterdam: Algemene Doopsgezinde Sociëteit, 1996), and Abraham Friesen, "Present at the Inception: Menno Simons and the Beginnings of Dutch Anabaptism," *Mennonite Quarterly Review* 72, no. 3 (July 1998): 351–88.

as demanded by civil authorities, which made them seem like dangerous radicals to most governments. Rather than reform whole communities, "radicals" like the Mennonites intentionally gathered only those who were truly repentant into separated churches, which clearly challenged the ideal of uniting the whole community religiously, but the model of the gathered or separated church proved to be especially suited to the survival of a variety of religious groups suffering active persecution.

Jean Calvin was a young law student in France when he first became interested and involved in the issues of religious reform.[7] In Paris in the early 1530s, he was closely associated with Nicolas Cop, rector of the university, and when Cop was forced to leave France for sanctuary in Basel after he openly called for religious reform in 1533, Calvin was also forced into hiding. Following the so-called "Affair of the Placards" in 1534 – named for placards calling for reform that were posted clandestinely throughout Paris and France more generally – Calvin fled to Basel, too, in the face of increased repression of all manner of religious dissent. In early 1536, Calvin published the first edition of his famous *Institutes of the Christian Religion*,[8] which earned him an international reputation as a reformer, and later that year he began assisting Guillaume Farel in his efforts to reform the church in the city-state of Geneva. Following a dispute with the city council, however, both Farel and Calvin were forced to leave Geneva, and in 1538 Calvin took a new position as pastor to the French exile community in Strasbourg. In 1541, the Council of Geneva invited Calvin to return and quickly adopted his Ecclesiastical Ordinances, which created a novel form of combined lay and clerical leadership for the Reformed Church.[9] From his position as both preacher and teacher, Calvin inspired religious dissidents and informed the creation of "Calvinist" churches throughout Europe and especially in France and the Netherlands.[10]

What was especially important for the survival of dissident religious movements in France and the Low Countries was the growth of committed exile communities abroad. In addition to the communities that Calvin served in

---

[7] See T. H. L. Parker, *John Calvin: A Biography* (Philadelphia: Westminster Press, 1975), and William J. Bouwsma, *John Calvin: A Sixteenth-Century Portrait* (New York: Oxford University Press, 1988).

[8] This first edition was in the form of a catechism, but later editions, which Calvin continued to work on throughout his life, were much longer and more systematic in their treatment of the principal issues of Reformed theology. For a modern English translation, see Jean Calvin, *Institutes of the Christian Religion*, ed. John T. McNeill, trans. Ford Lewis Battles, The Library of Christian Classics, vol. 20–21 (Philadelphia: Westminster Press, 1960).

[9] The Ecclesiastical Ordinances created four ordained offices in the Church, the first two clerical and the second two lay: preachers, teachers, elders, and deacons. For an introduction, see Philip Schaff, *Modern Christianity. The Swiss Reformation*, vol. 7 of *History of the Christian Church* (New York: C. Scribner's Sons, 1923), which is available online; the section on the Ecclesiastical Ordinances is at www.ccel.org/ccel/schaff/hcc8.iv.xiii.vii.html http://www .ccel.org/ccel/schaff/hcc8.

[10] For a general history of Calvinism, see Philip Benedict, *Christ's Churches Purely Reformed: A Social History of Calvinism* (New Haven: Yale University Press, 2002).

Strasbourg and Geneva, there were important exile communities in London and Emden (in northwest Germany) that provided clandestine religious communities not only with external allies and solidarity networks of support, but with a steady supply of trained preachers.[11] With this kind of external support, religious dissidents began building "churches under the cross" – that is, "gathered" churches of true believers separated from the established church – that looked a lot more like revolutionary cells than the officially reformed churches of Switzerland and Germany. Although such faith communities were theologically diverse, they frequently adopted the radically new institutional structure – the combined lay and clerical leadership model – of Reformed or Calvinist churches rather than Lutheran churches, which retained the integrative authority of professional clerics: pastors and bishops. And by the 1550s, these locally organized dissident communities had begun to institutionalize regional and even national networks by means of representative assemblies called synods.

Clearly the politicization of religious issues and the mobilization of popular religious movements produced decidedly different religious identity boundaries under these conditions. The determined repression of Charles V, Francis I, and their successors served effectively to *nationalize* the issue of religious reform, which had been addressed and largely resolved at the local and territorial level in Switzerland and Germany. By the same token, the reform movements and reformation coalitions that challenged the policy of repression developed national and even international networks of support and solidarity in the pursuit of religious reformation. In April 1559, these national contests for the religious future took on an additional international dimension when Habsburg Spain, now ruled by Philip II, and Valois France, now ruled by Henry II, concluded the Peace of Cateau-Cambrésis, ending a long series of Habsburg-Valois wars and binding "the Catholic monarchs in a joint endeavor to crush Protestantism."[12] Not surprisingly, then, under these conditions the mechanisms that recurrently led to religious war also produced decidedly different patterns of conflict.

HUGUENOTS, CATHOLICS, AND THE COMING OF THE FRENCH WARS

The early history of religious dissent in France and the Low Countries is difficult to excavate for the simple reason that in the face of official repression, the movements for religious reform were necessarily secretive and their activities

[11] Andrew Pettegree, *Emden and the Dutch Revolt: Exile and the Development of Reformed Protestantism* (Oxford: Clarendon Press, 1992); Philippe Denis, *Les églises d'étrangers en pays rhénans (1534–1564)*, Bibliothèque de la Faculté de Philosophie et Lettres de l'Université de Liège, 242 (Paris: Les Belles Lettres, 1984); A. Pettegree, *Foreign Protestant Communities in Sixteenth-Century London*, Oxford Historical Monographs (Oxford: Clarendon Press, 1986); R. M. Kingdon, *Geneva and the Coming of the Wars of Religion in France, 1555–1563* (Geneva: Librarie E. Droz, 1956).

[12] J. H. Salmon, *Society in Crisis: France in the Sixteenth Century* (New York: St. Martin's, 1975), 117.

clandestine. Nevertheless, by the 1550s religious dissenters in both places had become bolder and more visible and, for that reason they were seen as a growing threat by both French and Spanish authorities. In France, the pockets of clandestine Protestants had established contact with the French exile community and the Reformed Church in Geneva, which helped to create a network of Reformed churches. As popular preachers began attracting increasing numbers of followers, some of whom defied authorities by openly chanting psalms in the evangelical fashion or holding large outdoor services (*prêches*) outside the towns, the representatives of some of these "churches under the cross" met secretly in Paris in May 1559 to draft a Confession of Faith and adopt Articles of Discipline for a national church, just one month after the Peace of Cateau-Cambrésis was signed.[13] It was this network of fledgling churches, populated by a variety of social groups and connected with one another through their combined lay and clerical leadership, that served as the popular foundation of a broad coalition of challengers whose emergence set the stage for this new round of religious war.

Meanwhile, the planned repression of religious dissent did not get off to a good start in France. Henry II died suddenly in July 1559, shortly after being wounded during a jousting tournament celebrating the peace with Spain; he was succeeded by his fifteen-year-old son Francis II, who had recently married Mary, Queen of Scots. Not surprisingly, this succession set off fierce competition between factions at court for influence over the new king. On one side, the militantly Catholic Guise family, represented by Francis, duke of Guise, and Charles, duke of Lorraine, uncles of the new queen, immediately moved to dominate the court and take control of governmental administration. This certainly predicted the continuation of the policy of repression. On the other side, those who opposed Guise influence included the young king's mother, Catherine de Medici, and the Bourbon family, represented by Antoine, king of Navarre, and Louis, prince of Condé, both of whom had joined the Protestant cause.[14] In order to counter Guise influence, a broad conspiracy of Protestant nobles, including Louis de Bourbon, was organized in March 1560 to kidnap the king at his chateau in Amboise along the Loire and thus liberate him from the Guise influence at court. When the conspiracy was betrayed and several hundred of the noble conspirators were captured and summarily executed, it was clear that polarization over matters of religion had reached the highest levels of government as well.

The etymology of the term "Huguenot" to describe the broad coalition of Protestant forces in France is unclear. The most commonly accepted derivation is from the name applied to the Genevan partisans opposed to the Duke of

---

[13] Alastair Duke, Gillian Lewis, and Andrew Pettegree, eds., *Calvinism in Europe, 1540–1610: A Collection of Documents* (Manchester: Manchester University Press, 1992).

[14] I should note that Catherine's opposition to the Guise influence was not religious; her Catholicism was not in doubt, but her desire to protect her son's independence from noble influence was fierce.

Savoy in the 1520s and in favor of alliance with the Swiss *Eidgenossenschaft*; "Huguenot" would then be an alteration of *Eidgenoss* (confederate) and connote pejoratively the infidelity of the rebellious Swiss who had deposed their "legitimate" rulers. Other possibilities include allusions to Dutch/ Flemish *huisgenooten* (literally "housemates"), who clandestinely studied the Bible together, or an exclusively French derivation from the name of Hugh Capet, which may have been associated originally with the "little Hughes" who worshipped clandestinely in the Touraine.[15] In any case, the term came into general usage in the wake of the "Conspiracy of Amboise" in early 1560 and carried with it a whole host of pejorative political and religious connotations. That the Protestants nevertheless embraced the term to describe themselves makes it a particularly useful term to describe the broad coalition of ordinary people, pastors, magistrates, lawyers, and nobility – provincial nobles as well as princes of the blood – that emerged so dramatically in the early 1560s.

In early 1562 one of the movement's leaders, Admiral Gaspard de Coligny, tried to assemble a list of more than 2,000 churches, but even more conservative estimates of the numbers of adult Protestants suggest a Huguenot population of perhaps ten percent of the total population of France.[16] This broad Huguenot coalition represented a formidable challenge, at once religious and political, to the established Gallican Church and, by extension, the royal government that had so steadfastly defended it that it equated religious dissidence with political treason. The political situation became even more volatile and uncertain in December 1560, however, when Francis II died suddenly of an ear infection, and his mother, Catherine de Medici, established herself as regent for his brother and successor, Charles IX, who was only eleven years old.[17] Catherine quickly dismissed the Guises from court and released Louis de Bourbon, prince of Condé, from prison where he was awaiting execution for his role in the "Conspiracy." In her effort to find a middle course between the

---

[15] See Janet G. Gray, "The Origin of the Word Huguenot," *Sixteenth Century Journal* 14 (1983): 349–59, who discusses all the possibilities but favors the local French derivation. See also the article by Louis Jaucourt on "Huguenot" in the eighteenth-century *Encyclopédie*, which promotes the idea of a Swiss derivation: Jaucourt, Louis, chevalier de. "Huguenot." *The Encyclopedia of Diderot & d'Alembert Collaborative Translation Project*, trans. Susan Emanuel (Ann Arbor: Michigan Publishing, University of Michigan Library, 2005), http://hdl.handle.net/2027/spo.did2222.0000.428 (accessed June 6, 2014). Originally published as "Huguenot," *Encyclopédie ou Dictionnaire raisonné des sciences, des arts et des métiers*, 8:333 (Paris, 1765). When all is said and done, the Swiss origin seems the most compelling explanation from the comparative religious-political perspective that we are using here.

[16] Janine Garrisson, *Les Protestants du Midi, 1559–98* (Toulouse: Privat, 1980); Greengrass, *The French Reformation*; see also, Geoffrey Treasure, *The Huguenots* (New Haven: Yale University Press, 2013).

[17] My narrative vignettes of the French conflicts are based primarily and throughout on Arlette Jouanna, et al., *Histoire et dictionnaire des Guerres de Religion* (Paris: Robert Laffont, 1998), and Mack P. Holt, *The French Wars of Religion, 1562–1629*, New Approaches to European History (Cambridge: Cambridge University Press, 1995); cf. Salmon, *Society in Crisis* for a broad survey of the wars.

competing interests, Catherine convened two separate meetings of the Estates
General in December 1560 and August 1561 that nevertheless failed to resolve
the religious issue politically. Then, in September 1561, Catherine invited
religious leaders from both sides to a colloquy at Poissy. In contrast with the
disputations of the early German and Swiss Reformations, which dramatized
differences in order to choose for one or the other alternative, the Colloquy of
Poissy was intended to seek reconciliation and was thus similar to the earlier
colloquies at Marburg in 1529 and Regensburg in 1541 which had tried
unsuccessfully to reconcile theological and ecclesiological differences between
Luther and Zwingli and Protestants and Catholics, respectively. Like the
German negotiators before them, both sides refused to compromise, and the
Colloquy at Poissy, too, failed to achieve any form of reconciliation.

In late 1561, militant Catholics, fearful that Catherine might compromise
with the Huguenots, formed a military triumvirate to seek aid from Philip II of
Spain in order to "extirpate all those of the new religion."[18] Although earlier
edicts had begun to separate religious dissidence from political sedition, the
Catholics' worst fears were realized in January 1562 when Catherine issued the
Edict of Saint-Germain. For the first time, this edict granted limited recognition
and legality to Reformed worship by suspending "prohibitions and
punishments ... contained in previous edicts concerning assemblies made in
daylight outside the ... towns for preaching, prayers, and other practices of
their religion."[19] It was, then, the attack on March 1, 1562, on a public
Protestant worship service at Vassy by soldiers under the command of the
Catholic partisan, the duke of Guise, that sparked the first of the French civil/
religious wars.[20]

From the beginning, it was clear that this war would be very different from
the religious wars in Switzerland and Germany that had preceded it. Once the
national Reformed Synod proclaimed Louis de Bourbon, prince of Condé, the
protector of all Protestant churches in the kingdom, the movement for religious
reform was clearly linked with mobilization for war. The war began as
a widespread series of urban coups in which the Protestant forces seized
control locally, usually with a modest show of armed force and symbolic
violence like the "cleansing" of churches, as occurred at Rouen. The first of
these preemptive attacks came at Orleans, the center of Condé's operations,
on April 2, and was quickly followed in, among many other places, Angers in
the west, La Havre in the north, Valence in the south, and Lyon, the second city

[18] Quoted in Holt, *French Wars*, 65.
[19] The full French text of this edict is published in André Stegmann, ed., *Édits des guerres de religion*, Textes et documents de la Renaissance (Paris: J. Vrin, 1979), 8–14; a useful summary, along with summaries of its many precedents, many be found in N. M. Sutherland, *The Huguenot Struggle for Recognition* (New Haven: Yale University Press, 1980), appendix. The quotation is from David Potter, ed., *The French Wars of Religion: Selected Documents* (New York: St. Martin's Press, 1997), 31.
[20] On the start of the First French War, see Chapter 1, pp. 1–2, in this volume.

of the kingdom, with the largest concentration of Huguenot coups in the cities of the south and southwest. Although in a few places Catholics were able to repel the Protestants' action locally, as in the bloody urban warfare at Toulouse, a more formal military response was relatively slow in coming.[21] A few other cities, including Rouen, were recaptured by Catholic armies employing siege warfare in the late summer and autumn of 1562, and the Catholic forces won the only open battle of the war at Dreux in December. In the process, however, three of the four principal Catholic leaders were killed, and since the bulk of the Protestant cities remained unchallenged, there seemed to be little hope of defeating the Huguenot forces altogether. Thus, the government of Catherine de Medici sought a negotiated settlement, which was promulgated at Amboise in March 1563, just one year after the war began.

What is immediately striking about the first of the French Wars of Religion was the enormous explosion of direct popular engagement, both for and against the established Church. Indeed, the widespread pattern of communal violence, most pronounced in the first phase of the French wars, was the focus of very valuable historical research in the late twentieth century.[22] So who were these militant Catholics who were so fearful of Catherine's attempts to find peace and reconciliation through compromise – who actively countered both the Huguenots and the royal government, when necessary? To be sure, in addition to officials of the French or Gallican Church, the militant "Catholic" party included the courtly faction, led by the Guise family and supported from afar by Philip II of Spain. But it was also a good deal more than the agents of political and ecclesiastical authority, who had pursued and punished religious dissenters for decades. Indeed, we can probably say, in retrospect, that by the beginning of the French civil/religious wars, an unprecedented Catholic response to the challenges of Protestant reform had begun to build a broadly based coalition that mirrored the Huguenot coalition and proved capable not only of countering the Protestants' initial successes, but of prolonging the wars at critical junctures *until such time* as the survival of the established Gallican Church was assured.[23]

---

[21] Huguenot strikes were also repelled in Dijon, Aix-en-Provence, and Bordeaux.

[22] See especially Natalie Zemon Davis, *Society and Culture in Early Modern France* (Stanford, CA: Stanford University Press, 1975); Denis Crouzet, *Les guerriers de Dieu: la violence au temps des troubles de religion (vers 1525 – vers 1610)* (Seyssel: Champ Vallon, 1990); and Barbara B. Diefendorf, *Beneath the Cross: Catholics and Huguenots in Sixteenth-Century Paris* (New York: Oxford University Press, 1991). For a review of this literature, see Mark Greengrass, "The Psychology of Religious Violence," *French History* 5 (1991): 467–74; see also Luc Racaut, *Hatred in Print: Catholic Propaganda and Protestant Identity during the French Wars of Religion*, St. Andrews Studies in Reformation History (Aldershot, England; Burlington, VT: Ashgate, 2002), 23–37; David Nicholls, "The Theatre of Martyrdom in the French Reformation," *Past and Present*, 121 (1988): 49–73; and Kathleen A. Parrow, "From Defense to Resistance: Justification of Violence During the French Wars of Religion," *Transactions of the American Philosophical Society* 83, no. 6 (1993): i–vi, 1–79.

[23] Perhaps the only precedent for this anti-Protestant mobilization, including not just religious and political authorities but also popular mobilization, was the movement to restore Catholicism in

The emerging Catholic coalition in France was rooted, like its Huguenot counterpart, in a collaboration between popular preachers and ordinary people. In this, they were building on much older traditions of popular preaching and lay spirituality, which the Gallican Church had insistently invoked in opposition to the "Luther question" for decades. But as long as the Protestant movement remained clandestine and the authorities, both civil and religious, took the lead in indicting and executing "heretics," there was little room for popular mobilization and direct collective action/violence in defense of the established Church and its traditions; still, as Barbara Diefendorf notes, even early on, there was "a participatory element in the street theater of public executions."[24] In the late 1550s and beyond, however, as the Protestants became bolder and more openly defiant in their worship, there is also increasing evidence of a more robust collaboration between the Gallican Church and its most zealous defenders outside the institutions of church and state. On the one hand, popular preachers and polemicists not only continued to denounce the Protestants as heretics and "vermin" whose beliefs and practices polluted the sacred community, but they also began to promote the sort of active piety of the nascent Counter-Reformation associated with the Council of Trent. In this, they moved beyond mere criticism of the heretics to encourage the kind of figural action by which pious Catholics might clearly signal their allegiance to the true faith; this included frequent and very vivid calls for direct action to *exterminate* the Protestant heretics and to *eradicate* their ritual abominations.[25] On the other hand, there is evidence of a more organized popular response to Huguenot aggression and apparent success, which gave institutional shape to a popular Catholic coalition in places like Paris, where militia captains began to take an active role, and Toulouse, where a Catholic *syndicat* helped to drive the Huguenots from the city in 1562.[26] As Natalie Zemon Davis argues, the popular Catholic violence that so distinguished the

England under the leadership of Mary Tudor and Reginald Pole, Archbishop of Canterbury, between 1553 and 1558, which Eamon Duffy argues was critical to the "invention" of the Counter-Reformation; see Eamon Duffy, *Fires of Faith: Catholic England Under Mary Tudor* (New Haven: Yale University Press, 2009).

[24] Diefendorf, *Beneath the Cross*, 53; cf. Nicholls, "Theatre of Martyrdom."

[25] On the escalation of both polemical volume and popular action on the eve of the first war, see Diefendorf, *Beneath the Cross*, 49–63; G. Wylie Sypher, "'Faisant ce qu'il leur vient a plaisir': The Image of Protestantism in French Catholic Polemic on the Eve of the Religious Wars," *Sixteenth Century Journal* 11, no. 2 (1980): 59–84; and Racaut, *Hatred in Print*. On this score, the contrast with Germany could not be sharper: Bob Scribner argues that in Germany the overwhelming weight of propaganda was on the side of the Reformation; the Catholic response, by contrast, was "too meagre and too limited to have any large-scale or long-term impact." R. W. Scribner, *For the Sake of Simple Folk: Popular Propaganda for the German Reformation* (Oxford: Clarendon Press, 1994), 239.

[26] On Paris, see Diefendorf, *Beneath the Cross*; on Toulouse, see Mark Greengrass, "The Anatomy of a Religious Riot in Toulouse in May 1562," *Journal of Ecclesiastical History* 34 (1983): 367–91. See also, Stuart Carroll, "The Guise Affinity and Popular Protest during the Wars of Religion," *French History* 9, no. 2 (1995): 125–52.

start of the French civil wars from the earlier wars in Switzerland and Germany was deliberately imitative of official "justice" and was intended to compensate for perceived official inaction as a consequence of royal moderation.[27]

In the coming of the French wars, then, we can observe the same mechanisms that we saw in the first phase of the religious wars. New forms of religious *innovation* and *disputation* served to redefine and sharpen the differences between religious dissenters and defenders of the established Church with its elaborate hierarchy extending all the way to Rome, though in this phase the theology and ecclesiology of Jean Calvin generally eclipsed the Lutheran and Zwinglian "heresies" of the first phase. At the same time, the *politicization* of these issues by means of a determined pattern of state repression served effectively to "nationalize" the religious problem of theological and liturgical experimentation as a political problem of sedition, punishable by death. By extension, the clandestine *mobilization* of "churches under the cross" as well as the official promotion of Counter-Reformation lay piety served to produce a new set of politically salient "Huguenot" and "Catholic" religious identities. In short, under the new and changing conditions of the second half of the sixteenth century, the recurrent mechanisms of innovation, disputation, politicization, and mobilization accounted for decidedly different and new kinds of religious identity boundaries in the kingdom of France.

As the French Huguenots became bolder and more openly defiant and as the royal policy of repression became less certain in the midst of multiple successions to the French throne, the *activation* of these new religious identities and the boundaries that they entailed produced a number of instances of religious violence, especially in French cities, even before the outbreak of the French wars. In the context of virulent polemics that anathematized official attempts at compromise and reconciliation and accentuated *polarization* between the ever bolder proponents of religious reform and the equally zealous defenders of the "true" Church, then, the *brokerage* of national and even international alliances, including both violent specialists and noble patrons with ready access to arms and mercenaries, set the conditions for a widespread *escalation* of religious conflict by means of the clandestine networks of Huguenot religious solidarity following a Catholic attack on a Protestant worship service in Vassy. In short, under the new and changing conditions in a religiously divided kingdom of France, the recurrent mechanisms of activation, polarization, brokerage, and escalation accounted for the unprecedented explosion of both communal violence and coordinated destruction with which the first religious/civil war in France began in 1562.

Although the psychological shock and the physical toll of the communal violence were locally significant, the coordinated destruction of the First French

---

[27] Natalie Zemon Davis, "The Rites of Violence," in *Society and Culture in Early Modern France* (Stanford, CA: Stanford University Press, 1975), 152–87. See also Nicholls, "Theatre of Martyrdom."

War was limited, and the Peace/Edict of Amboise, which brought the war to an end in 1563, proved to be remarkably durable. In the face of sporadic religious violence locally and widespread Catholic opposition to the terms of the settlement, the royal government undertook a two-year tour of the kingdom that demonstrated its determination to enforce the peace and to overcome the opposition of the regional *parlements* – the sovereign royal courts at Paris, Rouen, Toulouse, Grenoble, Bordeaux, Dijon, Aix-en-Provence, and Rennes that were required to register the royal edict in order for it to take effect. Alarmed by the growing domination of the king's council by the Guise family – led now by Charles, cardinal of Lorraine, following the assassination of the duke of Guise during the first war – the military leaders of the Huguenots, Louis de Bourbon, prince of Condé, and the Admiral Gaspard de Coligny, nevertheless restarted the war in September 1567 by conspiring, again unsuccessfully, to capture the king and seizing a number of fortified cities, including Orleans, Nîmes, Mâcon, and Montpellier. By this time, however, the conflict in France had been complicated by a stunning explosion of religious violence in the Low Countries starting in the summer of 1566.

BEGGARS, SPANIARDS, AND THE COMING OF THE DUTCH WAR

In the Low Countries, the planned repression of dissent following the Peace of Cateau-Cambrésis in 1559 fared no better than it had in France. After concluding peace with France, Philip II soon departed his Low Countries provinces for Spain, leaving his half-sister, Margaret of Parma, as governor-general.[28] In order to strengthen the Church's response to the challenge of religious dissent, Philip had sought to reorganize the Church itself, and before he left, the papal bull *super universas* (1559), laid out a plan, originally devised by Charles V, to create fourteen new bishoprics and three new archbishoprics in the Netherlands. Although the Church in the Netherlands was clearly underinstitutionalized by comparison with the Gallican Church – there was just one bishopric in the northern provinces and four in the entire Habsburg Netherlands, by

---

[28] There are a number of broad surveys in English of the early history of the Eighty Years War and the Dutch Revolt, among them: Pieter Geyl, *The Revolt of the Netherlands (1555–1609)*, 2nd ed. (London: Ernest Benn, 1958), and Geoffrey Parker, *The Dutch Revolt*, rev. ed. (Harmondsworth: Penguin, 1985) are still useful. The first part of Jonathan I. Israel, *The Dutch Republic: Its Rise, Greatness, and Fall, 1477–1806*, The Oxford History of Early Modern Europe (Oxford: Clarendon Press, 1995) is more up to date; more recent yet, Graham Darby, ed., *The Origins and Development of the Dutch Revolt* (London; New York: Routledge, 2001), includes a very useful chronology and essays by leading scholars. A much-needed, new synthetic account, which expands the chronology to 1680, has just been published: Marjolein 't Hart, *The Dutch Wars of Independence: Warfare and Commerce in the Netherlands 1570–1680*, Modern Wars in Perspective (London and New York: Routledge, 2014). Leiden University is building a website dedicated to the revolt that includes English translations of some original sources, selected and translated by Alastair Duke: http://dutchrevolt.leiden.edu/dutch/Pages/default.aspx.

comparison with some 100 bishoprics in France[29] – the sudden introduction of so many new institutions, along with the concomitant redirection of fiscal resources to support them, awakened considerable resentment, suspicion, and resistance. Not surprisingly, much of that animosity was directed at Antoine Perrenot de Granvelle, Philip's trusted advisor, who was appointed cardinal primate of the new structure. Amid denunciations of "heresy-hunters and inquisitors," with whom the new bishoprics were associated, and only halting progress on the reorganization itself, Philip's regent, Margaret of Parma, requested the dismissal of Cardinal Granvelle and suspension of the church reform, which Philip granted finally in December 1564.

The dismissal of Cardinal Granvelle was widely perceived as a victory, not only for the noble magnates, such as William, prince of Orange, and Lamoraal, count of Egmond, who were Granvelle's principal challengers in the Grand Council at Brussels, but also for the widely dispersed evangelical movement that had in the period since 1559 become ever bolder in its defiance of the hated heresy laws. As local magistrates apparently relaxed their enforcement of the antiheresy laws, the theologically diverse secret conventicals of the religious dissidents had begun morphing into formal churches. The first Reformed or Calvinist church was formed in Antwerp in 1555, followed shortly by all the major towns in Flanders. In 1563 the first synod of Reformed churches was held in Antwerp under the tutelage of the "mother" church in Emden.[30] Emboldened by the new visibility of religious dissidents and Reformed churches in France, dissidents in the Low Countries also began holding outdoor worship services in the countryside (*hagepreken*, or "hedgepreaching," reminiscent of the French *prêches*), beyond the jurisdictions of the urban magistrates.[31] Amid a general expectation that the government in Brussels would soon relax enforcement of the heresy laws, however, Philip II unequivocally rejected the Grand Council's advice to do so in October 1565 and insisted that the heresy laws be strictly enforced.

In this increasingly uncertain environment, a group of lesser noblemen took the initiative in late 1565 by forming a league called the Compromise of the Nobility, which sought a religious peace along the lines of the peace that the Huguenots of France had recently negotiated with Catherine de Medici – that is to say, public recognition and legality, however limited, of Protestant worship. Led by Hendrik van Brederode, this movement, which grew to 400, included not only "Protestant and crypto-Protestant noblemen," as Jonathan Israel calls them, but also a number of moderate Catholics.[32] On April 5, 1566, an

---

[29] See the maps of the old and new bishoprics in Israel, *The Dutch Republic*, 142; on the bishoprics of France and their close relationship with political power, see Holt, *French Wars*, 13–14; Holt reports that of 101 incumbent bishops in 1559, only 19 resided regularly in their dioceses.

[30] Pettegree, *Emden and the Dutch Revolt*.

[31] Duke, *Reformation and Revolt*, 94, reports the first of these outdoor services, in imitation of the French *prêches*, in 1563; cf. Phyllis Mack Crew, *Calvinist Preaching and Iconoclasm in the Netherlands, 1544–1569* (Cambridge: Cambridge University Press, 1978).

[32] Israel, *The Dutch Republic*, 145, and Henk van Nierop, "A Beggar's Banquet: The Compromise of the Nobility and the Politics of Inversion," *European History Quarterly* 21 (1991): 419–43.

enormous delegation of more than 200 of these nobles, arrayed in a solemn and richly symbolic procession, "humbly petitioned" the regent, Margaret of Parma, for an end to religious repression. One of the regent's advisors, Charles, count of Berlaymont, allegedly mocked the assembled petitioners as "beggars," not worthy of her attention. For a whole host of reasons, the petitioners proudly embraced this term of derision, and in short order those who opposed the religious persecution and sought to preserve the "privileges" of the Low Countries provinces invoked the term "Beggars" to describe their emergent movement. But the submission of the compromise petition was important not only for its symbolism; it also had a stunning practical effect: In her reply three days later, Margaret promised to make a new appeal to Philip and to suspend enforcement of the heresy laws until further notice.[33]

This "victory" for the Compromise of the Nobility in early 1566 was only the start of what has been characterized retrospectively as the *wonderjaar* ("wonder" or "miracle" year) in both legend and history.[34] In May and into the early summer, popular evangelical preachers began leading ever more visible and openly defiant *hagepreken*, and by the end of June some of these attracted thousands of participants, especially in the southern provinces, where the religious reform movement was strongest. The largest of these demonstrations of popular support for religious reform may have been on July 14 at Laer, outside Antwerp, with 25,000 reported in attendance, but by the end of July, meetings of around 10,000 were also reported at Tournai and Valenciennes, and of 20,000 at Ghent. It is not clear how these very provocative and seemingly contagious enactments of dissident strength were coordinated or planned, but they were and are certainly compelling evidence of the potential for dynamic collaboration between popular preachers, many of whom had recently returned from exile in

---

[33] See Nierop, "A Beggar's Banquet"; Peter Arnade, "Beggars and Iconoclasts: The Political Culture of Iconoclasm on the Eve of the Revolt of the Netherlands," in *Power and the City in the Netherlandic World*, eds. Wayne Te Brake and Wim Klooster (Leiden: Brill, 2006), 59–83; and especially Peter Arnade, *Beggars, Iconoclasts, and Civic Patriots: The Political Culture of the Dutch Revolt* (Ithaca: Cornell University Press, 2008), which very skillfully sets this one incident (pp. 76–80) in a much larger political-cultural context of rising opposition to Philip II. Modern analysts invariably note the defiance of the petitioners' actions, which belies the rhetorical humility of the petition itself. For the text of the petition, as well as the regent's response, see G. Groen van Prinsterer, ed., *1566*, vol. II, *1e serie* of *Archives ou correspondence inedit de la maison d'Orange-Nassau* (Utrecht: Kemink et fils, 1835), 78–85; in English translation, see E. H. Kossmann and A. F. Mellink, eds., *Texts Concerning the Revolt of the Netherlands* (Cambridge: Cambridge University Press, 1974), 62–5.

[34] For good summaries in English, with full references to Dutch and French sources, see Phyllis Mack Crew, "The Wonderyear: Reformed Preaching and Iconoclasm in the Netherlands," in *Religion and the People, 800–1700*, ed. James Obelkevich (Chapel Hill: University of North Carolina Press, 1979), 191–220; Guido Marnef, "The Dynamics of Reformed Militancy in the Low Countries: The Wonderyear," in *The Education of a Christian Society: Humanism and the Reformation in Britain and the Netherlands*, eds. N. Scott Amos, Andrew Pettegree, and Henk van Nierop (Aldershot: Ashgate, 1999), 193–210; and chapter 5, "The Wonderyear" in Pettegree, *Emden and the Dutch Revolt*, 109–46.

Emden or London, and a wide variety of Philip II's ordinary subjects. In its response, the regent's government seemed timid if not paralyzed. The nobles who had formed the Compromise the previous year now seized the opportunity to submit a Second Request, to which Margaret responded with another appeal to Philip for relaxation of the heresy laws and a plea to her subjects to keep the peace and suspend the *hagepreken*.

This broad challenge to the religious policies of the Brussels and Spanish governments took on a startling new dimension in the late summer and fall of 1566 with an explosion of religious violence, often called the *beeldenstorm* or "iconoclastic fury." On August 10, Sebastian Matte, a minister who had recently returned from exile, preached a sermon outside the monastery of St. Laurence at Steenvoorde in the western district of Flanders, and in response, some twenty or so from his audience stormed the building and smashed all the religious images and objects. This call and response was repeated, with a different preacher, three days later at the monastery of St. Anthony nearby. There was another sermon by Matte with a larger audience at Poppering, two days later, after which some 100 people, many of them refugees who had recently returned from England, fanned out to destroy images in towns and villages throughout Flanders. In west Flanders alone, more than 400 churches, convents, and monasteries were damaged. By August 20, this wave of violence reached Antwerp, the great commercial center in Brabant, where more than twenty churches were "cleansed" with remarkable efficiency in a matter of just hours. On August 22: Ghent, Middelburg, 's-Hertogenbosch, and Breda were affected; on August 23: Mechelen, Amsterdam, Heusden, Tournai, and Turnhout; on August 24: Delft, Utrecht, and Valenciennes; and so on, though at a less dramatic pace, through late September (Groningen, Harderwijk, and Maastricht) and early October (Venlo and Delft, for a second time).[35]

Very few population centers in the Low Countries were spared, but in most provinces the iconoclastic destruction was largely restricted to the cities. There were also variations in the personnel – with returning refugees central early on and local zealots taking a greater role later – and the organization of the attacks – although Reformed ministers and municipal officials were frequently involved, at least implicitly, they often denied their participation or approval later. But in the end, two features of this *beeldenstorm* – a contemporary descriptor – stand out. On the one hand, there was an almost complete collapse of civil authority that compounded the collapse of religious authority; indeed, in most places the local militia, which was responsible for maintaining public order, either participated or refused to intervene, but where they did intervene, they often prevented attacks. On the other hand, there was precious little evidence of the sort of collective Catholic response that was so critical in France. Indeed, the iconoclasm of the summer and fall of 1566

---

[35] See the map of the spread of the iconoclasm in Parker, *The Dutch Revolt*, 77; cf. Pettegree, *Emden and the Dutch Revolt*, 118.

confirms Natalie Davis's astute observation that Calvinists attacked objects, images, and buildings whereas Catholics attacked persons; thus, in the absence of a popular Catholic counterattack in the Low Countries, the violence of the iconoclastic fury, however terrifying it must have seemed to devout Catholics, was largely directed at things rather than persons.

To date, historians have offered a variety of interesting, though only partial, explanations for the *relative absence* of a robust Catholic response to the Protestant violence – after all, explaining a negative is a difficult challenge even in the most elaborately documented cases.[36] To be sure, Philip II's unfailing determination to enforce strict heresy laws may have left even less room in the Netherlands than in France for "ordinary" Catholics to demonstrate their allegiance to the established Church through direct action. In addition, Judith Pollmann has underscored the *relative absence*, especially in this critical early stage, of clerical leadership, including the kind of Counter-Reformation preaching, and by extension, the virulent discourse of fear, urging direct action in defense of the "true" faith and a "pure" community of belief, that French historians have argued was essential to Catholic mobilization/violence in France.[37] Finally, it seems to me that the institutional "immaturity" of the established Church in the Habsburg Netherlands, which Philip's and Granvelle's reforms were designed to ameliorate, suggests not only fewer social investments in the power and prestige of clerical appointments but also fewer endowed institutions of popular piety, such as confraternities, that might have given organizational shape to a popular defense of the Church.[38]

In any case, the simultaneous collapse of civil and religious authority in the summer of 1566 and the relative absence of popular Catholic mobilization capable of countering Protestant violence are clearly related to the way the *wonderjaar* unfolded. Apparently stunned by this explosion of violence, Margaret of Parma signed an Accord on August 23, 1566 – that is, early on in the process – by which religious dissidents would enjoy freedom of worship wherever preaching had already taken place, but the noble league of the

---

[36] See Joke Spaans, "Catholicism and Resistance to the Reformation in the Northern Netherlands," in *Reformation, Revolt and Civil War in France and the Netherlands 1555–1585*, eds. Philip Benedict, et al. (Amsterdam: Koninklijke Nederlandse Akademie van Wetenschappen, 1999), 149–64; surveying the literature, Spaans suggests that the relative passivity of Dutch Catholics is comparable to that of English Catholics – and thus "normal" – and that the French case may be the exception that requires explanation.

[37] Judith Pollmann, "Countering the Reformation in France and the Netherlands: Clerical Leadership and Catholic Violence, 1560–1585," *Past and Present* 190 (2006): 83–120. See also, Judith Pollmann, *Catholic Identity and the Revolt of the Netherlands, 1520–1635*, The Past & Present Book Series (Oxford: Oxford University Press, 2011).

[38] I should point out that while the comparative analysis of the incidence of violence in the French and Dutch cases is important, our goal here is to shift the focus from understanding (the meaning or origins of) religious violence, as such, to understanding the way in which violence (or its absence) affects the possible trajectories of change and the long-term outcomes of the religious struggles.

Compromise would be dissolved. Enforcement of this Accord was left to provincial governors such as William of Orange and the Count of Egmond, who had favored moderation, and in early September, both Lutherans and Calvinists were permitted to construct new churches, two each, within the city of Antwerp, where Orange was governor. Local arrangements for Protestant worship were soon negotiated in Tournai and Ghent as well. By the end of September, Protestants in Amsterdam were allowed to use an existing church, and in many other places, in the absence of official leadership, Protestants simply commandeered existing (presumably cleansed) churches for their own use. Since the Accord only specified freedom of worship, and thus preaching, the construction or appropriation of churches clearly exceeded the regent's intentions. But soon the emboldened reform movements were offering the full range of religious services: baptisms, marriages, and communion. And it was the Calvinist or Reformed congregations, with their fledgling church organization combining lay and clerical leadership, that were in the best position to exploit the new opportunities provided by the collapse of authority. Indeed, they began to organize larger synodical meetings to coordinate and shape their common activities.

In all of this activity, we can see the emergence of a potentially powerful Beggar coalition, reminiscent of the Huguenot coalition in France: high nobles close to power in Brussels, such as Orange and Egmond; lesser nobles, such as Brederode and the Compromise of the Nobility; urban magistrates; and a broad network of nascent Reformed churches with a wide ranging social composition of intellectuals, preachers, lawyers, merchants, and artisans. At the same time, however, the government of Philip II urged Margaret of Parma to reassert government control and authorized/financed the raising of troops to counter the Beggars' challenge, which was at once political and religious. By mid-November, Margaret began to take the offensive: she issued orders for the strict enforcement of the Accord, insisting that the Protestant congregations cease "illegal" baptisms, marriages, and communion. She focused her attention on the "villes mauvaises" in the south where the Calvinists were the strongest: Antwerp, Valenciennes, and Tournai. Anticipating a military showdown, some Calvinist churches began collecting money to provide for a common defense and eventually to raise an army, but in mid-December Margaret ordered Tournai and Valenciennes to accept royal garrisons. Following some brief military skirmishes with armed Protestant bands, royal troops occupied Tournai on December 30 and laid siege to Valenciennes. But Orange and Egmond declined to join the open insurrection, affirmed their loyalty to the crown, and even assisted in the strict enforcement of the Accord, which meant that in some places the Calvinists had to give up their churches and once again worship in the open air. The hastily organized troops of Antwerp were surprised and decimated by a royal army on March 13, 1567, and on March 24 Valenciennes surrendered and the Calvinist leaders there were executed. What followed was a mass migration of religious dissidents and rebels abroad, which Geoffrey Parker estimates at 60,000.[39]

Thus, the *wonderjaar* ended as suddenly and dramatically as it had begun. Protestant churches were once again closed, and those dissident and rebel leaders who could sought refuge once again in exile. Hendrik van Brederode, who had been openly defiant, fled to safer haven in Germany, and even William of Orange, whose earlier opposition had compromised his position, retreated to his patrimonial estates in Germany. Meanwhile, Philip II convinced Don Fernandez Alvarez de Toledo, duke of Alva, to lead an army of 10,000 Spanish and Neapolitan soldiers, which arrived in the Low Countries finally in August 1567, having traveled northward from Italy along the long and difficult "Spanish Road." Acting out Philip's determination to eliminate political opposition and religious dissent once and for all, Alva created the so-called Council of Troubles that organized and quickly became the symbol of a particularly fierce repression.[40] In relatively short order, the Council of Troubles, which functioned much like an inquisitorial court, tried more than 12,000 people connected with the Beggars' rebellion, condemned some 9,000, including William of Orange, to forfeit some or all of their property, and most infamously ordered the execution of more than 1,000 for treason – including, among a mass execution of 60 noblemen in June 1568, the counts of Egmond and Horne, two prominent noble members of the Council of State, despite the fact that they had remained faithful to Catholicism.[41] Confident of his victory, Alva erected a statue of himself at Antwerp, with the motto "To the duke of Alva ... who extirpated sedition, reduced rebellion, restored religion, secured justice and established peace."[42]

Following the death of Brederode in early 1568, William of Orange emerged as the leader of the Beggar coalition in exile, which began raising troops in Germany. Louis of Nassau, William of Orange's brother, invaded Groningen in May 1568, but he was quickly defeated by Alva in July.[43] In October, William of Orange led a contingent of German soldiers across the Mass River, but he quickly withdrew again across the French border, there to disband his forces and to become part of the Third French War. Given the prominence of so many "foreign" troops under Alva's command, what remained of the Beggar coalition could reframe the emergent conflict as pitting the defenders of local "liberty" against the evil forces of Spanish "tyranny," thereby holding open the

---

[39] Parker, *The Dutch Revolt*, 119.

[40] Margaret of Parma was deeply opposed to Alva's repression, and she resigned her position as Philip's regent in the Low Countries; when she left Brussels in December 1567, she was replaced by Alva as governor-general. On the council, see Guido Marnef and Hugo de Schepper, "Raad van Beroerten (1567–1576)," in *De Centrale Overheidsinstellingen van de Habsburgse Nederlanden (1482–1795)* (Brussel: Algemeen Rijksarchief, 1994), I: 469–77.

[41] See Parker, *The Dutch Revolt*, 107–9, and Israel, *The Dutch Republic*, chapter 8.

[42] Quoted in Parker, *The Dutch Revolt*, 111.

[43] This invasion was to be part of a four-pronged attack from England, France, and Germany, most of which never materialized. See Parker, *The Dutch Revolt*, 108–10.

possibility of a future grand coalition of all Netherlanders, Catholic and Protestant alike. Still, these initial tokens of open revolt were hardly impressive or predictive of long-term success.

Like the First French War, then, this complex prologue to the Eighty Years War, which is conventionally dated from 1568, combined a widespread pattern of local religious violence with a limited amount of coordinated destruction. And in the coming of religious war in the Habsburg Netherlands, we can see the recurrence of the same mechanisms that accounted for the First French War. New forms of religious *innovation* served to sharpen the differences between religious dissenters and those who defended the established Church, though in the Low Countries the "peaceful" Anabaptists and the followers of Menno Simons, in particular, represented a more visible alternative to both the Lutherans of the German Reformation and the Calvinists of the French. As in France, the *politicization* of religious issues by means of a determined state policy of repression effectively "nationalized" the problem of religious reform and forced the religious dissidents underground, where their *mobilization* as "churches under the cross" was assisted by the Calvinist exile communities in Emden and London. Still, the variant concatenations of these familiar mechanisms may be said to have produced significant differences, even at this very early stage in these extended conflicts. At the official level, the French government used a formal *disputation* to support a policy of reconciliation, whereas the Spanish government of Philip II remained implacably opposed to any conversation with "heretics." And in the realm of popular mobilization, agents of the Gallican Church began building a powerful collaboration with pious Catholics that proved capable of countering Protestant aggression, whereas Catholic mobilization in the Low Countries was much weaker and comparable to the relatively weak Catholic response in Germany.[44] In the Low Countries, then, innovation, disputation, politicization, and mobilization accounted for a decidedly asymmetrical religious identity boundary separating a distant overlord and his authoritarian Catholic regime from a broad range of formerly clandestine, but increasingly organized, religious dissenters supported at least implicitly by all those who criticized the religious repression and the planned reorganization of the established Church.

The tumultuous events of the *wonderjaar* in 1566 seemed to *activate* this distinctive Netherlandic iteration of the generic Reform/Counter-Reform identity boundary nearly everywhere at once, and the dramatic explosion of both demonstrative worship services and iconoclastic violence revealed the social breadth, the political connections, and the geographical extent of the nascent Beggars' coalition, united above all by its opposition to Philip II's repressive policies. Despite all their local organizational advantages and the surprising numerical strength of the religious dissenters, the religious *polarization* did not translate into durable political alliances, as key political

---

[44] See Spaans, "Catholicism and Resistance," and Scribner, *For the Sake of Simple Folk.*

figures such as Orange, Egmond, and even Margaret of Parma sought to avoid open conflict through at least temporary moderation. Meanwhile the most zealous Beggars were unable, in the short term, to *broker* a military alliance capable of meeting the enormous military response of the Spanish authorities in 1567. By comparison with the much more durable and militarily resourceful Huguenot coalition in France, then, the Beggars' alliance appeared to crumble, not unlike the English Pilgrimage of Grace, and their first direct challenge to Spanish "tyranny" was short lived. Instead of achieving partial legality and public recognition like their French brethren, the religious dissenters of the Habsburg Netherlands were once again forced underground or into exile as the duke of Alva and the Council of Troubles reasserted an uncompromising regime of Catholic unity and purity.

CONNECTED STRUGGLES, RECURRENT WARS

In August of 1568, William of Orange, representing the Beggar movement in the Low Countries, and the prince of Condé and the Admiral Coligny, representing the Huguenots of France, concluded a formal treaty committing their movements to a common effort to defeat the "evil councilors" who were misleading their respective monarchs and seeking to crush the new religion. Meanwhile, Philip II was offering support to the cardinal of Lorraine, the leader of the Catholic Guise faction, in his effort to restart the conflict and undo the compromises that had ended the first two wars in France. Through these international solidarities, at once religious and political, the protracted struggles in France and the Low Countries remained linked for the next sixteen years, during which time these conflicts clearly began to transform the religious and political geography of Europe.

In France, the alternations between war and peace were frequent in the years between 1567 and 1580. As Table 5.1 indicates, there were six distinct wars ended by six different peace agreements in the space of just over thirteen years. The Huguenot leaders had restarted the war in September 1567 with their unsuccessful attempt to capture the king at Meaux; the Peace and Edict of Longjumeau followed after only six months of limited war in March 1568.[45] Just five months later, in August 1568, the Council of State, under the leadership of the cardinal of Lorraine, restarted war by revoking the Peace of Longjumeau and ordering the arrest of the Huguenot leaders: Condé and Coligny. This war – the third – was longer and more protracted in large measure because of foreign involvement, including incursions by William of Orange and his brother, Louis of Nassau, in 1568 and by the German Duke of Zweibrücken in 1569.[46] Although the Protestant forces suffered defeats at Jarnac in March 1569 – in which encounter the Huguenot leader Louis, prince of Condé, was killed – and at

---

[45] See Jouanna, et al., *Guerres de Religion*, 163–72.
[46] See Jouanna, et al., *Guerres de Religion*, 173–85.

TABLE 5.1 *Principal French religious conflicts and their settlements, 1559–1629*

Conflict	Dates	Settlement
Active Repression	June 1559–Jan. 1562	Edict of Saint-Germain, January 17, 1562
First War	Mar. 1562–Mar. 1563	Peace/Edict of Amboise, March 19,1563
Second War	Sept. 1567–Mar. 1568	Peace/Edict of Longjumeau, March 23, 1568
Third War	Aug. 1568–Aug. 1570	Peace/Edict of Saint-Germain, August 8, 1570
Fourth War	Nov. 1572–July 1573	Peace of La Rochelle, July 2, 1573 Edict of Boulogne, July 11, 1573
Fifth War	Oct. 1574–May 1576	Peace of Monsieur, May 6, 1576 Edict of Beaulieu, May 6, 1576
Sixth War	Dec. 1576–Sept. 1577	Peace of Bergerac, September 14, 1577 Edict of Poitiers, September 17, 1577
Seventh War	Mar. 1579–Mar. 1580	Peace/Edict of Fleix, November 26, 1580
Eighth War	Mar. 1585–Apr. 1598	Peace/Edict of Nantes, April 30, 1598
Ninth War	May 1621–June 1629	Peace/Edict of Alais, June 16, 1629

Moncontour in October 1569, they rallied under Coligny's leadership to defeat the royal army at Arnay-le-Duc in June 1570; in August 1570 the Peace and Edict of Saint-Germain granted civil rights to Huguenots and, having ended two years of war, provided for two years of peace.

The civil/religious conflicts in France took a more violent and destructive turn in 1572. In August, the royal wedding of the Protestant Henry de Bourbon, king of Navarre, to the Catholic Marguerite de Valois, King Charles's sister, brought a large number of Huguenot leaders to Paris. Following the wedding, an unsuccessful attempt on August 22 to assassinate the Huguenot leader, Admiral Coligny, led the King's Council, fearing a reprisal from the Huguenots, to approve a preemptive attack on the Huguenot leadership on August 24, St. Batholomew's Day. In the early morning, a troop of approximately 100 Swiss guards, led by Henry, duke of Guise, systematically murdered some three dozen Huguenot leaders, including Admiral Coligny, while they slept. There followed a more general, though less carefully organized, massacre of Protestants in Paris over the next three days, which was abetted by members of the civic militia but carried out, for the most part, by civilians. This paroxysm of popular and official violence, which claimed thousands of lives and was imitated in other French cities in the coming weeks, is of course known historically as the St. Bartholomew's Day Massacre, undoubtedly the most infamous campaign of annihilation in Europe during the era of the religious wars.[47]

---

[47] There is a large literature on the St. Bartholomew's Day massacres; see especially, Diefendorf, *Beneath the Cross*; Denis Crouzet, *La nuit de la Saint-Barthélemy: un rêve perdu de la*

The massacres of 1572 had a devastating impact on the Huguenot movement in France, depriving it of many of its noble leaders and halting its pattern of numerical growth over the previous two decades. But the Huguenots did not end their defiance. Sometime in late 1572, the regional leaders of the Huguenot "heartland" in the south and southwest devised a political organization to manage their common defense, and the first meetings of a general Protestant political assembly, which would continue to meet regularly until 1598, were held at Montauban and Millau in 1573 and 1574.[48] In addition, the city of La Rochelle, which had become a Protestant bastion during the third war, precipitated a brief renewal of coordinated destruction by refusing entry to its royal governor in September 1572. Charles IX declared war on La Rochelle in November, and royal forces began a very costly and destructive siege of the city in February. Amid (apparently false) rumors of an English armada on its way to relieve the Huguenots of La Rochelle, the royal government called off the siege in May, negotiated the Peace of La Rochelle, and promulgated the Edict of Boulogne in July 1573, which eliminated many of the privileges and guarantees that the previous edict had granted.[49] Before the start of a new round of war, however, the young king, Charles IX, died suddenly in May 1574 and was succeeded by his younger brother, Henry III.

Protestant discontent with the provisions of the Edict of Boulogne and troop movements on behalf of the reorganized and increasingly defiant Huguenot party threatened the peace again in the fall of 1574. During this "war," the fifth of the religious wars, there was, in fact, relatively little coordinated destruction; still, there were major political realignments and military incursions that once again changed the nature of Protestant/Catholic relations in France.[50] On the one hand, Francis, duke of Alençon, Henry III's younger brother, aligned himself with the Protestant forces and even presented a very aggressive set of demands on their behalf. On the other hand, the assorted military forces of the Huguenots were supported in the spring of 1576 by the arrival in France of 20,000 German mercenaries under the command of John Casimir, brother of the Calvinist Elector of the Palatinate. Once these forces were combined in central France, it was clear that the king was in no position to resist the 30,000 men under Huguenot command, and the royal government was forced to accept the Peace of Monsieur – so called in reference to "Monsieur," the duke of Alençon, who seemed to dictate its terms – and promulgate the Edict of Beaulieu on May 6, 1576. Under the terms of this Edict, which represented

Renaissance, Chroniques (Paris: Fayard, 1994); Janine Garrisson, *Tocsin pour un massacre, la saison des Saint-Barthélemy* (Paris: Le Centurion/Sciences humaines, 1968); and Philip Benedict, "The Saint Bartholemew's Massacres in the Provinces," *Historical Journal* 21 (1978): 205–25. See also the map in Holt, *French Wars*, 91. Some estimates of the casualties are as high as 10,000, but Benedict estimates conservatively 2,000 Protestants were killed in Paris and 3,000 elsewhere in France.

[48] See the organizational table in Jouanna, et al., *Guerres de Religion*, 224.

[49] See Jouanna, et al., *Guerres de Religion*, 205–14.

[50] See Jouanna, et al., *Guerres de Religion*, 228–40.

a dramatic recovery for the Huguenots, the French Protestants would enjoy the right of "a free, public, and general exercise of religion" everywhere in France except in Paris; the Huguenots were granted eight fortified cities for their protection; and their faith would henceforth be referred to in all official documents as the *religion prétendue réformée* (the "so-called reformed religion," or R. P. R. for short). In secret articles that were attached to the Edict of Beaulieu, the duke of Alençon was granted new titles – he now became duke of Anjou – and an enormous pension in order to gain, once again, his loyalty to the crown.

Henry III was under enormous pressure from Catholic partisans to undo the terms of the Edict of Beaulieu, however, and despite his desperate finances – the Estates General that met in late 1576 had refused the taxes he proposed – and a shortage of troops, his army began a campaign in December to retake the eight fortified cities that had been granted to the Huguenots in the edict. Although his forces captured two of the cities, the king accepted the Peace of Bergerac in September 1577 and issued the Edict of Poitiers, which put some limits on Protestant worship but otherwise renewed the terms of 1576.[51] In 1579 Protestant aggression in the southwest briefly restarted the war, but after a very limited engagement, this, the seventh war, was ended by the Peace and Edict of Fleix in November 1580.[52] Once again, the terms of the Edict of Beaulieu were, for the most part, reaffirmed.

In this recurrent alternation between war and peace, it is evident that political and religious polarization, extensive networks of popular religious solidarity and engagement, and domestic and international alliances that gave the religious factions ready access to military resources – that is to say, the dynamics that led recurrently to war – remained essentially undisturbed by the various treaties that were negotiated between the "Gallican" monarchy and its Huguenot challengers.[53] This is not to say, however, that nothing had changed since the beginning of the wars in 1562. On the contrary, episodic violence and low-intensity conflicts between Catholic and Protestant zealots in many cities and the devastating combination of popular and official violence in 1572 clearly exacerbated the mutual suspicions and polarization between ordinary Catholics and Protestants. At the same time, although these wars entailed relatively little in the way of conventional battles, the repeated mustering and deployment of troops on both sides took an enormous toll on the peasant populations that were expected to pay for their costs and that

---

[51] See Jouanna, et al., *Guerres de Religion*, 253–5.
[52] See Jouanna, et al., *Guerres de Religion*, 289–92.
[53] We will, of course, focus on the variations in these recurrent peace settlements in the next chapter. As Charles Tilly argued, coordinated destruction is more likely to occur when "parties on either side of the [identity] boundary polarize ... and/or when uncertainty about the other side's future actions increases on either or both sides." Charles Tilly, *The Politics of Collective Violence*, Cambridge Studies in Contentious Politics (Cambridge: Cambridge University Press, 2003), 103. Even this brief survey indicates how the various contenders took turns precipitating coordinated destruction under the enduring conditions of polarization and uncertainty.

sometimes lay in their paths, awaking popular insurrections opposed to the exactions of all kinds in Provence, Vivarais, and Dauphiné in 1579.[54] But more broadly, we can also discern a pattern of geographical segregation among the contending religious factions as a consequence of the struggles. The emergence of a separate Huguenot political organization, deeply republican and antimonarchical in its character according to some analysts,[55] certainly signals the Huguenots' essentially unchallenged domination in much of the southern and southwestern periphery of the kingdom, with Montauban, Nîmes, and La Rochelle emerging as their principal bastions of strength.[56] At the same time, Catholic dominance was steadily confirmed, not only in Paris where Protestant worship was consistently banned, but in places like Rouen, Amiens, and Dijon in the north and east where the spaces for Protestant difference were narrowed by aggressive Catholic action.[57] Still, the Edict of Fleix, recognizing and legitimating the coexistence of two highly mobilized and deeply antagonistic religious confessions, provided a framework for religious peace in France lasting nearly five years until 1585.

Meanwhile, following William of Orange's brief incursion into the Low Countries and his departure toward France to aid the Huguenots in December 1568, there was very little in the way of coordinated destruction at the beginning of what has come to be known as the Eighty Years War. After supporting the Huguenot cause in France during the Third French War, William of Orange and his brothers were recognized at the time of the Peace of Saint-Germain (August 1570) as "good relatives and friends" of King Charles IX.[58] With Coligny once again a part of the King's Council, William began planning

[54] See J. H. Salmon, "Peasant Revolt in Vivarais, 1575–1580," *French Historical Studies* 11 (1979): 1–28; E. Le Roy Ladurie, *Carnival in Romans*, trans. Mary Feeney (New York: G. Brazillier, 1979); and Daniel Hickey, *The Coming of French Absolutism; the Struggle for Tax Reform in the Province of Dauphiné, 1540–1640* (Toronto: University of Toronto Press, 1986).

[55] Garrisson, *Les Protestants du Midi, 1559–98*; Gordon Griffiths, *Representative Government in Western Europe in the Sixteenth Century: Commentary and Documents for the Study of Comparative Constitutional History* (Oxford: Clarendon Press, 1968); cf. Holt, *French Wars*, 98–101.

[56] Philip Conner, *Huguenot Heartland: Montauban and Southern French Calvinism During the Wars of Religion*, St. Andrews Studies in Reformation History (Aldershot, UK; Burlington, VT: Ashgate, 2002); Judith Chandler Pugh Meyer, *Reformation in La Rochelle: Tradition and Change in Early Modern Europe, 1500–1568*, Travaux d'Humanisme et Renaissance (Genève: Librairie Droz, 1996); Kevin C. Robbins, *City on the Ocean Sea, La Rochelle, 1530–1650: Urban Society, Religion, and Politics on the French Atlantic Frontier*, Studies in Medieval and Reformation Thought (Leiden; New York: Brill, 1997).

[57] David Lee Rosenberg, *Social Experience and Religious Choice: A Case Study, the Protestant Weavers and Woolcombers of Amiens in the Sixteenth Century* (Ph.D. diss., Yale University, 1978); Philip Benedict, *Rouen During the Wars of Religion* (Cambridge: Cambridge University Press, 1981); Holt, *French Wars*, 67–8.

[58] William and his brother, Louis of Nassau, had been part of military actions and sieges all over France, with Louis rising to become second in command of the Huguenot army. On their efforts to revive the Beggars' cause through their international efforts, see Parker, *The Dutch Revolt*, 120–4.

a coordinated invasion of the Netherlands involving the Netherlands exiles, England, and France. Earlier, in 1568, Louis of Nassau had helped to establish a naval force, quickly dubbed the Sea Beggars, which had proved capable of harassing the coastline and plundering monasteries.[59] As it happened, then, before the coordinated invasion could occur, it was this rag-tag naval force of Sea Beggars, which had been expelled from England, that attacked and held the small city of Den Briel in the province of Holland in April 1572, triggering what historians have come to call the (second) Dutch Revolt.[60] There followed a series of local insurrections in Vlissingen and Verre in the province of Zeeland, and in Enkhuizen, Hoorn, and Alkmaar in Holland. And so it went with most of the cities of Holland and Zeeland, with the notable exceptions of Middelburg and Amsterdam, falling into rebel hands.[61] In July 1572 the rebels organized the first independent meeting of the provincial Estates of Holland, which allocated money for the raising of troops and recognized Orange, in place of Alva, as governor-general. Capitalizing on the disruption in the north, Louis of Nassau also led an invasion of the southern province of Hainault from the south, capturing the city of Mons, while William of Orange prepared to lead an army of 16,000 into Brabant from Germany. In August, however, the St. Bartholomew's Day Massacre removed the threat of a large-scale Huguenot-backed invasion of the Habsburg Netherlands as envisioned by William of Orange.

The rebels of 1572 in many ways recreated the tentative Beggar coalition of 1566. Alva's repression and the autocratic tax policies associated with it had awakened opposition from many in the political elite, nobles as well as urban magistrates, while the hated "Tenth Penny" tax became a nearly universal symbol of "Spanish tyranny." The local insurrections also featured prominently the previously organized Reformed churches, supported by their extended networks in exile; not surprisingly, then, not only was Reformed worship once again established where the rebellion took hold, but churches were "cleansed," priests were harassed, and in some places the Catholic Mass was forbidden. But like the Beggars of 1566, the Beggars of 1572 were also confronted by a ferocious military response from Spanish authorities. First, Alva laid siege to Mons, and in September the city surrendered. Next, he moved on Mechelen, the principal city in Brabant that had declared for the revolt, and although the rebels fled and the city opened up its gates to the advancing forces, Alva allowed his men to sack the city, which resulted in a massacre. Then, having forced, by the example of Mechelen, the other southern cities to submit, Alva turned northward, perpetrating another

[59] J. C. A. de. Meij, *De Watergeuzen en de Nederlanden 1568–1572* (Amsterdam: Noord-Hollandsche Uitgevers Maatschappij, 1972).

[60] Parker, *The Dutch Revolt*, suggests the following rough chronology: First Revolt (1565–1568); Second Revolt (1569[1572]–1576); Third Revolt (1576–1581); Independence and Survival (1581–1589).

[61] See the map of the cities in revolt in 1572 in Parker, *The Dutch Revolt*, 139.

massacre at the city of Zutphen in Gelderland in November. Finally, turning west toward Holland, Alva on December 2, 1572, attacked the small town of Naarden, which was slow to submit, authorizing the exemplary slaughter of every man, woman, and child; only a handful its inhabitants escaped in the dark. Within days, Alva's army had marched west from Naarden past Amsterdam, which remained loyal, to lay siege to Haarlem, deep in rebel territory.

Once again, the Beggars' challenge was in peril of quick extinction, but this time the coalition survived a very bitter struggle between 1573 and 1576.[62] Although the people of Haarlem held out against the Spanish siege during the long winter months, the city finally fell to the Spanish in July 1573, which effectively split the province of Holland into two. In the north, the Spanish government's army besieged the city of Alkmaar, and in the south, they besieged Leiden, while in Zeeland, the Beggars besieged Middelburg, which had remained loyal to the Spanish regime. In the end, the rebels prevailed, by all accounts heroically, in all three places, and in the absence of any sustained military campaigns on either side, the Beggars' rebellion survived in Holland and Zeeland, establishing in the process the foundations for independent governance and asserting the public dominance of the Reformed churches.

The Beggars' survival was abetted, to be sure, by the simultaneous collapse of Spanish authority through a series of stunning calamities: very destructive mutinies by Spanish troops each year between 1573 and 1576; the financial weakness and eventual bankruptcy of the Spanish crown, due to very costly military operations simultaneously in the Low Countries and in the Mediterranean against the Ottoman Turks; and the death in 1576 of Don Luis de Requesens, who had succeeded Alva as governor-general in 1573. The cumulative effect was a growing, if uneasy, collaboration among Holland, Zeeland, and almost all of the other Low Countries provinces through the Estates General, which seized control of the government in Brussels in September 1576.[63] Together, the assembled provinces negotiated at Ghent the terms a peace agreement, which sought to end the war, to reaffirm local privileges, and to rid the Netherlands of Spanish troops. In early November, however, a brutal Spanish attack – known as the "Spanish Fury" – on the city of Antwerp destroyed more than 1,000 houses, killed some 8,000 people, and thoroughly discredited Don Juan of Austria, Philip II's new governor-general. On November 8, 1576, the Estates General, acting on its own authority, published the "Pacification of Ghent," which Don Juan was forced to accept, in principle at least ending the coordinated

---

[62] Perhaps the best account of the bitterness of this struggle, full of terror, deceit, and betrayal, is Henk van Nierop, *Treason in the Northern Quarter: War, Terror, and the Rule of Law in the Dutch Revolt*, trans. J. C. Grayson (Princeton, NJ: Princeton University Press, 2009).

[63] In the absence of an immediate successor to Requesens, the Grand Council had taken over direct control of Philip's government in Brussels; the Estates General, in turn, seized control by arresting the members of the Grand Council.

destruction of war and leaving the Beggars effectively in control of Holland and Zeeland.

In the absence of an agreement on "the matter of religion," however, the Pacification of Ghent appeared to have little chance of long-term success. Although enforcement of the heresy laws was again suspended and the Spanish soldiers were, in fact, ordered to leave the Netherlands in 1577, there appeared to be little room for negotiation or long-term collaboration across the Protestant/Catholic divide. On the one side, Philip II remained steadfastly opposed to any compromise that would allow Protestant worship, and on the other, the Beggars often moved forcefully to disestablish the Catholic Church, to assert a "public" monopoly for Reformed worship, and even to suppress Catholic worship altogether, wherever they held the upper hand.[64] Still, the Pacification of Ghent did commit the Estates General to further negotiations, and in June 1578 the young Archduke Matthias of Austria – whom the Estates General had recently recognized as governor-general and who would later be elected German emperor – working with William of Orange proposed a template for religious peace in the Low Countries – called *Paix de Religion* or *Religions-vrede*, in imitation of the German *Religionsfriede* – which the Estates General debated, published, and sent out for ratification by the several provinces in July 1578.[65] This *Paix de Religion* called for the restoration of Catholic worship where it had been suppressed in Holland and Zeeland as well as the introduction of Reformed worship where there was a minimum of local support, and in the coming months a number of local governments, including Brussels and Mechelen, formally adopted the Peace.

Despite these elite bargains, which might in principle have decreased elite *polarization* and disrupted the networks of solidarity and the military alliances that enabled re*escalation* of conflict, the Low Countries provinces were anything but pacified. In October 1577 a radical Calvinist movement had seized control of the city of Ghent, establishing a "Calvinist Republic," and sparking a broader civil war in the southern provinces between zealous Calvinists and the ardent defenders of both Catholicism and Spanish rule.[66]

---

[64] Despite some local agreements in 1572 allowing the continuation of Catholic worship after the establishment of public Reformed worship, the Estates of Holland formally abolished the Catholic Mass in 1573. A similar pattern of suppression of Catholic worship followed the establishment of Reformed worship in Friesland and Gelderland as well in 1577 and 1578; see Israel, *The Dutch Republic*, 187–92.

[65] P. J. H. Ubachs, "De Nederlandse Religievrede van 1578," *Nederlands archief voor kerkgeschiedenis* 77, no. 1 (1997): 41–61; see also Gerard van Gurp, *Reformatie in Brabant: protestanten en katholieken in de Meierij van 's-Hertogenbosch, 1523–1634* (Hilversum: Verloren, 2013), 161–4.

[66] Johan Decavele, ed., *Het einde van een rebelse droom: Opstellen over het calvinistisch bewind te Gent (1577–1584) en de terugkeer van de stad onder de gehoorzaamheid van de koning van Spanje (17 september 1584)* (Ghent: Stadsbestuur, 1984). In English, see the section on the "Calvinist Republic" in Johan Decavele and Paul van Peteghem, "Ghent 'Absolutely' Broken," in *Ghent. In Defence of a Rebellious City: History, Art, Culture*, ed. J. Decavele (Antwerp: Mercatorfonds, 1989), 107–33.

In early 1578 the Calvinist rebellion extended to a number of cities in the southwest, including the other principal cities of Flanders: Ypres and Bruges. In May 1578 a coup, known as the *Alteratie*, brought the city of Amsterdam, the last royalist holdout in the province of Holland, into the rebel fold, and by 1579, this pattern of local, piecemeal Calvinist-led insurrections extended as well to the principal cities of Brabant: Brussels and Antwerp. Meanwhile, Don Juan had quickly repudiated the Pacification and, supported by troops that Philip II once again deployed from Spain, renewed his attempts to reassert Spanish military dominance in the south, and the provincial Estates of Hainaut and Walloon Flanders declared that they would under no circumstances tolerate Protestant worship. Amid these signs of increasing *polarization*, the *brokerage* of two opposing military alliances in early 1579 signaled the beginning of a new phase of civil/religious wars in the Low Countries that would lead, within a decade, to the long-term bifurcation of the Netherlands.

On January 6, 1579, negotiators meeting at Arras (Atrecht) concluded an agreement, the "Articles of Peace," reconciling the Estates of Hainaut and Tournai, plus the cities of Lille, Douai, and Orchies, with their Spanish overlord. This Union of Arras, which was gradually extended to include all of the Walloon provinces plus parts of Brabant and Flanders, affirmed the political provisions of the Pacification of Ghent, especially with regard to provincial and municipal liberties as well as the expulsion of foreign troops. In exchange for these enormous political concessions, Philip II and his governor-general, Alexander Farnese, duke of Parma, demanded restoration of the Catholic Church and acceptance of Philip's sovereignty. Four months later, this bargain was reaffirmed and elaborated in the Treaty of Arras.[67]

Meanwhile, on January 23, 1579, negotiators meeting at Utrecht proclaimed articles of agreement for a separate union among the Estates of Holland, Zeeland, Utrecht, Gelderland, and the Ommelanden of Groningen.[68] This Union of Utrecht, which eventually included the cities of Brabant and Flanders as well as the provinces of Friesland, Overijssel, Drente, and the city of Groningen, bound or confederated the signatories "as if a single province"

[67] The French text of the twenty-seven "Articles de la Paix" is published in Jean Dumont, ed., *Corps universel diplomatique du droit des gens; contenant vn recueil des traitez d'alliance, de paix, de treve, de neutralité, de commerce, d'échange.. & autres contrats, qui ont été faits en Europe* (Amsterdam: P. Brunel, etc., 1726–31), vol. V, part i, 350–5; there is a partial English translation in Herbert H. Rowen, ed., *The Low Countries in Early Modern Times: A Documentary History*, Documentary History of Western Civilization (New York: Harper and Row, 1972), 261–6.

[68] The Dutch text of the "Verhandelinge van de Unie, Eeuwig Verbondt ende Eendracht" is published in Dumont, *Corps universel diplomatique*, vol V, part i, 322–7, as well as Cornelius Cau, ed., *Groot placaatboek, vervattende de placaaten, ordonnantien en edicten van de hoog mog. heeren Staaten generaal der Vereenigde Nederlanden; en van de edele groot mog. heeren Staaten van Holland en Westvriesland; mitsgaders van de edele mog heeren Staaten van Zeeland..*, vol. 1 ('s Gravenhage: H. I. van Wouw, 1658), 7ff. There is a complete English translation of the Union in Kossmann and Mellink, *Texts*, 165–73; there is a variant, partial translation in Rowen, *Low Countries*, 69–74.

for the general purpose of their common defense at the same time as it reaffirmed "the special and particular privileges" of "each province and of each town, member and inhabitant of those provinces." Article II of the Union of Utrecht explicitly bound the signatories to "assist each other with their lives and property against all acts of violence which anyone might perpetuate against them on behalf of … His Majesty the King," including specifically actions by the Spaniards "on the pretext of wanting to reestablish, restore or introduce the Roman Catholic religion by force of arms."[69]

Ironically, both of these unions claimed to strengthen and preserve the Pacification of Ghent and the general union based on it, but as separate and mutually exclusive political bargains they, in fact, undermined the unity of the Low Countries provinces and eventually helped to structure two strikingly different polities. In the Union of Arras, the confirmation of Habsburg overlordship and the reestablishment of the Catholic Church clearly came at a high political price for Philip II: both the reaffirmation of provincial and municipal privileges and the expulsion of "foreign" troops. Although the exigencies of the Eighty Years War kept those foreign troops around much longer than the Union envisioned, provincial and municipal privileges remained the bedrock of domestic politics in the southern provinces, effectively stunting the consolidation of centralized state power. Meanwhile, the reaffirmation of provincial and municipal privileges in the Union of Utrecht, which remained silent on the question of Habsburg overlordship, took on entirely different political meaning when just two years later, on July 26, 1581, that same Union, issuing the Act of Abjuration (*Plakkaat van Verlatinghe*), declared the king's sovereignty forfeit and willy-nilly set the northern provinces on a path toward republican independence via a long and very costly war of independence.[70]

In the near term, however, the leaders of United Provinces of the Northern Netherlands, as the rebel provinces would come to be known formally, were not at all prepared to make a go of it on their own. Indeed, in September 1580, prior to revoking Philip's claims to sovereignty, the Estates General, urged on by William of Orange, had offered limited sovereignty over the Netherlands to none other than the brother of the French king, Henry III. Francis, duke of Alençon/Anjou, who had earlier aligned himself with the Huguenots during the Fifth French War, now marched northward with French troops in support of the Beggars' cause, and having sworn to uphold their privileges, he was received by the Estates General as "prince and lord of the Netherlands" at Antwerp in February 1582. By this time, however, the conflicts in France and the Low

---

[69] Kossmann and Mellink, *Texts*, 167.
[70] The original Dutch text, as well as a French translation, of the "Plakkaat van Verlatinghe" is published in Dumont, *Corps universel diplomatique*, vol. 1, part i, 413–21; the Dutch text is also published in Cau, *Groot Placaatboek*, 25–36. There are English translations in Kossmann and Mellink, *Texts*, 216–28, and Rowen, *Low Countries*, 92–105.

Countries, though still obviously connected, appeared to be moving in very different directions.

DIVERGENT HISTORICAL TRAJECTORIES

In the Low Countries, the Beggars' piecemeal rebellion quickly morphed into an extended and more conventional war against a very formidable foe. Fortified by much better financing and as many as 60,000 Spanish, Italian, and German mercenaries, Alexander Farnese fought a long and generally successful campaign to reestablish Philip II's authority, especially where it was most recently losing ground in the southern provinces.[71] Having captured the Flemish cities of Ypres, Bruges, and Ghent in the course of 1584, Parma completed Spain's reconquest of the southern provinces in 1585 with the capitulations of Brussels in March and Antwerp in August. Farnese's successful campaign in the south avoided the vengeance of Alva's earlier campaigns; it nevertheless precipitated yet another forced migration of religious dissidents in the Low Countries – this time more than 150,000 Calvinists and Anabaptists, the largest such migration in the sixteenth-century wars, fled northward into the rebel provinces as well as to familiar sanctuaries abroad.[72]

By this time, however, the duke of Anjou had long since left the Netherlands. Continually frustrated by the limits placed on his authority and by the failure of the rebel provinces to provide him the financial resources he had been promised, Anjou was unable to perform his chosen role as peacemaker between Catholics and Protestants, and in June 1583, he left the Netherlands for good, although attempts at reconciliation continued until Anjou's untimely death in June 1584. Just a month later, amid the enormous pressures of Parma's steady reconquest of the rebellion's strongholds in the southern provinces, William of Orange, the unrivaled leader of the Beggars' Revolt, was assassinated in his home in Delft on July 10, 1584. The rebellious provinces initially hoped that Henry III would take up the mantle of his brother, but when he declined, the rebels turned to Queen Elizabeth of England to ensure their survival. By the Treaty of Nonsuch, signed on August 20, 1585, England would provide both military and financial assistance, and Elizabeth's trusted advisor, Robert Dudley, Earl of Leicester, was appointed governor-general and charged with the direction of the war effort and the coordination of its government.[73]

As it happened, England's open assistance of the United Provinces provided the rebellion with a much needed respite as Philip II, having reconquered the southern provinces and reestablished the supremacy of the Catholic Church,

---

[71] See the series of maps of the Spanish reconquest of the southern provinces in Parker, *The Dutch Revolt*, 210–12.

[72] J. Briels, *Zuid-Nederlandse immigratie 1572–1630* (Haarlem: Fibula-Van Dishoeck, 1978). See also Oscar Gelderblom, *Zuid-Nederlandse kooplieden en de opkomst van de Amsterdamse stapelmarkt (1578–1630)* (Hilversum: Verloren, 2000).

[73] Parker, *The Dutch Revolt*, 216–24; Israel, *The Dutch Republic*, 220–30.

now focused his resources on a massive invasion of England. But Leicester's attempts to create a more centralized government in the United Provinces served more clearly to divide the Netherlands rebels than to unite them, and dependence on the English proved to be as unsuccessful as dependence on the French. Indeed, by the time the Spanish Armada had been defeated in the summer of 1588, the leadership of Leicester had been discredited in the Netherlands, and he was recalled to England. By this time, however, the United Provinces of the Northern Netherlands were prepared to go it alone under the political leadership of Johan van Oldenbarnevelt, advocate of Holland, and the military leadership of Maurits, count of Nassau and son of William of Orange. During the 1590s, as renewed war in France once again deflected Spanish resources, the rebel provinces won their de facto, if not yet de jure, independence from Spain, and the United Provinces soon emerged as a major European power, with Reformed Protestantism as its "public" Church.[74]

By sharp contrast, as the Netherlands descended into a prolonged war, France was enjoying an extended period of relative peace in the early 1580s. By the terms of the Edict of Fleix (1580), which was in essence a renewal of the Edict of Poitiers (1577), Protestants were granted civil rights and integrated into the fabric of French society, eligible to hold office and serve in the military, and free to worship publicly in many parts of the kingdom. Indeed, despite the horrors of the recent past, the period from 1576 to 1585, as Mark Greengrass describes it, was characterized by extraordinary efforts, led by Henry III, both to sustain the peace and to reform the state by eliminating venality and corruption.[75] All of the promising signs of a durable peace were called into question, however, with the untimely death on June 10, 1584, of Francis, duke of Alençon and Anjou, the king's younger brother and next in line to the French throne. Should Henry III now die childless, as seemed likely, the succession of Valois kings would come to an end, and the next best claimant to the French throne was none other than the Protestant Henry de Bourbon, king of Navarre and "Protector" of the French Huguenots.

This new succession crisis, with the obvious "threat" of a Protestant succeeding to the French throne, precipitated the revival of an explicitly "Catholic" political coalition – the *Sainte Union* or "Holy League" – dedicated to undermining the peace and ridding the kingdom of Protestant heretics, which set the stage for the longest and most destructive of the French civil/religious wars (1585–1598).[76] The Catholic League, an extension of an earlier association in the 1570s dedicated to the preservation of the Gallican Church, was a loose amalgam of the courtly faction led by a new generation of

[74] See the map of the Dutch reconquest in Parker, *The Dutch Revolt*, 229; see also Israel, *The Dutch Republic*, 234–75.
[75] Mark Greengrass, *Governing Passions: Peace and Reform in the French Kingdom, 1576–1585* (Oxford; New York: Oxford University Press, 2007).
[76] See Jouanna, et al., *Guerres de Religion*, 305–440.

the Guise family[77] and widely dispersed local coalitions of municipal leaders supported by popular movements of Counter-Reformation piety. In December 1584, the aristocratic leaders of the Catholic League signed a formal treaty with Philip II of Spain, which provided for a monthly subsidy from Spain for the League to wage war against the Huguenots. Rejecting Henry of Navarre as heir to the throne, a manifesto issued by the League in March 1585 stated, "We have all solemnly sworn and promised to use force and take up arms to the end that the holy church of God may be restored to its dignity and [reunited in] the true and holy Catholic religion."[78] By July 1585, the League had compelled Henry III to agree to the Treaty of Nemours, which revoked all of the former edicts of pacification and forbade the practice of the "so-called reformed religion" everywhere in the kingdom.

As the French civil wars restarted, then, various forces of league noblemen sought to execute the Treaty of Nemours by force – that is, to eliminate the Huguenots and to reestablish the exclusive religious authority of the Gallican Church – especially in the north and east of the kingdom. At the same time, Henry of Navarre sought to maintain control of Huguenot fortifications in the south and southwest and to solicit foreign support from England and Germany. This peculiar constellation of forces might well have predicted a geographic bifurcation along religious lines of the kingdom of France, not unlike the division between north and south of the Habsburg Netherlands, but during the first phase of this extended war, the radical independence of the Catholic League, especially its local iteration under the leadership of the "Sixteen" in Paris, occasioned instead the unlikely collaboration of King Henry III and Henry of Navarre, the Huguenot leader, in defense of French unity.[79]

On May 12, 1588 – the "Day of the Barricades" – a popular revolt in Paris, combined with the open defiance of the leadership of the League, exposed the king's political weakness and forced him to flee the city.[80] In the summer, the king was also forced to accept virtually all of the League's demands – including the alternative succession to the throne of Charles, cardinal of Bourbon, Henry of Navarre's uncle – in the Edict of Union. But at the end of the year, during a meeting of the Estates General, which was dominated by League deputies, King Henry III ordered the arrest and execution of both Henry, duke of Guise, and his brother Louis, cardinal of Guise, in order to recover the initiative and

---

[77] Stuart Carroll, *Martyrs and Murderers: The Guise Family and the Making of Europe* (Oxford: Oxford University Press, 2009).

[78] Quoted in Salmon, *Society in Crisis*, 238.

[79] On the revolutionary "Sixteen" of Paris, see J. H. M. Salmon, "The Paris Sixteen, 1584–94; The Social Analysis of a Revolutionary Movement," *Journal of Modern History* 44 (1972): 540–76; R. Descimon, "La Ligue à Paris (1585–1594): une révision," *Annales E. S. C.* 37 (1982): 72–111; and Elie Barnavi, *Le parti de Dieu: Étude sociale et politique des chefs de la Ligue parisienne, 1585–1594*, Travaux du Centre de recherches sur la civilisation de l'Europe moderne (Bruxelles: Éditions Nauwelaerts, 1980).

[80] Stuart Carroll, "The Revolt of Paris, 1588: Aristocratic Insurgency and the Mobilization of Popular Support," *French Historical Studies* 23 (2000): 301–27.

authority he had lost to the Catholic League.[81] Now openly at war with the League, the king sought to make peace with Henry of Navarre, signing a formal agreement on April 3, 1589, that declared a cease-fire between the king and the Huguenots and restored many of the protections and privileges that the Huguenots had recently lost. By summer, the two kings had joined forces in a military campaign to wrest control of Paris from the Catholic League.

The course of the war changed dramatically, however, when a zealous monk assassinated King Henry III on August 1, 1589, as the royal army was poised to reclaim Paris. The second phase of the Eighth French War, then, consisted of a long series of campaigns by which Henry of Navarre sought to make good his claim to the French throne as Henry IV. In this phase, foreign involvement was again prominent: Philip II and Spain lent critical support to the Catholic League, especially in breaking Henry IV's siege of Paris in 1590, while Queen Elizabeth lent military support and German Protestant princes supplied mercenaries to Henry IV. As had been the case in the 1570s, there was also popular opposition to the continued strife, with peasant insurrections challenging the depredations of royalist and league armies alike in both Burgundy and the southwest.[82] Henry IV's dramatic abjuration of his Calvinist faith in July of 1593 was the essential prelude to his being consecrated and crowned king of France at Chartres on February 27, 1594.[83] Finally, on March 22, 1594, Henry IV reestablished royal authority in Paris for the first time in six years.

The last phase of this long war was characterized by Henry IV's attempts to pacify and appease the remaining opposition to his authority as the "most Catholic" king as well as the "Protector" of the Huguenots. In August 1595, Henry received absolution from Pope Clement VIII, which helped to ease some of the remaining Catholic opposition. Although some of his former Huguenot allies threatened open opposition, a new war beginning in 1595 with Spain – Philip II's fabled "Army of Flanders" seized Cambrai, Calais, and Amiens in the north – fostered some cooperation between Protestants and Catholics in opposition to a foreign enemy. Henry IV's recovery of Amiens in September of 1597 led to the surrender in January 1598 of the duke of Mercoeur, the last of the aristocratic Catholic League leaders to hold out against him. Finally, Henry reached a peace agreement with the Huguenot leaders and promulgated the Edict of Nantes in April 1598, ending more than thirty-six years of intermittent civil and religious war.

---

[81] Carroll, *Martyrs and Murderers: The Guise Family and the Making of Europe.*

[82] See Yves-Marie Bercé, *Histoire des Croquants*, Mémoires et documents, Société de l'École des Chartes, XXII (Geneva: Librairie Droz, 1974), which is partially translated into English: Yves-Marie Bercé, *History of Peasant Revolts*, trans. Amanda Whitmore (Ithaca: Cornell University Press, 1990); see also Henry Heller, *Iron and Blood: Civil Wars in Sixteenth-Century France* (Montreal: McGill-Queens University Press, 1991).

[83] Michael Wolfe, *The Conversion of Henri IV: Politics, Power, and Religious Belief in Early Modern France*, Harvard Historical Studies (Cambridge, Massachusetts; London: Harvard University Press, 1993).

By the end of the sixteenth century, then, three strikingly different trajectories of historical development had emerged from the religious wars in France and the Low Countries: (1) the Edict of Nantes restored the political unity of France by officially acknowledging and institutionalizing its religious diversity; meanwhile the protracted military struggle in the Low Countries yielded to the de facto division of (2) an officially Catholic south under Spanish rule from (3) an officially Protestant north as a confederated republic. Although these histories originated in similar patterns of official repression of religious dissent and the emergence of underground reform movements and were connected by means of international alliances and networks of support, the recurrent mechanisms that led to the creation of new, politically salient religious identities and, by extension, to the incidence of violent religious conflict and war combined differently under different circumstances to produce clearly divergent trajectories of change.

One of the principal differences that we have observed was in the relative strength, or weakness, of popular *mobilization* in support of the established Church. In many parts of France, a robust Catholic response, combining popular mobilization and strong clerical leadership, to the stunning growth of Reformed Protestantism yielded not only widespread communal violence in the 1560s and 1570s but also the revolutionary action of the Catholic League in the 1580s. By contrast, the relative weakness of the Catholic response in much of the Low Countries and in the south and southwest of France yielded relatively less interpersonal violence and the public dominance of Reformed Protestantism. In both conflicts, the recurrent *activation* of increasingly *polarized* religious identities combined with the recurrent *escalation* of local conflicts to produce national and international war rooted in (inter)national networks of religious solidarity. Over time, the relative strength of locally mobilized popular religious movements combined with the relative durability of brokered alliances, including specialists in coercive force, to transform the religious landscape of both France and the Low Countries. In this regard, the enormous constancy of Philip II's commitment to maintaining the "unity and purity" of the Catholic Church in the Netherlands at all costs contrasts with the remarkable consistency of the French royal government's commitment to a policy of pacification. It is, thus, to the contrasting histories and the relational dynamics of peacemaking, as opposed to war making, in France and the Low Countries that we will turn in the next two chapters in order to explain these divergent trajectories of historical change.

6

An Elusive Peace

> [W]e have, by this perpetual and irrevocable Edict, said, declared, and ordered, do say, declare, and order:
>
> 1. First that the memory of everything which has occurred between one side and the other since the beginning of the month of March 1585 up to our accession to the crown, and during the other preceding troubles and on account of them, shall remain extinct and dormant as though they never happened. And it shall not be allowable or permissible to our *procureurs-gënëraux*, or any other person whatever, public or private, at any time, or for whatever occasion there may be, to make mention of them, or institute a suit or prosecution in any courts or jurisdiction whatsoever.
> 2. We forbid all our subjects, of whatever estate or quality they may be, from renewing, injuring, or provoking one another by reproaches for what had occurred, for whatever cause and pretext there may be; from disputing these things, contesting, quarreling, or outraging or offending by word or deed; but they shall restrain themselves and live peaceably together like brothers, friends, and common citizens, under the penalty of being punished as infractors of the peace and disturbers of the public repose.
>
> *Edict of Nantes*, April 13, 1598[1]

Like the signatories of the Swiss *Landfrieden* more than six decades earlier, King Henry IV of France founded the famous Edict of Nantes, rhetorically at least, on the principles of amnesia and amnesty. Forgiving and forgetting is a recurrent, though hardly universal, theme in the history of peacemaking,[2]

---

[1] Richard L. Goodbar, ed., *The Edict of Nantes: Five Essays and a New Translation* (Bloomington, MN: The National Huguenot Society, 1998), 42.

[2] The alternative principles – remembering and forgiving – were, of course, the aspirational foundation of a very different strategy of peacemaking in recent memory in the remarkable

but it appears to have been a particularly significant element of Henry's remarkably successful strategy of appeasement and pacification that brought the French civil and religious wars to an end. Thus, in forgiving and forgetting the offenses of the past, the Edict of Nantes articulated a template for political reconciliation in which Catholics and Protestants might conceivably "live peaceably together as Brethren, Friends, and fellow-Citizens."

The difference in this respect with the history of peacemaking in the Low Countries could hardly be more striking. Philip II's steadfast refusal to accept any kind of compromise, or even conversation, with his enemies recurrently frustrated a wide variety of attempts to bring peace and reconciliation. Thus, Philip's death in September 1598, just months after the promulgation of the Edict of Nantes, opened up the possibility that his successor, Philip III, would seek a compromise in the very costly war with the United Provinces. Although Philip III and his regents in the Low Countries, Albert and Isabella, also frustrated hopes for a quick and comprehensive peace settlement, an armistice in 1607 eventually yielded to a Twelve Year Truce (1609–1621). In the truce agreement, Spain, for all practical purposes, recognized the independence and sovereignty of the United Provinces of the Northern Netherlands but failed to address the "problem" of religious differences. In the Low Countries, then, the coordinated destruction of religious war ended "temporarily" in a military stalemate and political estrangement, rather than reconciliation, much less the forgiving and forgetting of a comprehensive religious settlement.

What difference did these obvious differences make? Both the Edict of Nantes and the Twelve Year Truce marked the end of coordinated destruction for considerable periods of time in these very long and destructive religious wars and, thus, made religious peace possible. But how did these possibilities of religious peace differ in their origins as well as in their long-term consequences? The contrasting patterns of peacemaking, like the divergent histories of war making, in France and the Low Countries were evident from a very early date; indeed, despite their common commitment to the extirpation of heresy entailed in the Peace of Cateau-Cambrésis in 1559, the royal governments of France and Spain were clearly moving in different directions prior to the outbreak of war. As we saw in Chapter 5, the mechanisms that recurrently led to religious war produced decidedly different histories of coordinated destruction in France and the Low Countries; likewise, the mechanisms that recurrently led toward religious peace yielded decidedly different histories of religious coexistence. In this chapter we will examine the

history of post-apartheid South Africa. Cf. Barbara B. Diefendorf, "Waging Peace: Memory, Identity, and the Edict of Nantes," in *Religious Differences in France: Past and Present*, ed. Kathleen Perry Long, Sixteenth Century Essays & Studies (Kirksville, MO: Truman State University Press, 2006), 19–49.

early histories of peacemaking and the rather different possibilities of religious peace in France and the Low Countries from the 1560s to the 1580s before returning, in the next chapter, to a comparative analysis of the relational dynamics and the long-term consequences of the Edict of Nantes and the Twelve Year Truce.

THE PATH TOWARD RECONCILIATION IN FRANCE

The template of political reconciliation through the validation of religious coexistence that was at the heart of the Edict of Nantes was hardly new in 1598. As Olivier Christin has argued, the policy of the French government vis-à-vis French Protestantism moved clearly and decisively from repression to pacification in the period 1560 to 1563.[3] Following the untimely death of Henry II in 1559, this policy transformation became evident with a series of royal edicts in 1560 and 1561 that distinguished between religious heresy and political sedition by granting pardon to Protestants who did not create "scandal." Reserving questions of heretical belief to ecclesiastical courts, these edicts effectively decriminalized religious dissent, though that was not necessarily their specific intent.[4] This dramatic change in royal judicial policy was also consistent with Catherine de Medici's attempts, culminating in the Colloquy of Poissy, to promote a theological reconciliation between the religious dissenters, recently organized in the Reformed churches, and the established Church. In the absence of a religious reconciliation, then, the famous and controversial Edict of Saint-Germain in January 1562 opened the door to political reconciliation by granting limited legality to Reformed worship, specifically authorizing them to worship outside the cities (i.e., in the *faubourgs*) and in daylight.[5]

Although the Edict of Saint-Germain granted only a very limited space for Protestant worship, its central thrust was pacification in order to prevent greater disorder.[6] That the government viewed the situation, in general, and the Protestants, in particular, as deeply disorderly is evident in the injunction to

[3] Olivier Christin, "From Repression to Pacification: French Royal Policy in the Face of Protestantism," in *Reformation, Revolt and Civil War in France and the Netherlands 1555–1585*, eds. Philip Benedict, et al. (Amsterdam: Koninklijke Nederlandse Akademie van Wetenschappen, 1999), 201–14.

[4] The edicts in question – Edict of Amboise (March 1560), Edict of Romorantin (May 1560), Edict of Fontainebleau (April 1561), and Edict of Saint-Germain (July 1561) – are very usefully paraphrased, with citations of the original sources, in N. M. Sutherland, *The Huguenot Struggle for Recognition* (New Haven: Yale University Press, 1980), 347–53.

[5] A modern edition of the text of this edict may be found in André Stegmann, ed., *Édits des guerres de religion*, Textes et documents de la Renaissance (Paris: J. Vrin, 1979), 8–14; a partial English translation is in David Potter, ed., *The French Wars of Religion: Selected Documents* (New York: St. Martin's Press, 1997), 31–2; for a list of the principal French edicts and the conflicts they sought to end between 1562 and 1629, see Table 5.1.

[6] Cf. Denis Crouzet, "A Law of Difference in the History of Difference: The First Edict of 'Tolerance'," in *Religious Differences in France: Past and Present*, ed. Kathleen Perry Long, Sixteenth Century Essays & Studies (Kirksville, MO: Truman State University Press, 2006), 1–18.

"those of the new religion" that they vacate "the houses, property and revenues belonging to the clergy"; that they "return the reliquaries and ornaments they have taken from ... temples and churches"; neither should "they smash or demolish crosses and images, and do other scandalous and seditious acts, on pain of death."[7] Nevertheless, it forbade all "judges, magistrates and other persons of whatever quality" to molest or impede "those of the new Religion [when they] go to and return from and gather outside the towns for their religion."[8] In addition, the edict enjoined "all our subjects, of whatever religion, estate, quality and condition they be, that they make no assembly in arms, nor injure, reproach or provoke each other for the sake of religion, nor cause, move, favour or procure any sedition; but live and behave to each other gently and graciously."[9] Clearly, on the eve of the first religious war, the French royal government was abandoning Henry II's goal of extirpating heresy, opening up instead a space for religious coexistence by decriminalizing Protestant behavior and offering legitimacy and protection to "those of the new Religion."

That the Edict of Saint-Germain failed to disrupt the mechanisms that were leading France toward religious war is obvious enough: When a troop of soldiers under the command of the duke of Guise attacked a newly "legal" Protestant assembly at Vassy,[10] they *activated* the well-defined Huguenot/Catholic identity boundary, and the conflict quickly *escalated* via well-established and deeply *polarized* networks of Protestant and Catholic solidarity and engaged newly *brokered* military alliances on both sides of the religious identity boundary. In the face of zealous Catholic opposition, supported by Philip II of Spain, to any compromise with "heretics," the royal government was obviously powerless to fulfill its chosen role as mediator of the disputes and protector of religious dissidents, and having first been attacked, the leaders of the Huguenot party chose in the spring of 1562 for preemptive action across a broad terrain in their self-defense. Still, the coordinated destruction of the First French War was of relatively limited scope, and in early 1563 the royal government opened up peace negotiations with the Huguenots' military leaders, which resulted in the Peace and Edict of Amboise on March 19.[11]

In the preamble to this settlement – the first to result from direct negotiations between the crown and the dissidents – the young king, Charles IX, announced his delight that, with God's grace, he had found the means to pacify the kingdom of France. A remarkably brief and somewhat awkward document,

---

[7] Stegmann, *Édits*, 10; Potter, *Wars of Religion*, 31.

[8] Stegmann, *Édits*, 10; Potter, *Wars of Religion*, 31.

[9] Stegmann, *Édits*, 11; Potter, *Wars of Religion*, 31–2.

[10] On the technical legality of the site that the worshipers were using, a barn near a parish church, see Penny Roberts, "The Most Crucial Battle of the Wars of Religion? The Conflict over Sites for Reformed Worship in Sixteenth-Century France," *Archiv für Reformationsgeschichte* 89 (1998): 254.

[11] The French text is in Stegmann, *Édits*, 32–6; a partial English translation is in Potter, *Wars of Religion*, 82–4.

the Edict of Amboise was primarily concerned with addressing the deeply contentious issue of *where* public worship according to the new religion would be permitted and protected. In deference to the high nobility, who had negotiated the settlement, the edict first specified that Reformed worship would be permitted without constraint on the estates of those nobles who exercised "high justice"; a more restricted privilege of private worship was granted to the families of lesser nobles. In contrast with the Edict of Saint-Germain, which had allowed public worship outside the towns everywhere in the kingdom, the Edict of Amboise provided that within each administrative district – that is, each *bailliage* or *sénéchaussée*, of which there were approximately 100[12] – Reformed worship would be limited to the *faubourgs* of just one town. Reformed worship was also specifically prohibited in the vicinity of Paris and wherever the royal court resided. At the same time, however, the edict acknowledged the impressive gains that the Huguenots had made prior to and during the war, providing that "[i]n all towns in which the said Religion has been practiced prior to the 7th of the present month of March, in addition to the towns that will be, as is said above, specified in each *bailliage* and *sénéschaussée*, the same practice will continue in one or two places within the said town, as shall be ordained by us."[13] In the midst of the slightly tortured language that sorted out the limits on Reformed worship in public, however, the edict tempered those limitations by providing, in remarkably unambiguous language, a protected, private space for religious difference everywhere: "Nevertheless, everyone may live and dwell in his home everywhere without being pursued or molested, forced or constrained for matters of conscience."[14] To declare an individual right of free conscience, of course, was to place a profound limit on the authority of the Gallican Church's ecclesiastical courts to prosecute heresy.

Altogether more prescriptive of the desired parameters of religious diversity than it is descriptive of facts on the ground, the Edict of Amboise provided a simple template for the management of religious change and coexistence. Unlike the Swiss *Landfrieden* and the German *Religionsfriede*, the Edict of Amboise did not devolve decision-making authority over religious matters to localities and territories; rather the French negotiators placed critical decision making and active management of the religious peace exclusively in the hands of agents of the royal government. Also, in contrast with earlier French edicts as well as with the Swiss *Landfrieden* and the German *Religionsfriede*, the Edict of Amboise articulated a profound limit on the authority of ecclesiastical courts to pursue heresy. In protecting both corporate worship and private conscience, then, the Edict of Amboise confirmed and completed the royal government's transition from a policy of repression to a policy of pacification. Indeed, embracing religious coexistence as the foundation of a more peaceful future,

---

[12] Roberts, "Crucial Battle," 248.
[13] Stegmann, *Édits*, 34 This section also requires the Huguenots again to restore the "churches, houses, goods, possessions and revenues" that they had seized from the Catholic clergy.
[14] Stegmann, *Édits*, 34; quotation from Potter, *Wars of Religion*, 83.

the Edict of Amboise concluded with the same hopeful language of forgiving and forgetting that first appeared in the Second Swiss *Landfrieden*:

[T]hat all injuries and offenses that the iniquity of the time and the events that have happened have bred between our subjects, and all other things past and caused in these present tumults, should remain extinguished, as if dead and buried, and as if they had not happened; forbidding most strictly on pain of death all our subjects, of whatever estate or quality, to attack, injure or provoke each other by reproaches for things past, to dispute, quarrel or contest together over religion, offend or outrage by word or deed; but rather live peacefully together like brothers, friends and fellow citizens.[15]

So, was the young king's apparent confidence justified? How and how well did the Edict of Amboise pacify France? In retrospect, of course, it is tempting for historians to proclaim simply that, given the royal government's limitations, the Edict of Amboise was unenforceable and doomed to failure.[16] Nevertheless, the apparent determination of the royal government to enforce the peace and overcome the opposition of the sovereign courts is truly impressive, and despite some very difficult challenges, the peace did hold for four and a half years. Nationally, Catholic opposition to this agreement with "heretics" was focused on the refusal of some of the *parlements* – the eight sovereign royal courts in Paris and the major provincial capitals – to register the edict in order for it to take effect, but the two-year royal tour of these capitals clearly overcame this opposition.[17] The actual enforcement of the edict and the preservation of order were entrusted, in the first instance, to the three marshals of France, the highest military officials of the realm, as well as the provincial governors, many of whom were less than supportive of the edict. The real work of local and regional implementation and enforcement was entrusted, however, to thirteen pairs of royal commissioners, each with responsibility for specific provinces. These "commissioners of the peace" were formally charged in June 1563 with a wide range of responsibilities, including disarming the combatants, freeing religious prisoners, returning or compensating for seized property, reinstating Huguenots to office, and designating the sites for Reformed worship.[18]

---

[15] Stegmann, *Édits*, 35–6; Potter, *Wars of Religion*, 84.

[16] See, for example, Mack P. Holt, *The French Wars of Religion, 1562–1629*, New Approaches to European History (Cambridge: Cambridge University Press, 1995), 56: "The inevitable result was the continuation of the civil wars."

[17] See Chapter 5, p. 104, in this volume.

[18] The work of the commissioners is very well documented and affords us the opportunity to observe at close range the process by which the peace was implemented; in English see especially Jérémie Foa, "Making Peace: The Commissions for Enforcing the Pacification Edicts in the Reign of Charles IX," *French History* 18, no. 3 (2004): 256–74; Penny Roberts, "Religious Pluralism in Practice: The Enforcement of the Edicts of Pacification," in *The Adventure of Religious Pluralism in Early Modern France: Papers from the Exeter Conference, April 1999*, eds. Keith Cameron, Mark Greengrass, and Penny Roberts (Oxford: Peter Lang, 2000), 31–43; and Penny Roberts, *Peace and Authority during the French Religious Wars, c. 1560–1600*, Early Modern History (Houndmills, Basingstoke, Hampshire; New York: Palgrave Macmillan, 2013); on the specific provincial assignments, see Foa, "Making Peace," 259, and Roberts, *Peace and*

Any one of the many issues that the royal commissioners were charged with mediating had the potential to be deeply contentious in specific circumstances, but it is perhaps not surprising that some of the most significant challenges that the commissioners faced related to designating sites for Protestant worship.[19] By unambiguously validating religious coexistence as the foundation of domestic peace, the royal policy of pacification had effectively broken the close identification of religious purity with civic unity. Drawing a clear line between the religious authority of the Gallican Church to investigate heresy and the civic authority of the royal government to maintain public order was an enormous challenge to long-standing political and cultural assumptions, and nothing was more symbolic of the political-cultural realignment that this entailed than the visibility of Protestant worship. Still, the relatively vague prescriptions of the edict's language gave the commissioners significant room for maneuver as they sought to fashion a *modus vivendi* within the public domain for mutually antagonistic religious communities. And maneuver they certainly did, not infrequently defying powerful political figures and stretching the parameters of their mandate, as they successfully mediated conflicts over the location of Protestant worship in some fifty documented cases. Jérémie Foa argues that the remarkable effectiveness of the commissioners was rooted in their ability to present themselves as impartial outsiders, who eschewed religious bias.[20] Acting more clearly as independent mediators than as bureaucratic agents of the central state, the commissioners of the peace recurrently prevented the escalation of the local conflicts into renewed war by channeling the inevitable conflicts over interpretation and implementation of the edict into locally acceptable, though often messy, compromises.

In the formulation of the Edict of Amboise and in its subsequent implementation, then, we can discern some of the same basic principles and mechanisms that were also evident in the successful settlements in Switzerland and Germany. Like the Second Swiss *Landfrieden*, the king's edict explicitly recognized and validated the coexistence of two competitive religious communities within the same polity and established some basic rules and procedures by which their religious differences might be managed. Given the evident volatility of Huguenot-Catholic relations in many French cities – the most volatile being characterized by well-organized popular movements on both sides of the Huguenot/Catholic identity boundary – the edict's limitation of public Protestant worship to the *faubourgs* of certain designated cities appears to have been an attempt create a spatial *segregation* that might reduce

---

Authority, 190. For the French text of the commissions, see Roberts, *Peace and Authority*, 183–6.

[19] For a list of the designated sites, see Roberts, *Peace and Authority*, 188–9.

[20] Foa, "Making Peace." In 2008, Foa defended an unpublished dissertation, elaborating this impressive line of research, at the Université Lumière-Lyon 2, which was published as *Le tombeau de la paix: une histoire des edits de pacification, 1560–1572* (Limoges: Pulim, 2015), after I had completed this manuscript.

the occasions of direct confrontation. At the same time, restoring Huguenots to public office, returning or compensating for seized property, and releasing prisoners might well have reduced, over time, the effects of *polarization* and fostered a new civic culture in a religiously neutral public space. Although there was sporadic communal violence between the spring of 1563 and the fall of 1567, none of these locally violent activations of the Catholic/Huguenot identity boundary reignited coordinated destruction on a national scale. For a time, at least, determined application of the principles of mutual recognition and impartial mediation prevailed and preserved an improbable peace.

RECURRENT WAR, INTERMITTENT PEACE

What the Edict of Amboise most clearly failed to do, however, was to demobilize and demilitarize the broad national coalitions of zealous Huguenots and Catholics. To be sure, the commissioners of the peace were charged with disarming the combatants locally, but this was surely the least effective aspect of their work.[21] Meanwhile, it was the continued jostling and competition among the elite leaders of the religious factions – that is, those actors who had the most ready recourse to the force of arms – that provided the spark for the renewal of war. As it happened, the rising influence of the zealously Catholic Guise faction at court apparently awakened fear among Huguenot leaders that the king might be persuaded to repudiate the peace. Acting on their uncertainty regarding other national political actors, then, Condé and Coligny, the military leaders of the Huguenot faction, concocted and implemented another unsuccessful conspiracy to capture the king and to seize fortified cities, thereby restarting the war.[22]

After just six months of limited warfare, the Peace and Edict of Longjumeau (March 23, 1568) "purely and simply" restored the Edict of Amboise "in all points and articles in its original form."[23] In order to preempt the kind of official stalling that had slowed the implementation of the previous edict, the sovereign courts were ordered to publish the edict immediately (article 8). This time, too, the Huguenot armies were explicitly ordered to disarm and to withdraw from the towns and fortresses they had occupied (article 10). Finally, the king declared,

[article 12] To end all scruple and doubt, our subjects will abandon all Associations they have both within and without this kingdom, and will henceforth make no levies of

[21] Foa, "Making Peace," 267–8.
[22] Cf. Charles Tilly, *The Politics of Collective Violence*, Cambridge Studies in Contentious Politics (Cambridge: Cambridge University Press, 2003), 103, who argues that uncertainty about the future actions of other actors increases the likelihood of recourse to violent means and coordinated destruction in particular.
[23] French text in Stegmann, *Édits*, 53–8; there is a partial English translation in Potter, *Wars of Religion*, 105–6.

money, enrollments of men or any assemblies except those permitted by this Edict, and not in arms, on pain of punishment.[24]

These last two adjustments to the previous edict of pacification clearly indicate the negotiators' perception of the threat to religious peace to be elite factions, foreign alliances, and partisan military mobilizations. But simple prohibitions, without provisions for enforcement, could hardly complete the pacification process.

Just six months later, the worst fears of the Huguenot leaders were realized when the leader of the Guise faction, the cardinal of Lorraine, did persuade the young king to repudiate the peace: The Edict of St. Maur (September 28, 1568) nullified the previous edicts of pacification and forbade the exercise of any religion but the "Catholic, Apostolic and Roman."[25] The ensuing third civil war, which was highlighted by a large increase in foreign intervention, especially on the side of the Huguenots, was ended two years later by the Peace and Edict of Saint-Germain (August 8, 1570).[26] Rather than simply adjust the provisions of the previous edicts, however, this new Edict of Saint-Germain was a considerably more complex document, the product of a more thorough negotiation that reflects some of the lessons the negotiators evidently learned from previous failures; indeed, N. M. Sutherland describes this edict as a seminal document reflecting the increased military strength and influence of the Huguenots.[27]

Like the settlements that preceded it, this new edict of pacification was founded on the recognition of multiple religious communities within a single polity, and it restates at the outset the forgiving and forgetting clauses (articles 1–2) that had concluded the Edict of Amboise. On the whole, however, the Edict of Saint-Germain is much more clearly concerned with addressing the fears and guaranteeing the security of both religious communities. Indeed, in an apparent reflection of dramatic changes the previous wars had wrought, article 3 states:

We ordain that the Catholic and Romish Church be set up again and established in all places and quarters of this realm and country under our obedience, where the exercise of the same hath been left off, and that it may be freely and peaceably exercised without any trouble.[28]

Still, the dominant thrust of this revised template for religious peace was to prescribe more clearly a set of rules that might allay the fears and insecurities of the Protestant minority – those same fears that had disrupted the Peace of Amboise and had been amply confirmed by the Edict of St. Maur. Thus, article 4 reaffirms the complete freedom of religious conscience:

[24] Stegmann, *Édits*, 57; Potter, *Wars of Religion*, 106.   [25] Stegmann, *Édits*, 59–66.
[26] French text in Stegmann, *Édits*, 69–81; partial translation in Potter, *Wars of Religion*, 118–21.
[27] See her synopsis in Sutherland, *Huguenot Struggle*, 358–60.
[28] Stegmann, *Édits*, 70; Potter, *Wars of Religion*, 118.

And to the end that [no] occasion of trouble or contention be left among our said subjects, we have permitted and do permit them to live and dwell in all our towns and places of this our said realm ... without enquiry, vexing or molesting, or constraining to anything concerning religion against their consciences, neither by reason of the same to be searched in their homes.[29]

Abandoning the vague prescriptions of the Edict of Amboise, a series of eight articles (5–12) also specified precisely where Protestant worship would be permitted and protected while maintaining the prohibition of Protestant worship in the vicinity of Paris and the court.[30]

In a new departure, another series of articles specified the civil liberties that were to be guaranteed to Protestants. Not all of these were particularly generous: government officials were, for example, ordered in article 13 to provide for Protestant burials, but only by night! Still, article 15 prohibited discrimination on the basis of religion in admissions to institutions such as schools, universities, hospitals, and almshouses, and in article 22, "those of the said religion" were declared eligible to hold all public offices, deliberations, assemblies, and functions, "and not be in any way rejected or hindered from the enjoyment of them." Neither, according to article 23, should those of the "so-called Reformed religion" be "overburdened or oppressed with any ordinary or extraordinary charges [i.e., taxes or levies] than the Catholics." In all, article 26 declares,

We ordain, will and our pleasure is, that all those of the said Religion, as well generally as particularly, shall return and be conserved, maintained and kept under our protection and authority in all ... their goods, rights, actions, honours, estates, charges, pensions and dignities of what quality soever they be.

In addition, after rehabilitating specific individuals, including William, prince of Orange, and his brother, Louis of Nassau (article 30), who had fought in the third war on the side of the Huguenots, article 32 declared that

all sentences, judgments, arrests and proceedings, seizures, sales and decrees made and given against those of the so-called reformed religion, as well living as dead, since the departure of our most honoured lord and father King Henry, by occasion of the said religion, tumults and troubles ... to be henceforth broken, revoked and of no effect, which for this cause will be razed and put out of the registers of our courts.[31]

In sum, the Edict of Saint-Germain provided for the complete legal rehabilitation of all Protestants and guaranteed their basic civil liberties on a par, in most respects, with Catholics. Finally, addressing specifically their

[29] Stegmann, *Édits*, 71; Potter, *Wars of Religion*, 118.
[30] Article 8 names the *faubourgs* where Reformed worship will be permitted in Isle-de-France, Champagne, Burgundy, Picardy, Normandy, Lyonais, Languedoc, etc., where the earlier commissioners of the peace had apparently not yet designated them. Article 9 provides for public Reformed worship "in all such towns as it is publicly found to be used the first day of this present month of August."
[31] Stegmann, *Édits*, 75–7; quotations adapted from Potter, *Wars of Religion*, 120.

military insecurities, article 38 provided the Huguenot party, led by the king of Navarre and prince of Condé, with four fortified cities as *places de sûreté* for a period of two years.

Once again, the royal government of Charles IX both expressed and demonstrated its determination to enforce its edict of pacification. The closing articles of the Edict of Saint-Germain commanded the immediate registration, observation, and enforcement of the edict's provisions, and a new constellation of commissioners of the peace was dispatched throughout the kingdom to mediate the inevitable disagreements regarding the import and intended effect of the pacification.[32] Perhaps the clearest demonstration that the Edict of Saint-Germain was actually making peace possible is the fact that the noble leaders of the Huguenot coalition felt safe enough to congregate in large numbers in Paris for the politically symbolic interfaith wedding of the Protestant king of Navarre, Henry de Bourbon, to the Catholic sister of Charles IX, Marguerite de Valois. This time, however, it was a pair of Catholic conspiracies – the first, unsuccessful, to assassinate the Huguenot leader, Admiral Coligny, in broad daylight and then, amid fears and uncertainty regarding a possible Huguenot reprisal, the second, quite successful, to assassinate dozens of Huguenot leaders in their sleep – that subverted the peace, sparked the vicious communal violence of the St. Bartholomew's Day massacres, and restarted the French civil/religious wars.

The coordinated destruction of the fourth civil war, which focused on the open defiance and the subsequent siege of the city of La Rochelle, was brief and limited, and it was ended in July 1573 by the Peace of La Rochelle and the Edict of Boulogne. If the Edict of Saint-Germain in 1570 was a seminal document, the Edict of Boulogne was, according to N. M. Sutherland, "a disastrous edict, rashly concluded and crudely drafted."[33] Although it restated the freedom of religious conscience and reasserted the civil rights guaranteed to Protestants in 1570, it virtually eliminated public Reformed worship. The worship privileges of the nobility were curtailed, and public worship was banned in both the *faubourgs* that had been designated earlier and in the cities where it had previously been established. In only three cities – Montauban, La Rochelle, and Nîmes – were the Reformed allowed to worship collectively, but then only in homes and in private.[34] Little effort was actually made to enforce this edict, and following the sudden death of Charles IX and the succession of Henry III to the throne in May 1574, Protestant opposition to the Edict of Boulogne and massive troop movements on behalf of the Huguenot party restarted the civil wars again in the fall of 1574.

---

[32] See the maps of the extensive routes traveled by the commissioners dispatched to Guyenne, Languedoc, Provence, and Dauphiné in Foa, "Making Peace," 261.

[33] Sutherland, *Huguenot Struggle*, 360.

[34] Acceptance of this humiliating peace by only a segment of the Huguenot leadership opened up a split within the Huguenot coalition, with opposition to the edict concentrated in the southern heartland.

As we saw in Chapter 5, the fifth war resulted in a dramatic recovery of Huguenot power and influence even though there were few battles and relatively little coordinated destruction. A new alliance between Henry III's younger brother, Francis, duke of Alençon, and the Huguenot leadership, supported by a conglomeration of some 30,000 men under Huguenot command,[35] demonstrated the fundamental weakness of the king's position. Under this enormous threat, Henry III was forced to accept the Peace of Monsieur, which appeared to be dictated by "Monsieur," the king's own brother, and to promulgate the Edict of Beaulieu on May 6, 1576.[36]

The Edict of Beaulieu represented, after the Edict of Amboise (1563) and the Edict of Saint-Germain (1570), the third significant iteration of the basic template for a negotiated religious peace in France. Following a very brief prologue, the edict reiterated the opening articles of the Edict of Saint-Germain: the forgiving and forgetting clauses and the restoration of Catholic worship everywhere. The clear departure from precedent came in article 4:

> And to take away all occasion of trouble and disagreement among our subjects, we have granted and do grant free, public and general exercise of the so-called reformed religion [*religion prétendue réformée*] through all cities and places of our realm, and through all countries under our obedience and protection, without restraint of time, person or place. ... In which towns and places, the professors of the said religion may preach, pray, sing psalms, administer baptism and the Lord's Supper, ask the bands of matrimony and solemnize marriages, publicly catechize and read lectures, use discipline according to the said religion and do all other things belonging to the free and full exercise of the same. ... Nevertheless, we will and ordain that the professors of the said religion shall forbear the public exercise thereof in our city of Paris and in the suburbs thereof and within two leagues about the same.[37]

Clearly this represented a major "victory" for the Huguenot party: For this formerly clandestine movement, public, corporate worship in the Reformed manner was a kind of holy grail, and the "free, public and general exercise" clause was the most tangible token of their political success, just four years after the horrors of the St. Bartholomew's Day massacres. But this may have been a classic case of winning the battle but losing the war. For their Catholic enemies, public, corporate worship in the Reformed manner remained anathema and a visible token of the failure of the royal government to defend the Gallican Church and preserve the purity of faith. Thus, despite the edict's renewed prohibition of associations, Catholic militants immediately began creating the opposition leagues that would prolong the conflict, openly rebel against the crown, and initiate the most destructive of the sixteenth-century wars (1585–1598).

---

[35] Approximately 20,000 of these men were German mercenaries led by the brother of the Calvinist Elector of the Palatinate.

[36] The French text is in Stegmann, *Édits*, 97–120; there is a partial English translation in Potter, *Wars of Religion*, 163–8.

[37] Stegmann, *Édits*, 98; quotation adapted from Potter, *Wars of Religion*, 164.

The other major innovation of the Edict of Beaulieu had more staying power. This was the creation (articles 18–21), at the request of both Catholics and Protestants, of special *chambres mi-parties* (biconfessional courts within the various *parlements* consisting of equal numbers of Catholic and Protestant judges) to prevent discrimination in cases involving litigants of the different confessions.[38] In addition, the edict reaffirmed the civil liberties provisions of the Edict of Saint-Germain, restated the enforcement provisions, and increased from four to eight the number of *places de sûreté* that were permitted the Huguenot alliance. Finally, the edict forgave all acts of hostility associated with the St. Bartholomew's Day massacres and rehabilitated all those who had joined the Huguenot campaign, including specifically the king's brother, Francis, and his brother-in-law, Henry, king of Navarre. In a set of secret articles, moreover, the king's brother, Francis, who had forcefully advocated the Huguenots' grievances and negotiated their demands, was granted the duchies and revenues of Anjou, Touraine, and Berry, as well as a large annual pension, to secure his future loyalty to the royal government.[39]

The religious peace framed by the Edict of Beaulieu would last only a few months. In the fall, the meeting of the Estates General that the edict had called for was dominated by the members of the Catholic leagues; it repudiated the edict and called for the reestablishment of just one religion – "the Catholic, Apostolic and Roman" – though it refused the levies that the king requested. By December, the war had restarted, despite the king's desperate lack of finances and soldiers. In September 1577, the Edict of Poitiers, which ended the sixth war and marked the beginning of an extended period of relative peace and political renewal between 1577 and 1585,[40] retained most of the provisions of the Edict of Beaulieu, with the exception of the articles relating to freedom of worship, justice, and the *places de sûreté*.[41] The special courts would no longer be biconfessional, and public Reformed worship would be limited, as under the Edict of Amboise, to the *faubourgs* of one town in each administrative district as well as within those cities where it had been established as of September 17, 1577. In a long series of forty-eight secret articles, concluded with the king of Navarre and the prince of Condé, the king agreed to pay both the soldiers to guard the Huguenots' *places de sûreté* as well

---

[38] Mark Greengrass argues that the Edict of Beaulieu, instead of extending marginally the privileges of previous edicts, enunciates a new principle of equality in the freedom of worship it granted the Protestants and in the formation of the *chambres mi-parties*; see Mark Greengrass, "Pluralism and Equality: The Peace of Monsieur, May 1576," in *The Adventure of Religious Pluralism in Early Modern France: Papers from the Exeter Conference, April 1999*, eds. Keith Cameron, Mark Greengrass, and Penny Roberts (Oxford: Peter Lang, 2000), 45–63. Although the biconfessional courts were abandoned in the Edict of Poitiers (1577), they would be revived in the Edict of Nantes.

[39] Holt, *French Wars*, 105–6.

[40] See Mark Greengrass, *Governing Passions: Peace and Reform in the French Kingdom, 1576–1585* (Oxford; New York: Oxford University Press, 2007).

[41] French text in Stegmann, *Édits*, 131–53; Stegmann does not include the secret articles.

as Huguenots' German mercenaries.[42] A brief renewal of the war in the south – the seventh – was ended in November 1580 by the Edict of Fleix,[43] which confirmed the provisions of the Edict of Poitiers, including its secret articles, as well as the Treaty of Nérac (February 1579),[44] which had interpreted and amplified the Edict of Poitiers.

THE DYNAMICS OF RECONCILIATION

What can we learn about the dynamics of religious peacemaking from the French experience between 1560 and 1585? What kind of religious peace did the French edicts of pacification that preceded the Edict of Nantes make possible? On the one hand, it is clear that the French royal policy of embracing religious coexistence as the foundation of political reconciliation was remarkably constant. Despite the king's own brief repudiation of the peace in the Edict of St. Maur in 1568 and the Estates General's repudiation of the Edict of Beaulieu in 1576, the royal government's *default position* over the course of seven wars and as many edicts of pacification – that is, a period of approximately twenty-five years – was and remained the recognition of multiple confessions in a single polity as the essential foundation of religious peace and political reconciliation. This is not to say, of course, that those who negotiated the French settlements were mindlessly repeating the same actions in the insane expectation of achieving a different outcome. On the contrary, between the Edict of Amboise (1563) and the Edict of Fleix (1580), the parties to the peace treaties that served as the foundation of the edicts adjusted not only to changing circumstances, but to the evident shortcomings of previous agreements.

The most obvious change in French circumstances between 1560 and 1585 was the transformation of the Huguenots from a clandestine religious movement into a visible, institutionalized, and legitimate, albeit *minority*, element of French society and politics. To be sure, this was not an "outcome" that the leaders of either the Huguenot or the Catholic coalitions had envisioned or intended. Still, over time, the public visibility of the Protestant minority, the formal organization of both the Reformed churches and Protestant assemblies, and the integration of Reformed elites into public life became well-established facts on the ground that the various edicts of pacification sought to validate and preserve. This historical process was neither irreversible nor uniform, of course, and over time, a certain degree of local variation and geographic segregation emerged. In some parts of France, especially in the north and northeast, the position of the Huguenot minority remained fragile or deteriorated over time, while in other parts of the kingdom, especially in the south and southwest, the Huguenots established a dominant, even a majority, position. Such changes and variations, the cumulative residue of ongoing competition, episodic violence,

---

[42] Sutherland, *Huguenot Struggle*, 362–3.   [43] Stegmann, *Édits*, 192–203.
[44] Stegmann, *Édits*, 158–70.

and recurrent war, are reflected in the edicts' recurrent guarantees of free religious conscience, protections of a variously defined privilege of Reformed worship, and restoration of Catholic worship where it had ceased. Like the Swiss and German settlements, the French edicts did not bring religious coexistence into being; rather, their creators struggled mightily to find ways to validate the religious diversity that already existed and to adjust to changes in the religious landscape that had already taken place.

Although each of the French edicts of pacification eventually failed, they nevertheless enjoyed varying degrees of success as well. The most successful – the Edict of Amboise (1563) and the Edict of Fleix (1580) – each made more than four years of religious peace possible: Not only was there an absence of coordinated destruction, but there was a visible commitment to sustaining coexistence.[45] Thus, in the succession of edicts of pacification prior to the Edict of Nantes, we can see adjustments that reflect both success and failure. Following the evident success of the commissioners of the peace in enforcing the Edict of Amboise, for example, the commissions were reinvented to enforce the Edict of Saint-Germain (1570). Once the Edict of Saint-Germain introduced guarantees of specific civil liberties to Protestants – equal access to schools, universities, hospitals, and almshouses; eligibility for appointment to public offices; and the like – these guarantees were restated in subsequent edicts. Also, even before the debacle of the St. Bartholomew's Day massacres, the provision of *places de sûreté* to allay the fears of the Protestant minority became a recurrent feature of the edicts of pacification, beginning with the Edict of Saint-Germain. Over time, then, the edicts became increasingly complex and detailed documents, consisting of dozens of publicly registered articles as well as including secret articles intended to amplify or interpret the public articles.

At bottom, the most vexing problem faced by the putative French peacemakers was also the most basic, having fundamentally to do with recognition. The king's formal recognition of the Protestant minority, the foundation of his policy of pacification, recurrently entailed granting "those of the said religion" the privilege of public worship in the Reformed manner, and as long as there were zealous Catholics, with ready access to military resources, unwilling to accept any public Reformed worship, any peace settlement would remain fragile. Still, the authors of the various edicts struggled mightily to craft politically acceptable spaces for Protestant worship. The vague parameters of the Edict of Amboise (1563) were eventually replaced by the precise specificity of the Edict of Saint-Germain (1570); the almost complete prohibition of public Reformed worship in the Edict of Boulogne (1573) was precipitously supplanted by virtually unlimited Protestant worship in the Edict of Beaulieu (1576), only to be limited again, along the lines of the Edict of Amboise, in the Edicts of Poitiers (1577) and Fleix (1580). Perhaps the only lesson to be learned from this process of trial and error was that

---

[45] See especially Foa, "Making Peace"; Roberts, "Religious Pluralism in Practice"; and Greengrass, *Governing Passions*.

there was no "magic formula" that could balance the competing interests of mutually antagonistic religious groups in all circumstances. Yet the highly centralized, nationalized mode of French peacemaking seemed to demand a single, clearly defined set of rules to manage religious coexistence everywhere.

In this extended period of frequent alternations between war and peace in France, we can discern a familiar combination of the basic principles of religious peace agreements and the relational dynamics that make religious coexistence possible. As with the Swiss *Landfrieden* and the German *Religionsfriede*, all of the French edicts incorporated the basic principles of early modern peace settlements: recognition and validation of multiple religious groups in a single polity, provision of security to all parties, and a commitment to use mediation or legal processes to resolve outstanding issues. In the formal language of the French edicts, however, these were not the mutual commitments of the contending parties; rather, it was the king who formally recognized the Protestant minority, who promised them protection and security, and whose agents and agencies provided the mechanisms of ongoing mediation and impartial justice.

Likewise, in the practical experience and the active enforcement of the French edicts we can discern the combination of four relational mechanisms – negotiation, segregation, domination, and subversion – that combined to produce a distinctively French history of religious peace. The most obvious mechanism at work in the early history of French peacemaking is *negotiation*, which not only served as the foundation of the long series of royal edicts of pacification, but was also at the heart of local accommodations of religious difference that the commissioners of the peace and the special courts facilitated and maintained.[46] Less obvious perhaps, but equally important, is the dynamic of *segregation*. At the national level, the edicts recurrently sought to segregate the religious communities from the armed associations that made communal violence and the coordinated destruction of war possible. Similarly, at the local level, the edits recurrently sought to separate Protestant worshipers from the zealous Catholics who might attack them. Finally, a pattern of geographic segregation emerged willy-nilly over time, dividing the kingdom into separate zones of Protestant and Catholic strength.[47] Closely related to the local and national dynamics of physical segregation are the complementary dynamics of *domination* and *subversion*. Nationally, the Catholic majority had long

---

[46] Olivier Christin has discovered that a number of municipalities also negotiated their own local agreements when the national edicts failed to bring a stable peace; see Olivier Christin, "'Peace Must Come from Us': Friendship Pacts between the Confessions during the Wars of Religion," in *Toleration and Religious Identity: The Edict of Nantes and Its Implications in France, Britain and Ireland*, eds. Ruth Whelan and Carol Baxter (Dublin: Four Courts Press, 2003), 92–103, and Olivier Christin, *La paix de religion: L'autonomisation de la raison politique au xvie siècle*, Collection Liber (Paris: Éditions du Seuil, 1997), which includes the texts of several local pacts.

[47] See, for example, the description of these zones of strength and weakness in Gregory Hanlon, *Confession and Community in Seventeenth-Century France: Catholic and Protestant Coexistence in Aquitaine* (Philadelphia: University of Pennsylvania Press, 1993), introduction.

dominated the Protestant minority, especially prior to the edicts of pacification; by the same token, subversion had long been an essential part of the Protestant experience of repression. In the course of the French wars, the Huguenots gladly reversed those roles, seizing control of local communities, sometimes only briefly, as at Rouen, but for longer, sustained periods in many communities in the south and southwest, where Catholic religious practice ceased to be public and survived only clandestinely.[48] Still, in much of France, and especially in Paris and at the court, the Huguenots "survived" only discreetly, if not clandestinely, and their variably public or visible presence remained profoundly subversive of the long-standing ideal of Gallican unity and purity.

The essential point here is that prior to 1585 religious peace – that is, the absence of coordinated destruction and the sustained experience of religious coexistence – became as much a part of the routine experience of most French men and women of all ranks and regions as was the experience of communal violence and coordinated destruction. However traumatic the episodes of communal violence and the direct experience of coordinated destruction may have been, the early wars of religion in France were relatively limited in both time and place. In the many interstices, religious peace came to be, not the exception, but the rule. Thus, despite the best efforts of the king, his advisors, and the agents of his sovereign authority to establish a uniform pattern of peace informed by a single set of rules, the dynamics of negotiation, segregation, domination, and subversion recurrently combined to produce a religious peace that was, paradoxically, as variegated and messy in practice as any before or after.

A STILLBORN PEACE IN THE LOW COUNTRIES

Making peace was a rather different process in the Low Countries than it was in France. Whereas French royal policy vis-à-vis religious dissidents moved decisively from repression to pacification after 1560, Philip II, king of Spain and lord of the Netherlands, was in the early 1560s and would remain throughout his long reign steadfast in his policy of repression and his refusal to compromise with heretics. Indeed, as we saw in Chapter 5, faced with a rising tide of both demonstrative religious defiance and more formal political opposition, especially to his plan to reorganize and strengthen the Church, Philip might be persuaded to dismiss Granvelle, his trusted advisor, and suspend the church reforms in 1564. But amid widespread expectations and formal advice to the contrary, he unequivocally insisted, after a brief hesitation in October 1565, that the heresy laws be strictly enforced. Likewise, in 1566, amid the excitement and violence of the *wonderjaar*, Margaret of Parma, his regent, temporarily suspended enforcement of the heresy laws in response to the

---

[48] See especially, Philip Conner, *Huguenot Heartland: Montauban and Southern French Calvinism During the Wars of Religion*, St. Andrews Studies in Reformation History (Aldershot, England; Burlington, VT: Ashgate, 2002).

"humble" petition of the "beggar" nobles and even signed an accord allowing limited freedom of Protestant worship in response to the *beeldenstorm*. But Philip not only urged a military response by Margaret in late 1566, but in 1567, he dispatched the duke of Alva and 10,000 soldiers to eliminate political opposition and religious dissent once and for all, which resulted in perhaps the most violent and bitter repression of the sixteenth century.

In this situation, then, there would be no government-sponsored colloquies to foster theological reconciliation; nor would modest efforts to moderate royal policy, such as the Compromise of the Nobility, be treated in Madrid with much more than suspicion and contempt. Indeed, it is striking that the most public and promising attempts to make peace in the Low Countries, prior to the Twelve Year Truce – the Pacification of Ghent (1576) and the *Paix de Religion/Religions-vrede* (1578) – were fashioned in direct opposition to Philip II and his representatives in the Low Countries. Although these attempted settlements quickly gave way to renewed war, as so many others did elsewhere in Europe, they remained important reference points for later developments, and on closer examination they reveal for us some of the essential dynamics of the religious peace that would emerge in the Low Countries.

Recall that by 1576, the Beggar coalition had not only achieved its first military successes in Holland and Zeeland, but it had survived another ferocious military response by the duke of Alva. Following the death of Don Luis de Requesens, Alva's successor, the Estates General seized temporary control of the government in Brussels, and meeting together at Ghent, the Low Countries provinces negotiated the terms of a peace agreement: the so-called Pacification of Ghent, which was formally called a "treaty and confederation ... among the Estates of the Provinces of the Low Countries, the Prince of Orange, and the Estates of the Provinces of Holland and Zeeland."[49] As was common in the French edicts of pacification, the Pacification of Ghent began with a forgiving-and-forgetting clause: "[A]ll offenses, slanders, misdeeds, and damages occurring as a result of the troubles ... shall be forgiven, forgotten and considered as not having occurred, so that no mention shall ever be made of them and no one shall be called to account for them."[50] The foundation of this "lasting and unbreakable

---

[49] The Dutch and French texts of the "Pacification" may be found in Jean Dumont, ed., *Corps universel diplomatique du droit des gens; contenant vn recueil des traitez d'alliance, de paix, de treve, de neutralité, de commerce, d'échange.. & autres contrats, qui ont été faits en Europe* (Amsterdam: P. Brunel, etc., 1726–31), vol. 5, part 1, pp. 278–83; variant English translations may be found in E. H. Kossmann and A. F. Mellink, eds., *Texts Concerning the Revolt of the Netherlands* (Cambridge: Cambridge University Press, 1974), 126–32, and Herbert H. Rowen, ed., *The Low Countries in Early Modern Times: A Documentary History*, Documentary History of Western Civilization (New York: Harper and Row, 1972), 59–64, which are based on the Dutch and French texts, respectively.

[50] Dumont, *Corps universel diplomatique*, vol. 5, part 1, 280; quotation adapted from Rowen, *Low Countries*, 60.

friendship and peace," article II makes clear, was a common political opposition to Spanish tyranny; indeed, its principal purpose was

to drive and keep out of the country the Spanish soldiers and other foreigners who have attempted, without any recourse to law, to deprive Lords and Nobles of their lives, to appropriate the riches and wealth of the country, and to reduce and keep the common people in perpetual enslavement.[51]

In order to achieve their twin goals of internal concord and military liberation, the authors and signatories of the pacification had, like their Swiss, German, and French counterparts, to come to grips with less than pleasant facts on the ground, not the least of which concerned their religious differences. Notwithstanding William of Orange's personal preference and public advocacy for religious coexistence on the inclusive French model – that is, multiple officially recognized and protected faiths in a single polity[52] – the early military successes of the Beggars' coalition had entailed clearly exclusionary religious practices. Despite some local agreements to the contrary, the Estates of Holland had abolished the Catholic Mass in 1573, and in many places where local rebel victories brought (re)establishment of public Reformed worship, they had also brought renewed iconoclasm and active suppression of Catholic priests and spiritual practices. What's more, in the spring of 1576, the exclusionary practices of the local Beggar victories were validated by a formal union signed by the Estates of Holland and Zeeland. Article 25 stated:

And concerning Religion, their Excellencies shall admit and maintain the practice of the Reformed Evangelical Religion, staying and ceasing the exercise of all other Religions contrary to the Evangelical, providing that their Excellencies do not allow that anyone's belief or conscience be examined or that anyone, as a consequence, be caused difficulty, injury or harm.[53]

Sidestepping this deeply divisive issue, article III of the Pacification of Ghent committed the signatories to a convocation of the Estates General – "in the form and manner in which it was held during the time of the late emperor Charles, of praiseworthy memory" – in order "to put the affairs of the country generally and individually in good order, *concerning not only the exercise of religion in the provinces of Holland, Zeeland, and associated places*, but also the restitution of fortresses, artillery, ships, and other things belonging to His Majesty."[54] In the

---

[51] Dumont, *Corps universel diplomatique*, vol. 5, part 1, 280; Kossmann and Mellink, *Texts*, 126–27; Rowen, *Low Countries*, 61.

[52] See, for example, the Edict of Pacification that William published for the Principality of Orange in 1563, which may be found in Dumont, *Corps universel diplomatique*, vol. 5, part 1, 99; cf. K. W. Swart, *Willem van Oranje en de Nederlandse Opstand, 1572–1584*, introd. by Alastair Duke and Jonathan I. Israel (Den Haag: Sdu Uitgeverij, 1994).

[53] The Dutch and French texts of this union may be found in Dumont, *Corps universel diplomatique*, vol. 5, part 1, 256–64; quotation is from 263.

[54] Dumont, *Corps universel diplomatique*, vol. 5, part 1, 280; the quotations are adapted from Rowen, *Low Countries*, 61, emphasis mine.

near term, however, Article 4 provided that "the inhabitants on both sides, in any province of the Low Countries, no matter what their status, quality, or condition, will have the right to stay and reside, pass in and out, remain, and engage in trade everywhere ... in full freedom and security"; it went on to specify that persons from the rebel provinces of Holland and Zeeland "shall not be allowed or permitted to infringe in any way ... against the repose and public peace, notably against the Roman Catholic religion, or against its practices." Finally, in Article 5 the signatories declared in that "all ordinances heretofore made and published regarding heresy, as well as the criminal ordinances made by the Duke of Alva ... shall be suspended until the Estates General shall order otherwise."[55] For the rest, the pacification deals with a variety of practical matters such as the restitution of properties seized during the troubles, the release of prisoners without ransom, and even the destruction of "[t]he columns, trophies, inscriptions, and effigies erected by the Duke of Alva putting dishonor and blame on those named above."[56]

Clearly the proponents of concord in the Low Countries were counting on a broadly based opposition to Spanish tyranny, although they had to be mindful of the dangers of Reformed zealotry and Beggar tyranny as well. In the wake of the "Spanish Fury" at Antwerp, however, the Estates General were able to force Don Juan of Austria, Philip II's new designee as governor-general, to accept the pacification as a condition of their recognition of his authority. Although Philip quickly urged Don Juan to ignore his commitment to the pacification, the Spanish troops were actually ordered to leave the Low Countries, and the Estates General did eventually move to tackle the vexing problem of religion. In order for the process of pacification to continue, however, the Estates General had once again to oppose Philip directly: In 1577 they declared Don Juan forfeit of his office and proclaimed instead the young Austrian archduke, Matthias, to be governor-general, with William of Orange as his lieutenant-general. It was this new constellation of forces, then, that drafted and promulgated the *Paix de Religion/Religions-vrede* in July 1578.[57]

---

[55] Dumont, *Corps universel diplomatique*, vol. 5, part 1, 280–1; the quotations are adapted from Rowen, *Low Countries*, 61–2.

[56] Dumont, *Corps universel diplomatique*, vol. 5, part 1, 281; Rowen, *Low Countries*, 63.

[57] There is some confusion in the historical literature regarding the text of this agreement, between the draft of June 22 and the final text of July 12, 1578; see P. J. H. Ubachs, "De Nederlandse Religievrede van 1578," *Nederlands archief voor kerkgeschiedenis* 77, no. 1 (1997): 41–61. I have consulted both the French text published in Dumont, *Corps Universel Diplomatique*, vol. 5, part 1, 318–20, and the Dutch text published in Arthur C. Schrevel, ed., *Recueil de documents relatifs aux troubles religieux en Flandre, 1577–1584* (Bruges: L. de Planck, 1921), II, 492–503. See also the excellent summary of the articles (39–40) as well as a larger discussion of the context in O. J. de Jong, "Union and Religion," *Low Countries History Yearbook* (1981): 29–49, who uses yet another seventeenth-century published edition of the text, dated July 22, 1578. There is a very limited English translation, based on Dumont, in Rowen, *Low Countries*, 64–6. I wish to acknowledge the valuable assistance of my colleague Robert M. Stein in translating critical articles of this text.

The prologue to the *Paix de Religion* sets the agreement in the historical context of "the infringement of the privileges, rights, and laudable customs of the country and ... a despicable war undertaken by the enemies of the fatherland and [resulting] in our total ruin and enslavement." Confidently asserting both the possibility and the necessity of "an amicable agreement and peace in the matter of religion," the authors cited the recent positive examples of "Germany and France, who came to agreement in this respect and now live in peace and quiet, whereas previously they treated one another with mutual intolerance and enmity, and thus avoided the great perils, bloodshed, and other troubles which faced them." Implementing the agreement would not disrupt the unity of the provinces as provided for in the Pacification of Ghent, the prologue concluded, since no one would be required "to change his religion or to accept the liberty to do so if he does not approve of it."[58]

As was becoming conventional in these agreements, the first article stipulated "that all offenses and injuries committed since the Pacification of Ghent on account of religion shall be forgiven and forgotten as if they did not happen." The second article continues with an unequivocal, if somewhat awkward, assertion of the freedom of religious conscience:

And so that neither discord, nor contention may arise any longer with respect to the diversity of Religion (which can neither be maintained, established, nor oppressed by force of arms), it is decreed that each person shall remain free and unencumbered, regarding the two Religions, in the way that he wishes to answer before God, provided that they do not disturb one another, but that each person, whether religious or lay, may possess and retain his goods in peace and in tranquility, and serve God according to the conscience that has been given to him and according to the way that he would wish to answer for on the day of judgment, for so long and until such time as the two parties, having been freely heard in a General, or National, Council, may decide or determine otherwise.[59]

In order that this individual "freedom of religion" be properly and reasonably regulated on both sides, the *Paix de Religion* provided that the "Catholic and Roman Religion be reestablished in ... [all those places] where is has been abandoned, so that it might be exercised there peaceably and freely, without any trouble or hindrance, for those who wish for it" (article 3). Likewise, "the said religion known as reformed may be publicly exercised in all the cities and places of the Low Countries" (article 4). In both cases, however, the agreement specified that there be sufficient numbers of households – namely 100 households in the large cities and the larger part of smaller places – to warrant the (re)introduction of public worship; once the petitioners had presented themselves to the local authorities, the civil magistrates were

---

[58] Schrevel, *Recueil de documents*, vol. 2, 493–4; Dumont, *Corps universel diplomatique*, vol. 5, part 1, 318–19.

[59] Schrevel, *Recueil de documents*, vol. 2, 495–6; Dumont, *Corps universel diplomatique*, vol. 5, part 1, 319.

required immediately to designate suitable places of worship, provided that, in order to avoid contentions and quarrels, the Catholic places of worship were not too proximate to the Reformed (article 5). In those places where multiple forms of public worship were allowed, "they will be able respectively to observe, hear, and celebrate the divine services, sermons, prayers, chants, baptism, communion, burials, marriage, schools, and all that appertains to their respective religion." In addition, "[i]n those places where worship does not take place publicly, no one shall, on account of Religion, be examined or spoken to regarding what he may do in his home."[60]

The foundation of the *Paix de Religion* was, thus, an unlimited freedom of both *individual conscience* and *private worship* combined with an equivalently circumscribed liberty of *public worship* for both faith communities. Building on this foundation, the subsequent articles prohibited hindrance of another because of his religion, disturbance of his services, molestation of clergy, circulation of defamatory or satirical literature, defamatory preaching, and the like. Additionally, the *Paix* provided that anyone would be eligible for public office regardless of his religion, that there was to be no religious discrimination in admission to schools, universities, hospitals, or almshouses, and that Catholic feast days and fast days were to be observed by everyone outside Holland and Zeeland. Finally, there were a series of articles providing for the administration of impartial justice; compliance was to be monitored by special mixed commissions composed of "four sound and qualified persons."

In all, the *Paix de Religion* – the first formal attempt to negotiate a template for religious peace in the Low Countries – was a remarkably comprehensive and "mature" document. Although it borrowed its title from the German *Religionsfriede* (*Religions-vrede* in Dutch), it bore much closer resemblance – right down to the occasional use of the term *religion prétendue reformée* in the French edition of the text – to the most recent template for religious peace in France. Indeed, like the French edicts of pacification, this proposed settlement was "national" in scope, and rather than simply validating less than desirable and quite variable facts on the ground, as the German settlement had done, it prescribed a single set of clear rules for recognizing, protecting, and sustaining religious coexistence as the foundation for religious peace in all of the Netherlands. Like the Edict of Beaulieu (1576), it proposed very ambitious goals for recognition and coexistence of the two faiths – indeed, it cut both ways in rejecting the exclusionary practices of both the Beggars and the Spaniards – specifying universal freedom for the private exercise of both the Catholic and Reformed faiths and providing for political equality and social integration for individuals of both faiths. Like the Edict of Poitiers (1577), it placed significant limits on where the *public exercise* of the Reformed faith was

---

[60] Schrevel, *Recueil de documents*, vol. 2, 495–7; Dumont, *Corps universel diplomatique*, vol. 5, part 1, 319. From the fifth article onward, the numbering of the articles differs somewhat between the Dutch and French texts, though the substance remains equivalent.

to be introduced, but it applied the same threshold rules to where the public exercise of Catholicism was to be reintroduced.[61]

Taken together, the Pacification of Ghent and the *Paix de Religion* incorporated all of the essential components of an early modern religious settlement: recognition of multiple faiths in a single polity, provisions for the security of all parties to the agreement, and mechanisms for mediating future disagreements. Given Philip II's unwillingness to accept, much less enforce, its basic principles, however, the *Paix de Religion*'s ambitious vision for a "national" peace of religion was certainly doomed to failure, except as a revolutionary program; in any case, by the time it was sent to the provinces for their comments prior to final approval, Don Juan had already restarted the military campaign to reestablish Spanish control and radical Calvinists had established a revolutionary republic in Ghent. Still, in the period between 1578 and 1581, as P. J. H. Ubachs reports, at least twenty-seven cities in the Low Countries, both north and south, formally adopted the terms of the religious peace.[62] Thus, although it was never formally adopted at the national or provincial level, the *Paix de Religion* did serve for a time as a template for local reconciliation in places as diverse as Ghent (Flanders), Antwerp (Brabant), Haarlem (Holland), Wijk bij Duurstede (Utrecht), and Leeuwarden (Friesland).[63]

THE PATH TOWARD SEPARATION

As we saw in Chapter 5, the failure of the Pacification of Ghent and the *Paix de Religion* to bring a national peace was marked by the brokerage of two separate and partial military and political alliances in January 1579; although both alliances claimed to preserve and strengthen the Pacification of Ghent, they eventually helped to structure two separate polities: one loyal to its Spanish overlord (the Union of Arras) and the other in open rebellion against him (the Union of Utrecht). Coming in the midst of an escalating conflict, these strikingly different "bargains" were intended to mobilize and nurture mutually exclusive and equally bellicose coalitions in the midst of religious war. Thus, whereas both of these unions articulated in some detail the common vision of political decentralization, rooted in provincial self-regulation, that was the foundation of the Pacification of Ghent, they differed especially in their visions of religious peace, although articulating such a vision was hardly their primary purpose.

[61] See also Benjamin J. Kaplan, "'In Equality and Enjoying the Same Favor': Biconfessionalism in the Low Countries," in *A Companion to Multiconfessionalism in the Early Modern World*, ed. Thomas Max Safley, Brill's Companions to the Christian Tradition, vol. 28 (Leiden; Boston: Brill, 2011), 105–9.
[62] Ubachs, "Religievrede," 54–6.
[63] Ubachs, "Religievrede"; on its adoption in Antwerp, see Guido Marnef, "Multiconfessionalism in a Commercial Metropolis: The Case of 16th-Century Antwerp," in *A Companion to Multiconfessionalism in the Early Modern World*, ed. Thomas Max Safley, Brill's Companions to the Christian Tradition, vol. 28 (Leiden; Boston: Brill, 2011), 81–9.

The Union of Arras, which joined the Estates of Hainaut and Tournai with the cities of Lille, Douai, and Orchies on January 6, 1579, was followed by several months of hard bargaining with Alexander Farnese, duke of Parma, who had been appointed governor-general in the Netherlands, following the death of Don Juan in 1577. This culminated in the Treaty of Arras, which was signed on May 17, 1579, and eventually reconciled all of the Walloon provinces plus parts of Flanders and Brabant to Philip II. These "Articles of Peace" began by affirming that "the negotiations of the Pacification of Ghent ... will remain in full force and vigor" (article 1), and it continued with an amnesty clause (article 2) that pointedly linked "the preservation of the Roman, Apostolic, and Catholic religion" with "obedience to His Majesty," Philip II; it conspicuously provided that "rebels, exiles, whether in exile, or prison, or ordered to trial by the governors and magistrates of the contracting territories, ... will not be included in this present amnesty and pardon."[64] Following a series of articles requiring, again, the departure of foreign military forces, article 7 provided that

His Majesty and the United Lands will raise an army of natives of this country and others acceptable to His Majesty and to the Estates of the provinces which now enter into the present Treaty or may enter it later, at the expense of His Majesty, but with the understanding that the above-mentioned provinces will aid his majesty by payment of taxes ... in order to maintain the Roman Catholic religion and the obedience due to His Majesty.[65]

Amid more articles regarding political appointments, article 12 also required that "an oath shall be sworn by the contracting Estates, as well as by all persons in high office, governors, magistrates, burghers, and inhabitants ... to uphold both the Roman Catholic religion and the proper obedience due to the King."[66] Not surprisingly, the treaty makes no reference to either the Reformed religion or the more general freedom of religious conscience that was at the heart of the *Paix de Religion*.

Like the Union of Arras, the Union of Utrecht, which was concluded on January 23, 1579, brought a subset of the Low Countries provinces together in a political and military alliance: initially, just four provinces and part of a fifth, but eventually all eight northern provinces plus the cities of Brabant and Flanders.[67] The prologue, which accuses "the Spaniards" of

[64] Dumont, *Corps universel diplomatique*, vol. 5, part 1, 350; Rowen, *Low Countries*, 261–2.
[65] Dumont, *Corps universel diplomatique*, vol. 5, part 1, 351; Rowen, *Low Countries*, 263.
[66] Dumont, *Corps universel diplomatique*, vol. 5, part 1, 352; Rowen, *Low Countries*, 263–4.
[67] The original Dutch text is printed in Cornelius Cau, ed., *Groot placaatboek, vervattende de placaaten, ordonnantien en edicten van de hoog mog. heeren Staaten generaal der Vereenigde Nederlanden; en van de edele groot mog. heeren Staaten van Holland en Westvriesland; mitsgaders van de edele mog heeren Staaten van Zeeland ...*, vol. 1 ('s Gravenhage: H. I. van Wouw, 1658), col 7–26; the Dutch and French versions are published in parallel columns in Dumont, *Corps universel diplomatique*, vol. 5, part 1, 322–33; there are variant English translations in Kossmann and Mellink, *Texts*, 165–9, and Rowen, *Low Countries*, 69–73.

seeking the "ruin and destruction" of the provinces united under the Pacification of Ghent, explains that the members of this Union "have thought it advisable to ally and to unite more closely and specifically, not with the intention of withdrawing from the General Union set up at the Pacification of Ghent, but rather to strengthen it and to protect themselves against the wiles, attacks and violence of their enemies." Having thus reaffirmed the pacification, as did the Treaty of Arras, the first twelve articles of the Union of Utrecht spelled out the political, military, diplomatic, and fiscal specifics of what it meant for the signatories to "hold together eternally in all ways and forms as if they were but a single province ... without prejudice to the special and particular privileges, freedoms, exemptions, laws, statutes, laudable and particular customs, usages, and all other rights of each province."[68] In this case, however, the diversity of religion – both among the provinces and within them – demanded explicit attention, and the thirteenth article addressed this delicate issue in the tortured language of a multidimensional compromise:

Concerning the matter of religion: Holland and Zeeland shall act at their own discretion whereas the other provinces of this Union may conform to the contents of the Religious Peace, drafted by the archduke Matthias ... or else they may introduce (all together or each province independently), without being hindered or prevented from doing this by any other province, such regulations as they consider proper for the peace and welfare of the provinces, towns and their particular members and for the preservation of the properties and rights of all people, whether lay or clerical, provided that in accordance with the Pacification of Ghent, each individual enjoys freedom of religion and no one is persecuted or questioned about his religion.[69]

Two additional articles addressed the status and property of Catholic clergy, regular and secular, in the provinces of Holland and Zeeland, and of monks, in particular, in the other provinces. The remaining articles (15–36) provided for procedures for mediating disputes among the provinces, amending the Union, administering oaths to keep and preserve the Union, and the like.

"Concerning the matter of religion," then, the Unions of Arras and Utrecht could not, at first blush, be more dissimilar. Although they dealt primarily with the political, military, and fiscal issues of broad elite alliances mobilizing for war, their religious implications were abundantly clear and divergent. The members of the Union of Arras had bargained hard with their politically ambitious overlord for the preservation of their provincial privileges, which permanently frustrated Philip's hopes for a more efficient and centralized administration in the Low Countries. But in return, by the terms of the Treaty

[68] Cau, *Groot Placaatboek*, col. 7–10; the quotations are from Kossmann and Mellink, *Texts*, 165–6.
[69] Cau, *Groot Placaatboek*, col. 12–13; the quotation is adapted from Kossmann and Mellink, *Texts*, 169–70; cf. Rowen, *Low Countries*, 73–4. On the complex historical origins and context of this article, which was drafted and revised over a period of more than a year, see De Jong, "Union and Religion."

of Arras, they both acknowledged Philip's overlordship and accepted his *national* and thoroughly *prescriptive* solution to the "problem" of religion: the complete and exclusive restoration of the Roman Catholic Church. Indeed, these were the first negotiated "articles of peace" that embraced *religious exclusion* as a template for religious peace.

The members of the Union of Utrecht were equally keen to preserve their provincial privileges, but they formally abandoned all pretense of a national religious settlement: the powerful provinces of Holland and Zeeland were free, according to article 13, to "act at their own discretion," while the other provinces were free to act either alone or together, thereby devolving sovereign decision-making authority in the matter of religion to the provinces severally, as the *Religionsfriede* had done in Germany at the expense of Charles V's claims to enforce unity and purity. Although the *Paix de Religion*, by which the Prince of Orange had promoted his vision of a French-style national policy of *religious inclusion*, remained an option for the "other" provinces, Holland and Zeeland had bargained hard to exempt themselves from its requirement to restore Roman Catholic worship.[70] Still, there were important elements of the *Paix de Religion* that remained implicit in article 13 of the Union of Utrecht. On the one hand, article 13 enjoined the other provinces to choose either the *Paix de Religion* in its entirety or to adopt "such regulations as they consider proper for the peace and welfare of the provinces, towns, and their particular members and for *the preservation of the properties and rights of all people, whether lay or clerical*" [emphasis mine], as was the spirit of the *Paix*. On the other hand, the last clause of the article – that is, "provided that in accordance with the Pacification of Ghent, each individual enjoys freedom of religion and no one is persecuted or questioned about his religion" – was anything but an afterthought. Although this was a very generous gloss on the fifth article of the Pacification of Ghent, which had only suspended the heresy laws for a time, "freedom of religion" for "each individual" was the product of hard bargaining, and it eventually became the touchstone of the Dutch Republic's fabled history of religious pluralism.

At the time of their adoption, in 1579, no one could have imagined or intended that the Treaty of Arras and the Union of Utrecht would be the last official words "concerning the matter of religion" in the Low Countries. Yet by the time Farnese completed the conquest of the Calvinist "republics" in the cities of Flanders and Brabant in 1585, two distinct polities had begun to emerge in the Low Countries, each with its own distinctive template for religious peace. In the southern provinces, the reassertion and active enforcement of the exclusive position of the Roman Catholic Church, in accordance with the Treaty of Arras, entailed the revival of the hated inquisitorial courts to

---

[70] Indeed, William of Orange was so disappointed with article 13 that he refused to sign off on the Union of Utrecht for several months, until it was clear that there was little hope of reconciliation with the Catholic members of the Union of Arras; see De Jong, "Union and Religion," 44–5.

enforce religious unity and purity.[71] As we saw in Chapter 5, this precipitated yet another massive migration of religious dissidents, many of them to the north.

Meanwhile, in the United Provinces in the north, the consolidation of provincial authority "concerning the matter of religion" also produced, in the context of ongoing struggle, a formally exclusionary outcome. Although the Union of Utrecht enjoined all of the member provinces to ensure "freedom of religion" for individuals, the prospect of an exclusionary Protestant regime, on the Holland/Zeeland model, was clearly problematic for the rebel's efforts to build a broad political coalition against Spain. Thus, a supplementary explanation of article 13, adopted just three days after the Union was signed, insisted that "it has never been and is not now their purpose and intention to exclude from the union and alliance any towns or provinces which want to maintain the Roman Catholic religion exclusively and where the number of residents belonging to the Reformed religion is too small to enable them to enjoy, by virtue of the Religious Peace, the right to exercise the Reformed Religion."[72] The latter gesture toward inclusion, apparently intended to attract the Walloon provinces to the Union of Utrecht, was to no avail as the Spanish authorities consolidated their counteralignment with the southern provinces. Following the formal renunciation of Philip II's sovereignty in 1581, then, even the modest recommendation of the inclusive terms of the *Paix de Religion* was not, in fact, heeded in any of the northern provinces. One by one the provinces that joined the Union of Utrecht adopted instead the exclusionary model of Holland and Zeeland, thereby establishing the Reformed Church as the exclusive public church throughout the United Provinces.[73]

THE DYNAMICS OF SEPARATION

What can we learn about the dynamics of religious peacemaking from the experience of the Low Countries between 1560 and 1585? What kind of religious peace was possible in the absence of a comprehensive, negotiated settlement "concerning the matter of religion"? If the French royal government's default position in the course of seven wars and as many edicts of pacification was the recognition of multiple confessions in a single polity, the Spanish royal government's default position was its steadfast enforcement of

[71] Aline Goosens, *Les Inquisitions modernes dans les Pay-Bas méridionaux (1520–1633)*, 2 vols., Spiritualités et pensées libres (Bruxelles: Éditions de l'Université de Bruxelles, 1997–98).
[72] Cau, *Groot Placaatboek*, col. 17; the quotation is from Kossmann and Mellink, *Texts*, 153.
[73] See Jonathan I. Israel, *The Dutch Republic: Its Rise, Greatness, and Fall, 1477–1806*, The Oxford History of Early Modern Europe (Oxford: Clarendon Press, 1995), 196–205. For case studies of this process outside Holland, see W. Bergsma, *Tussen Gideonsbende en publieke kerk. Een studie over het gereformeerd protestantisme in Friesland, 1580–1650*, Fryske Histoaryske Rige 17 (Hilversum: Verloren, 1999), and Rients Reitsma, *Centrifugal and Centripetal Forces in the Early Dutch Republic. The States of Overijssel 1566–1600* (Amsterdam: Rodopi, 1982).

religious unity and purity. In the absence of a negotiated settlement, then, the people of the Low Countries were, in principle, at least, in a constant state of war, uninterrupted by the interludes of peace that the various French edicts had provided. Still, even as this long and bitter struggle changed the political and religious facts on the ground, the relational dynamics that recurrently made religious peace possible in Switzerland, Germany, and France were also operative in the Netherlands, especially in those areas where the ongoing war did not have a direct impact. In short, although Philip II's steadfast refusal to negotiate with "heretics" prevented the conclusion of a comprehensive agreement, the distinctive patterns of a religious peace in the Low Countries began to emerge well before the Twelve Year Truce was concluded.

The most obvious change in circumstances in the Low Countries between the 1560s and the 1580s was the institutionalized separation of the northern provinces from the southern provinces. Although the original strength of the evangelical reform movement had been in the cities of the south, the surprising military success and political survival of the Beggars in the cities of Holland and Zeeland in the 1570s began to shift the balance of both the resistance to "Spanish tyranny" and of the evangelical reform movement northward. The ratification of the Union of Utrecht in 1579 signaled the institutionalization of this geographic shift, but it still included the "Calvinist republic" in Ghent. The abjuration of Philip II's sovereignty by the northern provinces in 1581 formalized the divorce, though the rebels at first sought an alternative sovereign in France and England before going it alone in the late 1580s as the United Provinces of the Northern Netherlands. The other side of this complex interaction was, of course, the reconciliation of the southern provinces with Philip II by means of the Union and Treaty of Arras in 1579. The military success of the Spanish armies completed the consolidation of a delimited Spanish sovereignty in the south – that is, in the Walloon provinces of the southeast as well as the southern portions of Flanders and Brabant – with the conquest of the last of the rebellious Calvinist republics in 1584 and 1585 and the subsequent migration of evangelical "dissenters" to England, Germany, and especially the United Provinces of the Northern Netherlands.

Within the first twenty years of the Eighty Years War, then, clearly separate zones of Beggar and Spanish domination had begun to emerge in the Low Counties as a consequence of a war that brought neither victory nor defeat to either side. The borderlands between these zones and along the eastern frontier of the United Provinces remained the principal sites of coordinated destruction for many years to come, both before and after the Truce. Yet away from those frontiers, the dynamics that led recurrently toward (inter)national war did not necessarily negate or deflect the dynamics that might lead simultaneously toward religious peace, locally and regionally. Indeed, by the late 1580s, the distinctive patterns of religious peace in the Low Countries were becoming visible in both the northern provinces, where the Reformed Church was dominant, and the southern provinces, where the Catholic Church was dominant. Within the separate zones of Beggar/Reformed domination and Spanish/Catholic domination – that is, relatively removed from the coordinated destruction of the ongoing war – the familiar dynamics of negotiation, segregation, domination, and subversion combined differently than they had in Switzerland, Germany, and France to produce a distinctive framework for an enduring religious peace, even in the absence of a comprehensive agreement.

Clearly the primary mechanisms at work in the history of peacemaking in the Netherlands were *segregation* and *domination*. To be sure, the segregation of a Protestant north from a Catholic south as a consequence of an inconclusive international war was not what either side intended; on the contrary, those actors who recurrently pushed for the continuation of the war effort and eventual military victory – both the elite leaders of the broad military coalitions and the religious zealots on both sides of the enduring religious *polarization* – sought the political *and* religious reunification of all the provinces of Low Countries. Yet the broad, de facto segregation of the north from the south combined with the domination of a single religious confession in each zone to produce the basic framework for religious peace that was formally exclusionary throughout the Netherlands. This exclusionary template stood in sharp contrast, of course, with the formally inclusive framework for religious peace that had emerged simultaneously in France. As would become increasingly clear during and after the Twelve Year Truce, the domination of the Reformed Church in the United Provinces of the Northern Netherlands differed significantly in practice from the domination of the Catholic Church in southern provinces that remained subject to Spanish sovereignty. Still, it is striking that all of the Low Countries appeared to be moving toward a religious peace that was formally exclusionary.

As was also the case in France, *subversion* was a critical mechanism in the survival of subordinate religious groups in the Low Countries. Subversion had long been an essential part of the experience of the evangelical reform movement under nearly five decades of repression, and with the reestablishment of Spanish sovereignty in the southern provinces, this critical mechanism again became a routine counterpoint to the renewed domination of the Catholic Church. At the same time, when and where the Beggar coalition turned the tables and transformed the underground network of Reformed churches into an exclusive "public" church, subversion also recurrently and routinely abetted the "survival" of both Catholics and "other" Protestant or evangelical groups, such as Lutherans and Mennonites, who clearly remained outside the ranks of the Reformed faithful. We will return to a closer analysis of this "survival" process during and after the Truce in Chapter 8, but here it is important to note the peculiar combination of mechanisms – *segregation*, *domination*, and *subversion* – (re)producing separate zones of confessional domination simultaneously, not only in the north and the south in the Low Countries, but also in the northeast and southwest of France.

In retrospect, the principal difference in the dynamics of peacemaking in France and the Low Countries appears to be the relative prominence of direct national negotiations "concerning the matter of religion" in the French civil wars by comparison with the virtual absence of comparable negotiations in the Eighty Years War. Beginning in 1585, however, the recurrence of civil war in France and the continuation of war in the Low Countries obscured this fundamental difference and made it apparent that religious peace would remain elusive in both cases for more than a decade. In the next chapter, then, we will analyze the dynamics that finally brought these long-running conflicts to a more durable end around the turn of the seventeenth century and focus more clearly on the long-term consequences of these parallel yet strikingly different histories of peacemaking.

7

Ending War, Shaping Peace

> The war may last so long that not one of us will live to see peace, whatever our religion might be. With us it will be as it was with the children of Israel of whom few came to the promised land ... from this internal and civil war nothing good can come, but only destruction and the eclipse of the commonwealth.
>
> Henrich Knoppert, Zwolle, 1584

Durable peace was still a long time in coming in both France and the Low Countries in the mid-1580s. The death of Francis, duke of Alençon/Anjou, in June 1584 and the assassination of William of Orange just a month later signaled important transitions and intensifications in both the French and Dutch conflicts. The French wars, sparked by the uncompromising demands of the Catholic League, restarted in March 1585 with renewed intensity, and the Treaty of Nonsuch offered the Dutch rebels much-needed English support and a temporary reprieve from the Spanish counteroffensive in August 1585. To Henrich Knoppert, a learned patrician from Zwolle in the embattled Dutch province of Overijssel, it seemed as if death and destruction were the immediate fate and religious peace only the distant promise of a lost generation wandering in the desert of civil war.[1] Indeed, it would be another fourteen years and more than two decades until the fighting stopped in France and the Netherlands, respectively.

Still, the Peace and Edict of Nantes finally ended the eighth civil war in France in April 1598, and the Twelve Year Truce halted the long-running war in the Low Countries in April 1609. To be sure, even this cessation of coordinated destruction in France and the Low Countries was only temporary, inasmuch as the French wars resumed intermittently following the assassination of Henry IV in 1610, and the Dutch wars resumed following the expiration of the Truce in 1621. Nevertheless, the broad outlines of the Edict of

---

[1] Quoted in Rients Reitsma, *Centrifugal and Centripetal Forces in the Early Dutch Republic. The States of Overijssel 1566–1600* (Amsterdam: Rodopi, 1982), 204.

Nantes and the Twelve Year Truce were reaffirmed by the Peace/Edict of Alais (1629) and the first Treaty of Münster (1648). Together, then, these very different settlements – the Edict of Nantes and the Twelve Year Truce – afford us the opportunity to take stock of the dynamics of religious peacemaking in the second phase of Europe's religious wars – that is, prior to the Thirty Years War in Germany, beginning in 1618, and the civil wars in England, Scotland, and Ireland, beginning in 1638. So against the complex background of trial and error that we examined in Chapter 6, how did the Edict of Nantes and the Twelve Year Truce manage to disrupt or counteract the dynamics that sparked and sustained these seemingly endless wars? And what kind of religious peace did these critical bargains make possible?

PREPARING THE GROUND FOR PEACE

The Edict of Nantes was an enormously complex document, consisting of ninety-two public articles, amplified by fifty-six secret articles, and supplemented by two royal warrants (*brevets*).[2] According to the edict's prologue, the edict's overriding purpose was "to give to all our said subjects a general law, clear, pure, and absolute, by which they shall be governed with regard to all such differences which have hitherto sprung up, or may hereafter rise among them … and to establish among them a good and most lasting peace." The process by which the kingdom of France arrived at this "general law" was a long and difficult one, however. Noting "the frightful troubles, confusions, and disorders which prevailed at our accession to this kingdom," the edict's prologue actually describes, in Henry IV's royal voice, a two-staged process of pacification that produced it: "first, to undertake those things which

---

[2] There is a complete, modern, annotated edition of the text of the "Édit de Nantes en faveur de ceux de la religion prétendu réformée" and its supplements in Janine Garrisson, *L'Édit de Nantes. Texte présenté et annoté* (Biarritz: Atlantica/Société Henri IV, 1997). There is an English translation of the complete text in Roland Mousnier, *The Assassination of Henry IV: The Tyrannicide Problem and the Consolidation of the French Absolute Monarchy in the Early Seventeenth Century*, trans. Joan Spencer (New York: Scribner, 1973), appendix 4, 316–63; the translation of the public articles is from a seventeenth-century English publication (Edmund Everard, *The Great Pressures and Grievances of the Protestants in France* [London: T. Cockeril and R. Hartford, 1681]) while the secret articles and the royal *brevets* are newly translated. There is a new translation of the whole text in Richard L. Goodbar, ed., *The Edict of Nantes: Five Essays and a New Translation* (Bloomington, MN: The National Huguenot Society, 1998), 41–68.

In contrast with the previous French edicts, there is an enormous literature on the history and significance of the Edict of Nantes that this discussion can hardly do justice to. Among the many works occasioned by the 400th anniversary of the Edict in 1998, see for example Bernard Cottret, *L'Edit de Nantes: pour en finir avec les guerres de religion* (Paris: Perrin, 1997); Janine Garrisson, *L'Édit de Nantes. Chronique d'une paix attendue* (Paris: Fayard, 1998); Thierry Wanegffelen, *L'édit de Nantes: une histoire européenne de la tolérance du XVIe au XXe siècle* (Paris: Le Livre de poche, 1998); Michel Grandjean and Bernard Roussel, eds., *Coexister dans l'intolérance. L'édit de Nantes (1598)*, Histoire et Société, 37 (Geneva: Labor et Fides, 1998); and Ruth Whelan and Carol Baxter, eds., *Toleration and Religious Identity: The Edict of Nantes and Its Implications in France, Britain and Ireland* (Dublin: Four Courts Press, 2003).

could only be settled by force, and rather to suspend and put aside for a time all other matters which could and should be dealt with by reason and justice: such as the general differences of our subjects, and the particular ills of the more healthy parts of the state." Having "well and happily succeeded" in the first task, the king now expressed his "hope for equal success in what remains to be settled."[3] Before we consider how this "general law" made peace possible – that is, how it settled the "other matters which could and should be dealt with by reason and justice" – we will do well to explore the ways in which Henry had prepared the ground for "a good and most lasting peace" by addressing "those things that could only be settled by force."[4]

As we saw in Chapter 5, the last of the sixteenth-century wars in France was precipitated by the royal succession crisis following the death of Francis, duke of Anjou, in 1584, which left Henry of Navarre, the "Protector" of the broad Huguenot coalition, next in line to succeed the childless Henry III. By the summer of 1585, the Catholic partisans, who had joined together to form the *Sainte Union* (Catholic League), compelled Henry III to revoke all of the previous edicts of pacification and to forbid the practice of the "so-called Reformed religion" everywhere in France. In August 1589, after the king had executed the Guise-family leaders of the League and with the Catholic League in open revolt against the king, the succession crisis became dramatically more acute with the assassination of Henry III, which occasioned the Protestant Henry of Navarre's claim to the French throne as Henry IV. Clearly, making good on his claim to the throne and defeating his enemies in the *Sainte Union* ranked high among the matters that Henry thought "could only be settled by force" and thus had priority in the pacification process. But the coordinated destruction of war was not the only means by which Henry IV achieved these goals. On the contrary, in the years between 1590, when he was unable to force Paris, his capital, into submission, and 1598, when he concluded an agreement with the last of the leaders of the Catholic League to hold out against his authority, Henry very deliberately combined coercion with reconciliation to turn many of his religious enemies into allies or clients and, thus, to bring the coordinated destruction of the religious wars to an end.

Immediately following the death of Henry III, Henry of Navarre pledged to maintain the Catholic faith and to seek Catholic instruction, but he appeared to have little prospect of having his authority recognized by his Catholic enemies as long as he refused to renounce his Protestant faith. Amid the marginally shifting fortunes of an inconclusive war in July 1591, Henry may even have made matters worse when he issued the Edict of Mantes, which reinstated the previous edicts of pacification – the Edict of Poitiers (1577) as amended by the Edict of Fleix (1580) – recognizing freedom of conscience and limited freedom

[3] Garrisson, *L'Édit de Nantes*, 26–8; Goodbar, *Edict of Nantes*, 41–2.
[4] For a recent overview of this two-staged process, see Michel De Waele, *Réconcilier les français: Henri IV et la fin des troubles de religion, 1589–1598*, Les Collections de la République des lettres. Études (Québec: Presses de l'Université Laval, 2010).

of worship for the Protestants, although he simultaneously pledged again to maintain the Catholic faith.[5] The dynamics of the ongoing conflict changed dramatically, however, on July 25, 1593, when Henry IV renounced his Protestant faith and converted to Catholicism in a solemn ceremony in the cathedral at St. Denis.[6] Within days, he had concluded a general truce with Charles de Lorraine, duke of Mayenne, the new Guise-family leader of the Catholic League. Although the general truce quickly broke down and the war resumed, Henry IV was solemnly crowned king of France at Chartres on February 27, 1594, and he was able to reassert royal authority in Paris, for the first time since 1588, on March 22, 1594.

The remarkably lenient terms under which Henry IV accepted the submission of the city of Paris are emblematic of the policy of reconciliation that accompanied Henry's assertion of his royal authority vis-à-vis the power centers of the Catholic League. After the League-appointed governor of the city, Charles II, comte de Brissac, had opened the city's gates early in the morning of March 22, royal soldiers immediately occupied strategic positions throughout the city, and within hours the king entered the city in triumph and celebrated Mass at the cathedral of Notre Dame. He quickly assured League leaders who resided in the city that they would not be harmed if they did not resist, and he allowed several thousand soldiers under Spanish command to withdraw peacefully. In the coming days he not only performed acts of Catholic piety during Holy Week, but he reconfirmed the offices of most municipal officials and nearly all the officers of the *parlement*, which had opposed his succession to the throne. He even rewarded Brissac by promoting him to marshall of France. Only a small number of supposed ringleaders of the opposition were exiled from the city following its submission.[7] This pattern of leniency had emerged earlier with the submissions of Meaux (January 1) and Orleans (February 1), where the local Catholic League governors, who actively participated in the submission, were also rewarded with the marshall's baton; leniency would also recur in the submissions, in quick succession, of league cities such as Troyes, Rouen, and La Havre in March and April.

Henry IV applied the principle of "Peace with Honor" as well in his relations with the aristocratic leaders who had raised and/or commanded troops in opposition to his authority. Following the failure of the general truce with Mayenne, the royal government abandoned general negotiations with League leaders and instead confronted and/or negotiated with them *ad seriatim*, just as he did with the cities where the Catholic League had seized

---

[5] See N. M. Sutherland, *The Huguenot Struggle for Recognition* (New Haven: Yale University Press, 1980), 368–9; for the text of the Edict of Mantes, see André Stegmann, ed., *Édits des guerres de religion*, Textes et Documents de la Renaissance (Paris: J. Vrin, 1979), 229–36.

[6] Michael Wolfe, *The Conversion of Henri IV: Politics, Power, and Religious Belief in Early Modern France*, Harvard Historical Studies (Cambridge, MA; London: Harvard University Press, 1993).

[7] Wolfe, *Conversion of Henri IV*, 176–80.

power. According to Michael Wolfe, the many letters that Henry wrote to League leaders and the separate edicts that he issued following their submissions were infused with the language of *amitié* (friendship) and honor; indeed, the principal requirement of the peace treaties that Henry IV signed with his Catholic enemies was that they swear a public oath "before God and the king to observe the basic tenets of religion and morality established by the Crown." In return, his former enemies were usually confirmed in their honors and offices, offered exclusive guarantees for the Catholic faith in their immediate jurisdictions, and given enormous pensions or indemnities for their wartime losses.[8]

This is not to say that the process of pacification was entirely nonviolent and devoid of military peril. Appeasement worked to bring most League cities and many League nobles to submission, but not all. Among the League cities, Toulouse and Marseille, and among the League nobility, Philippe-Emmanuel de Lorraine, duke of Mercoeur, in Brittany and Jean-Louis de Nogaret de La Valette, duke of Epernon, in Provence, were prominent holdouts, at least for a time. But perhaps the most significant military threat to Henry IV was Philip II's open support of the Catholic League. Until its submission in 1594, the city of Paris, among others, had a significant garrison of Spanish soldiers, and in 1595, signs of a possible Spanish invasion from the Southern Netherlands provoked Henry to declare war on Spain. The Spanish occupation of the cities of Cambrai and Calais in 1596 and Amiens in the spring of 1597 represented a significant blow to Henry's military fortunes and caused him nearly to despair of finding peace. By the same token, the recovery of Amiens in September 1597 after a long and costly siege proved to be a turning point in the war and precipitated the submission of the duke of Mercoeur, the last of the Catholic League holdouts, in January 1598.[9]

The end of hostilities with the Catholic opposition to Henry's authority set the stage for the final negotiation of the Edict of Nantes with the Huguenot coalition. The Huguenots, too, represented a significant challenge for Henry and the pacification process, though his approach to them was strikingly different.[10] Henry of Navarre had been designated "Protector" of the Reformed churches and leader of the Huguenot coalition from 1576 onward, but in the midst of the royal succession crisis, that relationship obviously became strained. Henry's pledge to maintain Catholicism following the assassination of Henry III, his formal conversion to Catholicism and personal

---

[8] Wolfe, *Conversion of Henri IV*, 180–2. Wolfe notes, "Many of the treaties contained identically worded provisions worked out in earlier submissions, all of which demonstrated the king's decision after July 1593 to treat Catholics honorably after they swore him obedience" (181–2).

[9] Mack P. Holt, *The French Wars of Religion, 1562–1629*, New Approaches to European History (Cambridge: Cambridge University Press, 1995), 158–62; Sutherland, *Huguenot Struggle*, 311–20.

[10] See especially Sutherland, *Huguenot Struggle*, chapter 9: "The 'Protestant State' and the Edict of Nantes."

renunciation of Protestantism, and finally his coronation on February 27, 1594, as Henry IV, which included the traditional pledge to extirpate "heresy" – all of these steps were perceived as threats to their security by many Huguenot leaders. In 1591, Henry responded to the anxieties of his Protestant allies by issuing the Edict of Mantes, which reinstated the terms of the Edicts of Poitiers and Fleix, but the Protestants were soon demanding better terms and guarantees than those that had been offered and later revoked by Henry III. From 1593 onward, the Huguenot leadership, as represented in a series of Protestant assemblies – sometimes described as the Protestant "state within a state"[11] – began to insist on the negotiation of a new edict that would resolve the contradictions between the previous edicts and the many concessions that Henry was making to win the loyalty of his Catholic subjects.[12] Although the king tried to reassure the Protestants that he would deal with their urgent requests once he had defeated the challenges of the Catholic League and the king of Spain, the increasingly radical Protestant assemblies pushed back; they even declined to support Henry's efforts to retake Amiens in 1597, though they never openly broke with their "Protector" and never took up arms against him. Still, in the midst of this crisis in the relations between the Huguenot coalition and Henry IV, preliminary and secretive negotiations between representatives of the assembly and commissioners of the king laid the foundation for the provisions of the Edict of Nantes.[13]

In the course of the eighth civil war, then, we can see the operation of several of the by-now-familiar mechanisms that recurrently led toward religious peace. A very potent combination of military *domination* and amicable/honorable *negotiation* characterized Henry IV's pacification process vis-à-vis the Catholic League and its Spanish allies. Instead of treating the various municipal and noble leaders of the Catholic League as traitors who were in league with a traditional enemy of France, Henry hoped, in the words of Michael Wolfe, "to conquer the realm with kindness, which he meted out in measured doses" as he dealt with domestic enemies one by one over a period of years.[14] At the same time, he was uncompromising in his military efforts to remove Spanish garrisons from French territory. Although open military competition never characterized Henry's relations with the Huguenot coalition, political *domination* was clearly evident as Henry recurrently held off his Protestant "allies" with promises of future negotiations – once he had resolved "those things which could only be settled by force." At the same time, the leaders of the Huguenot coalition in the Protestant assembly worked hard to *subvert* the worst effects of the submission edicts that punctuated Henry's

---

[11] See Janine Garrisson, *Les Protestants du Midi, 1559–98* (Toulouse: Privat, 1980), and Henry Heller, *Iron and Blood: Civil Wars in Sixteenth-Century France* (Montreal: McGill-Queens University Press, 1991), especially chapter 3: "The Huguenot Republic."

[12] The Protestant Assembly at Sainte-Foy in June 1594 even seriously considered electing an alternative protector; see Sutherland, *Huguenot Struggle*, 303–5.

[13] Sutherland, *Huguenot Struggle*, 321–8.   [14] Wolfe, *Conversion of Henri IV*, 180.

pacification of the Catholic League, and recurrently demanded negotiations for new and better guarantees from their nominal "Protector." Finally, the forceful *segregation* of the remnants of the Catholic League from their Spanish patrons complemented the ongoing *segregation* of Protestants from Catholics in increasingly defined zones of relative strength.[15] Thus, the operation of all these mechanisms served mightily to prepare the ground for peace in the final negotiation of the Peace and Edict of Nantes in the spring of 1598.

"A GENERAL LAW, CLEAR, PURE AND ABSOLUTE"

Against the backdrop of nearly four decades of war making and peacemaking, it will hardly be surprising to suggest that the Edict of Nantes did not break dramatically new ground in addressing those "matters which could and should be dealt with by reason and justice." Indeed, in specifying "a general law, clear, pure and absolute," the public articles of the edict adhered closely to the model of the precedent edicts, especially the Edict of Poitiers (1577), plus its modifications in the Treaty of Nèrac (1579) and the Edict of Fleix (1580).[16] The first three articles of the Edict of Nantes echoed precisely the first three articles of the Edict of Poitiers: These consisted of the amnesty and amnesia clauses, quoted at the beginning of Chapter 6, as well as the article, repeated consistently since the Edict of Saint-Germain (1570), commanding the restoration of the "Catholic, Apostolic and Roman religion" where it had been discontinued. Likewise, the sixth article repeated the precise formulation of the freedom of conscience clause in the fourth article of the edicts of both Saint-Germain and Poitiers:

And in order to leave no occasion for troubles and differences among our subjects, we have permitted and do permit those of the so-called Reformed religion to live and dwell in all cities and places within this our kingdom ... without being questioned, vexed, or molested, nor constrained to do anything with regard to religion contrary to their conscience, nor on account of it to be searched out in their houses or places where they wish to dwell, bearing themselves otherwise according to what is in our present edict.[17]

Thus, it is clear from the outset that the royal policy of embracing religious coexistence as the foundation of political reconciliation remained firm and that there were to be no heresy trials or coercion of individuals in matters of religious belief.

[15] This was certainly the effect of Henry's assurances of exclusive Catholic worship in the immediate vicinity of former League strongholds, which as the Protestants were well aware undermined the guarantees of the edicts of Poitiers and Fleix.

[16] See Gregory Champeaud, "The Edict of Poitiers and the Treaty of Nérac, or Two Steps Towards the Edict of Nantes," *Sixteenth Century Journal* 32, no. 2 (2001): 319–34. Champeaud argues that the similarities between the Edict of Poitiers, plus the Treaty of Nérac, which clarified and confirmed it, and the Edict of Nantes were due, in part at least, to the personal involvement of Henry of Navarre (Henry IV) in these difficult negotiations.

[17] Garrisson, *L'Édit de Nantes*, 31; Goodbar, *Edict of Nantes*, 43.

Similarities of language are also evident in many of the articles concerning civil rights and the reconciliation of former combatants. For example, "those of the Reformed religion" were again granted equal access to all offices and ranks (Poiters: article 19; Nantes: article 27) as well as to educational institutions and hospitals (Poiters: article 15; Nantes: articles 13, 22). In addition, "Those of the said Religion may not in the future be surcharged or burdened more than the Catholics with any ordinary or extraordinary charges, according to their goods and faculties" (Poiters: article 45; Nantes: article 74).[18] Elaborating the amnesty and amnesia clauses, the Edict of Nantes also closely followed the precedents of the Edict of Poitiers, and other prior edicts, in establishing a kind of civil parity: the liberation of prisoners of war (Poiters: article 39; Nantes: article 73); the legal rehabilitation of various combatants and parties to the conflict (Poiters: article 38; Nantes: articles 58, 59); the cancellation of debts incurred by the Huguenots (Poiters: article 55; Nantes: article 76); and the return of stolen property (Poiters: articles 42, 43, 44; Nantes: article 69). Here the emphasis was, again, on eliminating obvious points of contention and sources of tension.

It is also hardly surprising that in 1598 the deeply contentious issue of public worship in the Reformed manner remained deeply contentious. Abandoning the extreme formulations of the Edict of Boulogne (1573) – no public Reformed worship, even where it had previously been established – and the Edict of Beaulieu (1576) – public Reformed worship everywhere, even where it had never before been established – the Edict of Nantes, like the Edicts of Amboise (1563), Saint-Germain (1570), and Poitiers (1577), tried to balance the prescriptions of "a general law" applicable throughout the kingdom with the acceptance of varied and often messy facts on the ground. The result was, once again, a complex but generally familiar template for the *limited* exercise of Reformed worship in public:

1. Unlimited worship on the estates of the high nobility; limited private worship on the estates of lesser nobles (articles 7, 8).
2. "We also permit those of the said religion to undertake and continue its exercise in all towns and places in our obedience where it had been established by them, and publicly performed at different times in the year 1596, and before the end of August 1597, notwithstanding all decisions and judgements to the contrary" (article 9).[19]
3. "Likewise the said exercise shall be established and re-established in all villages and places where it has been established or should have been established by the Edict of Pacification, passed in the year 1577 [Poitiers], by secret articles and the conferences of Nèrac and Fleix" (article 10).[20]

[18] Garrisson, *L'Édit de Nantes*, 60; Goodbar, *Edict of Nantes*, 54.
[19] Garrisson, *L'Édit de Nantes*, 32–3; the quotation is adapted from Goodbar, *Edict of Nantes*, 44.
[20] Garrisson, *L'Édit de Nantes*, 33; the quotation is adapted from Goodbar, *Edict of Nantes*, 44.

4. In each of the administrative districts (*bailliages* or *sénéchaussées*), "we ordain that in the faubourgs of one city, other than those which have been granted to them by the [previous agreements], and where there are not cities, in a small town or village, the exercise of the said so-called Reformed religion may be publicly performed by all those who may wish to go there" (article 11).[21]

The public articles of the Edict of Nantes retained the prohibition of public Reformed worship in the army (article 15), at court (article 14), and in the vicinity of Paris (article 14), but the edict opened up the limitations on public worship established in the Edict of Poitiers in two ways: by establishing two dates (1577 and 1596–1597) as reference points for the restoration or continuation of Reformed worship;[22] and by adding a second city per administrative district and allowing worship in any town or village where there was interest. Finally, although "they shall also be obliged to keep and observe the feasts prescribed in the Roman, Catholic, and Apostolic Church" (article 20) – that is, the Reformed could not open their shops or ply their trades on Catholic feast days – "we permit those of the said religion to build places for the exercise of it [i.e., churches or temples] in the towns and places where it has been granted them" (article 16).[23]

The Edict of Nantes also addressed the legal insecurities of the Huguenots at great length, and in this, it departed somewhat from precedent. The Edict of Beaulieu had introduced the concept of *chambres mi-parties* – special biconfessional courts comprised of equal numbers of Protestants and Catholic judges – to prevent discrimination in cases involving litigants of the different confessions (articles 18–21). The Edict of Poitiers had adopted the same strategy of creating special courts, but had abandoned the biconfessional principle by reducing the number of Protestant judges (articles 21–24), and the Treaty of Nérac continued to wrestle with the problem of impartial justice, devoting seven of its twenty-six articles to the problem.[24] The Edict of Nantes revived the biconfessional principle in the composition of the special courts, now called *chambres de l'Édit*, and took great care to resolve a variety of procedural and legal issues attendant to them. Indeed, the thirtieth article, which was the first of no less than thirty-eight articles devoted to the question of justice, asserted that "justice ... given and administered to our subjects without any suspicion, hatred or favor ... [is] one of the principal means of maintaining them in

[21] Garrisson, *L'Édit de Nantes*, 33–34; the quotation is adapted from Goodbar, *Edict of Nantes*, 44.
[22] In this sense, the Edict of Nantes was not merely an acceptance of facts on the ground, but a specification of principles that commanded adjustments of the (negative) effects of the last war.
[23] Garrisson, *L'Édit de Nantes*, 35–7; the quotations are adapted from Goodbar, *Edict of Nantes*, 45. Local authorities were also enjoined to provide the Reformed appropriate places for the burial of their dead.
[24] See Stegmann, *Édits*, 102–4, 137–8, 158–70; cf. Champeaud, "Edict of Poitiers," 329.

peace and concord."[25] As it happened, these *chambres de l'Édit*, combined with the special commissioners that the royal government revived from previous practice, were critical to the long-term enforcement of the pacification after 1598.

Like the Edicts of Beaulieu and Poitiers, the Edict of Nantes was supplemented by a series of secret articles. Generally, secret articles, according to N. M. Sutherland, "dealt with executive matters" and "tended to amplify the first set, often in terms favorable to the Protestants."[26] Their principal virtue was that they were not part of the public documents that were required to be published by the regional *parlements*, which frequently objected to important elements of the edicts of pacification that favored the Huguenots. As was usual, then, many of the fifty-six secret articles amplified the obligations, exemptions, and protections of the Reformed communities – freedom of conscience for Protestant clergy and teachers, ringing of church bells, operating schools, religious instruction of children, raising money for church expenses, providing adequate cemeteries, and the like – in response to concerns raised by the Huguenots. But a long series of twenty-three secret articles (articles 11–33, or some forty percent of the secret articles) also clarified the limits on public Reformed worship, apparently in response to Catholic demands. In the course of his military and diplomatic campaign against his foes in the Catholic League, as we have seen, Henry IV had negotiated agreements with many of the defeated leaders banning Reformed worship in their jurisdictions. In fact, article 12 of the public articles affirmed the continued validity of those agreements in general: "[T]he edicts and agreements formerly made for the submission of any princes, lords, gentlemen, and Catholic towns ... in what concerns the exercise of the said religion ... shall be kept and observed."[27] But the secret articles reaffirmed these agreements one by one, in effect instructing the commissioners enforcing the edict as the twelfth article had promised. In this sense, the secret articles were clearly responsive to the concerns of both religious communities.

The two royal *brevets*, by contrast, were dramatic concessions to the Huguenots: temporary, to be sure, but dramatic nevertheless. The first was dated the third day of April 1598, nearly a month before the public proclamation of the edict; in it, the king, "wishing to gratify his subjects of the so-called Reformed religion, and in order to aid them in meeting some great expenses they have to support," provided for a royal grant, payable quarterly, in "the sum of 45,000 *ecus*, to be employed in certain secret matters which concern them which His Majesty does not wish to be specified or declared."[28]

---

[25] Garrisson, *L'Édit de Nantes*, 40; the quotation is adapted from Goodbar, *Edict of Nantes*, 46. The articles (30–67) concerned with justice, and the *chambres de l'Édit* in particular, constituted more than forty percent of the ninety-two public articles in the edict.

[26] Sutherland, *Huguenot Struggle*, 371.

[27] Garrisson, *L'Édit de Nantes*, 34; Goodbar, *Edict of Nantes*, 44.

[28] Garrisson, *L'Édit de Nantes*, 91; Goodbar, *Edict of Nantes*, 65.

According to Janine Garrisson, this expenditure was not as "confidential" as the document's language suggested; rather, these funds were the product of a long negotiation between royal commissioners and the Protestant assembly and were intended to pay the salaries or stipends of Protestant pastors, professors, and students of theology.[29] Since the Protestants were required by the Edict of Nantes as well as earlier edicts to pay the tithe in support of the Catholic Church – much more an attribute of property relations than a pious contribution, even for Catholics – this royal grant was deemed a reasonable, if also volatile, concession, one that was surely objectionable to many Catholics.

The second *brevet*, which was dated on the last day of April 1598, was even more striking and costly to the king: It allowed a continued military presence in approximately 200 cities/towns held by the Huguenot coalition at the end of the war.[30] In approximately 100 of these cites, which had previously been garrisoned, the cost of the garrison would be paid for by an annual royal subsidy of 180,000 *ecus* (or 540,000 *livres tournois*, an enormous sum), with the provision of additional funding as necessary.[31] In all the others, urban militias, recruited from the local populations, would provide security. On the face of it, this *brevet* might seem to reinforce the reality of a Protestant "state within a state" inasmuch as the *places de sûreté*, which had recurrently been granted to the Huguenots since the Edict of Saint-Germain in 1570, clearly undermined the state's monopoly on coercive force. Now, however, they were not only reaffirmed but dramatically expanded in number. Still, on closer examination, this striking financial concession to the Huguenot also served to undermine the political independence of the Huguenot coalition.

Article 82 of the public articles had specifically addressed the issue of Protestant independence within the French state:

Also, those of the said religion shall cease and desist immediately from all illicit maneuvers, negotiations, and intelligence, both within and outside our kingdom, and the said assemblies and councils established in the provinces shall dissolve themselves promptly . . . ; forbidding our subjects very expressly to make henceforth any assessments and levies of funds without our permission, or fortifications, enrollments of men, congregations and assemblies, other than those permitted by our present edict, and without arms.[32]

Clearly this article was intended to dismantle the political and military institutions of the semi-independent "United Provinces of the Midi" – not only the assemblies that had recurrently bargained with the royal government, but the financial mechanisms by which the Huguenots had sustained their

---

[29] Garrisson, *L'Édit de Nantes*, 122–3, note 130.
[30] Garrisson, *L'Édit de Nantes*, 93–8; Goodbar, *Edict of Nantes*, 66–8.
[31] Even this provision of the second *brevet*, which on the face of it would have been anathema to zealous Catholics, was not entirely new. In fact, the secret articles of the Edict of Poitiers had also provided for royal financing of Huguenot garrisons as well as their German mercenaries; see Chapter 6, pp. 139–40, in this volume.
[32] Garrisson, *L'Édit de Nantes*, 66; Goodbar, *Edict of Nantes*, 56–7.

regional independence from the state. To provide, nevertheless, for 200 *places de sûreté* to allay the very real security concerns of the Protestants, as the second *brevet* did, would not undermine that goal as long as royal financing obviated the need for independent institutions and illicit levies. In this sense the second *brevet* complemented article 82 of the public articles and supported the process of segregating the Protestants' worshipping congregations, which the edict legitimated, from the political and military leadership that had sustained the civil wars, which the edict proscribed.[33]

Together, the two secret *brevets* represented significant financial concessions to the Huguenot negotiators, but they at the same time dramatically reinforced the Reformed churches' collective dependence on their royal protector. In this sense, they also clearly complemented the pacification strategy that Henry IV had used in relation to his former Catholic enemies: using (financial) generosity and attention to honor to establish their personal dependence on their royal patron. Thus, while the specific provisions of the Edict of Nantes did not break dramatically new ground – not even the secret articles or the *brevets* – the way they addressed "matters which could and should be dealt with by reason and justice" was a fitting culmination of a larger history of peacemaking, complete with an array of lessons learned, as well as an important complement to the process of pacification, which had addressed "those things which could only be settled by force."

In its broader comparative context, then, the Edict of Nantes made peace possible, in the first instance, by recreating or reaffirming the essential principles of peacemaking that had been evident in the Swiss and German settlements, as well as the earlier French edicts: recognition of multiple faith communities within a single polity, provision of security to all parties to the agreement, and commitment to legal processes and mediation to resolve outstanding issues and future disagreements. But in combination with Henry's pacification strategy, the Edict of Nantes also accomplished, at least for a time, what previous agreements had not succeeded in doing: it disrupted the specific mechanisms that had recurrently led back to war in France by dismantling the larger, *brokered* coalitions that had linked rival religious communities and networks with specialists in coercion. That the king had used "bribes," or more precisely enormous financial incentives, both personal and corporative, to accomplish the goal of neutralizing the Protestant and Catholic warlords should by no means diminish our appreciation of this effect.

In the wake of the Edict of Nantes, local conflicts continued to *activate* the Reformed/Catholic identity boundary on a regular basis, and the networks of religious solidarity could still enable the *escalation* of a local conflict into a larger regional or national cause, and *polarization* across the Reformed/

---

[33] The second *brevet* did secretly concede that a truncated Protestant Assembly of just ten delegates could continue to meet until the provisions of the Edict of Nantes were executed, though they were prohibited from making new demands beyond the execution of the edict. Garrisson, *L'Édit de Nantes*, 97–8; Goodbar, *Edict of Nantes*, 68.

Catholic identity boundary frequently made active cooperation or collaboration among local faith communities difficult, if not impossible. Yet, in addition to the negotiation and subversion that had been most evident in earlier, less successful edicts, the political *segregation* of the warlords – from one another and from the larger religious networks – in combination with the political and financial *domination* of the king served mightily to make a durable, if messy, national peace possible.

FROM SURVIVAL TO "INDEPENDENCE"

The process of ending war in the Low Countries was significantly different from the pacification process that Henry IV embarked on in France; indeed, in some senses it was both a simpler and a more difficult process. As was the case in France, there were a number of changes from the mid-1580s onward that altered the prospects for a negotiated settlement prior to the conclusion of a cease-fire agreement in 1607 and the Twelve Year Truce in 1609. In the Low Countries, however, these changes entailed, first, the survival of the rebel provinces in a long-running and costly war and, in the long run, their emergence as an independent republic and a military and economic power within and beyond Europe. In these changing circumstances, negotiating a settlement became a more straightforward process of bargaining between two independent state actors, but the issues that divided the parties to the agreement also expanded significantly.

As we saw in Chapter 5, following the departure of the Earl of Leicester in 1588, the United Provinces no longer sought a princely protector abroad and instead continued their military struggle with Spain on their own. Although their independence was anything but assured, the combined leadership of Johan van Oldenbarnevelt and Maurits of Nassau eventually brought both internal political stability and international military success. As *Advocaat* (chancellor or spokesperson) of the most populous and prosperous province of Holland, Oldenbarnevelt led the rebel provinces through the contentious process of establishing the stable institutions and political culture of republican governance – institutions and practices that balanced the interests of provincial autonomy with the leadership of Holland via the Estates General.[34] As military commander and *Stadhouder* (governor or viceroy) of the key provinces of Holland and Zeeland,[35] Maurits, the young son of William of Orange, led the

[34] For a general survey of this process of consolidation, see Jonathan I. Israel, *The Dutch Republic: Its Rise, Greatness, and Fall, 1477–1806*, The Oxford History of Early Modern Europe (Oxford: Clarendon Press, 1995), 233–40; see also Marjolein 't Hart, *The Making of a Bourgeois State: War, Politics and Finance During the Dutch Revolt* (Manchester: Manchester University Press, 1993), and Jan den Tex, *Oldenbarnevelt*, trans. R. B. Powell (Cambridge: Cambridge University Press, 1973). For an example of how this process unfolded in a relatively small and under-developed province, see Reitsma, *States of Overijssel*.

[35] Maurits was appointed *Stadhouder* of Holland and Zeeland in 1585 by the rebellious provincial estates as opposed to the royal sovereign who had created the position to streamline his relations

transformation of the Dutch army, doubling and eventually tripling the number of men under arms and emphasizing both mobility and discipline in their deployment.[36] Despite some serious military setbacks in 1588–1589, the new republic's armies gained considerable ground on the southern and eastern frontiers in the 1590s, capturing Breda in the south (1590), Groningen in the north (1594), and Grol and Lingen in the east (1597).[37]

By the time that Henry IV promulgated the Edict of Nantes in 1598, then, the loosely confederated United Provinces of the Northern Netherlands had emerged as a significant military power, capable of challenging Philip II's fabled Army of Flanders on its own terms. The death of Philip II in 1598, however, brought significant political changes to the "obedient provinces" in the southern Netherlands as well. Under the provisions of Philip's will, the southern provinces were assigned to Philip's sister Isabella and her husband Albert, the Austrian Archduke. As joint rulers in Brussels, the "Archdukes," as they were known, were nominally sovereign but remained fundamentally dependent on Spanish revenues and soldiers, which remained under the command of officers who swore their allegiance to Philip III of Spain. With the support of their Spanish patrons, Albert and Isabella began their reign with a stunning peace overture in 1599: they were willing to accept many of the political and religious changes in the northern provinces if the rebel provinces recognized the Archdukes' *de jure* sovereignty and made concessions to Catholic worship. Although Oldenbarnevelt and Maurits were opposed to any compromise on the questions of sovereignty and Catholic worship, they nevertheless engaged for a time in secret negotiations that made it seem as if peace might actually be possible.

At the same time, the United Provinces were undergoing a dramatic social and economic transformation, in many ways at the expense of the southern provinces, which culminated in their so-called Golden Age.[38] Between the 1560s and the 1620s more than 150,000 religious refugees, mostly from the provinces of Flanders and Brabant in the south migrating to the cities of the provinces of Holland and Zeeland in the north, reduced the populations of once-prosperous cities such as Antwerp, Ghent, Mechelen, and Bruges by half. On the receiving end, it helped to double and even treble the populations of

---

with the provinces; after 1590 Maurits was appointed *Stadhouder* of Utrecht, Overijssel, and Gelderland as well.

[36] The standing army increased from 21,000 in 1588 to 32,000 in 1595 and more than 60,000 in 1607, at the time of the cease fire; see figure 2.1 in Hart, *The Making of a Bourgeois State*, 43. See also Geoffrey Parker, *The Dutch Revolt*, rev. ed. (Harmondsworth: Penguin, 1985) and Geoffrey Parker, *The Military Revolution: Military Innovation and the Rise of the West, 1500–1800* (Cambridge: Cambridge University Press, 1988).

[37] See Israel, *The Dutch Republic*, 241–53, especially the map of recovered territory on p. 243.

[38] See especially Jan de Vries and Ad van der Woude, *The First Modern Economy: Success, Failure, and Perseverance of the Dutch Economy, 1500–1815* (Cambridge: Cambridge University Press, 1997) and Jonathan I. Israel, *Dutch Primacy in World Trade, 1585–1740* (Oxford: Clarendon Press, 1989).

Middelburg, Leiden, Haarlem, and Amsterdam; indeed, by 1600, one-third of the population of Amsterdam and as much as two-thirds of Leiden were migrants from the south.[39] This massive migration of people, capital, and skills from the south to the north, especially in the period 1585 to 1589, had two principal effects on the religious politics of the Low Countries. On the one hand, it accentuated the religious segregation of an officially Catholic south from an officially Protestant north, though the politically dominant Calvinists remained a minority in the Dutch Republic. On the other hand, the influx of so many religious refugees in the north bolstered the political constituency for the uncompromising policy goal of "liberating" the southern provinces militarily from Spanish "tyranny."

The simultaneous diversification and expansion of the Dutch economy was enabled as well by the rapid growth of maritime trade, often at the expense of Spanish, Portuguese, and Flemish traders, that helped to establish Dutch primacy in world trade for nearly a century and a half.[40] A renewed Spanish embargo in 1598 of Dutch ships, merchants, and goods in Spain and Portugal, in particular, spurred expansion of direct Dutch trade with the East Indies, which culminated in the chartering of the East India Company (*Verenigde Oostindische Compagnie*, or VOC) by the Estates General in 1602. Complementing the prosperous Dutch carrying trade with the Baltics, the stunning rise of the so-called rich trades with the East Indies, Africa, and the Americas firmly established the importance of the Dutch *entrepôt*, but at the same time greatly complicated the challenge of ending the war, which was becoming increasingly costly for both sides.

In the short term, the failure of the Archdukes' peace initiate was followed by a new Dutch military offensive into Flanders in the summer of 1600. A Dutch victory at Nieuwpoort, which confirmed the importance of their new military methods, was nevertheless followed by four years of military stalemate, and culminated in the loss of Ostend, the last Dutch stronghold on the Flemish coast, after a long Spanish siege, in 1604. In addition, a stunning counterattack by Ambrosio Spinola, commander of the Spanish Army of Flanders, captured the fortresses at Oldenzaal, Lingen, and Groll on the eastern frontier in 1605 and 1606. In September 1606, Oldenbarnevelt argued that the enormous costs of the war were making the financial position of the republic untenable, while Philip III, also under severe financial pressure, resolved to concede sovereignty to the rebel provinces and urged the Archdukes to undertake negotiations on that basis.[41]

Once the decision had been taken to treat the United Provinces "as if" they were independent, the process of ending the war became a good deal simpler.

---

[39] J. G. C. A. Briels, *Zuid-Nederlanders in de republiek 1572–1630: Een demographische en cultuurhistorische studie* (Sint-Niklaas: Uitgeverij Danthe, 1985), esp. chapter 3, 211–28.

[40] For a brief introduction to this remarkable transformation in European and world trade, see Israel, *The Dutch Republic*, 307–27.

[41] See Israel, *The Dutch Republic*, chapter 17.

Negotiators representing two statelike actors – Oldenbarnevelt for the United Provinces and Spinola for the Archdukes and Spain – could quickly arrange a cease fire in April 1607 based on the Archdukes' declared willingness (March 1607) "to negotiate with the Estates General of the United Netherlands ... considering them as free lands, provinces and States."[42] Although the cease-fire agreement entailed no specific, written concessions from the Dutch in exchange for their anticipated independence, formal talks resumed at The Hague in February 1608 in anticipation of the conclusion of a permanent peace, or at least an armistice or truce for a period of up to twenty years.

At this point, however, two major issues stood in the way of a durable end to the war: "the matter of religion," which remained a deeply contentious issue, had been seriously compounded by the question of trade with the Indies. From 1605 onward, the VOC had been making its first major inroads in the East Indies by countering or displacing the Spanish military presence in several key "Spice Islands" in the Moluccan archipelago, and plans were being made to form a new West India Company (WIC) to compete in the New World.[43] Meanwhile, the United Provinces had demonstrated their considerable naval power by sailing directly into the Bay of Gibraltar in April 1607 and destroying a fleet of more than twenty Spanish ships. In return for independence and a permanent peace, the Archdukes and the Spanish were demanding the dissolution of the VOC, the abortion of plans for the WIC, *and* toleration of public Catholic worship in the United Provinces. Given the political impossibility of gaining acceptance of these demands in the United Provinces, the negotiators had little choice but to bargain instead for a temporary truce. After direct talks in The Hague broke down in 1608, the negotiations resumed in Antwerp, with French and British mediation, leading finally to the promulgation of the Twelve Year Truce on April 9, 1609.[44]

THE DYNAMICS OF A "TEMPORARY" TRUCE

If the purpose of the French Edict of Nantes was to structure a durable religious peace, once the coordinated destruction of the Eighth War had ended, the purpose of the Twelve Year Truce was, quite simply, to bring more than four decades of intermittent and very costly war to an end, without specifying a clear template for the future. Consequently, the thirty-eight public articles of the Twelve Year Truce are as notable for what they do not specifically address as for

---

[42] Quoted in Israel, *The Dutch Republic*, 401.
[43] On the plans for a West India Company in 1606, see Henk den Heijer, "The Twelve Years' Truce and the Founding of the Dutch West India Company," *Halve Maen* 80, no. 4 (Winter 2007): 67–70; see also, Henk den Heijer, *De geschiedenis van de WIC* (Zutphen: Walburg, 1994).
[44] For an account of these negotiation, see Frances Gardiner Davenport, ed., *European Treaties Bearing on the History of the United States and Its Dependencies* (Washington, DC: Carnegie Institution of Washington, 1917–37), vol. 1, 258–63.

the principles they actually articulate.[45] Indeed, given the fact that the most contentious issues dividing the two parties to the negotiation – that is, the issues on which they had difficulty finding the kind of mutually acceptable compromise necessary to conclude a permanent peace – were the "matter of religion" and trade with the East and West Indies, it is perhaps not surprising that the text of this "temporary" agreement does not actually mention either "religion" or the "Indies."

In order to end the coordinated destruction of the war, the first four articles of the Twelve Year Truce addressed four basic issues. In the first, the Archdukes repeated their public declaration that they would negotiate with the Estates General of the United Provinces as "free lands, provinces, and Estates, against whom they make no claims." With the de facto independence of the United Provinces thus assured, the second article specified:

that the said truce will be in force and observed strictly, faithfully, and inviolably for the time of twelve years, during which there will be a halt to all acts of enmity between the said king, Archdukes, and the Estates General, at sea and in other waterways as well as on land in all their realms, provinces, lands, and lordships, and between all their subjects and residents of all conditions and qualities, with no exception of places or persons.

Article 3 articulated the essential political principle on which the Truce was founded: "Each party will remain in occupation and effective possession of the countries, towns, places, lands, and lordships which he holds and possesses at present." Derived from ancient Roman law, this possession principle – *uti possidetis, ita possideatis*, meaning roughly "as you possessed, you shall

---

[45] The Dutch text of the truce – "Tractaet van 't Bestant" – is printed in Cornelius Cau, ed., *Groot placaatboek, vervattende de placaaten, ordonnantien en edicten van de hoog mog. heeren Staaten generaal der Vereenigde Nederlanden; en van de edele groot mog. heeren Staaten van Holland en Westvriesland; mitsgaders van de edele mog heeren Staaten van Zeeland ...* ('s Gravenhage: H. I. van Wouw, 1658), vol. 1, col. 55–72; the French text – "Traité de Tréve" – is printed in Jean Dumont, ed., *Corps universel diplomatique du droit des gens; contenant vn recueil des traitez d'alliance, de paix, de treve, de neutralité, de commerce, d'échange.. & autres contrats, qui ont été faits en Europe* (Amsterdam: P. Brunel, etc., 1726–31), vol. 5, part 2, 99–102. The French text, which derives from publications by the French ambassador, Pierre Jeannin, includes in addition a secret agreement – "Traité particulier & secret, qui les Deputez des Etats [Estates General] ont demenadé au Roi d'Espagne, & qui a leur accordé en la forme qui ensuite" – as well as a "Certificat" and a "Déclaration" by the French and English ambassadors who served as mediators. For a bibliography of the texts and various historical commentaries, see Davenport, *European Treaties*, vol. 1, 263–64. There is an English translation of just the first five articles of the truce in Herbert H. Rowen, ed., *The Low Countries in Early Modern Times: A Documentary History*, Documentary History of Western Civilization (New York: Harper and Row, 1972), 112–13. There is an English translation of articles 2–4, the secret treaty, and the Certificate and of the French and English ambassadors in *British Guiana Boundary. Arbitration with the United States of Venezuela. The Counter-Case on Behalf of the Government of Her Britannic Majesty [and Appendix]* (London: Printed at the Foreign Office, by Harrison and sons, 1898), appendix, 322–4. There is an English translation of the king of Spain's ratification letter, dated July 7, 1609, in Davenport, *European Treaties*, 268–9. The translations here are mine, unless otherwise noted.

possess henceforth" – would be applied not only to the lines of political demarcation on the contested southern and eastern frontiers of the United Provinces, but also to the contested domain of maritime trade in the East and West Indies.[46] In a broader comparative context, the application of this common-sense principle is distinctive in the sense that the Swiss, German, and French agreements all sought to reunite polities that had been previously divided, whereas the Twelve Year Truce was validating the division of provinces that had been previously united. Neither application of this principle was, however, particularly straightforward.

With regard to the frontiers of the republic, which were not spelled out in the Truce itself, a "Certificat" that the French and English mediators appended to the Truce reported that "it has been agreed on by both sides, and has been so understood by us" that the possessions of the United Provinces in the divided provinces of Brabant and Flanders included the "marquisate of Bergen-op-Zoom, the baronies of Breda, Graves, and all that is bound up and united with the boroughs, villages and dependent therefrom."[47] In addition, a number of subsequent articles in the Truce articulated principles and procedures for the restoration of, or compensation for, properties and feudal rights that had been seized, and in some cases sold, on both sides of the military conflict since the year 1567 (articles 13–27); the right of return of refugees who had fled to "neutral countries" (article 28); the release of prisoners of war (article 34); and the like. Article 32 stated simply that "[a]ll disinheritances and dispossessions done in the hatred of the War are declared nul, and considered not to have happened." Not surprisingly, a number of territorial, commercial, and individual disputes, arising from the general possession principle, would be the subject of continuing negotiations between the Archdukes and the republic in 1609 and 1610, as provided for in the Truce.[48]

By comparison with the first three articles, article 4 of the Twelve Year Truce was remarkably convoluted and vague, suggesting an especially painful compromise.[49] It began with a variation on the amnesty and amnesia principle: "The subjects and inhabitants of the said king, archdukes and Estates will maintain on good terms of friendship and understanding with each other during this truce, without resentment for past offenses and damage that they have suffered." A second clause stipulated that "they shall also be able to travel and stay in each other's territories and conduct their business and commerce in them in full security, both on sea and on land." Freedom of

---

[46] See Davenport, *European Treaties*, vol. 1 260–1.

[47] See the French text of the "Certificat" and the English translation in *British Guiana Boundary*, 324. The French text is also printed in Dumont, *Corps universel diplomatique*, vol. 5, part 2, 102.

[48] See Rene Vermeir and Tomas Roggeman, "Implementing the Truce: Negotiations Between the Republic and the Archducal Netherlands, 1609–10," *European Review of History* 17 (2010): 817–33.

[49] Herbert Rowen's translation of this article (Rowen, *Low Countries*, 113) breaks it into several separate sentences, but in both French and Dutch it is one, very complex sentence.

movement and trade had been one of the principal demands of the northern provinces from the beginning of negotiations while the king of Spain had demanded the cessation of trade with the East and West Indies and the dissolution of both the *VOC* and the *WIC*; hence, the breakdown in the negotiations for a permanent treaty.[50] Here the *VOC* and the *WIC* were also not mentioned, and the principle of free trade was hedged by yet more run-on clauses: first, that "the said king nevertheless understands this to be restricted and limited to the kingdoms, territories, lands and lordships which he holds and possesses in Europe."[51] Beyond Europe, however, the king's understanding was that: (1) in those "places, cities, ports and harbors that he possesses," the Estates and their subjects "cannot carry out any trade without the expressed permission of the said King" and (2) they may nevertheless "conduct trade in the territories of other princes, potentates, and Peoples who allow them to . . . without the said King, his officers and subjects dependent on him offering and hindrance on that account."

Without explicitly mentioning either the East or West Indies, then, article 4 of the Twelve Year Truce applied the possession principle to designate the limits of free trade overseas: Where the Spanish actually "possessed" lands beyond Europe, Dutch traders would be excluded without express permission; where there was no actual possession, Dutch traders were free to make agreements with local potentates.[52] That the Dutch were still dissatisfied with the vague language of the fourth article is suggested by their insistence on a secret agreement, which should "be regarded as inserted in and forming part of the principal Treaty"; it affirmed:

That His Majesty will not obstruct in any way, either by sea or by land, the said Lords States [i.e., the Estates General of the United Provinces] or their subjects in the trade which they may carry on hereafter in the countries of all princes, potentates, and peoples who may permit them to do so, in whatever place that may be, even beyond the limits determined above and anywhere else . . . so that the said trade may be free and secured to them.[53]

---

[50] See the documents recounting the negotiations on maritime trade, both at The Hague, in 1608, and at Antwerp, in 1609, in *British Guiana Boundary*, 317–22.

[51] Within Europe, the king's understanding also included "other places and seas where the subjects of those kings and princes, who are his Friends and Allies, have the said commerce by mutual agreement." Articles 6–12 amplified the freedom of movement and commerce within Europe, specifying, for example, that the rights of inhabitants of the United Provinces should be commensurate with the rights enjoyed by the subject of the king of Great Britain under an Anglo-Spanish treaty since 1604 (article 7).

[52] The French ambassador Pierre Jeannin's account of the negotiations in Antwerp suggests why the king of Spain so insistently refused to name the Indies in the text of the truce: "the King of Spain was indeed willing to consent to this commerce in the said places [i.e., the Indies], but without expressing it: so that other kings and princes with whom he is in alliance and friendship may have no reason to make him the same demand in favour of their subjects." *British Guiana Boundary*, 320.

[53] *British Guiana Boundary*, 323–4.

It was only in the "Certificat" signed by the mediators that the Indies were specified, with the French and English ambassadors suggesting equal limitations – by explicit permission only – on Dutch and Spanish traders, depending on actual "possession."[54] Finally, article 5 of the Truce provided that "because a good long time is required to advise those outside the limits of Europe with troops and ships that they shall refrain from all acts of hostility, the Truce shall commence there a year from today." This, Pierre Jeannin, the French ambassador, reports, was an ingenious, but unmistakable reference to the Indies that the Dutch had insisted on inserting into the public articles of the treaty.[55]

Although maritime trade with the Indies was a relatively new issue that was deeply divisive, the negotiators were eventually able to fashion compromise language that applied to the Indies without actually mentioning the Indies. The silence on "matter of religion" in the Twelve Year Truce was much more profound. As we saw in Chapter 5, the failure of the Pacification of Ghent and the *Paix de religion/Religions-vrede* gave way in the 1570s to two separate political and military alliances – the Union of Arras and the Union of Utrecht – that not only sustained the seemingly unending and inconclusive war but, willy-nilly, also framed two divergent paths toward religious peace. The steady *segregation* of the Low Countries into two zones of religious *domination* – a "restored" Catholic Church in the south and a new "public" Reformed Church in the north – had moved most of the Netherlands – that is, except for the contested borderlands – in the direction of relatively stable, but formally exclusionary patterns of religious coexistence, in which subordinate religious groups survived, at least in part, by doggedly *subverting* each regime's exclusionary policies. The cease-fire agreement promised finally to add *negotiation* to that familiar mix of mechanisms to make a distinctive pattern of religious peace possible in the Low Countries.

From the start of the negotiations in The Hague, the king of Spain and the Archdukes had sought restoration of Catholic worship in the northern provinces, but on this critical point the Dutch remained unyielding. Even when he gave up on his demand for dissolution of the VOC, Philip still insisted on open and public toleration of Catholic worship in the northern provinces in exchange for Dutch independence. From Oldenbarnevelt's perspective, as the principal advocate of peace with Spain, however, this demand would be as difficult to concede as the issue of trade to the Indies.[56] In the end, Philip III had to consent to a truce agreement that remained officially

[54] Furthermore, the English and French ambassadors reported in their "Certificat" that the deputies of the United Provinces had repeatedly pledged to come to the aid of any of "their friends and allies" in the Indies, who might come under Spanish attack, without considering such action a violation of the treaty; *British Guiana Boundary*, 324.
[55] *British Guiana Boundary*, 321.
[56] On the dynamics of the negotiations in light of Dutch politics, see Israel, *The Dutch Republic*, 399–405.

silent on the religious question. Still, in his ratification letter of July 7, 1609, Philip expressed his "hope that during the truce the said States of the United Provinces will show good treatment to the Catholics who live among them."[57] Meanwhile, the only concession on the matter of religion that Spain and the Archdukes were able to achieve was expressed in a "Déclaration" from the French ambassadors, stating that:

the Gentlemen of the Estates and the Prince Maurits have promised us and given their word that there will be no innovations in Religion in Villages under the jurisdiction of the Cities of the United Provinces situated in Brabant; and as well that the exclusive exercise of the Catholic, Apostolic and Roman Religion that was done in the past will continue there without any change, and without bringing them any scandal.[58]

In the larger context of the Twelve Year Truce, this modest "Déclaration" may be the exception that confirms the rule. Indeed, the silence of the treaty on the matter of religion appears to have implied that the possession principle, expressed in article 3, applied as well to religious affairs: Except in contested rural borderlands in that part of Catholic Brabant "possessed" by the Dutch Republic, the exclusionary religious regimes that had emerged since the 1570s in the Catholic south and the Calvinist north would be maintained.[59]

So how, exactly, did the Twelve Year Truce make *religious peace* possible in the Low Countries? Although it bears little resemblance, in its silence on the matter of religion, to either the Swiss and German settlements or the Edict of Nantes, the Truce does incorporate all of the basic principles that we have seen thus far in early modern peace agreements: (1) mutual recognition (political, that is, and religious only by implication), (2) assurances of mutual security (embracing the possession principle and pledging nonaggression in both Europe and the Indies), and (3) mechanisms to resolve future disagreements, at least for the duration of the Truce (the Archdukes and the Estates General began formal supplemental negotiations almost immediately). By accepting the possession principle, the negotiators and the sovereigns they represented were accepting military, political, and religious facts on the ground that many on both sides of the struggle found less than desirable, if not abhorrent. In this way, the Truce represents a disruption of the coalitions between zealous religious movements (or establishments) and those who commanded and/or financed the military forces in conflict. For the time being, at least, political actors, such as Johan van Oldenbarnevelt and Ambrosio Spinola, who sought to reduce the crushing

---

[57] Davenport, *European Treaties*, 269.

[58] See the "Déclaration des Ambassadeurs de France à Anvers le 9. Avril 1609, que les Etats des Provinces-Unies des Païs-bas on promis qu'il ne sera rien innové en l'exercice de la Religion Catholique és Villages du Ressort des Villes desdites Provinces situées en Brabant," in Dumont, *Corps universel diplomatique*, vol. 5, part 2, 102.

[59] See also, Benjamin J. Kaplan, "'In Equality and Enjoying the Same Favor': Biconfessionalism in the Low Countries," in *A Companion to Multiconfessionalism in the Early Modern World*, ed. Thomas Max Safley, Brill's Companions to the Christian Tradition, vol. 28 (Leiden; Boston: Brill, 2011), 112–13.

financial burdens of seemingly unending war, were able to eclipse those who were willing to incur the enormous costs that military victory and/or religious unity and purity would undoubtedly require.

For the first time in the age of Europe's religious wars, then, a negotiated agreement – the Twelve Year Truce – helped to make *religious peace* possible without actually mentioning religion, much less articulating a template for the validation and management of the political relations among religiously diverse and often antagonistic groups within a common polity. Like the Swiss *Landfrieden*, the German *Religionsfriede*, and the French Edict of Nantes, the Truce validated important political (explicitly) and religious (implicitly) facts on the ground, and thus it highlights for us the extent to which the political and cultural landscape of the Low Countries had been transformed by nearly a century of religious conflict and more than four decades of intermittent and often very destructive war. To the extent that the forces engaged in the extended conflict in the Habsburg Netherlands were extraordinarily slow to accept a *negotiated* settlement, however, this case illustrates especially clearly the way in which other recurrent mechanisms – *domination, subversion*, and *segregation*, which were also evident in the Swiss *Eidgenossenschaft*, the German *Reich*, and the kingdom of France – could produce the essential characteristics of a variegated religious peace long before the war actually ended.

8

The Contours of Religious Peace II

Western Europe

Together the Edict of Nantes and the Twelve Year Truce, like the *Landfrieden* and *Religionsfriede* before them, served to make durable patterns of religious peace possible in northwestern Europe at the beginning of the seventeenth century. So what kind of peace did these settlements make possible? Would we recognize religious peace if we saw it at the beginning of the seventeenth century? As was the case in Switzerland and Germany, the peace settlements in France and the Low Countries validated and preserved patterns of religious diversity that were varied and more than a little messy. In this paired comparison, however, the negotiated settlements were on their face strikingly different from one another. Whereas the Edict of Nantes established a very detailed and broadly inclusive framework for the peaceful coexistence of two visible institutional churches, the Twelve Year Truce, in its silence on the matter of religion, implicitly validated two very different exclusionary outcomes, in which diversity was officially hidden from view in both the Dutch Republic and the Southern Netherlands. Despite these formal differences, we must nevertheless attend to at least one profound similarity: in all three cases, durable patterns of religious coexistence had emerged over time, and despite some serious challenges, religious diversity remained the hallmark of religious peace, even where it was under the most stress.

INCLUSION AND INTEGRATION

The Edict of Nantes clearly envisioned a broadly inclusive template for religious diversity in all of France, with **integration** (in the lower right of Figure 1.2) its dominant feature on the national scale. Indeed, the overall thrust of this agreement was to reduce the salience of religious differences, not just in the functioning of governmental institutions such as councils and courts, but in corporations of all kinds such as universities and guilds, and in public life generally. This vision of integration was not new to the Edict of Nantes, of course. As we saw in Chapter 6, the royal government, following decades of harsh repression, had begun to decriminalize religious difference even prior to the religious wars, but in 1563 the Edict of Amboise, for the first time, articulated an individual right of free religious conscience and devotions, privately "in his home." In addition to reaffirming and rearticulating the freedom of conscience clause, the Edict of Saint-Germain in 1570 also explicitly guaranteed the civil and political rights of Protestants. Despite the horrible strains of the St. Bartholomew's Day massacres and the subsequent wars, these basic principles of free conscience and civil and political equality remained the bedrock of each of the subsequent edicts of pacification, including the Edict of Nantes.

To be sure, there were elements of the French settlement that complicated this vision of integration on a national scale. The *Chambres de l'Edit*, for example, incorporated the principle of **parity** (in the upper right of Figure 1.2); in these critical institutions, the public salience of religious identities was an important element of the conflict-resolution processes that were intended to prevent reescalation of local or parochial disagreements into new rounds of civil war. In addition, the secret articles, some of which reaffirmed the specific agreements that Henry IV had negotiated with his former Catholic enemies, served to validate zones of exclusion that may best be described, in the absence of active repression, as confessional **privilege** (in upper left of the Figure 1.2). At the very least, then, the religious peace that the Edict of Nantes made possible incorporated a wide variety of experiences of religious coexistence – **integration, parity,** and **privilege** – simultaneously. Indeed, whereas the Edict of Nantes guaranteed an unlimited freedom of religious conscience – thus excluding formally the possibility of active **repression** (in the lower left of Figure 1.2) – it offered the Huguenots only a circumscribed freedom of public worship, as all the previous edicts of pacification had done.[1] And therein lay the principal messiness of the Edict of Nantes as well as one of the most challenging elements of its implementation.

Like the precedent agreements in Switzerland and Germany, the Edict of Nantes cannot be said to describe the actual patterns of religious diversity on the ground. Indeed, the varied patterns of religious peace that had emerged in France by the early 1580s were not appreciably altered by the thirteen years of war that followed the succession crisis of 1584; if anything, the geographic pattern of relative Huguenot strength in the south and southwest, in the so-called Huguenot Heartland, and of Catholic hegemony in the north and northeast had been reinforced in the course of the war. To the extent that the public articles of the Edict of Nantes prescribed a single set of rules regarding both public worship for Protestants and the restoration of Catholic worship where it had been repressed, it proposed to undo some of

---

[1] Even the Edict of Beaulieu (1576), which authorized public worship in the Reformed manner nearly everywhere in the kingdom, excluded public worship in Paris and its environs as well as in the vicinity of the court.

those regional variations. For our purposes, the cities of La Rochelle (on the Atlantic coast) and Metz (on the northeastern periphery) may be considered emblematic of the complicated and messy religious peace that the Edict of Nantes made possible.

In 1598, La Rochelle was, alongside Nîmes and Montauban, one of the most important anchors of the Huguenots' military and political cause, but that was not always the case.[2] In 1558, amid rapidly changing conditions, evangelical dissidents first organized a Reformed church in La Rochelle, and in that same year the first public Reformed worship service was held in the Église Saint-Barthélemy when the Protestant king of Navarre was in the city. The rapidly growing congregation quickly outgrew the house churches where they had been meeting privately, and in 1561, two *salles* were fitted for Reformed worship.[3] Later that same year, municipal authorities also facilitated an agreement by which the Reformed and Catholic communities of La Rochelle alternated worship services in the Église Saint-Barthélemy and the Église Saint-Sauveur. This locally arranged *simultaneum* – apparently sharing sacred space had, by this time, become an obvious strategy for accommodating religious diversity – was halted, however, after just a few months in 1562, by order of the royal government. Then, as civil war broke out following the "massacre" of Protestant worshipers at Vassy in March 1562, zealous iconoclasts demolished or damaged the interiors of La Rochelle's old Catholic churches. Still, the largely Protestant municipal government kept La Rochelle out of the larger Huguenot coalition and, by extension, out of the first civil war.

Since Reformed worship was well established within La Rochelle, implementation of the Edict of Amboise in 1563 did not require any mediated negotiations about when and where Reformed worship might be held, and the coexistence of two distinct worshiping communities within the city was very much consistent with the first national peace. Although Reformed domination of both the religious landscape and the civic government was well established by the beginning of the second war in 1567, La Rochelle again remained outside the formal Huguenot coalition, due in part, at least, to the city's long-standing policy of maintaining its independence by means of demonstrated loyalty to the crown, from whom it received its privileges. In early 1568, however, zealous Calvinists forced a temporary alliance with the Huguenots' cause, and later that year, following the ill-fated Peace of Longjumeau, even the "moderate" municipal government formally joined the Huguenots' national alliance during

---

[2] This brief sketch of La Rochelle's history is based primarily on Judith Chandler Pugh Meyer, *Reformation in La Rochelle: Tradition and Change in Early Modern Europe, 1500–1568*, Travaux d'Humanisme et Renaissance (Genève: Librairie Droz, 1996), and Kevin C. Robbins, *City on the Ocean Sea, La Rochelle, 1530–1650: Urban Society, Religion, and Politics on the French Atlantic Frontier*, Studies in Medieval and Reformation Thought (Leiden; New York: Brill, 1997). See also the Musee virtuel du Protestantisme (www.museeprotestant.org), which highlights critical episodes in the history of La Rochelle and includes an itinerary of historical sites of Protestant memory within the city.

[3] On the locations of Reformed worship, see Robbins, *La Rochelle*, chapter 3.

the third war.[4] At this point, most of the remaining Catholic clergy fled the city, and Catholic worship "survived" only informally or even clandestinely. In the wake of the St. Bartholomew's Day massacres in 1572, La Rochelle took center stage in the Huguenots' continued defiance when it refused to allow the city's royal governor entry. This precipitated the fourth war and a devastating three-month siege of La Rochelle in early 1573. Having survived the siege, however, La Rochelle now remained a cornerstone of the Huguenot alliance and a formidable *place de sûreté* through the end of the century. Meanwhile, the city repurposed a former Augustinian refectory for the use of the city's largest Reformed congregation in 1568, and in 1577, construction was started on the city's first purpose-built Reformed *grande temple*, designed to accommodate more than 3,000 worshipers, on the Place du Chateau at the center of the city.

When the Edict of Nantes was formally promulgated at La Rochelle on August 4, 1599, then, the principal challenge in implementing it was to restore Catholic worship in accordance with article 3. Earlier peace settlements had included the same requirement that the "Catholic, Apostolic and Roman religion" be restored where it had been discontinued, but popular protests had curtailed Catholic worship and impeded the work of priests in 1571, 1576, and 1577. After more than a week of tense negotiations among royal commissioners, urban authorities, and religious leaders, the mayor of La Rochelle finally announced on August 4, 1599, that the city would conform to the provisions of the Edict of Nantes.[5] As part of the agreement the commissioners had worked out, the *salle* Saint-Marguerite would be repurposed from Reformed to Catholic use, but this work was immediately disrupted when Calvinist protesters invaded the building, shattering windows, destroying the pulpit, and removing galleries. It was, nevertheless, a celebrated moment among French Catholics when, on August 6, 1599, the bishop of Saintes consecrated the Église Saint-Marguerite and celebrated Mass in La Rochelle for the first time in more than three decades.[6] The next day, the situation was very tense when the bishop symbolically took possession of and consecrated the ruins of the Église Saint-Barthélemy, which had been destroyed by iconoclasts in 1568 (see Illustration 8.1).

---

[4] This decision came largely in response to the king's plan to establish a royal garrison within the city, which the Protestant-dominated government perceived as a direct threat to the religious changes that were taking place. See especially, Meyer, *Reformation in La Rochelle*, 135–8.

[5] Daniel Hickey, "Enforcing the Edict of Nantes: The 1599 Commissions and Local Elites in Dauphiné and Poitou-Aunis," in *The Adventure of Religious Pluralism in Early Modern France: Papers from the Exeter Conference, April 1999*, eds. Keith Cameron, Mark Greengrass, and Penny Roberts (Oxford: Peter Lang, 2000), 75–82.

[6] See the broader reactions cited in Brian Sandberg, "'Re-Establishing the True Worship of God': Divinity and Religious Violence in France After the Edict of Nantes," *Renaissance & Reformation/Renaissance et Reforme* 29, no. 2/3 (2005): 139–82; Sandberg seems to conflate the celebration of the mass at Saint-Marguerite's with the later consecration of the ruins of the Église Saint-Barthélemy.

ILLUSTRATION 8.1: The tower is all that remains of the Église Saint–Barthélemy, which the Protestants destroyed in 1568. This was the place where the first Reformed service was held in 1558; the ruins were formally consecrated by the Bishop of Saintes in 1599. (Photo courtesy of Samuel Sy)

From the beginning, then, it was obvious that implementation of the religious peace in La Rochelle would be rife with competition and conflict, yet even episodic violence did not fundamentally alter the process of integrating two visible and mutually antagonistic worshiping communities within a common urban space. Indeed, in the first decade of the seventeenth century, the project of restoring Catholic worship made substantial progress throughout the Huguenot Heartland, although in Montauban the Mass was not celebrated before 1607. In the process of implementing the peace, the royal commissioners again played a critical role, as they had done in the 1560s and 1570s.[7] In La

---

[7] See especially Penny Roberts, *Peace and Authority during the French Religious Wars, c.1560–1600*, Early Modern History (Houndmills, Basingstoke, Hampshire; New York: Palgrave Macmillan, 2013).

Rochelle, the Reformed community nevertheless underscored their locally dominant position by finally completing the construction of and dedicating their *grande temple* in 1604.

In Metz, on the other side of the kingdom, the Edict of Nantes also made a visible and integrated religious peace possible.[8] In the late middle ages, Metz, an imperial free city within the German Empire, which styled itself as a republic, had emerged as an important center of commerce and a powerful bishopric. A highly choreographed visit to Metz by Emperor Charles V in 1544 underscored both its connection to the empire and its proud independence,[9] but in 1552, French military occupation of Metz in the context of the Second Schmalkaldic War in Germany began a steady process of political incorporation within the kingdom of France, which was finally confirmed officially in the Peace of Westphalia in 1648.[10] A dissenting church was first organized at Metz, with the help of Guillaume Farel, in 1542, but on Easter in 1543, a troop of soldiers, commanded by the duke of Guise, broke up a service of hundreds of evangelicals. As a consequence, Farel returned to Strasbourg, where he had been serving the French exile community, and religious dissent was expressly forbidden in Metz. Following the assertion of French control over Metz in 1552, Protestant worship was still not formally recognized, but nevertheless tolerated, if only for political reasons: in order to strengthen relations with Protestants in the empire. Then, as royal policy turned from persecution to pacification prior to the wars, an envoy from Geneva, Pierre de Cologne, helped to organize a specifically Reformed congregation in Metz, complete with a consistory and elders. After first meeting privately in the chateau of the baron de Clervant in Montoy, the fledgling congregation held its first "public" worship service on Pentecost in 1561 in the small Église Saint-Privat in Montigny, just south of the city (see Illustration 8.2).

Throughout the period of the civil/religious wars in France, Metz remained very much a Catholic stronghold, and the Reformed community struggled to become a visible presence within the city. With powerful bishops, a strong Jesuit presence, and a royal governor, the duke of Epernon, who was among the last

---

[8] This brief sketch of Metz' history is based primarily on Patricia Behre Miskimin, *One King, One Law, Three Faiths: Religion and the Rise of Absolutism in Seventeenth-Century Metz*, Contributions to the Study of World History, 90 (Westport, CT: Greenwood Press, 2002); Gérard Michaux and François-Yves Le Moigne, eds., *Protestants, Messins et Mosellans: XVIe–XXe Siècles: Actes Du Colloque de Metz (15–16 Novembre 1985)* (Metz: Serpenoise: Société d'histoire et d'archéologie de la Lorraine, 1988); and Pierre Bronn, ed., *Le protestantisme en pays messin: histoire et lieux de mémoire* (Metz: Serpenoise, 2007), which is very richly illustrated.

[9] See the description of this highly symbolic visitation in Miskimin, *One King, One Law, Three Faiths*, 7–9.

[10] In the Treaty of Chambord, the Lutheran princes of Germany ceded de facto control of Metz to Henry II in return for economic and military support against the emperor. Charles V attempted, but failed, to reclaim the city in 1552–1553. The defense of Metz against the emperor's siege was led by none other than the duke of Guise, who would be a leader of the Catholic cause at the beginning of the French civil wars.

ILLUSTRATION 8.2: The Calvinists of Metz held their first public worship service on Pentecost in 1562 in the small, ninth-century Église Saint-Privat, south of the city; the chapel has recently been restored to its earliest form. (Photo Wayne Te Brake)

opponents of Henry IV, Metz was also home to many powerful members of the Guise family. The Reformed community was nevertheless able to construct its first church inside the city's fortifications in 1562, although this "*temple du rétrachement*" was destroyed in 1569 by order of Charles IX, when he resided in the city during the third war.[11] Once again the Reformed were forced to worship privately or in villages outside the city. Following the fifth war and the Edict of Beaulieu in 1576, the Reformed were able to construct a new temple in the Rue de la Chèvre, near the city's commercial center, but again, within months, it was forced to close. Thus the Reformed community remained a largely "invisible" and still vulnerable presence within this majority-Catholic city. Then, in 1592, Henry IV issued letters patent that promised the "free exercise" of Reformed worship in the whole city of Metz and reaffirmed the offices and honorific positions of Protestants. By this time the Reformed community in Metz counted many important noble families, municipal officers, and wealthy merchants among its members and may have constituted as much as a third of the city's population; it was served by four pastors, and it had

[11] Charles ordered the destruction of the Reformed temple just days after learning of the royal victory at Jarnac, despite the prior entreaties of the Reformed community, who emphasized the biconfessional harmony of the city prior to the current war. See Penny Roberts, "One Town, Two Faiths: Unity and Exclusion during the French Religious Wars," in *A Companion to Multiconfessionalism in the Early Modern World*, ed. Thomas Max Safley, Brill's Companions to the Christian Tradition, vol. 28 (Leiden; Boston: Brill, 2011), 277–9.

created its own schools. Still, the temple on the Rue de la Chèvre reopened only briefly before it was forced again to close, the problem being that public Reformed worship was generally prohibited in cities that were the seats of bishops, as was the case in Metz. Instead, less formal worship spaces were provided at the *rétrenchement* (where the first temple had been destroyed) or developed further north in the Rue Chambière, just outside the city's fortifications.[12]

The Edict of Nantes did not radically alter this configuration of religious diversity in Metz, as it had done in reestablishing Catholic worship in La Rochelle. As an imperial free city, the edict's public articles did not formally apply to Metz, but article 9 of the secret articles explicitly reaffirmed the privileges granted to Metz's Reformed community in 1592, thereby extending the framework of religious integration to the kingdom's northeastern frontier, at least in principle. What changed the religious landscape of Metz more dramatically and made it truly distinctive was a visit by Henry IV in 1603. As "protector" of the Reformed community, the king attended to the grievances of the Reformed minority and helped to make their position more stable and secure; indeed, shortly after the king's visit, the Reformed community completed the construction of their large temple in Chambière, which continued to serve as a substantial and secure worship space just outside the city's walls for nearly sixty years.[13] At the same time, Henry IV issued letters patent to a small Jewish community that had begun to settle, once again, in Metz since the middle of the sixteenth century. Henry and his predecessors had been encouraging the resettlement of crypto-Jews from Iberia in a number of communities in France, but in Metz they were actually granted a measure of self-regulation as well as the privilege of living and worshiping publicly.[14] With this "privilege" – in the sense that a charter creates an exception to normally operative rules – Henry introduced a new kind of coexistence that was possible in the context of the Edict of Nantes: **ad hoc tolerance** (in the center of Figure 1.2). Despite the fears and protests of the local religious establishment, this Jewish enclave would flourish in the coming decades, becoming a focal

---

[12] The first public services were held in the originally open-air Chambière location in 1597; over time, the space was enclosed and galleries were added, and when it was completed after the turn of the century, it apparently could accommodate 4,000 worshipers. See the list of "Temples du pays Messin" in Jean Olry, *La persécution de l'église de Metz* (Paris: A. Franck, 1859), 2nd ed. (Reprint of 1690 Hanau ed.), https://archive.org/details/laperscutiondelooolrygoog, note C, 244–9. See also, Michaux and Le Moigne, *Protestants, Messins et Mosellans*, fig. 13, p. 32.

[13] See the reprint of an old engraving in Bronn, *Le protestantisme en pays messin: histoire et lieux de mémoire*, 56.

[14] On the broader context of Jewish history in France and more broadly in Europe, see Esther Benbassa, *The Jews of France: A History from Antiquity to the Present*, trans. M.B. DeBevoise (Princeton, NJ: Princeton University Press, 1999), and Jonathan I. Israel, *European Jewry in the Age of Mercantilism, 1550–1750* (Oxford: Oxford University Press, 1985). On the history of the Jewish community in seventeenth-century Metz, see Miskimin, *One King, One Law, Three Faiths*.

point of Jewish culture and commerce in France, and with the construction of a public synagogue in 1619, Metz became a visibly triconfessional city.[15]

As was the case in La Rochelle, the first decade of the religious peace in Metz was rife with contention and controversy, but this ongoing conflict did not materially alter the process of integrating multiple religious faith communities into the fabric of the local community. Just as Catholics learned quickly how to use the prescriptions of the Edict of Nantes to restore Catholic worship in La Rochelle and elsewhere throughout the Huguenot Heartland, so also Reformed minorities in areas of Catholic hegemony learned to use the edict and the local agreements that attended its implementation to their own advantage, or at least to their minimal disadvantage. Securing stable and convenient access to places of Protestant worship remained a challenge, but even in cities where Protestant worship was expressly forbidden, such as Paris and Metz, private worship and the construction of temples outside the zones of exclusion ensured that religious diversity was maintained or even expanded throughout the realm.[16] The regular commute that many French Protestants were forced to make in order to worship freely may, indeed, be considered the French variant on the eminently modular practice of *Auslauf*.

Although La Rochelle and Metz are both exceptional cases in many respects, they are nevertheless emblematic of the enormously complex and varied religious peace that the Edict of Nantes made possible in France. Against the backdrop of decades of deep *polarization* and recurrent episodes of coordinated destruction, the implementation of the Edict of Nantes was an enormous challenge, but in the first decades of the seventeenth century there can be no doubt that those responsible for the implementation of the edict made enormous progress in (1) institutionalizing the public recognition and visible presence of two antagonistic Christian confessions in a single unified state, (2) providing protection and security for both sides in a wide variety of circumstances, and (3) channeling the inevitable disagreements between the two faith communities into largely nonviolent patterns of religious competition and political contention.[17] The growing literature on the management of religious diversity

---

[15] There is a permanent exhibit on the history of the Jewish community in Metz in *Le Musée de la Cour d'Or*.

[16] On the special challenges of the location of Protestant worship spaces and the "sharing" of cemeteries after 1598, see Keith P. Luria, "Sharing Sacred Space: Protestant Temples and Religious Coexistence in the Seventeenth Century," in *Religious Differences in France: Past and Present*, ed. Kathleen Perry Long, Sixteenth Century Essays & Studies (Kirksville, MO: Truman State University Press, 2006), 51–72, and Keith P. Luria, "Cemeteries, Religious Difference, and the Creation of Cultural Boundaries in Seventeenth-Century French Communities," in *Memory and Identity: The Huguenots in France and the Atlantic Diaspora*, eds. Bertrand Van Ruymbeke and Randy J. Sparks (Columbia: University of South Carolina Press, 2003), 59–72. In both cases, the peace was far from uniform or fixed, but it for the most part represented a biconfessional outcome.

[17] The best overview in English of this progress, with citations of the growing literature, is Keith P. Luria, "France: An Overview," in *A Companion to Multiconfessionalism in the Early Modern World*, ed. Thomas Max Safley, Brill's Companions to the Christian Tradition, vol. 28 (Leiden;

in this biconfessional state underscores the local political dynamics that made the cases of La Rochelle and Metz so different from one another, but what distinguishes the Edict of Nantes most clearly from the Swiss *Landfrieden* and the *Religionsfriede* is the national scope of the settlement and the role of the reconstructed central government and its agents in implementing it. After all, the "universal" foundation of this biconfessional peace remained the individual's freedom of religious conscience and the guarantee of civil and political rights, which emanated clearly from the king, as did the new privileges of the Jewish community in Metz.

The stability of the French peace was sorely tested by the assassination of Henry IV by a Catholic zealot in May 1610.[18] His widow, Marie de Medici, became regent for her young son, the future Louis XIII, but this abrupt transition did not immediately alter royal policy regarding the implementation of the Edict of Nantes. The assassination did awaken the hopes of devout Catholics for complete restoration of Gallican Church at the same time as it stirred the worst fears of militant Calvinists. In La Rochelle, a popular coup in 1614, supported by the city's militias, displaced the old Calvinist elite and brought a new, more militant bourgeois Calvinist leadership to power, which greatly increased political tensions between this stubbornly independent city and the royal government.[19] But even this kind of political *polarization* did not immediately disrupt the regime or restart the wars. For the time being, at least, the religious peace held firm.

In retrospect, it is hard to visualize the religious peace in France at the beginning of the seventeenth century. On the one hand, a largely integrative peace is, by its nature, relatively invisible because the thrust of the settlement was to reduce the salience of religious diversity in public life. Still, the purpose-built "temples" that the Reformed congregations constructed, under the terms of the Edict of Nantes, to replace their less formal or private worship spaces might well be considered emblematic of the French peace. Unfortunately, these emblems of religious inclusion and **integration** within the French kingdom were systematically destroyed nearly a century later, around the time that Louis XIV officially revoked the edict in 1685; indeed, virtually all worship spaces that the Huguenots used during and after the wars were wiped off the religious landscape, with the notable exceptions of the tower of Église Saint-Barthélemy in La Rochelle (see Illustration 8.1) and the Église Saint-Privat outside Metz, which

Boston: Brill, 2011), 209–38. See also, Keith P. Luria, *Sacred Boundaries: Religious Coexistence and Conflict in Early Modern France* (Washington: Catholic University of America Press, 2005), which offers a sophisticated analysis of the dynamics of identity-boundary formation, transformation, and deformation in a range of circumstances in a thoroughly biconfessional state.

[18] The classic study is Roland Mousnier, *The Assassination of Henry IV: The Tyrannicide Problem and the Consolidation of the French Absolute Monarchy in the Early Seventeenth Century*, trans. Joan Spencer (New York: Scribner, 1973); see also, Mack P. Holt, *The French Wars of Religion, 1562–1629*, New Approaches to European History (Cambridge: Cambridge University Press, 1995).

[19] Robbins, *La Rochelle*, chapter 6.

was restored to Catholic use in 1610 (see Illustration 8.2).[20] Since the nineteenth century, however, *La Société de l'Histoire du Protestantisme Français*, with its beautiful *Bibliothèque* in the Rue des Saints-Pères in Paris, has been remarkably successful in recovering the history and preserving the documents and artifacts of the Reformed Church. In lieu of the former sites of Reformed worship, then, perhaps the "Musee virtuel du Protestantism fraiçaise," which is the twenty-first century heir of this effort, may be considered visually emblematic of the French peace.[21] This very extensive website offers a wide array of images, information, and virtual tours of the principal sites of Protestant historical memory, from the sixteenth century to the present, and it highlights the twenty-two very real regional and local museums devoted to Protestant history spread throughout France. A search for "La Rochelle," for example, will yield an extensive "Itinéraire protestant à La Rochelle," whereas a search for "Metz" yields nothing at all, which underscores the limitations of both popular and official historical memory.[22]

EXCLUSION AND SURVIVAL

Whereas the Edict of Nantes provided a framework for a nationally inclusive and integrative peace, the Twelve Year Truce provided nothing of the sort for the Low Countries. By ending nearly four decades of coordinated destruction, it of course made religious peace possible in two new polities-in-formation in the Southern Netherlands and the United Provinces of the Northern Netherlands. But in the absence of a formal, inclusive religious settlement, comparable to the *Landfrieden*, the *Religionsfriede*, or the Edict of Nantes, we encounter in the Low Countries patterns of religious coexistence that are formally exclusive and variously hidden. Although neither side "won," in the sense that they achieved their stated goals of reuniting the Low Countries provinces politically and religiously, the dominant coalitions in both north and south nevertheless claimed the religious privileges of "partial" victors. Let us start in the southern provinces where the historical trajectory after 1585 may be considered the polar opposite of the French path toward integration.

As we saw in Chapter 5, the formal agreement by which the Walloon (French-speaking) provinces reconciled with Philip II in 1579 – the Union of Arras – provided for the complete and exclusive restoration of the Roman Catholic

---

[20] The reason this small chapel has been preserved is undoubtedly its historical significance as the site of the first Christian worship in the area around Metz in the ninth century. Although it became obsolete for Catholic worship and was allowed to deteriorate after the seventeenth century, it has recently been restored to its early form. The official website for this restoration project only briefly mentions its use by the Protestants in the sixteenth century. See www .montigny-les-metz.fr/mobi/stprivat.htm.

[21] See www.museeprotestant.org.

[22] The omission of the history of Metz from this site is striking, but a wiki project on the website wiki-protestants.org is attempting to build such a tour of sites of Protestant historical memory for Metz. See www.wiki-protestants.org/wiki/Metz_(histoire).

Church, but it also guaranteed the privileges of the "obedient" provinces, and thus permanently frustrated Philip's hopes for a more consolidated governance of the Low Countries. The immediate task, however, was the restoration of Spanish military dominance in the southern provinces, where Philip's agents had nearly lost control in 1576. The recovery of lost territory began slowly between 1577 and 1583. But then it quickly accelerated, and by 1585, the Farnese had completed his reconquest of almost all of the territory that Spain would still hold at the time of the Truce.[23] Although traditional historiography emphasizes the seemingly inexorable "success" of the Counter-Reformation Church in the course of the seventeenth century, restoring the Catholic Church in those places where it had been badly damaged, if not eliminated, would prove to be a formidable challenge. Many churches were physically damaged, many parishes did not have priests, many priests were poorly trained and undisciplined – altogether, these difficult problems were hard to tackle in a time of war, uncertainty, and limited resources.[24] Indeed, the physical and spiritual rebuilding project did not really get underway until the beginning of the seventeenth century, in part because a deeply divided clerical establishment did not fully embrace the reforms of the Council of Trent until a critical meeting of the provincial synod in 1607.

Meanwhile, eradicating Protestant "heresies" turned out to be a losing battle, not unlike the Reformed battle against Anabaptists in Bern. On the one hand, active **repression** of religious dissent is hard work and brings with it significant costs. To be sure, the religious and civic authorities in the "obedient" provinces revived the infamous inquisitorial courts,[25] and, wherever they reestablished Spanish/Catholic control, they issued orders that "dissenters" either abjure their heretical beliefs and reconcile with the established Church or emigrate. This, of course, occasioned the largest forced migration of the sixteenth century, which depopulated many important cities and crippled the economy of the southern provinces. But unlike the severe repression prior to the Eighty Years War and under the duke of Alva, judicial executions were, in fact, relatively rare; they focused on Mennonites, not Calvinists, and ended altogether in 1597.[26] In 1609, on the eve of the formal Truce, the Archdukes formally lowered the maximum penalty for heresy from death to expulsion. On the other hand, there is considerable evidence of the ongoing *subversion* of religious dissenters, whose *secrecy, dissimulation,* and rugged determination combined with the *indifference* and active *connivance* of

---

[23] See the maps of this military transformation in Geoffrey Parker, *The Dutch Revolt*, rev. ed. (Harmondsworth: Penguin, 1985), 210–12; for a map of the boundary between 1607 and 1621, see p. 229.

[24] For an overview of the situation, see L. E. Halkin, "Het katholiek herstel in de Zuidelijke Nederlanden 1579–1609," in *Algemene Geschiedenis der Nederlanden, vol 6, Nieuwe tijd* (Haarlem: Fibula-Van Dishoeck, 1979), 344–51.

[25] Aline Goosens, *Les Inquisitions modernes dans les Pay-Bas méridionaux (1520–1633),* 2 vols., Spiritualités et pensées libres (Bruxelles: Éditions de l'Université de Bruxelles, 1997–98).

[26] Halkin, "Katholiek herstel," 346.

"others" (see Table 4.1) to assure the survival of religious diversity, even in this, the most extreme case of religious exclusion and active **repression** at the beginning of the seventeenth century. Consider the relational dynamics of this story of repression and survival in the very different examples of the city of Antwerp and the village of St. Maria-Horebeke.

The commercial metropolis of Antwerp had become one of the most important centers of evangelical religious dissent in the Low Countries by the middle of the sixteenth century, and in 1566 and 1567, during the "wonderyear," it was one of the first cities to sanction evangelical worship officially for both Lutherans and Calvinists.[27] After falling to the duke of Alva and the "Spanish fury" in 1567, the city once again became a prominent example of religious diversity when it adopted a "provisional" version of the *Paix de Religion* in 1578 and an "eternal" version of the Peace in 1579.[28] Both of these local agreements provided for public worship for Catholics, Calvinists, and Lutherans, although not Anabaptists, who were considered politically dangerous, but by 1581, the increasingly radical city administration, dominated by Calvinists, had banished the public exercise of Catholic worship altogether. At the time Antwerp once again capitulated to Spanish control in 1585, an estimated forty to forty-five percent of the city's population was Protestant.[29] After some hard bargaining by the city's magistrates, the city's capitulation agreement allowed Protestants a period of four years during which they could live within the city without being troubled as long as they did not create public scandal; by the end of that period they would either have to be reconciled with the Catholic Church or leave the city.[30]

Not surprisingly, the reassertion of Spanish control under Alexander Farnese, the duke of Parma, while not as brutal as that of the duke of Alva in 1567, precipitated a significant emigration from Antwerp, as it did in many cities.[31] In the first year alone, perhaps 32,000 of the city's 80,000 inhabitants left, and after a lull for two years there was another surge, as the period of grace

---

[27] See Chapter 5, p. 109, in this volume. On the history of religious diversity in Antwerp prior to the Spanish reconquest, see Guido Marnef, *Antwerp in the Age of Reformation: Underground Protestantism in a Commercial Metropolis, 1550–1577* (Baltimore: Johns Hopkins University Press, 1996), and Guido Marnef, "Multiconfessionalism in a Commercial Metropolis: The Case of 16th-Century Antwerp," in *A Companion to Multiconfessionalism in the Early Modern World*, ed. Thomas Max Safley, Brill's Companions to the Christian Tradition, vol. 28 (Leiden; Boston: Brill, 2011), 75–97, in addition to a large number of articles in both English and Dutch by the same author.

[28] See Chapter 6, pp. 149, in this volume.

[29] These estimates are much higher than those at the same time for most cities in the northern provinces.

[30] By comparison, the Protestants of Ghent and Brussels were allowed only two years, and Mechelen just seven months; see Marnef, "Multiconfessionalism," 96.

[31] On the history of religious diversity in Antwerp after 1585, see Marie Juliette Marinus, "De protestanten te Antwerpen (1585–1700)," *Trajecta. Tijdschrift voor de geschiedenis van het katholiek leven in de Nederlanden* 2 (1993): 327–43, and Marie Juliette Marinus, *De Contrareformatie te Antwerpen (1585–1676). Kerelijk leven in een grootstad*, Verhandelingen

expired, that brought the total as high as one-half of the city's population. At the same time, the reestablished Catholic Church recorded some 3,000 conversions to Catholicism.[32] To be sure, not all of those emigrating were Protestants leaving because of their faith; likewise, a number of those formal conversions to Catholicism were undoubtedly insincere, as Catholic religious authorities feared. Still, it is clear that in a very short period of time, Antwerp became, once again, an overwhelmingly Catholic, but much diminished, city.

In the period between 1589, when the grace period expired, and 1607, when the preliminary Truce took hold, the Protestants who remained were once again forced to regroup as "churches under the cross." That they nevertheless survived is evident from a variety of sources, including the loud complaints in Catholic clerical reports. At least two factors appear to have aided and abetted the persistence of clandestine religious diversity and even formal Protestant worship in Antwerp. In the first place, in a commercial metropolis, it was readily apparent to local authorities that strict exclusion of Protestant worship would be bad for commerce, inasmuch as many "foreign" diplomats, merchants, and commercial agents within the city were from officially Protestant territories elsewhere in Europe. Much to the chagrin of zealous Catholics, **ad hoc tolerance** of Protestant worship within foreign merchant and diplomatic communities also provided cover for local Protestant devotion.[33] In addition, proximity to the "border" with the United Provinces of the Northern Netherlands made it possible for Protestants to travel outside the city for worship services, baptisms, weddings, and the like. The originally military frontier, which became a political fixture by the possession principle in article 3 of the Truce, was made all the more porous by the provisions in article 4 that guaranteed freedom of travel across the frontier. As Maria Marinus reports, "The Antwerp Protestants interpreted this personal freedom of travel as an acceptance of religious freedom."[34] Thus she describes a well-organized weekly commute in 1609 of ten to twelve canal-boatloads of dissenters to worship publicly as Protestants at the nearby fort at Lillo.[35] Despite formal condemnations of this strategy, clearly the Low Countries equivalent of *Auslauf*, the practice continued, in part because of the fear on the

van de Koninklijke Academie voor Wetenschappen, Letteren en Schone Kunsten van België, Klasse der Letteren, jg. 57, nr. 155 (Brussel: Paleis der Academiën, 1995).

[32] Marinus, "De protestanten," 128; Marnef reports a much lower figure of 1,600: Marnef, "Multiconfessionalism," 96. See also, Guido Marnef, "Protestant Conversions in an Age of Catholic Reformation: The Case of Sixteenth-Century Antwerp," *Intersections. Yearbook for Early Modern Studies* 3 (2004): 33–47.

[33] On the broader history of this ad hoc tolerance of foreign residents in both Protestant and Catholic territories, see Benjamin J. Kaplan, "Diplomacy and Domestic Devotion: Embassy Chapels and the Toleration of Dissent in Early Modern Europe," *Journal of Early Modern History* 6 (2002): 341–61, and Benjamin J. Kaplan, *Divided by Faith: Religious Conflict and the Practice of Toleration in Early Modern Europe* (Cambridge, MA: Harvard University Press, 2007).

[34] Marinus, "De protestanten," 329.

[35] On the widespread practice of crossing political borders to worship freely in another jurisdiction, see Kaplan, *Divided by Faith*, esp. Chapter 6. See also Chapter 4, pp. 72–73, in this volume.

part of civic authorities that too-stringent enforcement of the policy of religious exclusion might precipitate even more costly emigration. Consequently religious diversity remained a distinct feature of the urban landscape in Antwerp, well beyond the expiration of the Truce and the resumption of coordinated destruction in 1621.[36]

Reformed Protestants in the small village of St. Maria-Horebeke did not enjoy the relative advantages of Protestants in a commercial metropolis near the frontier with the officially Protestant north. South of Ghent and east of Oudenaarde, some fifty kilometers away from the nearest frontier with the United Provinces, St. Maria-Horebeke has the distinction of having a continuously organized Reformed Church from the sixteenth century to the present. Indeed, although the traditional wisdom on the history of the Southern Netherlands suggests that Protestantism was effectively eliminated from the interior, their story of repression and survival is proudly remembered and commemorated at a rural intersection just outside the village, which is pointedly called "Beggars' Corner" (*Geuzenhoek*).[37] Imagine my surprise when I first traveled to St. Maria-Horebeke and found not only a Reformed community worshiping in a lovely nineteenth-century brick church, but a "hidden" eighteenth-century worship space attached to the current parsonage, a private burial ground, and a substantial museum, which contains both historical artifacts of local Protestant history and a large collection of documents (see Illustration 8.3). Today, there is even an inn down the street called the Haegepreeck, in reference to the illegal hedge preaching of the 1560s.

St. Maria-Horebeke was one of seven villages in the rolling hills of East Flanders where Calvinism was well established in the 1560s. Following the reconsolidation of Spanish control in East Flanders, these Reformed congregations, collectively known as the "Flemish Mount of Olives" (*Olijfberg*), adapted to their radically changed circumstances by adopting the survival strategies of persecuted minorities everywhere: worshiping clandestinely, pretending to conform by occasionally attending the Catholic Mass, having their children baptized by the local priest if a Protestant pastor

---

[36] See the impressive map of "The Protestant Presence in Antwerp (1611–1632)" in Marinus, "De protestanten," 330, which marks the location of Protestant households and Protestant assemblies spread throughout the city. On the later perseverance of clandestine Protestantism in Antwerp, see B. Du Buy, *De geschiedenis van den Brabandschen Olijfberg* (Brussels: Vereeniging voor de geschiedenis van het Belgisch Protestantism, 1960).

[37] On the history of this Reformed congregation from the sixteenth century to the present, see Arnold J. de Jonge, *De Geuzenhoek te Horebeke van geslacht tot geslacht*, pamphlet (Horebeke: Protestants Historisch Museum, 1993); on the broader history of the "Olijfberg," see C. de Rammelaere, "Bijdrage tot de geschiedenis van het Protestantisme in het Oudenaardse gedurende de moderne periode," *Handelingen der Maatschappij voor Geschiedenis en Oudheidkunde te Gent* n.r. 14 (1960): 103–15. For a more extended discussion of the dynamics of their survival, see Wayne Te Brake, "Emblems of Coexistence in a Confessional World," in *Living with Religious Diversity in Early Modern Europe*, eds. C. Scott Dixon, Dagmar Freist, and Mark Greengrass (Farnham, England: Ashgate Publishing, 2009), 53–79.

ILLUSTRATION 8.3: Arial view of "Beggars' Corner" in St. Maria-Horebeke. The "hidden" church dates from the eighteenth century. (Image adapted from the cover of A. J. de Jonge, *De Geuzenhoek te Horebeke* [Horebeke: Protestants Historisch Museum, 1993])

was not available. Sometimes they even traveled to the Protestant parts of Flanders in the Dutch Republic for special worship occasions or to celebrate Protestant marriage ceremonies without the threat of disturbance or persecution. To be sure, the Reformed congregations in East Flanders did not escape the attention of religious authorities; indeed, local priests recurrently complained to their superiors about the continuing problem of "heretics" in their midst; they also betrayed their awareness of the problem of dissimulation by noting in their baptismal records that the children of suspected Protestants were "illegitimate," presumably because their parents were not married as Catholics. So how did Reformed Protestantism survive in the *Olijfberg*?

Protestants in rural East Flanders may have had the distinct advantage of relative obscurity – of being in small, seemingly insignificant places that were hardly worthy of the considerable effort that complete repression of religious dissent would require. And here, too, as in the Emmental, local authorities appear to have been less than consistent or vigilant in enforcing exclusionary rules. Still, the history that is recorded at Beggars' Corner in St. Maria-Horebeke is also illustrative of the importance of the political leverage of external allies and even distant strangers in the survival of diversity. From the

1590s onward, the four district organizations (classes) of the Reformed churches in the province of Zeeland in the United Provinces provided an essential lifeline to these Flemish churches "under the cross," sending them, when possible, trained pastors who provided "education in the Word of God." That task became considerably easier under the Truce, which allowed for freedom of movement between north and south, explicitly for merchants, but also surreptitiously for Protestant pastors. At times of duress, however, external support might take more overtly political forms, as when political authorities in the Dutch Republic threatened reprisals against Catholics to forestall repressive measures against the Reformed congregations of the *Olijfberg*.[38] The records of the Reformed congregation in St. Maria-Horebeke also include a formal commitment from a group of Catholics across the border in the United Provinces to continue to advocate for the peaceful continuation of Reformed worship in Horebeke; indeed, they described a "certain agreement" between themselves and the Reformed pastor at St. Maria-Horebeke to do everything in their power to assure or maintain freedom of worship on both sides.[39] In short, survival under repression is hardly a solo performance; it is invariably the *subversive* work of many hands (see Table 4.1).

Although the cases of Antwerp and St. Maria-Horebeke are exceptional in the sense that their histories have survived quite vividly in both scholarship and popular memory, they are likely only the tip of a larger iceberg, most of which remains invisible under the water line of incomplete documentation and limited memory. A broader catalogue of the pockets of secretive Protestantism in the Southern Provinces is still a long way off, but there are nevertheless widely scattered indications of "discreet" Reformed worship throughout the early modern period in the cities of Ghent, Brussels, Namur, and Tournai, the province of Limburg, and the independent Prince-Bishopric of Liege.[40] Like the history of Anabaptists in the Emmental, their stories suggest the profound limits of official intolerance in the face of popular resistance and network-based subversion.

PRIVILEGE AND THE MULTIPLICATION OF DISSIDENT VOICES

Just as the Twelve Year Truce implicitly validated the exclusive restoration of the Catholic Church in the Southern Netherlands, it implicitly validated a very different kind of religious exclusion in the United Provinces of the Northern Netherlands. In the north, the political future had been shaped by a defensive

---

[38] For specific examples, see Jonge, *De Geuzenhoek te Horebeke*, 11–15.

[39] "Aantekening Boek van den Flaamschen Olijfberg," fols. 2–3, in the Protestant Historical Museum. See also, Te Brake, "Emblems of Coexistence," 67.

[40] See E. M. Braekman, *Le Protestantisme belge au 17e siècle: Belgique, nord de la France, refuge*, Terres protestantes (Carrières-sous-Poissy, France: La Cause, 2001), and Charles Everitt Self, "The Tragedy of Belgian Protestantism: Subversion and Survival" (Ph.D. diss., University of California Santa Cruz, 1995).

military and political alliance, the Union of Utrecht (1579), which willy-nilly
came to serve as the constitutional framework for the newly independent Dutch
Republic. As we saw in Chapter 6, the Union of Utrecht was studiously
ambiguous about the religious future of this defensive political and military
alliance: Article 13 specified that "concerning the matter of religion," the
provinces of Holland and Zeeland were free to act at their own discretion,
while the other provinces might either conform to the provisions of the
Religious Peace (1578) or introduce such regulations as they consider proper
for their peace and welfare, "provided that … each individual enjoys freedom of
religion and no one is persecuted or questioned about his religion."[41] Although
this was hardly a blueprint for the religious future, this universal guarantee of
the freedom of religious conscience did establish the parameters of a distinctive
religious peace in the Northern Netherlands.

   In the 1570s, the Beggars' piecemeal military successes in Holland and
Zeeland had already resulted in the abolition of the Catholic Mass and the
designation of the Reformed Church as the exclusive "public" church in most
cities, and during the negotiations for the Union of Utrecht, these provinces had
resisted any compromise with the old order. Those who favored an inclusive
model, including William of Orange, hoped that the other signatories might
adopt the French-style, biconfessional framework of the *Paix de Religion*,
allowing equally limited opportunities for public worship for Protestants and
Catholics alike. As it happened, however, over the next decades, as the rebels
struggled to consolidate their control, all of the other provinces chose the
exclusive model of Holland and Zeeland, privileging the Reformed Church as
the public church. But at the same time, all of the United Provinces of the
Northern Netherlands, including Holland and Zeeland, had agreed in the
Union of Utrecht to the provision that "each individual enjoys freedom of
religion," thereby rejecting, like the all French edicts since 1563, the
possibility of heresy trials and enforced conformity.

   From the 1580s onward, then, it was clear that the new Dutch Republic was
charting a distinctive course, quite unlike the Southern Netherlands.
The clearest difference was that in the south, the exclusive Catholic Church
was empowered to pursue the idealized authoritarian goal of "unity and purity"
by means of coercion and active repression, while in the north, the exclusive
Reformed Church was prevented, in principle, from pursuing the same goal,
even if its leaders had desired it. But what did it mean to combine an exclusive
"public" church with the individual freedom of religious choice? Once again,
there were no established scripts or well-known strategies for accommodating
religious differences under these rules, but clear patterns had begun to emerge
well before the Twelve Year Truce implicitly validated some very complex and
messy facts on the ground. In the broadest sense, the transformation of the

---

[41] E. H. Kossmann and A. F. Mellink, eds., *Texts Concerning the Revolt of the Netherlands*
(Cambridge: Cambridge University Press, 1974), 169–70.

religious landscape that had begun as part of a revolutionary change of political regime entailed significant challenges and required serious adjustments for a wide spectrum of religious actors – both the Catholic Church and the various dissident groups that had taken root in the northern provinces.

That the Reformed (Calvinist) churches had benefited most clearly from the political changes underway in the second half of the sixteenth century is not surprising. Among the dissident groups who defied the determined repression of the Spanish regime in the Low Countries – Lutherans, Calvinists, and Mennonites – the Calvinists were often the best organized, many were well connected politically, they were the beneficiaries of significant external support from exile communities abroad, and they had attracted a strong and very zealous popular base of support, especially in the cities, where the political revolution also had its roots. Thus where the Beggar alliance won its local battles en route to political domination and eventual self-determination in the various provinces – first in Holland and Zeeland, then Utrecht, the northern provinces (Friesland and Groningen), and the eastern provinces (Gelderland and Overijssel) – the Reformed congregations typically were emboldened and authorized to occupy the existing Catholic churches, although even this could take time as local authorities resisted sudden or disruptive changes.

But becoming **privileged** churches did not mean that these former "churches under the cross" were necessarily ready or even willing to constitute a dominant, much less universal, church once the Spanish forces had been defeated and the Catholic Church disestablished. One often-cited estimate from 1587 suggests that, early on, only ten percent of the population in the aggressively Calvinist province of Holland was affiliated with the Reformed Church, which is comparable to the estimates of the Huguenots' share of the population of France in the early 1570s. Over time, their proportion of the Dutch population would grow steadily, but in the aggregate, the Reformed church would remain a minority church.[42] One obvious reason is that membership in the Reformed Church had always been and would always be voluntary, not automatic;[43] indeed, the requirements for formal membership – which included not only "pure" belief, but submission to church discipline – were often a deterrent to rapid growth in membership.

In addition, like the Dutch Mennonites,[44] the Dutch Calvinists were susceptible to theological cleavages and ecclesiastical differences that had

---

[42] Hans Knippenberg, *De religieuze kaart van Nederland: omvang en geografische spreiding van de godsdienstige gezindten vanaf de Reformatie tot heden* (Assen: Van Gorcum, 1992) and J. A. de Kok, *Nederland op de breuklijn Rome-Reformatie: Numerieke aspecten van protestantisering en katholieke herleving in de noordelijke Nederlanden, 1580–1880* (Assen: Van Gorcum, 1964).

[43] This was a clear departure from the existing models of established Calvinist churches in Geneva, a Reformed city-state since the 1540s, and Scotland, a Presbyterian kingdom since the 1560s, where membership was automatic and conformity was established in law, though not necessarily enforced coercively.

[44] In the 1560s, for example, the Mennonite movement divided between the so-called Frisian and Flemish factions, which were, in turn subdivided into no less than six factions by the 1590s – all

important implications not only for the shape of the religious community but also in the realm of public policy. Since the early years of the Eighty Years War, the Calvinists had been divided between the strictly "orthodox," who emphasized the theological purity as well as institutional independence of the "true" church, and the "libertines," who envisioned a more capacious church closely monitored by civic authorities.[45] During the Truce, however, this cleavage took on clearer theological definition as a conflict over the doctrine of predestination between the supporters of two rival theologians at the new University of Leiden: the latitudinarian "Aminians" and orthodox "Gomarists."[46] Theological *innovation* and academic *disputation* combined, as they had recurrently in the sixteenth century, with *politicization* and *mobilization* when Maurits of Nassau, the military leader of the republic, allied with Orthodox Calvinists, and Johan van Oldenbarnevelt, the political leader of the province of Holland, allied with the so-called Remonstrants, whose formal appeal (remonstrance) to the Estates of Holland gave them their "identity." This very volatile political conflict culminated in the trial and execution of Oldenbarnevelt for treason in 1618 and the extra-legal purging of many town councils in the province of Holland as Prince Maurits and his allies, the so-called Counter-Remonstrants, consolidated their control; it was also closely linked to the condemnation of Arminian theology in the Synod of Dordrecht in 1619. Consequently, the Remonstrants, who represented a sizable or even dominant group in some cities, were expelled from the public Reformed Church.

Establishing and maintaining Reformed **privilege** was, at bottom, a contentious political process that varied considerably from place to place and province to province, and it was very much a work in progress at the time of the Truce.[47] There were many decisions to be made regarding the ownership

---

of which clearly undermined their coherence as a religious movement. See, in English, I. B. Horst, ed., *The Dutch Dissenters: A Critical Companion to Their History and Ideas* (Leiden: E. J. Brill, 1986); Cornelis Krahn, *Dutch Anabaptism: Origins, Spread, Life and Thought* (The Hague, 1968); Alastair Hamilton, Sjouke Voolstra, and Piet Visser, eds., *From Martyr to Muppy. A Historical Introduction to Cultural Assimilation Processes of a Religious Minority in the Netherlands: The Mennonites* (Amsterdam: Amsterdam University Press, 1994).

[45] See, for example, Benjamin J. Kaplan, "Dutch Particularlism and the Calvinst Quest for 'Holy Uniformity'," *Archiv Für Reformationsgeschichte* 82 (1991): 239–55; Kaplan underscores the political dimensions of this conflict in terms of local control vs. more coordinated provincial or even national policies.

[46] For an overview of this conflict, which threatened the political stability of the new Republic, see Jonathan I. Israel, *The Dutch Republic: Its Rise, Greatness, and Fall, 1477–1806*, The Oxford History of Early Modern Europe (Oxford: Clarendon Press, 1995), 421–74.

[47] See the ground-breaking essays by Alastair Duke on this complex process of adaptation, especially in the province of Holland, reprinted in Alastair Duke, *Reformation and Revolt in the Low Countries* (London: Hambledon Press, 1990), 199–293; see also, Andrew Pettegree, "Coming to Terms with Victory: The Upbuilding of a Calvinist Church in Holland, 1572–1590," in *Calvinism in Europe, 1540–1620*, eds. Alastair Duke, Gillian Lewis, and Andrew Pettegree (Cambridge: Cambridge University Press, 1994), 160–80. The most thorough provincial-level study is on

and maintenance of church property, the authority of clergy and church institutions vis-à-vis civil authorities, and the proper place of religious rituals in public life. In the cities where the Reformed Church was the most thoroughly established, membership in the town councils might eventually overlap considerably with membership in the Reformed consistory;[48] in most places, public officials were required to be at least "*liefhebbers*" of the Reformed Church – that is, they needed to demonstrate their "affection" for the Church by attending services, though full membership was not required – but even this requirement might be only laxly enforced. What the Calvinists most jealously guarded, however, was their exclusive privilege of *public* worship, even in those places where their services were poorly attended and they were vastly outnumbered by other religious groups.[49] Indeed, the exclusive publicity of Reformed worship quickly became the hallmark of religious coexistence in the Dutch Republic as Catholics and other religious "dissenters," who continued to assert their own religious identities, were required to worship clandestinely or at least discreetly in accommodations (*schuilkerken*, or nominally hidden churches) that did not look like houses of worship.[50]

The significant proportion of the Dutch population that remained faithful to the Catholic Church faced by far the most formidable challenge in adapting to the dramatic political changes that attended the founding of the Dutch Republic.[51] On the one hand, they were faced with a flood of legislation, which varied from place to place, prohibiting a broad array of traditional religious practices: public celebration of the Mass, worship assemblies of all kinds, processions, pilgrimages, and the like. Although the freedom of conscience clause of the Union of Utrecht protected their individual choices to remain Catholic, their clergy were subject, at least episodically, to harassment, arrest, and fines, and their clandestine worship services were sometimes broken up violently. On the other hand, the establishment of a new public Reformed Church entailed the seizure of their churches and the secularization of a great deal of church property as well as the sources of revenue that had previously

Friesland; see W. Bergsma, *Tussen Gideonsbende en publieke kerk. Een studie over het gereformeerd protestantisme in Friesland, 1580–1650*, Fryske Histoaryske Rige 17 (Hilversum: Verloren, 1999).

[48] See, for example, Frank van der Pol, "Religious Diversity and Everyday Ethics in the Seventeenth-Century Dutch City Kampen," *Church History* 71 (2002): 16–62.

[49] See, for example, H. ten Boom, "De Vestiging van het Gereforeerde Kerk in het Land van Maas en Waal en de aangrezende dorpen van het Rijk van Nijmegen in het begin van de 17e eeuw. Een mislukte reformatie," *Nederlandsch archief voor kerkgeschiedenis* 50, no. 2 (1970): 197–229.

[50] For a broader analysis of the phenomenon of nominally hidden churches, see Benjamin J. Kaplan, "Fictions of Privacy: House Chapels and the Spatial Accommodation of Religious Dissent in Early Modern Europe," *American Historical Review* 107 (2002): 1031–64, and Kaplan, *Divided by Faith*.

[51] On the enormity of this challenge, see especially the introductory chapter of Charles H. Parker, *Faith on the Margins: Catholics and Catholicism in the Dutch Golden Age* (Cambridge, Mass.: Harvard University Press, 2008); see also Christine Kooi, *Calvinists and Catholics During Holland's Golden Age: Heretics and Idolaters* (Cambridge: Cambridge University Press, 2012).

supported the established Church. In the early days of the transition, many Catholic clergy fled, as they had in the Huguenot Heartland in France, and the episcopal hierarchy quickly ceased to function; indeed, the Church at Rome officially abolished the church hierarchy in 1592 with the appointment of the first *vicar apostolic*, Sasbout Vosmeer, who was to head what eventually came to be known as the "Holland Mission." Over the course of the seventeenth century, the Catholic Church would eventually make a remarkable recovery, both spiritually and organizationally, as a very different kind of church; still, it would take several decades before the Catholic faithful even worked out a *modus vivendi* with local authorities. Again, these arrangements varied from place to place, but they often involved the payment of significant bribes to local authorities that were eventually institutionalized as "recognition" payments.[52] At the time of the Truce, of course, these enormous adjustments to the religious experience of Catholics were still very much in process.

At the same time, the other evangelical dissenters, who in some places outnumbered the Calvinists, were also forced to adjust to the new political realities in the Dutch republican state-in-formation. The largest of these were the Mennonites, who had prospered in the Dutch-speaking provinces as the "peaceful" Anabaptists following the debacle at Münster in the 1530s. They were still often condemned as schismatics by other Protestants for the way they rebaptized and separated the "faithful" from the "godless" in their "gathered" churches, and they were considered deeply suspicious by the political elite for their refusal to bear arms and their repudiation of civil authority more generally. Still, they demonstrated a significant appeal to the religiously devout and emerged as the largest evangelical "competitor" to the Reformed Church in the new republic.[53] For them, in contrast to the Catholic faithful, worshiping clandestinely, or at least discreetly, in deference to the new dominance of the Reformed Church required relatively little adjustment. The same was true for the generally smaller and less common Lutheran congregations, which were viewed with considerably less suspicion by both civil and religious authorities, but nevertheless were required to worship discreetly in accommodations that did not resemble churches. Compared to the bitter repression of the past, accepting the exclusive privilege of the Reformed Church may have seemed relatively easy, but for both of these groups, the longer-range challenge was to gain a more public acceptance and to move out of the shadows.[54]

---

[52] See Christine Kooi, "Paying Off the Sheriff: Strategies of Catholic Toleration in Golden Age Holland," in *Calvinism and Religious Toleration in the Dutch Golden Age*, eds. R. Po-Chia Hsia and H. F. K. van Nierop (Cambridge: Cambridge University Press, 2002), 87–101, and Charles H. Parker, "Paying for the Privilege: The Management of Public Order and Religious Pluralism in Two Early Modern Societies," *Journal of World History* 17, no. 3 (2006): 267–96.

[53] On the appeal of Mennonite congregations to disgruntled Calvinists, see Wiebe Bergsma, "Gereformeerden en doopsgezinden: van concurrentie tot gedwongen acceptatie," *Doopsgezinde Bijdragen* 20 (1994): 129–56.

[54] See, for example, Joke Spaans, "De lutherse lobby voor vrijheid van godsdienstoefening in Friesland," *De zeventiende Eeuw* 20 (2004): 38–52, and Troy David Osborne, "Worthy of the

So what did religious peace actually look like in the United Provinces of the Northern Netherlands? In the absence of a formal religious settlement and given the importance of local and provincial decision making, it was, of course, enormously complex and varied, and in light of the remarkable range of confessional "choices" that were available in many urban communities – Reformed (Orthodox Calvinist), Remonstrant (Arminian), Catholic, Mennonite, and Lutheran, to name only the most prominent – it was more than a little messy, though hardly in the same ways as the Swiss, German, and French cases we have already seen. Indeed, some key local studies have suggested, it is likely that at the time of the Truce, the largest segment of the Dutch population remained "undecided" – that is, they did not affiliate immediately with any confession in this very fluid religious environment.[55] Still, in retrospect, we can say that, despite a wealth of variation in numbers, proportions, and relationships that were the historical residue of locally contentious political processes, the Dutch Republic had by 1609 already developed a remarkably "national" pattern of **privileged** religious diversity (in the upper left of Figure 1.2) of which a multitude of "hidden churches" (*schuilkerken*) are most clearly emblematic.[56] Let me offer two very early examples.

Just outside the small village of Loenen, which is located between the cities of Apeldoorn and Arnhem in the eastern province of Gelderland, there is a lovely manor house with an equally lovely array of outbuildings: the house or castle "ter Horst."[57] In 1557, amid rising religious competition and tension in the Low Countries, Wijnand Hackfort, the descendent of a noble lineage who was serving as a *burgemeester* (ruling magistrate) in Arnhem, began construction of the existing estate house, which was nominally fortified by a drawbridge and a moat, as was befitting a traditional noble estate (see Illustration 8.4). Among the outbuildings is a substantial step-gabled structure that predates the estate house and has served variously as a barn, a carriage house, and an *orangerie*; prior to the Reformation it may also have served as a private chapel for the

Tolerance They'd Been Given: Dutch Mennonites, Reputation, and Political Persuasion in the Seventeenth and Eighteenth Centuries," *Archiv für Reformationsgeschichte* 99 (2008): 256–97.

[55] The strongest assertion of this argument is in Joke Spaans, *Haarlem na de Reformatie: Stedelijke cultuur en kerkelijk leven, 1577–1620*, Hollandse Historische Reeks 11 ('s-Gravenhage: Stichting Hollandse Historische Reeks, 1989); she estimates the Reformed population at twenty percent, the Mennonite fourteen percent, Catholic twelve percent, and Lutheran and Walloon (French-speaking Reformed) each one percent.

[56] For broad descriptions of Dutch pluralism, in English, see Willem Frijhoff and Marijke Spies, *1650: Hard-Won Unity*, vol. 1 of *Dutch Culture in a European Perspective* (Assen: Royal Van Gorcum; New York: Palgrave Macmillan, 2004), 349–427, and Maarten Prak, *The Dutch Republic in the Seventeenth Century: The Golden Age*, in *Dutch Republic*, trans. Diane Webb (Cambridge, UK; New York: Cambridge University Press, 2005), 201–21. The term "*schuilkerk*" is actually an anachronism, born in the nineteenth century, but it has nevertheless proven to be a useful shorthand accepted by most Dutch historians.

[57] C. C. de Kool-Verhoog, *Kasteel ter Horst: Een lagchend landhuis in Loenen* (Loenen: Stichting Wijnand Hacfort, 2002).

ILLUSTRATION 8.4: The sixteenth-century Huize ter Horst, just outside Loenen in the Province of Gelderland, has a moat as befits a noble's estate. (Photo Wayne Te Brake)

ILLUSTRATION 8.5: The *orangerie* at Huize ter Horst served as a Catholic *schuilkerk* after the Church in Loenen was closed for Catholic worship in the 1590s. (Photo Wayne Te Brake)

ILLUSTRATION 8.6: In the eighteenth century, a purpose-built *schuilkerk* was built into the new carriage house, hidden behind the closed shutters. (Photo Wayne Te Brake)

resident family, but in any case, in the seventeenth and eighteenth centuries it served as a Roman Catholic *schuilkerk* (see Illustration 8.5).

The formal establishment of the Reformed Church that accompanied Dutch political independence was relatively slow to come to villages such as Loenen, and the nearby village chapel, which had also been built by Wijnand Hackfort in the 1550s, was still being served by a Catholic priest in the early 1590s. When the incumbent priest passed away in 1595, however, local authorities would not replace him with another priest, and the chapel was simply dismantled and closed; sometime later it was put to use as a Reformed church. Consequently, Roman Catholic worship was relocated to the privacy of the barn/chapel/ *schuilkerk* at Huize ter Horst, and worship services were led by an itinerant priest who was responsible for a cluster of seven chapels in the area; in order to ensure the safety and security of this arrangement, the Catholic landlords who sheltered these chapels apparently paid "recognition" fees to local authorities. Today, the *orangerie* bears no clear markings of its service as a place of religious worship, but its long, sloping roof and high ceiling suggest how it may have been particularly well suited for that purpose. Toward the end of the eighteenth century a purpose-built chapel with a lovely altar was "hidden" behind the shutters of a larger building complex on the estate (see Illustrations 8.6 and 8.7), but the original *schuilkerk/orangerie* remains a very early token of a remarkably stable

ILLUSTRATION 8.7: The interior of the modest eighteenth-century *schuilkerk* at Huize ter Horst. (Photo Wayne Te Brake)

and durable kind of Protestant-Catholic coexistence that was possible behind the public façade of an exclusive, privileged Reformed Church.

In the small village of Pingjum – some 150 kilometers north of Loenen in the province of Friesland, near the modern *Afsluitdijk* that encloses the Zuider Zee, and not far from the village of Witmarsum where Menno Simons served as a priest in the 1530s – there is an equally compelling emblem of Calvinist-Mennonite coexistence. In the street called Kleine Buren, behind the façade of a typical residence (see Illustration 8.8), there is a small *doopsgezind* or Mennonite church, which is for all practical purposes hidden or invisible. This purpose-built structure was constructed around 1600, with the typical Mennonite arrangement where women and children were seated in the center and a lectern for the pastor and seating for the men were arranged around the periphery (see Illustration 8.9). But given the fact that this modest church stands in close proximity to the official Reformed Church in the center of the village (see Illustration 8.10), it is obvious that it was hidden only in the token sense that it was made to look like something other than a house of worship. Not surprisingly, Pingjum and the nearby village of Witmarsum, like the Anabaptist sites in the Emmental in Switzerland, are important stops on Mennonite discovery tours today.

ILLUSTRATION 8.8: A Mennonite Church was constructed around 1600 behind the façade of this typical village house in Pingjum, Friesland. (Photo Wayne Te Brake)

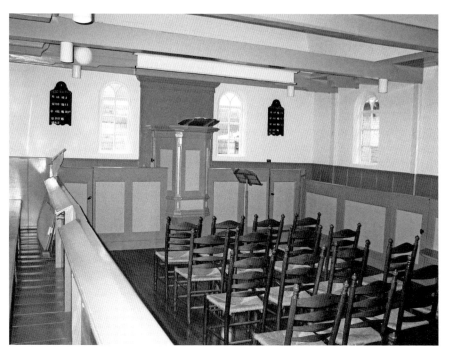

ILLUSTRATION 8.9: The Mennonite *schuilkerk* in Pingjum has seating for women and children in the center and for men around the periphery. (Photo Wayne Te Brake)

ILLUSTRATION 8.10: The Mennonite Church at Pingjum was built in close proximity to the Reformed Church in the center of the village. (Photo Wayne Te Brake)

In the city of Gouda – with a population of around 10,000, it is the smallest of the six "big" cities in the province of Holland – we can see in surprising detail how the adjustments to a new political/religious reality unfolded in an urban landscape. Gouda officially declared for the rebellious Beggar alliance in June of 1572, as a consequence of a shadowy internal conspiracy whose leader quickly negotiated a "religious peace" with local magistrates that declared freedom of religion for both Protestants and Catholics.[58] Given the increasing religious polarization that accompanied the first successes of the rebel coalition and the frequent intervention of rebel armies and militias in support of zealous Calvinists in local affairs, this locally brokered religious peace appears to have had relatively little prospect of living up to its core promise of peaceful coexistence on equal terms. But as it happened, it took more than a year of fits and starts before Calvinist zealots turned the tide against the local political elite, which sought doggedly to retain public Catholic worship in this rebel city. The establishment of a new religious order was, thus, a long and often tortured process.

[58] For this early history, see C. C. Hibben, *Gouda in Revolt; Particularism and Pacifism in the Revolt of the Netherlands, 1572–1588* (Utrecht: HES Publishers, 1983).

Like the mid-sized cities of Bautzen and Biberach in Germany, Gouda had only one parish, and its parish church, the *Janskerk* (Church of St. John the Baptist), dominated the urban landscape; there were, in addition, some twenty-five chapels associated with various religious orders and civic institutions.[59] Under the terms of the religious peace in 1572, the Catholics continued to worship in the *Janskerk*, while the Reformed organized their first public worship services in July in two of the chapels: the *Gasthuiskerk* and the *Onze Lieve Vrouw* chapel. Following a radical attack on and a threat to destroy the *Janskerk*, local authorities, in order to forestall additional violence, reluctantly closed the *Janskerk* to Catholic worship (especially the Mass, which the Calvinists considered idolatrous) and thereby opened up an extended struggle for control of the church and the city's religious future. After a forced entry, the first Reformed service was held in the *Janskerk* in February of 1573, but regular services did not begin until later in the spring. In the meantime, the Catholic community worked hard to hide and preserve the many valuable objects within the church from either confiscation (to fund the rebel war effort) or destruction by iconoclasts; Catholic worship continued for a time in the city's smaller chapels, though many were attacked and ransacked by zealous Calvinists and rebel soldiers.[60] Still, municipal authorities did not enforce explicitly anti-Catholic legislation until 1574, when they expelled all Catholic religious who would not take an oath of loyalty to the new regime, leaving the Catholic faithful largely devoid of clerical leadership.

As Gouda's Catholics lost control of, first, the *Janskerk* and eventually all of the medieval chapels, which were either destroyed or repurposed in the coming decades, the leaders of the Catholic community who remained began laying the foundations for a much less prominent future. Almost immediately, they organized worship in two houses that were adapted for formal worship in very close proximity to the *Janskerk*, and by 1600, they had begun paying some 400 guilders per year in "recognition" fees to the local sheriff, who nevertheless used episodic harassment to extract even higher payments.[61] In 1630, Petrus Purmerent, who was appointed in 1615 to lead the Holland Mission effort in Gouda, began buying a number of contiguous properties nearby that allowed construction in 1632 of a new purpose-built, largely "hidden" *schuilkerk* of St. John the Baptist, inside a block of buildings between the Hoge Gouwe and the Raam (see Illustration 8.11). Reflecting the enormous institutional adjustments taking place, this new Church of St. John the Baptist was not considered a traditional "parish" church, but rather, a *statie* (station) within the larger Holland Mission; it was expanded several times in the seventeenth century and

---

[59] For an architectural and historical review of Gouda's urban landscape, see Wim Denslagen, ed., *Gouda*, De Nederlandse monumenten van geschiedenis en kunst (Zeist: Rijksdienst voor de Monumentenzorg; Zwolle: Waanders, 2001), www.dbnl.org/tekst/dens002goud01_01.

[60] On the history and decoration of Gouda's Catholic *schuilkerken*, in particular, see Xander van Eck, *Kunst, twist en devotie: Goudse katholieke schuilkerken 1572–1795* (Delft: Eburon, 1994).

[61] Kooi, "Paying Off the Sheriff."

ILLUSTRATION 8.11: Even the modern entrance to the Church of St. John the Baptist on the Hoge Gouwe in Gouda fits unobtrusively into the urban environment. (Photo courtesy of Thomas Rouw)

fundamentally redesigned in the nineteenth century, but it is still used as an "Oud Katholiek" church today (see Illustration 8.12). A second Catholic *statie*, known as "De Tol," was created by private initiative in 1634. Meanwhile, Jesuit and Franciscan "missionaries" established their own *staties* in the 1630s and 1640s, giving devout Catholics their own "choice" of worship experiences, both within and alongside the official Holland Mission effort.

During the Truce, the effects of the conflicts playing out within the Reformed Church were clearly evident in the changing religious landscape of Gouda as well.[62] In the larger conflict between Remonstrants (Arminians) and Counter-Remonstrants (Gomarists), the Remonstrants were dominant in the political elite of Gouda, with the result that the orthodox Counter-Remonstrants were forced to worship clandestinely, but in 1618 they petitioned the provincial Estates and were granted use of the *Gasthuiskerk*, which had been used for military storage during the war. Shortly thereafter, however, the Remonstrants were purged from the municipal administration; the Counter-Remonstrants quickly seized control of the *Janskerk* and expelled the Remonstrants. The

[62] Denslagen, *Gouda*, 290–321.

ILLUSTRATION 8.12: Even though the interior of the St. John the Baptist Church has been expanded and redesigned several times since the seventeenth century, it remains a modest worship space by comparison with the original Janskerk. (Photo courtesy of Thomas Rouw)

Gasthuiskerk was subsequently made available to the Walloon (French-speaking) Reformed congregation, which had sided with the Counter-Remonstrants. The Remonstrants were forced to worship clandestinely, but by 1629, they had constructed a purpose-built *schuilkerk*, which remained in use until the nineteenth century, when it was replaced.

The Catholic and Mennonite *schuilkerken* in Loenen and Pingjum are perhaps the oldest of these iconic "hidden" churches to survive in the northern provinces of the Low Countries. Over time, however, they would appear with remarkable variety, as the case of Gouda suggests, nearly everywhere in the republic; today an intrepid traveler can find interesting, even beautiful examples of "hidden" worship spaces in many Dutch cities, although most of those that survive are from a later date. By the middle of the seventeenth century, for example, the rapidly growing city of Amsterdam had substantial purpose-built Lutheran (1633) and Mennonite (1639) churches alongside as many as sixty smaller Catholic worship spaces.[63] The most famous of these Catholic chapels, and one of the rare survivors, is the private chapel built in the 1660s into the top three floors of a beautiful canal house only

---

[63] See Frederick F. Barends, *Geloven in de Schaduw: Schuilkerken in Amsterdam* (Gent: Snoeck-Dacaju & Zoon, 1996).

ILLUSTRATION 8.13: The Catholic schuilkerk, known affectionately as "Our Dear Lord in the Attic," is built into the top three floors of a merchant's canal house, just a stone's throw from Oude Kerk in the center of Amsterdam. (Photo Wayne Te Brake)

a stone's throw from the massive Oude Kerk; known affectionately as "Ons' Lieve Heer op Solder" (Our Dear Lord in the Attic), it is preserved today as a museum (see Illustration 8.13), is highlighted in most tour guides for the city, and also has a substantial online presence.[64]

The new purpose-built Lutheran church in Amsterdam, which now serves as the ceremonial Aula (auditorium) of the University of Amsterdam, is actually emblematic of a slightly different dimension of religious coexistence in the Dutch Republic. While the Mennonite church, on the opposite side of the Singel canal

---

[64] See www.opsolder.nl/eng/home.php. There is also a purpose-built Catholic chapel that is still in use in the famous Begijnhof; after worshiping first in the sacristy of the Begijnhof's "English" church (a kind of *simultaneum*), and various houses within the complex, the Catholic community designed and built this lovely chapel in the 1670s. See www.begijnhofamsterdam.nl.

from the Lutheran church, was formally hidden within a block of houses,[65] the Lutheran church was prominently visible as a church, reflecting a formal **ad hoc tolerance** granted by the municipal administration to the largely German Lutheran community, with its significant commercial connections to the empire.[66] Similar to the ad hoc tolerance granted to Jews in Metz and foreign Protestants in Antwerp, this Lutheran exception to the normally operative rules regarding the publicity of non-Reformed worship was actually preceded by a less formal ad hoc tolerance that the city of Amsterdam had granted to Sephardic Jews. Like the French, several Dutch cities had been welcoming Crypto-Jewish refugees from Portugal in the last decades of the sixteenth century, and in 1602 the growing Jewish community in Amsterdam installed their first rabbi, marking their important transition from clandestine dissimulation as "new" Christians to initially private worship as Jews.[67] By 1612, construction of a public synagogue had begun, and in 1649 a second was added; in 1660 and 1671 synagogues were also built for the growing Polish and German communities of Ashkenazi Jews. In contrast to the Jews of Metz, whose public worship was formally protected by royal letters patent, the acceptance of public Jewish worship in Amsterdam was piecemeal, a series of incremental adjustments by local authorities, often in competition with other cities, such as Rotterdam, Alkmaar, and Haarlem, which also sought the benefit of their commercial activities.[68] Together, the public worship of the Lutheran and Jewish communities in Amsterdam exemplified the political possibility and economic utility of **ad hoc tolerance** – that is, local adjustments to normally operative rules limiting religious diversity.

We should also take note of one more example of **ad hoc tolerance** that grew out of the negotiations that led to the Truce. Recall that in an unofficial *Déclaration* from the French ambassadors who mediated the final agreement, the Dutch authorities pledged "that there will be no innovations in Religion in Villages under the jurisdiction of the Cities of the United Provinces situated in Brabant."[69] There, in the contested borderlands in the northern parts of Catholic Brabant that were "possessed" by the United Provinces and subsequently ruled as Generality Lands, the *Déclaration* continues, "the exclusive exercise of the Catholic, Apostolic and Roman Religion that was done in the past will continue there without any change, and without bringing them any scandal." This was an obvious exception to the normally

---

[65] See the aerial photo of this church in Kaplan, *Divided by Faith*, 181.

[66] The relatively large Lutheran community in Amsterdam may have constituted fifteen percent of the city's population. This new church was built on the site of an earlier "house church," in a former warehouse. For a broader context, see Frijhoff and Spies, *1650: Hard-Won Unity*, 394–9.

[67] See J. C. H. Blom and Renate G. Fuks-Mansfeld, eds., *History of the Jews in the Netherlands*, trans. Arnold J. Pomerans and Erica Pomerans (Portland, OR: Littman Library of Jewish Civilization, 2002), and Miriam Bodian, *Hebrews of the Portuguese Nation: Conversos and Community in Early Modern Amsterdam* (Bloomington: Indiana University Press, 1997).

[68] Cf. Prak, *The Dutch Republic in the Seventeenth Century: The Golden Age*, 216–19.

[69] See Chapter 7, note 58, in this volume.

exclusionary rules regarding Catholic worship, and it would continue to be a contentious issue as the borders changed again following the expiration of the Truce in 1621.[70]

What made the Dutch peace distinctive in a larger comparative sense was the local accommodation of multiple "dissident" identities in a national context that promised and largely delivered on the individual's freedom of religious conscience. By the time of the Twelve Year Truce in 1609, the disestablishment of the Catholic Church, and the simultaneous establishment of a privileged, but not universal, Reformed Church had produced the basic contours of a distinctive religious peace that went well beyond the generic evangelical/Catholic identity boundaries of the early sixteenth century. To be sure, the Catholic/Reformed role reversal that attended the de facto independence of the Dutch Republic was fraught with tension, intimidation, more than a little coercion, and even occasional violence. But compared with the active **repression** of the sixteenth century, this was a relatively nonviolent process, with most of the violence directed at churches and religious objects rather than human beings; in broad outline, it was a fait accompli by the second decade of the seventeenth century. Indeed, the most dramatic and portentous religious conflicts during the Truce and beyond took place *within* the Reformed Church and continued the larger pattern of multiplication of religious identities/choices, rather than the simplification or limitation of religious choices that attended negotiated settlements in Switzerland, Germany, and France.

THE NEW DIMENSIONS OF DIVERSITY

Just as the religious wars in France and the Low Countries in the second half of the sixteenth century were decidedly different from the wars in Switzerland and Germany in the first half of the century, so also the religious peace that blossomed in France and the Low Countries at the beginning of the seventeenth century incorporated new dimensions to the patterns of religious diversity we found in Switzerland and Germany. The Edict of Nantes, like the *Landfrieden* and the *Religionsfriede*, validated and extended a remarkably inclusive religious regime in France, but the Twelve Year Truce silently validated two very different forms of religious exclusion in the Southern Netherlands and the Dutch Republic. Indeed, if we add the specific examples I have highlighted in this chapter to the basic template of Figure 1.2, we will see a rather different range of variation than was evident in Figure 4.1.

While La Rochelle and Metz are illustrative of the complexity of France's national experiment in the **integration** of Reformed alongside Catholics in

---

[70] See Benjamin J. Kaplan, "'In Equality and Enjoying the Same Favor': Biconfessionalism in the Low Countries," in *A Companion to Multiconfessionalism in the Early Modern World*, ed. Thomas Max Safley, Brill's Companions to the Christian Tradition, vol. 28 (Leiden; Boston: Brill, 2011), 99–126.

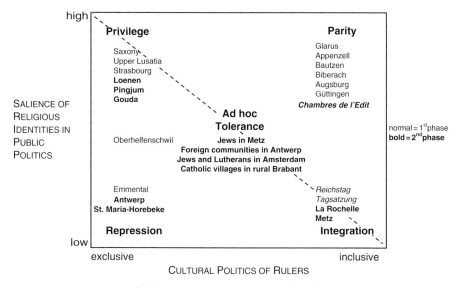

FIGURE 8.1: Patterns of religious coexistence in central and western Europe

public life, Antwerp and St. Maria-Horebeke are emblematic of the survival of diversity under conditions of active **repression** on a "national" scale. Loenen, Pingjum, and Gouda are illustrative of the multiplicity of religious voices and choices under the broad umbrella of **privilege** in the United Provinces, whereas Metz, Antwerp, Amsterdam, and rural Brabant provide examples of the way **ad hoc tolerance** could offer exceptional spaces for religious difference within very different "national" templates. The parity that was built into the French *Chambres de l'Edit* is the rare exception that highlights a broader contrast. Indeed, it is striking that the principal variations we found in France and the Low Countries were arranged to the left of and below an imaginary diagonal line running from privilege through ad hoc tolerance to integration in Figure 8.1. This, of course, is a sharp contrast with the principal variations we found in Switzerland and Germany, which were, on the whole, to the right of and above that diagonal. These contrasting patterns of religious coexistence and diversity are not, of course, mutually exclusive; neither are they strictly sequential. Instead they may be considered cumulative overlays on the conceptual map that is represented graphically in Figure 1.2.

When we turn our attention to the last phase of religious war that began in 1618, we will encounter two very different histories of war – one, a thoroughly international conflict that started out as a civil war and was fought almost entirely within the German-Roman Empire; and the other, a series of interconnected civil wars within a composite monarchy – that may be considered the climax and denouement within the larger drama of Europe's age of religious wars. As we might expect, the mechanisms that led recurrently to religious conflict, violence, and war yielded, under new conditions in the first half of the seventeenth century, visibly different variations on by-now familiar themes. In turn, in their very different settlements – one, the result of a broadly international negotiation and the other, the cumulative result of a series of inconclusive military and political "victories" – we will encounter both new themes and familiar variations that may be said to represent the extent to which those who claimed political and religious authority in Europe gave their grudging consent to the obvious facts of religious diversity among the ordinary people who were nominally subject to their authority. Indeed, the mechanisms that led away from religious violence and war yielded, under new conditions in the second half of the seventeenth century, remarkably durable patterns of religious peace that were both familiar and surprisingly modern.

PHASE III

1618–1651

9

Climax and Denouement

In the first half of the sixteenth century, the relatively limited religious wars in Switzerland and Germany were predicated on the sudden explosion of the "Luther question," the drama and destruction of the Peasants' War, and the piecemeal success of Reformation coalitions in constituent members of the Swiss *Eidgenossenschaft* and the German *Reich*. In the second half of the sixteenth century, the much longer and more destructive religious wars in France and the Low Countries were predicated on more than three decades of repression of religious dissent, the development of underground "churches under the cross," and the (inter)nationalization of networks of religious solidarity, both Catholic and evangelical. In the first half of the seventeenth century, the very different religious wars in Germany and Great Britain were predicated on all of that – the many decades of religious conflict, violence, and war – as well as a remarkable legacy of religious peace. Indeed, at the beginning of the seventeenth century, there was a moment when it appeared as if the era of religious wars in central and western Europe might be coming to an end. Consider the evidence we have seen so far.

In Switzerland, as we saw in Chapter 3, religious conflicts continued to bedevil the *Eidgenossenschaft* at both the local and territorial level for decades, but none of them – not even the deep polarization within both Glarus (in the 1560s) and Appenzell (as late as 1597) – reignited the religious wars. In Germany, too, there were significant challenges and adjustments to the terms of the *Religionsfriede* – such as princely conversions, disagreements over ecclesiastical properties, and popular challenges to their rulers' claims of *ius reformandi* – but the peace held firm. In France, as we saw in Chapter 8, the determined efforts of Henry IV and his royal commissioners to implement the provisions of the Edict of Nantes – both to restore Catholic worship and to secure Reformed integration – even survived the assassination of the king in 1610. Meanwhile, in the Low Countries, following the cease fire in 1607 and the Twelve Year Truce in 1609, both the Southern Netherlands and the United

Provinces settled into durable, if strikingly different, patterns of religious coexistence. Indeed, throughout western and central Europe durable patterns of religious diversity had replaced the "unity and purity" that had characterized Latin Christendom just a century earlier. Even in the composite British monarchy, which had known its share of religious upheaval – the Pilgrimage of Grace (1536), the restoration of Catholicism under Mary I (1553), the restoration and extension of Protestant Reformation under Elizabeth (1558), the establishment of an official Calvinist reformation in Scotland (1560), and the Tudor conquest and "plantation" of Protestant settlers in Ireland (1550s onward) – the first decades of the seventeenth century were remarkably peaceful under the capacious umbrella of the established churches of England, Scotland, and Ireland.[1]

This peace did not last, of course, and when it failed, it failed spectacularly: The Thirty Years War, the most destructive in European history prior to World War I, started in 1618; both the Eighty Years War and the French civil/religious wars restarted in the 1620s; and the civil wars in Scotland, Ireland, and England began in 1638. This remarkable confluence of conflicts – all engaging religious identities as critical markers of political enmity and alliance – may be considered the climax of Europe's era of religious wars. In retrospect, it is tempting to see the general peace that had emerged prior to the wars as particularly fragile and to argue that renewed war was inevitable. But for our purposes, it is critical to recognize the contingency of each of these struggles; to identify the mechanisms that led from religious peace back to religious war in Germany, France, and the Low Countries, but not Switzerland; and to disentangle the multiple religious identities/enmities that continued to frame these conflicts, even when *political* motives and intentions seemed to guide many of the most famous and bellicose actors.

FROM LOCAL RESISTANCE TO INTERNATIONAL WAR

The coming of the Thirty Years War underscores two insights relevant to this broadly comparative account of religious war and religious peace in early modern Europe: that implementing and maintaining a formal religious peace requires hard work, commitment, and adaptation to change (as we saw in

---

[1] See, for example, Patrick Collinson, *The Religion of Protestants. The Church in English Society 1559–1625*, The Ford Lectures 1979 (Oxford: Clarendon Press, 1982), and Diarmaid MacCulloch, *The Reformation* (New York: Viking, 2004), 513–20: "Early Stuart England: The Church's Golden Age?" See also, Ute Lotz-Heumann, *Die doppelte Konfessionalisierung in Irland. Konflikt und Koexistenz im 16. und in der ersten Hälfte des 17. Jahrhunderts*, Spätmittelalter und Reformation (Tübingen: Mohr Siebeck, 2000), and Ute Lotz-Heumann, "Between Conflict and Coexistence: The Catholic Community in Ireland as a 'visible Underground Church' in the Late Sixteenth and Early Seventeenth Centuries," in *Catholic Communities in Protestant States: Britain and the Netherlands c.1570–1720*, eds. Benjamin J. Kaplan, et al., Studies in Early Modern European History (Manchester, UK; New York: Manchester University Press, 2009), 168–82.

France); and that starting a religious war is a complex process that involves the concatenation of many complex mechanisms, which suggests that it is actually not very easy to do (think of the Pilgrimage of Grace). As it happened, the Thirty Years War was famously sparked by a bold act of political defiance in Bohemia on May 23, 1618: the so-called Defenestration of Prague.[2] But the conditions for a rapid escalation from local resistance to international war had been a long time in the making, and even then, this infamous conflagration, in which as many as eight million people may have lost their lives, was by no means an inevitable consequence.

In the *Religionsfriede*, as we saw in Chapter 3, the political elites of the German-Roman Empire had very reluctantly agreed, after nearly four decades of controversy and conflict, to accept the obvious fact of their religious differences as the necessary foundation for a common and more peaceful future. The prescriptive language of this elite bargain served to validate relatively stable "facts on the ground" by means of pledges of mutual recognition and to preserve the status quo by prohibiting cross-territorial interference in religious affairs. Still, as we saw in Chapter 4, the actual patterns of religious diversity and coexistence that emerged in the empire both before and after 1555 were a good deal more complex, messy, and subject to change over time than the agreement seemed to allow or envision. It was precisely this disconnect between the authoritarian conservatism of Germany's rulers, as expressed in the *Religionsfriede*, and the ongoing and dynamic process of religious diversification – one that engaged a much broader array of political actors – that made keeping the peace so difficult and demanding. As Thomas Brady suggests, however, the "skilled pragmatism" of emperors Ferdinand I (1558–1564) and Maximilian II (1564–1576) and Elector August I of Saxony (1553–1586) had served both to establish firmly the empire's religious peace and to demonstrate how it might be used to accommodate change.[3] Indeed, in 1556, Ferdinand had founded the Landsberg Alliance that was, according to Peter Wilson, "expressly dedicated to upholding the Augsburg settlement and renounced religion as a ground for violence."[4]

Historians whose specific purpose is to describe and account for the resumption of religious war in the empire usually attend to the kinds of official changes or actions that seemed to challenge or contravene specific

---

[2] For a recent description and analysis of this infamous event, see Peter H. Wilson, *The Thirty Years War: Europe's Tragedy* (Cambridge: Harvard University Press, 2009), 3–4, 269ff.

[3] Thomas A. Brady, Jr., "Settlements: The Holy Roman Empire," in *Visions, Programs and Outcomes*, vol. 2 of *Handbook of European History, 1400–1600*, eds. Thomas A. Brady, Heiko A. Oberman, and James D. Tracy (Leiden: E. J. Brill, 1995), 253. On the intellectual foundations of the Habsburg policy of finding the "via media" in this period, see Howard Louthan, *The Quest for Compromise: Peacemakers in Counter-Reformation Vienna*, Cambridge Studies in Early Modern History (Cambridge; New York: Cambridge University Press, 1997).

[4] Wilson, *Thirty Years War*, 198.

provisions of the peace agreement.[5] Princely conversions to Calvinism, for example, presumably violated the exclusion, in the fifth paragraph, of "other" Christians, but as it happened, such attempts to establish a Reformed church order were more likely to run seriously afoul of the rulers' subjects than of their political peers; they certainly did not precipitate war. Catholic clerical conversions to Protestantism were, by contrast, more clearly threatening to the political and religious status quo to the extent that they entailed the confiscation or secularization of ecclesiastical properties and incomes. The controversial sixth paragraph of the *Religionsfriede* – the so-called Ecclesiastical Reservation – sought to prevent such confiscations, but the Protestants had not agreed to it and thus did not honor it. In the first decades of the peace, the conversion of lower-level clerics to Protestantism was deemed acceptable as long as the Protestant converts were considered temporary (nonhereditary) "administrators" of their benefices. But the conversion of the Archbishop/ Elector of Cologne, Gebhard Truchess von Waldburg, to Calvinism in 1582, following his marriage to a nun, threatened the political balance within the empire, with roughly equal numbers of spiritual (Catholic) and lay (Protestant) electors;[6] it precipitated military mobilizations by various Protestant and Catholic forces in the Rhineland, but in the end Truchess, who had been formally deposed by the pope, fled to Holland and was replaced by his Catholic rival. As it happened, neither side had brokered firm enough military alliances to hazard a war effort.[7]

The ongoing process of religious diversification, however, presented more subtle and deeply subversive challenges to the status quo of the *Religionsfriede*. Prior to the religious wars, many of Germany's imperial free cities had adopted a Lutheran church order, and in the decades after 1555, a number of self-governing cities, such as Colmar in Alsace, followed suit, using the *Religionsfriede*'s devolution of religious sovereignty to the territorial and local level – what came to be called the *ius reformandi* – to authorize their change of the status quo.[8] In the composite territories of the Austrian Habsburgs,

---

[5] In addition to Peter Wilson's massive survey, see, in English, Geoffrey Parker, ed., *The Thirty Years' War* (London: Routledge, 1987); J. V. Polisensky, *The Thirty Years War* (Berkeley: University of California Press, 1971); and C. V. Wedgewood, *The Thirty Years War* (London: J. Cape, 1938).

[6] The "election" of German-Roman emperors was formalized by the Golden Bull of 1356; the translated text may be found at http://avalon.law.yale.edu/medieval/golden.asp. There were three spiritual electors: the archbishops of Mainz, Trier, and Cologne; there were four lay electors: the Count Palatine of the Rhine, the Duke of Saxony, and the Margrave of Brandenburg were princes of the empire, while the fourth, the king of Bohemia, was a neighboring monarch, with a restricted role in imperial affairs.

[7] See Wilson, *Thirty Years War*, 207–11.

[8] Kaspar von Greyerz, *The Late City Reformation in Germany. The Case of Colmar, 1522–1628* (Wiesbaden: Steiner, 1980). On the history of this concept, see Bernd Christian Schneider, *Ius reformandi: die Entwicklung eines Staatskirchenrechts von seinen Aufängen bis zum Ende des Alten Reiches*, Jus ecclesiasticum, vol. 68 (Tübingen: Mohr Siebeck, 2001), and much more briefly, Bernd Christian Schneider, "Ius Reformandi," in *Religion Past & Present:*

however – in the various lordships of Austria, and the elective kingdoms of Hungary and Bohemia – the process of religious diversification also continued apace, outside the privileged spaces of self-regulating imperial free cities. On an imaginary map of evangelical and Catholic territories in the 1550s, these Habsburg territories, along with Bavaria and the prince-bishoprics of the empire, would undoubtedly be colored solidly Catholic because of Ferdinand's stalwart adherence to Catholicism, alongside his brother, Charles V. But as we saw in Chapter 4, in the case of Bautzen and Upper Lusatia, the contentious political processes that were initiated by the Luther question could result in the institutionalization of Lutheran reforms in provincial cities and even rural communities, quite contrary to the wishes of their Habsburg territorial overlords. How this process unfolded in Bohemia is directly relevant to the coming of the Thirty Years War.

In the kingdom of Bohemia, which was incorporated into the Habsburg domain in 1526, religious diversity was, of course, nothing new, not even in 1517. The heartland of the Hussite revolution between 1419 and 1436, the kingdom of Bohemia-Moravia became officially multiconfessional when the moderate Utraquists, who had defeated the radical Taborites, gained formal recognition in 1436 by the emperor, the Council of Basel, and the Bohemian Catholics.[9] In 1485, the Utraquist Church became an established church in both Bohemia and Moravia, and subsequently their elective kings had to swear to uphold both the Utraquist and the Catholic churches. Catholicism was further marginalized when Bohemian nobles seized church properties, the Bohemian Estates abolished the clerical estate, and the Utraquist Church eliminated clerical benefices. A third "confession" also emerged in the second half of the fifteenth century when the Bohemian Brethren revived the religious traditions of the radical Taborites; they rejected the priesthood and the Mass and lived as pacifists, observing a strict moral discipline.[10] Although Lutheran preachers had some influence in the formation of a "new Utraquist" movement, King Ferdinand worked hard to prevent further religious innovations after his coronation in 1526. A network of Lutheran churches emerged nevertheless in northern Bohemia (in the territory of Upper Lusatia), and in 1546, a combined opposition of Lutheran and Brethren nobles even tried to prevent King

---

Encyclopedia of Theology and Religion, ed. Hans Dieter Betz (Leiden; Boston: Brill, 2007–13), vol. 6, 627.

[9] For a brief introduction to this pre-Reformation history, see Winfried Eberhard, "Reformation and Counter-Reformation in East Central Europe," in *Visions, Programs and Outcomes*, vol. 2 of *Handbook of European History, 1400–1600*, eds. Thomas A. Brady, Heiko A. Oberman, and James D. Tracy (Leiden: E. J. Brill, 1995), 553–5; more specifically on the Hussite revolution, see F. M. Bartos, *The Hussite Revolution, 1424–1437* (Boulder, CO: East European Monographs, 1986). The term "Utraquist" comes from their sacramental practice, in sharp contrast with general Catholic practice, of giving both the communion bread and the wine to the laity (*sub utraque specie*); they also rejected papal claims to universal jurisdiction and authority.

[10] In Moravia, it was the Brethren communities who offered shelter to persecuted Swiss Anabaptists in the sixteenth century; see Chapter 4, p. 85, in this volume.

Ferdinand from mobilizing troops in Bohemia in support of Charles V's campaign against the Evangelical forces in the First Schmalkaldic War.

Under the *Religionsfriede*, then, Bohemia was a uniquely multiconfessional constituent of the officially biconfessional empire, a complex mixture of Lutheran, Utraquist (with both "Old" and "New" factions), Brethren, and Catholic faith communities.[11] Under Emperor/King Maximilian II, the non-Catholic political class of Bohemia, nobles, and urban delegates increasingly under Lutheran leadership in the nobility, sought unsuccessfully to gain formal recognition of a common Bohemian Confession, but the emperor did concede their right to elect noble "Defenders" of the evangelical Estates and churches. Under the long reign of Emperor/King Rudolf II (1576–1612), the array of diverse religious voices in Bohemia increased even more when Calvinism attracted a number of "converts" among the noble elite, much as it did among the princes of the empire. Finally, in 1609, taking advantage of a moment of political opportunity,[12] this dominant and increasingly confident multiconfessional coalition, represented by Calvinist nobles in the Bohemian Estates, pressured Rudolf II, who had relocated the imperial court to Prague, to issue the "Letter of Majesty"; this royal edict granted extensive religious freedoms to the various evangelical religious communities, under the umbrella of the Bohemian Confession, and confirmed the independent role of the evangelical Defenders within the Bohemian Estates, which constituted, according to Winfried Eberhard, a kind of shadow government in Bohemia.[13] It was this religious freedom, which went well beyond the conservative biconfessional vision of the *Religionsfriede*, that the Bohemian rebels were defending in 1618.

The remarkable advance of a very diverse Protestantism in the kingdom of Bohemia was exceptional, to be sure, but it was not unique: a variety of Protestants also gained adherents and even a degree of formal recognition in the other Habsburg dominions in Austria and Hungary.[14] But it was also not without opposition; indeed, the essential counterpoint to the theme of Protestant "advance" in the empire as well as the composite Habsburg

[11] Zdeněk V. David, "Confessional Accommodation in Early Modern Bohemia: Shifting Relations Between Catholics and Utraquists," in *Conciliation and Confession: The Struggle for Unity in the Age of Reform, 1415–1648*, eds. Howard P. Louthan and Randall C. Zachman (Notre Dame, IN: University of Notre Dame Press, 2004), 173–98.

[12] The moment of opportunity was provided by a conflict among the Austrian Habsburg arch-dukes, known as the "Brothers' Quarrel"; see Wilson, *Thirty Years War*, 106–15.

[13] Eberhard, "Reformation and Counter-Reformation in East Central Europe," 561. The text of the Letter of Majesty as well as a parallel agreement between the Bohemian Catholics and evangelicals may be found at www.germanhistorydocs.ghi-dc.org/sub_document.cfm?document_id=4501.

[14] For brief introduction to these developments in Austria and Hungary, see Brady, "Settlements: The Holy Roman Empire," and Eberhard, "Reformation and Counter-Reformation in East Central Europe." More broadly see R. J. W. Evans, *The Making of the Habsburg Monarchy, 1500–1700: An Interpretation* (Oxford: Oxford University Press, 1979).

kingdoms, was a broad crescendo of Catholic "revival." The cutting edge of the Catholic response to the ongoing process of religious diversification was, of course, the development of a specifically Catholic vision of reform at the Council of Trent – the so-called Tridentine reforms – and the creation of newly militant Catholic orders, especially the Jesuits and Capuchins, which did much to revitalize lay Catholic piety.[15] Not unlike the theological innovations of the early Protestant reformers, the theological and ecclesiastical *innovations* of the Tridentine reformers combined with new rounds of *disputation, politicization,* and *mobilization* and yielded a variety of new, politically salient religious identities and boundaries; these, in turn, served to mark the new round of religious warfare in the seventeenth century. As the whole of Europe moved beyond the generic Protestant/Catholic oppositions and alliances of the early sixteenth century, it was the Austrian branch of the House of Habsburg that gave shape and definition to the political forces of Catholic revival in Central and Eastern Europe.

Ever since Charles V's confrontation with Martin Luther at the Diet of Worms, the Habsburgs had been closely aligned with the political defense of papal orthodoxy and the advancement of "unity and purity" within the Catholic Church. The dynastic politics of the Austrian branch of the Habsburgs had shifted dramatically, however, following the decisive defeat of Charles's claim to religious sovereignty within the empire. Indeed, in the first decades after 1555, emperors Ferdinand I and Maximilian II quite pragmatically linked the reputation and fortunes of Austrian Habsburgs to the effective implementation the *Religionsfriede* and the development of imperial institutions and mechanisms to prevent the (re)escalation of local religious conflicts into the coordinated destruction of religious war. Emperor Rudolf II, who has a well-deserved reputation for unpredictability and erratic, even bizarre, behavior, continued to present himself as an impartial peacemaker in imperial politics, but at the same time, he began to link the dynastic interests of the House of Habsburg with a general institutional revival of the Catholic Church, especially in his patrimonial lands.[16]

The Austrian Habsburgs were not alone in linking their political futures to the exclusive "restoration" of Catholic unity and purity; in the 1580s, their Spanish cousins were certainly undertaking the same project in the Southern Netherlands as were the spiritual electors and the dukes of Bavaria within the empire.[17] Clearly the Letter of Majesty represented a setback to the revival of Catholic and Habsburg authority in Bohemia in 1609, but Rudolf's successors as king of

---

[15] For a general survey, see Michael A. Mullett, *The Catholic Reformation* (London; New York: Routledge, 1999).

[16] See Wilson, *Thirty Years War*, esp. chapter 7: "From Rudolph to Mathias, 1582–1612."

[17] Peter Wilson argues that Bavaria, the lone Catholic exception among the largely Protestant secular principalities of the empire, "had already consolidated political authority on the basis of Catholic conformity before the Habsburg archdukes attempted this on their own lands;" Wilson, *Thirty Years War*, 199.

Bohemia, Mathias (1612–1617) and Ferdinand II (1617–1637), decisively undid that policy reversal, and very provocatively set about restricting Protestant worship, and closing Protestant churches in the kingdom of Bohemia.[18] These actions, which sought to reverse the effects of the process of religious diversification, may be considered emblematic of the new, starkly authoritarian, Catholic interpretation of the *Religionsfriede* – recall that the notion of *cuius regio eius religio*, as an authoritarian political claim, was only invented by Lutheran jurists at the end of the sixteenth century.[19] Not surprisingly, these actions were the proximate cause of the bold Bohemian challenge to Habsburg authority in 1618: The "defenestration" of two of Ferdinand's regents, plus one of their servants, by armed agents of the Bohemian Defenders at Hradschin castle in Prague on May 23. Although the three men survived their fall – miraculously, according to Catholic legend, or ignominiously, according to Protestant accounts – this deliberate act of defiance clearly activated a new Bohemian version of the generic Protestant/Catholic identity boundary, but it did not immediately start an international war.

In the Bohemian challenge to Habsburg authority, then, we can see the combination of some, but not yet all, of the mechanisms that helped us to describe and account for the first two clusters of religious war in Europe. In the last decades of the sixteenth century and the first two of the seventeenth, a variety of contentious confrontations – among religiously competitive rulers as well as between rulers and their religiously diverse subjects – recurrently *activated* new, more complex versions of the generic Protestant/Catholic identity boundary. At the same time, there is evidence of increasingly polarized relations among the ruling elites of the German-Roman Empire and of its constituent parts. In fact, an important token of serious *polarization* was the virtual paralysis of the *Reichskamergericht* (Imperial Chamber Court, with a balance of Protestant and Catholic judges in sensitive religious cases), which had been an important venue for the mediation of Protestant/Catholic disputes under the *Religionsfriede*.[20] Instead, more cases were being adjudicated by the *Riechshofrat* (Imperial Court Council or Aulic Council); with a preponderance of Catholic members appointed by the emperor, this body issued a series of partisan verdicts in religious disputes between 1604 and 1608 that, according to Peter Wilson,

attempted to restore the Catholic interpretation of the Augsburg settlement in the imperial cities. While the Protestants argued the terms permitted freedom of conscience, Catholics pointed to other clauses suggesting the cities' religion had to remain as it had been in 1555.[21]

---

[18] On the provocative nature of their policies and their implementation by the newly appointed archbishop (the post had been vacant for decades), see Wilson, *Thirty Years War*, 270. Cf. Parker, *The Thirty Years' War*, 83–8.

[19] See Chapter 1, note 20, in this volume.   [20] Wilson, *Thirty Years War*, 216–19.

[21] Wilson, *Thirty Years War*, 221.

In other words, instead of mediating between conflicting interpretations of the *Religionsfriede*, the Aulic Council began to advance a partisan program of interpreting the *Religionsfriede* to the Protestants' maximum disadvantage. One such verdict in the case of the Swabian city of Donauwörth resulted in the mobilization of Bavarian troops to enforce an imperial ban and led in 1608 and 1609 to the creation of a Protestant Union, followed by a Catholic League, which threatened once again to divide the ruling elite of the empire along the generic Protestant/Catholic identity boundary.[22] In short, without the active support of the emperor and in the absence of "impartial" or mediative action by imperial institutions, the religious peace became perceptibly more fragile.

Still, even the forceful reversal of the Protestant "advance" in Donauwörth – there were apparently only sixteen Catholic households left in a population of 4,000, and the only remaining Catholic church was a Benedictine chapel, protected by the bishop of Augsburg – did not precipitate a more general *escalation* of this local contest into a categorical struggle between militarized Protestant and Catholic alliances within the empire. And so the religious peace held firm, in part because the opposing alliances were fragile and the *brokerage* of militants on either side of the conflict had failed to militarize the relations of Protestant and Catholic elites. A year later, there was also considerable saber rattling around a disputed succession in the duchies of Cleves and Jülich, but this confrontation was resolved, at least temporarily, by a negotiated compromise.[23] Following the "Defenestration" of Prague, however, *activation* of the Bohemian variation on the Protestant/Catholic identity boundary and political *polarization* of the imperial political elites finally did combine with network-based *escalation* and with the *brokerage* of broader military alliances to bring the coordinated destruction of war. But the militarization of this new round of religious confrontation turned out to be decidedly incomplete and unbalanced, and the first phase of the war was over almost before it started.

In its first year, the Bohemian revolt against King Ferdinand failed to attract external support from the fractious Protestant Union within the empire or to win any military campaigns, such as an unsuccessful attempt to capture Vienna. But prior to King Ferdinand's election to the imperial throne in August 1619, succeeding Matthias, the rebel leaders formed a revolutionary Confederation in July – consisting of the territories of Bohemia, Silesia, Moravia, and Upper and Lower Lusatia – which abolished Catholic spiritual authority and rejected Ferdinand as king. In his stead, the Confederation elected the young Calvinist elector of the Rhine Palatinate, Frederick V, whose father had created the Protestant Union of the empire and whose dynastic and religious/political connections with both England and the Dutch Republic might have promised

---

[22] Wilson, *Thirty Years War*, 221–8; see also, C. Scott Dixon, "Urban Order and Religious Coexistence in the German Imperial City: Augsburg and Donauwörth, 1548–1608," *Central European History* 40 (2007): 1–33.

[23] Wilson, *Thirty Years War*, 229–38.

a broadly international network of religious solidarity and military support. Over the next year, however, the Bohemians were able to garner little military support within the empire and more broadly in Europe, except in Hungary, where the Transylvanian prince Bethlen Gabor, who promised to be "a crusader of the righteous against Habsburg Catholic tyranny,"[24] was elected king, replacing Ferdinand. For his part, Ferdinand benefited from a revitalized Catholic League, under the leadership of Duke Maximilian of Bavaria, and in the decisive battle at White Mountain, just outside Prague, the combined forces of the emperor and the League crushed the Bohemian forces on November 8, 1620. Frederick V, who was later mocked for the brevity of his reign as the "winter king," quickly fled Prague; subsequently, the Bohemian Revolt, and with it the Bohemian Confederation, collapsed.

The defeat of the Bohemian Revolt had a devastating impact on the Protestants of Bohemia, who constituted the vast majority of the population, not unlike the impact of the Spanish Habsburg reconquest on the Protestants of the Southern Netherlands. The principal beneficiary of what many Catholics saw as a providential deliverance, Ferdinand II was now free to pursue his vision of what R. J. W. Evans calls "confessional absolutism," the foundation of which was the simple equation of Protestantism with disloyalty.[25] As one might expect, this new phase of the Counter-Reformation began with a thoroughgoing political *and* religious purge in Bohemia: twenty-seven leaders of the revolt were executed in June 1621 and the rest had all their property confiscated; the historic concession to the Utraquist Church of communion of both kinds was promptly withdrawn; first, in 1621, Calvinist and, somewhat later, Lutheran preachers were branded with sedition and expelled, and within three or four years public Protestant worship ceased; in 1627, Ferdinand decreed a new constitution that revoked traditional Bohemian "freedoms" and established a one-confession state; finally, a few months later, all Protestants were given the command either to conform to this new political and religious regime or to leave. Not surprisingly, this occasioned the second massive forced migration of the post-Reformation era.[26]

Although the Battle of White Mountain brought the Bohemian war to an end, it did not end the larger contest, at once dynastic and religious, between the

---

[24] Wilson, *Thirty Years War*, 290; see also his broader account of the military/political complexity of the Bohemian Revolt, 269–313.

[25] See Evans, *The Making of the Habsburg Monarchy, 1500–1700: An Interpretation*, 67–73. Evans describes Ferdinand's "theory" of confessional absolutism, which may be considered an extreme expression of *cuius regio eius religio*, as follows: "the Catholic monarch, prostrate before God, must become all-powerful over his subjects" (68).

[26] Peter Wilson reports a total of perhaps 350,000 refugees from Austria, Silesia, and Bohemia/ Moravia in the wake of this Habsburg victory; 150,000 are estimated to have left Bohemia/ Moravia, most in the years immediately following the defeat of the Bohemian Revolt: *Thirty Years War*, 360. On the long-term process of Catholic Reformation, see Howard Louthan, *Converting Bohemia: Force and Persuasion in the Catholic Reformation*, New Studies in European History (Cambridge; New York: Cambridge University Press, 2009).

Calvinist Frederick V and the Catholic Ferdinand II, plus their assorted allies. Instead, the action shifted westward to the Rhine valley, where Frederick's authority in the Palatinate was most obviously at stake. It was soon clear that here, too, Emperor Ferdinand and his allies – including prominently Bavaria and the revitalized Catholic League as well as Spain, and Poland – were in a strong position to press their advantage against Frederick, who fled into exile in the Dutch Republic and whose alliance was much diminished by the dissolution of the Protestant Union in 1621, amid dissension in its very diverse ranks. At the same time, however, both the French civil/religious wars and the Eighty Years War were restarting, and it was clear that Europe's era of religious war was entering a new, more international and comprehensive phase.

UNFINISHED BUSINESS

In retrospect, we can perhaps conclude that the religious peace in Germany was undermined by two broadly structural or environmental changes: (1) the long-term growth and internal diversification of Protestantism in both the empire and the patrimonial lands of the Austrian Habsburgs, and (2) amid the broadly European revival of Counter-Reformation Catholicism, the gradual but pronounced shift of Habsburg policy away from impartial implementation of the *Religionsfriede* to the forceful promotion of a starkly authoritarian interpretation of the peace. By contrast, the religious peace in France and the Low Countries was undermined by two sudden political changes: (1) the assassination of Henry IV, the principal architect of pacification and integration in France, and (2) the trial and execution of Johan van Oldenbarnevelt, the principal Dutch architect of the Twelve Year Truce, and the simultaneous political revolution of Maurits and the Counter-Remonstrants in the United Provinces. Although the same mechanisms made renewed war possible in each of these cases, under these new conditions in the 1620s, the wars were all significantly different from their earlier iterations.

As noted in Chapter 8, the death of Henry IV in 1610 did not immediately restart the French civil/religious wars, although the regency government of Marie de Medici, under the tutelage of her Italian confidant, the fiercely anti-Huguenot Concino Concini, did awaken the fears of many elite leaders of the former Huguenot coalition, who anticipated a dramatic reversal of Henry's commitment to religious peace. Still, a new round of Protestant/Catholic polarization was forestalled for the better part of a decade by a more general elite opposition to Marie's regency, the so-called Revolt of the Princes, which cut across Protestant/Catholic divisions in the political elite and culminated in a convocation of the Estates General (the last such meeting before the French Revolution), shortly after Louis XIII reached the age of majority in 1614.[27]

---

[27] See J. Michael Hayden, *France and the Estates General of 1614*, Cambridge Studies in Early Modern History (London: Cambridge University Press, 1974).

These elite political tensions remained unresolved until Louis decided to assert his own authority in 1617 (at the age of 17!), imprisoned Concini, dismissed all his mother's advisors, and consigned his mother to the royal chateau at Blois. The specific issue that clearly reactivated the Protestant/Catholic identity boundary in French politics was the unfinished business, from the perspective of the royal government, of the small Protestant principality of Béarn on the southern periphery of the kingdom in the Pyrenees.

Before becoming Henry IV, king of France, Henry de Bourbon had been Henry III, king of Navarre and, by extension, the sovereign of Béarn. Indeed, Henry had been raised as a Protestant in Pau, the capital of Béarn, by his mother, Queen Jeanne III of Navarre, who also formally established the Reformed Church in Béarn in 1561.[28] Henry succeeded her in 1572 as king of Navarre, the same year his marriage to Marguerite de Valois was the setting for the St. Bartholomew's Day Massacre in Paris. As a nominally sovereign principality, however, Béarn was not formally included in the Edict of Nantes, and although Henry IV issued a special edict of toleration to Béarn's Catholics in 1599, it remained officially Reformed under Henry's successor, Louis II.[29] Thus, when Louis XIII issued an Edict of Restitution in 1617, requiring that all church property be restored to the Catholic Church, it set up a confrontation with Béarn, the only jurisdiction, nominally subject to the king of France, that had officially disestablished the Catholic Church. Béarnese opposition to the edict first surfaced in 1618, at the same time as the Bohemian Estates were challenging Habsburg authority, but it took until the summer of 1620 before Louis XIII's government mobilized a military expedition to enforce his royal claims on the southern periphery. As it happened, the governor of Béarn decided against military resistance, and in October, Louis XIII entered the city of Pau, establishing, once and for all, French royal authority and restoring Catholicism without any bloodshed.

In response to the submission of Béarn, what remained of the political and military leadership of the Huguenot coalition convened an Assembly at La Rochelle in November 1620, which the royal government declared to be illegal under the Edict of Nantes (article 82).[30] The militant wing of the Huguenot community, which dominated the Assembly, nevertheless tried to recreate the Protestant "state within the state" of the war years, levying taxes, creating defensive zones based on their *places de sûreté*, and forbidding their leaders to make any peace agreements or truces without the Assembly's assent. These acts of defiance clearly represented a new level of elite *polarization*, but as

---

[28] See Mark Greengrass, "The Calvinist Experiment in Béarn," in *Calvinism in Europe, 1540–1620*, eds. Andrew Pettegree, Alastair Duke, and Gillian Lewis (Cambridge: Cambridge University Press, 1994), 119–42.

[29] Christian Desplat, "Louis XIII and the Union of Béarn to France," in *Conquest and Coalescence: The Shaping of the State in Early Modern Europe*, ed. Mark Greengrass (London: Edward Arnold, 1991), 68–83.

[30] See Chapter 7, pp. 167–8, in this volume.

was the case in Bohemia, the *escalation* was incomplete and the alliance that the Huguenot leaders *brokered* was only a shadow of its earlier iterations. Thus, when Louis XIII's government mounted a new military expedition in the summer of 1621, it encountered significant military opposition, especially at St-Jean d'Angély, near La Rochelle, where the royal forces prevailed after a month-long siege, and at Montauban, where the Huguenots resisted a siege successfully. In the following summer, however, royal forces confronted a dwindling number of the Huguenot's fortified towns – *ad seriatim*, much like Henry IV had done with the cities of the Catholic League – until, faced with a siege at Montpellier, the Huguenot Assembly allowed its military leader, the duke de Rohan, to sue for peace. The Peace/Edict of Montpellier (1622) essentially dismantled the Huguenots' defenses, forcing them to give up immediately all of the *places de sûreté* that had already submitted and guaranteeing that the rest would expire in 1625.[31] The only remaining site of Huguenot resistance was the city of La Rochelle, which was emboldened by the prospect of naval support from England, but La Rochelle finally submitted in October 1628 after a desperate and devastating fourteen-month siege that cost the lives of perhaps half the city's population.[32]

In retrospect, this reprise of the religious wars in France hardly seems like a fair fight. Indeed, the militant Huguenot leadership, mostly noble warlords, failed to recreate the national religious/political/military coalition that had sustained them in the sixteenth-century wars; this may be said to underscore the effectiveness of the Edict of Nantes in (1) segregating the Huguenot military leadership from the widely scattered network of worshiping congregations in the Reformed Church and (2) integrating the bulk of the French Calvinist population into public life. Meanwhile, as the royal armies forced the submission of the Huguenots' fortified cities, Louis XIII emulated his father's lenient policy of reconciliation, confirming the honors of his former enemies and frequently offering them important positions in the service of the royal government. Underscoring the limited political and military nature of the Huguenots' resistance and defeat, the Peace/Edict of Alais (Alès), which was concluded by Cardinal Richelieu and the duke de Rohan on June 16, 1629, simply reaffirmed all of the formal articles of the Edict of Nantes, without revision, except for the royal *brevets* that had provided enormous, but temporary, royal subsidies to sustain the fortified cities and the Reformed clerical leadership. In combination, the royal policy of reconciliation and the terms of the Edict of Alais demonstrate the government's ongoing commitment to the difficult compromises that made religious peace both possible and

---

[31] An English translation of the edict is in Elie Benoist, *The History of the Famous Edict of Nantes: Containing an Account of All the Persecutions, That Have Been in France from Its First Publication to This Present Time*, 2 vol. (London: Printed for John Dunton, 1694), 521–4.

[32] For a fuller account of the ninth civil war, see Mack P. Holt, *The French Wars of Religion, 1562–1629*, New Approaches to European History (Cambridge: Cambridge University Press, 1995), chapter 7.

sustainable in France.[33] Unlike the defeat of the Bohemian Revolt, then, the definitive end of Huguenot resistance in France did not result in a religious purge or another wave of forced migration.

In the United Provinces, the climax of the conflict between Remonstrants and Counter-Remonstrants in 1618–1619 coincided with the Bohemian Revolt and the resurgence of Huguenot resistance in France, and its outcome – the execution of Oldenbarnevelt and the "revolutionary" triumph of the Counter-Remonstrants in alliance with Prince Maurits – certainly enhanced the likelihood that peace negotiations with Spain would fail and their long-running war would resume after the expiration of the Truce in 1621.[34] Meanwhile, the Dutch were directly involved in the start of the Thirty Years War in Germany, financing the mobilization of an assortment of Protestant forces, deploying Dutch troops to the Rhineland, and offering refuge to Frederick V and his family at The Hague, following his multiple defeats in Bohemia and the Palatinate. Still, while the Eighty Years War did not resume immediately in 1621, when it did in 1622, the Dutch were very much on the defensive, in the Spanish siege of Bergen-op-Zoom, their critical frontier fortress in north Brabant, and in the Duchy of Jülich, where the Dutch had a military garrison. In other words, while domestic religious *polarization, escalation*, and the *brokerage* of national religious alliances are relevant to any explanation of why the Truce failed to yield to lasting peace, it is international religious *polarization*, network-based *escalation*, and diplomatic *brokerage* that we must attend to in order to account for the resumption and long-term continuation of coordinated destruction in what had long since become an international war for Dutch independence, no longer bearing much resemblance to the civil/religious strife of the 1560s and 1570s.[35]

In the early years of this last, climactic phase of Europe's religious wars, neither the Dutch nor their German Protestant allies fared very well. Where the Dutch and German wars clearly overlapped in the early 1620s, Spanish forces expelled the Dutch garrison in Jülich in 1622, and although their siege of

---

[33] Although Christian Desplat reports that Louis XIII had vowed earlier to "work towards the destruction of the Huguenots, if given the opportunity," his reaffirmation, working now with Cardinal Richelieu as his chief minister, of the Edict of Nantes appears to underscore the essentially political nature of that destruction; cf. Desplat, "Union of Béarn," 69.

[34] The principal stumbling blocks remained, as they had been in 1607, overseas trade as well as religious "freedom," and the triumph of the orthodox Calvinists, who were supported by many of the Protestant refugees from the south, made it unlikely that the Republic would give up either its long-standing goal of reuniting the Netherlands provinces or its stubborn refusal to grant freedom of worship to Catholics in the north. For background, see Jonathan I. Israel, *The Dutch Republic: Its Rise, Greatness, and Fall, 1477–1806*, The Oxford History of Early Modern Europe (Oxford: Clarendon Press, 1995), 421–77.

[35] For a novel analysis of the military, political, economic, and social dimensions of this larger international struggle, see Marjolein 't Hart, *The Dutch Wars of Independence: Warfare and Commerce in the Netherlands 1570–1680*, Modern Wars in Perspective (London and New York: Routledge, 2014).

Bergen-op-Zoom eventually failed, the Spanish captured Breda in 1625.[36] Meanwhile, the military forces of the Catholic League in Germany, under the command of Count Jean Tserclaes de Tilly (a Walloon Brabanter who had served under Parma in the 1580s), overwhelmed the scattered and poorly coordinated Protestant allies of Frederick V in a series of battles, culminating at Stadtlohn in 1622; as a reward for his efforts, the leader of the Catholic League, Maximilian of Bavaria, was given the electoral office of the formerly Protestant Palatinate by Emperor Ferdinand in 1623. Still, the war did not end, as Tilly's forces turned north toward Westphalia, where what remained of the Protestant forces offered little resistance. It was this pattern of Catholic military success, accompanied by an aggressive policy of "re-Catholicization,"[37] that precipitated the brief, direct military intervention of the Lutheran king of Denmark, Christian IV. Despite this international *escalation* on behalf of the embattled Protestants of the empire, the military struggle continued to go badly for the fragile Protestant coalition. By the time Christian signed a peace with Ferdinand in 1629, by the terms of which Christian recovered territories he had lost but withdrew permanently from imperial politics, the Protestant cause, according to Geoffrey Parker, was "in ruins."[38] As if to punctuate his military domination in the empire, as in his patrimonial lands, Ferdinand issued the infamous Edict of Restitution in March 1629, which ordered the restitution of all Church lands secularized since the *Religionsfriede*, declared that ecclesiastical princes had the right to enforce religious conformity,[39] and specifically banned all Protestant sects besides Lutheranism – the maximal expression, perhaps, of Ferdinand's vision of confessional absolutism.[40]

From this point onward, the scale of this originally limited conflict, the complexity of the international enmities and alliances, the size of the armies involved, and the sheer magnitude of the destruction inflicted on Germany gave entirely new meaning to Europe's ongoing "religious wars." In the 1630s and 1640s, Swedish and French intervention – a strange combination of support for the Protestant cause and dynastic opposition to the Habsburgs – ensured that the conflict within the empire and over the empire's political and religious future would continue for many more years, but as the destruction continued, neither side ever prevailed militarily. Finally, after a series of failed attempts to make peace, including the Peace of Prague in 1635, the Peace of Westphalia formally brought the conflict to an end in 1648. The famous Westphalian settlement, as we will see in the next chapter, addressed at enormous length

---

[36] This event was celebrated in the monumental painting by Diego Velázquez, "The Surrender of Breda," which is in the Prado Museum in Madrid.

[37] See Parker, *The Thirty Years' War*, 88–94.

[38] Parker, *The Thirty Years' War*, 81; on the "Danish intermezzo" more broadly, 71–81.

[39] This effectively nullified the controversial "Declaration," granting freedom of religious practice to Protestants in Ecclesiastical jurisdictions, appended by Ferdinand I to the *Religionsfriede*; see Chapter 3, p. 62, in this volume.

[40] As it happened, the execution of the edict was even more extreme than the letter of its text; see Parker, *The Thirty Years' War*, 98–9.

the various political and dynastic interests at stake, but it also, finally, addressed the "problem" of religious diversity – that is, its potential for the recurrent concatenation of *activation, polarization, escalation,* and *brokerage* marked by religious identity boundaries – which was so prominent at the beginning and remained the most difficult issue to resolve until the very end.

   Still, the Thirty Years War, for all its international dimensions was hardly the only religious contest involving the coordinated destruction of war. Although clearly overlapping and engaging some of the same violent actors, the ongoing Dutch War of Independence had a life of its own. In fact, while Protestant "resistance" was being recurrently defeated in France and Germany in the 1620s, the Dutch Republic gradually regained its military swagger and enjoyed some success against the fabled Spanish Army of Flanders. Following the death of Prince Maurits in 1525, Frederik Hendrik, his younger brother who succeed him as captain-general of the Republic's armies, captured important towns in eastern Overijssel (1626) and Gelderland (1627); the Dutch admiral Piet Heyn took the Spanish silver fleet near Cuba (1628); and Dutch forces besieged and captured the city of 's-Hertogenbosch in Brabant (1629). In 1630, the Dutch conquered significant portions of Brazil,[41] and in the summer of 1632, having taken Venlo and Roermond on his way south, Frederik Hendrik besieged and captured the important city of Masstricht, deep in Spanish-held territory. By this time, however, both the Dutch and the Spanish armies had grown enormously, and the problems of pay, provision, and supply frequently frustrated ambitious military goals on both sides.[42] Consequently, the ongoing war looks, in retrospect, like a series of stalemates in the 1630s and 1640s, until fiscal pressures, war weariness, and political changes finally resulted in a cease fire in 1647 and the completion of peace negotiations at the German city of Münster in 1648.

   In the nearly simultaneous restart of the religious wars in the German Empire, France, and the Low Countries, we encounter the relational dynamics that recurrently made religious war possible in early modern Europe: the *activation* of (new) politically salient religious identities, the *polarization* of political actors on either side of those boundaries, the *escalation* of the conflict via networks of religious solidarity, and the *brokerage* of (inter)national alliances that prominently include specialists in coercive violence. What is largely absent in all three cases, however, is the sustained *mobilization* of popular religious movements and the direct political engagement of ordinary people that had characterized the urban reformations in Germany and Switzerland, the communal violence in France, and the revolutionary reformations in the Low Countries. Instead, this new round of religious war in central and western Europe primarily engaged a diverse, but limited, set of military entrepreneurs, dynasts, and warlords. As the scale of diplomatic and

---

[41] Brazil was of course a Portuguese colony, but Portugal was ruled by the Spanish crown from 1580 to 1640. See Israel, *The Dutch Republic,* 518.

[42] See Hart, *Dutch Wars,* 25–8.

military engagement increased so did the potential for large-scale destruction and the difficulties of finding the kind of political compromises that recurrently made negotiated settlements, and by extension, religious peace possible. Still, peace was possible, as the maintenance of peace in Switzerland, the relatively limited reprise of religious war within France, and the Westphalian settlement suggest. When we turn our attention to the composite British monarchy – England, Scotland, and Ireland – we once again encounter volatile combinations of elite polarization and popular engagement, not unlike those that characterized the earlier religious wars in central and western Europe. In these cases, however, the coordinated destruction of religious/civil war ended in military victories rather than political compromises.

THE RELIGIOUS WARS OF THREE KINGDOMS

As we saw in Chapter 5, the kingdom of England, under Elizabeth, was directly involved in the second phase of Europe's religious wars on the continent, offering military aid to both the Dutch Beggars and the French Huguenots; indeed, for a brief period, following the deaths of François, duke of Anjou, and William, prince of Orange, in 1584, Elizabeth's trusted advisor, Robert Dudley, earl of Leicester, was appointed governor-general of the rebellious Dutch provinces and charged with the direction of their war effort. The English defeat of the Spanish Armada in 1588 was also indirectly a powerful aid to the Dutch Beggars. As the religious/civil/international wars restarted in Germany, France, and the Netherlands in the early seventeenth century, however, Elizabeth's successor in 1603, James VI, the Stewart king of Scotland, who ruled the composite monarchy of Scotland, England, and Ireland as James I, largely avoided direct involvement in the continent's religious wars, even though the embattled Frederick V, elector of the Palatinate, was his son-in-law.[43] Although James's son and successor in 1525, Charles I, offered naval support, under the command of the duke of Buckingham, to the French Huguenots in the defiant city of La Rochelle in 1527, he, too, avoided direct or sustained engagement in the Thirty Years War.

When a series of three civil wars did break out sequentially in the composite British monarchy – first in Scotland in 1638–1639, then in Ireland in 1641, and finally in England in 1642 – they had remarkably little to do with simultaneous conflicts on the continent, but they did bear a strong family resemblance to the civil/religious wars in France and the Low Countries in the sense that they were profoundly religious and revolutionary at the same time.[44] Indeed, all three grew out of a combination of popular and elite resistance to the authoritarian

---

[43] On James's limited support for the Bohemian Revolt and German Protestants, see Wilson, *Thirty Years War.*

[44] For a more extended analysis of the popular politics of these essentially "revolutionary" conflicts, see Wayne Te Brake, *Shaping History: Ordinary People in European Politics, 1500–1700* (Berkeley and Los Angeles: University of California Press, 1998), 137–49. For general surveys of

and exclusionary religious policies of their common sovereign, Charles I. Still, the recurrent mechanisms of *activation, polarization, escalation*, and *brokerage* combined differently in these three very different kingdoms, and consequently the interconnected and eventually conjoined religious wars took very different forms and had very different religious outcomes in Scotland, Ireland, and England. Their differences are especially visible in the (new) politically salient religious identities that were activated in the specific conflicts and sparked larger escalations in each case.

In Scotland, where the civil wars began, a conflict over the authority of bishops within the Church of Scotland pitted Scottish Presbyterian "Covenanters" against the agents of "Anglican" liturgy and episcopacy. Ever since its establishment in 1560 by the Scottish Parliament, in defiance of French Catholic influence in Edinburgh Castle, the Church of Scotland (the Kirk), which was decidedly Calvinist in both theology and ecclesiology, had wrestled with the contradictions inherent in the coexistence of a "presbyterian" authority structure – with its fusion of lay and clerical leadership culminating in a national General Assembly – and the various remnants of an earlier episcopal authority.[45] These contradictions were exacerbated by the dynastic union of Scotland and England after 1603, which made the Stewart king, James VI/I, the "Supreme Governor" of the episcopal Church of England, but not of the presbyterian Church of Scotland, although by the Concordat of Leith (1572), he was allowed to appoint bishops in Scotland with the Kirk's approval.

In the 1630s, Charles I, having pulled back from his European military ventures, began ever more insistently to demand, not unlike his Catholic counterparts on the continent, religious conformity from all of his political subjects, and in 1637, working in concert with Anglican Archbishop William Laud, he forcefully introduced a slightly modified Scottish version of the Anglican *Book of Common Prayer* as the exclusive basis for Protestant religious worship in Scotland. This was met with a howl of official Presbyterian protest as well as popular demonstrations in Glasgow and Edinburgh, and faced with the royal government's refusal to compromise, Scottish political opposition took the form of a national "covenant," protesting the liturgical innovation, which was signed initially by hundreds of

---

the civil wars, see Austin Woolrych, *Britain in Revolution, 1625–1660* (Oxford: Oxford University Press, 2002); Martyn Bennett, *The Civil Wars in Britain and Ireland, 1638–1651* (Oxford: Blackwell Publishers, 1997); and Allan I. Macinnes, *The British Revolution, 1629–1660*, British Studies Series (Houndmills, Basingstoke, Hampshire; New York: Palgrave Macmillan, 2005). For those who are not familiar with the particulars of British history or are simply bewildered by the enormous historiography, the timelines, biographies, and short articles of the British Civil War Project, covering the whole period 1638 to 1700, may be useful: http://bcw-project.org.

[45] On the background and early history of the Bishops War, see David Stevenson, *The Scottish Revolution 1637–1644. The Triumph of the Covenanters* (Newton Abbot: David and Charles, 1973) and Keith M. Brown, *Kingdom or Province? Scotland and the Regal Union, 1603–1715*, British History in Prespective (Houndmills, UK: Macmillan, 1992).

political and religious leaders, but popularized by evangelical preaching.[46] The growth of a broadly based popular "Covenant" movement, organized informally in conventicals and private churches where they could not control existing structures, forced the king to call a General Assembly of the Scottish Kirk in 1638. It was this Assembly, dominated by "Covenanters," that directly challenged the king's claim to ecclesiastical authority, undoing his liturgical changes, and abolishing the episcopal structure through which he enforced conformity to Anglican practice. As the confrontation escalated, the Covenanters consolidated their control of churches and presbyteries, and mobilized a national army, 18,000 strong, which was led by Scottish soldiers with mercenary experience on the continent. Eventually the Scottish Parliament also met, without royal permission, and fashioned a new constitutional structure to sustain itself independently. Anticipating a royal attack, following some minor skirmishes, the Scottish Covenanter army eventually crossed the border with England and easily defeated the king's poorly equipped forces in August 1640. Charles had little option but to offer the Covenanters "incentives" to halt their invasion of northern England.

Once again, the *activation*, in specific circumstances, of religious identities and the boundaries they entailed had combined with *polarization* along those identity boundaries, network-based *escalation*, and the *brokerage* of larger coalitions that included military specialists to make religious war possible, only this time the coordinated destruction pitted Covenanters against Anglicans rather than the generic Protestants against Catholics. These relatively new and distinctly parochial identities are emblematic of the peculiarities of Scottish and English history, of course, but they are also emblematic of the ongoing proliferation of religious identities and diversity across the formerly uniform religious landscape of Latin Christendom; this process had also occasioned division and controversy between Lutherans and Calvinists in Germany and between Remonstrants (also known as Arminians) and Orthodox Calvinists in the Dutch Republic. Only in relatively rare circumstances did such divisions and controversies among proponents of variously conceived theological, liturgical, and ecclesiastical reforms, outside the Church of Rome, lead to the militarization of religious factions and the coordinated destruction of war. Locally distinct variations on these themes in Ireland and England nevertheless followed quickly on the Scottish "Bishops War."

In Ireland, the civil war was framed by the British colonial policy of "planting" English and Scottish settlers and religion on Irish land; it pitted a broad alliance of "Old" or Gaelic Irish and "Old" English "Confederates" against an "Anglican" alliance of "New" English settlers and the Anglo-Irish colonial administration. Ever since Henry VIII had established himself as

---

[46] For context, see John Morrill, ed., *The Scottish National Covenant in Its British Context, 1638–1651* (Edinburgh: Edinburgh University Press, 1990).

Supreme Head of the Church of Ireland in 1536, even before he had managed to
elevate his deeply contested "sovereignty" in Ireland from a lordship to
a monarchy in 1541, the English "conquest" of Ireland had been marked by
politically salient religious identity boundaries – generically Protestant vs.
Catholic – that intersected only imperfectly with national or ethnic identities
such as Irish and English.[47] To be sure, the political salience of the religious
identities was briefly disrupted in the 1550s, when Queen Mary (1553–1558)
reestablished the Catholic Church and its connection to Rome, but under her
successor, Elizabeth, from 1558 onward, the assertion of English political
authority and law was again conjoined with the establishment of Anglican
religious practice and more broadly with "British civilization."[48] Faced with
a long series of regional rebellions, the English military conquest of Ireland was
not completed until the early seventeenth century with the "flight of the earls"
in 1607, under James VI/I. In the meantime, both Mary and Elizabeth had
employed the strategy of "planting" English settlers on lands seized from
(rebellious) Irish landowners in order to secure loyalty to English
colonization.[49] By the beginning of the seventeenth century, inasmuch as the
vast majority of the native Irish population resisted the government's ever more
insistent attempts to convert them to Anglican spirituality and religious
practice, both "Irish" and "Catholic" identities came to be equated with
political disloyalty, much like "Bohemian" and "Protestant" identities were
being equated with disloyalty on the continent.

Under the relatively peaceful conditions of the first decades of the
seventeenth century, the English colonial authorities undertook a radical
transformation of the northern Irish province of Ulster. A joint public and
private initiative on a much broader scale than earlier plantation efforts, the
Ulster plantation, between 1610 and 1640, involved the migration of tens of
thousands of mostly Protestant Scottish and English settlers, who were
supposed to supplant the native Irish Catholic population, but instead came,
in most places, to be thoroughly mingled with them. The appointment of
Thomas Wentworth as Charles I's lord deputy in Ireland in 1631 marked the
beginning of a steady and forceful promotion of England's fiscal, political, and
religious authority in Ireland at the expense of not just the native Irish, but of all
Catholics, including the "Old" English settlers, who had benefited from the first

---

[47] For background, see Colm Lennon, *Sixteenth-Century Ireland: The Incomplete Conquest*
(New York: St. Martin's Press, 1995), and Steven G. Ellis, *Ireland in the Age of the Tudors,
1447–1603: English Expansion and the End of Gaelic Rule*, Longman History of Ireland
(New York: Addison Wesley Longman, 1998).
[48] See especially Nicholas P. Canny, *The Elizabethan Conquest of Ireland: A Pattern Established,
1565–76* (Hassocks: Harvester Press, 1976), and Nicholas Canny, *Making Ireland British,
1580–1650* (Oxford: Oxford University Press, 2001).
[49] The first "plantations" were concentrated just outside the Pale – the zone of direct English
control around Dublin – in Leix and Offaly and in the southwest in Munster; see the map of
Tudor and Stuart plantations in Thomas Bartlett, *Ireland: A History* (Cambridge; New York:
Cambridge University Press, 2010), 102.

plantations, but had remained Catholic. Wentworth's heavy-handed regime not only threatened the Old English Catholics with fines and confiscation of their lands for failing to conform religiously, but also imposed fines on "dissenting" Protestant settlers, such as the Presbyterians from Scotland, for failing to attend worship in the Church of Ireland. Drawing inspiration from the Scottish Covenanter's challenge to "Laudian" intolerance in Presbyterian Scotland, a coalition of Irish Catholics – including Catholic military exiles, who had fought for the Spanish in Flanders, and supported by Counter-Reformation Catholics on the continent – hatched a conspiracy in the summer of 1641 to seize Dublin Castle, the seat and symbol of English authority in Ireland, and to organize simultaneously a popular rebellion against the "British" – that is, the combined Scottish and English – Plantation in Ulster.

The seizure of Dublin Castle failed to materialize, but a popular rebellion in Ulster in October 1641 resulted in what Thomas Bartlett describes as "a pitiless onslaught by the native Irish on the settler population and their possessions,"[50] which plunged Ireland into nearly twenty years of conflict, frequent massacres, and the coordinated destruction of a war in which religious identities were the most reliable, if also confusing, markers of political enmity and alignment. In the short term, the popular uprising and organized military action in Ulster led to both Scottish and English intervention in Ireland as well as the creation, in 1642, of a formal Confederation, which brought together the rebels of Ulster and the Old English aristocracy, who had been alienated by the authoritarian policies of Wentworth, but nevertheless professed loyalty to King Charles.[51] Modeled on the Irish Parliament, the Irish Confederation, with its headquarters in Kilkenny, functioned as a revolutionary government in Ireland for some eight years, raising taxes and recruiting armies, organizing a navy and conducting diplomatic relations with the chief Catholic powers of Europe. But their ongoing attempt to win concessions for Irish Catholics from Dublin Castle and sign an agreement with Charles I eventually foundered on the collapse of Charles's authority in the face of Parliamentary opposition in England.

In England, the civil war was precipitated, in part at least, by the revolutionary challenges that Charles I was facing simultaneously in Scotland and Ireland, and it pitted a broad range of religious "dissenters," including "presbyterians," "baptists," and "independents," collectively known as "puritans," against the agents of royal autocracy and "Anglican" or "Laudian" religious conformity. Ever since King Henry VIII, working with the Parliament, established himself as Supreme Head the Church of England in 1531, the kingdom of England, which

---

[50] Bartlett, *Ireland: A History*, 115.

[51] The apparent irony of the Irish Confederates proclaiming loyalty to Charles I at the same time as their insurrection was threatening his government in Ireland needs, undoubtedly, to be understood against the backdrop of a broadly accepted rumor/suspicion – credible to radical Protestant "dissenters" in England, Presbyterians in Scotland, and Catholics in Ireland alike – that Charles was a secret or closeted Catholic, who might any day restore Catholicism in all of his kingdoms.

also legally incorporated Wales between 1535 and 1542, had struggled with the issue of religious conformity. As we saw in Chapter 2, Henry's Church began some modest reforms of religious ritual and dogma, which combined with the largely negative, confiscatory actions of his royal commissioners to spark the popular, but still-born, Catholic revolt, known as the Pilgrimage of Grace, in the fall of 1536.[52] After 1547, the government of Henry's successor, his nine-year-old son, Edward VI, pushed official religious reform considerably farther in England, abolishing the Mass and clerical celibacy, closing monasteries, and instituting compulsory services in English, using Thomas Cranmer's *Book of Common Prayer*. After Edward's untimely death at the age of 15 in 1553, his half-sister Mary I officially restored Catholicism and the connection to Rome; her execution of nearly 300 Protestant "heretics" earned her the epithet "Bloody Mary," but she also enjoyed considerable popular support among the large population that remained loyal to traditional Catholic spirituality and ritual practice.[53]

Elizabeth succeeded her half-sister in 1558 and officially returned England to Protestantism with the Act of Supremacy in 1559, which was accompanied by an Act of Uniformity, making attendance at the Church of England mandatory. Under the Elizabethan Settlement, Catholic recusancy – that is, refusal to attend the services of the Church of England – was defined as a *political* problem, and Catholic missionaries were considered *traitors*. Indeed, in the 1580s and 1590s, Diarmaid MacCulloch reports, England also executed some 200 Catholic priests and laypeople, more than any other country in Europe.[54] At the same time, the Church of England faced criticism and resistance from Protestants, often Calvinists, who argued that the reforms of the Church had not gone far enough – that the *Book of Common Prayer* emphasized scripted liturgy over the preaching of the Word and that the authoritarian power of episcopacy was at odds with "true" reformation, along the lines of Geneva and Scotland. The Protestant critics of the Anglican Church, dubbed "puritans," sometimes segregated themselves in private devotional practice, and they, too, elicited a crackdown from the official conformists when three separatist leaders were executed for sedition in 1593.[55] What is striking here is that the issues that divided Protestant separatists from conformists had relatively little to do with formal theology, but more clearly had to do with ritual practice and the nature of ecclesiastical authority.[56]

[52] For an overview of religious change under the Tudors, see Christopher Haigh, *English Reformations: Religion, Politics, and Society Under the Tudors* (Oxford: Clarendon Press, 1993).

[53] For a significant revision of the largely negative historiography of Mary's reign, see Eamon Duffy, *Fires of Faith: Catholic England Under Mary Tudor* (New Haven: Yale University Press, 2009).

[54] MacCulloch, *The Reformation*, 392.   [55] See MacCulloch, *The Reformation*, 382–93.

[56] Christopher Marsh provides a very useable survey of the dimensions of religious diversity at the end of the sixteenth century in *Popular Religion in Sixteenth-Century England: Holding Their Peace* (New York: St. Martin's Press, 1998), especially chapter 4.

At the beginning of the seventeenth century, with the dynastic union of Scotland and England under James VI/I, there may have been greater space for religious diversity in England as both "church papists" and "puritans" practiced the *dissimulation* of "occasional conformity," supported by a degree of unofficial *casuistry*, to avoid unwanted notice from Church authorities.[57] Meanwhile, English participation in the international Synod at Dordrecht, which condemned the theology of Jacobus Arminius in 1619, introduced to English polemics the term "Arminian," which zealous "puritans" used to smear the "latitudinarian" theology of the official Church. Still the recurrent *activation* of such relatively new religious identities did not combine with political and religious *polarization*, network-based *escalation*, and the *brokerage* of militarized religious/political alliances within England until well after Charles I succeeded James VI/I in 1625. When Charles dissolved a particularly contentious session of the English Parliament in 1629, the same autocratic policies – the aggressive assertion of the "divine right" of both kings and bishops and the active enforcement of religious conformity – that had fostered *polarization, escalation*, and the *brokerage* of revolutionary coalitions in Scotland and Ireland, not to mention Bohemia, served to alienate a broad range of his subjects in England as well.[58] Still, it was not until the Covenanters' revolutionary challenge in Scotland forced Charles to reconvene the English Parliament after eleven years of "personal rule" in 1640 – first the contentious "Short" Parliament in April, which was dissolved after just three weeks, and then the "Long" Parliament in November, which was not formally dissolved until 1660 – that a clearer pattern of religious and political *polarization* and network-based *escalation* set the stage for revolutionary conflict and religious war in England as well. Even so, it took the revolutionary challenge of the Irish insurrection to precipitate the *brokerage* of opposing military/political/religious alliances that made civil and religious wars possible in England.[59]

The first phase of the English Civil War, which began in August 1642, pitted a composite Puritan coalition, organized by a Committee of Safety in

---

[57] See Alexandra Walsham, *Church Papists: Catholicism, Conformity, and Confessional Polemic in Early Modern England*, Royal Historical Society Studies in History (Woodbridge, Suffolk, UK; Rochester, NY, USA: Boydell Press, 1993), and Patrick Collinson, "The Cohabitation of the Faithful with the Unfaithful," in *From Persecution to Toleration: The Glorious Revolution and Religion in England*, ed. Ole Peter Grell, Jonathan Israel, and Nicholas Tyacke (Oxford: Clarendon Press, 1991), 51–76. See also, table 4.1, "Mechanisms in the Survival of Religious Diversity."

[58] On the broad range of issues that alienated both the elite and ordinary political subjects of England, David Underdown, *Revel, Riot and Rebellion: Popular Politics and Culture in England, 1603–1660* (Oxford University Press, 1985) is especially useful; see also the important revisions of Conrad Russell, *The Fall of the British Monarchies, 1637–42* (Oxford: Clarendon Press, 1991).

[59] For broad surveys of the English wars in the context of the larger Wars of Three Kingdoms, see Woolrych, *Britain in Revolution*, and Bennett, *Civil Wars*.

Parliament, against the Royalist forces of the king, supported by the Anglican Church. Fearing the intervention of Irish Catholic troops on the side of the Royalist forces, the English Puritans negotiated a "Solemn League and Covenant" with the Scottish Covenanters in 1643, which resulted in the creation of a Committee of Both Kingdoms to organize their common war effort and to manage eventual peace initiatives. In 1645, the joint committee authorized the creation of a professional army, to replace locally mobilized militias, which came to be known as the New Model Army.[60] The last major battle of the first war in March 1646 was a victory for the New Model Army, and in May, Charles surrendered to a Scottish army; over the next months, a series of Royalist garrisons surrendered in England and Wales, and the Scots handed King Charles over to the English Parliament, which imprisoned him, bringing the first war to an end.

As war broke out in all three kingdoms, then, it is clear that religious identities were the most important or reliable makers of political enmity and alliance in each of the kingdoms and across the composite monarchy. To be sure, there were extremely important social, economic, fiscal, and political issues at stake in these struggles,[61] but like the simultaneous wars on the continent – principally, the Eighty Years War and the Thirty Years War – the wars of the three kingdoms were religious in their origins in the very real sense that the combatants identified their enemies as well as their allies in terms of their religious beliefs, practices, or affiliations. Although at times, the generic identity boundary between Catholics and Protestants was activated and served to identify networks of solidarity and support, especially internationally, what is especially striking in this last cluster of religious wars is the proliferation of relatively new and locally specific identities among those whom we might call Protestant. We have, of course, encountered an analogous proliferation of Protestant identities and subcultures on the continent, especially in Bohemia and the United Provinces, but in the composite British monarchies, the older, broadly theological distinctions among Lutherans, Calvinists, and Anabaptists/Mennonites are not particularly useful or evident. Instead, we encounter distinctions rooted in *innovation* and *disputation* in the realm of ecclesiastical authority: episcopalian (maintaining the authority of the hierarchy of bishops), presbyterian (integrating the blended authority of clergy and "elders"), or independent (underscoring the fundamental integrity of "gathered" or separated congregations). To some extent, such distinctions might be considered congruent with the Lutheran/Calvinist/Anabaptist

---

[60] See Ian Gentles, *The New Model Army in England, Ireland, and Scotland, 1645–1653* (Oxford: Blackwell Publishers, 1992).

[61] On the social interpretation of the English Revolution, see especially Christopher Hill, *The World Turned Upside Down: Radical Ideas During the English Revolution,* (New York: Viking Press, 1972), and Brian Manning, *The English People and the English Revolution, 1640–1649,* 2nd ed. (London: Bookmarks, 1991); on popular politics, in particular, in a broader comparative context, see also Te Brake, *Shaping History.*

distinctions, but the problem of religious authority or "sovereignty" – that is, the question of who can make final decisions in matters of religious belief, ritual behavior, and community membership or affiliation – was at critical moments preeminent politically in this confluence of religious wars in England, Scotland, and Ireland.

We have already seen the critical importance of the division between episcopalians and presbyterians in the Bishops Wars in Scotland, and we have also noted the alienation of Scottish presbyterians from the episcopal Church of Ireland. In the course of the first English civil war, however, the division, within the composite Puritan alliance, between Presbyterians and Independents became both visible and salient. Although it is safe to say that all Presbyterians were Puritans, clearly not all Puritans were Presbyterian. Indeed, during the 1640s, as the authority of the Church of England began to crumble, there was an explosion of new worshipping communities, some of them presbyterian but many of them "gathered" or stubbornly independent, alongside (or in the place of) the parish churches of the established Church – not unlike what occurred in France and the Low Countries in the 1560s as the authority of the established Church crumbled.[62] Within the Long Parliament, the groupings of Independents and Presbyterians were fluid, but the question of how to treat the king served to polarize them: while the Presbyterians favored "peace" with the king, the Independents wanted to bring him to "justice." As the Presbyterians gained strength in the Parliament, the Independents gained strength in the New Model Army, both within the officer corps and in the rank and file. After the king escaped from his captivity in November 1647, he signed an "Engagement" with a group of Scottish Presbyterian Covenanters, who feared the Independents in the New Model Army more than the king. By the terms of the Engagement, the king promised to impose presbyterian reforms within England in return for the support of a Scottish army.[63] And so the second phase of the civil war began, with the division between Presbyterians and Independents on full display.

The brief, but bitter, second civil war in England and Scotland culminated in August 1648 with the defeat of the Scottish/Royalist "Engager" Army by the New Model Army, under the command of the fiercely Independent Oliver Cromwell, in the Battle of Preston. Then, in December, a troop of soldiers under the command of Thomas Pride excluded 186 and actually detained 51 Presbyterian members of Parliament who still favored making peace with the king, and "Pride's Purge," as this coup has come to be known, cleared the way politically for the "Rump" Parliament, now dominated by Independents, to

---

[62] On the place of these churches in the religious landscape of England, see Chapter 12 in this volume.

[63] The imposition of presbyterian reform was to be provisional for a period of three years, pending a broader agreement on reform in the Assembly of Divines, which had been created by Parliament in 1643. The engagement agreement was opposed by the Scottish Kirk, and thus served to divide the Scottish Covenanters as well as the English Puritans.

bring the king to justice.[64] On January 20, 1649, King Charles I stood trial for treason before a High Court of Justice, appointed by the Rump Parliament; a week later he was condemned to death; and on January 30, 1649, he was beheaded as a tyrant and a traitor.

The military/political coup of the Independents in 1648 followed by the execution of Charles I in 1649 clearly constituted a watershed in British history – in the following months and years, the Rump Parliament abolished both the monarchy and the nobility, disestablished the Church of England, and created a new republican Commonwealth – but it did not end the religious wars of the three kingdoms. In addition to pockets of Royalist opposition in England, there were still significant Royalist political coalitions and armies in Ireland and Scotland, and the leaders of the new revolutionary government were in no mood for negotiations or peace settlements. Thus, in June 1649, Oliver Cromwell was appointed lord-lieutenant of Ireland, and in August he landed in Ireland as commander-in-chief of a military force of 20,000. In January of 1649, a treaty had created a military alliance between the Royalist forces of the colonial government in Dublin and the Irish Confederation in Kilkenny, but this broad Irish resistance to the English Commonwealth was no match for the professional soldiers of the New Model Army. Cromwell's sieges of Drogheda and Wexford in September and October 1649 culminated in the indiscriminate slaughter of thousands of Royalist soldiers as well as Catholic townspeople. In March 1650, Cromwell besieged and occupied the confederate capital at Kilkenny, and by May, departing for England, he had left his Irish expedition in the hands of Harry Ireton, who conducted more campaigns in Leinster and Munster in 1650 and continued some mop-up operations in Connaught in 1651.

Following the execution of Charles I and the creation of the republican Commonwealth in England, Charles II had been declared king in Scotland. In May of 1650, the young king, who was in exile on the continent, signed the Treaty of Breda with the Covenanter government of Scotland, by which he promised, as his father had, to impose presbyterian reform in England in exchange for a Scottish army to assert his claims to the hereditary succession of his father. At about the same time as Charles II landed in Scotland in July, Cromwell was appointed commander of a Commonwealth army to invade Scotland. Following a decisive battle against the Covenanter army at Dunbar in southern Scotland in September, Cromwell's forces finally occupied Edinburgh Castle in December 1650. During the winter and spring, Cromwell was occupied for months trying to consolidate Commonwealth control in northern Scotland; finally Charles's Royalist armies moved southward into England, with Cromwell and the Commonwealth's armies in pursuit in August 1651. The conclusive battle of the last of the civil/religious wars

---

[64] The classic study of this event is David Underdown, *Pride's Purge: Politics in the Puritan Revolution* (Oxford: Clarendon Press, 1971).

was won by Cromwell's forces at Worcester in September, and with the consolidation of the Commonwealth in all three kingdoms, Charles II fled into exile in France.

A WAR OF ALL AGAINST ALL?

When the political philosopher Thomas Hobbes coined and elaborated the notion of a "war of all against all" in the second quarter of the seventeenth century, he was engaged in a thought experiment regarding the origins and nature of civil society and the state, not an attempt to describe and account for actual events. Still, for the historian trying to characterize the history of Europe in the decades immediately preceding the publication of Hobbes's *Leviathan* in 1651, there is a very strong temptation to pull his classic elaboration of that notion out of its philosophical context and deploy it as a characterization of Europe's experience during the last clusters of religious war between 1620 and 1650.

Hereby it is manifest that during the time men live without a common Power to keep them all in awe, they are in that condition which is called War; and such a war as is of every man against every man. . . . In such condition there is no place for Industry, because the fruit thereof is uncertain: and consequently no Culture of the Earth; no Navigation, nor use of the commodities that may be imported by Sea; no commodious Building; no Instruments of moving and removing such things as require much force; no Knowledge of the face of the Earth; no account of Time; no Arts; no Letters; no Society; and which is worst of all, continual Fear, and danger of violent death; And the life of man solitary, poor, nasty, brutish, and short.[65]

In assessing the quality of human life in the absence of awesome power, Hobbes underscores the disincentives to industry and agriculture; the apparent futility of enterprise; the absence of constructive effort, of accumulating knowledge, artistic creativity, and literary production; and, above all, the omnipresence of both fear and actual danger.

Thomas Hobbes's powerful language is clearly over the top as description, but it may nevertheless be useful as a corrective to the relatively stale, dispassionate language that has seemed more appropriate to this mechanistic account of the last clusters of religious war in early modern Europe.[66] Indeed, it pains me that this very synoptic account of the religious wars has attended so little to the very real human costs they entailed. Historians of early modern Europe have long ago identified a "general crisis" of the seventeenth century – featuring many of the elements of Hobbes's speculation – that clearly interrupted the remarkable

---

[65] Thomas Hobbes, *Leviathan, or the Matter, Forms & Power of a Commonwealth Ecclesiastical and Civil* (Neeland Media LLC. Kindle Edition, 2014), 35.

[66] Michael Howard characterized this as "a period in which warfare seemed to escape from rational control; to cease indeed to be 'war' in the sense of politically-motivated use of force by generally recognized authorities, and to degenerate instead into universal, anarchic, and self-perpetuating violence." Michael Howard, *War in European History* (London; New York: Oxford University Press, 1976), 37.

economic and demographic growth of the previous century.[67] To be sure, there were broad, structural mechanisms at work in bringing about this crisis, but the violence and disruption of the religious wars were certainly prominent elements within this toxic mix. For the thousands of people who found themselves directly in harm's way – such as the people of Magdeburg in 1631 or of Drogheda in 1649[68] – Hobbes's characterization of the deleterious consequences of a war of all against all might have seemed all too apt.

As we have seen throughout this work, a broad range of political actors in early modern Europe responded to the "problems" associated with the transnational process of religious diversification by deploying violence and unleashing the coordinated destruction of war. In doing so, however, they recurrently demonstrated, quite unintentionally, of course, that "religious" war – that is, war in which religious identities serve as the markers of both enmity and alliance – was not the solution, but an extension or an intensification of the problem. Furthermore, as the organization, technology, and strategy of warfare "modernized" during this period, the deleterious effects of religious war became ever more pronounced, making peace ever more difficult to achieve. Yet peace was possible, even after the coincidence and confluence of so many wars. Thus, in the next three chapters, we will turn our attention, first, to the strikingly different ways the last clusters of religious war ended in continental Europe and the Great Britain, and then, to the contours of the religious peace that these endings made possible.

---

[67] See, for example, Hugh Trevor-Roper, *The Crisis of the Seventeenth Century: Religion, the Reformation, and Social Change* (New York: Harper & Row, 1967); G. Parker and L. M. Smith, eds., *The General Crisis of the Seventeenth Century* (London; Boston: Routledge & Kegan Paul, 1978); and T. K. Rabb, *The Struggle for Stability in Early Modern Europe* (Oxford: Oxford University Press, 1975).

[68] In 1631, in one of the most notorious massacres of the Thirty Years War, the Protestant city of Magdeburg was sacked by the combined forces of the emperor and the Catholic League; some 20,000 defenders and civilians were estimated to have died, and a year later the city had only 449 inhabitants. See Wilson, *Thirty Years War*, 468–70. In the polemical literature of the time, the Cromwellian atrocities against Catholics at Drogheda and Wexford in 1649 were immediately compared to the slaughter at Magdeburg.

10

Grudging Consent

On December 25, 1641, representatives of the principal European military powers – France, Spain, Sweden, the Dutch Republic, and the German Empire – signed the Treaty of Hamburg by which they agreed to convene a congress to negotiate a general peace in Europe. More than six years later, the Congress of Westphalia bore its historically unprecedented fruit in a cluster of three international peace settlements.[1] In January of 1648, the representatives of Spain and the Dutch Republic signed, and on May 15, 1648, they solemnly swore the Oath of Ratification of the Peace of Münster that ended the Eighty Years War and recognized the independence of the United Provinces of the Northern Netherlands; it was the latter ceremony that formally ended their hostilities and was commemorated in a celebrated painting by Gerard ter Borch.[2] In August of 1648, the preliminary articles of a treaty between the German Empire and the kingdom of Sweden, along with her allies, were agreed at Osnabrück, and on October 24, 1648, this treaty and a complementary treaty that had been concluded earlier between the German Empire and the kingdom of France, along with her allies, were signed and promulgated simultaneously, although at different locations, in the city

---

[1] The best work in English on the Peace of Westphalia is Derek Croxton, *Westphalia: The Last Christian Peace* (New York: Palgrave Macmillan, 2013). The standard works on the Congress and Peace of Westphalia are Fritz Dickmann, *Der Westfälische Frieden*, 7th ed., ed. Konrad Repgen (Münster: Aschendorff, 1998), and Jan Joseph Poelhekke, *De Vrede Van Munster* ('s-Gravenhage: M. Nijhoff, 1948); see also Heinz Duchhardt, ed., *Der Westfälische Friede: Diplomatie, politische Zäsur, kulturelles Umfeld, Receptionsgeschichte*, Historische Zeitschrift, Beiheft 26 (München: R. Oldenburg, 1998). Excellent summaries in English of recent research can also be found in Klaus Bussmann and Heinz Schilling, eds., *Politics, Religion, Law and Society*, vol. 1 of *1648: War and Peace in Europe* (Münster/Osnabrück: Veranstaltungsgesellschaft 350 Jahre Westfälischer Friede, 1998).

[2] See Klaus Bussmann and Heinz Schilling, eds., *Exhibition Catalogue*, vol. 3 of *1648: War and Peace in Europe* (Münster/Osnabrück: Veranstaltungsgesellschaft 350 Jahre Westfälischer Friede, 1998), 213, fig. 615.

of Münster. The eventual ratification of these two documents officially brought an end to the hostilities of the Thirty Years War. Together, the Treaties of Münster and the Treaty of Osnabrück constitute the Peace of Westphalia, which the treaties describe as a "Christian, universal and perpetual Peace." The Peace of Westphalia stands even today as one of the greatest achievements in European diplomatic history.[3]

Unfortunately for the people of Bohemia, whose political defiance in the infamous "defenestration" of Prague had ignited the coordinated destruction of the Thirty Years War, the Treaty of Hamburg in 1641 did not include a truce or cease fire agreement, and the fighting continued apace while the negotiations dragged on. Swedish forces had been making intermittent forays in Czech lands since 1639, but in 1647 the Swedish commander Wrangel began a new offensive that was eventually rewarded by the occupation on July 26, 1648, of the town of Hradschin and the famous castle, together with the Lesser Town of Prague.[4] Intermittent plunder and months of waiting followed, as both the Swedish and the Imperial commanders built up their forces; at last, the Swedish forces launched their first attack on the Old Town starting on October 11. Amidst a lull in the fighting, negotiations began on the fourteenth, but the Swedes launched a new attack on October 25. Armed citizens, including a student militia company, fought valiantly alongside the Imperial army during the Battle of Prague, which culminated on October 30 with a Swedish demand for the city's surrender. When this was refused, the Swedish forces, fearing the arrival of Imperial reinforcements, began retreating, though they continued sporadic attacks until November 8. A definitive truce was finally arranged at the end of November, but the Swedish commanders still celebrated the Christmas of 1648 at Hradschin Castle. The last Swedish soldiers finally left Prague at the end of September 1649, though they stayed on in other parts of Bohemia until July 1650.

The sad irony for the people of Prague was that the last heavy offensive against the Bohemian capital occurred *after* the signing of the Peace of Westphalia on October 24, 1648. According to Zdenek Hojda, "News that the peace had been declared reached both sides several days before the fighting ended, but the Swedes only stopped the siege when reinforcements of the Imperial army reached the town. The temptation to take booty remained until

---

[3] Despite the claims of its authors, the Peace of Westphalia was not a universal peace within Europe inasmuch as it failed to end the ongoing war between France and Spain; cf. Konrad Repgen, "Negotiating the Peace of Westphalia: A Survey with an Examination of the Major Problems," in *Politics, Religion, Law and Society*, vol. 1 of *1648: War and Peace in Europe*, eds. Klaus Bussmann and Heinz Schilling (Münster/Osnabrück: Veranstaltungsgesellschaft 350 Jahre Westfälischer Friede, 1998), 355–72. Repgen reports that in the end, only points of secondary and tertiary importance remained when the negotiators broke off the negotiations.

[4] Zdenek Hojda, "The Battle of Prague in 1648 and the End of the Thirty Years War," in *Politics, Religion, Law and Society*, vol. 1 of *1648: War and Peace in Europe*, eds. Klaus Bussmann and Heinz Schilling (Münster/Osnabrück: Veranstaltungsgesellschaft 350 Jahre Westfälischer Friede, 1998), 403–11.

the end."[5] But much had changed since 1618. At the beginning of this bitter war, the "Protestant" people of Prague had mobilized to demand religious liberty in defiance of their king and emperor, but following the Protestants' defeat at White Mountain (1620), there was a massive repression and emigration of the remarkably diverse Protestant population in Bohemia. Thus, by the end, the "Catholic" people of Prague reportedly fought alongside the emperor's forces in defiance of the Protestant Swedes.

Although historians are accustomed to thinking of the Peace of Westphalia as singular and exceptional – indeed, the first token of the modern international system of sovereign states – it is critically important for our purposes to situate it squarely within the comparative historical context of more than a century of both religious war and religious peace in early modern Europe. Just as the Thirty Years War was an extension of earlier episodes of religious war, so also the Treaties of Münster and Osnabrück, which officially brought it to an end, were extensions or elaborations of earlier templates for religious peace. In fact, the Westphalian religious settlement for Germany was one of three very different negotiated settlements in the first half of the seventeenth century, alongside the Edict of Alais for France and the First Treaty of Münster for the Low Countries, that revised or extended prior agreements. All of these stand in sharp contrast, however, to the Cromwellian military victories that established a common political hegemony – the Commonwealth – but very different religious "settlements" in the composite British state. So what difference did these differences make? How did the possibilities of religious peace differ in these very different histories? Here we will attend to the ways in which the mechanisms that recurrently led away from religious war toward religious peace in the sixteenth century – *domination, subversion, negotiation*, and *segregation* – combined differently in very different circumstances in the middle of the seventeenth century to make durable and distinctive patterns of religious peace possible.

PEACEMAKING 2.0

As we saw in the previous chapter, religious war restarted nearly simultaneously in Germany, France, and the Low Countries. In France, the ninth and last civil war was a limited engagement that focused on the remnants of Huguenot political and military independence in the Huguenot Heartland. The peace agreement that was negotiated in the summer of 1629 marks the rise to prominence, as chief minister in the court of Louis XIII, of Cardinal Richelieu, who negotiated on behalf of the royal government. Although the war had ended in a decisive victory/defeat, the terms of the Edict of Alais were remarkably consistent with the royal government's earlier policies of pacification and reconciliation.[6] To be sure, the

---

[5] Hojda, "The Battle of Prague," 408.
[6] The text of the Edict of Alais is printed in Elie Benoist, *Histoire de l'Édit de Nantes: contenant les choses les plus remarquables qui se sont passées en France avant & après sa publication, à*

Huguenot "party" had to give up its subsidies and its remaining *places de sûreté*; indeed, the preamble specified that each of the fortified cities was to give to the royal commissioners hostages, who would be held until the destruction of their fortifications was complete. But article IV also forgave, pardoned, and "burri'd in Oblivion … all things past," and article V reaffirmed the king's commitment "to maintain all our Subjects professing the Pretended Reformed Religion in the free Exercise of the said Religion, and in the Enjoyment of the Edicts to them granted";[7] thus it confirmed both the public and the secret articles of the Edict of Nantes that had provided for freedom of religious conscience and private devotions, civil and political equality for Calvinists, and a delimited space for public Reformed worship throughout the kingdom. Even in the defiant and devastated city of La Rochelle, the Reformed community remained a visible presence, which was assured of the protection of the king.[8] By stripping away the last vestiges of Huguenot independence, this new iteration of the religious peace in France accentuated the dependence of the Reformed Church on the royal government's commitment to pacification and integration. In this case, then, the *segregation* of the Reformed Church from its military allies combined with royal *domination* and formal *negotiation* to renew the terms of religious peace set forth in the Edict of Nantes.

In the Low Countries, by contrast, the renewal of the war between the Dutch Republic and Spain in 1622 was much more than a limited reengagement; it would last for another quarter of a century before it, too, ended in a negotiated settlement. Inasmuch as this last stage of the Eighty Years War was effectively an international war among state actors, the negotiations to bring it, at long last, to an end were also thoroughly international. Although there had been some resistance initially, the Dutch were included as signatories of the Treaty of Hamburg that set the stage for the Congress of Westphalia, and thus their negotiations were bound up in the endless squabbles, technicalities, diplomatic rituals, and intrigues that attended the birth of the Peace of Westphalia. Despite the international context and foreign venue, however, the

---

l'ocasion de la diversité des religions, et principalement les contraventions, inexecutions, chi-canes, artifices, violences, & autres injustices, que les reformez se plaignent d'y avoir souffertes, jusques à l'édit de revocation, en octobre 1685; avec ce qui a suivi ce nouvel édit jusques à présent, 3 vol. (Delft: Beman, 1693–95), 2: Recueil, 92–8; there is an English translation in Elie Benoist, *The History of the Famous Edict of Nantes: Containing an Account of All the Persecutions, That Have Been in France from Its First Publication to This Present Time*, 2 vol. (London: Printed for John Dunton, 1694), 553–61. Both of these publications are available as digital scans from multiple online collections. Cf. Mack P. Holt, *The French Wars of Religion, 1562–1629*, New Approaches to European History (Cambridge: Cambridge University Press, 1995), 186–7, and N. M. Sutherland, "The Crown, the Huguenots, and the Edict of Nantes," in *The Huguenot Connection: The Edict of Nantes, Its Revocation, and Early French Migration to South Carolina* (Dordrecht; Boston: Kluwer, 1988), 45–8.

[7] Benoist, *The History of the Famous Edict of Nantes*, 556, 558.

[8] On the fate of La Rochelle's Protestants, see David Parker, *La Rochelle and the French Monarchy: Conflict and Order in Seventeenth-Century France*, Royal Historical Society Studies in History Series, no. 19 (London: Royal Historical Society, 1980), esp. chapter 5.

issues that were most clearly at stake in the negotiations between Spain and the United Provinces of the Northern Netherlands were the same as they had been four decades earlier: sovereignty and political boundaries, international trade, and religious diversity. These issues remained deeply divisive, not only separating north from south in the Low Countries, but exposing political divisions between hawks and doves within the two polities. Indeed, internal divisions in the Dutch Republic had scuttled peace negotiations in 1632–1633, and in 1648, the provinces of Utrecht and Zeeland opposed the negotiations while Zeeland even refused to endorse and promulgate the Peace of Münster for three weeks after it had been formally ratified.[9] Still, the treaty's text gives voice to the kind of war weariness that recurrently made difficult political compromises acceptable in early modern Europe: as the preamble expressed it, the signatories,

moved by Christian pity, desire to end the general misery and prevent the dreadful consequences, calamity, harm, and danger which the further continuation of the aforesaid wars in the Low Countries would bring in their train.[10]

Not surprisingly, the Treaty and Peace of Münster between Spain and the United Provinces built on the template established by the Twelve Year Truce, but as a formal treaty it was a rather different document. In the first place, of course, it recognized the United Provinces, in article I, as "free and sovereign states, provinces and lands" with whom the king of Spain "is satisfied to negotiate … , as he does by these presents, a *perpetual peace*."[11] Like the Truce, the Peace resolved the question of boundaries by adopting the possession principle (*uti possidetis, ita possideatis*, or "as you possessed, you shall possess henceforth"), and accordingly, article III articulates the territorial changes since 1609, especially reflecting the military gains by the Republic in the divided provinces of Flanders, Brabant, including 's-Hertogenbosch and the

---

[9] Under the political norms of the Dutch Republic, decisions regarding the declaration of war and the ratification of peace treaties in the Estates General required unanimous decisions among the seven member provinces, but in this exceptional case, ratification was accomplished with only six votes, with Zeeland refusing to concur. On the Dutch politics of peace in the 1630s and 1640s, see Jonathan I. Israel, *The Dutch Republic: Its Rise, Greatness, and Fall, 1477–1806*, The Oxford History of Early Modern Europe (Oxford: Clarendon Press, 1995), 518–23, 595–609.

[10] The Latin text, plus a French translation, of the Treaty of Münster are reproduced in Clive Parry, ed., *The Consolidated Treaty Series*, 231 vols. (Dobbs Ferry, NY: Oceana Publications, 1969–81), vol. 1, 3–117. There is a modern edition of the Dutch text in C. Smit, *Het Vredesverdrag van Munster, 30 January 1648* (Leiden: Brill, 1948), 30–60; there is a partial English translation in Herbert H. Rowen, ed., *The Low Countries in Early Modern Times: A Documentary History*, Documentary History of Western Civilization (New York: Harper and Row, 1972), 178–87; quotation at 179.

[11] Smit, *Vredesverdrag van Munster*, 30, and Rowen, *Low Countries*, 181. The emphasis is in the original text. For a thoughtful analysis of how difficult even this basic compromise was for the Spanish authorities, see Laura Manzano Baena, *Conflicting Words: The Peace Treaty of Münster (1648) and the Political Culture of the Dutch Republic and the Spanish Monarchy*, Avisos de Flandes (Leuven: Leuven University Press, 2011).

surrounding Meijerij, the Lands of Overmaas, and Limburg, including the city of Maastricht.[12] In order to resolve eventual disputes regarding territories, boundaries, taxes, duties, and the like, the agreement created, undoubtedly following French examples, a "Chambre mi-parti," with equal judicial representation (article XXI). Unlike the Truce, which had carefully avoided any direct mention of the East or West Indies, where economic and political competition was fierce and volatile, this "perpetual peace" necessarily addressed questions of trade and administration both within and beyond Europe; again, the possession principle was applied, including the portions of Brazil controlled by the Dutch West India Company (WIC) since 1641 (articles V and VI). In short, the First Peace of Münster, like the earlier agreements in Switzerland, Germany, and France, made peace possible by incorporating mutual (political) recognition, assuring future security on both sides, and providing a mechanism for the resolution of future disputes short of recourse to coercive means.

Unlike the formal political compromises that explicitly shaped the religious peace elsewhere in Europe, the Peace of Münster, like the Truce before it, did not address or resolve the difficult religious issues that were such an important part of the war's origin; only article 19 specified that in the exercise of religion when traveling across the newly established boundaries, all parties should avoid conduct that might lead to scandal. This is not to say that religious issues were no longer contentious in the 1640s. In fact, the Treaty remained silent on the religious issues precisely because the negotiators could not reach agreement on them: the Spanish negotiators refused to accept freedom of worship for "heretics" in the Southern Netherlands while the Dutch negotiators refused to accept freedom of worship for "papists" in the United Provinces.[13] Nevertheless, the grudging consent they gave to the political, legal, and economic provisions of the Treaty did bring a definitive end to the coordinated destruction of the religious war that began in the Low Countries in the 1560s, and so it made enduring religious peace possible. As we saw earlier, during the Truce, *negotiation* combined with *segregation* between two new polities and *domination* within each to renew the distinctive peace that was, in turn, shaped and reshaped by the *subversion* of religious "dissenters" on both sides of the border (see Chapter 8).

In France in 1629 and in the Low Countries in 1648, then, negotiated settlements revised or adapted earlier settlements in accordance with changed military and political circumstances, but they did not fundamentally alter the terms of the religious peace that had emerged by the first decades of the seventeenth century. Much the same can be said about the German-Roman

---

[12] In three small territories of "Over-Mass," near the border with Germany to the east of Maastricht, the signatories left in place a joint administration with the prince-bishop of Liege that had been created in the 1630s.

[13] For the war of words that made compromise on "the matter of religion" so very difficult, see Baena, *Conflicting Words*, chapter 5, 197–234.

Empire and the Peace of Westphalia in 1648, but the story of how the signatories to this agreement came to give their grudging consent to what might seem to be only minor adjustments to the original *Religionsfriede* of 1555 is neither direct nor obvious. Indeed, in the 1630s the first attempt to "revise" the *Religionsfriede* in the Peace of Prague might have predicted a very different religious future for Germany, in particular, and Europe, as a whole.

Like the Augsburg Interim (1548), which preceded the German *Religionsfriede* (1555), the Peace of Prague (1635) was an imperial initiative that reflected both the emperor's temporary military advantage and the emperor's political and religious aspirations. Indeed, this template for peace reflected the dynamic of *domination* more clearly than *negotiation* and compromise. The Peace of Prague followed a major imperial victory over Swedish forces at Nördlingen in 1634, which turned back Swedish penetration all the way into southern Germany, and the negotiations that led to it were limited to the emperor and the elector of Saxony, who was a staunch Lutheran, but feared "foreign" interference within Germany. The elector won some softening of the terms of the very divisive Edict of Restitution (its terms would be suspended for forty years) and some concessions to Lutheran religious practice, in line with the *Religionsfriede*, as well as confirmation of Saxon authority in Lusatia (which had initially followed the defeat of the Bohemian Revolt).[14] What the emperor achieved was the exclusion of his patrimonial lands from the religious peace and at least nominal unification of all military forces in the empire under his command; the latter entailed the dissolution of the Catholic League, which had operated independently under Bavarian leadership, and sought to redefine the war as a conflict between "foreign" enemies and a "united" Germany.

Without further negotiation, the limited agreement between the emperor and the elector of Saxony was expanded to include other electors and estates, who were granted amnesty if they had opposed the emperor since 1630. But those who refused to adopt the Peace of Prague were declared outlaws subject to legal confiscation of their territories. Although the emperor claimed to be seeking a proper restoration of the constitutional order within the empire, this was, as Peter Wilson suggests, a "monarchical solution," which "conveniently reserved peace-making as an imperial prerogative."[15] Had it actually been implemented, the Peace of Prague would likely have made the empire safe for the maximization of the Habsburg vision of "confessional absolutism."

Although the Peace of Prague won the piecemeal and grudging consent of many in the political elite of the empire, it failed to unite Germany against its

---

[14] The German text of the Peace of Prague, which is a very complex document comprising ninety-four articles, is printed in J. J. Schmauss and H. C. von Senckenberg, eds., *Neue und vollständigere Sammlung der Reichs-Abschiede*, 4 vol. (Franckfurt am Mayn: E. A. Koch, 1747), III, 534–48; a digital scan of this document collection is available from Google Books.

[15] Peter H. Wilson, *The Thirty Years War: Europe's Tragedy* (Cambridge: Harvard University Press, 2009), 566.

"foreign" enemies, namely Sweden and France, in large measure because of the exclusion of so many Protestant leaders – including the rulers of the Palatinate, Hessen-Kassel and Württemberg – from the amnesty provision. Despite the temporary suspension of the Edict of Restitution for ecclesiastical lands, the legal confiscation and, by extension, re-Catholicization of these "outlaw" Protestant territories would clearly have furthered the Habsburgs' Counter-Reformation ambition of turning back the tide of religious diversification. As a decidedly authoritarian initiative, the Peace of Prague had little chance of actually redefining the war, much less actually bringing peace; instead it set the stage for what may have been the most anarchic and destructive phase of the Thirty Years War in the early 1640s.[16] Thus, the coordinated destruction of war, now thoroughly international, would continue unabated until all the combatants, and Emperor Ferdinand III (1637–1657) in particular, gave up the goal of military victory and agreed to the kinds of political and religious concessions that made enduring peace possible.

A UNIVERSAL AND PERPETUAL PEACE?

How did the treaties negotiated in the Congress of Westphalia finally bring the continent's religious wars to an end in 1648? As we have seen in the earlier phases of religious war, the challenge of religious peacemaking was twofold: to deflect or reverse the mechanisms – *activation, polarization, escalation*, and *brokerage* – that recurrently led to violence and war and to manage the "problem" of religious diversity and/or to mitigate the effects of religious competition, short of further recourse to violent means. The Swiss *Landfrieden*, the German *Religionsfriede*, and the French edicts of pacification addressed both of these challenges explicitly, combining *negotiation* with acceptance of the facts of local or territorial *domination* and/or *segregation*, while leaving enough ambiguous space for *subversion* and informal adaptation to changing circumstances. The Twelve Year Truce failed to address the question of religious diversity in the Low Countries, but it nevertheless demonstrated that a purely political settlement could at least interrupt a long-standing war and make durable peace possible.

At the Congress of Westphalia, many participants, including especially the representatives of Ferdinand III, envisioned an international *political* agreement to end all the international wars – including the wars between Spain and the Dutch Republic and between Spain and France – without addressing the religious issues that divided the empire.[17] As it happened, the war between Spain and France remained unresolved for another eleven years, and, as we have already seen, the first Treaty of Münster addressed only the international political issues between Spain and the Dutch Republic; likewise, the second

[16] See Wilson, *Thirty Years War*, 622–70.
[17] Since the Peace of Prague, the emperor had claimed that the religious divisions of the empire had been replaced by imperial unity and he, alone, could negotiate a political settlement to bring the international war within Germany to an end on behalf of the empire as a whole.

Treaty of Münster addressed explicitly just the international political issues between France and the empire. Only the Treaty of Osnabrück addressed both the international political issues between Sweden and the empire *and* the domestic religious issues of the original conflict within the German-Roman Empire. Because it was the more comprehensive of the two treaties signed in October and it included a broader range of adherents, including England, Denmark, Poland-Lithuania, and Russia, the Treaty of Osnabrück, according to the *Consolidated Treaty Series*, was the primary instrument, which was officially incorporated by multiple references into the second Treaty of Münster.[18]

How the Congress of Westphalia reached this unprecedented, if not quite universal, conclusion is a complex story of formal diplomacy and back-door intrigue, amid changing battlefield conditions, that has neither a clear beginning nor a definitive end. According to Conrad Repgen, a total of 109 delegations, representing a total of 140 imperial estates and 38 other "interested parties," participated in the peace conference, and since the delegates arrived and departed at different times and their preliminary agreements required both formal signatures and official ratifications, not to mention further amplification and actual implementation, the Peace of Westphalia was more clearly a process than a singular event.[19] The details of this process need not detain us here, but an important turning point came when Emperor Ferdinand III, following a "catastrophic defeat" at the hands of Swedish troops in the Battle of Jankau in Bohemia in 1645, was forced to relinquish his claim to represent the empire as a whole and, instead, to summon the empire's constituent members – the so-called estates, including territorial lords and imperial cities – to participate as independent parties in the peace process. Like Charles V's decision to turn over negotiations with his Protestant "enemies" to his brother, the inclusion of the imperial estates, to negotiate with and alongside the emperor, had far-reaching effects; indeed, Repgen

---

[18] See Parry, *The Consolidated Treaty Series*, 1, 119. Volume 1 of the *Consolidated Treaty Series* – its 231 printed volumes are available in many law-school libraries – contains the full Latin text plus eighteenth-century English translations of both the Münster and Osnabrück treaties, but thanks to the herculean efforts of the *Vereinigung zur Erforschung der Neueren Geschichte* (VENG) to edit and publish an enormous range of official documents and correspondence relating to the Congress of Westphalia in a forty-volume series, these documents and a wide range of images are available, as of 2014, without restriction online at www.digitale-sammlun gen.de/index.html?c=sammlung&projekt=1290080792&ordnung=sig&ab=&suchbegriff=&kl =&l=de&l=en&l=de. The treaty texts, in particular, plus translations from the official Latin into German, English, and French, among other languages, are available at www.pax-westphalica .de/ipmipo/index.html. There is also a website called "Everything Peace of Westphalia," created and maintained by Derek Croxton, which very conveniently offers links to a variety of resources, images, and texts at http://peaceofwestphalia.org.

[19] Repgen, "Negotiating the Peace of Westphalia," 356. For a fuller and more recent account in English of the negotiations, complete with references to the enormous literature, see Croxton, *Westphalia: The Last Christian Peace*, especially chapters 7 and 8, which divide the issues of "foreign satisfaction" from the "German issues."

terms it the "first important political result" of the peace process, which was reinforced by Sweden's dogged and ultimately successful linkage of domestic religious issues, claiming to represent the interests of Germany's Protestants, to the "satisfaction" of foreign, great-power interests.[20] Although it could have ended the war differently, the Peace of Westphalia, like the precedent *Landfrieden, Religionsfriede,* and Edict of Nantes, not only ended the coordinated destruction of the Thirty Years War, but articulated a template for a "Christian," if not quite universal peace.

As noted earlier, the two treaties signed in October 1648 at Münster were very different documents – the Osnabrück treaty is much longer, nearly one-quarter of its text addresses religious issues, and it has a broader range of signatories – but these treaties were nevertheless intended to be complementary: They have a similar internal logic and have substantial passages in common, and the Münster treaty (the IPM) explicitly incorporates, in paragraphs 47/49, all of articles V and VII of the Osnabrück treaty (the IPO), which address issues of religious law, "as if the words of the abovesaid Instrument were reported here verbatim."[21] They also have much in common, of course, with the earlier negotiated settlements we have examined. Indeed, like the Swiss *Landfrieden* (1531) and the French Edict of Nantes (1598), the Peace of Westphalia is founded rhetorically on the principles of amnesia and amnesty.

That there be on both sides a perpetual Oblivion and Amnesty of all that has been done since the beginning of these Troubles, in what Place or in what Manner soever Hostilities may have been exercis'd by the one or the other Party; so that neither for any of those things, nor upon any other Account or Pretext whatsoever, any Act of Hostility or Enmity, Vexation or Hindrance shall be exercis'd or suffer'd, or caus'd to be exercis'd, either as to Persons, Condition, Goods or Security, either by one's self or by others, in private or openly, directly or indirectly, under form of Right of Law, or by open Deed, either within, or in any Place whatsoever without the Empire, notwithstanding all former Compacts to the contrary; but that all Injuries, Violences, Hostilities and Damages, and all Expences that either side has been oblig'd to be at, as well before as during the War, and all Libels by Words or Writing shall be entirely forgotten, without any regard to Persons or Things; so that whatever might be demanded or pretended by one against another upon this account, shall be bury'd in perpetual Oblivion.[22]

[20] Repgen, "Negotiating the Peace of Westphalia," 357.

[21] All references to the text of the second Münster (IPM) and Osnabrück (IPO) treaties will be to Vereinigung zur Erforschung der Neueren Geschichte, *Wesfälischen Friedenverträge von 24. Oktober 1648. Texte und Üersetzungen. Acta* (Internet publication, 2004) (www.pax-westphalica.de/ipmipo/index.html). References to the IPM will cite the paragraph numbers of the texts (Latin original/English translation when they are different) and references to the IPO will cite the article number, plus the subparagraph numbers, where necessary, of the texts (Latin original/English translation when they are different). The Acta Pacis Westphalicae website has a whole host of useful capabilities and reader aids, including side-by-side translations, a detailed overview of the articles and paragraphs of the treaties, and comprehensive cross-references between the two treaties.

[22] Paragraph 2 IPM, article II IPO; quotation from the English translation of the IPO.

In the Swiss *Landfrieden*, the principles of forgiving and forgetting were tied to the acceptance of facts on the ground and implicitly, at least, to the possession principle (*uti possidetis, ita possideatis*) that, we noted earlier, served as the foundation of the Twelve Year Truce and the first Treaty of Münster. The acceptance of facts on the ground was also implicit in the mutual recognition that was at the heart of the German *Religionsfriede* (1555).[23] In this new German settlement, however, "amnesty" was tied explicitly to the principle of "restitution" – which is to say, to the undoing of changes that had occurred during the war:

> According to this Foundation of a general and unlimited Amnesty, all and every[one] . . ., who upon occasion of the Troubles of Bohemia and Germany, or upon the account of Alliances contracted on one side and another, may have suffer'd any Prejudice or Damage from either Party, in any manner, or under any pretext whatsoever, . . . shall be fully re-establish'd on both sides, in the same State, . . . notwithstanding all the Changes made to the contrary, which shall be annul'd and remain void.[24]

This promise of general restitution is stunning, of course, but it is not unlike the way the Edict of Nantes, in articles 9 and 10, also explicitly voided changes that had taken place "during the precedent troubles," restoring, for example, both Catholic worship, wherever it had been eliminated, and Protestant worship were it had existed in either 1577 or in 1596–1597.[25] Not surprisingly, in the empire the general principle of restitution required considerable amplification and specification; indeed, substantial sections of both the IPM and the IPO are devoted to the elaboration of specific, presumably the most contentious, restitutions of authority, both political and "spiritual."[26]

To specify the restitution of changes wrought by some thirty years of coordinated destruction is, of course, to identify the difficult compromises that were required in order to stop the violence of war. For our purposes, the provisions for religious "restitution" are of primary interest, but these were often impacted by the broader political compromises that made peace possible. Take, for example, the fate of the Palatinate. As we saw in Chapter 9, following the Bohemian Revolt, both the Upper Palatinate and the Lower or Rhineland Palatinate, the patrimony of the elector Frederick V, were overrun by the forces of the Catholic League; this resulted in the exile of Frederick and his family, the

---

[23] In the enforcement of the German peace after 1555, the facts on the ground that the *Religionsfriede* implicitly accepted were taken to be the state of affairs that existed as of the signing of the Treaty of Passau, which ended the fighting in 1552.

[24] Article III, 1 IPO, paragraph 5 IPM; quotation from the English translation of the IPO.

[25] See Chapter 7, pp. 163–5, in this volume.

[26] See article IV in the IPO, which runs to no less than 57 subparagraphs, and paragraphs 7–46 in the IPM (no less than one-third of the treaty's 120 paragraphs), including paragraph 35 which simply incorporates, as if "word by word," article IV, subparagraphs 28–45 IPO. Many subparagraphs in article V of the IPO also explicate the meaning of "ecclesiastical restitution." On the relationship of "amnesty" to "restitution," see Repgen, "Negotiating the Peace of Westphalia," 262–3.

confiscation of his territory, the transfer of the office of elector to Maximilian of Bavaria, and the effective return of this critical Protestant territory to Catholicism.[27] Under the Westphalian settlement, "restitution" entailed the restoration of the political claims of Frederick's son, Karl Ludwig, only in the Rhineland, while the Upper Palatinate was permanently alienated to the Duchy of Bavaria and the electoral title was retained by Duke Maximillian; a new, less senior, electoral office was created to compensate Karl Ludwig and his branch of the Wittelsbach family.[28] In other words, while a Protestant ruler was restored in the Rhineland Palatinate, Catholic authority was validated in the Upper Palatinate. Clearly, restitution, which may be considered compensation for those who had suffered losses during the war, had its very real limits.[29] The other glaring exception to the principle of restitution was an explicit exemption of the Habsburg confiscations of rebel property in Bohemia and Austria (article IV, subparagraphs 53/51 IPO; paragraph 42 IPM).

There was another major component of the Westphalian political settlement that also had potential implications for the future of religious diversity in Germany: the "satisfactions" in favor of France and Sweden as well as their German allies. Quite unlike anything that had been part of the earlier settlements in Europe, these foreign "satisfactions" and domestic "compensations" were quite different in the two treaties, but together they constitute a considerable proportion of the text of the combined treaties and may be said to represent the political price that the emperor and his allies within the empire had to pay for peace, and especially for the evacuation of "foreign" armies from the empire. In the Osnabrück treaty, the principal territorial satisfaction was made to the small kingdom of Sweden (article X IPO), whose troops occupied important positions in both Bohemia and the empire. Most important, Sweden acquired western Pommerania as well as the port city of Wismar and secularized ecclesiastical territories in Bremen and Verden – all of these were territories they already occupied – and by virtue of these new acquisitions, the Swedish monarchy became a constituent member (estate) of the empire. Sweden also bargained hard for a special monetary satisfaction to underwrite the enormous costs of demobilizing the thousands of Swedish soldiers still stationed in Bohemia and elsewhere in central and northern Germany (article XVI, subparagraphs 8–12, IPO). The IPO also included political compensations for Sweden's Protestant allies: Mecklenburg, Braunschweig-Lüneburg, and Electoral Brandenburg, which acquired eastern Pommerania as well as various secularized (arch)bishoprics (articles XI–XIII

---

[27] Prior to the war, Heidelberg, the capital of the Rhineland Palatinate, had become an important center of international Calvinism, of which the Heidelberg Catechism (1563), one of the core "confessions" of international Calvinism to this day, is emblematic.

[28] Paragraphs 10–46 IPM, and article IV, subparagraphs 2–22 IPO.

[29] The other restitutions specified in both treaties involved the princely houses of Baden and Württemberg, and the families of sixteen imperial counts, all of whom had suffered losses because of their exclusion from the limited amnesty in the Peace of Prague.

IPO); both treaties included the same complex political and military satisfaction for Hessen-Kassel (article XV IPO; paragraphs 48–60 IPM). On the whole, these adjustments to the political geography of the empire in the IPO did not promise to have a significant impact on the geography of religious diversity in Germany, inasmuch as the political changes affected jurisdictions that were already Protestant.[30] In the Münster treaty, the principal territorial satisfaction was made to the kingdom of France, whose troops occupied important positions in southern and southwestern Germany. Whereas the IPM validated France's long-standing incorporation of most of Lorraine, including the episcopal city of Metz, it also gave France a new, but delimited "sovereignty" over Alsace, on the western side of the Rhine, in exchange for a considerable monetary payment to the House of Austria and the withdrawal of its troops further east.[31] In this case, then, territorial satisfaction involved the transfer of political authority over the Lutheran population of Alsace to a Catholic sovereign, without specifying the religious consequences for the local population.

In all, then, the legal amnesty, political restitution, foreign satisfaction, and domestic compensation provisions, which constitute the bulk of the Münster and Osnabrück treaties, represent the political compromises that the principal combatants, the German estates, and the various "interested parties" were grudgingly willing to accept in order to end the coordinated destruction of the Thirty Years War.[32] Here we see especially clearly how the mechanism of *negotiation* and political compromise combined with *segregation* – both the withdrawal and the demobilization of armies and the dissolution of international coalitions – to reverse or deflect the mechanisms, especially network-based *escalation* and political *brokerage*, that had for so many years made the coordinated destruction of war possible. But what of the deep religious *polarization* that had so clearly informed the beginning of the Thirty Years War and had remained a particularly contentious feature of the negotiations that brought it to an end? As we saw in the negotiated settlement between Spain and the Dutch Republic, a purely political settlement can under some circumstances bring a long-standing religious war to an end, but in this case, Sweden refused to agree to its political and military "satisfactions" without first resolving the religious grievances of its Protestant allies. Consequently, the political bargains of the international elite that were more or less in place by the fall of 1647 had to await the final resolution of the deeply

[30] Pommerania had become Protestant prior to the Schmalkaldic wars, but the ecclesiastical jurisdictions had been secularized after 1555 in defiance of the Ecclesiastical Reservation, which the Evangelical estates disputed.

[31] Although the cities were to retain their privileges as imperial cities, the incorporation of the Habsburg territories of Upper and Lower Alsace into the kingdom of France was termed unconditional. On the legal complexity, if not contradictions, of this satisfaction, see Repgen, "Negotiating the Peace of Westphalia," 366–9.

[32] Some of the "interested parties," such as the papacy, were deeply opposed to the Westphalian settlement, but could not prevent its ratification or stop its implementation.

contentious religious issues in the spring of 1648. This, of course, brings us to article V of the Treaty of Osnabrück, which addresses "the Grievances of the one and the other Religion, which ... have been partly the Cause and the Occasion of the present War."

A CHRISTIAN PEACE

Whereas the Peace of Westphalia, as a whole, is founded on amnesty and amnesia regarding "all that has been committed since the beginning of these Troubles," the religious settlement that became the *sine qua non* of the general peace was rooted, first and foremost, in the memory of the religious peace that had preceded the war. Indeed, the first subparagraph of article V states that the *Religionsfriede* of 1555,

in all its Points and Articles agreed and concluded by the unanimous Consent of the Emperor and Electors, Princes and States of both Religions, shall be maintain'd in its Force and Vigour, and sacredly and inviolably observ'd.

But much had changed in the empire since 1555, and accordingly, the signatories declared that

those things that are appointed by this Treaty with Consent of both Parties, touching certain Articles in the said Transaction [i.e., the *Religionsfriede*] which are troublesom and litigious shall be look'd upon to ... [be] a perpetual Declaration of the said Pacification, ... and that all which Oppositions are by virtue of these Presents declar'd null and void. (article V, subparagraph 1 IPO)

In principle, then, the other paragraphs of article V, nearly 10,000 words in English translation, represent a series of footnotes on the *Religionsfriede*, the specific language of which is not actually included in this settlement, presumably because, after more than nine decades of experience, its text was very well known and readily available.

As we saw in Chapter 3, the central thrust of the opening articles of the original *Religionsfriede* in 1555 was an explicit recognition and validation by the members of the imperial diet of their obvious religious differences. To this mutual recognition, however, this new settlement adds, also by way of introduction, an important clarification:

And as to all other things [presumably, those things that were not "troublesom and litigious"], That there be an exact and reciprocal Equality amongst all the Electors, Princes and States of both Religions, conformably to the State of the Commonweal, the Constitutions of the Empire, and the present Convention: so that what is just of one side shall be so of the other, all Violence and Force between the two Parties being for ever prohibited. (article V, subparagraph 1 IPO)

Indeed, "exact and reciprocal Equality" had not been specified in 1555, and as we saw in Chapter 9, many elements of the *Religionsfriede* only became "troublesom and litigious" when partisanship and unequal "justice" began to characterize the enforcement of the religious peace. In order to revive the religious peace that had been obtained in the past, then, the signatories embraced "exact and reciprocal Equality" within the political elite as the essential foundation of a more durable peace.

In the context of this complex combination of amnesty regarding the war, memory regarding the peace, and "exact and reciprocal Equality" among the "two Parties," the second subparagraph of article V introduces the deeply contentious question of "Restitution in Ecclesiastical Affairs." As an elite political bargain, the original *Religionsfriede* was, above all, concerned with the preservation of the religiously diverse status quo within the German-Roman Empire, which was generally understood to be the situation at the time of the Treaty of Passau in 1552 as the foundation for a durable peace. Clearly, both the piecemeal adaptations we observed during the peace (1555–1618) and the coordinated destruction of the war (1618–1648) had brought profound changes to the religious landscape of the empire, and deciding how to define a new "status quo" – that is, fixing the chronological reference point for eventual restitutions – under this renewal of the *Religionsfriede* was extremely difficult. No one appears to have imaged or proposed a return to the situation in 1552 or 1555, but the Protestants generally favored a return to 1618, that is, prior to the Bohemian Revolt; the Catholics – at least those who were willing to consider any kind of compromise – generally favored a later date, say 1630, prior to Sweden's entry into the war but after the Edict of Restitution, or 1627, which was the "normative" year that was fixed in the Peace of Prague. How the negotiators at the Congress of Westphalia eventually agreed to the "normative year" of 1524 remains something of a mystery, but the second subparagraph announces, without explanation, that January 1, 1624, is to be "the Term from which Restitution in Ecclesiastical Affairs is to begin" (article V, subparagraph 2 IPO). Certainly this date makes sense in the context of Emperor Ferdinand III's insistence that his patrimonial lands in Austria and the kingdom of Bohemia be exempt from any religious compromises that might undo or compromise the program of re-Catholicization that he undertook in Bohemia and Austria following the Bohemian Revolt. From the Protestants' perspective, 1624 was perhaps acceptable because it predates the major efforts at re-Catholicization elsewhere in the empire.

Altogether, balancing the requirements of amnesty, memory, parity, and restitution was a tall order, and the specific emendations that were included in this settlement are eloquent testimony to the transformation of the religious landscape and the political culture of the German-Roman Empire, not just since 1517, but also since 1555. Like the *Religionsfriede*, the religious peace of Westphalia embraced religious diversity, as opposed to authoritarian uniformity, as the foundation for an enduring peace within the empire, and as an elite bargain that sought especially to restore comity and cooperation among the constituent members of the empire, it was concerned with specifying the assets, privileges, prerogatives, and immunities of Germany's powerful elites with regard to the thorniest issues that had divided them since 1555. Take, for example, the deeply contentious issue of ecclesiastical property. In the *Religionsfriede*, Ferdinand I had unilaterally included the "Ecclesiastical Reservation," limiting further secularization of ecclesiastical properties and incomes, in order to gain Catholic consent, but the evangelicals had refused to honor it, and secularization continued in a number of places after 1555, though it was prevented famously in the case of the Archbishopric of Cologne. In the Osnabrück treaty, article V, subparagraphs 14–27/10–22 address these thorny issues in the often-tortured detail of a difficult compromise, essentially validating secularizations that had occurred prior to 1624, limiting them after that date, and making awkward exceptions in particularly contentious cases; additional subparagraphs (48–49/40) regulated competing claims to ecclesiastical income and authority.

In 1555, the *Religionsfriede* had also warmly endorsed the status quo in biconfessional cities, providing that the "citizens and inhabitants of the same free and imperial cities ... shall peacefully and quietly dwell with and among one another, and no party shall venture to abolish the religion, church-customs or ceremonies of another, or persecute them therefor."[33] In the decades prior to the Thirty Years War, however, this biconfessional ideal broke down in several places, and article V, subparagraphs 3–12/4–8, articulated new rules for the composition and operation of municipal authorities in four biconfessional cities, including the complex case of Augsburg, where religious divisions had been particularly corrosive of local government. In these cases, the settlement mandated a strict **parity** – that is, equal numbers of local magistrates of the different confessions – in order to restore comity and cooperation. Similarly, in order to mitigate the effects of religious polarization and unequal representation at the imperial level, the IPO (article V, subparagraph 51–58/42–45) articulated new rules for the operation and composition of imperial institutions and, in particular, the *Reichskamergericht* (Imperial Chamber Court) and the *Reichshofrat* (Aulic Council), which had been compromised as the principal institutions for the adjudication of legal disputes in the implementation of the *Religionsfriede*. In the courts as well as the diets, the settlement imposed strict **parity** rules for those involved in the adjudication of religious disputes. In addition, subparagraph 52/43 specifically mandated "amicable resolution," strictly forbidding majority decision making:

In matters of Religion, and in all other Affairs, wherein the States cannot be consider'd as one Body, and when the Catholick States and those of the Confession of Augsburg are divided into two Parties; the Difference shall be decided in an amicable way only, without any side's being tied down by a Plurality of Voices.

---

[33] Karl Brandi, ed., *Der Augsburger Religionsfriede vom 25 Sept. 1555: Kritische Ausgabe des Textes* (München: Rieger'sche Universitäts-Buchhandlung, 1896), 35; Henry Clay Vedder, ed., *The Peace of Augsburg*, Historical Leaflets, no. 5 (Chester, PA: Crozer Theological Seminary, 1901), 8–9.

Among those matters that had proven to be the most "troublesom and litigious" in the implementation of the *Religionsfriede* was what jurists called the *ius reformandi* (the "right of reformation"), by which the constituent members of the empire – that is, the territorial rulers and imperial cities as opposed to the emperor – claimed the authority to determine and regulate religious practice in their jurisdictions.[34] Although this claim to religious "sovereignty" had only been implied, and at the same time qualified, in the *Religionsfriede*, evangelical rulers, jurists, and polemicists had asserted it forcefully in order to validate further changes to the religious landscape of the empire after 1555.[35] Eventually, Catholic authorities, including the Habsburgs as territorial rulers in Bohemia and Austria, also asserted this same putative "right of reformation" to validate their efforts to enforce conformity to Catholicism. Since neither the evangelical nor the Catholic claims went uncontested, this new peace of religion necessarily sought both to clarify the scope and to qualify the practice of *ius reformandi*; indeed the IPO, by clarifying and limiting it, gave the concept a new legal status that it had not had previously.[36] But the theoretical concept and the actual exercise of *ius reformandi* affected much more than the "troublesom and litigious" relationships among the political elites of the empire; more fundamentally, it shaped the relationships of a very diverse set of rulers to their religiously diverse and equally contentious subjects. Despite the ruler-centered concerns of its authors, what is striking about the provisions of the Westphalian settlement with regard to the *ius reformandi* is the profound respect it articulates for the religious "autonomy" – that is, discretion or freedom of choice – of their subjects, both as groups and as individuals.[37]

Perhaps the most obvious limit that the IPO placed on the ruler's putative "right of reformation" was entailed in the designation of the "normative" year, 1624. In principle, whatever religious authority existed as of January 1, 1624, was to be restored – in addition to the either/or choice of "the old religion" or the "religion of the Confession of Augsburg" (as the *Religionsfriede* had described it), there was also the coexistence of multiple religious authorities, especially in biconfessional cities – and since this was to remain so in perpetuity,

---

[34] For an exhaustive technical "biography" of this legal concept, as distinct from "cuius regio eius religio," see Bernd Christian Schneider, *Ius reformandi: die Entwicklung eines Staatskirchenrechts von seinen Aufängen bis zum Ende des Alten Reiches*, Jus ecclesiasticum, vol. 68 (Tübingen: Mohr Siebeck, 2001). There is a brief, but very useful synopsis of his analysis in Bernd Christian Schneider, "Ius Reformandi," in *Religion Past & Present: Encyclopedia of Theology and Religion*, ed. Hans Dieter Betz (Leiden; Boston: Brill, 2007–13), vol. 6, 627.

[35] See Chapter 3, pp. 58–63 and Chapter 9, pp. 219–22, this volume.

[36] Among the clarifications, for example, subparagraph 28/23 declared that imperial knights should have "the same Right in matter of Religion" as electors, princes, and estates, and subparagraph 29/24 declared that for imperial free cities, the *ius reformandi* extended to their surrounding jursidictions as well as the immediate urban core.

[37] On the Protestant negotiators' understanding of the notion of "autonomy" and their assertion of it among their initial list of grievances, see Croxton, *Westphalia: The Last Christian Peace*, 274.

the new rules implied that rulers could no longer choose to adopt new church regulations at will. In addition, "dissenting," or subordinate, religious groups that could prove they had worshiped either publicly or privately in any jurisdiction at any time in 1624 would be able to do so again and in perpetuity. Like the *Religionsfriede*, the IPO explicitly prohibited cross-boundary interference in religious affairs; it

ordain'd, in order to preserve a more perfect Concord among the States, That no Person should entice to his Religion the Subjects of others … [and] that the same thing shall be observ'd by the States of the one and the other Religion. (article V, subparagraph 30/25)

At the same time, however, the IPO updated and formalized the controversial "Declaration," protecting Protestants within Catholic jurisdictions, which Ferdinand I had appended unilaterally to the *Religionsfriede*, but Catholic authorities had refused to recognize. Article V, subparagraph 31/25 now granted "the Vassals and Subjects" of "Catholick" or ecclesiastical states "the publick or private exercise of the Religion of the Confession of Augsburg" if they had done so at any time in the year 1624, "either by a certain Agreement and Privilege, or by long Usage, or in fine by the sole Observance of the said Religion only for that Year." This passage concludes emphatically with a robust endorsement of diversity:

[A]ll which things shall be observ'd for ever and in all Places, till it shall [b]e otherwise agreed with relation to the Christian Religion, whether in general, or among the immediate States and their Subjects by mutual Consent; so that no Person may be molested by any one whatsoever, nor in any way or manner whatsoever; but on the contrary, that such as have been molested, or in any manner depriv'd of their Right, may be simply and fully restor'd to the State wherein they were in the year 1624, without any exception. The same thing shall be observ'd with regard to the Catholick Subjects, who are in the States of the Confession of Augsburg, where they had the publick or private Use and Exercise of the Catholick Religion in the year 1624. (subparagraphs 31–32/26)

In other words, Protestants and Catholics were to enjoy the same protections when they were subordinate to authorities of the other confession.

Thus, mandating "Ecclesiastical Restitution" in relation to the year 1624 clearly entailed profound limits on the religious sovereignty that Germany's territorial rulers had claimed for themselves.[38] Like the authors of the *Religionsfriede* nearly a century earlier, the authors of the IPO most readily expressed these limits in the familiar language of old-regime privileges that adhered to corporative groups, but they also, at critical points, specifically limited state authority vis-à-vis "Persons … without any exception." This attention to the interests of individual persons was largely absent in the original *Religionsfriede*, except in the right of individuals to emigrate without

[38] Peter Wilson even argues that Germany's rulers retained the putative right of reformation only "as supervision of their territorial churches. They were no longer able to impose their own theological beliefs on their subjects." *Thirty Years War*, 759.

penalty or molestation from jurisdictions that were exclusive of their religious preferences. In the IPO, the so-called *ius emigrandi* was both renewed and amplified:

That if any Subject, who had not the publick or private Exercise of his Religion in the year 1624, or who, after the Publication of the Peace, shall have a mind to change his Religion, or be willing to change his Abode, or be order'd by the Lord of the Mannor to remove, he shall be at liberty to do it, to keep or sell his Goods, and ... to visit them with all Freedom. (article V, subparagraph 36/24)

Some historians have mistakenly construed the *ius emigrandi* to be the privilege of authoritarian rulers to force dissenting subjects to leave if they refused to conform; here, however, it is clearly presented as a liberty, or a limit on the authority of the intolerant ruler.[39]

This new, sometimes awkward, attention to the interests and discretion of individuals – to "any Subject" who "shall have a mind to change his Religion" – is certainly consistent with a broader shift, since 1555, toward the embrace of individual "liberty of conscience," as in France and the United Provinces. It receives its fullest expression, I believe, in article V, subparagraphs 34 and 35/28, which warrant quotation in full:

It has moreover been found good, that those of the Confession of Augsburg, who are Subjects of the Catholicks, and the Catholick Subjects of the States of the Confession of Augsburg, who had not the publick or private Exercise of their Religion in any time of the year 1624. and who after the Publication of the Peace shall profess and embrace a Religion different from that of the Lord of the Territory, shall in consequence of the said Peace be patiently suffer'd and tolerated, without any Hindrance or Impediment to attend their Devotions in their Houses and in private, with all Liberty of Conscience, and without any Inquisition or Trouble, and even to assist in their Neighbourhood, as often as they have a mind, at the publick Exercise of their Religion, or send their Children to foreign Schools of their Religion, or have them instructed in their Families by private Masters; provided the said Vassals and Subjects do their Duty in all other things, and hold themselves in due Obedience and Subjection, without giving occasion to any Disturbance or Commotion.

In like manner Subjects, whether they be Catholicks, or of the Confession of Augsburg, shall not be despis'd any where upon account of their Religion, nor excluded from the Community of Merchants, Artizans or Companies, nor depriv'd of Successions, Legacies, Hospitals, Lazar-Houses, or Alms-Houses, and other Privileges or Rights, and far less of Church-yards, and the Honour of Burial; nor shall any more be exacted of them for the Expence of their Funerals, than the Dues usually paid for Burying-Places in Parish-Churches: so that in these and all other the like things they shall be treated in the same manner as Brethren and Sisters, with equal Justice and Protection.

---

[39] See the brief discussion of the history of this concept in Hans Dieter Betz and et al., eds., *Religion Past & Present: Encyclopedia of Theology and Religion* (Leiden; Boston: Brill, 2007–13), vol. 6, 626.

In these critical passages, the IPO comes close to embracing the combined principles of freedom of religious conscience and civil equality, which, as we saw in Chapter 8, were the foundation of the bold vision of religious inclusion and integration in France.

As close as the IPO comes to declaring a recognizably modern "right" of free religious conscience and civil equality for all religious "dissenters," it nevertheless remains thoroughly entangled in the older language, deriving from the *Religionsfriede*, of binary oppositions between "the two Parties," between the adherents of "the old Religion" and of the "Confession of Augsburg." Article V of the IPO does, without explanation but very consistently, update the awkward sixteenth-century designation of the "old religion" with the more modern terminology of "Catholick" and "Catholicks," yet it clings to the equally anachronistic and awkward expression "those of the Confession of Augsburg" to designate what had become a very diverse group of Protestant authorities who were, in fact, signatories to the treaty. In order to accommodate all of the signatories, then, article VII functions as a necessary footnote to article V, and declares:

It has likewise been thought good, by the unanimous Consent ... That the same Right or Advantage, which all the other Imperial Constitutions, the Peace of Religion, this present Transaction, and the Decision of Grievances therein contain'd, grant to the Catholick States and Subjects, and to those of the Confession of Augsburg, ought also to be granted to those who call themselves the Reform'd; saving nevertheless for ever the ... Regulations which the States that call themselves Protestants have stipulated among themselves, and with their Subjects, whereby care has hitherto been taken of the States and Subjects of every place, as to Religion and the Exercise thereof ... saving also the Liberty of Conscience of every one.

Article VII goes on, of course, to spell out the practical implications of this dramatic transformation of a biconfessional agreement into a multiconfessional agreement among the "Catholicks," "the Reform'd" (Calvinists) and "those of the Confession of Augsburg" (Lutherans); this elaboration centers on the provision that those rulers "who call themselves Protestants," who might "go over to the Religion of another Party," can only do so privately and that it "shall not be lawful to change the Exercise of Religion, or the Ecclesiastical Laws and Customs which shall have been receiv'd formerly." It concludes, however, on a starkly exclusive note: "But besides these Religions no other shall be receiv'd or tolerated in the Sacred Roman Empire." One would almost think that the dreaded Anabaptists of the sixteenth century were still an imminent threat!

All in all, then, it is easy to understand how the very diverse "Protestants" throughout Europe could celebrate the Peace of Westphalia as an enormous victory for "religious liberty," for "dissenting" subjects as well as authoritative, but not authoritarian, rulers. Still, this religious settlement was, at bottom, a difficult compromise, not unlike the compromises we examined in earlier phases. For some Catholics, such as Emperor Ferdinand III who had resisted, on the advice of his religious advisors, the inclusion of a religious settlement in the Westphalian negotiations, any religious compromise with "heretics" could be seen as unacceptable, even morally reprehensible.[40] As for the Protestant signatories, their deep disappointment with the Westphalian religious settlement is expressed in the text itself.

Throughout the negotiations, Ferdinand III had insisted that where he exercised immediate authority – that is, as a territorial ruler, rather than as emperor, in Austria and in Bohemia – he be exempted from the limitations imposed on all other territorial rulers by the religious peace. Article V of the IPO does not explicitly grant that principle, except by implication in creating specific protections and privileges for Lutherans in several duchies and the city of Breslau in Silesia, which were part of the composite kingdom of Bohemia (see subparagraphs 38–40/31). In the immediately following section, however, their disappointment is evident:

And forasmuch as a greater Liberty of the Exercise of Religion has been several times endeavour'd to be agreed during the present Negotiation in the said Dutchies, and the other Kingdoms and Provinces belonging to his said Imperial Majesty and the House of Austria, and that nevertheless it could not be obtain'd because of the Opposition made by the Imperial Plenipotentiaries: Her Royal Majesty of Sweden, and the States of the Confession of Augsburg, reserve to themselves, and to every one of them in particular, the liberty of mediating amicably, and interceding humbly for that effect with his Imperial Majesty in the next Dyet and elsewhere; the Peace always subsisting nevertheless, and all Violence and Force remaining unlawful and forbidden. (article V, subparagraph 41/31 IPO)

Claiming only a modest mediating prerogative for themselves, the Protestant signatories implicitly and awkwardly acknowledged the painful truth that they had not been able to undo or modulate the dramatic effects of Emperor Ferdinand's "confessional absolutism" in Bohemia and Austria.[41]

Altogether, then, the religious peace, which was the *sine qua non* of the broader Peace of Westphalia, looks very much like the *Augsburger Religionsfriede* that served as its foundation: it reduced the salience of religious identities in the political affairs of the empire by means of pledges of mutual recognition and security; in its acknowledgment and limitation of the concept of *ius reformandi*, it once again shifted the scale of religious sovereignty – which is to say, final decision-making authority with respect to religious belief and practice – to the local level; it also sought to prevent the (re)escalation of local and parochial conflicts by channeling future disagreements over religious authority into institutions and processes that were reformed to assure "exact and reciprocal Equality" and "amicable" resolution. What was stikingly novel in this religious

---

[40] See Croxton, *Westphalia: The Last Christian Peace*, 301–5.

[41] The Protestant signatories expressed the same regret in accepting the specific exemption of these territories from the political amnesty/restitution provisions in article IV, subparagraph 53/51, in the IPO.

settlement was the clearer definition it gave to the "autonomy" of subjects vis-à-vis the authoritarian claims of rulers. Not only was there no specific mention anywhere in either of these settlements of the authoritarian principle *cuius regio eius religio* (whose the rule, his the religion), but even where it may have been implied in the concessions that the Protestants were forced to make in the face of Emperor Ferdinand's confessional absolutism, it was clearly framed as an exception to the more tolerant and inclusive rules that applied to everyone else. To be sure, the two very lengthy treaties that constituted the German Peace of Westphalia updated and emended the *Religionsfriede* in important ways, but like the Edict of Alais and the first Treaty of Münster, these treaties did not fundamentally alter the essential terms of the original, which had been, after all, a remarkably successful peace.

Ratifying and implementing the Peace of Westphalia were not easy or straightforward tasks, and it would take until 1654 for the last foreign troops to leave.[42] Meanwhile, the war between Spain and France continued, there were new Swedish wars in the Baltic, and there was a quick succession of three Anglo-Dutch wars between the 1650s and the 1670s. So this was hardly a universal or perpetual peace. But there can be no doubt that the Westphalian resolution of "the Grievances of the one and the other Religion, which . . . have been partly the Cause and the Occasion of the present War," made durable religious peace possible, and the institutions and judicial processes that it (re)created sustained the religious peace within the empire until the empire itself ceased to exist in the beginning of the nineteenth century, which is no mean achievement. To be sure, there would be plenty of religious contention, litigation, and even a few direct challenges to the spirit if not the letter of the religious settlement,[43] but none of these *reactivations* of familiar religious identities/boundaries combined with *polarization* among the political elites, broad, network-based *escalation*, and the *brokerage* of militarized religious coalitions to reignite religious war.

IN SEARCH OF DURABLE RELIGIOUS PEACE

As we saw in Chapter 9, the civil/religious wars in Ireland, Scotland, and England ended with military conquest and the consolidation of the republican Commonwealth under the leadership of Oliver Cromwell at about the same time as the Peace of Westphalia was being implemented and the last foreign armies were leaving Germany. But on the face of it, the Wars of the Three Kingdoms and the Thirty Years War could not have ended more differently. In Germany it took six years of diplomatic effort and hundreds of pages of text to end the fighting and to establish a template for a durable religious peace, while in the three kingdoms there were neither negotiations nor formal

---

[42] See Wilson, *Thirty Years War*, 751–78.
[43] The most sensational challenge to the religious peace may have been the expulsion of Lutherans from the archbishopric of Salzburg in the 1680s and the 1730s. We will return to these examples of "repression" in the next chapter.

settlements. In the Low Countries, of course, we encountered lengthy negotiations and a formal political settlement that ended the coordinated destruction of the Eighty Years War, but the first Treaty of Münster failed to address the religious issues on which the combatants could not reach agreement. So in this broader comparative context, the case of the three kingdoms presents us with new questions: In the absence of any official negotiation whatsoever, where does religious peace come from? And what does religious peace look like? We will address the second question in Chapter 12, where we will find that, like the other cases we have examined, religious peace was complicated, messy, and subject to change over time. Here we will attend to the ways in which the familiar dynamics of *segregation, domination*, and *subversion* worked to shape that complex and messy peace, even in the absence of a formal negotiated settlement.

In order to describe and account for religious peace in Great Britain, it is important to recall that the negotiated settlements we have examined did not create the "facts" of religious diversity on which religious peace was founded, although both the Edict of Nantes and the Peace of Westphalia attempted to recreate situations of religious coexistence that had been disrupted or eliminated as a consequence of religious warfare. Rather, formally inclusive religious peace settlements generally validated and sought to preserve religious diversity that was already in place in order to achieve religious peace; in the absence of a religious settlement, the "new" political regimes in both the Southern Netherlands and the United Provinces of the Northern Netherlands worked within formally exclusionary templates, but willy-nilly preserved a portion of the religious diversity that was already in place, though under decidedly different terms. In the absence of a religious settlement in Great Britain, then, we can also expect that changes in their political regimes would necessarily preserve or modulate religious diversity that was already in place, but under decidedly different terms in the three kingdoms. In these cases, however, the political context of the religious peace proved to be devilishly unstable for many decades. Let us begin, however, with a review of the status quo ante.

In the first decades of the seventeenth century, when James VI/I's personal rule brought the three kingdoms together in a composite monarchy, religious diversity was clearly evident, though variously constituted, in all of his dominions. In England, a theologically capacious, but authoritarian episcopal, Church of England coexisted with a small, well-connected remnant of faithful Catholics as well as an assortment of "puritan" dissidents, who might practice "occasional conformity" while meeting clandestinely in "conventicals" or "gathered churches." In Scotland, a presbyterian Kirk base coexisted nervously with an episcopal Church hierarchy as well as a remnant of devout, but marginalized Catholics. In Ireland, an officially episcopal Church of Ireland coexisted with a growing population of Scottish Presbyterians as well as a majority population of Catholics. In all three kingdoms, legislation compelled conformity to the established church, though enforcement varied in time and place. As might be expected, the simultaneous collapse of both political and religious authority during the civil wars opened up new spaces for religious difference and new opportunities for the assertion of alternative claims to religious authority. The result was the emergence of an occasionally chaotic "religious marketplace," quite unlike anything on the continent, with the possible exception of the Dutch Republic, and an unstable sequence of transient political outcomes with variable implications for the religious future in the three kingdoms.[44]

During the war years, as both civil and religious authority collapsed, the cacophony of dissident voices may at times have been deafening, especially in London and more generally in England. Among those who were promoting new claims to religious authority, the allied challengers to Charles I in Scotland and England, who created the "Solemn League and Covenant" (1644), pledged to undertake:

the reformation of religion in the kingdoms of England and Ireland, in doctrine, worship, discipline and government, according to the Word of God, and the example of the best reformed Churches [i.e., the Scottish presbyterian system]; and we shall endeavour to bring the Churches of God in the three kingdoms to the nearest conjunction and uniformity in religion, confession of faith, form of Church government, directory for worship and catechising.[45]

In addition to presbyterian authority and uniform religious practice, these revolutionary allies committed themselves to

the extirpation of Popery, prelacy (that is, Church government by Archbishops, Bishops, their Chancellors and Commissaries, Deans, Deans and Chapters, Archdeacons, and all other ecclesiastical officers depending on that hierarchy), superstition, heresy, schism, profaneness, and whatsoever shall be found to be contrary to sound doctrine and the power of godliness.[46]

Meanwhile, in Ireland, the revolutionary government created by the Confederation in Kilkenny restored Catholic religious authority and sought permanent concessions from the colonial government in Dublin.

[44] On the religious marketplace in England, see Bernard Capp, "The Religious Marketplace: Public Disputations in Civil War and Interregnum England," *English Historical Review* 129, no. 2 (2014): 47–78, and the many sources cited there. For a broader survey of the whole period of instability, see John Coffey, *Persecution and Toleration in Protestant England, 1558–1689*, Studies in Modern History (Harlow, England; New York: Longman, 2000).

[45] Many of the critical documents relating to the "Puritan" revolution were published more than a century ago in Samuel Rawson Gardiner, ed., *The Constitutional Documents of the Puritan Revolution, 1628–1660* (Oxford: Clarendon Press, 1889). This very useful collection has been both scanned and digitized, and is now available in a variety of online formats, including a facsimile of the original in Google Books and a digitized and searchable version at www .constitution.org/eng/conpur_.htm. Here I will identify quotations by the document numbers and paragraph numbers in the original edition. This quote is from doc. 58, paragraph 1.

[46] Gardiner, *Constitutional Documents*, doc. 58, paragraph II; the parenthetical definition of "prelacy" is in the original.

As his political and religious authority crumbled around him, the previously intransigent Charles I did demonstrate a willingness to compromise with his adversaries. In his "Engagement" with the Scots in 1647, for example, he accepted the implementation of the presbyterian system in England, in accord with the Solemn League and Covenant, for a provisional term of three years, while an assembly of experts worked out a permanent solution; in doing so, he also committed himself to the goal of "suppressing the opinions and practices of Anti-Trinitarians, Anabaptists, Antinomians, Arminians, Familists, Brownists, Separatists, Independents, Libertines, and Seekers"[47] – this laundry list of "outsiders" to be excluded reflecting, of course, the cacophony of "new" voices that the crisis of authority had unleashed. At the same time, his representatives in Dublin came close to reaching an accommodation with those "papists" in Confederate Ireland, who saw him as an ally rather than an enemy.

In a particularly vivid confirmation of the principle that the stated intentions of the principal actors are unreliable predictors of the outcomes of revolutionary conflicts, it was a collection of "outsiders" – "(Ana)baptists," "Separatists," "Independents" and the like – who actually "won" the key battles in 1648, purged the Parliament in England, tried and executed the king, created the Commonwealth, and consolidated its authority in all three kingdoms. In early 1649, the so-called Rump Parliament, dominated by those outsiders, passed, in quick succession, a series of acts that together represent their new political settlement: an act abolishing the office of King (March 17), an act abolishing the House of Lords (March 19), and an act declaring England to be a Commonwealth (May 19).[48] Because of dissension within this triumphant coalition, however, it took another year and a half before the new government addressed the question of religious authority, and then only obliquely in an act repealing the Elizabethan statutes, which had imposed penalties for not attending the Church of England (September 1650). In their place, they declared that

all and every person and persons within this Commonwealth and the territories thereof, shall (having no reasonable excuse for their absence) upon every Lord's day, days of public thanksgiving and humiliation, diligently resort to some public place where the service and worship of God is exercised, or shall be present at some other place in the practice of some religious duty, either of prayer, preaching, reading or expounding the scriptures, or conferring upon the same.[49]

This constituted, of course, a stunning reversal of the authoritarian policies of the recent past, but it also left a lot of questions unanswered. In the meantime, the king's "Engagement" to install a presbyterian system of church authority

---

[47] Gardiner, *Constitutional Documents*, doc. 76.
[48] Gardiner, *Constitutional Documents*, doc. 88, 89, 90.
[49] Gardiner, *Constitutional Documents*, doc. 93. For an American of my generation, this evokes memories of the 1950s liberal exhortation to attend "the church of your choice."

provisionally was still, technically, in effect, though it does not appear to have been enforced in most places. In the absence of a clarification or new definition of ecclesiastical authority, then, the conditions of an open religious "marketplace," which had been the unintended consequence of the revolutionary crisis, were under this new regime left in place as a new normal.

This revolutionary religious settlement by silent proclamation did not last long. After completing the consolidation of the Commonwealth's authority militarily in Ireland and Scotland, Oliver Cromwell, now Lord General, dissolved the Rump Parliament and called a new "Council-Chamber at Whitehall" (the so-called Barebones Parliament), which eventually dissolved itself, leaving governmental authority to Cromwell as "Lord Protector." On December 16, 1653, the Protectorate issued the "Instrument of Government," Britain's first written constitution, which represented a revolutionary political settlement, not just for England, but by extension, Scotland and Ireland, which were incorporated into the Commonwealth and empowered to delegate representatives to its Parliament.[50]

The Instrument of Government was above all concerned with defining and limiting the civil authority of the new government, which consisted of the Lord Protector, a Council, and a single-chamber Parliament; it addressed the questions of religious authority and religious liberty only briefly in a series of four articles near the end. Article XXXV stated simply "[t]hat the Christian religion, as contained in the Scriptures, be held forth and recommended as the public profession of these nations"; it went on to call for a system for the provision of able teachers of religion without specifying what that might look like. Article XXXVI added "[t]hat to the public profession held forth none shall be compelled by penalties or otherwise; but that endeavours be used to win them by sound doctrine and the example of a good conversation." Having thus rejected the established church and the coerced conformity of the past, the Instrument went on, in article XXXVII to promise protection and freedom of worship to all "such as profess faith in God by Jesus Christ (though differing in judgment from the doctrine, worship or discipline publicly held forth)", but with a notable exception: "provided this liberty be not extended to Popery [Catholicism] or Prelacy [Anglicanism], nor to such as, under the profession of Christ, hold forth and practise licentiousness." Finally, article XXXVIII provided "[t]hat all laws, statutes and ordinances, and clauses in any law, statute or ordinance to the contrary of the aforesaid liberty, shall be esteemed as null and void."

These constitutional provisions, quite unlike any other religious settlement we have seen, clearly represent the victory of the religious "outsiders" who controlled the revolutionary government. Having disestablished the coercive religious authority of the past, the leaders of the new Commonwealth – the

---

[50] Gardiner, *Constitutional Documents*, doc. 97. The new Parliament would consist of 400 members from England and Wales and just 30 from Scotland and 30 from Ireland.

various Independents, Separatists, and Baptists, who had fought for "religious liberty" – declined to designate an alternative, not even the provincially fragmented and decentralized "public" Reformed Church, with its classes and synods, in the United Provinces. As we have seen in earlier cases, "freedom of religious conscience" is the often elusive ideal of religious "dissenters" who seek to limit the coercive power of established churches and the political regimes that are allied with them;[51] the "religious liberty" that England's "dissenters" enshrined in the Instrument of Government effectively eliminated the coercive power, in matters of religion, of both church and state, but for the exemption of those who advocated "Popery," "Prelacy" and "licentiousness."[52]

Exclusions, if they are meaningful, entail enforcement, of course, and enforcement requires authority. It is not clear how the revolutionary regime would have managed the tensions they built into their own constitution of government in the long term,[53] but the simultaneous embrace of disestablishment and exclusion had clearly differential implications for the three constituent parts of the Commonwealth in the short term. In England, disestablishment of the episcopal hierarchy of the Church of England kept the religious marketplace of civil war years alive and well, though the prosecution of notable Quakers and other radicals for blasphemy demonstrated that there were limits and served to clarify what the Instrument of Government may have meant by "licentiousness."[54] By comparison with "Prelacy," which enjoyed a broad base of support among those who were devoted to their Anglican parishes and local religious traditions, "Popery" was a less obvious or immediate threat to the new Puritan regime, and England's Catholic faithful, a small but still well connected number, may even have enjoyed a measure of benign neglect under the Commonwealth. The new regime's policies nevertheless alienated both the Anglicans and the Presbyterians who had been

---

[51] Indeed, Andrew Pettegree goes so far as to characterize "tolerance," the frequent complement to "freedom of conscience," as the "party cry of the disappointed, the dispossessed, or the seriously confused." He goes on to conclude that "in the early modern period it was only ever a loser's creed." Andrew Pettegree, "The Politics of Toleration in the Free Netherlands, 1572–1620," in *Tolerance and Intolerance in the European Reformation*, eds. Ole Peter Grell and Bob Scribner (Cambridge: Cambridge University Press, 1996), 198.

[52] For a continental view of "liberty" and "free conscience," see Robert von Friedeburg, "The Juridification of Natural Law: Christoph Beshold's Claim for a Natural Right to Believe What One Wants," *The Historical Journal* 53, no. 1 (2010), 1–19.

[53] In 1657, the "Humble Petition and Advice" clarified the limits of religious liberty, providing that clergy who received public support were to conform to a confession of faith, but the Protector and the Parliament never promulgated such a document. See Gardiner, Constitutional Documents, doc. 102, paragraph 11.

[54] For overviews of this very fluid situation, see Bernard Capp, "Multiculturalism in Early Modern Britain," in *A Companion to Multiconfessionalism in the Early Modern World*, ed. Thomas Max Safley, Brill's Companions to the Christian Tradition, vol. 28 (Leiden; Boston: Brill, 2011), 289–315, and Coffey, *Persecution and Toleration*, 134–65. See also, Christopher Durston and Judith Maltby, eds., *Religion in Revolutionary England* (Manchester; New York: Manchester University Press, 2006).

allied, alternately, with Charles I and Charles II. In Scotland, disestablishment of the official Kirk meant not only the definitive end of "Prelacy," which had disintegrated during the wars, but also the loss of presbyterian integration or "connection" in favor of local independence. There, too, Catholics may have experienced some relief in the short term, while "new" voices, such as Quakers and Baptists, enjoyed new opportunities.

In Ireland, too, the disestablishment of "Prelacy" in the Church of Ireland, the explicit exclusion of the "Popery" of the civil war Confederacy, and the implicit rejection of even presbyterian connection opened up new opportunities for "the propagation of the Gospel" by a variety of new dissident voices, including Quakers and Baptists.[55] But following the devastation of the civil war, in which between twenty and forty percent of the population may have died, the years of "Cromwellian" rule in the 1650s stand out in popular Irish memory as being synonymous "with religious persecution, political outlawry, legal dispossession and forced transplantation of population."[56] In very quick succession, legislation in both England and Ireland renewed, for example, the "Settlement of Ireland" (August 1652), expelled Catholic priests (January 1653), and ordered the transplantation of all native Irish from east of the Shannon River to the western province of Connaught (July 1653).[57] Although the actual transfer of population did not occur on the massive scale envisioned by the legislation, the confiscation and transfer of property reduced Catholic ownership of Irish land from approximately sixty percent in 1640 to as little as ten percent by 1660. In short, for the Catholic majority population of Ireland, the advent of "religious liberty" under the Cromwellian "settlement" was profoundly repressive and devastating, not unlike the repression and devastation inflicted on Bohemian Protestants just a few decades earlier.

So how different were these variant religious outcomes – in the wake of military victory and in the absence of formal negotiations – from the negotiated settlements we have seen on the continent? While, in the absence of formal *negotiation*, these top-down settlements by proclamation did clearly open up new, even unprecedented, spaces for religious diversity, they did not provide the formal recognition of specific groups that characterized the continental settlements, and as a consequence, they could not provide the kind of security that the formally recognized signatories of a negotiated peace might enjoy.

---

[55] Phil Kilroy, "Radical Religion in Ireland, 1641–1660," in *Ireland from Independence to Occupation, 1641–1660*, ed. Jane Ohlmeyer (Cambridge: Cambridge University Press, 1995), 201–17.

[56] Thomas Bartlett, *Ireland: A History* (Cambridge; New York: Cambridge University Press, 2010), 128. See also, T. C. Barnard, *Cromwellian Ireland: English Government and Reform in Ireland 1649–1660*, Oxford Historical Monographs (London: Oxford University Press, 1975), and T. C. Barnard, "Conclusion. Settling and Unsettling Ireland: The Cromwellian and Williamite Revolutions," in *Ireland from Independence to Occupation, 1641–1660*, ed. Jane Ohlmeyer (Cambridge: Cambridge University Press, 1995), 265–91.

[57] See the very useful "Chronology of Events, 1639–1660," in *Ireland from Independence to Occupation, 1641–1660*, ed. Jane Ohlmeyer (Cambridge: Cambridge University Press, 1995), xv–l.

Neither did they provide political or legal processes to resolve future conflicts between competitive and often mutually intolerant religious communities. Indeed, what is striking about these authoritarian settlements is that they were shaped almost exclusively by the complementary dynamics of political and military *domination* and political and religious *subversion*. Even in Ireland, where geographic *segregation* of Catholics from Protestants was the explicit goal of the confiscation and resettlement policies, the different "confessions" continued to be thoroughly mixed with one another in most places; meanwhile, the *segregation* of religious activists from the specialists in coercion who had been their allies was decidedly one-sided, creating conditions that were more clearly conducive to campaigns of annihilation than religious peace.

The revolutionary political and religious settlement of the Commonwealth and Protectorate did not endure, of course, but it is striking that the political instability that followed the death of the Lord Protector, Oliver Cromwell, in 1658 did not yield to a new round of religious war. On the contrary, in 1659, Cromwell's son and successor, Richard Cromwell, resigned, leaving the way open for the largely peaceful restoration of the monarchy in 1660. In April, before his return from exile on the continent, Charles II issued the "Declaration of Breda," which included a statement of his intentions regarding the matter of religion:

And because the passion and uncharitableness of the times have produced several opinions in religion, by which men are engaged in parties and animosities against each other ... , we do declare a liberty to tender consciences, and that no man shall be disquieted or called in question for differences of opinion in matter of religion, which do not disturb the peace of the kingdom.

He went on to express his willingness to consent to any act of Parliament "for the full granting that indulgence."[58] The king's restoration nevertheless entailed the "restoration" of the Anglican churches of England, Scotland, and Ireland, complete with their episcopal hierarchies, and despite the king's declaration of "liberty to tender consciences," the new "Cavalier" Parliament, elected in 1661, passed a series of four laws, known as the Clarendon Code, which were intended to turn back the tide of religious "nonconformity."[59]

This new Restoration settlement, the top-down result of another partisan "victory," also had different effects on the three kingdoms. In England, it resulted in the removal of perhaps 2,000 clergy who refused to conform, while

[58] Gardiner, *Constitutional Documents*, doc. 105.
[59] The Corporation Act (1661) required office holders to take the Anglican communion and renounce the "Solemn League and Covenant"; the Act of Uniformity (1662) required the use of the "Book of Common Prayer" in all worship services; the Conventicle Act (1662, revised 1670) made meetings for Nonconformist worship illegal, even in private houses; and the Five-Mile Act (1665) forbade Nonconformist ministers to live, teach, or visit within five miles of a town or any other place where they had ministered. Cf. Tim Harris, Paul Seaward, and Mark Goldie, eds., *The Politics of Religion in Restoration England* (Oxford: Basil Blackwell, 1990).

in Scotland hundreds of Presbyterian pastors resigned their positions and worked, instead, to organize and lead a new "Covenanter" movement that worshiped clandestinely in illegal "conventicles." In Ireland, Charles confirmed most of the massive land transfers of the 1650s, but offered some relief to "innocent papists" who could prove their title to confiscated land; in consequence, Catholic land ownership may have again increased from ten to twenty percent, though it came nowhere near the prewar level of sixty percent.[60] Although the Restoration of the monarchy proved to be a more durable political settlement than the Commonwealth had been, the religious settlements that flowed from it were far from stable or uncontested. In March 1672, while the Cavalier Parliament was not in session, Charles II issued a "Declaration of Indulgence" that suspended the laws penalizing Protestant nonconformists and Catholic recusants and established a system for licensing nonconformist preachers and meeting places. Although Catholics were still not allowed to worship publicly, in very short order more than 1,500 licenses were issued to a range of Presbyterian, Independent, and Baptist preachers.[61] After only a year, however, the Parliament reconvened and forced the king to revoke the Declaration, and the new Test Act (March 1673) reinforced the penalties against nonconformity, requiring all office holders to take oaths of supremacy and allegiance; in 1678 a revised Test Act applied even to the Parliament, and henceforth Catholic peers could no longer sit in the House of Lords.[62]

The last decade of Charles II's reign came to be known as the "Great Persecution," first of Catholics, in the late 1670s because of recurrent fears of a "Popish plot," and later in the early 1680s of Protestant nonconformists, with Quakers, especially, being jailed by the thousands.[63] The death of Charles II and the succession of James II, an avowed Catholic, in 1685 signaled a new era of political instability and religious uncertainty in all of the three monarchies. James made it abundantly clear that he wanted to secure civil equality for Catholics throughout his kingdoms; he not only appointed Catholics to important offices but also tried to persuade the Parliament to repeal anti-Catholic legislation. At first suspicious of Protestant dissenters, he changed course in 1686, when he pardoned dissenters, including 1,200 Quakers, who had been imprisoned under the Clarendon Code. But the benefits of an openly Catholic monarch were undoubtedly most evident to the majority Catholic population of Ireland; indeed, in relatively short order, Catholics were given control of most of the high offices of the Irish state, and the Catholic Lord Tyrconnel was appointed

---

[60] Bartlett, *Ireland: A History*, 132–7.
[61] Frank Bate, *The Declaration of Indulgence, 1672: A Study in the Rise of Organised Dissent* (London: Pub. for the University Press of Liverpool by A. Constable, 1908). The text of the declaration is printed, pp. 76–8, and the full list of licensed meeting places and preachers is in appendix VII. See also, Andrew Browning, ed., *1660–1714*, vol. 8 of *English Historical Documents* (New York: Oxford University Press, 1953), 387–8.
[62] Browning, *English Hist. Doc.*, 389–94.
[63] For details and examples, see Coffey, *Persecution and Toleration*, 169–79.

Lord-Lieutenant of Ireland. For Scotland, King James VII issued a new "Declaration of Indulgence" in February 1687, granting freedom of worship to nonconformists; in the face of objections, the declaration was amended in June to grant moderate Presbyterians liberties equal to Catholics, while specifically prohibiting the demonstrative outdoor assemblies of the more radical "Covenanters."[64]

In April 1687, James, having dissolved the English Parliament, also issued a new "Declaration of Indulgence" for England, which suspended the penal laws and the Test Act. Explaining this abrupt departure from the recent past, the prologue explained that

> there is nothing now that we so earnestly desire as to establish our government on such a foundation as may make our subjects happy, and unite them to us by inclination as well as duty; which we think can be done by no means so effectually as by granting to them the free exercise of their religion for the time to come.

Perhaps more controversially, this royal declaration expressed the king's wish "that all the people of our dominions were members of the Catholic Church." He nevertheless embraced the principle

> that conscience ought not to be constrained nor people forced in matters of mere religion; it has ever been directly contrary to our inclination, as we think it is to the interest of government, which it destroys by spoiling trade, depopulating countries, and discouraging strangers, and finally, that it never obtained the end for which it was employed. And in this we are the more confirmed by the reflections we have made upon the conduct of the four last reigns. For after all the frequent and pressing endeavours that were used in each of them to reduce this kingdom to an exact conformity in religion, it is visible the success has not answered the design, and that the difficulty is invincible.

Having thus acknowledged the futility of coerced conformity, the king pledged, first of all, that "we will protect and maintain the archbishops, bishops, and clergy, and all other our subjects of the Church of England, in the free exercise of their religion." With regard to both Protestant nonconformists and Catholic recusants, James granted "all our loving subjects" the liberty "to meet and serve God after their own way and manner, be it in private houses or in places purposely hired or built for that use," providing "that their meetings and assemblies be peaceably, openly, and publicly held, and all persons freely admitted to them."[65] A year later, he reaffirmed the Indulgence and pledged to "establish liberty of conscience on such just and equal foundation as will render it unalterable, and secure to all people the free exercise of their religion for ever, by which future ages may reap the benefit of what is so undoubtedly for the general good of the whole kingdom."[66]

In the broader comparative context of the religious settlements we have analyzed, these Declarations authorizing "liberty of conscience" and public

---

[64] The text of the June amendment is printed in Browning, *English Hist. Doc.*, 621–22.
[65] Browning, *English Hist. Doc.*, 395–7.   [66] Browning, *English Hist. Doc.*, 399.

worship for both Catholics and Protestant dissenters stand out as by far the most inclusive: Even though they do not disestablish the established churches, they are exclusive of no one; what's more they suspend all legislation requiring church attendance. Still, James's declarations were no more durable or effective than the various proclamations and enactments that preceded them, in large measure because of the autocratic manner in which they were issued. Thus, opposition to "arbitrary power" combined with long-standing fears of "Popery" to animate what Steven Pincus describes as the "First Modern Revolution" in 1688–1689,[67] better known in England as the "Glorious Revolution," which deposed the king and of course nullified his proposed religious settlement. To make a very long story short, in June 1688, after the birth of a male heir, which promised a succession of Catholic monarchs after James, a group of just seven political notables, including the bishop of London, invited William III, prince of Orange, Stadhouder of the United Provinces, and husband of Mary, James's Protestant daughter, to intervene in English politics by force.[68] In October, William published a "Declaration" of his reasons for intervention,[69] and in November he invaded England. By December, James II had, like his brother Charles II in 1651, fled England for exile in France. In February 1689, William III and his wife Mary II formally accepted what is commonly known as the "Bill of Rights,"[70] which had been enacted by a revolutionary "Convention" Parliament to limit royal authority and to reset the royal succession; only then were they crowned as dual monarchs of England.

Whereas the Bill of Rights provided a stable foundation for a more durable royal government in England, it did not automatically apply to Scotland and Ireland, much less did it provide a durable religious settlement for any of the kingdoms. In Scotland, the "Claim of Right Act," enacted in April 1689, provided an equivalent political settlement preliminary to the coronation of William and Mary.[71] In Ireland, however, the Irish Parliament, which was called to meet in May 1689 for the first time since 1666 by the exile James II, passed the "Act of Recognition," which recognized James II as king of Ireland, and the "Declaratory Act," which declared acts of the English Parliament to have no validity in Ireland.[72] This opened up a rather different and more treacherous revolutionary situation than obtained in England, in which *activation* of the Protestant/Catholic identity boundary combined with political *polarization*, network-based *escalation*, and the *brokerage* of an international "Catholic" military alliance. The combination of these mechanisms yielded yet another

---

[67] Steven C. A. Pincus, *1688: The First Modern Revolution* (New Haven: Yale University Press, 2009).

[68] Browning, *English Hist. Doc.*, 120–2.

[69] The text of the Declaration is available at www.jacobite.ca/documents/16881010.htm. See also Tony Claydon, "William III's Declaration of Reasons and the Glorious Revolution," *The Historical Journal* 39, no. 1 (1996): 87–108.

[70] Browning, *English Hist. Doc.*, 122–8.   [71] Browning, *English Hist. Doc.*, 635–9.

[72] Browning, *English Hist. Doc.*, 747–50.

round of destructive religious war in Ireland: the so-called Williamite Wars, from 1689 to 1691, which ended with the defeat and exile of James II from Ireland, too, and the negotiation of the Treaty of Limerick in October 1691.[73] In the end, then, the dual monarchy of William and Mary was recognized in all three kingdoms, but under very different political terms, which were combined with very different religious settlements.

In England, the new religious settlement under William and Mary took the form of "An Act for Exempting their Majestyes Protestant Subjects dissenting from the Church of England from the Penalties of certaine Lawes," better known as the Toleration Act of May 1689.[74] In his Declaration of Reasons in 1688, William III had pledged to secure religious dissenters "from all persecution upon the account of their religion, even papists themselves not excepted."[75] But according to John Coffey, "The depth of Protestant prejudice against Catholics meant that William's plan to grant them toleration was doomed from the start."[76] Even passing legislation in favor of Protestant dissenters proved to be difficult. A Comprehension Act to incorporate dissenters into the established church, for example, failed in the face of Anglican opposition, and a proposal to allow dissenters to take up public office met a similar fate. The cumbersome compromise that was eventually passed in May 1689 merely exempted dissenters from the penalties imposed by the Elizabethan Act of Uniformity and the Clarendon Code (article IV), neither of which was actually repealed; it allowed dissenting preachers to be licensed, provided they swore an oath of political allegiance, and granted them freedom of worship in licensed meeting houses, much as Charles II's "Indulgence" had done, if only briefly, in 1672. In this case, even (Ana)Baptist ministers could be licensed, due to an exception they were granted regarding infant baptism (article X), and Quakers were allowed to make a declaration of allegiance rather than swear an oath (article XIII). As a consequence, within a year, some 1,200 dissenter meetinghouses were again licensed in England.[77] Still, with its deliberate exclusion of Catholics, this compromise, to which enough members of the revolutionary Parliament finally gave their grudging consent in May 1689, fell far short of the freedom of conscience that James II had promised.

In Scotland, the revolutionary religious settlement took the form of a series of Acts of Parliament that William III was forced to accept. The first rescinded the Act of Supremacy (1669) by which Charles II had claimed supreme authority in "all causes ecclesiastical";[78] the second was an "Act restoring the Presbyterian ministers who were thrust from their churches" since 1661;[79] and the third was

---

[73] Browning, *English Hist. Doc.*, 765–9.   [74] Browning, *English Hist. Doc.*, 400–3.
[75] See www.jacobite.ca/documents/16881010.htm.
[76] Coffey, *Persecution and Toleration*, 198.
[77] Capp, "Multiculturalism in Early Modern Britain," 313.
[78] Browning, *English Hist. Doc.*, 639. See also, for Scotland, the University of St. Andrews website "Records of the Parliaments of Scotland to 1707": www.rps.ac.uk.
[79] Browning, *English Hist. Doc.*, 639–40.

an "Act ratifying the Confession of Faith and settling Presbyterian Church government,"[80] which restored the General Assembly as the highest authority in the Kirk of Scotland. Although William had hoped to promote toleration for Episcopalians, many Anglican ministers were expelled from their offices, and in some places, those who promoted "Prelacy" were now forced to worship in "illegal" conventicles, as the Covenanters had done for nearly three decades.[81]

In Ireland, the Treaty of Limerick (October 1691) completed the establishment of William's royal authority, eliminating the last vestiges of Irish/"Jacobite" resistance in the western counties. Not surprisingly, the treaty required the Catholic gentry to take an oath of loyalty to William and Mary; those who did not were immediately suspect. It began, however, with a tone of religious conciliation, not unlike the Edict of Alais in France:

The Roman Catholics of this kingdom shall enjoy such privileges in the exercise of their religion as are consistent with the laws of Ireland, or as they did enjoy in the reign of king Charles the second: and their majesties, as soon as their affairs will permit them to summon a parliament in this kingdom, will endeavour to procure the said Roman Catholics such farther security in that particular, as may preserve them from any disturbance upon the account of their said religion.[82]

As noted earlier, the restoration of Charles II had offered some relief from the repression of Catholics under the Commonwealth, but even this promise to "preserve them from any disturbance" was undercut by an infamous series of "penal" laws passed by the Protestant-dominated Irish Parliament between 1695 and 1704 that were intended, as the act of 1704 stated, "to Prevent the Further Growth of Popery."[83] In effect, the Penal Laws prevented Catholics from holding public office, being seated in parliament, or even owning property, though they did not criminalize Catholic religious worship, as the Commonwealth legislation had done.

Thus, the consolidation of the new political regime of William and Mary, after some sixty years of conflict, violence, war, and instability, entailed very different religious settlements in the three kingdoms. These settlements were unlike the intermediate, authoritarian settlements – the Commonwealth, under Cromwell; the Restoration, under Charles II; and even the Catholic "pre-revolution," under James II – in that they flowed from separate "negotiations" in the three kingdoms, and they reflected and validated, at least partially, the very different "facts on the ground" in the three kingdoms. The specific features of these settlements were still subject to contestation and change, as we will see in the Chapter 12, but in broad outline they finally established the political, institutional, and legal frameworks within which very different patterns of religious diversity became permanent and visible features of the religious landscapes of the three kingdoms. The durability of these settlements was related, I believe, to the fact that *negotiation* and

---

[80] Browning, *English Hist. Doc.*, 640–2.
[81] Capp, "Multiculturalism in Early Modern Britain," 313–14.
[82] Browning, *English Hist. Doc.*, 765–9.   [83] Browning, *English Hist. Doc.*, 781–3.

compromise was finally combined with a more universal *segregation* of religious activists from the commanders of militias and armies; although these settlements still clearly entailed the *domination* of established churches, they also opened up considerable space for the *subversion* of the harshest consequences of "defeat" by religious dissidents and nonconformists.

MAKING RELIGIOUS PEACE POSSIBLE

By now it should be obvious that making durable religious peace possible is no easy task. Negotiated settlements can be very helpful, though as we have seen in earlier chapters, they can quite readily fail if they are not accompanied by the demobilization of armies or the demilitarization of religious movements. Negotiations that are preceded by a cease-fire agreement are even more helpful because they halt the destruction and the accumulation of grievances that make agreement "on the matter of religion" more difficult. Still, as we have seen in this chapter, negotiations that are not preceded by cease-fire agreements and wars that end without negotiated settlements can also make religious peace possible. The religious wars that we have analyzed ended in very different ways, but in all cases, the first step toward making peace possible was ending the wars.

For those who prosecuted the wars, "victory" would have been considered, without a doubt, the optimal way to end the religious wars. But just as it is possible to win crucial battles without winning wars, so also it is possible to win wars without making durable peace possible. Winning wars or even decisive political victories, short of the coordinated destruction of war, does not automatically make durable peace possible, though "victory," like a cease fire, can be an important step if it stops the fighting. The seventeenth century religious wars on the continent and in Great Britain ended very differently, but the different paths toward religious peace had one critical ingredient in common: grudging consent.[84] On one level, the forces in conflict agreed, reluctantly in all cases, that more war would be fruitless – that the ongoing coordinated destruction was the problem, not the solution. On a more fundamental level, the grudging consent was that of an array of very diverse subjects and rulers accepting both facts on the ground and different forms of bargained compliance to political authority – compliance that entailed a multiplicity of religious voices, limits on the religious sovereignty of rulers, and protection from arbitrary action by rulers or their agents. In the next two chapters we will explore the broad contours of the religious peace this grudging consent made possible.

---

[84] I borrow the notion of "grudging consent" from Charles Tilly, who applied it to the parallel problems of democratization and de-democratization: Charles Tilly, "Grudging Consent," *The American Interest*, no. 3 (September/October 2007): 17–23. Like democratization, religious peace is reversible; as Tilly's logic suggests, religious peace, like democracy, is more like a verb than a state of being.

11

The Contours of Religious Peace III

The Continent

Together, the Peace/Edict of Alais, the Peace of Westphalia, and the political settlements in the composite British monarchy, like the *Landfrieden*, the *Religionsfriede*, and the Edict of Nantes before them, made durable patterns of religious peace possible in both continental Europe and Great Britain in the second half of the seventeenth century. What kind of peace did these settlements make possible? Would we recognize religious peace if we saw it at the end of the seventeenth century? Like the earlier settlements in Germany, Switzerland, France, and the Low Countries, these settlements validated and preserved patterns of religious diversity that were complex, varied, and more than a little messy. In this paired comparison, the last of three, we will encounter the kinds of variation and messiness in the patterns of religious diversity that are by now more or less familiar, but in this exploration of the contours of religious peace, I should also like to emphasize the ways in which religious diversity became more firmly embedded in both legal structures and everyday experience. In the short term, the Peace of Westphalia validated a number of political and religious adjustments, both within the German-Roman Empire and in the borderlands to the east and the west. In the longer term, political instability within the composite British state prolonged the emergence of a durable religious peace, but by the 1690s the three kingdoms had developed relatively stable, strikingly different, and visibly diverse forms of religious peace. Once again, it will not be possible to offer a complete catalogue of the varieties of religious peace, but a series of local or regional examples will serve to illustrate the range of variation and the overall direction of change.

We begin on the continent where we will see a broad range of contentious political actors adapting old strategies to new situations in order to accommodate their differences more durably and peacefully. As we saw in Chapter 10, the *religious* Peace of Westphalia – that is, the portions of the Treaty of Osnabrück that addressed religious issues – rested firmly on the foundation of the *Religionsfriede* of 1555, which "shall be maintained in its

Force and Vigour, and sacredly and inviolably observed" (article V, subparagraph 1, IPO). Thus, it is not surprising that the religious peace after 1648 bears a very strong resemblance to the complicated and messy religious peace that emerged within the empire after 1555. That resemblance is visible, in the first place, in the territorial differentiation – the now triconfessional patchwork quilt of official churches: evangelical (Lutheran), Reformed (Calvinist), and Catholic – that the elite signatories built into the agreement itself. It is visible as well in the varieties of internal religious differentiation that resulted from the contentious political interactions of authoritative rulers and their often religiously diverse subjects; indeed, the diverse religious landscape of Germany continued to defy "confessional" mapmaking after 1648 as it had before. Finally, the resemblance is also visible in the practical strategies that the various actors recurrently used to accommodate religious differences both within communities and across political boundaries: indeed, the practices of sharing sacred spaces (*Simultankirche*) as well as political spaces, of traveling from one jurisdiction to another to worship freely (*Auslauf*), and of deliberately *hiding* diversity, through *secrecy, dissimulation*, and the like, were as useful and effective in the second half of the seventeenth century as they had been in the second half of the sixteenth.

Still, the three treaties that ended the last major spasms of religious war on the European continent – the Eighty and Thirty Years wars – also entailed significant adjustments to new and changing facts of religious diversity on the ground, both within the German-Roman Empire and in the borderlands to the east and the west of the empire. Undoubtedly the most complicated and messy adjustments within the empire were entailed in the application of the parity, restitution, and autonomy principles that were new to the Treaty of Osnabrück, but at the same time the most dramatic adjustments were entailed in the implicit exemption from those very principles of the emperor's territorial sovereignties in Austria and Bohemia, the eastern borderlands of the empire. Meanwhile, in the empire's western borderlands, important adjustments were also entailed in the application of the possession principle in the first Treaty of Münster and the French "satisfactions" in the second Treaty of Münster. Let's begin with Bohemia in the east and work our way toward the west.

TESTING THE LIMITS OF CONFESSIONAL ABSOLUTISM

The kingdom of Bohemia, which included the territories of Lusatia, Silesia, and Moravia, was undoubtedly the most religiously diverse polity in the Habsburgs' massive political orbit prior to the Thirty Years War. Then, as we saw in Chapter 9, the defeat of the Bohemian Revolt in the first phase of the war precipitated a long and sustained process of re-Catholicization – much like the reestablishment of the Catholic Church in the Southern Netherlands beginning in the 1580s – the most immediate effect of which was the second major wave of forced religious migration in early modern Europe. The closure or destruction of Protestant churches, the confiscation of Protestant properties, and the permanent relocation of hundreds of thousands of Protestant households utterly transformed the religious landscape of Bohemia in the long term, as the exceptional **integration** of a wide variety of religious groups into public life in prewar Bohemia was replaced by an active **repression** of religious dissent during and after the war. During the war, the assertion of Habsburg confessional absolutism throughout Bohemia and Austria was especially coercive, but over time, force and violence gave way to persuasion and "missionary" activity.[1]

But this dramatic top-down transformation of the religious landscape of Bohemia was not without resistance, interruptions, and ad hoc exceptions. As a reward for Saxon support during the Bohemian Revolt, for example, Emperor/King Ferdinand II ceded authority over Upper Lusatia, which as we saw in Chapter 4 was largely Lutheran, to the Lutheran Elector of Saxony. This cession, which was confirmed both by the Peace of Prague and by the Treaty of Osnabrück, effectively exported the "problem" of Lusatia's religious diversity and validated the originally subversive, but long-standing prominence of Lutherans in Upper Lusatia (**privilege**) as well as the equally subversive *Simultankirche* in the St. Petri Dom in Bautzen (**parity**). At various times during the war, Swedish forces also penetrated other Bohemian territories, and when they occupied Prague, for example, they found there were still large numbers of dissenters who eagerly attended their Protestant services. Then, at the end of the war, the Treaty of Osnabrück also specifically provided for **ad-hoc toleration** of evangelical worship in specific noble jurisdictions in Silesia and within the city of Breslau (article V, subparagraphs 38–40/31 IPO).

Under these varied conditions, then, Protestantism was much less visible in what remained of Bohemia, of course, but Protestant worship and religious practices nevertheless survived. Aside from the specific pockets of **ad hoc tolerance** granted to Lutherans in Silesia, there was a more formal institutionalization of the practice of *Auslauf* in areas near the boundary with Saxony, now augmented to include Lusatia; thousands of Lutherans routinely crossed into Saxony to attend worship services where a number of churches were dedicated to their use.[2] Also, just outside the Silesian cities of Glogau, Jauer, and Scheidnitz, Lutherans were allowed to build *Friedenkirchen* (peace churches), to which dissenters would travel long distances to attend services.[3] In Bohemia and Moravia, where the **repression** of Protestantism was most severe, the profoundly

---

[1] See, Howard Louthan, *Converting Bohemia: Force and Persuasion in the Catholic Reformation*, New Studies in European History (Cambridge; New York: Cambridge University Press, 2009).

[2] Benjamin J. Kaplan, *Divided by Faith: Religious Conflict and the Practice of Toleration in Early Modern Europe* (Cambridge, MA: Harvard University Press, 2007), 166.

[3] Kaplan, *Divided by Faith*, 209; Anton Schindling, "Neighbours of a Different Faith: Confessional Coexistence and Parity in the Territorial States and Towns of the Empire," in *Politics, Religion, Law and Society*, vol. 1 of *1648: War and Peace in Europe*, ed. Klaus Bussmann and Heinz Schilling (Münster/Osnabrück: Veranstaltungsgesellschaft 350 Jahre Westfälischer Friede, 1998), 465.

subversive survival of religious dissent and "heretical" worship depended more clearly on *secrecy* and the relative invisibility of *dissimulation*, which, as we have seen in earlier cases, dissidents recurrently turned to in order to avoid persecution.[4] Unfortunately, I have had neither the time nor the linguistic skills to explore the local histories of the *Geheimprotestanten* (secret Protestants) in these territories, but ongoing research is revealing a remarkable, if largely hidden, history of Protestant survival, of which the impressive maps of documented Protestant communities that Ondřej Macek has developed are surely emblematic.[5] In a variety of both visible and invisible ways, then, religious dissenters in the kingdom of Bohemia managed to test the limits of confessional absolutism and to keep evangelical religious practices alive into the eighteenth century, when they reemerged at the cutting edge of a Protestant evangelical awakening.[6]

There was a parallel process of re-Catholicization within the empire in the Upper Palatinate (Oberpfaltz).[7] The Palatinate did not have the same rich history of religious diversity as Bohemia did prior to the sixteenth century, yet Lutheran preachers found receptive audiences and even built significant reform movements in several small cities of the Upper Palatinate – Amberg, Neunberg, Neumarkt, and Weiden – prior to the adoption of the *Religionsfriede* in 1555. An official territorial reformation did not occur until 1556, when Elector Ottheinrich introduced a formal Lutheran reform settlement. His successor, Frederick III, "the Pious," attempted, however, to introduce the Reformed theology of the "Heidelberg Catechism" in the face of Lutheran opposition in the 1560s, which resulted in occasionally fierce inter-Protestant conflict, until Lutheranism was restored by Ludwig VI in 1576. Reformed Calvinism was finally reintroduced in the Palatinate in 1583, and under Frederick IV and Frederick V, the Palatinate as a whole became a highly visible token of the advance of international Calvinism and the Elector became the leader of the Protestant Union of the empire. As we saw in Chapter 9, however, Frederick V's

---

[4] On the survival of clandestine Protestantism, see the broad range of research collected in Rudolf Leeb, Martin Scheutz, and Dietmar Weikl, eds., *Geheimprotestantismus und evangelische Kirchen in der Habsburgermonarchie und im Erzstift Salzburg (17./18. Jahrhundert)*, Veröffentlichungen des Instituts für Österreichische Geschichtsforschung, vol. 51 (Wien: Böhlau; München: Oldenbourg, 2009).

[5] Ondřej Macek, "Geheimprotestanten in Böhmen und Mähren im 17. und 18. Jahrhundert," in *Geheimprotestantismus und evangelische Kirchen in der Habsburgermonarchie und im Erzstift Salzburg (17./18. Jahrhundert)*, in *Geheimprotestantismus und evangelische Kirchen*, ed. Rudolf Leeb, Martin Scheutz, and Dietmar Weikl, Veröffentlichungen des Instituts für Österreichische Geschichtsforschung, vol. 51 (Wien: Böhlau; München: Oldenbourg, 2009), 237–69; see the maps on pages 249 and 250.

[6] On the vitality and variety of evangelical religious practices in the eighteenth century, see W. Reginald Ward, *The Protestant Evangelical Awakening* (Cambridge: Cambridge University Press, 1992), especially chapter 2.

[7] The following account of the Upper Palatinate is based on the excellent study of Trevor Johnson, *Magistrates, Madonnas and Miracles: The Counter Reformation in the Upper Palatinate*, St. Andrews Studies in Reformation History (Farnham, England; Burlington, VT: Ashgate, 2009).

involvement in the Bohemian Revolt ended in disaster, and in 1621 the Upper Palatinate was occupied by Duke Maximilian of Bavaria, leader of the Catholic League.

Although there was little doubt about Maximilian's intentions, the formal reintroduction of Catholicism began slowly, at least until such time as Maximilian was confirmed in the office of Elector by the emperor and his temporary authority over the Upper Palatinate was made permanent in 1628.[8] At first Protestant pastors were removed gradually, and the agents of Maximilian's new authority sought to exploit differences between Lutherans and Calvinists to open up opportunities for voluntary conversions, but in 1628, after seven years of de facto multiconfessionalism, the *Religionspatent* published by Maximilian's government required that the entire population convert to Catholicism, in line with the *ius reformandi* that Catholic rulers, like their Protestant counterparts, had begun to claim for themselves. Although there was political resistance, especially among the rural nobility, and a significant emigration of the political, intellectual, and financial elite, especially from the capital, Amberg, in the long term, the process of re-Catholicization may have been more thorough-going, perhaps because it was less coercive, in the Upper Palatinate than it was in Bohemia. Nevertheless, Trevor Johnson concludes:

> Nicodemism, the secret attachment of New-Catholics to the Protestant faith of their parents and grandparents, may have been widespread, particularly in the early years of conversion, but its failure to threaten the new regime exposed its political irrelevance.[9]

In other words, like religious dissidents who faced active **repression** in Bern and the Southern Netherlands, the *subversive* crypto-Protestants of the Upper Palatinate survived precisely because they did not threaten the new regime. By remaining formally invisible, and thus not a salient feature of public politics, they might be politically irrelevant, but they kept religious diversity alive, even under difficult conditions.

VALIDATING DISSENT AND INSTITUTIONALIZING DIVERSITY

Now, if religious diversity became significantly less visible in Bohemia and the Upper Paltinate, during and after the war, religious diversity became, routinely and formally, a more visible feature of public life in the empire as a whole, following the Peace of Westphalia. Like the other religious settlements we have already examined, the Peace of Westphalia does not actually describe for us the "facts" of religious diversity that the Treaties of Münster and Osnabrück explicitly validated and sought to maintain as the foundation of a more

---

[8] A more forceful attempt by Maximilian to re-Catholicize Upper Austria, where he also exercised temporary jurisdiction, had provoked open resistance and rebellion, which Maximilian was keen to avoid in the Upper Palatinate; see Johnson, *Magistrates, Madonnas and Miracles*, 69.

[9] Johnson, *Magistrates, Madonnas and Miracles*, 314.

peaceful future. As we saw in Chapter 10, however, the Treaty of Osnabrück specified three important principles – parity, restitution, and autonomy – that had far-reaching implications for the character and legal status of the religious diversity that was already well embedded in the German cultural landscape. Let's look at each of these in turn.

"Parity," as a relational principle, was neither defined nor mandated in the *Religionsfriede* of 1555, though it was certainly implied in the mutual recognition that was the foundation of the agreement; it may also have been implicitly endorsed in the paragraph which stated that in imperial free cities, where both confessions were established, the

citizens and inhabitants of the same free and imperial cities, spiritual ranks and secular, shall peacefully and quietly dwell with and among one another, and no party shall venture to abolish the religion, church-customs or ceremonies of another, or persecute them therefor.[10]

Parity nevertheless came to be a prominent feature, not only of the implementation regime, but more broadly of the practice of religious coexistence in the early decades of the religious peace in Germany. Thus, Protestant and Catholic judges were balanced in the *Reichskamergericht* (though not in the *Reichshofrat*) for the adjudication of cases regarding religion, and even the imperial diet began to organize its work and operations in relation to the newly organized Protestant and Catholic factions among the Estates. More broadly, we encountered a variety of parity arrangements, characterized by equivalence and mutuality regardless of comparative size, in the organization of religious diversity in places as diverse as Bautzen, Güttingen, and Glarus. Indeed, the widespread phenomenon of sharing sacred spaces is especially emblematic of the principle of parity among competitive religious groups in local settings. More formally, perhaps, it had become critical to the implementation of the religious peace in four biconfessional cities in the south: Augsburg, Biberach, Ravensburg, and Dinkelsbühl.[11]

Thus, it is hardly surprising that parity figures prominently, though variously, in the Peace of Westphalia. As we saw in Chapter 9, in the run-up to the Thirty Years War, religious polarization had compromised the judicial processes that were intended to mediate religious conflicts as well as the routine functioning of the imperial diet. In order to restore comity and collaboration at this elite level, the very first subparagraph of article V in the Treaty of Osnabrück mandated

---

[10] Karl Brandi, ed., *Der Augsburger Religionsfriede Vom 25 Sept. 1555: Kritische Ausgabe Des Textes* (München: Rieger'sche Universitäts-Buchhandlung, 1896), 35; Henry Clay Vedder, ed., *The Peace of Augsburg*, Historical Leaflets, no. 5 (Chester, PA: Crozer Theological Seminary, 1901), 8–9.

[11] See Paul Warmbrunn, *Zwei Konfessionen in einer Stadt: Das Zusammenleben von Katholiken und Protestanten in den paritätischen Reichsstädten Augsburg, Biberach, Ravensburg, und Dinkelsbühl von 1548 bis 1648*, Veröffentlichungen des Instituts für Europäische Geschichte Mainz (Wiesbaden: Steiner, 1983).

[t]hat there be an exact and reciprocal Equality amongst all the Electors, Princes and States of both Religions, conformably to the State of the Commonweal, the Constitutions of the Empire, and the present Convention: so that what is just of one side shall be so of the other, all Violence and Force between the two Parties being for ever prohibited.[12]

More specifically, article V, subparagraphs 51–58/42–45, of the Treaty imposed strict rules of parity on those involved in the adjudication of religious disputes in both the courts and the diets, with subparagraph 52/43 specifically mandating "amicable resolution" and strictly forbidding majority decision making. Meanwhile, at the territorial level, a subcontract of the Peace of Westphalia, the *Capitulatio Perpetua*, concluded in 1650, mandated a peculiar parity arrangement by which territorial jurisdiction over the prince-bishopric of Osnabrück would alternate between the Catholic archbishop of Cologne and the Lutheran duke of Braunschweig-Lüneburg, both of whom were obliged to guarantee the biconfessional status quo.[13] Finally, at the local level, article V, subparagraphs 3–12/4–8, rearticulated and specifically mandated strict parity arrangements in order to preserve religious coexistence in the biconfessional cities of Augsburg, Biberach, Ravensburg, and Dinkelsbühl, where the religious peace had broken down in the atmosphere of religious polarization prior to and during the second round of war. Besides restoring Protestant-Catholic collaboration in the governance of Augsburg, the Peace enabled the reconstruction of the Lutheran Holy Cross Church, which had been destroyed in 1629 by authority of the Edict of Restitution.[14]

As a remedy for deep and seemingly intractable polarization, then, parity actually worked quite well, at the imperial level, at the territorial level, and at the local level. To be sure, its newly precise legal definitions following Westphalia served to make imperial politics more cumbersome and to make the empire look less like a "state," but parity may also have led unintentionally, in some places, to the formation of an "invisible frontier" that increasingly separated Protestants from Catholics in social life.[15] As a locally generated

---

[12] Article V, subparagraph 1 IPO.

[13] The prince-bishopric of Osnabrück was officially Lutheran between 1543 and 1548, and while it officially returned to Catholicism prior to the *Religionsfriede*, it remained religiously diverse. See Dagmar Freist, "Religious Violence in Early Modern Germany," *Leidschrift* 20, no. 1 (2005): 144–5, and Dagmar Freist, "Crossing Religious Borders: The Experience of Religious Difference and Its Impact on Mixed Marriages in Eighteenth-Century Germany," in *Living with Diversity in Early Modern Europe*, eds. C. Scott Dixon, Dagmar Freist, and Mark Greengrass, St. Andrews Studies in Reformation History (Farnham, England: Ashgate, 2009), 210–14. This agreement also allocated control over local churches, according to a rather puzzling and sometimes unjust formula, to either Evangelicals or Catholics; cf. Schindling, "Neighbours of a Different Faith," 471–2.

[14] Emily Fisher Gray, "Good Neighbors: Architecture and Confession in Augsburg's Lutheran Church of Holy Cross, 1525–1661" (Ph.D. diss., University of Pennsylvania, 2004). A remarkable fund-raising campaign brought in financial contributions from Protestants throughout Europe. On the origins of this rare form of *simultaneum*, see Chapter 4, pp. 75–7, in this volume.

[15] See Etienne François, *Die unsichtbare Grenze: Protestanten und Katholiken in Augsburg 1648–1806* (Sigmaringen: Jan Thorbeke Verlag, 1991).

improvisation, of course, it continued to inform the creation and preservation of *Simultankirchen*, some of which were now more than a century old.

"Restitution," as a remedy for the depredations and confessional changes wrought by war, was definitely not part of the vocabulary or the culture of the *Religionsfriede*, but it entered the official discourse of the empire very dramatically and controversially in the "Edict of Restitution" of 1629. Riding the high tide of his military successes in Bohemia, in the Palatinate, and in his campaign against Danish intervention, Emperor Ferdinand II had used the concept of restitution to articulate his vision of "confessional absolutism": that is, to order the restitution of all Church land secularized since 1555, to declare that ecclesiastical princes had the right to enforce religious uniformity, and to ban all Protestant sects besides Lutheranism. As it reappeared in the texts of the Peace of Westphalia, however, "restitution" had a more balanced, though limited, application in both articles IV (political) and V (ecclesiastical) of the Treaty of Osnabrück and paragraphs 7–46 of the second Treaty of Münster. As we saw in Chapter 10, ecclesiastical restitution in relation to the "normal year" of 1624 imposed profound limits, at least in principle, on the religious authority of Germany's many rulers: henceforth rulers were required to permit religious worship that could be shown to have been practiced, either publicly or privately/secretively, at any time in that year, while their subjects now had protection/sanction in imperial law to emerge from the shadows cast by the exclusive, authoritarian religious policies of their rulers. Clearly, "restitution," as it was articulated in the Osnabrück treaty, represented a good deal more than a clarification of the *Religionsfriede*; indeed, it entailed an enormous expansion of the space for visible and salient differences among religious groups in public life.

"Autonomy," as an individual remedy for official intolerance, was clearly a novel and deeply contested feature of the Peace of Westphalia.[16] To be sure, the *Religionsfriede* had asserted the so-called *ius emigrandi*: the right of individuals to move to another political jurisdiction "for the sake of their religion." As a bargain among political elites, however, this first German peace did not come close to articulating anything like a freedom of individual religious conscience for their subjects – something that was perhaps implicit in the first Swiss *Landfrieden* of 1529 ("no one should be coerced into the faith") and became explicit in the French Edict of Amboise (1563) and all subsequent edicts of pacification in France. According to Derek Croxton, the concept of autonomy, as it was understood by the Protestants who promoted it in the Westphalian negotiations, rested on the controversial "Declaration" that Ferdinand had appended to the *Religionsfriede*, which promised that Protestants would be tolerated in their private worship within Catholic ecclesiastical jurisdictions, but did not make the same guarantees for

---

[16] See Ronald G. Asch, "Religious Toleration, the Peace of Westphalia and the German Territorial Estates," *Parliaments, Estates and Representation* 20, no. 1 (2000): 75–89.

Catholics in Protestant jurisdictions.[17] By contrast, the autonomy provisions that were incorporated in the Osnabrück treaty were not confession-specific; indeed, just as ecclesiastical restitution applied equally to Catholics and Protestants – both established rulers and their dissenting subjects – and *ius emigrandi* applied to "any Subject ... , who after the Publication of the Peace shall have a mind to change his religion," so also article V, subparagraphs 34 and 35, provide that both Catholic and Protestant dissenters – even "those who had not the publick or private Exercise of their Religion in any time of the year 1624" – should be patiently tolerated "with all Liberty of Conscience" and that "they shall be treated in the same manner as Brethren and Sisters, with equal Justice and Protection." Although some Protestant advocates insisted that "autonomy," understood as the right of individuals to practice their chosen religion, also entailed a right to public worship, at the very least it opened up a universal space for private devotions and worship, just as the freedom of religious conscience had done in France and the Dutch Republic.

Clearly the parity, restitution, and autonomy provisions of the Osnabrück treaty did not create religious diversity where it had not existed before. Rather, in the wake of thirty years of very destructive warfare, the parity, restitution, and autonomy provisions of the Peace of Westphalia established a more clearly defined framework and a more elaborate set of rules for reviving, managing, and maintaining durable patterns of religious diversity at both the territorial and local levels; more fundamentally, these principles offered "dissenters" in particular – that is, political subjects whose religious choices differed from those of their putative sovereigns – a new and altogether firmer foundation in imperial law for resistance to their rulers' attempts to enforce confessional conformity. Over time, then, parity and "amicable resolution" became deeply embedded in the political culture of both the imperial diet and the reconstituted imperial courts where religious disputes were adjudicated. To be sure, imperial politics became considerably more cumbersome, as the main actors routinely divided into separate religious bodies, the *corpus Catholicorum* and the *corpus Evangelicorum*, that would meet separately before they met to resolve their differences in a process called *itio in partes* (separating into parts), while one of the most pronounced effects of the judicial reforms was the thorough-going "juridification" of religious disputes whereby confessional antagonisms were recurrently channeled into often decades-long legal processes. In order to explore the adjustments that were framed by the Westphalian settlement at the territorial and local levels, consider the complicated and messy examples of the Electorate of Saxony and the city of Hamburg.

As we saw in Chapter 4, Saxony, the home of Martin Luther, was in many ways the prototype for a Lutheran reformation at the territorial level. Although the process was attenuated and incomplete, in the second half of the sixteenth

---

[17] Derek Croxton, *Westphalia: The Last Christian Peace* (New York: Palgrave Macmillan, 2013), 274.

century, Electoral Saxony, which had been reunited with Albertine Saxony, was a paragon of orthodox Lutheran stability and probity. In the run-up to the Thirty Years War, Elector Johann Georg, who contended that the Bohemians falsely portrayed their struggle with the emperor as religious, was deeply suspicious of the more confrontational policies of the Calvinist electors of the Palatinate, who ultimately led the weak and divided Protestant Union into support of the Bohemian Revolt.[18] In the event, the Lutheran elector supported the Catholic emperor in the Bohemian phase of the war by intervening "to restore order" in the neighboring territory of Upper Lusatia, and as we saw earlier, he was rewarded with the cession of jurisdiction over Upper Lusatia, which was reaffirmed by both the Peace of Prague and the Peace of Westphalia.[19] The absorption of Lusatia brought with it, of course, the Catholic minority that was a well-established part of the *Simultankirche* at Bautzen and was protected by the Cathedral chapter of the Petri Dom. At the same time, however, Saxony absorbed a significant flood of Protestant refugees who were fleeing the forceful re-Catholicization of the rest of Bohemia. In very short order, the religious landscape of Saxony underwent a significant transformation, and the stolidly Lutheran rulers of Saxony were forced to accommodate a wide variety of Protestant "guests" – not just Lutherans, but Calvinists, Utraquists, and Bohemian Brethren as well.[20] In other words, the early years of the Thirty Years War brought unanticipated changes in the religious landscape of Lutheran Saxony that required long-term adjustments by both the political and religious establishments and their religiously diverse subjects.

How the Saxons made these adjustments was clearly framed by the *religious* Peace of Westphalia in a number of ways. Soon after the implementation of the Peace, for example, Lutheran pastors, the face of the religious establishment in Saxony, began articulating their concerns in formal complaints sent to the elector about the "infiltration" of non-Lutheran exiles who represented, from their perspective, a real and present danger to "the salvation of souls" within the electorate.[21] The specific documentation they submitted in support of their

---

[18] See Peter H. Wilson, *The Thirty Years War: Europe's Tragedy* (Cambridge: Harvard University Press, 2009), chapter 9.

[19] The initial grant of jurisdiction over Lusatia was until such time as Ferdinand refunded the elector's expenses; inasmuch as the refund was not made, the cession of authority over Upper Lusatia became permanent.

[20] See Alexander Schunka, *Gäste, die bleiben: Zuwanderer in Kursachsen und der Oberlausitz im 17. und frühen 18. Jahrhundert* (Münster: LIT, 2006).

[21] The following section is based on Dagmar Freist, "Religionssicherheiten und Gefahren für das 'Seelenheil.' Religiös-politische Befindlichkeiten in Kursachsen seit dem Übertritt Augusts des Starken zum Katholizismus," in *Konfession und Konflikt. Religiöse Pluralisierung in Sachsen im 18. und 19. Jahrhundert* (München: Achendorff, 2012), 35–53; see also Dagmar Freist, "*Social Sites*, Practices and Contested Religious Space in 17th and 18th Century Saxony," paper presented at the conference on "Religious Wars in Early Modern Europe and Contemporary Islam" (City University of New York; Columbia University, 2014).

claim suggests they had for decades been carefully monitoring the activities of their many non-Lutheran "guests," and one of their specific concerns was the "problem" of mixed marriages between partners with different religious beliefs and affiliations.[22] Since the Peace, conversions to Catholicism were also particularly worrisome, and these, like mixed marriages, raised questions regarding the traditional authority of fathers vis-à-vis their wives and children. In the 1670s, the elector consulted a range of secular and religious experts, who concluded, with regard to conversions, that the spiritual welfare of Lutheran women and children overrode the traditional authority of the father; in the matter of mixed marriages, the elector instructed pastors to discourage mixed marriages, but in the event they occurred nevertheless, he mandated that the non-Lutheran partners be required to pay a monetary security (*Sicherheit*) to guarantee that all children be brought up Lutheran. Together, the pastors' concerns and the elector's official actions betray a consensus on two important points: that the restitution provisions in the Peace of Westphalia guaranteed the religious status quo of Lutheran **privilege** and that "[r]ulers were not only responsible for the physical well-being of their subjects but also for their spiritual well-being and salvation."[23] Thus in 1694, Elector Georg III declared that "[a]ll measures have to be taken and policies introduced to prevent the public exercise of foreign religions or the introduction of dangerous [radicals]."[24]

Meanwhile, the non-Lutheran "guests" within Saxony were learning to advance their own interests using both the restitution and autonomy provisions of the Peace of Westphalia. There had long been a limited amount of non-Lutheran worship, both Catholic and Protestant, under the **ad hoc tolerance** accorded to foreign merchant communities in the larger cities, such as Dresden and Leipzig. But after the Peace, as the religious diversity of the Saxon population was becoming more keenly felt and, indeed, feared by the "orthodox" Lutheran establishment, these "dissenters," whose religion differed from the one established by their ruler, were able to advocate for greater security and visibility in public life; citing either the restitution provisions of

---

[22] Mixed marriages were perceived as a problem throughout Germany; see especially Dagmar Freist, "One Body, Two Confessions: Mixed Marriages in Germany," in *Gender in Early Modern German History*, Ulinka Rublack (Cambridge: Cambridge University Press, 2002), 295–97; Dagmar Freist, "Between Conscience and Coercion: Mixed Marriages, Church, Secular Authority, and Family," in *Mixed Matches: Transgressive Unions in Germany from the Reformation to the Enlightenment*, ed. David M Luebke and Mary Lindemann (New York: Berghahn Books, 2014), 101–18; and the forthcoming publication of her *habilitation* thesis, Dagmar Freist, *Glaube – Liebe – Zwietracht: Konfessionell gemischte Ehen in Deutschland in der Frühen Neuzeit* (München: Oldenbourg, 2015). Prof. Freist's important comparative research treats mixed marriages as a particularly important site of tension, after Westphalia, between coercion and conscience and as a token of the long-term process of religious "pluralization."

[23] Freist, "Mixed Marriages in Germany," 296.

[24] Quoted in Freist, "Religionssicherheiten," 36.

the Treaty of Osnabrück, in the case of Saxony's modest residual population of Catholics, or the autonomy provisions, in the case of Reformed exiles, they crafted petitions and appeals to the same civil authorities who considered themselves responsible for the religious safety of their subjects. This growing tension between religious diversity and the official urge to maintain the status quo came to a head, however, in 1697 when the elector, Friedrich August, converted to Catholicism in order to be elected king of the Polish-Lithuanian Commonwealth as August II.

Elector Friedrich August was neither the first nor the last German imperial "prince" to convert to Catholicism after the Peace of Westphalia – one tabulation counted forty-two such conversions between 1648 and 1786 – but the experience of Saxony is particularly instructive.[25] Following this "personal" conversion, Lutheran fears of forced re-Catholicization were heightened, of course, but what is striking is how little the official political and religious situation in Saxony actually changed. Government officials were still required to swear an oath to uphold the Augsburg Confession, and the elector continued for decades to be the director of the imperial *Corpus Evangelicorum* through an arrangement which delegated the responsibility to a Lutheran duke. In order to forestall trouble at home, Friedrich August promised not to appoint Catholic officials, that he would not attempt to convert anyone to the Catholic faith, and that the pledges his predecessor had made in 1694 would remain valid and in force; he also guaranteed freedom of religious conscience. In other words, Saxony remained officially Lutheran (**privilege**) even though the religious facts on the ground continued to change in the direction of more visible diversity. In particular, missionaries sent by Rome worked hard to create an informal infrastructure for the Catholic Church in the vicinity of the now Catholic court, and in 1708, the elector guaranteed that Catholics should even have the right to worship publicly, which clearly undermined any Lutheran understanding of the status quo, but was nevertheless permissible under the restitution and autonomy provisions of the Treaty of Osnabrück. As Dagmar Freist's research shows, the increasing familiarity of religious differences in daily experience within Saxony surely gave rise to tensions, mutual irritation, and especially formal disputes revolving around mixed marriages, but it did not lead to conflict that could not be peacefully adjudicated within the rules and structures of the Peace of Westphalia.[26]

The Lutheran city of Hamburg is emblematic of the same long-term trend toward increasingly visible religious diversity within the empire, but with some distinctive variations on the theme. Like the Electorate of Saxony, Hamburg became a paragon Lutheran stability and probity in the sixteenth century, but by the beginning of the seventeenth century it had become an increasingly

---

[25] David M. Luebke, "A Multiconfessional Empire," in *A Companion to Multiconfessionalism in the Early Modern World*, ed. Thomas Max Safley, Brill's Companions to the Christian Tradition, vol. 28 (Leiden; Boston: Brill, 2011), 149–50.

[26] See especially Freist, "Religionssicherheiten."

diverse mercantile metropolis. This religious diversification was, in large measure, made possible by the simultaneous growth of the town of Altona, just a few kilometers to the west along the Elbe River and within easy walking distance from Hamburg. Altona was under the political jurisdiction of the duke of Schaumburg – and after 1640, the kings of Denmark – whose mercantile objective, ultimately unsuccessful, of promoting Altona's harbor and commercial facilities at the expense of Hamburg gave rise to an extraordinary degree of **ad hoc tolerance** of religious "dissenters" in the beginning of the seventeenth century. Although Altona was officially Lutheran, Catholics, Calvinists, Mennonites, and Jews were all granted freedom to worship there, and as the small fishing village grew into a substantial town, their worshiping congregations grew dramatically.[27] Many of the economically successful non-Lutherans who worshiped in Altona, however, preferred to live and work in Hamburg, which resulted in a particularly vivid and large-scale example of the practice of *Auslauf* in order to worship freely in another jurisdiction. In short, while Hamburg and Altona remained fierce economic competitors, especially under Danish policies after 1640, in their growing religious diversity, they were joined at the hip.

After 1648, the Peace of Westphalia opened up the very real possibility of official recognition of private, discreet worship for Calvinists and Catholics, if not Mennonites and Jews, within Hamburg itself. This set up an ongoing competition between the "dissenters," who sought both a firmer foothold and greater visibility, and the Lutheran establishment, which fought a dogged and largely successful rearguard campaign to prevent exactly that, well into the eighteenth century.[28] In this contentious and often bitter competition, the Hamburg Senate was recurrently called on to be the political arbiter between two very different claims based on the Peace of Westpahalia, but caution generally prevailed among the Lutheran elite until well into the eighteenth century. Over time, the determined practice of *Auslauf* gradually gave way to discreet, private worship and eventually public worship after 1785. In short, there was no shortage of religious controversy, competition, and conflict within Hamburg, as in the empire as a whole, following the Peace of Westphalia, but it is striking that the updated framework and mechanisms provided for by the Osnabrück treaty kept the religious peace until the dissolution of the empire itself in 1806.

[27] This account of religious diversification in Hamburg and Altona is based on Joachim Whaley, *Religious Toleration and Social Change in Hamburg, 1529–1819* (Cambridge: Cambridge University Press, 1985).
[28] On the different histories of the Catholic, Jewish (both Sephardic and Ashkenazi), and Calvinist communities, see Whaley, *Religious Toleration and Social Change in Hamburg, 1529–1819*, chapters 2, 3, and 4, respectively. On the complicated experience of the Mennonites, in particular, see Michael Driedger, *Obedient Heretics: Mennonite Identities in Lutheran Hamburg and Altona During the Confessional Age* (Aldershot, England: Ashgate, 2002).

BOUNDARIES, BORDERLANDS, AND BICONFESSIONALISM

If we shift our focus to the western borderlands of the empire, we see a different set of adjustments that were entailed in the two treaties of Münster, between Spain and the United Provinces and between the empire and France. In its silence on the "matter of religion," the first Treaty of Münster did nothing specifically to alter the basic contours of religious peace in the Low Countries that had emerged by the early decades of the seventeenth century and were more or less solidified during the Twelve Year Truce (see Chapter 8). Thus, in the United Provinces of the Northern Netherlands, local authorities provided variable spaces for religious difference alongside the exclusive public Reformed churches (**privilege**) and under the umbrella of a "national" commitment to freedom of religious conscience; a multitude of *schuilkerken* (nominally hidden churches), representing a cacophony of dissident voices, both Catholic and Protestant, were most clearly emblematic of this trajectory. By comparison, in the absence of any guarantee of religious freedom in the Southern Netherlands, religious differences were variously hidden under an officially **repressive** Catholic regime, which nevertheless accommodated religious differences under the cloak of secrecy, *Auslauf*, and **ad hoc tolerance**.

Still, the Treaty of Münster entailed some visible adjustments to these divergent patterns of historical development, especially in the boundary changes, resulting from the possession principle, which the treaty formally validated. On the one hand, Dutch forces had recovered fortresses and territory they had lost in the eastern provinces of Overijssel and Gelderland just prior to the Truce, and as a consequence they had to accommodate their majority-Catholic populations, not as conquered Generality Lands, but as constituent parts of the United Provinces, where Catholic religious practice was the public norm. On the other hand, Frederik Hendrik enjoyed considerable military success in 1629 in the divided province of Brabant, with the conquest of 's-Hertogenbosch and the surrounding Meierij, and again in 1632, along the Mass River, with the conquest of parts of Upper Gelderland, the city of Maastricht, the Lands of Overmaas, and Limburg. It was especially in these largely Catholic areas that the Peace of Westphalia validated some new departures in the complexity and messiness of religious peace in the Low Countries.

As we saw in Chapter 8, rural Catholics in the divided province of Brabant were granted an **ad hoc tolerance**, protecting their traditional worship practices, in a *Déclaration* signed by the French ambassador, Pierre Jeannin, who had brokered the Twelve Year Truce. With the expiration of the Truce in 1621, the *Déclaration* also presumably became a moot point, and in any case it would not necessarily apply to the territories the republic gained in 1629. In the city of 's-Hertogenbosch, the campaign's real prize, the republic's military victory occasioned a large exodus of Catholic clerics, though the city's nuns were allowed to stay; public Catholic worship was banned, Church properties and resources were confiscated, Reformed worship was begun in the enormous

St-Janskerk, and a new Reformed Church structure was organized.[29] In both the city and the countryside, the newly dominant Reformed Church could build on the remnants of earlier attempts at Calvinist evangelization in the sixteenth century and during episodes of military occupation in the seventeenth. Still, the real impetus in creating an exclusive public Reformed Church came from pastors and officials who had migrated or been recruited from elsewhere in the republic. As it happened, then, despite some limited success in implanting Calvinism in the cities, the countryside in the Meierij, which was deeply contested militarily during the remainder of the war but was "possessed" by the republic at the time of the Peace of Westphalia, remained *subversively* and overwhelmingly, though discreetly, Catholic, no longer enjoying even the limited protections of a revocable ad hoc tolerance that had distinguished Brabant's Catholics from Catholics elsewhere in the republic.

Farther south and east, the successful military campaign of 1632 unfolded differently. In the hope of still attracting support for the project of reuniting the whole of the Netherlands, the Estates General assured the religious and political leaders of the southern provinces that, if they joined, they could order their religious affairs as they saw best. Thus, as their army moved south from Venlo, through the major prize, Maastricht, and on to Limburg, the Estates General issued an open call for a southern rebellion, guaranteeing traditional political privileges and "the public exercise of Roman Catholic religion."[30] Although their campaign stalled, and they soon gave up some of their gains, the leaders of the republic kept their word by not formally abolishing public Catholic worship. And in doing so, they introduced forms of religious inclusion that were modeled on German and French experience, but were not accepted elsewhere in the republic.[31] In the city of Maastricht, which had been jointly ruled by the dukes of Brabant and the prince-bishops of Liège, the Estates General promised to continue the condominium of authority in place of Brabant, and in that capacity they created a **parity** regime, very much like the

---

[29] See further Peter Toebak, "Het kerkelijk-godsdienstige en culturele leven binnen het noordwes-telijke deel van het hertogdom Brabant (1587–1609): een typering," *Trajecta. Tijdschrift voor de geschiedenis van het katholiek leven in de Nederlanden* 1 (1992): 124–43; Gerard van Gurp, *Reformatie in Brabant: protestanten en katholieken in de Meierij van 's-Hertogenbosch, 1523–1634* (Hilversum: Verloren, 2013); and Charles de Mooij, *Geloof kan bergen verzetten: reformatie en katholieke herleving te Bergen op Zoom, 1577–1795* (Hilversum: Verloren, 1998). Cf. Benjamin J. Kaplan, "'In Equality and Enjoying the Same Favor': Biconfessionalism in the Low Countries," in *A Companion to Multiconfessionalism in the Early Modern World*, ed. Thomas Max Safley, Brill's Companions to the Christian Tradition, vol. 28 (Leiden; Boston: Brill, 2011), 110–11.

[30] Quoted in Kaplan, "Biconfessionalism," 111.

[31] The importance of the French model of religious inclusion goes back to William of Orange and the *Paix de Religion* of 1578; as Benjamin Kaplan suggests, the French example remains influential in the background as it was Henry IV's representative, Pierre Jeannin, who had urged the ad hoc tolerance of Brabant's Catholics in the Twelve Year Truce, and it was French pressure in the 1630s that opened the Dutch to forms of inclusion that they had refused to consider at the end of the sixteenth century. See Kaplan, "Biconfessionalism," passim.

ILLUSTRATION 11.1: On the central square of Maastricht, the Vrijthof, the Protestant Janskerk (left) is located immediately across a small passage from the much larger Catholic Basilica of St. Servaas. (Euku/Wikipedia Commons/CC BY-SA 3.0)

biconfessional cities of Germany.[32] Municipal offices were equally divided between Protestants and Catholics, and despite their numerical inferiority, Calvinists were allotted two of Maastricht's four churches, and half of the communal resources. Still Catholic religious institutions, like the Chapter of St. Servaas, and Catholic schools and charities remained in place. Today, the location of the Reformed St. Janskerk next to the enormous Catholic Basilica of St. Servaas on the Vrijthoff, Maastricht's central square, is still fittingly emblematic of this durable form of religious coexistence in the Dutch Republic's most significant biconfessional city (see Illustration 11.1).

The biconfessional arrangements in the nearby Lands of Overmaas – the three small lordships (*Heerlijkheid*) of Valkenburg, 's-Hertogenrade, and Dalhem, which were linked to the Duchy of Limburg – were a good deal more complicated and messier.[33] The Dutch commitment not to abolish Catholic

---

[32] See P. J. H. Ubachs, *Twee heren, twee confessies: De verhouding van staat en kerk te Maastricht, 1632–1673* (Assen: Van Gorcum, 1975), and Kaplan, "Biconfessionalism." Note that these apparently modular biconfessional arrangements were adopted and adapted to Maastricht prior the formalization of comparable "parity" arrangements in Germany in the IPO; this Low Countries variation was validated, in turn, by the first Treaty of Münster.

[33] See W. A. J. Munier, *Het simultaneum in de landen van Overmaas: een uniek instituut in de nederlandse kerkgeschiedenis (1632–1878)*, Maaslandse monografieën (Leeuwarden: Eisma B.V., 1998), and Kaplan, "Biconfessionalism," 120–3.

ILLUSTRATION 11.2: The Church of Sts. Nicholas and Barbara in Valkenburg was shared by Calvinists and Catholics between the 1630s and 1661 and, after a period of exclusive Calvinist use, between 1680 and 1819. (Photo Wayne Te Brake)

worship in these territories was linked to the capitulation of Limburg; though the Dutch again lost control of Limburg, they maintained their commitment in the Lands of Overmaas. The capitulation of Limburg in 1632 had urged the sharing of sacred space (now Latinized from the German original as *simultaneum*) in villages with only one church, which apparently occurred in villages where a Reformed pastor was actually posted – that is, in just under half of the villages in these territories. In the first Treaty of Münster, however, the Dutch agreed to divide sovereignty over the three lordships of Overmaas with Spain, which they finally accomplished in a complex patchwork fashion, in a Partition Treaty in 1661,[34] and under this agreement, the Dutch demonstrated their "sovereignty" by replacing Catholic officials and formally abolishing Catholic worship in the territories they controlled. Following a period of French occupation during the Franco-Dutch War, between 1673 and 1678, they quietly revived the practice of *simultaneum* in those villages where Calvinists had an active congregation. Thus, the previously shared Church of Sts. Nicholas and Barbara in Valkenburg was appropriated for

---

[34] See the map of this patchwork of religious and political authority in Benjamin J. Kaplan, *Cunegonde's Kidnapping: A Story of Religious Conflict in the Age of Enlightenment*, The Lewis Walpole Series in Eighteenth-Century Culture and History (New Haven: Yale University Press, 2014), 68–9.

ILLUSTRATION 11.3: The shared village church of Olne, deep in French-speaking Limburg to the southeast of Liege, served as an Auslauf destination for Calvinists from other parts of the Southern Netherlands between the 1630s and the end of the old regime. (Photo Wayne Te Brake)

exclusive Reformed worship in 1661, but by 1680, the Protestants and Catholics of Valkenburg had once again agreed to share the church – a *simultaneum* that lasted until 1819 (see Illustration 11.2).[35] Likewise, in the small village of Olne, located in a small patch Dutch sovereignty in Dahlem to the southeast of Liège in modern French-speaking Belgium, Reformed Protestants and Catholics shared the village church through the end of the old regime (see Illustration 11.3).[36]

Undoubtedly the most fascinating case of the ingenious, recurrently conflicted, yet durable complexity of religious coexistence in this region is the exceedingly messy case of the village of Vaals, which Benjamin Kaplan has expertly and creatively excavated in *Cunegonde's Kidnapping*. Kaplan tells a story of recurrent conflict that culminated tragically in violence in the 1760s, but for our purposes it can be seen, by the same token, as a story of durable, if deeply contentious, coexistence.[37] Vaals was located in the small eastern-most patch of Dutch sovereignty in 's-Hertogenrade, just a few kilometers to the west of the

---

[35] Similarly, the Church of St. Pancrus in Heerlen, in a small, isolated piece of the lordship to the east of Valkenburg, was shared by Protestants and Catholics until the 1830s, when the Reformed built their own worship space.

[36] On the history of Olne, see Munier, *Het Simultaneum in de Landen Van Overmaas*, passim.

[37] See especially chapter 3, "On this Soil," in Kaplan, *Cunegonde's Kidnapping*, 59–90.

fortifications of the German city of Aachen, where Protestants, both Lutherans and Calvinists, had suffered under official repression prior to and during the Thirty Years War. Although there were only a handful of Calvinists living in Vaals, Dutch authorities organized a Dutch/German Reformed congregation in 1649 expressly in order to offer refuge for Protestants in Aachen and nearby Burtscheid, who under the autonomy provisions of the Treaty of Osnabrück were free to practice *Auslauf* in order to worship freely and publicly in Vaals.[38] At the same time, French-speaking Calvinists, from nearby Germany as well as from Limburg and Liège, formed their own congregation and for a time both groups shared the parish church with local Catholics.

Under these crowded conditions, the French-speaking congregation soon moved out to worship in a barn and later in a more suitable space. Also in 1669, Dutch authorities began construction of a new purpose-built Reformed church to accommodate the rapidly growing congregation of German Calvinists; this new church was built perpendicular to and shared a medieval tower with the original parish church, which was retained by the Catholic congregation.[39] Thus their "typical" *simultaneum* morphed into a new hybrid form, which is reminiscent of the immediately proximate evangelical and Catholic churches in the Priory of the Holy Cross in Augsburg. Eventually, Lutherans and Mennonites, mainly from Germany, also organized congregations in this crossroads of religious commutation, though they worshiped "privately" in structures (*schuilkerken*) that were nominally hidden, unlike the Catholics who enjoyed the very special privilege of worshipping publicly in this island of Dutch sovereignty in the eastern borderlands of the empire. If nothing else, the remarkable case of Vaals is emblematic of the modularity of the whole gamut of practices by which a wide variety of actors in both the empire and beyond recurrently managed to accommodate their religious differences: sharing sacred spaces (*simultaneum*), crossing boundaries (*Auslauf*), and worshipping "privately" in structures that did not look like churches (*schuilkerken*). Complex and messy, to be sure, but effective nevertheless!

MANDATING PARITY

The second Treaty of Münster, between France and the empire, also entailed significant adjustments in the structures and experience of religious diversity in the western borderlands of the empire. As we saw in Chapter 10, French control of the bishopric of Metz, along with Verdun and Toul, which had begun a century earlier in the Second Schmalkaldic War, was confirmed as part of the French "satisfactions." In addition, France was ceded "supreme authority" in the

---

[38] As a congregation created for the purpose of providing *Ausluaf* opportunities for Aachen's Protestants, the Reformed Church in Vaals is comparable to the *Friedenkirchen* that served Bohemian Lutherans in Saxony.

[39] See the floor plan of this unusual construction in Kaplan, *Cunegonde's Kidnapping*, 87.

Habsburg Margravates of Upper and Lower Alsace, the city of Breisach, and the ten small cities of the "Decapolis," including Obernai, Colmar, and Mulhouse, which were to retain their traditional privileges as part of the empire. Since the treaty transferred authority from the aggressively Catholic Habsburgs to the "most Christian" and Catholic king of France, this did not entail an immediate change in the formal religious policies of the various regimes in largely Lutheran Alsace; in any case, the religious "rights" of both Protestants and Catholics were protected, in principle, by article V of the Treaty of Osnabrück, which was incorporated, "as if ... verbatim," in the Münster treaty.[40]

Still, as they rebuilt their new acquisitions in the first decades following the Peace, French authorities worked cautiously to open up new opportunities for Catholic religious practices where Protestants were **privileged** and had long dominated public life. Then, as part of the same Franco-Dutch War that resulted in their occupation of the Lands of Overmaas, the French established direct control over those parts of Alsace where their authority had been conditional, and by the Treaty of Nijmegen (1679), the whole of Alsace, with the exception of Strasbourg, was annexed to France. At this point, French authorities began to advance much more aggressively the interest of Catholics in Protestant Alsace, which brought important changes to the religious landscape of Alsace. Consider the complex histories of Colmar, Hunawihr, and Dettwiller, which are emblematic, I believe, of the kind of religious peace that emerged in Alsace under French rule.

Religious diversity was well established in Colmar: Ever since the 1530s, evangelicals had been practicing *Auslauf* to the neighboring village of Horbourg, but it was not until 1575 that Colmar's magistracy appealed to their putative *ius reformandi* as an imperial city and made it officially Lutheran; still, Colmar's political authorities did not abolish Catholic worship.[41] Thereafter, as Peter Wallace describes it, visible "multiconfessionalism" was a consistent, but ever-changing experience as shifts in theological orientation among the city's elites moved it from Lutheranism to Reformed Calvinism. There was a brief interruption of multiconfessional practices when Habsburg authorities imposed a top-down Catholic Reformation at the high tide of Catholic military fortunes in 1627: They officially banned Protestant worship, and disestablished the Evangelical Church. In 1632, however, Swedish occupation reversed the

---

[40] On the possibly deliberate ambiguities of the French satisfaction with regard to its new authority in Alsace, see Konrad Repgen, "Negotiating the Peace of Westphalia: A Survey with an Examination of the Major Problems," in *Politics, Religion, Law and Society*, vol. 1 of *1648: War and Peace in Europe*, eds. Klaus Bussmann and Heinz Schilling (Münster/Osnabrück: Veranstaltungsgesellschaft 350 Jahre Westfälischer Friede, 1998), 356–9.

[41] See Chapter 9, p. 320, in this volume. My account here is based on Peter G. Wallace, "Multiconfessionalism in the Holy Roman Empire: The Case of Colmar, 1550–1750," in *A Companion to Multiconfessionalism in the Early Modern World*, ed. Thomas Max Safley, Brill's Companions to the Christian Tradition, vol. 28 (Leiden; Boston: Brill, 2011), 179–205; see also Kaspar von Greyerz, *The Late City Reformation in Germany. The Case of Colmar, 1522–1628* (Wiesbaden: Steiner, 1980).

Catholic domination and restored "orthodox" Lutheranism, but still allowed Catholic worship. Finally, in 1634, French armies replaced the Swedes as Colmar's "protectors," and in line with Louis XIII's stated purpose of protecting "Germany's liberty," the French retained the biconfessional arrangement negotiated by the Swedes, which was confirmed in the Treaty of Reuil in 1635. Thus, the cession of authority over Upper and Lower Alsace and the decapolis in the Peace of Westphalia followed from this French occupation. After the Treaty of Nijmegen confirmed France's direct control of Colmar in 1679, however, the French *intendant* (royal administrator) in Alsace ordered the city's Lutheran officials to appoint Catholics to fill vacancies in the upcoming election in 1680, and when they resisted, the French authorities imposed a parity arrangement like those installed in Maastricht and mandated in the four Swabian cities in the Treaty of Osnabrück. In other words, German-style confessional **parity** became "the foundation of Louis XIV's counter-reform at Colmar."[42]

A parallel story unfolded in the small village of Hunawihr, some fifteen kilometers to the northwest of Colmar. Hunawihr, which is beautifully situated along the modern Alsatian "wine route," has the curious, but altogether lovely "fortified" Church of St. Jacques-le-Majeur, which became a pilgrimage site for St. Huna on the eve of the Reformation (see Illustration 11.4).[43] In the 1530s the counts of Montbéliard-Wurtemberg, the territorial rulers at the time, introduced a formal Lutheran reformation, as they had done more generally in their various lordships in the region. The village remained officially Lutheran under the *Religionsfriede* and through the Thirty Years War, when it, too, was occupied by French armies. Under the Peace of Westphalia, Hunawihr was only "indirectly" ruled by the king of France because it was part of a Württemberg dependence, not a Habsburg lordship; still, after 1673 it became fully part of France along with the rest of Upper Alsace. Thus, in 1684, it was subject to a decree issued by the *intendant* of Alsace that in all villages with more than seven Catholic families, the local Protestant churches were to be shared equally with Catholics in a German-style *simultaneum* (the French term is *église simultanée*), with the specific requirement that the Catholics have exclusive use of the choir (see Illustration 11.5).[44] In the next four years, seventy-eight Protestant

---

[42] Peter G. Wallace, "Multiconfessionalism," 196. The biconfessional political regime in Colmar had long included Catholics, but now they were to enjoy equal numbers of representatives despite their numerical inferiority in the general population.

[43] See Association des Amis de l'église historique de Hunawihr, *L'Église Fortifieé de Hunawihr* (Colmar: Editions SAEP, 1990). Much of the text of this lovely brochure is reproduced on the French Wikipedia site at https://fr.wikipedia.org/wiki/Hunawihr. The fortification of this lovely church was something of a historical accident: the fortification initially protected a noble estate with a modest chapel; over time the church grew substantially and eventually crowded out the noble residence, while the protective wall remained intact. There is a small display at the base of the church tower today that reconstructs this historical evolution.

[44] See Bernard Vogler, "Le Simultaneum," in *Protestants d'Alsace et de Moselle: Lieux de Mémoire et de Vie*, ed. Antoine Pfeiffer (Strasbourg /Ingersheim: Oberlin/SAEP, 2006), 297–8.

ILLUSTRATION 11.4: The "fortified" Church of St. Jacques-le-Majeur in Hunawihr sits high above the vineyards of the wine route in Upper Alsace. (Photo Wayne Te Brake)

village churches in Upper and Lower Alsace became *églises simultanées*, with another forty-five in the next decade. In the course of the eighteenth century, as Alsace became a more visibly multiconfessional part of the kingdom of France, another forty churches were added for a total of 163. The Church of St. Jacques-le-Majeur did not become an *église simultanée* until 1687, but it is still proudly shared by Protestants and Catholics today (see Illustration 11.6), as are eight other village churches in Upper Alsace and forty-two in Lower Alsace.[45]

In the village of Dettwiller, approximately thirty kilometers northwest of Strasbourg in Lower Alsace, another variant of this story of religious adaptation unfolded at roughly the same time. Dettwiller was part of the territory of the imperial free city of Strasbourg, and in 1530, Protestant reform was introduced officially in Dettwiller, but Dettwiller, like Strasbourg, became biconfessional, and from then until 1547, Protestants and Catholics probably shared the village church, which was, like the church in Hunawihr, dedicated to St. Jacques-le-Majeur (see Illustration 11.7); in 1547, Strasbourg officially imposed, though it did not enforce, Lutheran uniformity on its territory.[46]

[45] See also the lovely Church of St. Urbain in Muntzenheim, which is, like the "fortified" church at Hunawihr, a national historical monument.

[46] See Club Patrimoine de Dettwiller, ed., *Dettwiller, Rosenwiller: Bachknippe Gèscht un Hit*, Collection Mémoire de vies (Strasbourg: Carré Blanc Éditions, 2006), 56–8, 158–91. I am deeply

ILLUSTRATION 11.5: After the Church of St. Jacques-le-Majeur became an église simultanée in 1687, the apse was reserved for the exclusive use of Catholics; the nave was shared. (Photo Wayne Te Brake)

Meanwhile, in the 1530s, the Catholic parish was officially dissolved, and Dettwiller became part of the Catholic parish of Wilwisheim, which provided services to the dwindling number of Catholics who remained, but were considerably less visible. Still, this **privileged** coexistence enjoyed a long and stable history; it was implicitly validated by the *Religionsfriede*, and although it was repeatedly occupied by foreign troops, the church and the village survived the ravages of the Thirty Years War.[47] Because it belonged to Strasbourg, Dettwiller did not fall under French control in either 1648 (the Treaty of Münster) or in the 1670s. After 1650, a Reformed Calvinist community, possibly consisting of refugees recruited to replace the population losses of the war, was also formed in Dettwiller; in spite of the opposition of the Lutheran pastor, they even constructed

grateful to a local Catholic priest who helped me to find one of the few remaining copies of this wonderful piece of local history; he also very proudly helped me to "discover," much to my surprise and delight, the history of the local synagogue.

[47] One chronicler of this period wrote, "Dettwiller was almost destroyed at the beginning of the Thirty Years War. In 1621 by Mansfield [the Portestant commander]; in 1634 by Poles and Croats under Count van Gallas [Catholic]; in 1641, 1643, and 1645 worse came to worst. At the end, there were only 20 citizens left." Quoted in *Dettwiller*, 10.

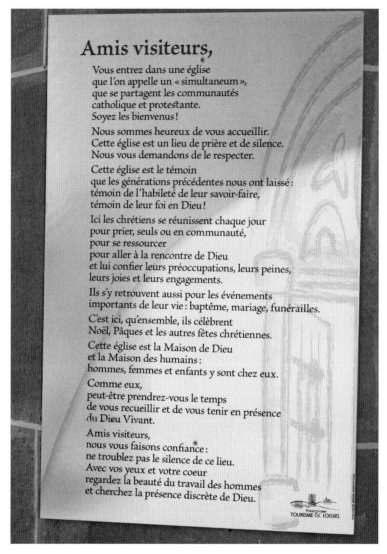

ILLUSTRATION 11.6: A poster inside the Hunawihr church proudly introduces and explains the significance of shared sacred space to the modern visitor, without betraying the mandate that brought it into being. (Photo Wayne Te Brake)

their own "temple" in 1655.[48] In 1681, however, Strasbourg was finally besieged and taken by French armies in yet another French invasion, and although it was not finally confirmed until the Treaty of Rijswijk in 1697, Strasbourg and, with it

[48] *Dettwiller*, 161.

ILLUSTRATION 11.7: The *église simultanée* in Detwiller in Lower Alsace, also dedicated to St. Jacques-le-Majeur, has been shared by Lutherans and Catholics intermittently since the 1530s. (Photo Wayne Te Brake)

Dettwiller, came under French control.[49] Thus, Dettwiller, like Hunawihr, was subject to the mandate that in villages where there were at least seven Catholic families, a formal *église simultanée* be created; in Dettwiller, this did not occur officially until 1692, even though the practice was hardly new.[50]

What is equally striking in the religious landscape of Dettwiller, however, is that just down the street and around the corner from the Church of St. Jacques-le-Majeur, there is a small Jewish synagogue, set back from the street and only partially hidden from view by the surrounding buildings (see Illustration 11.8). In Dettwiller, as in places throughout the territories of Alsace and Lorraine, there is evidence of the growth of small Jewish communities, not unlike the one we saw earlier in Metz, from the middle of the sixteenth century onward. Throughout the county of Hanau-Lichtenberg as well as the territory of Strasbourg, Jews were "tolerated," subject to the payment of a *Schirmgeld* (patronage fee) – yet another example of **ad hoc tolerance**. At the end of the

---

[49] Although Strasbourg remained a multiconfessional city under French rule, the Cathedral of Notre Dame was immediately assigned to Catholic use, exclusively.

[50] When I visited this church, the sexton proudly informed me that Protestants and Catholics have always shared the baptismal font in Dettwiller.

ILLUSTRATION 11.8: The modern synagogue at Dettwiller, no longer in use, served a Jewish community that grew slowly from the middle of the sixteenth century and built its first synagogue at this location in the early eighteenth century. (Photo Wayne Te Brake)

seventeenth century there were only five Jewish families in Dettwiller, but during the eighteenth century, when they built their first synagogue, the community grew to eighteen families and had a population of nearly 100. The "new" synagogue, which was constructed in 1854, when the Jewish population exceeded 150, occupies the same location as the original.[51] This modest synagogue is particularly emblematic, I believe, of the robust religious pluralism that was made possible by the Peace of Westphalia even in places where one might least expect it.

In all three cases, then – in Colmar, Hunawihr, and Dettwiller, as throughout Alsace – Louis XIV and his agents deliberately used the religious terms of the Peace of Westphalia to advance the confessional interests of Catholics, while his Protestant subjects could use those same provisions to defend and preserve their own confessional interests. In his hands, those eminently modular practices of civic **parity** and shared sacred spaces (*Simultankirchen, simultaneum*, and *églises simultanées*) became instruments of power: cudgels with which he could beat back his "enemies" in places where Protestants were previously

[51] See *Dettwiller*, 163 and https://fr.wikipedia.org/wiki/Dettwiller. On the broader history of the Jewish communities throughout the region, see http://judaisme.sdv.fr/today/shial/index.htm.

dominant. Indeed, in the 1680s and 1690s, the agents of French absolutism and dynastic expansion deployed the same weapons that they used in Alsace to advance the cause of international Catholic reform in territories they invaded and at least temporarily occupied on the left bank of the Rhine.[52] Louis XIV's unmistakably and aggressively partisan actions contributed, of course, to a heightened anxiety among Protestants who feared that France and its allies were promoting a wholesale re-Catholicization in the western borderlands of the empire, just as the Habsburgs and their allies had done in the east. Despite the obvious confessional intentions evident here, however, the stories of Colmar, Hunawihr, and Dettwiller indicate that while the standing and visibility of Catholics in public life was certainly enhanced, the outcome in Alsace, as well as throughout the western borderlands, was the strengthening and institutionalization, rather than the diminution or eclipse, of religious pluralism and the growth of what Laurent Jalabert calls a rough and ready "toleration" and mutual respect in daily life.

THE NEW DIMENSIONS OF DIVERSITY AFTER WESTPHALIA

All in all, then, the contours of the religious peace that the Westphalian settlement made possible were at once strikingly familiar and distinctively new. On the familiar side of the coin, we have seen a spectacular diffusion of the eminently modular practices by which a variety of contentious political actors in or near the German-Roman Empire accommodated their religious differences in public life and in daily experience: sharing spaces (*simultaneum* and political parity), traveling or commuting to worship freely (*Auslauf*), and deliberately hiding religious differences to avoid trouble. On the new side of the coin, we have seen the practical effect of the updated institutional framework and the much more elaborate set of rules that the Peace of Westphalia set in place: especially in the implementation of the parity, restitution, and autonomy provisions in the Treaty of Osnabrück. Thanks to an implicit exemption from these principles, the Austrian Habsburgs were able to pursue their vision of "confessional absolutism" in their territorial domains with relatively fewer legal and political restrictions, though even there it is clear that they failed to achieve anything that even approaches the "unity and purity" that are implied in the putative principle of *cuius regio eius religio*. On the contrary, as the evidence from the rest of the empire and its western borderlands suggests, the political "modernity" that the Peace of Westphalia helped to codify and promote was more clearly one in which the religious sovereignty of even the most authoritarian rulers was profoundly limited and the legitimacy and

---

[52] See, in a growing literature, the very helpful research of Laurent Jalabert, *Catholiques et protestants sur la rive gauche du Rhin: droits, confessions et coexistence religieuse de 1648 à 1789* (Bruxelles; New York: P.I.E. Peter Lang, 2009). See also Helmut Neumaier, "Simultaneum und Religionsfrieden im Alten Reich. Zu Phänomenologie und Typologie eines umkämpften Rechtsinstituts," *Historisches Jahrbuch* 128, no. 1 (2008): 137–76.

visibility of religious "dissenters," both organized groups and newly autonomous individuals, were greatly enhanced.

If we enter the illustrative cases we have explored in this chapter as a new overlay on the template of the variable forms of religious coexistence in Figure 1.2, we see an increasingly complex and messy peace in continental Europe that warrants a larger scale for Figure 11.1. In addition to the numerous examples of **parity** (in the upper right) that were exemplary of the first phase of war and peace in Germany and Switzerland, I have now added a diverse set of new examples: Osnabrück with its distinctive parity structure at the territorial level as mandated by the Peace of Westphalia, and a wide variety of cities and smaller villages mainly in the western borderlands of the empire, which underscore the utility and modularity of familiar forms of sharing community and sacred space under diverse political conditions. In the lower left, I have added the new examples of active **repression** in Bohemia and the Upper Palatinate during and, as exceptions to the restitution and autonomy provisions, after the Peace of Westphalia. In the upper left, I have added just one new example of **privilege** – alongside long-established, but changing patterns of **privilege** in Saxony, Upper Lusatia, and Strasbourg – in the city of Hamburg, where the Lutheran establishment clung doggedly to the traditional forms of local exclusion, despite the growing diversity of their local population. As very important exceptions to the politics of religious exclusion, I have added the **ad hoc tolerance** that was granted to Lutherans in Silesia; Catholics, Calvinists, Mennonites, and Jews in Altona; and Jews in Dettwiller. At the same time I have noted the *loss* of **ad hoc tolerance** in the Catholic villages of Brabant, where Catholics in both the cities and the countryside had to worship more discreetly in the face of the Dutch Republic's assertion of the **privilege** of the Reformed Church.

Although it does not represent a complete catalogue, what is perhaps most striking about this new layer on the template of variation is that most of the new examples in Figure 11.1 are situated in the top half of the diagram. We have explored official policies of both inclusion and exclusion, but the dynamics of contentious religious politics in the bulk of the cases resulted in the increased visibility and salience of religious identities in public life following the Peace of Westphalia. Just as striking, perhaps, as the exceptional cases of active **repression** in the Upper Palatinate and Bohemia is the absence of any new forms of **integration** (lower right). In what historians have called the "age of confessionalization," the deliberate reduction of the salience of religious identities for the sake of comity and cooperation in public life does not seem to have been an option or an aspiration for most political actors.

DISTURBING THE PEACE: A CODA

As we have seen throughout this work, religious peace does not mean the absence of religious contention or conflict; rather, conflict and coexistence

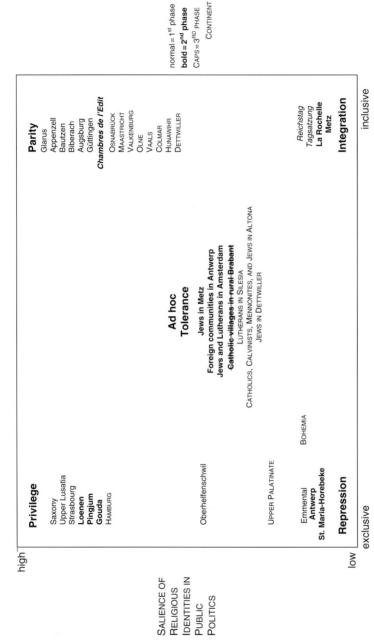

FIGURE 11.1: Patterns of religious coexistence in continental Europe

Privilege
Saxony
Upper Lusatia
Strasbourg
Loenen
Pingjum
Gouda
HAMBURG

Parity
Glarus
Appenzell
Bautzen
Biberach
Augsburg
Güttingen
Chambres de l'Edit
OSNABRÜCK
MAASTRICHT
VALKENBURG
OLNE
VAALS
COLMAR
HUNAWIHR
DETTWILLER

**Ad hoc
Tolerance**

Jews in Metz
Foreign communities in Antwerp
Jews and Lutherans in Amsterdam
~~Catholic villages in rural Brabant~~
LUTHERANS IN SILESIA
CATHOLICS, CALVINISTS, MENNONITES, AND JEWS IN ALTONA
JEWS IN DETTWILLER

Oberhelfenschwil

UPPER PALATINATE

BOHEMIA

Emmental
Antwerp
St. Maria-Horebeke
Repression

Reichstag
Tagsatzung
La Rochelle
Metz
Integration

SALIENCE OF
RELIGIOUS
IDENTITIES IN
PUBLIC
POLITICS

high

low

exclusive

inclusive

CULTURAL POLITICS OF RULERS

normal = 1st phase
bold = 2nd phase
CAPS = 3RD PHASE
CONTINENT

were inextricably entangled in the larger history of accommodating religious differences in early modern Europe, or any time and place, for that matter. In some exceptional cases, however, local or parochial conflicts did escalate, when outsiders or third parties intervened, polarization made routine collaboration difficult, or larger militarized alliances were brokered in support of the forces in conflict. Like the peace settlements we explored in the first two phases of religious war and peace, the Peace that emerged during and after this last spasm of religious war on the continent was also vulnerable to the resumption of coordinated destruction in which religious identities were the principal markers of both enmity and alliance. Here let me look briefly at several very different disturbances of the religious peace in Switzerland, France, and the German-Roman Empire.

As we saw in Chapter 10, the basic elements of the political settlements that made religious peace possible in the second half of the seventeenth century were essentially the same as the basic provisions we found in the second Swiss *Landfrieden* in 1531: mutual recognition, pledges of security, and mechanisms to resolve future disagreements short of war. In the comparative context of the later seventeenth century, however, the fate of the ground-breaking Swiss peace settlement in the seventeenth century is instructive. As noted at the beginning of Chapter 9, the Swiss *Landfrieden* was the only sixteenth-century settlement that did not give way to a resumption of religious war in the first half of the seventeenth century; indeed, as Randolph Head suggests, "From the perspective of war-ravaged Germany … the Swiss Confederation seemed to be a haven of peace and prosperity."[53] This is not to say that maintaining a religious peace on the basis of these principles was easy. Already in the sixteenth century we saw disturbances, such as the polarization within Glarus that threatened the peace, but by the 1630s, resolution of even the most minor religious disputes in the *Gemeine Herrschaften* (where Catholic and Reformed confederates shared jurisdiction) was becoming difficult. Still, a protracted legal struggle over the mechanisms for preserving peace in Rheintal was ended peacefully when the Catholic confederates reluctantly accepted the introduction of the parity principle – equal numbers of Protestants and Catholics – in commissions to resolve religious conflicts.[54] Shortly after the Peace of Westphalia was concluded, the Swiss Peasants' War broke out in 1653 when peasants in Luzern and Bern revolted against the corruption of their urban overlords; in this case, Catholic and Reformed

---

[53] Randolph C. Head, "Thinking with the Thurgau: Political Pamphlets from the Vilmergerkrieg and the Construction of Biconfessional Politics in Switzerland and Europe," in *Politics and Reformations: Communities, Polities, Nations, and Empires. Essays in Honor of Thomas A. Brady Jr.*, eds. Christopher Ocker, et al., Studies in Medieval and Reformation Traditions, 128 (Leiden; Boston: Brill, 2007), 239. See also, Thomas Lau, "Villmergerkrieg, Erster," in *Historicher Lexikon der Schweiz* (www.hls-dhs-dss.ch/textes/d/D8910.php, 2014).

[54] Head, "Thinking with the Thurgau," 240, note 5.

confederates would cooperate in the suppression of the popular revolt, not unlike the Peasants' War 125 years earlier.[55]

Just two years later, however, the "discovery" and subsequent repression of the group of dissimulating Protestants (see Chapter 4) in Catholic Schwyz once again *polarized* the Reformed and Catholic confederates (mainly Zurich and Bern against Schwyz and Luzern).[56] There followed a partial, but rapid *escalation* from a "domestic" religious problem to coordinated destruction – a new round of religious war among Swiss confederates with easy access to violent means. The First War of Villmergen began in January 1656 when Zurich occupied Thurgau, and Luzern quickly moved to block the movement of troops from Bern. After Zurich's forces failed in a siege of Rapperswil (another *Gemeine Herrschaft*), they suffered a humiliating defeat by troops from the much smaller Schwyz. A peace agreement, signed on February 1656, just thirty-eight days later, nevertheless reconfirmed the *Landfrieden* of 1531, which required the grudging consent of the Swiss confederates to live once again according to the template for religious peace that they had devised 125 years earlier.

A half century later, there was another dangerous escalation of local religious conflict within the Swiss *Eidgenossenschaft* when the majority Protestant population of Toggenburg resisted the increasingly autocratic politics of their overlord, the Catholic Abbey of St. Gallen.[57] At first the Toggenburger rebels enjoyed support from both Protestant and Catholic confederates who feared an international escalation, specifically an alliance of the Abbey of St. Gallen with the Habsburg emperor, Leopold II, in violation of the Swiss policy of strict neutrality, which had kept them out of the Thirty Years War. By the time a new war broke out in April of 1712 – this one called either the Second War of Villmergen or the Toggenburg War – the Habsburg connection had disappeared and the principal forces in conflict consisted of Protestants – Zurich and Bern plus Protestant troops from Thurgau and Toggenburg, supported by Geneva – against Catholics – the *V Orte* (the five Catholic confederates) plus the Abbey of St. Gallen supported by Wallis. The first attempt to make a peace settlement failed in July, but on August 11, 1712, the combatants agreed to the Peace of Aarau, which reduced the political hegemony of the Catholic confederates in

---

[55] Andreas Suter, *Der schweizerische Bauernkrieg von 1653: Politische Sozialgeschichte – Sozialgeschichte eines politischen Ereignisses* (Tübingen: Biblioteca Academica Verlag, 1997).

[56] See Mark Furner, "The 'Nicodemites' in Arth, Canton Schwyz, 1530–1698" (Master's thesis, University of Warwick, 1994), and Head, "Thinking with the Thurgau," 244, note 15. These underground Protestant families had a long history, dating back to the 1530s, but in 1655, the Schwyz authorities began actively to prosecute them. Some were sent to Milan to the Inquisitorial Court, and those who fled to Zürich for safety had their property confiscated.

[57] See Thomas Lau, "Villmergerkrieg, Zweiter," in *Historicher Lexikon der Schweiz* (www.hls-dhs-dss.ch/textes/d/D8911.php, 2013) and the sources cited there. There is a similar article called "Toggenburg War" at https://en.wikipedia.org/w/index.php?title=Toggenburg_War&oldid=605 597403. On religious relations within Toggenburg in the sixteenth century, see Chapter 4, pp. 78–80.

relation to the governance of the *Gemeine Herrschaften* and formally instituted the **parity** principle in commissions adjudicating religious matters, but otherwise reaffirmed the basic principles of the *Landfrieden* of 1531. In short, despite these serious disturbances of the peace, the religious peace of 1531 proved to be the durable foundation for peaceful religious coexistence in the *Eidgenossenschaft* into the modern era.

There was, of course, a much more dramatic disturbance of the post-Westphalia religious peace in France in 1685 when Louis XIV formally revoked the Edict of Nantes by means of the Edict of Fontainebleau. As we saw in Chapter 10, the Edict of Alais, which ended the last of the civil wars in 1629, eliminated the political and military independence of the old Huguenot coalition, but reaffirmed both the public and secret articles of the Edict of Nantes, which provided for the **integration** of Calvinists and Catholics in public life. During both the Thirty Years War and the so-called Fronde rebellion (1648–1653) that followed in its wake, the Reformed population of France proved to be loyal subjects of their kings – first Louis XIII, during the early years of the war, and the boy king Louis XIV during the Fronde – whom they recognized as their "protectors" in accordance with the Edict of Nantes. Under the personal rule of Louis XIV, following the death of Mazarin in 1661, however, the royal agents and courts that were charged with the maintenance of the religious peace began ever more aggressively to interpret the text of the Edict to the maximum disadvantage of the kingdom's Reformed churches.[58] In particular, Catholic plaintiffs were recurrently successful in reducing the Huguenots' opportunities for public worship, based on narrow and partisan interpretations the Edict's carefully specified limits on Reformed worship as well as its provisions in article 3, ordering the restoration of Catholic worship "without any disturbance or impediment."[59] By 1680, the number of Reformed "temples" that existed in 1598 had been reduced by half, and following a decree from the royal council in 1681, ordering the destruction of temples that received back Huguenots who had converted to Catholicism, the number of destroyed temples spiked even higher. Keith Luria describes the dynamic,

Changing royal policies, the rising tide of Catholic-Reformation militancy, the influence of religious orders, such as Jesuits and Capuchins, the draining away of the Reformed population through conversions – all of these contributed to disabling peaceful

---

[58] Prior to this, the Huguenots had successfully used the edict to protect their interests; see especially Keith P. Luria, "France: An Overview," in *A Companion to Multiconfessionalism in the Early Modern World*, ed. Thomas Max Safley, Brill's Companions to the Christian Tradition, vol. 28 (Leiden; Boston: Brill, 2011), 209–38.

[59] On the partisan interpretation of these provisions, see Luria, "France: An Overview," 235–7, and Keith P. Luria, "Sharing Sacred Space: Protestant Temples and Religious Coexistence in the Seventeenth Century," in *Religious Differences in France: Past and Present*, ed. Kathleen Perry Long, Sixteenth Century Essays & Studies (Kirksville, MO: Truman State University Press, 2006), 51–72.

confessional relations that careful negotiations or simple practical coexistence had created in biconfessional French communities.

Luria goes on to argue that not all relations between Catholics and Protestants were soured; rather, when they came into conflict, "there was no longer any way to negotiate a peaceful result. The monarchy, its officials and its courts no longer mediated or arbitrated; they persecuted."[60] Indeed, at the same time, the royal government had begun deploying special detachments of soldiers (the hated dragoons) to intimidate Protestants into converting to Catholicism.

Although this rising tide of persecution had already deprived the Reformed churches of many, if not most, of their venues for public worship, including the large purpose-built temples at La Rochelle and Metz (see Chapter 8), and set off the third major episode of forced migration of the post-Reformation era, the actual revocation of the Edict of Nantes in 1685 was still much more than a mere formality. Under French law, those of the "so-called reformed religion" (R. P. R., for short) still enjoyed unlimited freedom of religious conscience, a broad range of civil and political rights, and were fully integrated into French social and educational institutions. With the Edict of Fontainebleau, Louis XIV aimed for nothing less than "to obliterate the memory of the troubles, the confusion, and the evils which the progress of this false religion has caused in this kingdom."[61] Having asserted in the preamble the fatuous claim that the number of Reformed faithful was now so small that the Edict of Nantes was no longer necessary, the king's edict mandated the immediate destruction of the remaining temples (article 1), forbad the practice of the Reformed religion anywhere in the kingdom, even privately (articles 2 and 3), ordered all Reformed pastors who would not convert to Catholicism to leave the kingdom within fourteen days (article 4), forbad private instruction in the Reformed religion (article 7), ordered that the children of Protestants be baptized by Catholic priests, and prohibited all Reformed families, other than pastors, from leaving the kingdom (article 10). Article 12 still granted individual, nonclerical dissenters the "liberty" to remain in France, "without ... molestation or hindrance on account of the said R. P. R. [the so-called reformed religion]" – though their marriages were annulled and their children were to be put in the care of Catholic families! – but the Edict of Fontainebleau put a definitive end to France's bold experiment in religious **integration** as well as the king's formal obligation to "protect" his Reformed subjects.

Like authoritarian claims of *cuius regio eius religio*, more generally, Louis XIV's confessional absolutism cannot be taken at face value as a description of

---

[60] Luria, "France: An Overview," 237.
[61] There is a scan of the printed text of the Edict of Fontainebleau (Paris, 1685) available from the Biblioteque Nationale de France at http://gallica.bnf.fr/ark:/12148/btv1b86224359/f3.image.r =edit%20fontainebleau%201685.langFR. An English translation is available at http://hugue notsweb.free.fr/english/edict_1685.htm. This quotation is from the preamble.

ILLUSTRATION 11.9: The Museum of the Desert in Le Mas-Soubeyran preserves a wide variety of material and documentary evidence of the survival of Protestantism in France after the revocation of the Edict of Nantes. (Photo Wayne Te Brake)

or a reliable guide to lived experience. On the contrary, while all remaining Reformed temples (with just a few exceptions) were quickly destroyed, the practice of the Reformed religion continued, the Reformed pastors did not all leave, private education in the Reformed religion did not end, not all children of Reformed parents were baptized as Catholics, and a lot more Huguenots did leave France.[62] As they saw it, the Reformed population of France entered into their "time of trial in the desert," much like the ancient people of Israel. Indeed, although the Huguenots' side of this dramatic story is reflected, usually negatively, in official archives, the best place to recover it is undoubtedly the Musée du Désert (Museum of the Desert), in the small village of Le Mas-Soubeyran in the Cevennes in southern France, near Alès (see Illustration 11.9). Today nearly the whole village is given over to the museum, which, like the Protestant Historical Museum in St. Maria-Horebeke in Flanders, is chock full of evidence, both material and documentary, of the survival of religious diversity under severe

---

[62] For an introduction to the history of the Huguenots' "survival" in France and the Huguenot diaspora, see Bertrand Van Ruymbeke and Randy J. Sparks, eds., *Memory and Identity: The Huguenots in France and the Atlantic Diaspora*, The Carolina Lowcountry and the Atlantic World (Columbia: University of South Carolina Press, 2003).

repression.[63] As it happened, the Huguenots of the Cevennes, known as the "Camisards," were especially defiant after the revocation of the Edict of Nantes, and in 1702 the royal government began a two-year military campaign to crush the Camisards' "rebellion" and eliminate the "problem" of religious dissent.[64] In the absence of a more general escalation, and after two years of guerrilla warfare, sporadic fighting continued until 1710, when it faded away without a definitive settlement. Following the death of Louis XIV in 1715, the Reformed faithful were reorganized in clandestine churches led by itinerant preachers and enjoyed a considerable revival under the leadership of Antoine Court.

In sum, Louis XIV's forceful repression of the French Huguenots at the same time as he was mandating biconfessional structures in Alsace – *églises simultanées* and parity governance – proved to be a very costly failure. Like the active **repression** of Protestants in the Southern Netherlands and Bohemia and of Catholics in Ireland (see Chapter 12), Louis's bold experiment in confessional absolutism failed to solve the perceived problem of religious diversity or to achieve the unity and purity of the imagined Christian community of the past. To be sure, the revocation of the Edict of Nantes disrupted the religious peace in France – indeed it substituted **repression** for **integration** – but it did not destroy the religious peace of post-Westphalian Europe: It did not restart the religious wars, and it did not eliminate the diversity that is at the heart of our definition of religious peace. Indeed, as Keith Luria concludes, "Despite royal persecution, France had become a permanently biconfessional country."[65]

A final example of the disturbance of the post-Westphalian peace differs from the others in that it did not entail even a token renewal of coordinated destruction. Like most polities in central Europe, the officially Catholic Prince-Bishopric of Salzburg contained a considerable number of religious dissenters, in this case, mainly Lutherans, whose religious practices and beliefs differed from those of their rulers.[66] These were, however, mainly located in remote alpine valleys some distance from the metropolitan center of the archbishopric.

---

[63] See www.museedudesert.com/article5759.html. The Musée du Désert is of course affiliated with the larger network of Protestant museums, some twenty-two in all; see www.museeprotestant .org. Unfortunately, the museum does not permit photography, but my personal favorite artifact is a portable pulpit for the preaching of the Word, which could be disguised as a wine barrel in the "Assemblies Room"; for a "virtual visit" see www.museedudesert.com/article23.html. See also the wonderful analysis of this "lieu de mémoire" in Philippe Joutard, "The Museum of the Desert: The Protestant Minority," in *Realms of Memory: Rethinking the French Past*, ed. Pierre Nora (New York: Columbia University Press, 1996), 353–77, and Wayne Te Brake, "Emblems of Coexistence in a Confessional World," in *Living with Religious Diversity in Early Modern Europe*, eds. C. Scott Dixon, Dagmar Freist, and Mark Greengrass (Farnham, England: Ashgate Publishing, 2009), 53–79.

[64] See Liliane Crété, *Les Camisards* (Paris: Perrin, 1992), and Philippe Joutard, ed., *Les Camisards*, Collection Folio/Histoire (Paris: Editions Gallimard/Julliard, 1994).

[65] Luria, "France: An Overview," 238.

[66] The following account is based primarily on Mack Walker, *The Salzburg Transaction: Expulsion and Redemption in Eighteenth-Century Germany* (Ithaca, NY: Cornell University Press, 1992); Walker examines this remarkable "transaction" from five different perspectives:

In the 1680s, around the time of heightened tensions elsewhere in Europe, especially France, the Salzburg authorities "discovered" and then banished about a thousand Protestants from the remote Defereggental, in east Tyrol, despite the autonomy provisions that had been offered to dissenters in the Peace of Westphalia. What is striking here is that, in sharp contrast with Louis XIV's policies, the archbishop chose banishment or expulsion rather than enforced conformity. In any case, this disturbance of the religious peace had few reverberations beyond its local context.

Nearly fifty years later, however, the discovery of widespread Lutheranism among the independent farmsteads of the Pongau involved a much higher order of magnitude, and the story of their subsequent expulsion engaged a much broader range of actors. On October 31, 1731, Archbishop Leopold Anton von Firmian issued an expulsion decree affecting some 20,000 Lutherans, which set off a storm of controversy in the empire and more broadly in Europe: The independent farmers were required to sell their property and leave within three months; laborers, miners, and craftsmen who had no land were to leave in just eight days. In the highest echelons of imperial politics, almost everyone seemed to agree that, because Salzburg had always been officially Catholic, the archbishop was technically justified in insisting on uniformity; after all, from a ruler's perspective religious dissent looks a lot more like treason than liberty.

In the event, the Protestant estates in the *corpus evangeloricum* (the evangleical faction in the diet) urged emigration rather than forced conformity, and in February 1732, King Friedrich Wilhelm of Prussia helped to resolve the crisis when he officially invited the Salzburg Lutherans to settle in Prussian Lithuania, which nearly 16,000 eventually did; others ended up in Saxony on their way to Prussia, and some went as far as the new English colony of Georgia in North America, where they established the first Lutheran church in 1734.[67] For our purposes, what is striking about the "Salzburg Transaction" is that this disturbance of the peace, which *activated* the generic Protestant-Catholic identity boundary both locally and more broadly in Europe, did not invoke the other familiar mechanisms – *polarization, escalation*, and *brokerage* – that had recurrently led to war in earlier generations; instead *negotiation* and *segregation*, in particular, helped to account for the durability of the religious peace.

Taken together, these diverse disturbances of the post-Westphalian peace teach us a good deal about both the fragility and the durability of religious peace in continental Europe. Against the backdrop of a century and a half of intermittent religious war, serious conflicts that *activated* religious identities and the boundaries associated with them could and, on relatively rare occasions, did combine with political *polarization*, network-based *escalation*, and the *brokerage*

---

the archbishopric; the kingdom of Prussia; the empire; the migrants themselves; and the legends that have grown up around it. See also, Luebke, "Multiconfessional Empire," 152.

[67] In the end, as Mack Walker suggests, nearly everyone involved in this episode got what they wanted, with the exception, of course, of the Lutheran peasants, laborers, miners, and artisans of the Pongau.

of larger militarized alliances rooted in religious solidarity to produce brief, but very limited, episodes of coordinated destruction in which religious identities served as the principal markers of enmity and alliance. These religious wars in Switzerland and France may, however, be considered the exceptions that confirmed the new normal in continental Europe: The era of religious war had passed and the religious peace proved to be durable. In addition, what all of these disturbances of the religious peace had in common – whether they resulted in war or whether war was averted – was that they were sparked by the attempts of either territorial or national rulers to impose or enforce norms of "unity and purity" on subject populations that were, in fact, diverse and had been for some time. These authoritarian attempts to turn the clock back to an imagined time in the now distant past threatened once again to criminalize religious differences by equating religious differences with sedition or treason;[68] thus, it was official intolerance, rather than popular intolerance, that constituted the most serious threat to religious peace. In all of these cases, the very officials who were entrusted with maintenance of the peace simply abdicated their responsibility.

Whereas the post-Westphalian peace proved to be durable, it was also clearly subject to change over time. We have seen remarkable but incremental patterns of change over time in the contours of the religious peace in situations as diverse as Saxony, Hamburg, Limburg, and Alsace, but the most dramatic changes undoubtedly came in France and Salzburg. What is particularly instructive about all of these cases is that it was in the realm of contentious politics – that is, in the contentious interactions of often intolerant rulers (sometimes territorial, as in Switzerland and Germany, and sometimes national, as in France) and their religiously diverse and often intolerant subjects – that the actual contours and lived experience of religious peace was shaped and reshaped in early modern Europe. Thus, while the infrapolitics of elite bargaining recurrently made peace possible, the contentious politics of rulers and subjects accounted for the variations in what religious peace actually looked like.

When we turn our attention finally to the composite British monarchy, we will find a common historical trajectory toward the legalization of religious diversity. Still the contentious political interactions of the religiously diverse populations of the three very different kingdoms with the rulers they had in common, produced new variations on familiar themes, and strikingly different experiences of religious peace among them.

---

[68] In the sixteenth century, this brutal equation had resulted in thousands of heresy trials and executions in France and the Low Countries, but in the seventeenth century, in Bohemia and France, for example, it appears no longer to have been possible to punish religious difference by public executions, though the eighteenth-century example of the execution of Jean Calas in Toulouse comes close. On the latter see, in a large and often polemical literature, David D. Bien, *The Calas Affair: Persecution, Toleration, and Heresy in Eighteenth-Century Toulouse* (Princeton, NJ: Princeton University Press, 1960).

12

The Contours of Religious Peace IV

Great Britain

As we saw in Chapters 9 and 10, a long period of political instability prolonged the emergence of religious peace in England, Scotland, and Ireland. In the absence of a negotiated political settlement, a series of transient and contested military and political "victories" proved to be a weak foundation for religious peace. Still, by the end of the seventeenth century the contours of a durable religious peace were visible in all three kingdoms. Each had experienced differently the religious tumults of the sixteenth century – the Henrican and Edwardian Reformations, the Marian Counter-Reformation, and the Elizabethan Settlement – and each kingdom had experienced the political tumults of the seventeenth century – the Puritan Revolution, the Commonwealth, the Restoration, and the Glorious Revolution – differently. Consequently the contours of the religious peace that were made possible by the political stability and the variously "negotiated" religious settlements under the joint monarchy of William and Mary were strikingly different in the three kingdoms. Still, the challenge of surveying the range of variation and selecting specific examples of what religious peace actually looked like in England, Scotland, and Ireland is significantly easier than the survey we have just conducted on the continent; indeed, although there were important local and regional variations, the relatively consolidated sovereignties of the three monarchies stand in sharp contrast to the fragmented sovereignties that characterized the German-Roman Empire and helped to make the religious peace there so complex and messy. We will begin, perhaps a bit too conventionally, by looking at the core of the composite monarchy: England.

ENGLAND: TOLERATING THE DISSENTERS

To review the historical context briefly, both Catholics and "Puritans" were part of the religious landscape of England prior to the civil war, but they remained largely hidden by noble protection (Catholics) and "occasional conformity"

(Church Papists as well as Puritans).[1] The collapse of religious and political authority in the 1640s, however, opened up a robust "religious marketplace" comparable to the expansion of religious choices offered in the United Provinces, and the disestablishment of the Anglican Church under the Commonwealth kept that marketplace open and visible in the 1650s. Although the restoration of the monarchy in 1660 entailed the renewal of compelled conformity to the **privileged** Anglican Church, the government and the Church could not put the genie of religious nonconformity or dissent back into the bottle. In 1672, Charles II, and after 1685, James II opened up space for the accommodation of dissenters of all sorts, including Catholics, but conservative reaction reversed these initiatives or limited their effect. Finally, in 1689, the Glorious Revolution in England produced both the "Bill of Rights," limiting royal authority, and the "Toleration Act," offering **ad hoc toleration**, via a licensing process, to Protestant nonconformists, but not to Catholics. Today, the English landscape is still filled with emblems of the vigorous diversity that first exploded in the 1640s and was finally "tolerated" in the 1690s.[2] Consider the following examples, each of which has a distinctive story that connects the Protestant dissent of 1640s to the tolerated dissenters of the 1690s.

In the dispersed settlements of Suffolk County in East Anglia, near the North Sea coast, there is a modified sixteenth-century barn known as the Walpole Old Chapel that is emblematic of the instability of the period of political tumult as well as the relative security of the new era of toleration (see Illustration 12.1).[3] Puritan "Separatists" and "Independents" were especially strong in East Anglia before and during the civil wars, and an "Independent" congregation was formally organized at Walpole in 1649, six months after the execution of the king. The leader of the Suffolk Independents, who rejected any external authority, was a pastor ordained in the established church who had fled to the United Provinces in the 1630s to serve the exiled Puritan community in Rotterdam, but returned in 1642 to become a leader of the Puritan Revolution. The fledgling Walpole congregation, in particular, was served by three Independent parish pastors under the Commonwealth.[4] The last of these was Samuel Manning, who was expelled

---

[1] For an account of religious diversity and coexistence in England, in terms of the dialectic of tolerance and intolerance, see Alexandra Walsham, *Charitable Hatred: Tolerance and Intolerance in England, 1500–1700*, Politics, Culture, and Society in Early Modern Britain (Manchester; New York: Manchester University Press, 2006); for a brief introduction to the religious "minorities" that were in evidence, see pp. 20–6.

[2] See, for example, the very comprehensive and beautifully illustrated volumes published by the Royal Commission on Historical Monuments: Christopher Stell, ed., *An Inventory of Nonconformist Chapels and Meeting-Houses*, 4 Vol. (London: H. M. S. O., 1986–2002): Central England (1986), Southwest England (1991), North of England (1994), Eastern England (2002). Most of the chapels and meetinghouses in this inventory were constructed after the period we are surveying here, but they are nevertheless emblematic of the early history of nonconformity in England.

[3] See www.walpoleoldchapel.co.uk and www.hct.org.uk/chapels/east-england/walpole-old-chapel/23.

[4] Although there was no established church in England under the Commonwealth, many parish churches were served by Puritan pastors, both Presbyterians and Independents, who replaced

ILLUSTRATION 12.1: The Walpole Old Chapel in East Anglia served a congregation of "Independents," which was formed in 1649, until 1970; the originally clandestine barn church was licensed for public worship after the Act of Toleration in 1690. (Photo Wayne Te Brake)

from his parish "living" under the Anglican restoration, but remained the leader of his Independent congregation, which worshiped discreetly in various houses, until it was finally licensed under the Toleration Act in 1690. It is not clear when the Walpole Independents began to use the barn for worship services, but it was probably in 1689, prior to its licensure, that it was expanded to its current form, in which the preaching pulpit is the focal point of the worship space (see Illustration 12.2).[5]

In the town of Macclesfield in Cheshire, just south of Manchester, there is a purpose-built Presbyterian chapel, set back from King Edward Street behind a wrought-iron gate, that is emblematic of a parallel development (see Illustration 12.3). Presbyterians were the "Puritans" who organized their congregations within a larger Reformed or Presbyterian/Synodical authority structure and who were willing to negotiate with King Charles I under terms of the Solemn League and Covenant; thus, it was their political allies who were

priests who were tainted by "episcopacy," but these were expelled from their positions after the restoration of the **privileged** Anglican Church after 1660.

[5] Independent or Congregational worship services were maintained at the Walpole Old Chapel until 1970, when the congregation was disbanded; today the chapel is maintained by the Historic Chapels Trust and is used for occasional Quaker meetings.

ILLUSTRATION 12.2: The well-preserved interior of the Walpole Old Chapel features prominently the pulpit for the preaching of the Word; the main level has ample seating in pew boxes while the balcony has open seating in rows. (Photo Wayne Te Brake)

purged from Parliament in 1648, prior to the trial and execution of Charles I. During and after the civil wars, many Presbyterian pastors, like the Independents in Walpole, came to lead "reformed" congregations within the disaggregated parochial structure of England, but following the Restoration, they, too, were purged from their official positions and were forced to leave the parish churches to lead clandestine worship services, known as illegal "conventicles," in urban houses or rural barns. Following this period of repression, the King Edward Street Chapel, known originally as the Back Street Chapel, was built in 1689 and licensed in1690; it was designed, in the form of a "conventical" barn, for a large Presbyterian congregation of perhaps 450, with an impressive pulpit in the middle of the long side of the sanctuary for the preaching of the Word (see Illustration 12.4). In 1764, its pastor, John Palmer, led the transformation of the Presbyterian congregation into a Unitarian fellowship; it remains a Unitarian chapel today, but the worship space retains most of the architectural features of its original use.[6]

---

[6] The King Edward Street Unitarian Chapel distributes a brochure of "Historical Notes" to visitors; see also, www.maccunitarians.co.uk/about-us and http://list.historicengland.org.uk/resultsingle .aspx?uid=1291252.

ILLUSTRATION 12.3: The King Edward Street Chapel in Macclesfield, a purpose-built Presbyterian worship space, was set off from the street inside a block of buildings, though it was not formally required to be "hidden." (Photo courtesy of Roger Graham)

Not far to the west of Macclesfield in the Cheshire countryside, the Great Warford Baptist Chapel offers yet another variation on the theme (see Illustration 12.5).[7] Early English Baptists were also known as "Puritans"

[7] See O. Knott, *Great Warford Baptist Chapel* (no date), biblicalstudies.org.uk/pdf/tbhs/06-1_025 .pdf; see also, www.warfordhistory.co.uk/?page_id=7 and www.greatwarfordpc.org.uk/history.

ILLUSTRATION 12.4: The surprisingly capacious interior of the King Edward Street Chapel, which is now a Unitarian Church, was designed in 1690 to accommodate 450 Presbyterian worshipers; its form recalls the barns where these dissenters used to worship clandestinely. (Photo courtesy of Roger Graham)

ILLUSTRATION 12.5: The Great Warford Baptist Chapel, a modest structure, is a converted barn that is still used for religious services; the congregation originated in 1642 and worshiped discretely in various houses until it was officially licensed under the Act of Toleration in 1690. (Photo courtesy of Roger Graham)

ILLUSTRATION 12.6: The small Quaker Meeting House in Burford was probably built in the 1688 and is one of the oldest purpose-built Quaker Meeting Houses still in use in England. (Photo Wayne Te Brake)

who, like the Independents at Walpole, had connections to the United Provinces and were "Separatists," worshiping in "gathered" congregations outside any larger authority structure; unlike the other Puritans, but like the Dutch Anabaptists with whom they were connected, the English Baptists rejected infant baptism and practiced adult or "believer" baptism. The earliest Baptist congregation was created in 1611 at Spitalfields in London, and they proliferated more broadly in the 1620s. The congregation in Warford was organized in 1642, at the start of the civil war, and met "privately" in what are known as the Norbury Houses. The Warford Baptists, who did not occupy a "reformed" parish church under the Commonwealth, may have begun worshiping clandestinely in the repurposed barn that is still the Great Warford Baptist Chapel as early as 1668, though they were not deeded the property until 1712. In any case, the chapel, which is still used for Baptist worship, though now slightly smaller, may well be the oldest Baptist worship space in continuous use in England. Unlike their counterparts on the continent, where they were often reviled, the Baptists in Great Warford enjoyed the same **ad hoc tolerance** as other Protestant dissenters after 1690, with article X of the Toleration Act providing them a special exemption regarding infant baptism.

Finally, let me offer the rather different example of the Friends Meeting House in Pytts Lane, Burford, to the west of Oxford and on the southern edge of the Cotswolds (see Illustration.12.6)[8] The Religious Society of Friends, also known as the Quakers, were among the many dissident voices and movements – including the Seekers, Ranters, Adamites, and Muggletonians – that emerged during the Revolution and flourished at times under the Commonwealth. George Fox, the founder of the Friends, began preaching in 1647, and his followers acquired the derisive title of "Quakers" in the 1650s. The first Friends meeting was organized in 1652, and in time, like the Beggars and Huguenots we encountered earlier, the Friends came to embrace the name Quakers, which may have seemed appropriate to both their anti-authoritarian politics – they rejected all religious authority, refused to take oaths, and refused to bear arms – and their unorthodox style of worship.[9] Although Fox was able to establish a mutually respectful relationship with Oliver Cromwell, he and his followers were persecuted by Puritans and Anglicans alike.[10] **Repression** was worst under the Restoration, when in 1662 the Cavalier Parliament passed the so-called Quaker Act which required all subjects to swear an oath of allegiance to the king, which the Quakers refused to do. Again, Quakers were arrested and imprisoned by the thousands, but in a striking reversal, James II pardoned some 1,200 imprisoned Quakers in 1686 and included the Friends among the Protestant dissidents for whom he issued a "Declaration of Indulgence" in 1687. This opening to the Quakers was continued when the Quakers, too, were granted exemption from coerced conformity by article XIII of the Toleration Act, which allowed them to declare allegiance rather than swear an oath. In Burford, an early Friends meeting was broken up by authorities in 1662. Construction of the Friends Meeting House in Pytts Lane may have started as early as 1688, making it one of the oldest Quaker meetinghouses in England; in any case, it was licensed in 1690 and is still in use today.

In addition to these examples of Protestant "nonconformity" – a term that entered common usage in the 1660s, first as an illegal practice and after 1690 as a "tolerated" practice – there are at least two other histories of religious difference in England that became part of the religious peace in England at the end of the seventeenth century. Alongside the descendants of the medieval Lollards, Catholics were, of course, the original "dissenters" or noncomformists whose resistance to and subversion of top-down reform in the sixteenth century resulted in the Pilgrimage of Grace in 1536. Following the brief restoration of Catholicism

---

[8] See http://ohct.org.uk/church/friends-meeting-house-3 and www.victoriacountyhistory.ac.uk/explore/items/friends-meeting-house-pytts-lane.

[9] See, on the latter, Tom Webster, "On Shaky Ground: Quakers, Puritans, Possession and High Spirits," in *The Experience of Revolution in Stuart Britain and Ireland: Essays for John Morrill*, ed. Michael J. Braddick and David L. Smith (Cambridge, UK; New York: Cambridge University Press, 2011), 172–89.

[10] See John Coffey, *Persecution and Toleration in Protestant England, 1558–1689*, Studies in Modern History (Harlow, England; New York: Longman, 2000), 169–79.

under Queen Mary, the Elizabethan Settlement after 1558 required regular church attendance under the Act of Uniformity (1559). Thereafter, those Catholics who refused to attend the established Church of England and participate in its sacraments were known as "recusants" and were subject to increasingly heavy fines; priests were liable to much more severe punishments as traitors.[11] Meanwhile, some of the Catholic faithful hid their Crypto-Catholicism under the veneer of "occasional conformity" and thereby increased the anxieties of Anglican ecclesiastical authorities as well as the spiritual concerns of the Catholic missionaries who were sent from the continent to guide and nurture their faith.[12] For the most part, formal Catholic worship and the celebration of the Mass were kept alive under the protection of the Catholic nobility, whose private chapels served the laity at least episodically; indeed, the "priest holes" – hiding places analogous to the Anabaptist "*Täuferversteck*" in the Swiss Emmental – they built to hide their priests are the stuff of popular legend and modern tourism in England.[13]

The survival of Catholic spiritual practices, more generally, had much to do with both private devotions, which were kept secret and out of sight, and pilgrimages to traditional sacred sites, which were more visibly *subversive* of official attempts to enforce the public monopoly of the Church of England.[14] During the period of political tumult and instability, beginning with the civil war and ending finally with the Glorious Revolution, England's Catholics were recurrently subject to fierce Protestant "hatred" and violence, but there were also moments when "liberation" and restoration might have seemed possible, none so pregnant with possibility as the succession of the avowedly Catholic James II to the throne in 1685. Still, after James was replaced by William and Mary in 1689, there was some hope for relief from compelled conformity, inasmuch as William had promised, in his "Declaration of Reasons," to secure "even papists" from "all persecution upon the account of their religion."[15] In the end, however, England's Catholics were explicitly

---

[11] On the parameters of "Fraternal correction and holy violence," including the division of labor between spiritual and civil authorities, see Walsham, *Charitable Hatred*, 39–105.

[12] See Alexandra Walsham, *Church Papists: Catholicism, Conformity, and Confessional Polemic in Early Modern England*, Royal Historical Society Studies in History (Woodbridge, Suffolk, UK; Rochester, NY, USA: Boydell Press, 1993), and Alexandra Walsham, "Beads, Books and Bare Ruined Choirs: Transmutations of Catholic Ritual Life in Protestant England," in *Catholic Communities in Protestant States: Britain and the Netherlands c.1570–1720*, eds. Benjamin J. Kaplan, et al., Studies in Early Modern European History (Manchester, UK; New York: Manchester University Press, 2009), 103–22.

[13] See, for example, www.gutenberg.org/files/13918/13918-h/13918-h.htm, www.historic-uk .com/HistoryUK/HistoryofEngland/Priests-Holes, and http://britainexplorer.com/articles/item/ 192-harvington-hall-priest-holes-and-hides.

[14] See, for example, Lisa McClain, "Without Church, Cathedral, or Shrine: The Search for Religious Space Among Catholics in England, 1559–1625," *Sixteenth Century Journal* 33, no. 2 (Summer 2002): 381–99, and Lisa McClain, *Lest We Be Damned: Practical Innovation and Lived Experience Among Catholics in Protestant England, 1559–1642* (New York: Routledge, 2004).

[15] See Chapter 10, pp. 276–7, in this volume.

ILLUSTRATION 12.7: St. Winefride's Well, with structures dating from the sixteenth century, is emblematic of the endurance of Catholic religious practices despite the recurrent fears of "Popery" that excluded them from the Act of Toleration in 1690. (Photo Wayne Te Brake)

exempted from the provisions of the Toleration Act, which meant that their worship had to remain clandestine and private, while in public they remained subject to episodic spasms of **repression** in the form of popular "anti-Popery" and official harassment.

As an emblem of the long-term perseverance of the small English Catholic minority through the religious and political tumults of the Reformation to the Glorious Revolution and beyond, let me suggest the pilgrimage shrine at St. Winefride's Well in Holywell, Flintshire, North Wales (see Illustration 12.7).[16] According to legend, St. Winefride was a seventh-century virgin whose gruesome martyrdom by decapitation was undone by her saintly

---

[16] See especially Alexandra Walsham, "Holywell: Contesting Sacred Space in Post-Reformation Wales," in *Sacred Space in Early Modern Europe*, eds. Will Coster and Andrew Spicer (Cambridge: Cambridge University Press, 2005), 211–36; and for the broader context of both pre-Reformation Catholic spirituality and the struggle to reform the landscape during and after the Reformation, see her impressively comprehensive study, *The Reformation of the Landscape: Religion, Identity, and Memory in Early Modern Britain and Ireland* (Oxford; New York: Oxford University Press, 2011).

uncle, Beuno, and the place where her severed head is said to have landed is the site of a prodigious well spring that became an important pilgrimage shrine in the twelfth century. By the end of the fifteenth century, St. Winefride's Well, which was a dependency of a nearby Cistercian house, had begun to attract noble and royal patronage. Its chapel was rebuilt in the 1490s in the Perpendicular style that it still has today. Despite Protestant theological attacks on the cult of miracles and saints, the shrine at St. Winefride's Well not only survived occasional physical attacks largely intact, but it remained an important pilgrimage destination. Indeed, pilgrimage to St. Winefride's shrine at Holywell – which developed a significant infrastructure to support the large number of visitors, like similar shrines on the continent – was actively promoted by the Counter-Reformation priesthood and Church. By the 1620s, Holywell "seems to have become the focus of increasingly overt and audacious assemblies of recusants, often *en masse*."[17] One manuscript account from the 1670s compiled fifty examples of persons restored to health by the well's healing waters. Alexandra Walsham sums up this remarkable history: "Bearing the wounds of repeated spasms of evangelical zeal, it was a visible testimony to the defiance and courage of an embattled community and to the resurgent Church at Rome to which it proudly owed its allegiance."[18] Given the exclusion of the Catholics from the Toleration Act, the visible presence of St. Winefride's Well is emblematic, then, of the discreet and nominally hidden worship and spiritual practices of Catholics as part of the religious peace even after 1688.

Together, then, these emblems of Protestant nonconformity and Catholic survival underscore the **ad hoc** quality of the religious **tolerance** that characterized the religious peace in England. Whereas the exclusion of Catholics was categorical, the tolerance accorded to Protestant dissenters was piecemeal, as some 1,200 dissenter chapels were licensed within the space of a year, one congregation at a time. One final example will serve to confirm the distinctive character of the English government's use of the eminently modular practice of **ad hoc tolerance**, which we have encountered in variant circumstances on the continent as well: the readmission of Jews.[19] Although Jews had been expelled from England in 1290, small numbers of Jews began to filter back, as they did on the continent, nominally as *conversos* ("new Christians") but possibly retaining secretive Jewish religious practices, following their expulsions from Iberia at the end of the fifteenth century. By 1655, the Crypto-Jewish colony in London had been augmented by new, openly Jewish immigrants coming from the Dutch Republic, and the influential

---

[17] Walsham, "Holywell," 227.   [18] Walsham, "Holywell," 232.

[19] See Coffey, *Persecution and Toleration*, 155–7; Bernard Capp, "Multiculturalism in Early Modern Britain," in *A Companion to Multiconfessionalism in the Early Modern World*, ed. Thomas Max Safley, Brill's Companions to the Christian Tradition, vol. 28 (Leiden; Boston: Brill, 2011), 289–315; and David S. Katz, *The Jews in the History of England, 1485–1850* (Oxford; New York: Clarendon Press, 1994).

Jewish rabbi from Amsterdam, Menasseh ben Israel, submitted a formal petition to Cromwell's Council of State asking for readmission. Although Cromwell did not formally grant the petition, he informally allowed the Jewish community in London to emerge from the shadows, as they had done fifty years earlier in Amsterdam, and to worship publicly; by 1657, they had acquired a cemetery and built a synagogue. Following the Restoration, Charles II gave them a written promise of protection in 1664, with further royal commitments coming in 1674 and 1685. In the 1690s, when the population of Jews was around 400, new immigrants from Germany established an Ashkenazi synagogue and cemetery. In this gradual and informal process, the Jews of England, like the much larger Jewish community of Amsterdam, were afforded an **ad hoc tolerance** that was denied to Catholics.

SCOTLAND: VINDICATING THE DISSIDENTS?

In Scotland, where the British civil wars had begun in the 1630s as a struggle against compelled conformity to Anglican episcopacy and liturgical practice, the contours of the religious peace that emerged in the 1690s were in large measure a vindication of that struggle. As we saw in Chapters 9 and 10, the "National Covenant" that shaped the Scottish Presbyterian opposition to Charles I's authoritarian political and religious practices had three rather different lives. In its first iteration, the Covenant was emblematic of the successful revolution that abolished Anglican episcopacy and liturgy and firmly established the Presbyterian Kirk, free of civil control. In its second iteration, as the "Solemn League and Covenant," it united the Presbyterians of Scotland and England – first in opposition to Charles I (1644) and later in an uncomfortable and divisive alliance with him (1647) and his son (1649) – and promised to export the Scottish Presbyterian model of Calvinist theology and ecclesiastical politics to both England and Ireland. That promise was extinguished with the Purge of the English Parliament in 1648 and the consolidation of the Commonwealth under Cromwell's leadership. Following the Restoration in 1660, the National Covenant was reborn as the emblem of a "radical" movement of Presbyterian "dissenters" who refused to accept the reestablishment of Anglican episcopacy, left the established Kirk, and took their movement underground.[20] It is in this third iteration that the Covenant became

---

[20] On the origins of the Covenanters under Charles I, see Allan I. Macinnes, *Charles I and the Making of the Covenanting Movement, 1625–1641* (Edinburgh: J. Donald Publishers, 1991); on the institutionalization of the covenant during the civil wars, see John Morrill, ed., *The Scottish National Covenant in Its British Context, 1638–1651* (Edinburgh: Edinburgh University Press, 1990); on the Covenanters under the Restoration, see Ian B. Cowan, *The Scottish Covenanters, 1660–1688* (London: V. Gollancz, 1976). On the travails of the Scottish Presbyterians in a broader international context, see Philip Benedict, *Christ's Churches Purely Reformed: A Social History of Calvinism* (New Haven: Yale University Press, 2002), esp. chapter 12, "British Schisms."

especially divisive among Scottish Presbyterians, and the stolid "Covenanters" became not only religious malcontents but enemies of the state.

The Restoration was a particularly difficult period for all dissenters in Scotland, including both Catholic recusants and Quakers, for whom persecution was nothing new.[21] But for the Covenanters, the Restoration entailed a complete role reversal; indeed, in 1661 the Cavalier Parliament in England ordered the hangman to publicly burn the "Solemn League and Covenant." In 1662, in response to the reestablishment of episcopal authority in Restoration Scotland, some 268 Presbyterian ministers, or approximately one-fourth of the Scottish clergy (mostly in the southwest of Scotland where they constituted half of the clergy), refused to swear the oaths that were now required of pastors, and they were "ejected" from their positions. Many of these pastors continued to minister to their followers privately in homes, barns, and larger outdoor worship services. The latter came to be known as "conventicles" – that is, illegal or unlicensed worship services that recall the "hedgepreaching" and *prêches* of the early Dutch and French Calvinists respectively – in large measure because of the **repressive** response of the Scottish authorities who specifically outlawed them as "seminaries of treason" and identified worship outside the structure of the established church as an act of treason, potentially punishable by death. In fact, conventicles were not exactly unprecedented in Scottish history, but in the 1660s and 1670s, these sometimes large, demonstrative and politically defiant assemblies of ejected pastors and thousands of voluntary faithful became practically synonymous with the Scottish Covenanters. Typically they included many of the elements of orthodox Presbyterian worship services – prayers, the singing of psalms and hymns, Bible reading, biblical preaching, and when possible, communion – and as they became larger, the illegal assemblies of this new iteration of the covenanting movement left the homes and barns of dissenting families and were relocated to remote places in the hills that were inaccessible except to those with local knowledge.[22]

One such remote place, in Irongray parish just west of Dumfries, is emblematic of the heroic popular image that the Covenanter conventicles have long enjoyed (see Illustration 12.8).[23] A brisk one-mile hike up Skeoch Hill from Maxwelltown Farm, set in a small hollow, is a memorial

---

[21] See Gordon DesBrisay, "Catholics, Quakers, and Religious Persecution in Restoration Aberdeen," *Innes Review* 47 (1996): 136–68; Allan Macinnes, "Catholic Recusancy and the Penal Laws, 1603–1707," *Records of the Scottish Church History Society* 23 (1987): 27–63; and Allan I. Macinnes, "Repression and Concilliation: The Highland Dimension 1660–1688," *The Scottish Historical Review* 65, no. 2 (1986): 176–95.

[22] See David Morton, "Covenanters and Conventicles in South West Scotland," [MPhil(R) thesis, University of Glasgow, 2012], http://theses.gla.ac.uk/id/eprint/3767. Although flawed, I found this somewhat primitive master's thesis invaluable in my own exploration of the Covenanter movement, especially Morton's description of the conventicles and his exploration of modern memorials.

[23] One source of this popular reputation is Robert Wodrow, ed., *The History of the Sufferings of the Church of Scotland, From the Restauration to the Revolution* (Edinburgh: Printed by James

ILLUSTRATION 12.8: The Communion Stones Monument is located on top of Skeoch Hill, near Dumfries, where in 1678, some 3,000 communicants were served at stone tables; the monument is dedicated to those who fought for religious liberty. (Photo Wayne Te Brake)

constructed in 1870 to mark the spot "where a large number of Covenanters met in the summer of 1678 to worship God and where about 3000 communicants celebrated the sacrament of the Lord's Supper."[24] While "only" 3,000 are said to have taken communion, served by four "ejected" pastors, Ian Cowan reports that a crowd of 14,000 may have been in attendance, though it seems doubtful to me that the site could accommodate that many people and avoid detection.[25] In any case, adjacent to the monument are the remnants of four rows of eleven "communion stones" – primitive stone tables that were used to serve the

Watson, 1721–22), which is available online at www.puritanboard.com/showthread.php/22214-History-of-the-Sufferings-of-the-Church-of-Scotland-Robert-Wodrow.

[24] I can personally attest to the remoteness of the location and the importance of local knowledge in order to locate it; without the help of a bass fisherman, who loaned me his map in order to find Maxwelltown Farm, on whose property the site is located, and without the specific instructions of the farm's owner, Pat Hyslop, I would never have found the route to the top. There is a digital version of the detailed map I used at www.streetmap.co.uk/idld.srf ?x=285910&y=579050&z=120&sv=285910,579050&st=4&mapp=idld.srf&searchp=s.srf& dn=677&ax=285910&ay=579050&lm=o.

[25] See Cowan, *Scottish Covenanters*, 92; Philip Benedict repeats this estimate.

large numbers of communicants – which the monument states "are significant memorials to those troublous times in which our fathers contended for the great principle of civil and religious freedom."[26] As useful as this place is as a testimony to the Covenanters' resistance to civil and religious "tyranny," the story of this third iteration of the Covenanter movement is a good deal more complicated than this and other modern memorials might suggest.

The government's reaction to the Covenanter movement was unambiguous and persecutory, to be sure, but its enforcement was inconsistent, and when it was strenuous, it tended, for a time at least, to increase popular support and participation rather than tamp it down.[27] For example, in 1666, in reaction to heavy fines reinforced by the punitive quartering of troops, a group of Covenanters mobilized a march of some 1,000 people toward Edinburgh, but this "Pentland Rising" was halted militarily, and thirty-six Covenanters were executed. Subsequently, a less militarized approach to enforcement of church attendance and two declarations of indulgence in 1669 and 1672 brought some of the ejected pastors back into the established Kirk. But in the late 1670s, a new governmental crackdown on conventicles once again swelled the Covenanter movement. Now enormous conventicles were protected from military interference by armed guards, as was the case on Skeoch Hill in 1678. Then, in 1679, the capture and execution of the archbishop of St. Andrews by armed Covenanters, and in the early 1680s, the organization of the new, more radical "Cameronian" movement precipitated what Ian Cowan calls the "Killing Times," resulting in more than 100 deaths in episodic skirmishes and summary executions.[28] After 1686, the conventicles virtually ceased, while the "indulgences" of James II opened up new space for religious dissenters, first for Catholics and Quakers, and later for "dissenting" Presbyterians, though Covenanters' conventicles were still specifically excluded. In retrospect, in this long and deeply contentious interaction, the Covenanters can hardly be said to have won; in fact, on the eve the Glorious Revolution they were bereft of influential allies and they were vilified by their enemies, as well as moderate Presbyterians, for having undermined the possibility of religious peace. By this time, thousands of Covenanters had also left Scotland for Ireland.

In retrospect, the dispirited Covenanters could have seen the Glorious Revolution as a providential liberation, but in any case, they were neither part of the revolution nor part of the contentious process by which the political and religious implications of the revolution for Scotland were hammered out in the

---

[26] This site is still used occasionally for commemorative services; indeed, Pat Hyslop, the farm's owner, reported that her two oldest children were baptized on Skeoch Hill.

[27] For a brief survey of the cycles of active repression and moderation, see Benedict, *Christ's Churches*, 412–14.

[28] Cowan, *Scottish Covenanters*, 122–33.

Revolution Settlement in 1689 and 1690.[29] As we saw in Chapter 10, following the coronation of William and Mary, subject to the Claim of Right, the Scottish Parliament repealed the Act of Supremacy of 1669, by which Charles II claimed the right to establish episcopal authority over the Presbyterian Kirk, restored "the Presbyterian ministers who were thrust from their churches," and reaffirmed the sixteenth-century Confession of Faith and the independent authority of the presbyteries, synods, and general assemblies of the Kirk. In short order, then, the dissenters of the Restoration period were once again free to worship publicly in their old churches, while a goodly number of the masters of the Restoration Church became Scotland's newest dissenters. Indeed, what the Glorious Revolution restored was an exclusive religious regime, with a **privileged** Kirk that repeatedly sought to renew the so-called Penal Laws that punished nonconforming dissenters, Catholic recusants, Quakers, and Anglicans alike. In this sense, the religious peace in Scotland represented the vindication not only of the dissenting Covenanter's uncompromising opposition to "Prelacy," but also, in the short run at least, of their intolerance of religious diversity. Apparently the "religious freedom" that the Convenanter "fathers" contended for at Skeoch Hill was *theirs* alone! And although their pastors returned to the established Presbyterian Kirk, some Covenanters broke away to form their own Reformed Presbyterian Church.

On the face of it, then, Scotland remained the least diverse of the three British kingdoms at the end of the seventeenth century. Catholicism survived especially in Edinburgh, where it had enjoyed royal patronage at critical moments, and in the remote Highlands, where aristocratic patronage was protective against periodic renewal and enforcement of the Penal Laws.[30] Quakers persevered mainly in the cities, though their numbers were in decline by the eighteenth century.[31] In sharp contrast with both England and Ireland, however, the Revolution in Scottish politics had suddenly transformed the Anglican faithful into dissenters, whose pastoral leaders were now "ejected" from their livings and who now were forced, in some places, to worship discreetly in homes or other clandestine accommodations in order to avoid trouble. The active persecution of Scottish Anglicans was diminished and ended, however, in the early eighteenth century following the Act of Union in 1707, which brought the end of Scottish political independence as the English and Scottish parliaments were fused. In 1712, this new Parliament passed an Act of Toleration, over the strenuous objections of Scottish Presbyterian leaders, which permitted public

[29] See Ian B. Cowan, "Church and State Reformed? The Revolution of 1688–9 in Scotland," in *The Anglo-Dutch Moment: Essays on the Glorious Revolution and Its World Impact*, ed. Jonathan I. Israel (Cambridge: Cambridge University Press, 1991), 163–83.

[30] See Allan Macinnes, "Catholic Recusancy," who argues that the frequent renewals of the Penal Laws were political gestures more than sincere attempts to compel conformity.

[31] See George B. Burnet, *The Story of Quakerism in Scotland, 1650–1850. With an Epilogue on the Period 1850–1950 by William H. Marwick* (London: J. Clarke, 1952).

Anglican worship and introduced **ad hoc tolerance** of Protestant differences into an otherwise exclusive Scottish religious landscape.[32]

IRELAND: SECURING THE "PROTESTANT ASCENDANCY"

At the end of the seventeenth century, Ireland had by far the largest proportion of dissenters, both Catholic and Protestant, of the three British kingdoms or of any polity in Europe, though as we saw in Chapters 9 and 10, that diversity was deeply contentious and had most recently been tested by the coordinated destruction of the Williamite Wars. The Catholic majority population, which doggedly resisted conversion to Protestantism, had been subject to periodic **repression** from the 1560s onward, with the most serious episode coming in the 1650s under the Commonwealth. The restoration of the monarchy in 1660 brought a measure of relief from the worst spasms of repression and "transportation," but having once again chosen the "wrong" side by recognizing and supporting James II in the Glorious Revolution, Ireland's Catholics "negotiated," in the Treaty of Limerick, a modicum of security "from any disturbance upon account of their said religion." But these assurances were undercut by the infamous series of Penal Laws that the Irish Parliament enacted between 1695 and 1704. By preventing Catholics from holding public office, from being seated in Parliament, or even from owning property which might afford them the franchise in parliamentary elections, the Penal Laws secured what is called the Protestant Ascendency in Irish politics for a century and more. Still, inasmuch as the Penal Laws did not criminalize Catholic spiritual practices, as the Commonwealth legislation had done, the religious peace that emerged in Ireland at the end of the seventeenth century gave a new visibility and security to religious diversity in all its dimensions. So what did religious diversity actually look like in Ireland under the Protestant Ascendency in politics?

Catholic religious services and spiritual practices, which were deeply *subversive* of Anglican hegemony, were maintained throughout Ireland, even in the most difficult periods of persecution, at a variety of sites and in a variety of modes, both formal and informal. Indeed, it is the informality of many Catholic spiritual practices that makes Ireland an especially "hard" case to recover in the documentary record. In some periods, of course, Catholic religious observance was necessarily *secretive* because of the peril of persecution and prosecution. In addition, however, unlike the Anabaptists of the Emmental, the Calvinists of the Southern Netherlands and France, or the Catholics of the United Provinces, early modern Irish Catholics and their descendants have not been encouraged to tell and retell their stories of ingenious adaptation and heroic resistance under adversity, much less have they institutionalized the memories of their oppression in national museums, either real or virtual. As it happened, the agents of the institutional Catholic Church with its hierarchy of priests and bishops, which was gradually reconstructed in the course of the eighteenth and nineteenth centuries,

---

[32] See Benedict, *Christ's Churches*, 418–22.

often disapproved of the informal religious practices and devotional "patterns" that Irish Catholics used to keep their faith alive in the absence of priests and routine celebrations of the Mass. Still, despite the very real dangers of active **repression** and the limits of official clerical (dis)approval, the Irish landscape is still dotted with emblems of the informal and improvised Catholic spirituality of the most difficult years.[33] Here we can only sample the very rich and diverse evidence, but in general early modern Irish Catholicism appears to have combined two important threads: (1) practices that descended from and related to traditional pilgrimage and devotional sites, and (2) newly invented practices related to improvised places of worship, once they were denied the use of Ireland's churches.

Undoubtedly the most famous example of the former is located in the midst of the Ultster Plantation at Lough Derg, County Donegal. Station Island, in the middle of Lough Derg, is the home of an important medieval pilgrimage site, popularly known as St. Patrick's Purgatory. As the name suggests, St. Patrick's Purgatory commemorates the period of self-examination and denial that St. Patrick is said to have committed himself to in the midst of his missionary activity in the fifth century. From the twelfth century onward, Lough Derg and St. Patrick's Purgatory attracted famous pilgrims from the continent, but like St. Winefride's Well at Holywell in Wales, St. Patrick's Purgatory took on new significance in the post-Reformation era, now as a pilgrimage site for Irish Catholics. Although Station Island sustained more significant damage in 1632 and the 1680s than the shrine at Holywell, the pilgrimages continued under the Commonwealth and beyond; at the beginning of the eighteenth century it was reported to receive an average of 5,000 pilgrims a year who undertook a nine-day period of severe fasting and prayer. Today Station Island still attracts some 10,000 pilgrims annually, though the "patterns" are less severe, and includes a large complex of buildings to accommodate the pilgrims.[34]

There was another famous pilgrimage destination on the other side of Ireland at Glendalough, County Wicklow, in the mountains south of Dublin. There, the ruins of a medieval monastery devoted to St. Kevin – which was destroyed during the Norman Conquest in the thirteenth century, not as a result of the Reformation – offered a more accessible and less rigorous pilgrimage experience in a very beautiful setting. In the early seventeenth century, Glendalough was

---

[33] For an argumentative, yet very compelling survey of popular Catholic spirituality prior to the nineteenth-century famine, see Michael P. Carroll, *Irish Pilgrimage: Holy Wells and Popular Catholic Devotion.* (Baltimore: Johns Hopkins University Press, 1999). I have benefited enormously from his work in my own explorations of the patterns of Irish religious diversity. See also Patrick J. Corish, *The Catholic Community in the Seventeenth and Eighteenth Centuries* (Dublin: Helicon, 1981).

[34] I am very grateful to Mgr. Richard Mohan, who allowed me to visit the island in the midst of the pilgrimage season in 2007, even though I was not a pilgrim. For the context of the modern pilgrimage, which remains a severe test for many people, see Lawrence J. Taylor, *Occasions of Faith: An Anthropology of Irish Catholics*, Series in Contemporary Ethnography (Philadelphia: University of Pennsylvania Press, 1995).

counted, along with Lough Derg, among the five most important pilgrimage sites in Ireland, and in the early eighteenth century, soldiers broke up a very large encampment of pilgrims who were celebrating St. Kevin's Day.[35]

Much more common than a pilgrimage to St. Patrick's Purgatory or Glendalough, for ordinary Irish Catholics, was a visit to a holy well, of which there were hundreds, perhaps thousands at one time or another.[36] Holy wells are often found at sites of pre-Christian, Celtic spirituality, which were later adapted or appropriated for specifically Christian purposes, and consequently, there is considerable disagreement about whether the early modern practices of Irish Catholics at these sites were "pagan" holdovers in need of reform or sincerely and legitimately Christian. For our purposes, however, it is clear that the popular use of such sites, both during and after the worst periods of active **repression** of Catholicism, represented an adaptation and appropriation that is typical of the mechanisms of dissenter "survival" we found elsewhere in Europe (see Table 4.1). In particular, the relative invisibility or *secrecy* of the devotional practices at holy wells appears to have combined with a considerable dose of "lay *casuistry*" as the Catholic faithful devised and performed complex "patterns" they saw as both penitential and worshipful.

If we focus instead on the second thread of early modern Irish Catholicism – that is, newly invented practices related to improvised places of worship – we can discern more clearly, I believe, the specific history of religious coexistence in early modern Ireland. "Mass rocks" and "penal chapels" are legendary in popular memory, and examples of commemorative sites and memorials can easily be located via online searches.[37] Here let me offer just two variant

---

[35] See, Carroll, *Irish Pilgrimage*, 111–17, and Walsham, *The Reformation of the Landscape: Religion, Identity, and Memory in Early Modern Britain and Ireland*, 146, 203. See also, for example, www.catholicireland.net/glendalough-a-celtic-pilgrimage and www.google.com/url? sa=t&rct=j&q=&esrc=s&source=web&cd=8&ved=0CE4QFjAH&url=http%3A%2F%2Fprese ntationsociety.org.au%2Fwp-content%2Fuploads%2F2012%2F08%2FP4-Glendalough.pdf& ei=xSGVVduED82ZyATKn4ngDA&usg=AFQjCNE9mHuQPCHV3PWWcgg4Zunx_RDpxA& sig2=Y6XnfSjmqTV8JzuCmpE2Pg&bvm=bv.96952980,d.aWw.

[36] On the geography of holy wells, see Carroll, *Irish Pilgrimage*, 19–25; for a succinct introduction to the "uses" of holy wells and the devotional "patterns" – often known as "making the rounds" – associated with them, see Michael P. Carroll, "Rethinking Popular Catholicism in Pre-Famine Ireland," *Journal for the Scientific Study of Religion* 34, no. 3 (0354–65 1995): 356–8. There is much to be found online about Ireland's holy wells, although the information provided by tourist agencies, and the like, is often unreliable. See, for example, www.irishcultureandcustoms.com /ALandmks/HolyWells.html and www.google.com/#q=the+holy+wells+of+ireland.

[37] There is, for example, a modern scalan and "mass rock," alongside a nineteenth-cenutry statue of St. Patrick, as well as recently installed Stations of the Cross at Tobercurry, County Sligo; see www.sligotourism.ie/attractions/mass-rock. There is also a large memorial at Ballaghaderreen, County Roscommon, called the Four Altars Monument, which seems to me to be of questionable authenticity; see www.loughgaralakesandlegends.ie/north-roscommon/the-four-altars-2. Some, like the mass rock in Doneraile, have only recently been rediscovered; see http://homepage .eircom.net/~neillod/massrock.html.

ILLUSTRATION 12.9: The remote site for clandestine worship at Disert in county
Donegal includes a modest megalith that apparently marks the burial site of a Druid
chieftain. (Photo Wayne Te Brake)

examples on opposite ends of the island: in Donegal in the far northwest and
Wexford in the southeast.[38]

Not far from St. Patrick's Purgatory in rural Donegal, at the foot of the
Bluestack Mountains, there is a complex religious site known variously as the
Disert Graveyard and St. Colmcille's Well.[39] In fact, there are many layers of
spiritual history at this site. First, there is a modest, prehistoric megalith –
consisting of two upright stones connected by a lintel stone which has
a pyramid of smaller stones on top of it (see Illustration 12.9).[40] Nearby,
within a small enclosure, there is a primitive holy well dedicated to the sixth-
century missionary St. Colmcille; this well is undoubtedly pre-Reformation in
origin, but like many of these old sites, it is now covered and nearly grown over

---

[38] On the importance of these two examples in the larger history of the contentious politics of
religious diversity, see Wayne Te Brake, "The Contentious Politics of Religious Diversity," in
Cities, States, Trust, and Rule: New Departures from the Work of Charles Tilly, ed.
Michael Hanagan and Chris Tilly (New York: Springer, 2011), 237–8.

[39] There is very little documentation regarding this site, though the site itself speaks volumes. For
online desctriptions, see http://pilgrimagemedievalireland.com/2013/06/09/st-colmcilles-well-
disert-donegal and www.walkingireland.ie/walks/The-Disert-Circular-Walk.

[40] According to a sign at the site, erected with funding from the Heritage Council of Ireland, the
megalith marked the burial site of a Druid chieftain.

ILLUSTRATION 12.10: At the Disert site, St. Colmcille's Well, the mass rock and the Graveyard are located in close proximity to one another; the megalith is out of the frame perhaps 100 feet to the right. (Photo Wayne Te Brake)

ILLUSTRATION 12.11: Though it is still used commemoratively, the improvised altar at Dissert is in poor repair. The ballaun stones on the altar are said to have various curative powers; the metal cross above and to the right is undoubtedly of a later date. (Photo Wayne Te Brake)

ILLUSTRATION 12.12: The Church of St. Anne at Tomhaggard, County Wexford, was destroyed along with forty five other churches by Oliver Cromwell's forces in 1649. The cemetery has been in continuous use. (Photo Wayne Te Brake)

with vegetation. Close to the well, there is a graveyard, which is (was) defined by the stone wall and was in use as late as the 1930s; and between the well and graveyard is a makeshift altar, or Mass rock (see Illustrations 12.10 and 12.11).

The graveyard and altar bear silent testimony to the history of religious coexistence in Ulster following the Reformation. In the early years, Protestants and Catholics shared the cemetery in nearby Inver, but with the implementation of the Ulster Plantation scheme after 1610, the parish church was seized for Protestant worship and the Catholic priests were denied access to the cemetery, hence, the makeshift altar and the graveyard at Disert. Although we do not know precisely when this "ancient" sacred site was repurposed for regular use as an improvised Catholic worship site, the remoteness of this site suggests the urgent need for *secrecy* during the long and difficult seventeenth century in Ulster. The Disert altar continued to be used regularly as a worship site until the end of the eighteenth century; today it is still used commemoratively on the first Sunday in June.[41]

In the small village of Tomhaggard, near the Celtic Sea, in County Wexford, a complex mix of sacred sites tells a slightly different version of the story of Irish

---

[41] The graveyard was used for the burial of adults until 1840, when a new Catholic graveyard was opened in nearby Fosses, where a "Mass house" had also been built in 1808; it was used for the burial of unbaptized infants until the 1930s. I am deeply grateful to John Burke, a nearby resident, who stopped to aid a pair of confused foreigners on a quiet Sunday morning and ended up sharing the history of the Disert graveyard, as well as the directions to the very well-hidden site.

ILLUSTRATION 12.13: The improvised altar, or "mass rock," at Tomhaggard is "hidden" along a hedge row on the Devereaux farm, less than a quarter of a mile from the ruins of St. Anne's Church. (Photo Wayne Te Brake)

Catholic perseverance.[42] In a small park in the center of the village are two holy wells, dedicated to St. Anne and St. James, in close proximity to one another; indeed the water from the two wells flows today into a common channel. Just across the street from the park are the ruins of a beautiful thirteenth-century parish church dedicated also to St. Anne, and a Catholic graveyard (see Illustration 12.12).

The ruins of the church bring us to a specific moment in the middle of the seventeenth century when Oliver Cromwell's military campaign to crush the Irish Confederacy brought him south from Drogheda to Wexford, both of which were sites of terrible carnage. Up to that point, the Catholics of Tomhaggard had simply continued to use their parish church, but in 1649 the Church of St. Anne was one of forty-six churches in the baronies of Forth and Bargy that were destroyed by Cromwell's army; in the absence of Protestant

---

[42] See www.kilmoreparish.ie/t_history.htm, www.kilmoreparish.ie/t_penal.htm, and www.kilmore parish.ie/monasteries.htm, which are separate pages on the history of Tomhaggard on the website of the Parish of Kilmore, of which Tomhaggard is now a part. See also, Danny McDonald, ed., *Tomhaggard: A Sacred Place* (Tomhaggard, Co. Wexford: Tomhaggard Heritage Group, 2002).

ILLUSTRATION 12.14: Above the Tommhaggard mass rock there is a stone marker commemorating the death of Fr. Nicholas Mayler in 1653, which was installed in 1999; to the left of the altar there is a stone from a window in the ruined church. (Photo Wayne Te Brake)

ILLUSTRATION 12.15: In the center of Tomhaggard, across the street from the ruins of the Church, a modest penal chapel was built above St. Anne's Well. The modern stone altar and pulpit on the right are used for outdoor worship services in the summertime. (Photo Wayne Te Brake)

congregations, the authorities simply destroyed these churches in order to prevent their continued use by Catholics.

Having been deprived of their parish church, the Catholic faithful of Tomhaggard began worshiping at an improvised altar hidden in a hedgerow on the property of Lord Devereaux, just a couple hundred meters from the ruins of the church (see Illustration 12.13).[43] Then, on Christmas morning in 1653, a detachment of Cromwell's "red coats" attacked the worshipers at the Tomhaggard Mass rock and killed Father Nicholas Mayler while he was serving Mass; today, a painted stone placed above the altar commemorates that traumatic event, and the local parishioners now celebrate Mass at the site each Christmas at dawn, rain or shine (see Illustration 12.14).[44]

The Mass rock site remained in regular use as a worship site until the early eighteenth century, when Lord Devereaux, who had temporarily lost his land under the Commonwealth, was able to build a simple scalan – an open-sided construction with a thatched roof to cover an altar and to protect the priest – on his property just above St. Anne's Well (see Illustration 12.15). Later the scalan was fully enclosed to make a small "penal chapel," which remained in use until the community was able to build its current chapel in 1813.[45]

Together, the examples of Disert and Tomhaggard teach us a great deal about the contours of the religious peace that emerged in Ireland at the end of the seventeenth century. Perhaps the most important lesson is that different parts of Ireland experienced the tribulations of the seventeenth century differently, though the dynamics of the locally variable, contentious political processes that shaped the peace are strikingly similar and familiar. In Ulster, Donegal, and at the Disert site, we see that the active **repression** of Catholicism entailed in the plantation scheme forced the local Catholic faithful to make the painful shift from public worship to clandestine worship sometime in the first decades of the seventeenth century, whereas they abandoned their secret worship site and built a "mass house" only in the beginning of the nineteenth century.[46] By contrast, in Leinster, Wexford, and at Tomhaggard, which was not touched by the plantations and forced removals of the seventeenth century,

---

[43] I am deeply grateful to Tommy Devereaux, the current owner of the property, for allowing me access – indeed, personally showing me the site, when I could not find it on my own – and sharing the history of his family as well as of the Mass rock.

[44] To the left of the altar slab, there is a stone, now nearly overgrown, that appears to come from the ruins of the parish church – a part of the arch above one of the windows. In 1951 and again in 1999, on the 350th anniversary of the destruction of the church, when the memorial stone was installed, the local community performed a reenactment of the 1653 attack, complete with red-coated soldiers.

[45] The Tomhaggard "penal chapel" is one of the few that have been preserved, in this case perhaps because it was converted to use for potato storage once the new chapel was built. Above the door, there is another stone from the ruined parish church built into the scalan, one that matches the stone at the Mass rock.

[46] There is a wonderful example of a later eighteenth-century Mass house, originally from Tullyallen in County Armagh, that has been preserved as part of the Ulster American Folk Park, which is an open-air museum in Castletown, just outside Omagh, County Tyrone,

public worship only ceased with the destruction of the parish church in 1649, and despite the terrible trauma of the murder of their priest, the local community was able to reemerge from the shadows of secrecy required by active **repression** at a much earlier date, apparently able to benefit from the **ad hoc tolerance** of "visible" worship provided for in the Treaty of Limerick a full century earlier than in Ulster.[47] Still, the dynamics of "survival" and even the specific practices of clandestine worship were essentially the same in these two very different places and were typical of the survival of dissenters under active **repression**, more generally in Great Britain and on the continent.

At the same time, these two examples, as emblematic of the broader exit of Catholics from the shadows of secrecy and oppression, alert us to the long-term consequences of the experience of exclusion: of **privilege, repression,** and even **ad hoc tolerance.** Because neither the Treaty of Limerick nor the infamous Penal Laws criminalized Catholic religious practices as the punitive religious legislation under the Commonwealth had done, all Irish Catholics were able, eventually, to escape the worst privations of the seventeenth century, with regard to their religious worship. Still, the explicitly punitive Penal Laws of the late seventeenth century underscore the way exclusion entails the formation of what Charles Tilly called "durable inequality."[48] In terms of the religious boundaries and identities we have been concerned with in this study, durable inequality develops when identity differences or inequalities that are at first "merely" religious come to be reinforced by other kinds of political, social, economic, educational, and even geographic inequalities/differences. As Tilly demonstrated in his work, once they are in place, durable inequalities are hard to unpack and undo. Ireland, under the Penal Laws, may be considered a textbook case or at least an explicit example of the durability of the religious inequalties that were a visible token of the religious peace. After a century and more of plantations, forced removals, violence, and the selective and deliberate destruction of the sacred symbols, worship spaces, and devotional practices of Irish Catholics, as well as their schools, the Penal Laws sealed the inequalities with an eye to making them permanent by excluding "dissenters" from the political arena: that is, by excluding them from public offices of all kinds, from sitting in Parliament, and from exercising the franchise. Removing the worst obstacles preventing public worship must have been a huge relief for the Catholic faithful, but unpacking the rest of the durable inequalities – in education, land ownership, wealth, and the like – that were still very clearly marked by their religious identities remained a formidable challenge and, by extension, the lasting

Northern Ireland. See http://nmni.com/uafp/Collections/Buildings/Ulster-Buildings/Tullyallen-Masshouse.

[47] Although I know of no documentation to that effect, I think we can assume that the priest who served Tomhaggard and the scalan that they used for the "public" celebration of the Mass after Limerick were officially "licensed."

[48] See Charles Tilly, *Durable Inequality* (Berkeley: University of California Press, 1998).

legacy of the long and difficult seventeenth century. We will return to the problem of durable inequalities in the final chapter.

Whereas the Catholics were the most numerous, they were by no means the only religious dissenters in Ireland. In fact, during the seventeenth century both the numbers and the diversity of non-Catholic "dissenters" increased. As we saw in Chapters 9 and 10, the Ulster Plantation in the first half of the century brought large numbers of Presbyterian and Independent "nonconformists" from Scotland and England to the northern province of Ulster, and although they were at first "accommodated" within the established Church, most of these also resisted the requirements of conformity to the Church of Ireland they were subject to in Ireland from the 1630s onward. Then, during the Commonwealth, as such requirements fell away, new sorts of nonconformists – mainly Baptists and Quakers – settled in Ireland, especially in the cities. And after the Restoration, there was a new migration of Huguenot refugees from France, many of them settling in County Laois, west of Dublin, as the increasingly autocratic regime of Louis XIV deployed the terms of the Edict of Nantes to the maximum disadvantage of the *religion pretendu reformé* until he finally revoked the Edict in 1685. Prior to the Glorious Revolution and the Williamite Wars, the **privilege** of the Anglican Church of Ireland forced this wide assortment of dissenters to worship "privately." But under the new regime established by William and Mary, Protestant dissenters, too, could emerge from the shadows, and in 1719, in the Act of Toleration, the Protestant "dissenters" of Ireland were granted freedom of worship, though they still were excluded from participation in politics, like Catholics, under the exclusively Anglican Protestant Ascendancy.[49] At the Ulster American Folk Park, there is a replica of a Presbyterian meetinghouse in Mountjoy, a hamlet in County Tyrone, that may be considered emblematic of their nominally hidden "meetinghouses," not unlike those of Protestant dissenters in England and the *schuilkerken* in the Dutch Republic.[50]

THE NEW DIMENSIONS OF DIVERSITY

All in all, even though the three British monarchies shared the same royal sovereigns at the end of the seventeenth century, William and Mary presided over three very different versions of the religious peace that were the cumulative residue of nearly eight decades of religious conflict and political instability,

---

[49] Some of the recent Covenanter immigrants from Scotland, like the radical Covenanters in Scotland, broke away and formed the small Reformed Presbyterian Church in Ireland.

[50] See http://nmni.com/uafp/Collections/Buildings/Ulster-Buildings/Meeting-House. The interior of this meetinghouse, which has a barnlike form, like the King Edward Street Chapel in Macclesfield, has the pulpit positioned in the middle of the long side of the sanctuary. There is another Presbyterian meetinghouse from Omagh, County Tyrone, preserved at the Ulster Folk and Transport Museum near Belfast: http://nmni.com/uftm/Collections/buildings/Town-Area-% 281%29/Presbyterian-House.

punctuated by the coordinated destruction of religious war. In the end, three very different elite bargains reflecting very different facts on the ground made durable religious peace possible, but as we have seen throughout this study, the essential facts of religious diversity were not new; rather, what was new was the grudging consent of both the rulers and their very diverse subjects to settlements that were neither imaginable at the beginning of the process nor ideal at the end; they were quite simply, in each case, an acceptable foundation for a more peaceful future.

Although I have taken pains to emphasize their differences, what all three kingdoms had in common, of course, was the basic framework of an established or **privileged** church. In this, the British were not inventing anything entirely new; indeed, the basic structures of religious peace in Great Britain are similar to the formally exclusive structures of religious coexistence that we encountered in the Low Countries, also in the absence of a fully articulated religious peace settlement, such as the Peace of Westphalia. England, with its broad array of Protestant nonconformists and Catholic recusants, recalls the cacophony of sectarian voices that were subordinate to the public Reformed Church in the United Provinces; in both places, which came to enjoy international reputations for "tolerance," Protestant dissenters were evident nearly everywhere, but were required to worship in buildings that did not look like churches, whereas Catholics were explicitly excluded from public life. Ireland, with its majority Catholic and nonconforming Protestant populations under the domination of the strictly Anglican Protestant Ascendancy, comports well with the subordination of the majority Catholic populations of the Dutch Generality Lands to a minority and culturally "foreign" Reformed Church; in these places, rigidly discriminatory rules in politics belied the reality of a surprisingly visible religious diversity. Scotland, with its small Anglican, Catholic, and Quaker minorities, is perhaps most like the provinces of the Southern Netherlands, once the worst era of repression had passed; Presbyterian unity and purity proved to be no more attainable than Catholic unity and purity. In all of these places, formal religious exclusion that reflected the domination of one group over all others proved, nevertheless, to be compatible with robust, if often hidden or private, practices of religious diversity, without all the rules and formal institutional structures that characterized the religious peace in Germany under the Peace of Westphalia.

These similarities are quite clearly evident if we situate the very diverse illustrative cases we have explored in this chapter as a final overlay on the now very densely populated template of the variable forms of religious coexistence. Although at this point our typological map threatens to become almost unintelligible because it is so complex and messy, it is nevertheless evident that all the new entries in Figure 12.1 are located on the left or exclusive side of the diagram, just as all of the Low Countries examples were in the beginning of the seventeenth century. If this were a complete catalogue, all of the United Provinces of the Northern Netherlands would be clustered in the upper-left quadrant (**privilege**) along with all three of the British kingdoms. (For

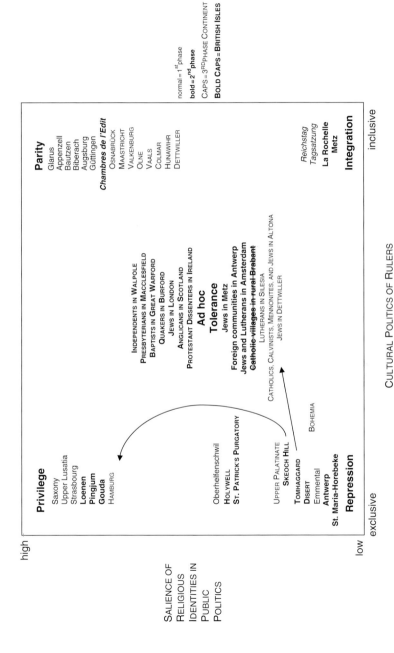

CULTURAL POLITICS OF RULERS

FIGURE 12.1: Patterns of religious coexistence in continental Europe and Great Britain

the sake of legibility, we will have to imagine that they could all fit!) In the lower-left quadrant, in the realm of active repression, I have located both Skeoch Hill in Scotland and Disert and Tomhaggard in Ireland, near Antwerp and St. Maria-Horebeke. Also on the far left, I have located Holywell and St. Patrick's Purgatory, the Catholic pilgrimage sites in England and Ireland, respectively, in the indeterminate middle, such as Oberhelfenschwil in Toggenburg: officially illegal, but only intermittently or ineffectively disturbed. But the largest number of new entries are clustered in the middle of the diagram, indicating how the officially intolerant rulers of all three kingdoms deployed the increasingly common practice of **ad hoc tolerance** to open new, if limited, spaces for a very diverse assortment of "dissenters" in public life, just as their counterparts were doing on the continent. Worship under these circumstances still usually had to take place in structures that did not look like churches, but a formal charter or even a license offered a good deal more visibility and security than their formerly clandestine worship, usually by connivance, which was always vulnerable to disturbance, if not prosecution. In this way, we can see that, as was also the case on the continent, even formally exclusive outcomes could contribute to the larger trend toward increasingly visible, and thus salient, forms of religious coexistence.

The two arrows I have drawn are meant to indicate that, at the end of the century, the Covenanters of Skeoch Hill in Scotland were afforded the opportunity to become, once again, part of the Presbyterian establishment (**privilege**) and that the Catholics of Tomhaggard in Ireland were able to emerge from the shadows in a form of **ad hoc tolerance**; by contrast, the Catholics at Disert in the Ulster Plantation continued to worship clandestinely for another century. I could also have indicated the very different transition at the end of the century of La Rochelle and Metz, as emblematic of France as a whole, except for Alsace, from **integration** to active **repression** as a consequence of the revocation of the Edict of Nantes. But, if we were to extend the scope of this study into the eighteenth century, we would actually witness the radical depopulation of the bottom half of the diagram.

On the continent, both the Austrian Habsburgs and the French Bourbons steadily relaxed the harsh limits they had placed on religious diversity in the early decades of the eighteenth century, but in 1781, Emperor Joseph II issued the Patent of Toleration, which granted **ad hoc tolerance** to his Protestant populations in Bohemia and Austria as well as the Southern Netherlands.[51]

---

[51] This long-awaited edict applied not only in his territorial jurisdictions in Austria and Bohemia, but also to the provinces of the Southern Netherlands, where the indirect authority of the Spanish had passed to the Austrian branch of the house of Habsburg at the beginning of the century. For the German text of the Patent of Toleration, see Peter Barton, ed., "'Das' Toleranzpatent von 1781. Edition der wichtigsten Fassungen," in *Im Ziechen der Toleranz. Aufzätze zur Toleranzgesetzgebung de 18. Jahrhunderts in den Reichen Joseph II, ihren Voraussetzungen und irhen Folgen*, ed. Peter Barton (Wien: Institut für protestanische Kirchengeschichte, 1981), 152–202. This was followed in 1782 by the Edict of Toleration, which applied to Jews in Inner Austria.

Only then were the Calvinists of St. Maria-Horebeke empowered to build the "hidden" church at Beggars' Corner. Likewise, in 1787, Louis XVI issued an Edict of Toleration granting **ad hoc tolerance** for discreet worship and civil rights to Calvinists in all of France.[52] In doing so, the most prominent and aggressive experiments in confessional absolutism in post-Westphalian Europe were officially ended. At almost the same time, the leaders of the Protestant Ascendancy in Ireland also passed a series of Catholic Relief Acts to undo the harsh edges of the Penal Laws, without granting Catholics political rights.[53] Only then did the Catholics of Disert emerge from the shadows. Whereas historians have sometimes seen the Edicts of Toleration as a product of Enlightenment culture, these tortured documents more clearly represent a very belated form of grudging consent by authoritarian rulers to the **ad hoc tolerance** of their dissenting subjects; they were validating, at long last, the facts of religious diversity on the ground; acknowledging the practical limits of their ancestors' claims to religious sovereignty; and hoping to reduce the obvious costs of official repression.[54]

As noted throughout this study, religious peace in early modern Europe was, at each phase of the cycles of religious war and religious peace, terribly complicated and more than a bit messy. Indeed, there was throughout this history a fundamental disconnect between the pronouncements of Europe's diverse rulers and the practical experiences of their even more diverse subjects. Taking the perspective of the diverse and often dissenting subjects seriously into account nevertheless allowed us to construct a new and more dynamic account of the origins and character of religious pluralism in modern Europe. Neither the historical processes nor their variant outcomes were necessarily pretty, but at each stage difficult compromises and accommodations, both formal and informal, validated, managed, or in some way ensured the survival of an ever-expanding range of religious beliefs, practices, and institutions; these compromises recurrently helped to relieve the burdens of those ordinary Europeans who had the temerity to challenge the religious choices that Europe's rulers – plus the claimants to religious authority who were allied with them – recurrently insisted were in their best interest. How this complex historical record can help us to envision religious peace, now and in the future, will be the focus of the final chapter.

---

[52] The French text of the Edict of Toleration is available at www.museeprotestant.org/en/notice/the-edict-of-toleration-november-29th-1787; there is a partial English translation at https://chnm.gmu.edu/revolution/d/276.

[53] The text of the Catholic Relief Acts of 1778, 1782, and 1793 are available at http://members.pcug.org.au/~ppmay/acts/relief_acts.htm.

[54] See also Ben Kaplan's analysis of Joseph's Patent of Toleration in Benjamin J. Kaplan, *Divided by Faith: Religious Conflict and the Practice of Toleration in Early Modern Europe* (Cambridge, MA: Harvard University Press, 2007), 194–95. This distinction underscores, I would like to think, the value of relational accounts of political outcomes, as opposed to traditional cognitive arguments oriented to rulers alone.

CONCLUSION

13

Envisioning Religious Peace

By now the intrepid reader will no doubt have noticed that for eleven long chapters I have tried to keep my historian's hat firmly on my head. Although I have deployed the social-scientific language of mechanisms and processes, the strategies of contentious political analysis, and the heuristic of a typological map, I have above all been concerned, not with proposing or refining social-scientific theory, but with getting the story straight. The comparative historical analyses I have offered were designed to answer three basic questions about early modern Europe: (1) How did the religious wars start, and why did they look the way they did? (2) How did the various clusters of religious war end, and what did their peace settlements look like? And (3) What did religious peace actually look like?

ANSWERING THE BIG QUESTIONS

With regard to the first question, I have been at pains to show that a limited number of relational mechanisms – activation, polarization, escalation, and brokerage – help us to describe and account for six clusters of religious war in European history. Since my definition of religious war highlights the way religious identities are used by the forces in conflict to mark both their enmities and their alliances, I have also been at pains to show how a limited set of relational and cognitive mechanisms – innovation, disputation, politicization, and mobilization – help us to describe and account for the ever-expanding range of politically salient religious identities and affiliations in early modern Europe. With regard to the second question, I have been at pains to show that a limited number of relational mechanisms – negotiation, segregation, domination, and subversion – help us to describe and account for a limited range of peace settlements, both formal and informal, that ended Europe's principal clusters of religious war. These are the clusters of mechanisms that I identified in Figure 1.1 to guide our historical investigation, broken down into three paired comparisons, of (1) the origins of new religious identities, which historians often call "sectarian" at least until they are fully embedded in new cultural institutions; (2) what made a very diverse set of religious wars possible, not all of which historians have considered "real" religious wars; and (3) what made a very diverse set of peace settlements possible, many of which the historians who generalize about the nature of religious peace have never actually examined.

The reader, and my scholarly critics, in particular, will have to decide how effective my comparative historical analyses are, but the logic of the social-scientific arguments I have made is that, while these lists of mechanisms may not be exhaustive, the recurrent concatenation of these mechanisms under different historical conditions helps us to understand or explain a limited range of historical outcomes. In broadest outline, we can now be clearer about the explicandum: Over a period of roughly two centuries, Europeans – that is a wide variety of political actors, rulers and subjects as well as claimants to religious authority – replaced the relative cultural unity, if not purity, of late-medieval Latin Christendom with a very durable, but limited, range of political settlements that institutionalized and legalized a rich pattern of religious diversity – not authoritarian uniformity! – as the new normal in European culture, thereby making religious peace possible. This was, in fact, a stunning transformation, surely one of the BIG changes in European history! It is not Max Weber's story of inexorable secularization, but it is, at bottom, a story of religious diversification that a new generation of post-Reformation historians has recovered and identified. This book has not been about the process of religious diversification, per se, but about how the results of that process became embedded in political, legal, and cultural institutions.

Historians, for better or worse, are accustomed to teaching historical method by example, rather than precept. As I said at the outset of this book, however, I believe that it is one of the fundamental moral challenges of our time to use historical research to connect the beginnings of religious wars with possible endings in order to imagine how a world engulfed in religious conflict might once again find peace. The first step, I believe, is to think comparatively, not at the end of an investigation, whether scholarly or journalistic, but at the beginning, when larger comparisons can inform and sharpen the questions we ask about particular cases. Instead of asking the BIG questions implicitly, we need to ask them explicitly, fully intending the answers we find in investigating particular cases of religious controversy and conflict – historically, or in the present – will bear on how we answer the BIG questions.

At the risk of minimizing the enormous intellectual challenge of answering just one of these questions in any particular case, I have summarized in Figure 13.1 what we should be looking for, when we try to investigate the BIG questions: what might plausibly allow us to connect the beginnings of violent religious conflicts and war with how they might end, and what those endings might look like. I call it a "simple guide," but I am well aware from my

---

Where do politically salient religious identities come from?

- **Innovation**, often based on appeals to an idealized distant past, opens new questions regarding religious beliefs, ritual practices, and religious authority.

- **Disputation**, whether formal or informal, serves to clarify the issues at stake and their larger implications.

- **Politicization** increases the stakes of religious disagreements when political actors, outside the debate, choose sides.

- **Mobilization** inserts religious issues into the political arena when political actors organize for action on behalf of one side or the other.

What makes religious war possible?

- **Activation** of religious identities/boundaries in specific settings serves to make those identities politically salient.

- **Escalation** transforms local disputes into larger categorical conflicts when broader networks of religious solidarity identify local or parochial conflicts as their own.

- **Polarization** makes cross-boundary cooperation more difficult when actors on either side of the identity boundary police that boundary.

- **Brokerage** of larger coalitions and alliances, including specialists in coercion, facilitates the militarization of religious conflict.

What make religious peace possible?

- **Negotiation**, both formal and informal, local and national, can lead to mutual recognition, security guarantees, and provisions for the non-violent resolution of future disputes.

- **Segregation**, political, social, or physical, can reduce the likelihood of violent encounters and/or disrupt coalitions (including violent specialists) that enable violent conflict.

- **Domination** can bring order to otherwise violent or chaotic situations.

- **Subversion** can open up spaces for diversity where formal agreement or domination would seem to exclude them.

Figure 13.1: How to answer the BIG questions: a simple guide

own long and sometimes frustrating experience how difficult it is to answer – even briefly, as I have done, by the standards of my historical colleagues – the BIG questions in early modern Europe. The "simple" point is that anyone can reasonably hope to contribute to meaningful answers to the BIG questions, if we always have that moral and intellectual goal in mind. In addition, the practical lesson that I think I have learned is that what we are looking for is how these mechanisms cluster or concatenate in different settings rather how they operate in isolation. In the previous chapters of this book, I have tried to suggest how different concatenations produced different outcomes in early modern Europe, fully realizing that the investigation of European history will not produce universal causal sequences, but rather valuable lessons about what to look for, where to find it, and how to understand it as part of a larger historical process.

A COMPLEX AND MESSY PEACE

With regard to the third question – What did religious peace actually look like? – I have offered a typological or conceptual map (Figure 1.2) that I think helps us to describe the range of variation, and I have used contentious political analysis to account for how the various forms of peace came into being, usually long before, but sometimes also after, formal elite bargains made religious peace possible. This turned out to be by far the most difficult question to answer, for a variety of reasons, but it is, to my mind, the most important question to answer. It was a number of years ago, after I had benefited from a broad international scholarly collaboration on the theme of accommodating religious differences, that I realized that the traditional sources of historical research – the documentary evidence contained in archives and libraries – were not helping us to understand what religious peace actually looked like. And so I began a serious, if limited, effort both to find and to figure out how to use the kinds of visual and material evidence that have become part of this book. By way of conclusion, then, I should like to summarize briefly what I think we have *seen*, and how we might use some larger lessons derived from European experience to envision religious peace today and in the future. The essential point, I believe, is that in order for us to seek, to promote, or actually to make religious peace in our currently tumultuous and deeply divided world, we have to imagine more realistically what that peace might look like.

The simplest and perhaps best answer that I have recurrently given to the question of what peace looked like in early modern Europe is that it was complex and messy, and even subject to change over time, but not simply random. This is not meant to be flippant, but reflective of the perennial difficulty we face in describing and accounting for religious diversity in European history: Despite the often prescriptive language of elite bargains expressed in national or international settlements, the actual patterns of religious diversity that we find in local and regional histories were both more improvised and less regulated or constrained than the official documents contained in governmental archives would suggest. In general, we can say that in Germany, Switzerland, and France, negotiated national settlements of the matter of religion located the center of gravity on the inclusive (right) side of Figure 1.2. Still, within specific territories and cities, there were often established churches, especially in the constituent parts of the Swiss Confederation and German-Roman Empire, and less formal patterns of cohabitation at the local or parochial level. In the absence of negotiated settlements or specifically religious treaties or edicts, in the Low Countries and Great Britain, the center of gravity was on the exclusive (left) side of Figure 1.2, though in these cases, especially, **ad hoc tolerance** created a whole host of exceptions to the formally exclusive outcomes. Finally, in parts of Switzerland, the Southern Netherlands, Bohemia, and Ireland, there were (in)famous examples of authoritarian confessionalism and episodes of active **repression** of religious differences, which in every case proved to be ineffective in eliminating religious diversity where it had already taken root.

So what did that complex and messy peace actually look like? Unfortunately, the best, most comprehensive visual representation I could come up with is Figure 12.1, which is complex and messy to be sure, but it borders on being illegible and can hardly be considered visually evocative, much less inspirational! Fortunately, the challenge of finding a suitable illustration for the cover of this book brought me back to a painting by Edward Hicks, called "The Peaceable Kingdom." Hicks, who was a sign painter in Pennsylvania in the nineteenth century and not an artist of the first rank, actually produced more than 100 paintings of his vision of the peaceable kingdom; as a Quaker, his vision of peace was informed by the prophecy of Isaiah:

> The wolf will live with the lamb,
>> the leopard will lie down with the goat,
> the calf and the lion and the yearling together;
>> and a little child will lead them.
> The cow will feed with the bear,
>> their young will lie down together,
>> and the lion will eat straw like the ox.
> The infant will play near the cobra's den,
>> and the young child will put its hand into the viper's nest.
> They will neither harm nor destroy
>> on all my holy mountain,
> for the earth will be filled with the knowledge of the Lord
>> as the waters cover the sea.[1]

What I like about the image I have selected from Hick's painting is its literal adherence to the sacred text, with its improbable and counterintuitive collection of characters arranged on an apparently steep slope in a "natural" setting where gravity does not seem to be fully in force. It is complex and messy, just like early modern European experience, and full of the surprises and incongruities that characterized our exploration of the contours of religious peace in Europe. But to my taste, at least, it is also not a particularly pretty picture; neither is it devoid of tension and danger.[2]

Now, there are other biblical prophecies that might also be usefully evocative in the hands of someone more creative than I am. I am sure, for example, that

---

[1] Isaiah 11: 6–9 (New International Version).

[2] In fact, the left side of the original painting, which has been cropped out, is a bit too pretty for my taste: It is an image, from a distance, of William Penn making peace with a group of Native Americans. We now know, of course, that such stories in American history did not end well. There is an image of the whole painting at www.worcesterart.org/collection/American/1934.65 .html.

I am not the only one to have wondered what it would be like to beat swords into plowshares and spears into pruning hooks.[3] While creative imagination can be clarifying and even inspirational, the envisioning I have in mind is an historically informed imagination of the possibilities of religious peace. As I have pointed out in previous chapters, some of the most important practices by which early modern Europeans learned to live with their obvious religious differences – sharing sacred spaces, traveling to worship more freely, and hiding to avoid trouble – were eminently modular and adaptable to a wide variety of situations.[4] What is critical, when we try to make sense of situations of religious conflict and try to imagine a more peaceful future, is that we actually look for evidence of such practices, as well as the stories about how they came into being. These practices almost invariably predate the elite bargains that make peace possible; they both establish peaceful facts on the ground and serve as the foundation of a durable peace in the future, whether or not they are bottom-up and subversive or top-down and official in origin. Thus is it also important to remember that whereas elite bargains can make peace possible, they do not constitute the peace; they validate, manage, or sometimes reshape what others have created, but they do not bring it into being.

Although the stories I have told to illustrate the various forms of religious coexistence are usefully informative about Europe and even inspirational in some cases, they also illuminate and underscore what I expect to be the essential characteristics of religious peace, regardless of time and place. First of all, religious peace is the work of many hands: of often competitive rulers and their religiously diverse subjects as well as of multiple claimants to religious authority. One of the most important reasons that earlier generations of historians failed to appreciate the deeply contentious and often subversive origins of religious pluralism in Europe is that they failed to take the dissenting subjects seriously into account as both intentional and consequential actors. The prospects for religious peace in our own time will also seem dim, if not nil, unless and until we incorporate a broader vision of the informal peace that precedes the formal peace and serves as the foundation for durable patterns of religious coexistence.

---

[3] The image of beating swords into plowshares and spears into pruning hooks comes from both Isaiah 2:4 and Micah 4:3. In Joel 3:10, however, the image and injunction are reversed: "Beat your plowshares into swords, and your pruning hooks into spears; let the weakling say, 'I am a warrior'" (New Revised Standard Version). A more dramatic example of the sometimes contradictory nature of biblical literature can hardly be imagined.

[4] Imagine how proud I was of myself when I found, during a teaching collaboration at Koç University, the "hidden" Church of Saints Peter and Paul in the heart of old Istanbul, just down the hill from the Galata Tower; today, like many of the sites of coexistence we explored in central and western Europe, this marvelous example of religious coexistence in the context of established privilege is also mentioned in tourist guides to the city. See, for example, www.lonelyplanet.com/turkey/istanbul/sights/religious/church-ss-peter-paul. There is a picture of the entrance to the church courtyard at: https://en.wikipedia.org/wiki/Church_of_SS_Peter_and_Paul,_Istanbul.

Secondly, it is important to understand that religious peace is very hard work. Especially in the so-called Abrahamic faith traditions (Judaism, Christianity, and Islam), disagreements about the nature of religious authority are often more difficult to resolve than disagreements about theology – that is, the formal understanding of God, of humankind, and of the relationship between them. As a consequence, as we have seen throughout this work, reconciliation, which might have been the best possible foundation for peace, proved to be impossible among political actors who were convinced that they knew what God wanted.[5] Religious peace agreements, as we have seen, require compromise or at least grudging consent to rules and accommodations – basically, mutual recognition, security guarantees, and procedures, including mediation, for resolving future disputes – that may seem, on their face, unacceptable. In addition, it is often the case, though not necessarily, that rulers of a variety of sorts – civil authorities and their agents plus, indirectly, the religious authorities with whom they may be allied – are entrusted with the implementation and maintenance of religious peace settlements. When, as we have seen, those actors, for whatever political or ideological reasons, abdicate that responsibility or simply stop the impartial enforcement of rules and accommodations, religious peace settlements are especially fragile. Sometimes, as in the case of Henry IV of France, it is even mortally dangerous to implement and maintain the peace.

Finally, it is important to recognize that peace is not free. The costs of religious war – in terms of the destruction of human life, material objects, and even the environment; the enormous expenditures required to coordinate that destruction; and the steady accumulation of grievances – might seem to be obvious, but the perceived benefits of a military victory or the perceived need of self-defense recurrently seem to outweigh the obvious costs, as political actors of a variety of sorts choose to deploy the instruments of coordinated destruction in the service of some higher good. Against that backdrop, the benefits of peace may seem obvious, while we sometimes willfully ignore or simply overlook the obvious costs of peace. Although I have not undertaken any kind of objective cost-benefit analysis of religious peace, let me at least point out what I see as some of the obvious costs of the different forms of religious peace we found in early modern Europe. If the typological map represented by Figure 1.2 is a useful heuristic, it can also help us to organize a discussion of the possible or even likely costs of different forms of religious coexistence as the foundation for a durable peace. The following brief reflections are based primarily on my reading of European history, but I believe this sort of understanding is critically important if we are to develop a realistic vision of religious peace today.

---

[5] Indeed, it is perhaps true that societies without doubt are inherently dangerous places; still, in European history, as we have seen, peace among fervently convinced believers proved to be possible.

COUNTING THE COSTS OF PEACE

Let's begin in the lower left of Figure 1.2, in the realm of active repression and "mere" survival, where the cost of religious peace might seem to be the greatest – indeed, where the obvious costs might seem to preclude regarding **repression** as a form of peaceful coexistence. Repression was a recurrent theme in all three phases of religious war in early modern Europe, but inasmuch as it proved to be ineffective in eliminating diversity in every case we have found – with the possible exception of the prince-bishopric of Salzburg, where the "problem" of religious diversity was exported to other polities, by international consent and active collaboration – it was, in fact, a durable form of religious peace. As a short-term strategy of domination, repression could have enormous costs for dissenters, of course, but as a long-term relationship, public domination combined with private survival required the grudging consent of authorities, often by connivance, to hidden practices of dissenting subjects and the necessity, among dissenters, of secrecy and dissimulation to avoid trouble. Some of the unintended benefits of this difficult relationship may be that "ordinary" disssenting believers, practicing "lay casuisty," are able to adapt the norms of orthodox religious belief and ritual practice to their specific needs, while the need for private religious education often gives women new leadership roles within the household and the community of faith. Indeed, it is under conditions of repression that one discovers the enormous spiritual ingenuity, improvisation, and courage that often worries religious authorities, but empowers ordinary believers. Who knows how many situations of religious repression are affecting the same trade-offs today?

In the lower right of Figure 1.2, in the realm of **integration**, the benefits of religious peace may seem more obvious while the costs would seem to be negligible. As it happened, integration, which is officially inclusive but limits the visibility and salience of religious identities in public life, was a relatively rare experience in early modern Europe, whereas many today might see it as ideal. After all, it would seem to be the polar opposite of **privilege**, and the establishment or privileging of a dominant form of religious faith and ritual practice is expressly forbidden in the first amendment to United States Constitution.[6] We did find important examples of integration in the first phase of religious war and peace, in the Swiss *Tagsatzung* and the German *Reichstag*, where the reduced salience of religious differences made comity and collaboration possible, though not permanent; we also found integration on a much larger scale at the beginning of the seventeenth century, in France, where a bold experiment in integration was the foundation of a durable peace in the wake of recurrent and very destructive religious and civil wars. The costs of integration, however, are subtle and can be significant for believers whose faith

---

[6] The First Amendment reads, in part, "Congress shall make no law respecting an establishment of religion." For modern interpretations of this quintessentially early modern clause, see, for example, www.firstamendmentcenter.org/establishment-clause.

and ritual practices would seem to require publicity and visibility/salience. For French Calvinists, (re)integration into civil and political life may have seemed ideal, even when it was paired with serious limits on the publicity of their worship, since they were used to worshiping discreetly; for French Catholics (as opposed, say, to Dutch or English Catholics), by contrast, any limitation on the publicity of their ritual processions and feast days, which were often disruptive or impinged on Calvinists, seemed to be anathema.[7] Constitutional mandates of religious integration meet with similar sorts of objections from the religiously devout today, in Turkey as well as France and the United States.

In the upper right of Figure 1.2, we encounter one of the most varied and pervasive forms of durable religious coexistence: **parity**, which in a variety of iterations proved to be both modular and scalable from the local and territorial to the national and imperial levels. The sharing of sacred and public spaces and the careful balancing of judicial and political representation among multiple faith communities often required complicated agreements and elaborate rules that made religious peace durable and sustainable, especially in Germany and Switzerland, where it was especially compatible with their religiously inclusive political regimes. Over time, however, the rules and complex arrangements could become inflexible, resistant to change, and thus problematic. Whether it involved the sharing of baptismal fonts, the sharing of a priory courtyard, or the careful balancing of political interests in cities and territories, parity could lead as readily to estrangement as to harmony. The formal parity arrangements that were designed to bring religious peace following very violent and destructive civil wars in twentieth-century Lebanon and Bosnia have exhibited the same costly tendencies.

In the upper left of Figure 1.2, **privilege** institutionalizes the domination of one confession or faith community over all others, in the absence of active persecution; it is probably the most common form of religious coexistence we find in early modern Europe. In the constituent members of the German *Reich* and the Swiss Confederation, it was the locally and territorially exclusive counterpoint to inclusive templates on the national level, but over time, durable patterns of dissent and nonconformity belied the rulers' new claims of religious sovereignty (*ius reformandi*). In England and the United Provinces, privilege proved to be compatible with very vibrant and robust patterns of religious diversity that did not limit the range of dissident or nonconforming voices as long as they acknowledged and practiced the conventions – for example, worshiping in structures that did not look like churches – that were built into these formally exclusive regimes. For those who had previously or might otherwise have been subjected to active persecution, privilege would have seemed like a reasonable bargain in the short term at least, but in the longer term privileged regimes with established or "public" churches institutionalize

---

[7] See especially, Keith P. Luria, *Sacred Boundaries: Religious Coexistence and Conflict in Early Modern France* (Washington: Catholic University of America Press, 2005).

religious inequalities that easily become durable when they coincide with other forms of inequality: unequal access to public welfare, education, certain professions, even residential locations. These durable inequalities have proven to be particularly intractable, even when limitations on religious practice are reduced, and they are particularly problematic when they are perceived as "injustices."

Finally, in the middle of Figure 1.2, **ad hoc tolerance**, which grants specific exemptions to otherwise generally operative rules of exclusion, came to be a very prominent feature of the religious peace in various parts of Europe in the second half of the seventeenth century and beyond. In a particularly unfortunate turn of phrase, Andrew Pettegree, one of my generation's finest early modern historians, once declared that tolerance "was only ever a loser's creed."[8] As we have encountered it here, however, tolerance was not a creed at all, but a political practice by which otherwise intolerant rulers could step back from the harshest consequences of their official policies of exclusion, give relief to "worthy" or at least influential dissenters, and thereby reduce the political and economic costs of their own intolerance. In this sense, it might be considered a win-win practice at first blush. In most situations, however, these partial exemptions from the disabilities of religious exclusion do not undo the larger nexus of the durable inequalities that exclusion gives rise to. In addition, the plain fact is that these ad hoc exemptions are also and forever vulnerable to revocation by the "sovereign" authority who granted them.

In other words, all of the variable patterns of religious coexistence we have encountered in early modern Europe entail both costs and benefits. None of them is perfect, but together they represent the variety of ways that it is possible both to imagine and to devise a more peaceful future in the context of religious strife and war. At the beginning of this work, you may recall, I resisted the temptation to build the criterion of justice into our working definition of religious peace. As we have found, religious peace – that is, the durable presence of religious diversity in the absence of war – was indeed possible even in the wake of very long and destructive wars. But it was neither easy nor free. Thus, one of the very real dangers of some of the most prominent forms of religious peace – privilege, repression, and ad hoc tolerance – is the institutionalization of durable inequalities which may be regarded as profoundly unjust. Indeed, one of the important challenges for those who seek to make religious peace more sustainable is to unpack and undo the injustices that flow from regimes of religious domination and formal exclusion. The political, social, and economic emancipation of religious minorities can be a very slow process, but many polities in Europe moved successfully, if fitfully, in that direction between the eighteenth and twentieth centuries without experiencing new rounds of religious violence and war. The modern

---

[8] Andrew Pettegree, "The Politics of Toleration in the Free Netherlands, 1572–1620," in *Tolerance and Intolerance in the European Reformation*, eds. Ole Peter Grell and Bob Scribner (Cambridge: Cambridge University Press, 1996), 198.

history of Ireland reminds us, however, that in the very difficult cases, the injustices built into the durable inequalities of religious exclusion can haunt public politics long after religious worship is free and the outsiders are officially "emancipated." While there can be peace without justice, eliminating injustice, where it has been institutionalized as durable inequality, is undoubtedly one of the biggest reasons why peace is so hard.

OF PRIVILEGES AND RIGHTS

However useful it is to think in terms of recurrent mechanisms and large-scale historical processes, perhaps one of the most important lessons to learn from the cycles of religious war and religious peace in early modern Europe is that some of the most important changes are subtle, incremental, and hardly visible. In old-regime Europe, one's place in society was generally defined in terms of privileges – the corporative privileges of parliaments or estates, of cities, universities, and guilds, of cathedral chapters, monasteries, peasant villages, and the like. In some meaningful sense, the only people without privilege were social outcasts. Indeed, privileges served as the principal linkages between subjects and sovereigns, and in political terms, privileges were the principal limitations on sovereign authority, which is to say they carved out spaces for self-regulation, without the fear of interference from above, where the privileges originated. It is hardly surprising, then, in this world of pervasive, sometimes cross-cutting and contradictory, privileges, that religious diversity, too, came to be defined, validated, and managed in terms of corporative or group privileges – that is, collective exemptions from normally operative rules, collective representation within parity arrangements, or collective obligations in exchange for recognition. But in the long history of religious conflict and coexistence in early modern Europe, we can also see the origins and development of something more clearly "modern": the individual's freedom of religious conscience.

We saw the beginning of that thread in the slightly awkward language of the first article of the first Swiss *Landfrieden* in 1529: "since no one should be coerced into faith, that therefore the *Orte* [territories] and their subjects should also not be coerced." It reemerges in the more famous *Religionsfriede* of Augsburg (1555) when it assures the individual subjects of otherwise intolerant rulers that they may leave for another jurisdiction: "and on our honor and faith shall in no way be punished." It appears more explicitly in the fourth article of the Edict of Amboise, which ended the First French War in 1563 – following a specification of the limited opportunities for public Reformed worship, this crucial article asserts: "Nevertheless, everyone may live and dwell everywhere without being pursued or molested, forced or constrained for matters of conscience" – and some version of that assurance was repeated in all subsequent edicts of pacification, including, of course, the Edict of Nantes. It also figures prominently in the Low Countries, in the (unsuccessful) *Paix de Religion* (1578) and, by extension, in the Union of Utrecht (1579), where article 13 provides that "each inhabitant enjoys freedom of religion and no one is persecuted or questioned about his religion." Indeed, by the first quarter of the seventeenth century, freedom of religious conscience had become, at least implicitly, very much a part of the European cultural and political landscape, even in the Southern Netherlands where the Inquisition was ended.

Against this background, then, we can say that the freedom of religious conscience reached a kind of public maturity in the Peace of Westphalia in 1648. Article V, subparagraph 34–35/28, of the Treaty of Osnabrück stipulates that anyone who "shall profess and embrace a Religion different from that of the Lord of the Territory, shall in consequence of the said Peace be patiently suffer'd and tolerated, without any Hindrance or Impediment to attend their Devotions in their Homes and in private, with all Liberty of Conscience, and without any Inquisition or Trouble." After declaring that no one shall "be despised anywhere upon account of their Religion," the paragraph concludes "that in these and all other the like things they shall be treated in the same manner as Brethren and Sisters, with equal Justice and Protection." Recall that this agreement was signed by the representatives of some 180 polities and became, thereby, a part of international law. Thus, freedom of religious conscience, which first emerged in the sixteenth century as the holy grail of a wide variety of persecuted and vulnerable "dissenters," had clearly become, after more than a century of struggle, one of the hallmarks of a radically new and visibly diverse religious landscape. In fact, even though there were periods of serious repression after the last spasms of religious war, none of them was accompanied by heresy trials or the judicial examination of individual consciences.

What are we to make of this "freedom of religious conscience"? Was it a privilege or a right? And how is it related to the modern notion of freedom of religion as a universal human right? In some contexts, the freedom of religious conscience may be a privilege, as would seem to have been the case when the elector of Brandenburg or the elector of Saxony granted freedom of religious conscience to their subjects. In France, too, it might have seemed to be a privilege inasmuch as the edicts of pacification, which established an unlimited freedom of religious conscience, were proclamations issued by the king; in these cases, however, it was clearly the product of hard bargaining among the king and his religiously diverse subjects in an effort to find politically acceptable compromises and bring peace to a troubled land. As it reappeared in various articulations in the Swiss *Landfrieden*, the German *Religionsfriede*, the Dutch Union of Utrecht, and the Treaty of Osnabrück, however, the freedom of religious conscience was clearly the product of hard bargaining and not a privilege granted by a "beneficent" sovereign. But does that make it a right?

Today we are inclined to see "rights" as philosophical absolutes, inherent in nature if not given to us by God. The United Nations, for example, in its "Universal Declaration of Human Rights" (1948), presents "freedom of religion" as something very robust and expansive, a right to which all human beings are inherently entitled:

Art. 18: Everyone has the right to freedom of thought, conscience and religion; this right includes freedom to change his religion or belief, and freedom, either alone or in community with others and in public or private, to manifest his religion or belief in teaching, practice, worship and observance.[9]

This the early modern freedom of religious conscience was surely not. But in a seminal, though unfortunately obscure article, Charles Tilly offers a definition of "rights" – as *enforceable* claims that citizens (or subjects) can make on their governments – and an account of where they come from – they come from *struggle* – that is particularly useful, I believe, for historians, and perhaps for all students of religious conflict and coexistence.[10] By Tilly's definition, then, rights that are simply announced by international declarations, national constitutions, or philosophical consensus, are not necessarily *enforceable*; indeed, it is the historical *struggle* that reveals them to be meaningful/effective or not. By these relational criteria, which philosophical "realists" will surely quibble with, the freedom of religious conscience that we have found in early modern Europe was most certainly one of the earliest of the modern "human" rights, though it is also among the most contested, even today.

But even if it may be considered a "right," isn't freedom of religious conscience an awfully meager reward for a whole lot of struggle? As we have seen in this study, the freedom of religious conscience was sometimes as small as a simple right to emigrate without threat of punitive consequences (*ius emigrandi*), but at other times, it could also entail or be accompanied by the right to worship discreetly or even the right to worship publicly, whether in a structure that didn't look like a house of worship or one that did and was equipped with a bell. These very significant variations were the product of recurrent concatenations of familiar mechanisms – *negotiation, domination, segregation,* and *subversion* – within the larger historical process of accommodating religious differences. A universally declared "freedom of religion" is a wonderful goal to work for, but extremely difficult to attain in real historical situations. By comparison, whereas the freedom of religious conscience may seem meager to modern Europeans and neo-Europeans who are the beneficiaries of centuries

---

[9] See www.un.org/en/documents/udhr for the full text of the declaration.

[10] This important essay was first published as "Where Do Rights Come From?" in *Contributions to the Comparative Study of Development*, vol. 2 of *Proceedings from Vilhelm Aubert Memorial Symposion 1990*, ed. Lars Mjøset (Oslo: Institute for Social Research, 1992), 9–36; it was later republished under the same title as Charles Tilly, "Where Do Rights Come From?" in *Contributions to the Comparative Study of Development*, vol. 2 of *Democracy, Revolution and History*, eds. Lars Mjøset and Theda Skocpol (Ithaca: Cornell University Press, 1998).

of historical struggle, it would be an invaluable first step for millions of people around the world who are still subject to blasphemy laws, who are forbidden to change religions, or who face the mortal peril of forced migrations because they have been expelled from their homes on account of the matter of their religion. For them, the simple practice of **ad hoc tolerance** (an old-regime exemption from normally operative rules of exclusion) might be an enormous blessing.[11]

If this long historical exploration offers us just one final, pithy lesson to those who seek religious peace in the twenty-first century, it may be the echo of an aphorism that apparently originated in town-planning circles in the early twentieth century and became the watchword of the environmental movements in the 1970s: Think Globally, Act Locally! Although it is important that we seek to realize "freedom of religion" for everyone, the surest path to that noble end – an *enforceable* set of claims on governments everywhere – is likely to be via a whole host of local or parochial *struggles*.

---

[11] Today, of course, we may not be as modern in our enjoyment of religious freedoms as the notion that old-regime privileges have been superseded by natural or God-given rights, à la the American or French revolutions, might suggest; indeed, we still often grant legal standing and tax exemptions to specific religious organizations, for example, as ad hoc privileges or exemptions to normally operative rules.

Bibliography

Abray, Lorna Jane. "Confession, Conscience, and Honor: The Limits of Magisterial Tolerance in Sixteenth-Century Strassburg." In *Tolerance and Intolerance in the European Reformation*, edited by Ole Peter Grell and Bob Scribner, 94–107. Cambridge: Cambridge University Press, 1996.

The People's Reformation; Magistrates, Clergy and Commons in Strasbourg, 1500–1598. Ithaca, NY: Cornell University Press, 1985.

Althusius, Johannes. *The Politics of Johannes Althusius*. Translated and edited by Frederick S. Carney. London: Eyre & Spottiswoode, 1964.

Arnade, Peter. "Beggars and Iconoclasts: The Political Culture of Iconoclasm on the Eve of the Revolt of the Netherlands." In *Power and the City in the Netherlandic World*, edited by Wayne Te Brake and Wim Klooster, 59–83. Leiden: Brill, 2006.

Beggars, Iconoclasts, and Civic Patriots: The Political Culture of the Dutch Revolt. Ithaca, NY: Cornell University Press, 2008.

Asch, Ronald G. "Religious Toleration, the Peace of Westphalia and the German Territorial Estates." *Parliaments, Estates and Representation* 20, no. 1 (2000): 75–89.

Association des Amis de l'église historique de Hunawihr. *L'Église Fortifieé de Hunawihr*. Colmar: Editions SAEP, 1990.

Audisio, Gabriel. *Les Vaudois de Luberon: une minorité de Provence, 1460–1560*. Gap: Mérindol, 1984.

The Waldensian Dissent: Persecution and Survival, c. 1170–c.1570. Translated by Clair Davison. Cambridge Medieval Textbooks. Cambridge: Cambridge University Press, 1999.

Ayoob, Mohammed. *The Many Faces of Political Islam: Religion and Politics in the Muslim World*. Ann Arbor: University of Michigan Press, 2008.

Backus, Irena. "The Disputations of Baden, 1526 and Berne, 1528: Neutralizing the Early Church." *Studies in Reformed Theology and History* 1 (1993): 1–69.

Baena, Laura Manzano. *Conflicting Words: The Peace Treaty of Münster (1648) and the Political Culture of the Dutch Republic and the Spanish Monarchy*. Avisos de Flandes. Leuven: Leuven University Press, 2011.

Bainton, Roland. *Here I Stand: A Life of Martin Luther*. New York: Abingdon-Cokesbury Press, 1950.

Barends, Frederick F. *Geloven in de Schaduw: Schuilkerken in Amsterdam.* Gent: Snoeck-Dacaju & Zoon, 1996.

Barkey, Karen. *Empire of Difference: The Ottomans in Comparative Perspective.* Cambridge; New York: Cambridge University Press, 2008.

Barnard, T. C. "Conclusion. Settling and Unsettling Ireland: The Cromwellian and Williamite Revolutions." In *Ireland from Independence to Occupation, 1641–1660,* edited by Jane Ohlmeyer, 265–91. Cambridge: Cambridge University Press, 1995.

Cromwellian Ireland: English Government and Reform in Ireland 1649–1660. Oxford Historical Monographs. London: Oxford University Press, 1975.

Barnavi, Elie. *Le parti de Dieu: Étude sociale et politique des chefs de la Ligue parisienne, 1585–1594.* Travaux du Centre de recherches sur la civilisation de l'Europe moderne. Bruxelles: Éditions Nauwelaerts, 1980.

Bartlett, Thomas. *Ireland: A History.* Cambridge; New York: Cambridge University Press, 2010.

Barton, Peter, ed. "'Das' Toleranzpatent von 1781. Edition der wichtigsten Fassungen." In *Im Ziechen der Toleranz. Aufzätze zur Toleranzgesetzgebung de 18. Jahrhunderts in den Reichen Joseph II, ihren Voraussetzungen und irhen Folgen,* edited by Peter Barton, 152–202. Wien: Institut für protestanische Kirchengeschichte, 1981.

Bartos, F. M. *The Hussite Revolution, 1424–1437.* Boulder, CO: East European Monographs, 1986.

Bate, Frank. *The Declaration of Indulgence, 1672: A Study in the Rise of Organised Dissent.* London: Pub. for the University Press of Liverpool by A. Constable, 1908.

Benbassa, Esther. *The Jews of France: A History from Antiquity to the Present.* Translated by M. B. DeBevoise. Princeton, NJ: Princeton University Press, 1999.

Benedict, Philip. *Christ's Churches Purely Reformed: A Social History of Calvinism.* New Haven, CT: Yale University Press, 2002.

Rouen During the Wars of Religion. Cambridge: Cambridge University Press, 1981.

"Settlements: France." In *Visions, Programs and Outcomes. Vol. 2 of Handbook of European History, 1400–1600,* edited by Thomas A. Brady, Heiko A. Oberman, and James D. Tracy, 417–54. Leiden: E. J. Brill, 1995.

"The Saint Bartholemew's Massacres in the Provinces." *Historical Journal* 21 (1978): 205–25.

Benedict, Philip, Guido Marnef, Henk van Nierop, and Marc Venard, eds. *Reformation, Revolt and Civil War in France and the Netherlands 1555–1585.* Amsterdam: Koninklijke Nederlandse Akademie van Wetenschappen, 1999.

Bennett, Martyn. *The Civil Wars in Britain and Ireland, 1638–1651.* Oxford: Blackwell Publishers, 1997.

Benoist, Elie. *Histoire de l'Édit de Nantes: contenant les choses les plus remarquables qui se sont passées en France avant & après sa publication, à l'ocasion de la diversité des religions, et principalement les contraventions, inexecutions, chicanes, artifices, violences, & autres injustices, que les reformez se plaignent d'y avoir souffertes, jusques à l'édit de revocation, en octobre 1685; avec ce qui a suivi ce nouvel édit jusques à présent.* 3 vol. Delft: Beman, 1693–5.

The History of the Famous Edict of Nantes: Containing an Account of All the Persecutions That Have Been in France from Its First Publication to This Present Time. 2 vol. London: Printed for John Dunton, 1694.

Bercé, Yves-Marie. *Histoire des Croquants*. Mémoires et documents, Société de l'École des Chartes, XXII. Geneva: Librairie Droz, 1974.
  History of Peasant Revolts. Translated by Amanda Whitmore. Ithaca, NY: Cornell University Press, 1990.
Bergsma, Wiebe. "Gereformeerden en doopsgezinden: van concurrentie tot gedwongen acceptatie." *Doopsgezinde Bijdragen* 20 (1994): 129–56.
  Tussen Gideonsbende en publieke kerk. Een studie over het gereformeerd protestantisme in Friesland, 1580–1650. Fryske Histoaryske Rige 17. Hilversum: Verloren, 1999.
Berner, Hans. *"Die gute Correspondenz": die Politik der Stadt Basel gegenüber dem Fürstbistum Basel in den Jahren 1525–1585*. Basler Beiträge zur Geschichtswissenschaft, vol. 158. Basel: Helbing & Lichtenhahn, 1989.
Betz, Hans Dieter, et al., eds. *Religion Past & Present: Encyclopedia of Theology and Religion*. Leiden; Boston: Brill, 2007–13.
Bien, David D. *The Calas Affair: Persecution, Toleration, and Heresy in Eighteenth-Century Toulouse*. Princeton, NJ: Princeton University Press, 1960.
Blickle, Peter. *Communal Reformation: The Quest for Salvation in Sixteenth-Century Germany*. Translated by Thomas Dunlap. Atlantic Highlands, NJ: Humanities Press, 1992.
  "Peasant Revolts in the German Empire in the Late Middle Ages." *Social History* 4 (1979): 223–39.
  The Revolution of 1525: The German Peasants' War from a New Perspective. Translated by Thomas A. Brady Jr. and H. C. Erik Midelfort. Baltimore: Johns Hopkins University Press, 1981.
Blockmans, Wim. *Keizer Karel V: De utopie van het keizerschap*. Leuven: Van Halewyck, 2000.
Blom, J. C. H., and Renate G. Fuks-Mansfeld, eds. *History of the Jews in the Netherlands*. Translated by Arnold J. Pomerans and Erica Pomerans. Portland, OR: Littman Library of Jewish Civilization, 2002.
Bodian, Miriam. *Hebrews of the Portuguese Nation: Conversos and Community in Early Modern Amsterdam*. Bloomington: Indiana University Press, 1997.
Bodin, Jean. *The Six Books of a Commonweale*. Edited and translated by Kenneth Douglas McRae. Cambridge, MA: Harvard University Press, 1962.
Bohnstedt, John W. "The Infidel Scourge of God: The Turkish Menace as Seen by German Pamphleteers of the Reformation Era." *Transactions of the American Philosophical Society* New Series 58, part 9 (1968).
Bonjour, Edgar. *Swiss Neutrality, Its History and Meaning*. Translated by Mary Hottinger. London: G. Allen & Unwin, 1946.
Boom, H. ten. "De Vestiging van het Gereforeerde Kerk in het Land van Maas en Waal en de aangrezende dorpen van het Rijk van Nijmegen in het begin van de 17e eeuw. Een mislukte reformatie." *Nederlandsch archief voor kerkgeschiedenis* 50, no. 2 (1970): 197–229.
Bouwsma, William J. *John Calvin: A Sixteenth-Century Portrait*. New York: Oxford University Press, 1988.
Brady, Thomas A., Jr. "Settlements: The Holy Roman Empire." In *Visions, Programs and Outcomes*. Vol. 2 of *Handbook of European History, 1400–1600*, edited by Thomas A. Brady, Heiko A. Oberman, and James D. Tracy, 349–83. Leiden: E. J. Brill, 1995.

The Politics of the Reformation in Germany: Jacob Sturm (1489–1553) of Strasbourg.
Atlantic Highlands, NJ: Humanities Press, 1997.

Turning Swiss: Cities and Empire, 1450–1550. Cambridge: Cambridge University
Press, 1985.

Braekman, E. M. *Le Protestantisme belge au 17e siècle: Belgique, nord de la France,
refuge.* Terres protestantes. Carrières-sous-Poissy, France: La Cause, 2001.

Brandi, Karl, ed. *Der Augsburger Religionsfriede vom 25 Sept. 1555: Kritische Ausgabe
des Textes.* München: Rieger'sche Universitäts-Buchhandlung, 1896.

Briels, J. G. C. A. *Zuid-Nederlanders in de republiek 1572–1630: Een demographische
en cultuurhistorische studie.* Sint-Niklaas: Uitgeverij Danthe, 1985.

Zuid-Nederlandse immigratie 1572–1630. Haarlem: Fibula-Van Dishoeck, 1978.

Broadhead, P. "Politics and Expediency in the Augburg Reformation." In *Reformation
Principle and Practice; Essays in Honour of A. G. Dickens*, edited by P. N. Brooks.
London: Scolar Press, 1980.

"Popular Pressure for Reform in Augsburg, 1524–1534." In *Stadtbürgertum und Adel
in der Reformation*, edited by W. J. Mommsen, P. Alter, and R. W. Scribner, 80–7.
Stuttgart: Klett-Cotta, 1979.

Bronn, Pierre, ed. *Le protestantisme en pays messin: histoire et lieux de mémoire.* Metz:
Serpenoise, 2007.

Brown, Keith M. *Kingdom or Province? Scotland and the Regal Union, 1603–1715.*
British History in Prespective. Houndsmills, UK: Macmillan, 1992.

Browning, Andrew, ed. *1660–1714. Vol. 8 of English Historical Documents.* New York:
Oxford University Press, 1953.

Burnet, George B. *The Story of Quakerism in Scotland, 1650–1850. With an Epilogue
on the Period 1850–1950 by William H. Marwick.* London: J. Clarke, 1952.

Bush, Michael. *The Pilgrimage of Grace: A Study of the Rebel Armies of October 1536.*
Manchester, UK: Manchester University Press, 1996.

Bussmann, Klaus, and Heinz Schilling, eds. *Exhibition Catalogue. Vol. 3 of 1648: War
and Peace in Europe.* Münster/Osnabrück: Veranstaltungsgesellschaft 350 Jahre
Westfälischer Friede, 1998.

eds. *Politics, Religion, Law and Society. Vol. 1 of 1648: War and Peace in Europe.*
Münster/Osnabrück: Veranstaltungsgesellschaft 350 Jahre Westfälischer Friede,
1998.

Calvin, Jean. *Institutes of the Christian Religion.* Edited by John T. McNeill. Translated
by Ford Lewis Battles. The Library of Christian Classics, vol. 20–21. Philadelphia:
Westminster Press, 1960.

Cameron, Euan. *The European Reformation.* Oxford: Clarendon Press, 1991.

The Reformation of the Heretics: The Waldenes of the Alps 1480–1580. Oxford:
Clarendon Press, 1984.

Canny, Nicholas P. *The Elizabethan Conquest of Ireland: A Pattern Established,
1565–76.* Hassocks: Harvester Press, 1976.

Making Ireland British, 1580–1650. Oxford: Oxford University Press, 2001.

Capp, Bernard. "Multiculturalism in Early Modern Britain." In *A Companion to
Multiconfessionalism in the Early Modern World*, edited by Thomas Max Safley.
Brill's Companions to the Christian Tradition, vol. 28, 289–315. Leiden; Boston:
Brill, 2011.

"The Religious Marketplace: Public Disputations in Civil War and Interregnum
England." *English Historical Review* 129, no. 2 (2014): 47–78.

Carroll, Michael P. *Irish Pilgrimage: Holy Wells and Popular Catholic Devotion.* Baltimore: Johns Hopkins University Press, 1999.

"Rethinking Popular Catholicism in Pre-Famine Ireland." *Journal for the Scientific Study of Religion* 34, no. 3 (1995): 354–65.

Carroll, Stuart. *Martyrs and Murderers: The Guise Family and the Making of Europe.* Oxford: Oxford University Press, 2009.

"The Guise Affinity and Popular Protest during the Wars of Religion." *French History* 9, no. 2 (1995): 125–52.

"The Revolt of Paris, 1588: Aristocratic Insurgency and the Mobilization of Popular Support." *French Historical Studies* 23 (2000): 301–27.

Cau, Cornelius, ed. *Groot placaatboek, vervattende de placaaten, ordonnantien en edicten van de hoog mog. heeren Staaten generaal der Vereenigde Nederlanden; en van de edele groot mog. heeren Staaten van Holland en Westvriesland; mitsgaders van de edele mog heeren Staaten van Zeeland ...* vol. 1. 's Gravenhage: H. I. van Wouw, 1658.

Champeaud, Gregory. "The Edict of Poitiers and the Treaty of Nérac, or Two Steps Towards the Edict of Nantes." *Sixteenth Century Journal* 32, no. 2 (2001): 319–34.

Christin, Olivier. "From Repression to Pacification: French Royal Policy in the Face of Protestantism." In *Reformation, Revolt and Civil War in France and the Netherlands 1555–1585*, edited by Philip Benedict, Guido Marnef, Henk van Nierop, and Marc Venard, 201–14. Amsterdam: Koninklijke Nederlandse Akademie van Wetenschappen, 1999.

La paix de religion: L'autonomisation de la raison politique au xvie siècle. Collection Liber. Paris: Éditions du Seuil, 1997.

"'Peace Must Come from Us': Friendship Pacts Between the Confessions During the Wars of Religion." In *Toleration and Religious Identity: The Edict of Nantes and Its Implications in France, Britain and Ireland*, edited by Ruth Whelan and Carol Baxter, 92–103. Dublin: Four Courts Press, 2003.

Clasen, Claus-Peter. *Anabaptism: A Social History, 1525–1618.* Ithaca, NY: Cornell University Press, 1972.

"Executions of Anabaptists, 1525–1618; A Research Report." *Mennonite Quarterly Review* 47 (1973): 115–52.

Claydon, Tony. "William III's Declaration of Reasons and the Glorious Revolution." *The Historical Journal* 39, no. 1 (1996): 87–108.

Close, Christopher W. *The Negotiated Reformation: Imperial Cities and the Politics of Urban Reform, 1525–1550.* Cambridge; New York: Cambridge University Press, 2009.

Club Patrimoine de Dettwiller, ed. *Dettwiller, Rosenwiller: Bachknippe Gèscht un Hit.* Collection Mémoire de vies. Strasbourg: Carré Blanc Éditions, 2006.

Coffey, John. *Persecution and Toleration in Protestant England, 1558–1689.* Studies in Modern History. Harlow, England; New York: Longman, 2000.

Collinson, Patrick. "The Cohabitation of the Faithful with the Unfaithful." In *From Persecution to Toleration: The Glorious Revolution and Religion in England*, edited by Ole Peter Grell, Jonathan Israel, and Nicholas Tyacke, 51–76. Oxford: Clarendon Press, 1991.

The Religion of Protestants. The Church in English Society 1559–1625. The Ford Lectures 1979. Oxford: Clarendon Press, 1982.

Conner, Philip. *Huguenot Heartland: Montauban and Southern French Calvinism During the Wars of Religion.* St. Andrews Studies in Reformation History. Aldershot, England; Burlington, VT: Ashgate, 2002.

Corish, Patrick J. *The Catholic Community in the Seventeenth and Eighteenth Centuries.* Dublin: Helicon, 1981.

Cottret, Bernard. *L'Edit de Nantes: pour en finir avec les guerres de religion.* Paris: Perrin, 1997.

Cowan, Ian B. "Church and State Reformed? The Revolution of 1688–9 in Scotland." In *The Anglo-Dutch Moment: Essays on the Glorious Revolution and Its World Impact,* edited by Jonathan I. Israel, 163–83. Cambridge: Cambridge University Press, 1991.

The Scottish Covenanters, 1660–1688. London: V. Gollancz, 1976.

Crew, Phyllis Mack. *Calvinist Preaching and Iconoclasm in the Netherlands, 1544–1569.* Cambridge: Cambridge University Press, 1978.

"The Wonderyear: Reformed Preaching and Iconoclasm in the Netherlands." In *Religion and the People, 800–1700,* edited by James Obelkevich, 191–220. Chapel Hill: University of North Carolina Press, 1979.

Crété, Liliane. *Les Camisards.* Paris: Perrin, 1992.

Crouzet, Denis. "A Law of Difference in the History of Difference: The First Edict of 'Tolerance'." In *Religious Differences in France: Past and Present,* edited by Kathleen Perry Long. Sixteenth Century Essays & Studies, 1–18. Kirksville, MO: Truman State University Press, 2006.

La nuit de la Saint-Barthélemy: un rêve perdu de la Renaissance. Chroniques. Paris: Fayard, 1994.

Les guerriers de Dieu: la violence au temps des troubles de religion (vers 1525 – vers 1610). Seyssel: Champ Vallon, 1990.

Croxton, Derek. *Westphalia: The Last Christian Peace.* New York: Palgrave Macmillan, 2013.

Darby, Graham, ed. *The Origins and Development of the Dutch Revolt.* London; New York: Routledge, 2001.

Davenport, Frances Gardiner, ed. *European Treaties Bearing on the History of the United States and Its Dependencies.* Washington, DC: Carnegie Institution of Washington, 1917–37.

David, Zdeněk V. "Confessional Accommodation in Early Modern Bohemia: Shifting Relations Between Catholics and Utraquists." In *Conciliation and Confession: The Struggle for Unity in the Age of Reform, 1415–1648,* edited by Howard P. Louthan and Randall C. Zachman, 173–98. Notre Dame, IN: University of Notre Dame Press, 2004.

Davies, C. S. L. "Popular Religion and the Pilgrimage of Grace." In *Order and Disorder in Early Modern England,* edited by Anthony Fletcher and John Stevenson, 58–91. Cambridge: Cambridge University Press, 1985.

"The Pilgrimage of Grace Reconsidered." In *Popular Protest and the Social Order in Early Modern England,* edited by P. Slack, 16–38. Cambridge: Cambridge University Press, 1984.

Davies, Joan. "Persecution and Protestantism: Toulouse, 1562–1575." *The Historical Journal* 22 (1979): 31–51.

Davis, Natalie Zemon. *Society and Culture in Early Modern France.* Stanford, CA: Stanford University Press, 1975.

"The Rites of Violence." In *Society and Culture in Early Modern France*, 152–87. Stanford, CA: Stanford University Press, 1975.

De Waele, Michel. *Réconcilier les français: Henri IV et la fin des troubles de religion, 1589–1598*. Les Collections de la République des lettres. Études. Québec: Presses de l'Université Laval, 2010.

Decavele, Johan, ed. *Het einde van een rebelse droom: Opstellen over het calvinistisch bewind te Gent (1577–1584) en de terugkeer van de stad onder de gehoorzaamheid van de koning van Spanje (17 september 1584)*. Ghent: Stadsbestuur, 1984.

Decavele, Johan, and Paul van Peteghem. "Ghent 'Absolutely' Broken." In *Ghent. In Defence of a Rebellious City: History, Art, Culture*, edited by J. Decavele, 107–33. Antwerp: Mercatorfonds, 1989.

Denis, Philippe. *Les églises d'étrangers en pays rhénans (1534–1564)*. Bibliothèque de la Faculté de Philosophie et Lettres de l'Université de Liège, 242. Paris: Les Belles Lettres, 1984.

Denslagen, Wim, ed. *Gouda*. De Nederlandse monumenten van geschiedenis en kunst. Zeist: Rijksdienst voor de Monumentenzorg. Zwolle: Waanders, 2001. www.dbnl.org/tekst/dens002goud01_01.

DesBrisay, Gordon. "Catholics, Quakers, and Religious Persecution in Restoration Aberdeen." *Innes Review* 47 (1996): 136–68.

Descimon, R. "La Ligue à Paris (1585–1594): une révision." *Annales E. S. C.* 37 (1982): 72–111.

Desplat, Christian. "Louis XIII and the Union of Béarn to France." In *Conquest and Coalescence: The Shaping of the State in Early Modern Europe*, edited by Mark Greengrass, 68–83. London: Edward Arnold, 1991.

Dickmann, Fritz. *Der Westfälische Frieden*. 7th ed. Edited by Konrad Repgen. Münster: Aschendorff, 1998.

Diefendorf, Barbara B. *Beneath the Cross: Catholics and Huguenots in Sixteenth-Century Paris*. New York: Oxford University Press, 1991.

"Waging Peace: Memory, Identity, and the Edict of Nantes." In *Religious Differences in France: Past and Present*, edited by Kathleen Perry Long. Sixteenth Century Essays & Studies, 19–49. Kirksville, MO: Truman State University Press, 2006.

Dixon, C. Scott. *The Reformation and Rural Society; The Parishes of Brandenburg-Ansbach-Kulmbach, 1528–1603*. Cambridge: Cambridge University Press, 1996.

The Reformation in Germany. Historical Association Studies. Oxford, UK; Malden, MA: Blackwell Publishers, 2002.

"Urban Order and Religious Coexistence in the German Imperial City: Augsburg and Donauwörth, 1548–1608." *Central European History* 40 (2007): 1–33.

Dixon, C. Scott, Dagmar Freist, and Mark Greengrass, eds. *Living with Religious Diversity in Early Modern Europe*. Farnham, England: Ashgate Publishing, 2009.

Driedger, Michael. *Obedient Heretics: Mennonite Identities in Lutheran Hamburg and Altona during the Confessional Age*. Aldershot, England: Ashgate, 2002.

Du Buy, B. *De geschiedenis van den Brabandschen Olijfberg*. Brussel: Vereeniging voor de geschiedenis van het Belgisch Protestantism, 1960.

Duchhardt, Heinz, ed. *Der Westfälische Friede: Diplomatie, politische Zäsur, kulturelles Umfeld, Receptionsgeschichte*. Historische Zeitschrift, Beiheft 26. München: R. Oldenburg, 1998.

Duffy, Eamon. *Fires of Faith: Catholic England under Mary Tudor*. New Haven, CT: Yale University Press, 2009.

Duke, Alastair. *Reformation and Revolt in the Low Countries*. London: Hambledon Press, 1990.

"The Face of Popular Religious Dissent, 1520–30." In *Reformation and Revolt in the Low Countries*, 29–59. London: Hambledon Press, 1990.

Duke, Alastair, Gillian Lewis, and Andrew Pettegree, eds. *Calvinism in Europe, 1540–1610: A Collection of Documents*. Manchester, UK: Manchester University Press, 1992.

Dumont, Jean, ed. *Corps universel diplomatique du droit des gens; contenant vn recueil des traitez d'alliance, de paix, de treve, de neutralité, de commerce, d'échange. & autres contrats, qui ont été faits en Europe*. Amsterdam: P. Brunel, etc., 1726–31.

Dunn, Richard S. *The Age of Religious Wars, 1559–1715*. The Norton History of Modern Europe. New York: Norton, 1979.

Durston, Christopher, and Judith Maltby, eds. *Religion in Revolutionary England*. Manchester, UK; New York: Manchester University Press, 2006.

Eberhard, Winfried. "Reformation and Counter-Reformation in East Central Europe." In *Visions, Programs and Outcomes*. Vol. 2 of *Handbook of European History, 1400–1600*, edited by Thomas A. Brady, Heiko A. Oberman, and James D. Tracy, 551–605. Leiden: E. J. Brill, 1995.

Eck, Xander van. *Kunst, twist en devotie: Goudse katholieke schuilkerken 1572–1795*. Delft: Eburon, 1994.

Ellis, Steven G. *Ireland in the Age of the Tudors, 1447–1603: English Expansion and the End of Gaelic Rule*. Longman History of Ireland. New York: Addison Wesley Longman, 1998.

Evans, R. J. W. *The Making of the Habsburg Monarchy, 1500–1700: An Interpretation*. Oxford: Oxford University Press, 1979.

Everard, Edmund. *The Great Pressures and Grievances of the Protestants in France*. London: T. Cockeril and R. Hartford, 1681.

Fischer, P. Rainhald, Walter Schläpfer, and Franz Stark. *Das ungeteilte Land (Von der Urzeit bis 1597)*. Vol. 1 of *Appenzeller Geschichte*. Appenzell: Regierungen der beiden Halbkantone Appenzell, 1964.

Fletcher, Anthony. *Tudor Rebellions*. 3rd ed. London: Longman, 1983.

Foa, Jérémie. "Making Peace: The Commissions for Enforcing the Pacification Edicts in the Reign of Charles IX." *French History* 18, no. 3 (2004): 256–74.

Foord, Archibald S. "Historical Revisions: The Peace of Augsburg." *New England Social Studies Bulletin* 9 (1952): 1–7.

François, Etienne. *Die unsichtbare Grenze: Protestanten und Katholiken in Augsburg 1648–1806*. Sigmaringen: Jan Thorbeke Verlag, 1991.

Freist, Dagmar. "Between Conscience and Coercion: Mixed Marriages, Church, Secular Authority, and Family." In *Mixed Matches: Transgressive Unions in Germany from the Reformation to the Enlightenment*, edited by David M. Luebke and Mary Lindemann, 101–18. New York: Berghahn Books, 2014.

"Crossing Religious Borders: The Experience of Religious Difference and Its Impact on Mixed Marriages in Eighteenth-Century Germany." In *Living with Diversity in Early Modern Europe*, edited by C. Scott Dixon, Dagmar Freist, and Mark Greengrass. St. Andrews Studies in Reformation History, 203–24. Farnham, England: Ashgate, 2009.

Glaube – Liebe – Zwietracht: Konfessionell gemischte Ehen in Deutschland in der Frühen Neuzeit. München: Oldenbourg, 2015.

"One Body, Two Confessions: Mixed Marriages in Germany." In *Gender in Early Modern German History*, edited by Ulinka Rublack. 275–304. Cambridge: Cambridge University Press, 2002.

"Religionssicherheiten und Gefahren für das 'Seelenheil.' Religiös-politische Befindlichkeiten in Kursachsen seit dem Übertritt Augusts des Starken zum Katholizismus." In *Konfession und Konflikt. Religiöse Pluralisierung in Sachsen im 18. und 19. Jahrhundert*, 35–53. München: Achendorff, 2012.

"Religious Violence in Early Modern Germany." *Leidschrift* 20, no. 1 (2005): 141–52.

"*Social Sites*, Practices and Contested Religious Space in 17th and 18th Century Saxony." Paper presented at the conference on "Religious Wars in Early Modern Europe and Contemporary Islam." City University of New York; Columbia University, 2014.

Friesen, Abraham. "Present at the Inception: Menno Simons and the Beginnings of Dutch Anabaptism." *Mennonite Quarterly Review* 72, no. 3 (July 1998): 351–88.

Frijhoff, Willem, and Marijke Spies. *1650: Hard-Won Unity. Vol. 1 of Dutch Culture in a European Perspective*. Assen: Royal Van Gorcum; New York: Palgrave Macmillan, 2004.

Furner, Mark. "Lay Casuistry and the Survival of Later Anabaptists in Bern." *Mennonite Quarterly Review* 75 (2001): 429–70.

"The 'Nicodemites' in Arth, Canton Schwyz, 1530–1698." Master's thesis, University of Warwick, 1994.

"The Repression and Survival of Anabaptism in the Emmental, Switzerland, 1659–1743." Ph.D. diss., Cambridge University, 1998.

Gardiner, Samuel Rawson, ed. *The Constitutional Documents of the Puritan Revolution, 1628–1660*. Oxford: Clarendon Press, 1889.

Garrisson, Janine. *L'Édit de Nantes. Chronique d'une paix attendue*. Paris: Fayard, 1998.

L'Édit de Nantes. Texte présenté et annoté. Biarritz: Atlantica/Société Henri IV, 1997.

Les Protestants du Midi, 1559–98. Toulouse: Privat, 1980.

Tocsin pour un massacre, la saison des Saint-Barthélemy. Paris: Le Centurion/Sciences humaines, 1968.

Gelderblom, Oscar. *Zuid-Nederlandse kooplieden en de opkomst van de Amsterdamse stapelmarkt (1578–1630)*. Hilversum: Verloren, 2000.

Gentles, Ian. *The New Model Army in England, Ireland, and Scotland, 1645–1653*. Oxford: Blackwell Publishers, 1992.

Geyl, Pieter. *The Revolt of the Netherlands (1555–1609)*. 2nd ed. London: Ernest Benn, 1958.

Goodbar, Richard L., ed. *The Edict of Nantes: Five Essays and a New Translation*. Bloomington, MN: The National Huguenot Society, 1998.

Goosens, Aline. *Les Inquisitions modernes dans les Pay-Bas méridionaux (1520–1633)*. 2 vols. Spiritualités et pensées libres. Bruxelles: Éditions de l'Université de Bruxelles, 1997–8.

Gordon, Bruce. *The Swiss Reformation*. Manchester, UK: Manchester University Press, 2002.

Gorski, Philip S. *The Disciplinary Revolution: Calvinism and the Rise of the State in Early Modern Europe*. Chicago: University of Chicago Press, 2003.

Grandjean, Michel, and Bernard Roussel, eds. *Coexister dans l'intolerance. L'édit de Nantes (1598)*. Histoire et Société, 37. Geneva: Labor et Fides, 1998.

Gray, Emily Fisher. "Good Neighbors: Architecture and Confession in Augsburg's Lutheran Church of Holy Cross, 1525–1661." Ph.D. diss., University of Pennsylvania, 2004.

Gray, Janet G. "The Origin of the Word Huguenot." *Sixteenth Century Journal* 14 (1983): 349–59.

Great Britain. *British Guiana Boundary. Arbitration with the United States of Venezuela. The Counter-Case on Behalf of the Government of Her Britannic Majesty [and Appendix]*. London: Printed at the Foreign Office, by Harrison and Sons, 1898.

Greengrass, Mark. *Christendom Destroyed: Europe 1517–1648*. New York: Viking Penguin, 2014.

———. *Governing Passions: Peace and Reform in the French Kingdom, 1576–1585*. Oxford; New York: Oxford University Press, 2007.

———. "Pluralism and Equality: The Peace of Monsieur, May 1576." In *The Adventure of Religious Pluralism in Early Modern France: Papers from the Exeter Conference, April 1999*, edited by Keith Cameron, Mark Greengrass, and Penny Roberts, 45–63. Oxford: Peter Lang, 2000.

———. "The Anatomy of a Religious Riot in Toulouse in May 1562." *Journal of Ecclesiastical History* 34 (1983): 367–91.

———. "The Calvinist Experiment in Béarn." In *Calvinism in Europe, 1540–1620*, edited by Andrew Pettegree, Alastair Duke, and Gillian Lewis, 119–42. Cambridge: Cambridge University Press, 1994.

———. *The French Reformation*. Historical Association Studies. Oxford: Blackwell, 1987.

———. "The Psychology of Religious Violence." *French History* 5 (1991): 467–74.

Greyerz, Kaspar von. *The Late City Reformation in Germany. The Case of Colmar, 1522–1628*. Wiesbaden: Steiner, 1980.

Griffiths, Gordon. *Representative Government in Western Europe in the Sixteenth Century: Commentary and Documents for the Study of Comparative Constitutional History*. Oxford: Clarendon Press, 1968.

Groen van Prinsterer, G., ed. *1566. Vol. II, 1e serie of Archives ou correspondence inedit de la maison d'Orange-Nassau*. Utrecht: Kemink et fils, 1835.

Gurp, Gerard van. *Reformatie in Brabant: protestanten en katholieken in de Meierij van 's-Hertogenbosch, 1523–1634*. Hilversum: Verloren, 2013.

Haeke, Daniela. "Chruch, Space and Conflict: Religious Co-Existence and Political Communication in Seventeenth-Century Switzerland." *German History* 25, no. 3 (2007): 286–312.

Haigh, Christopher. *English Reformations: Religion, Politics, and Society Under the Tudors*. Oxford: Clarendon Press, 1993.

Halkin, L. E. "Het katholiek herstel in de Zuidelijke Nederlanden 1579–1609." In *Algemene Geschiedenis der Nederlanden, vol 6, Nieuwe tijd*, 344–51. Haarlem: Fibula-Van Dishoeck, 1979.

Hamilton, Alastair, Sjouke Voolstra, and Piet Visser, eds. *From Martyr to Muppy. A Historical Introduction to Cultural Assimilation Processes of a Religious Minority in the Netherlands: The Mennonites*. Amsterdam: Amsterdam University Press, 1994.

Hanlon, Gregory. *Confession and Community in Seventeenth-Century France: Catholic and Protestant Coexistence in Aquitaine*. Philadelphia: University of Pennsylvania Press, 1993.

Harris, Tim, Paul Seaward, and Mark Goldie, eds. *The Politics of Religion in Restoration England*. Oxford: Basil Blackwell, 1990.

Hart, Marjolein 't. *The Dutch Wars of Independence: Warfare and Commerce in the Netherlands 1570–1680*. Modern Wars in Perspective. London and New York: Routledge, 2014.

  The Making of a Bourgeois State: War, Politics and Finance during the Dutch Revolt. Manchester, UK: Manchester University Press, 1993.

Haude, Sigrun. *In the Shadow of "Savage Wolves": Anabaptist Münster and the German Reformation during the 1530s*. Studies in Central European Histories. Boston: Humanities Press, 2000.

Hayden, J. Michael. *France and the Estates General of 1614*. Cambridge Studies in Early Modern History. London: Cambridge University Press, 1974.

Head, Randolph C. *Early Modern Democracy in the Grisons: Social Order and Political Language in a Swiss Mountain Canton, 1470–1620*. Cambridge Studies in Early Modern History. Cambridge: Cambridge University Press, 1995.

  "Fragmented dominion, fragmented churches: The institutionalization of the *Landfrieden* in the Thurgau, 1460–1600." *Archiv für Reformationsgeschichte* 96 (2005): 117–44.

  "Negotiating Co-Existence through Institutions and Practice in Early Modern Europe: The Thurgau, 1520–1712." Paper presented to a conference on "Accommodating Difference: The Politics of Cultural Pluralism in Europe" at the Netherlands Institute for Advanced Study. Wassenaar, The Netherlands, 2001.

  "Shared Lordship, Authority, and Administration: The Exercise of Dominion in the *Gemeine Herrschaften* of the Swiss Confederation, 1417–1600." *Central European History* 30 (1997): 489–512.

  "Thinking with the Thurgau: Political Pamphlets from the Vilmergerkrieg and the Construction of Biconfessional Politics in Switzerland and Europe." In *Politics and Reformations: Communities, Polities, Nations, and Empires. Essays in Honor of Thomas A. Brady Jr.*, edited by Christopher Ocker, Michael Printy, Peter Starenko, and Peter Wallace. Studies in Medieval and Reformation Traditions, 128, 239–58. Leiden; Boston: Brill, 2007.

Heckel, Martin. *Staat und Kirche nach den Lehren der evangelischen Juristen Deutschlands in der ersten Hälfte des 17. Jahrhunderts*. Jus ecclesiasticum, vol. 6. München: Claudius-Verlag, 1968.

Heijer, Henk den. *De geschiedenis van de WIC*. Zutphen: Walburg, 1994.

  "The Twelve Years' Truce and the Founding of the Dutch West India Company." *Halve Maen* 80, no. 4 (Winter 2007): 67–70.

Heller, Henry. *Iron and Blood: Civil Wars in Sixteenth-Century France*. Montreal: McGill-Queens University Press, 1991.

Hibben, C. C. *Gouda in Revolt; Particularism and Pacifism in the Revolt of the Netherlands, 1572–1588*. Utrecht: HES Publishers, 1983.

Hickey, Daniel. "Enforcing the Edict of Nantes: The 1599 Commissions and Local Elites in Dauphiné and Poitou-Aunis." In *The Adventure of Religious Pluralism in Early Modern France: Papers from the Exeter Conference, April 1999*, edited by

Keith Cameron, Mark Greengrass, and Penny Roberts, 65–83. Oxford: Peter Lang, 2000.

The Coming of French Absolutism; the Struggle for Tax Reform in the Province of Dauphiné, 1540–1640. Toronto: University of Toronto Press, 1986.

Hill, Christopher. *The World Turned Upside Down: Radical Ideas during the English Revolution.* New York: Viking Press, 1972.

Hobbes, Thomas. *Leviathan, or the Matter, Forms & Power of a Commonwealth Ecclesiastical and Civil.* Neeland Media LLC. Kindle Edition, 2014.

Hojda, Zdenek. "The Battle of Prague in 1648 and the End of the Thirty Years War." In *Politics, Religion, Law and Society. Vol. 1* of *1648: War and Peace in Europe,* edited by Klaus Bussmann and Heinz Schilling, 403–11. Münster/Osnabrück: Veranstaltungsgesellschaft 350 Jahre Westfälischer Friede, 1998.

Holt, Mack P. *The French Wars of Religion, 1562–1629.* New Approaches to European History. Cambridge: Cambridge University Press, 1995.

Horsch, John. *Menno Simons, His Life, Labors, and Teachings.* Scottdale, PA: Mennonite Publishing House, 1916.

Horst, I. B., ed. *The Dutch Dissenters: A Critical Companion to Their History and Ideas.* Leiden: E. J. Brill, 1986.

Housley, Norman. *Religious Warfare in Europe, 1400–1536.* Oxford: Oxford University Press, 2002.

Howard, Michael. *War in European History.* London; New York: Oxford University Press, 1976.

Hsia, R. Po-Chia. "Münster and the Anabaptists." In *The German People and the Reformation,* edited by R. Po-Chia Hsia, 51–69. Ithaca, NY: Cornell University Press, 1988.

Israel, Jonathan I. *Dutch Primacy in World Trade, 1585–1740.* Oxford: Clarendon Press, 1989.

European Jewry in the Age of Mercantilism, 1550–1750. Oxford: Oxford University Press, 1985.

The Dutch Republic: Its Rise, Greatness, and Fall, 1477–1806. The Oxford History of Early Modern Europe. Oxford: Clarendon Press, 1995.

Jalabert, Laurent. *Catholiques et protestants sur la rive gauche du Rhin: droits, confessions et coexistence religieuse de 1648 à 1789.* Bruxelles; New York: P.I.E. Peter Lang, 2009.

Jedin, Hubert. *A History of the Council of Trent.* 2 vols. Translated by Dom Ernest Graf. Edinburgh: Thomas Nelson and Sons, 1957.

Johnson, Trevor. *Magistrates, Madonnas and Miracles: The Counter Reformation in the Upper Palatinate.* St. Andrews Studies in Reformation History. Farnham, England; Burlington, VT: Ashgate, 2009.

Jong, O. J. de. "Union and Religion." *Low Countries History Yearbook* (1981), 29–49.

Jonge, Arnold J. de. *De Geuzenhoek te Horebeke van geslacht tot geslacht.* Pamphlet. Horebeke: Protestants Historisch Museum, 1993.

Jouanna, Arlette, Jacqueline Boucher, Dominique Biloghi, and Guy Le Thiec. *Histoire et dictionaire des Guerres de Religion.* Paris: Robert Laffont, 1998.

Joutard, Philippe, ed. *Les Camisards.* Collection Folio/Histoire. Paris: Editions Gallimard/Julliard, 1994.

"The Museum of the Desert: The Protestant Minority." In *Realms of Memory: Rethinking the French Past*, edited by Pierre Nora, 353–77. New York: Columbia University Press, 1996.

Juergensmeyer, Mark. *Terror in the Mind of God: The Global Rise of Religious Violence*. Berkeley: University of California Press, 2000.

Kaplan, Benjamin J. *Cunegonde's Kidnapping: A Story of Religious Conflict in the Age of Enlightenment*. The Lewis Walpole Series in Eighteenth-Century Culture and History. New Haven, CT: Yale University Press, 2014.

"Diplomacy and Domestic Devotion: Embassy Chapels and the Toleration of Dissent in Early Modern Europe." *Journal of Early Modern History* 6 (2002): 341–61.

Divided by Faith: Religious Conflict and the Practice of Toleration in Early Modern Europe. Cambridge, MA: Harvard University Press, 2007.

"Dutch Particularlism and the Calvinst Quest for 'Holy Uniformity'." *Archiv Für Reformationsgeschichte* 82 (1991): 239–55.

"Fictions of Privacy: House Chapels and the Spatial Accommodation of Religious Dissent in Early Modern Europe." *American Historical Review* 107 (2002): 1031–64.

"'In Equality and Enjoying the Same Favor': Biconfessionalism in the Low Countries." In *A Companion to Multiconfessionalism in the Early Modern World*, edited by Thomas Max Safley. Brill's Companions to the Christian Tradition, vol. 28, 99–126. Leiden; Boston: Brill, 2011.

Muslims in the Dutch Golden Age: Representations and Realities of Religious Toleration. Fourth Golden Age Lecture. Amsterdam: Universiteit van Amsterdam, 2007.

Katz, David S. *The Jews in the History of England, 1485–1850*. Oxford; New York: Clarendon Press, 1994.

Kidd, B. J., ed. *Documents Illustrative of the Contintental Reformation*. Oxford: Clarendon Press, 1911.

Kilroy, Phil. "Radical Religion in Ireland, 1641–1660." In *Ireland from Independence to Occupation, 1641–1660*, edited by Jane Ohlmeyer, 201–17. Cambridge: Cambridge University Press, 1995.

Kingdon, R. M. *Geneva and the Coming of the Wars of Religion in France, 1555–1563*. Geneva: Librarie E. Droz, 1956.

Knippenberg, Hans. *De religieuze kaart van Nederland: omvang en geografische spreiding van de godsdienstige gezindten vanaf de Reformatie tot heden*. Assen: Van Gorcum, 1992.

Knott, O. *Great Warford Baptist Chapel*, no date. Biblicalstudies.org.uk/pdf/tbhs/06-1_025.pdf.

Kok, J. A. de. *Nederland op de breuklijn Rome-Reformatie: Numerieke aspecten van protestantisering en katholieke herleving in de noordelijke Nederlanden, 1580–1880*. Assen: Van Gorcum, 1964.

Konnert, Mark. *Early Modern Europe: The Age of Religious War, 1559–1715*. Peterborough, Ont., Canada; Orchard Park, NY, USA: Broadview Press, 2006.

Kooi, Christine. *Calvinists and Catholics During Holland's Golden Age: Heretics and Idolaters*. Cambridge: Cambridge University Press, 2012.

"Paying Off the Sheriff: Strategies of Catholic Toleration in Golden Age Holland." In *Calvinism and Religious Toleration in the Dutch Golden Age*, edited by R. Po-Chia Hsia and H. F. K. van Nierop, 87–101. Cambridge: Cambridge University Press, 2002.

Kool-Verhoog, C. C. de. *Kasteel ter Horst: Een lagchend landhuis in Loenen.* Loenen: Stichting Wijnand Hacfort, 2002.

Kossmann, E. H., and A. F. Mellink, eds. *Texts Concerning the Revolt of the Netherlands.* Cambridge: Cambridge University Press, 1974.

Krahn, Cornelis. *Dutch Anabaptism: Origins, Spread, Life and Thought.* The Hague: Martinus Nijhoff, 1968.

Lau, Thomas. "Villmergerkrieg, Erster." In *Historicher Lexikon der Schweiz.* www.hls-dhs-dss.ch/textes/d/D8910.php, 2014.

"Villmergerkrieg, Zweiter." In *Historicher Lexikon der Schweiz.* www.hls-dhs-dss.ch/textes/d/D8911.php, 2013.

Le Roy Ladurie, E. *Carnival in Romans.* Translated by Mary Feeney. New York: G. Brazillier, 1979.

Leaver, Robin A. *Luther's Liturgical Music: Principles and Implications.* Lutheran Quarterly Books. Grand Rapids, MI: William B. Eerdmans Pub. Co., 2007.

Leeb, Rudolf, Martin Scheutz, and Dietmar Weikl, eds. *Geheimprotestantismus und evangelische Kirchen in der Habsburgermonarchie und im Erzstift Salzburg (17./18. Jahrhundert).* Veröffentlichungen des Instituts für Österreichische Geschichtsforschung, vol. 51. Wien: Böhlau; München: Oldenbourg, 2009.

Lehmann, Christoph. *De pace religionis acta publica et originalia, das ist, Reichs-Handlungen, Schriften und Protocollen über die Reichs-Constitution des Religion-Friedens.* 3. vol. Franckfurt am Main: Christian Genschens Buchhandlung, 1707–10.

Lennon, Colm. *Sixteenth-Century Ireland: The Incomplete Conquest.* New York: St. Martin's Press, 1995.

Link, Christoph. "Ius Emigrandi." In *Religion Past & Present: Encyclopedia of Theology and Religion*, edited by Hans Dieter Betz, vol. 6, 626. Leiden; Boston: Brill, 2007–13.

Lotz-Heumann, Ute. "Between Conflict and Coexistence: The Catholic Community in Ireland as a 'Visible Underground Church' in the Late Sixteenth and Early Seventeenth Centuries." In *Catholic Communities in Protestant States: Britain and the Netherlands c.1570–1720*, edited by Benjamin J. Kaplan, Bob Moore, Henk van Nierop, and Judith Pollmann. Studies in Early Modern European History, 168–82. Manchester, UK; New York: Manchester University Press, 2009.

"The Concept of 'Confessionalization': A Historiographical Paradigm in Dispute." *Memoria y Civilizacion* 4 (2001): 93–201.

Die doppelte Konfessionalisierung in Irland. Konflikt und Koexistenz im 16. und in der ersten Hälfte des 17. Jahrhunderts. Spätmittelalter und Reformation. Tübingen: Mohr Siebeck, 2000.

Louthan, Howard. *Converting Bohemia: Force and Persuasion in the Catholic Reformation.* New Studies in European History. Cambridge, UK; New York: Cambridge University Press, 2009.

The Quest for Compromise: Peacemakers in Counter-Reformation Vienna. Cambridge Studies in Early Modern History. Cambridge, UK; New York: Cambridge University Press, 1997.

Luebke, David M. "A Multiconfessional Empire." In *A Companion to Multiconfessionalism in the Early Modern World*, edited by Thomas Max Safley.

Brill's Companions to the Christian Tradition, vol. 28, 129–54. Leiden; Boston: Brill, 2011.

Luria, Keith P. "Cemeteries, Religious Difference, and the Creation of Cultural Boundaries in Seventeenth-Century French Communities." In *Memory and Identity: The Huguenots in France and the Atlantic Diaspora*, edited by Bertrand Van Ruymbeke and Randy J. Sparks, 59–72. Columbia: University of South Carolina Press, 2003.

"France: An Overview." In *A Companion to Multiconfessionalism in the Early Modern World*, edited by Thomas Max Safley. Brill's Companions to the Christian Tradition, vol. 28, 209–38. Leiden; Boston: Brill, 2011.

Sacred Boundaries: Religious Coexistence and Conflict in Early Modern France. Washington, DC: Catholic University of America Press, 2005.

"Sharing Sacred Space: Protestant Temples and Religious Coexistence in the Seventeenth Century." In *Religious Differences in France: Past and Present*, edited by Kathleen Perry Long. Sixteenth Century Essays & Studies, 51–72. Kirksville, MO: Truman State University Press, 2006.

Luther, Martin. *Luther: Selected Political Writings.* Edited and translated by J. M. Porter. Philadelphia: Fortress Press, 1974.

Maarbjerg, John. "Iconoclasm in the Thurgau: Two Related Incidents in the Summer of 1524." *Sixteenth Century Journal* 24 (1993): 577–93.

MacCulloch, Diarmaid. *The Reformation.* New York: Viking, 2004.

Macek, Ondřej. "Geheimprotestanten in Böhmen und Mähren im 17. und 18. Jahrhundert." In *Geheimprotestantismus und evangelische Kirchen in der Habsburgermonarchie und im Erzstift Salzburg (17./18. Jahrhundert). In Geheimprotestantismus und evangelische Kirchen*, edited by Rudolf Leeb, Martin Scheutz, and Dietmar Weikl. Veröffentlichungen des Instituts für Österreichische Geschichtsforschung, vol. 51, 237–69. Wien: Böhlau; München: Oldenbourg, 2009.

Macinnes, Allan I. "Catholic Recusancy and the Penal Laws, 1603–1707." *Records of the Scottish Church History Society* 23 (1987): 27–63.

Charles I and the Making of the Covenanting Movement, 1625–1641. Edinburgh: J. Donald Publishers, 1991.

"Repression and Conciliation: The Highland Dimension 1660–1688." *The Scottish Historical Review* 65, no. 2 (1986): 176–195.

The British Revolution, 1629–1660. British Studies Series. Houndmills, Basingstoke, Hampshire; New York, NY: Palgrave Macmillan, 2005.

Mahling, Jan. "Die evangelishe Kirche – Gemeindegeschichte seit 1523." In *Von Budissin nach Bautzen: Beiträge zur Geschichte der Stadt Bautzen*, edited by Manfred Thiemann, 122–33. Bautzen: Lusatia Verlag, 2002.

Manning, Brian. *The English People and the English Revolution, 1640–1649.* 2nd ed. London: Bookmarks, 1991.

Marinus, Marie Juliette. *De Contrareformatie te Antwerpen (1585–1676). Kerelijk leven in een grootstad.* Verhandelingen van de Koninklijke Academie voor Wetenschappen, Letteren en Schone Kunsten van België, Klasse der Letteren, jg. 57, nr. 155. Brussel: Paleis der Academiën, 1995.

"De protestanten te Antwerpen (1585–1700)." *Trajecta. Tijdschrift voor de geschiedenis van het katholiek leven in de Nederlanden* 2 (1993): 327–43.

Marnef, Guido. *Antwerp in the Age of Reformation: Underground Protestantism in a Commercial Metropolis, 1550–1577.* Baltimore: Johns Hopkins University Press, 1996.

"Multiconfessionalism in a Commeercial Metropolis: The Case of 16th-Century Antwerp." In *A Companion to Multiconfessionalism in the Early Modern World,* edited by Thomas Max Safley. Brill's Companions to the Christian Tradition, vol. 28, 75–97. Leiden; Boston: Brill, 2011.

"Protestant Conversions in an Age of Catholic Reformation: The Case of Sixteenth-Century Antwerp." *Intersections. Yearbook for Early Modern Studies* 3 (2004): 33–47.

"The Dynamics of Reformed Militancy in the Low Countries: The Wonderyear." In *The Education of a Christian Society: Humanism and the Reformation in Britain and the Netherlands,* edited by N. Scott Amos, Andrew Pettegree, and Henk van Nierop, 193–210. Aldershot: Ashgate, 1999.

Marnef, Guido, and Hugo de Schepper. "Raad van Beroerten (1567–1576)." In *De Centrale Overheidsinstellingen van de Habsburgse Nederlanden (1482–1795),* I: 469–77. Brussel: Algemeen Rijksarchief, 1994.

Marsh, Christopher. *Popular Religion in Sixteenth-Century England: Holding Their Peace.* New York: St. Martin's Press, 1998.

McAdam, Doug, Sidney Tarrow, and Charles Tilly. *Dynamics of Contention.* New York: Cambridge University Press, 2001.

"Methods of Measuring Mechanisms of Contention." *Qualitative Sociology* 31, no. 4 (December 2008): 307–31.

McClain, Lisa. *Lest We Be Damned: Practical Innovation and Lived Experience among Catholics in Protestant England, 1559–1642.* New York: Routledge, 2004.

"Without Church, Cathedral, or Shrine: The Search for Religious Space among Catholics in England, 1559–1625." *Sixteenth Century Journal* 33, no. 2 (Summer 2002): 381–99.

McDonald, Danny, ed. *Tomhaggard: A Sacred Place.* Tomhaggard, Co. Wexford: Tomhaggard Heritage Group, 2002.

Mehlhausen, Joachim, ed. *Das Augsburger Interim von 1548.* Texte zur Geschichte der evangelischen Theologie. Neukirchen-Vluyn: Neukirchener Verlag, 1970.

Meij, J. C. A. de. *De Watergeuzen en de Nederlanden 1568–1572.* Amsterdam: Noord-Hollandsche Uitgevers Maatschappij, 1972.

Meyer, Judith Chandler Pugh. *Reformation in La Rochelle: Tradition and Change in Early Modern Europe, 1500–1568.* Travaux d'Humanisme et Renaissance. Genève: Librairie Droz, 1996.

Michaux, Gérard, and François-Yves Le Moigne, eds. *Protestants, Messins et Mosellans: XVIe-XXe Siècles: Actes Du Colloque de Metz (15–16 Novembre 1985).* Metz: Serpenoise: Société d'histoire et d'archéologie de la Lorraine, 1988.

Miller, Douglas. *Armies of the German Peasants' War 1524–26.* Illustrated by Angus McBride. Men-at-Arms Series. Oxford: Osprey, 2003.

Miskimin, Patricia Behre. *One King, One Law, Three Faiths: Religion and the Rise of Absolutism in Seventeenth-Century Metz.* Contributions to the Study of World History, 90. Westport, CT: Greenwood Press, 2002.

Moeller, Bernd. *Imperial Cities and the Reformation: Three Essays.* Edited by H. C. E. Midelfort and M. U. Edwards. Philadelphia: Fortress Press, 1972.

Monge, Mathilde. "Clandestinité, dissimulation, détachement du monde. Les anabaptistes en Europe occidentale, des xvie-xviie siècles." *Hypothèses* (2006), 35–44.

Mooij, Charles de. *Geloof kan bergen verzetten: reformatie en katholieke herleving te Bergen op Zoom, 1577–1795*. Hilversum: Verloren, 1998.

Morrill, John, ed. *The Scottish National Covenant in Its British Context, 1638–1651*. Edinburgh: Edinburgh University Press, 1990.

Morton, David. "Covenanters and Conventicles in South West Scotland." MPhil(R) thesis, University of Glasgow, 2012. http://theses.gla.ac.uk/id/eprint/3767.

Mousnier, Roland. *The Assassination of Henry IV: The Tyrannicide Problem and the Consolidation of the French Absolute Monarchy in the Early Seventeenth Century*. Translated by Joan Spencer. New York: Scribner, 1973.

Mullett, Michael A. *The Catholic Reformation*. London; New York: Routledge, 1999.

Munier, W. A. J. *Het simultaneum in de landen van Overmaas: een uniek instituut in de nederlandse kerkgeschiedenis (1632–1878)*. Maaslandse monografieën. Leeuwarden: Eisma B.V., 1998.

Neumaier, Helmut. "Simultaneum und Religionsfrieden im Alten Reich. Zu Phänomenologie und Typologie eines umkämpten Rechtsinstituts." *Historisches Jahrbuch* 128, no. 1 (2008): 137–76.

Nicholls, David. "France." In *The Early Reformation in Europe*, edited by Andrew Pettegree, 120–41. Cambridge: Cambridge University Press, 1992.

"The Theatre of Martyrdom in the French Reformation." *Past and Present* 121 (1988): 49–73.

Nierop, Henk van. "A Beggar's Banquet: The Compromise of the Nobility and the Politics of Inversion." *European History Quarterly* 21 (1991): 419–43.

"Similar Problems, Different Outcomes: The Revolt of the Netherlands and the Wars of Religion in France." In *A Miracle Mirrored: The Dutch Republic in European Perspective*, edited by Karel Davids and Jan Lucassen, 26–56. Cambridge: Cambridge University Press, 1995.

Treason in the Northern Quarter: War, Terror, and the Rule of Law in the Dutch Revolt. Translated by J. C. Grayson. Princeton, NJ: Princeton University Press, 2009.

Nischan, Bodo. *Prince, People and Confession: The Second Reformation in Brandenburg*. Philadelphia: University of Pennsylvania Press, 1994.

Ohlmeyer, Jane, ed. "Chronology of Events, 1639–1660." In *Ireland from Independence to Occupation, 1641–1660*, xv–l. Cambridge: Cambridge University Press, 1995.

Olry, Jean. *La persécution de l'église de Metz*. Paris: A. Franck, 1859. 2nd ed. (Reprint of 1690 Hanau ed.). https://archive.org/details/laperscutiondelooolrygoog.

Osborne, Troy David. "Worthy of the Tolerance They'd Been Given: Dutch Mennonites, Reputation, and Political Persuasion in the Seventeenth and Eighteenth Centuries." *Archiv für Reformationsgeschichte* 99 (2008): 256–97.

Parker, Charles H. *Faith on the Margins: Catholics and Catholicism in the Dutch Golden Age*. Cambridge, MA: Harvard University Press, 2008.

"Paying for the Privilege: The Management of Public Order and Religious Pluralism in Two Early Modern Societies." *Journal of World History* 17, no. 3 (2006): 267–96.

Parker, David. *La Rochelle and the French Monarchy: Conflict and Order in Seventeenth-Century France*. Royal Historical Society Studies in History Series, no. 19. London: Royal Historical Society, 1980.

Parker, G., and L. M. Smith, eds. *The General Crisis of the Seventeenth Century*. London; Boston: Routledge & Kegan Paul, 1978.

Parker, Geoffrey, ed. *The Thirty Years' War*. London: Routledge, 1987.

    The Dutch Revolt. Rev. ed. Harmondsworth: Penguin, 1985.

    The Military Revolution: Military Innovation and the Rise of the West, 1500–1800. Cambridge: Cambridge University Press, 1988.

Parker, T. H. L. *John Calvin: A Biography*. Philadelphia: Westminster Press, 1975.

Parrow, Kathleen A. "From Defense to Resistance: Justification of Violence during the French Wars of Religion." *Transactions of the American Philosophical Society* 83, no. 6 (1993): i–vi, 1–79.

Parry, Clive, ed. *The Consolidated Treaty Series*. 231 vols. Dobbs Ferry, NY: Oceana Publications, 1969–81.

Pettegree, Andrew. "Coming to Terms with Victory: The Upbuilding of a Calvinist Church in Holland, 1572–1590." In *Calvinism in Europe, 1540–1620*, edited by Alastair Duke, Gillian Lewis, and Andrew Pettegree, 160–80. Cambridge: Cambridge University Press, 1994.

    Emden and the Dutch Revolt: Exile and the Development of Reformed Protestantism. Oxford: Clarendon Press, 1992.

    Foreign Protestant Communities in Sixteenth-Century London. Oxford Historical Monographs. Oxford: Clarendon Press, 1986.

    "The Politics of Toleration in the Free Netherlands, 1572–1620." In *Tolerance and Intolerance in the European Reformation*, edited by Ole Peter Grell and Bob Scribner, 182–97. Cambridge: Cambridge University Press, 1996.

Peyer, Hans Conrad. *Verfassungsgeschichte der alten Schweiz*. Zürich: Schultheis Polygraphischer Verlag, 1978.

Pincus, Steven C. A. *1688: The First Modern Revolution*. New Haven, CT: Yale University Press, 2009.

Poelhekke, Jan Joseph. *De Vrede Van Munster*. 's-Gravenhage: M. Nijhoff, 1948.

Pol, Frank van der. "Religious Diversity and Everyday Ethics in the Seventeenth-Century Dutch City Kampen." *Church History* 71 (2002): 16–62.

Polisensky, J. V. *The Thirty Years War*. Berkeley: University of California Press, 1971.

Pollard, A. F. "The Conflict of Creeds and Parties in Germany." In *The Reformation. Vol. 2 of The Cambridge Modern History*, edited by A. W. Ward, Prothero, and Stanley Leathes. 1934, 206–45. Cambridge: Cambridge University Press, 1903.

Pollmann, Judith. *Catholic Identity and the Revolt of the Netherlands, 1520–1635*. The Past & Present Book Series. Oxford: Oxford University Press, 2011.

    "Countering the Reformation in France and the Netherlands: Clerical Leadership and Catholic Violence, 1560–1585." *Past and Present* 190 (2006): 83–120.

Potter, David, ed. *The French Wars of Religion: Selected Documents*. New York: St. Martin's Press, 1997.

Prak, Maarten. *The Dutch Republic in the Seventeenth Century: The Golden Age*. Translated by Diane Webb. Cambridge, UK; New York: Cambridge University Press, 2005.

Rabb, T. K. *The Struggle for Stability in Early Modern Europe*. Oxford: Oxford University Press, 1975.

Racaut, Luc. *Hatred in Print: Catholic Propaganda and Protestant Identity During the French Wars of Religion*. St. Andrews Studies in Reformation History. Aldershot, UK; Burlington, VT: Ashgate, 2002.

Rademaker-Helfferich, B, and S. Zijlstra. *Een leven vol gevaar: Menno Simons (1496–1561) leidsman der dopers.* Catalogue of an exhibit at the Fries Museum, Leeuwarden. Amsterdam: Algemene Doopsgezinde Sociëteit, 1996.

Rammelaere, C. de. "Bijdrage tot de geschiedenis van het Protestantisme in het Oudenaardse gedurende de moderne periode." *Handelingen der Maatschappij voor Geschiedenis en Oudheidkunde te Gent* n.r. 14 (1960): 103–15.

Reitsma, Rients. *Centrifugal and Centripetal Forces in the Early Dutch Republic. The States of Overijssel 1566–1600.* Amsterdam: Rodopi, 1982.

Repgen, Konrad. "Negotiating the Peace of Westphalia: A Survey with an Examination of the Major Problems." In *Politics, Religion, Law and Society. Vol. 1 of 1648: War and Peace in Europe*, edited by Klaus Bussmann and Heinz Schilling, 355–72. Münster/Osnabrück: Veranstaltungsgesellschaft 350 Jahre Westfälischer Friede, 1998.

"What Is a 'Religious War'?" In *Politics and Society in Reformation Europe. Essays for Sir Geoffrey Elton on His Sixty-Fifth Birthday*, edited by E. I. Kouri and Tom Scott, 311–28. London: Macmillan Press, 1987.

Robbins, Kevin C. *City on the Ocean Sea, La Rochelle, 1530–1650: Urban Society, Religion, and Politics on the French Atlantic Frontier.* Studies in Medieval and Reformation Thought. Leiden; New York: Brill, 1997.

Roberts, Penny. "One Town, Two Faiths: Unity and Exclusion During the Franch Religious Wars." In *A Companion to Multiconfessionalism in the Early Modern World*, edited by Thomas Max Safley. Brill's Companions to the Christian Tradition, vol. 28, 265–85. Leiden; Boston: Brill, 2011.

Peace and Authority During the French Religious Wars, c.1560–1600. Early Modern History. Houndmills, Basingstoke, Hampshire; New York: Palgrave Macmillan, 2013.

"Religious Pluralism in Practice: The Enforcement of the Edicts of Pacification." In *The Adventure of Religious Pluralism in Early Modern France: Papers from the Exeter Conference, April 1999*, edited by Keith Cameron, Mark Greengrass, and Penny Roberts, 31–43. Oxford: Peter Lang, 2000.

"The Languages of Peace during the French Religious Wars." *Cultural and Social History* 4, no. 3 (2007): 297–315.

"The Most Crucial Battle of the Wars of Religion? The Conflict over Sites for Reformed Worship in Sixteenth-Century France." *Archiv für Reformationsgeschichte* 89 (1998): 247–67.

Rosenberg, David Lee. *Social Experience and Religious Choice: A Case Study, the Protestant Weavers and Woolcombers of Amiens in the Sixteenth Century.* Ph.D. diss., Yale University, 1978.

Rowen, Herbert H., ed. *The Low Countries in Early Modern Times: A Documentary History.* Documentary History of Western Civilization. New York: Harper and Row, 1972.

Russell, Conrad. *The Fall of the British Monarchies, 1637–42.* Oxford: Clarendon Press, 1991.

Ruymbeke, Bertrand Van, and Randy J. Sparks, eds. *Memory and Identity: The Huguenots in France and the Atlantic Diaspora.* The Carolina Lowcountry and the Atlantic World. Columbia: University of South Carolina Press, 2003.

Safley, Thomas Max, ed. *A Companion to Multiconfessionalism in the Early Modern World*. Brill's Companions to the Christian Tradition, vol. 28. Leiden; Boston: Brill, 2011.

Salmon, J. H. M. "Peasant Revolt in Vivarais, 1575–1580." *French Historical Studies* 11 (1979): 1–28.

Society in Crisis: France in the Sixteenth Century. New York: St. Martin's, 1975.

"The Paris Sixteen, 1584–94; The Social Analysis of a Revolutionary Movement." *Journal of Modern History* 44 (1972): 540–76.

Sandberg, Brian. "'Re-Establishing the True Worship of God': Divinity and Religious Violence in France after the Edict of Nantes." *Renaissance & Reformation/ Renaissance et Reforme* 29, no. 2/3 (2005): 139–82.

Schaff, Philip. *Modern Christianity. The Swiss Reformation*. Vol. 7 of *History of the Christian Church*. New York: C. Scribner's Sons, 1923.

Schiess, Traugott, ed. *Von der Aufname Appenzells in den Eidgenössischen Bund bis zur Landesteilung, 1514–1597*. Vol. 2 of *Appenzeller Urkundenbuch*. Trogen: O. Kübler, 1934.

Schilling, Heinz. "Between Territorial State and Urban Liberty. Lutheranism and Calvinism in the County of Lippe." In *The German People and the Reformation*, edited by R. Po-Chia Hsia, 263–83. Ithaca, NY: Cornell University Press, 1988.

Civic Calvinism in Northwestern Germany and the Netherlands: Sixteenth to Nineteenth Centuries. Sixteenth Century Essays and Studies, vol. 17. Kirkville, MO: Sixteenth Century Journal Publishers, 1991.

"Confessional Europe." In *Visions, Programs and Outcomes. Vol. 2 of Handbook of European History, 1400–1600*, edited by Thomas A. Brady, Heiko A. Oberman, and James D. Tracy, 641–81. Leiden: E. J. Brill, 1995.

Schindling, Anton. "Neighbours of a Different Faith: Confessional Coexistence and Parity in the Territorial States and Towns of the Empire." In *Politics, Religion, Law and Society. Vol. 1 of 1648: War and Peace in Europe*, edited by Klaus Bussmann and Heinz Schilling, 465–73. Münster/Osnabrück: Veranstaltungsgesellschaft 350 Jahre Westfälischer Friede, 1998.

Schindling, Anton, and Walter Ziegler, eds. *Die Territorien des Reichs im Zeitalter der Reformation und Konfessionalisierung: Land und Konfession 1500–1650*. Katholisches Leben und Kirchenreform in Zeitalter der Glaubensspaltung, vol. 49–53, 57. Münster: Aschendorff, 1989–97.

Schmauss, J. J., and H.C. von Senckenberg, eds. *Neue und vollständigere Sammlung der Reichs-Abschiede*. 4 vol. Franckfurt am Mayn: E. A. Koch, 1747.

Schmidt, Heinrich Richard. *Dorf und Religion: Reformierte Sittenzucht in Berner Landgemeinden der Frühen Neuzeit*. Quellen und Forschungen Zür Agrargeschichte. Stuttgart: Gustav Fischer, 1995.

"Morals Courts in Rural Berne During the Early Modern Period." In *The Reformation in Eastern and Central Europe*, edited by Karin Maag, 155–81. London: Scolar Press, 1997.

Schneider, Bernd Christian. "Ius Reformandi." In *Religion Past & Present: Encyclopedia of Theology and Religion*, edited by Hans Dieter Betz, vol. 6, 627. Leiden; Boston: Brill, 2007–13.

Ius reformandi: die Entwicklung eines Staatskirchenrechts von seinen Aufängen bis zum Ende des Alten Reiches. Jus ecclesiasticum, vol. 68. Tübingen: Mohr Siebeck, 2001.

Schrevel, Arthur C., ed. *Recueil de documents relatifs aux troubles religieux en Flandre, 1577–1584*. Bruges: L. de Planck, 1921.

Schroeder, Henry, ed. and trans. *Canons and Decrees of the Council of Trent*. Rockford, IL: Tan Books and Publishers, 1978.

Schunka, Alexander. *Gäste, die bleiben: Zuwanderer in Kursachsen und der Oberlausitz im 17. und frühen 18. Jahrhundert*. Münster: LIT, 2006.

Schwartz, Stuart B. *All Can Be Saved: Religious Tolerance and Salvation in the Iberian Atlantic World*. New Haven, CT: Yale University Press, 2008.

Scott, James C. *Domination and the Arts of Resistance: Hidden Transcripts*. New Haven, CT: Yale University Press, 1990.

Scott, Tom, and Bob Scribner, trans. and eds. *The German Peasants' War: A History in Documents*. Atlantic Highlands, NJ: Humanities Press, 1991.

Scribner, R. W. *For the Sake of Simple Folk: Popular Propaganda for the German Reformation*. Oxford: Clarendon Press, 1994.

Popular Culture and Popular Movements in Reformation Germany. London: Hambledon Press, 1987.

The German Reformation. Atlantic Highlands, NJ: Humanities Press, 1986.

Scribner, R. W., and Gerhard Benecke, eds. *The German Peasant War of 1525: New Viewpoints*. London: George Allen and Unwin, 1979.

Seifert, Siegfried. "Die katholische Kirche nach der Reformation." In *Von Budissin nach Bautzen: Beiträge zur Geschichte der Stadt Bautzen*, edited by Manfred Thiemann, 110–21. Bautzen: Lusatia Verlag, 2002.

Self, Charles Everitt. "The Tragedy of Belgian Protestantism: Subversion and Survival." Ph.D. diss., University of California Santa Cruz, 1995.

Smit, C. *Het Vredesverdrag van Munster, 30 januany 1648*. Leiden: Brill, 1948.

Spaans, Joke. "Catholicism and Resistance to the Reformation in the Northern Netherlands." In *Reformation, Revolt and Civil War in France and the Netherlands 1555–1585*, edited by Philip Benedict, Guido Marnef, Henk van Nierop, and Marc Venard, 149–64. Amsterdam: Koninklijke Nederlandse Akademie van Wetenschappen, 1999.

"De lutherse lobby voor vrijheid van godsdienstoefening in Friesland." *De zeventiende Eeuw* 20 (2004): 38–52.

Haarlem na de Reformatie: Stedelijke cultuur en kerkelijk leven, 1577–1620. Hollandse Historische Reeks 11. 's-Gravenhage: Stichting Hollandse Historische Reeks, 1989.

Stayer, James M. "The Passing of the Radical Moment in the Radical Reformation." *Mennonite Quarterly Review* 71, no. 1 (1997): 147–52.

"The Swiss Brethren: An Exercise in Historical Definition." *Church History* 47, no. 2 (1978): 174–95.

Stegmann, André, ed. *Édits des guerres de religion*. Textes et documents de la Renaissance. Paris: J. Vrin, 1979.

Stell, Christopher, ed. *An Inventory of Nonconformist Chapels and Meeting-Houses*. 4 vol. London: H. M. S. O., 1986–2002.

Stevenson, David. *The Scottish Revolution 1637–1644. The Triumph of the Covenanters*. Newton Abbot: David and Charles, 1973.

Strickler, Johannes, ed. *Eidgenössischen Abschiede aus dem Zeitraume von 1529 bis 1532. Vol. 4, part 1b of Amtliche Sammlung der älteren Eidgenössischen Abschiede*. Edited by Johannes Strickler. Zürich: J. Schabeliz, 1876.

Sullivan, Andrew. "This Is Religious War." *The New York Times Magazine*, 7 October 2001.

Suter, Andreas. *Der schweizerische Bauernkrieg von 1653: Politische Sozialgeschichte – Sozialgeschichte eines politischen Ereignisses.* Tübingen: Biblioteca Academica Verlag, 1997.

Sutherland, N. M. "The Crown, the Huguenots, and the Edict of Nantes." In *The Huguenot Connection: The Edict of Nantes, Its Revocation, and Early French Migration to South Carolina.* Dordrecht; Boston: Kluwer, 1988.

The Huguenot Struggle for Recognition. New Haven, CT: Yale University Press, 1980.

Swart, K. W. *Willem van Oranje en de Nederlandse Opstand, 1572–1584.* With an introduction by Alastair Duke and Jonathan I. Israel. Den Haag: Sdu Uitgeverij, 1994.

Sypher, G. Wylie. "'Faisant ce qu'il leur vient a plaisir': The Image of Protestantism in French Catholic Polemic on the Eve of the Religious Wars." *Sixteenth Century Journal* 11, no. 2 (1980): 59–84.

Tarrow, Sidney. *Power in Movement. Social Movements, Collective Action and Politics*, 2nd ed. Cambridge Studies in Comparative Politics. Cambridge: Cambridge University Press, 1997.

"The Strategy of Paired Comparison: Toward a Theory of Practice." *Comparative Political Studies* 43, no. 2 (2010): 230–59.

Taylor, Lawrence J. *Occasions of Faith: An Anthropology of Irish Catholics.* Series in Contemporary Ethnography. Philadelphia: University of Pennsylvania Press, 1995.

Te Brake, Wayne. "Emblems of Coexistence in a Confessional World." In *Living with Religious Diversity in Early Modern Europe*, edited by C. Scott Dixon, Dagmar Freist, and Mark Greengrass, 53–79. Farnham, England: Ashgate Publishing, 2009.

Shaping History: Ordinary People in European Politics, 1500–1700. Berkeley and Los Angeles: University of California Press, 1998.

"The Contentious Politics of Religious Diversity." In *Cities, States, Trust, and Rule: New Departures from the Work of Charles Tilly*, edited by Michael Hanagan and Chris Tilly, 229–48. New York: Springer, 2011.

Tex, Jan den. *Oldenbarnevelt.* Translated by R. B. Powell. Cambridge: Cambridge University Press, 1973.

Tilly, Charles. "Collective Violence in European Perspective." In *The History of Violence in America: Historical and Comparative Perspectives*, edited by Hugh Davis Graham and Ted Robert Gurr. New York: F. A. Praeger, 1969.

Durable Inequality. Berkeley: University of California Press, 1998.

"Grudging Consent." *The American Interest*, no. 3 (September/October 2007): 17–23.

"Political Identities in Changing Polities." *Social Research* 70 (2003): 1301–15.

The Politics of Collective Violence. Cambridge Studies in Contentious Politics. Cambridge: Cambridge University Press, 2003.

"Where Do Rights Come From?" In *Contributions to the Comparative Study of Development. Vol. 2 of Democracy, Revolution and History*, edited by Lars Mjøset and Theda Skocpol. Ithaca, NY: Cornell University Press, 1998.

Toebak, Peter. "Het kerkelijk-godsdienstige en culturele leven binnen het noordwestelijke deel van het hertogdom Brabant (1587–1609): een typering." *Trajecta. Tijdschrift voor de geschiedenis van het katholiek leven in de Nederlanden* 1 (1992): 124–43.

Tracy, James D. *Europe's Reformations, 1450–1650*. Critical Issues in History. Lanham, MD: Rowman and Littlefield, 1999.

Treasure, Geoffrey. *The Huguenots*. New Haven, CT: Yale University Press, 2013.

Trevor-Roper, Hugh. *The Crisis of the Seventeenth Century: Religion, the Reformation, and Social Change*. New York: Harper & Row, 1967.

Ubachs, P. J. H. "De Nederlandse Religievrede van 1578." *Nederlands archief voor kerkgeschiedenis* 77, no. 1 (1997): 41–61.

Twee heren, twee confessies: De verhouding van staat en kerk te Maastricht, 1632–1673. Assen: Van Gorcum, 1975.

Underdown, David. *Pride's Purge: Politics in the Puritan Revolution*. Oxford: Clarendon Press, 1971.

Revel, Riot and Rebellion: Popular Politics and Culture in England, 1603–1660. Oxford: Oxford University Press, 1985.

Vedder, Henry Clay, ed. *The Decree of Worms*. Historical Leaflets, no. 3. Chester, PA: Crozer Theological Seminary, 1901.

ed. *The Peace of Augsburg*. Historical Leaflets, no. 5. Chester, PA: Crozer Theological Seminary, 1901.

Vereinigung zur Erforschung der Neueren Geschichte. *Wesfälischen Friedenverträge von 24. Oktober 1648. Texte und Üersetzungen*. Acta. www.pax-westphalica.de/ipmipo/index.html.

Vermeir, Rene, and Tomas Roggeman. "Implementing the Truce: Negotiations between the Republic and the Archducal Netherlands, 1609–10." *European Review of History* 17 (2010): 817–33.

Vogler, Bernard. "Le Simultaneum." In *Protestants d'Alsace et de Moselle: Lieux de Mémoire et de Vie*, edited by Antoine Pfeiffer, 297–98. Strasbourg /Ingersheim: Oberlin/SAEP, 2006.

Volkland, Frauke. "Katholieken und Reformierte im Toggenburg und im Rheintal." In *Frühe Neuzeit. Vol.* 4, 131–46. St. Gallen: Amt für Kultur des Kantons St. Gallen, 2003.

"Konfessionelle Abgrenzung Zwischen Gewalt, Stereotypenbildung und Symbolik: Gemischtkonfessionelle Gebiete der Ostschweiz und die Kurfalz Im Vergleich." In *Religion und Gewalt: Konflicte, Rituale, Deutungen (1500–1800)*, edited by Kaspar von Greyerz and Kim Siebenhüner, 343–65. Göttingen: Vandenhoek & Reprecht, 2006.

"Reformiert sein 'unter' Katholiken. Zur religiösen Praxis reformiert Gläubiger in gemischtkonfessionellen Gemeinden der Alten Eidgenossenschaft im 17. Jahrhundert." In *Ländliche Frömmigkeit. Konfessionskulturen und Lebenswelten 1500–1850*, edited by Norbert Haag, Sabine Holtz, and Wolfgang Zimmermann, 159–77. Stuttgart: Thorbeke, 2002.

Vos, Karel. *Menno Simons, 1496–1561, Zijn Leven en Werken en Zijne Reformatorische Denkbeelden*. Leiden: E. J. Brill, 1914.

Vries, Jan de, and Ad van der Woude. *The First Modern Economy: Success, Failure, and Perseverance of the Dutch Economy, 1500–1815*. Cambridge: Cambridge University Press, 1997.

Walder, Ernst, ed. *Religionsvergleiche des 16. Jahrhunderts. Vol. 7–8 of Quellen zur neueren Geschichte.* Bern: Verlag Herbert Lang, 1960–61.

Walker, Mack. *The Salzburg Transaction: Expulsion and Redemption in Eighteenth-Century Germany.* Ithaca, NY: Cornell University Press, 1992.

Wallace, Peter G. "Multiconfessionalism in the Holy Roman Empire: The Case of Colmar, 1550–1750." In *A Companion to Multiconfessionalism in the Early Modern World,* edited by Thomas Max Safley. Brill's Companions to the Christian Tradition, vol. 28, 179–205. Leiden; Boston: Brill, 2011.

The Long European Reformation: Religion, Political Conflict, and the Search for Conformity, 1350–1750. European History in Perspective. Houndmills, Basingstoke, Hampshire; New York: Palgrave Macmillan, 2004.

Walsham, Alexandra. "Beads, Books and Bare Ruined Choirs: Transmutations of Catholic Ritual Life in Protestant England." In *Catholic Communities in Protestant States: Britain and the Netherlands c.1570–1720,* edited by Benjamin J. Kaplan, Bob Moore, Henk van Nierop, and Judith Pollmann. Studies in Early Modern European History, 103–22. Manchester, UK; New York: Manchester University Press, 2009.

Charitable Hatred: Tolerance and Intolerance in England, 1500–1700. Politics, Culture, and Society in Early Modern Britain. Manchester, UK; New York: Manchester University Press, 2006.

Church Papists: Catholicism, Conformity, and Confessional Polemic in Early Modern England. Royal Historical Society Studies in History. Woodbridge, Suffolk, UK; Rochester, NY, USA: Boydell Press, 1993.

"Holywell: Contesting Sacred Space in Post-Reformation Wales." In *Sacred Space in Early Modern Europe,* edited by Will Coster and Andrew Spicer, 211–36. Cambridge: Cambridge University Press, 2005.

The Reformation of the Landscape: Religion, Identity, and Memory in Early Modern Britain and Ireland. Oxford; New York: Oxford University Press, 2011.

Walter, Barbara F. *Committing to Peace: The Successful Settlement of Civil Wars.* Princeton, NJ: Princeton University Press, 2002.

Wandel, Lee Palmer. "Strubelhans and the Singing Monks." In *Krisenbewusstsein und Krisenbewältigung in der frühen Neuzeit: Festschrift für Hans-Christolph Rublack,* edited by Monika Hagenmaier and Sabine Holtz, 307–15. Frankfurt am Main: Peter Lang, 1992.

Voracious Idols and Violent Hands. Iconoclasm in Reformation Zurich, Strasbourg, and Basel. Cambridge: Cambridge University Press, 1995.

Wanegffelen, Thierry. *L'édit de Nantes: une histoire européenne de la tolérance du XVIe au XXe siècle.* Paris: Le Livre de poche, 1998.

Ward, W. Reginald. *The Protestant Evangelical Awakening.* Cambridge: Cambridge University Press, 1992.

Warmbrunn, Paul. *Zwei Konfessionen in einer Stadt: Das Zusammenleben von Katholiken und Protestanten in den paritätischen Reichsstädten Augsburg, Biberach, Ravensburg, und Dinkelsbühl von 1548 bis 1648.* Veröffentlichungen des Instituts für Europäische Geschichte Mainz. Wiesbaden: Steiner, 1983.

Webster, Tom. "On Shaky Ground: Quakers, Puritans, Possession and High Spirits." In *The Experience of Revolution in Stuart Britain and Ireland: Essays for John Morrill,* edited by Michael J. Braddick and David L. Smith, 172–89. Cambridge; New York: Cambridge University Press, 2011.

Wedgewood, C. V. *The Thirty Years War*. London: J. Cape, 1938.

Whaley, Joachim. *Religious Toleration and Social Change in Hamburg, 1529–1819*. Cambridge: Cambridge University Press, 1985.

Whelan, Ruth, and Carol Baxter, eds. *Toleration and Religious Identity: The Edict of Nantes and Its Implications in France, Britain and Ireland*. Dublin: Four Courts Press, 2003.

Wick, Markus René. "Der 'Glarnerhandel,' Strukturgeschichte und konflictsoziologische Hypothesen zum Glarner Konfessionsgegensatz." Diss., Universität Bern. *Jahrbuch des Historischen Vereins Glarus* 69 (1982): 49–240.

Wilson, Peter H. *The Thirty Years War: Europe's Tragedy*. Cambridge, MA: Harvard University Press, 2009.

Wodrow, Robert, ed. *The History of the Sufferings of the Church of Scotland: From the Restauration to the Revolution*. Edinburgh: Printed by James Watson, 1721–22.

Wolfe, Michael. *The Conversion of Henri IV: Politics, Power, and Religious Belief in Early Modern France*. Harvard Historical Studies. Cambridge, MA; London: Harvard University Press, 1993.

Woltjer, J. J. "Violence during the Wars of Religion in France and the Netherlands: A Comparison." *Nederlands Archief Voor Kerkgeschiedenis* 76, no. 1 (1996): 26–45.

Woolrych, Austin. *Britain in Revolution, 1625–1660*. Oxford: Oxford University Press, 2002.

Wuthnow, Robert. *Communities of Discourse: Ideology and Social Structure in the Reformation, the Enlightenment, and European Socialism*. Cambridge, MA: Harvard University Press, 1989.

Z'Graggen, Bruno. *Tyrannenmord im Toggenburg. Fürstäbtische Herrschaft und protestantischer Widerstand um 1600*. Zürich: Chronos Verlag, 1999

Index

Books in the Series